CW00819739

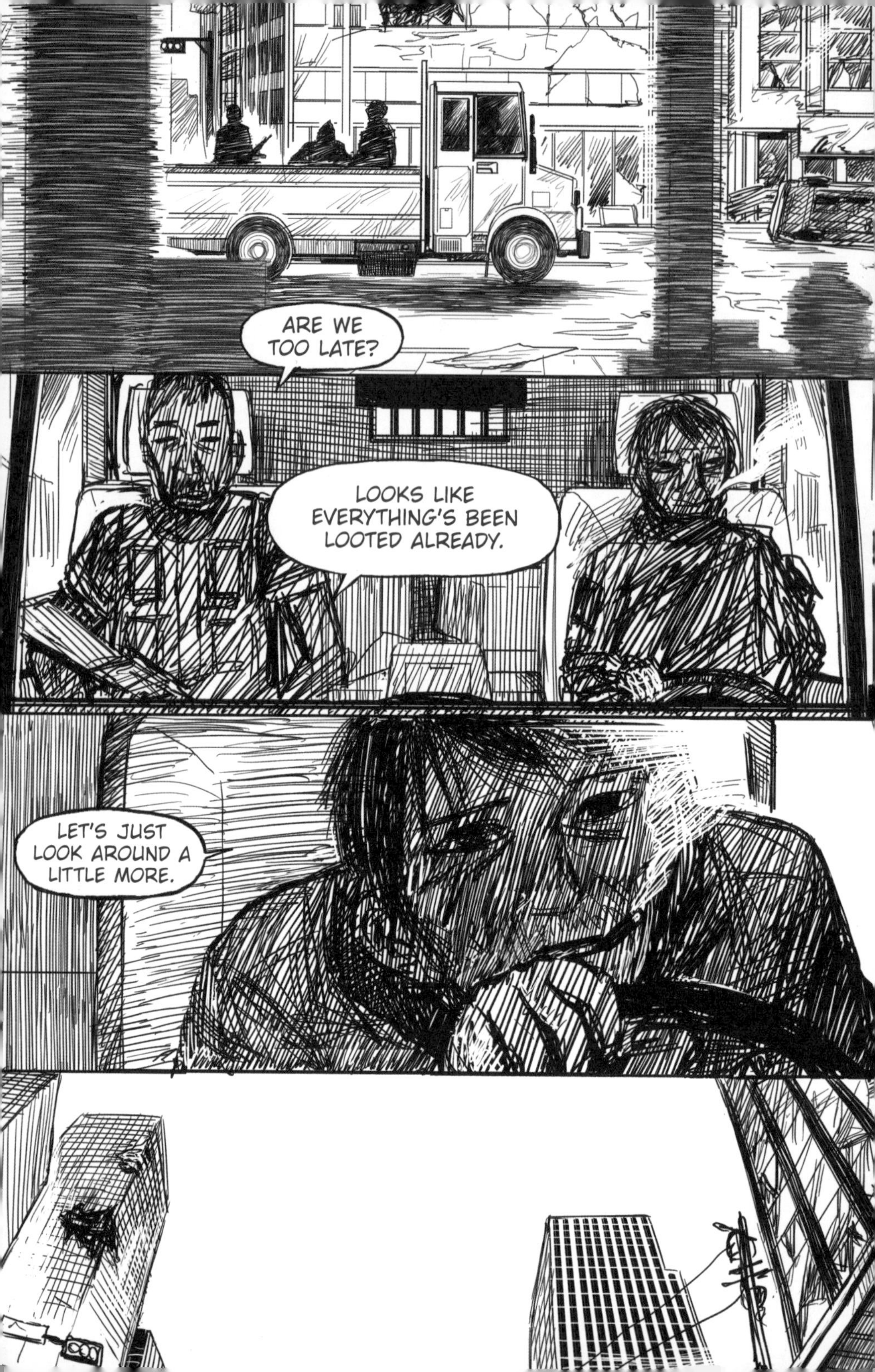
ARE WE TOO LATE?
LOOKS LIKE EVERYTHING'S BEEN LOOTED ALREADY.
LET'S JUST LOOK AROUND A LITTLE MORE.

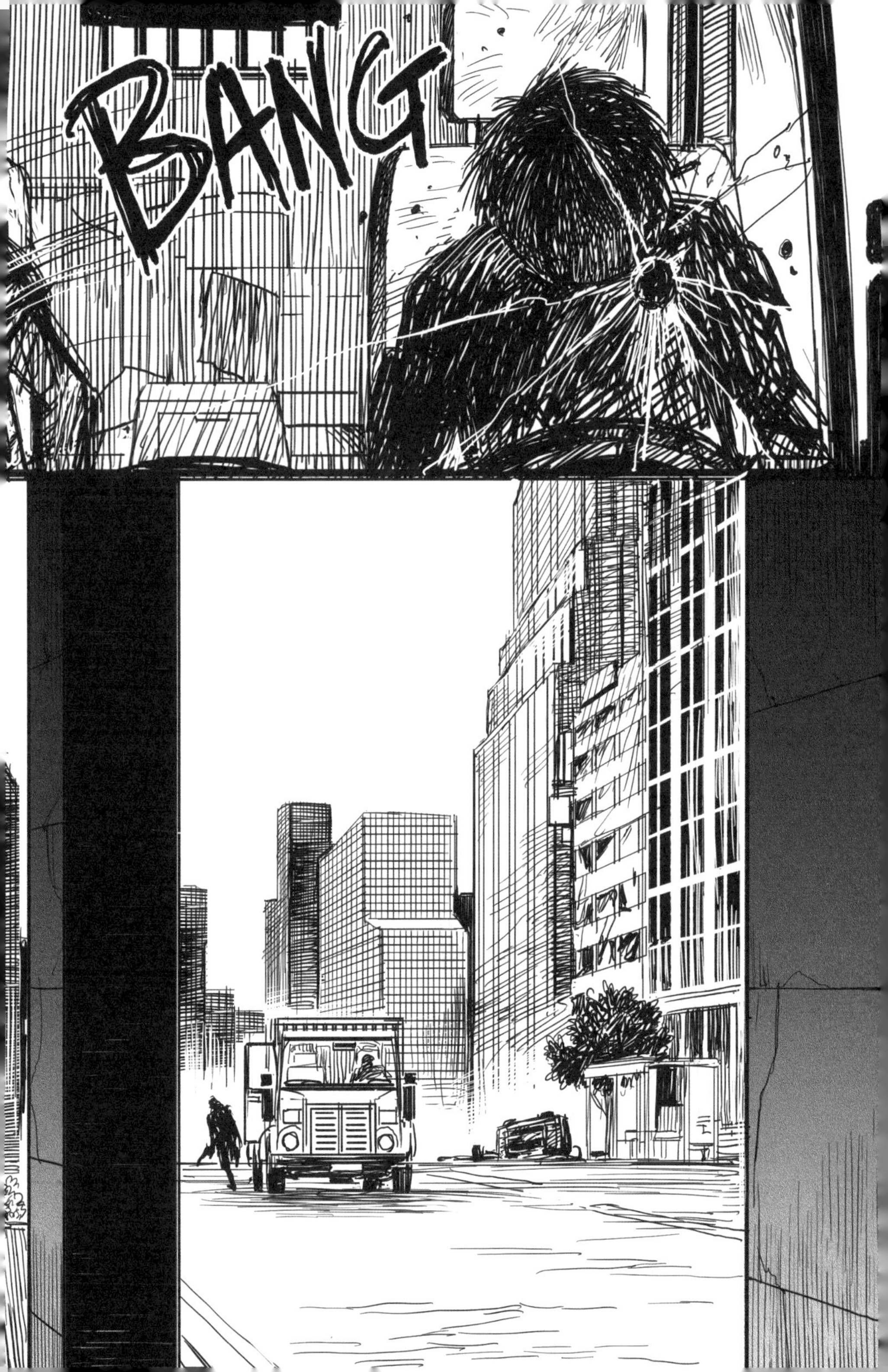
BANG

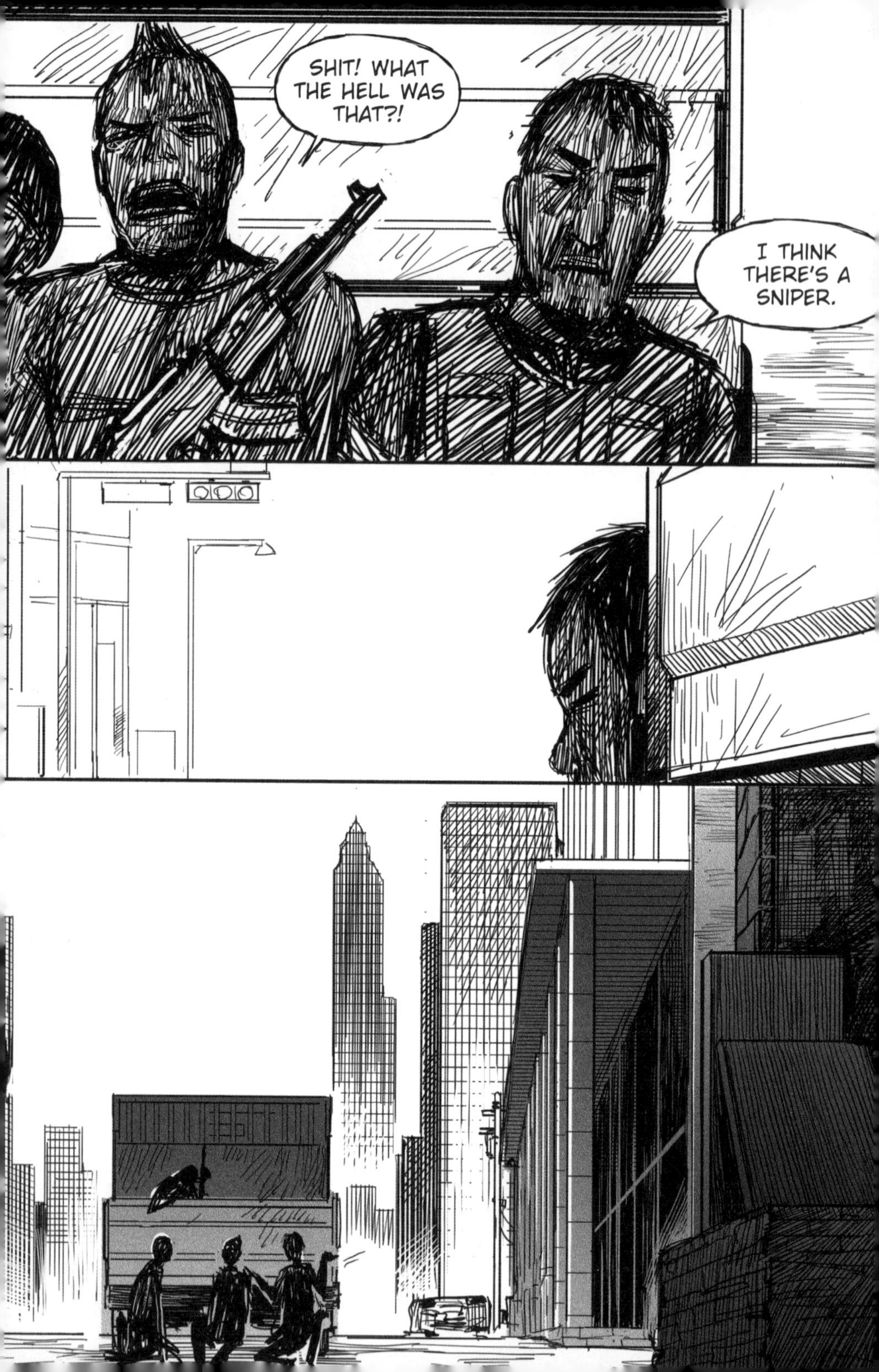
SHIT! WHAT THE HELL WAS THAT?!
I THINK THERE'S A SNIPER.

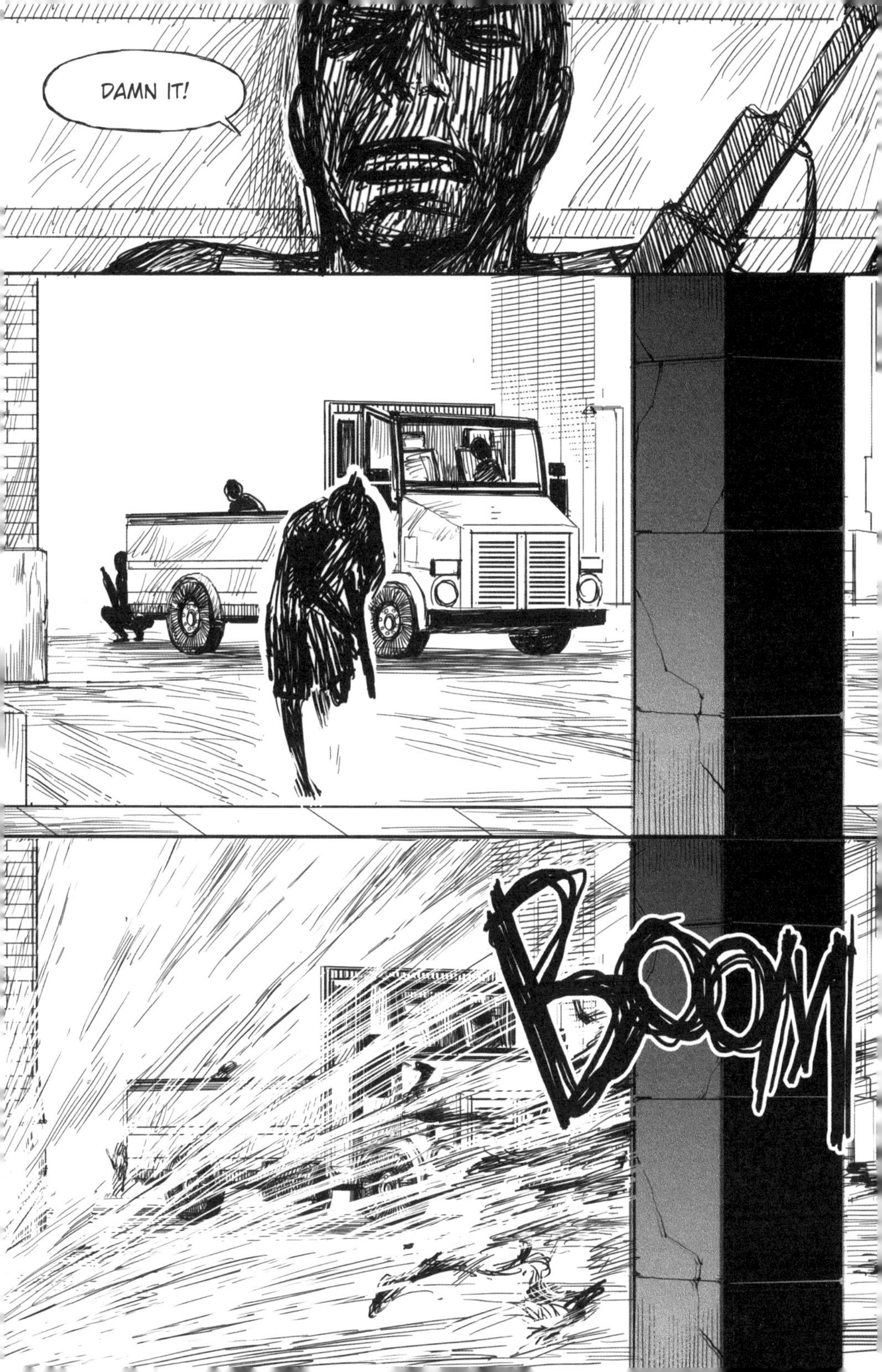
DAMN IT!
BOOM

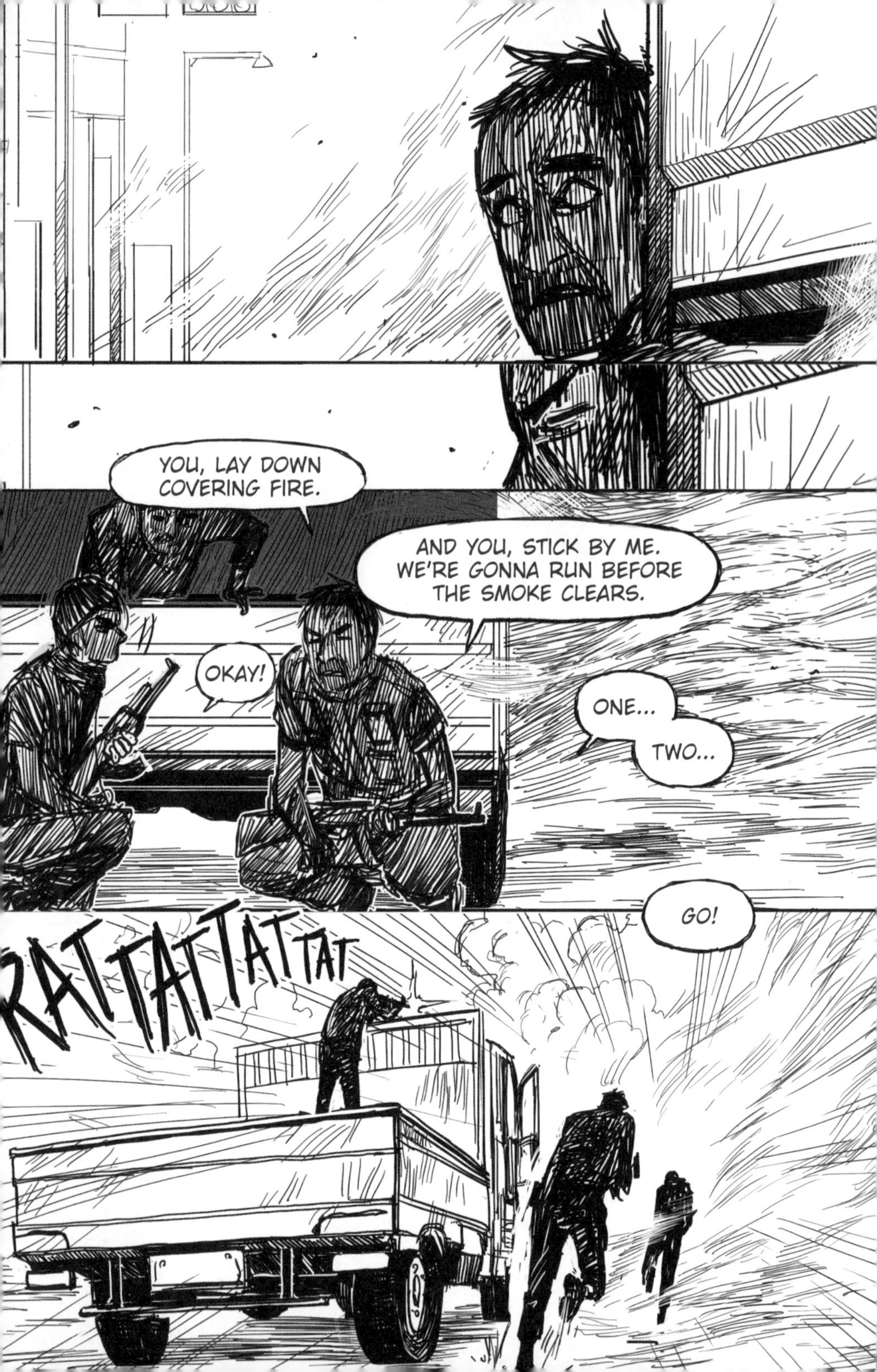
YOU, LAY DOWN COVERING FIRE.
AND YOU, STICK BY ME. WE'RE GONNA RUN BEFORE THE SMOKE CLEARS.
OKAY!
ONE...
TWO...
GO!
RATTATTATTAT

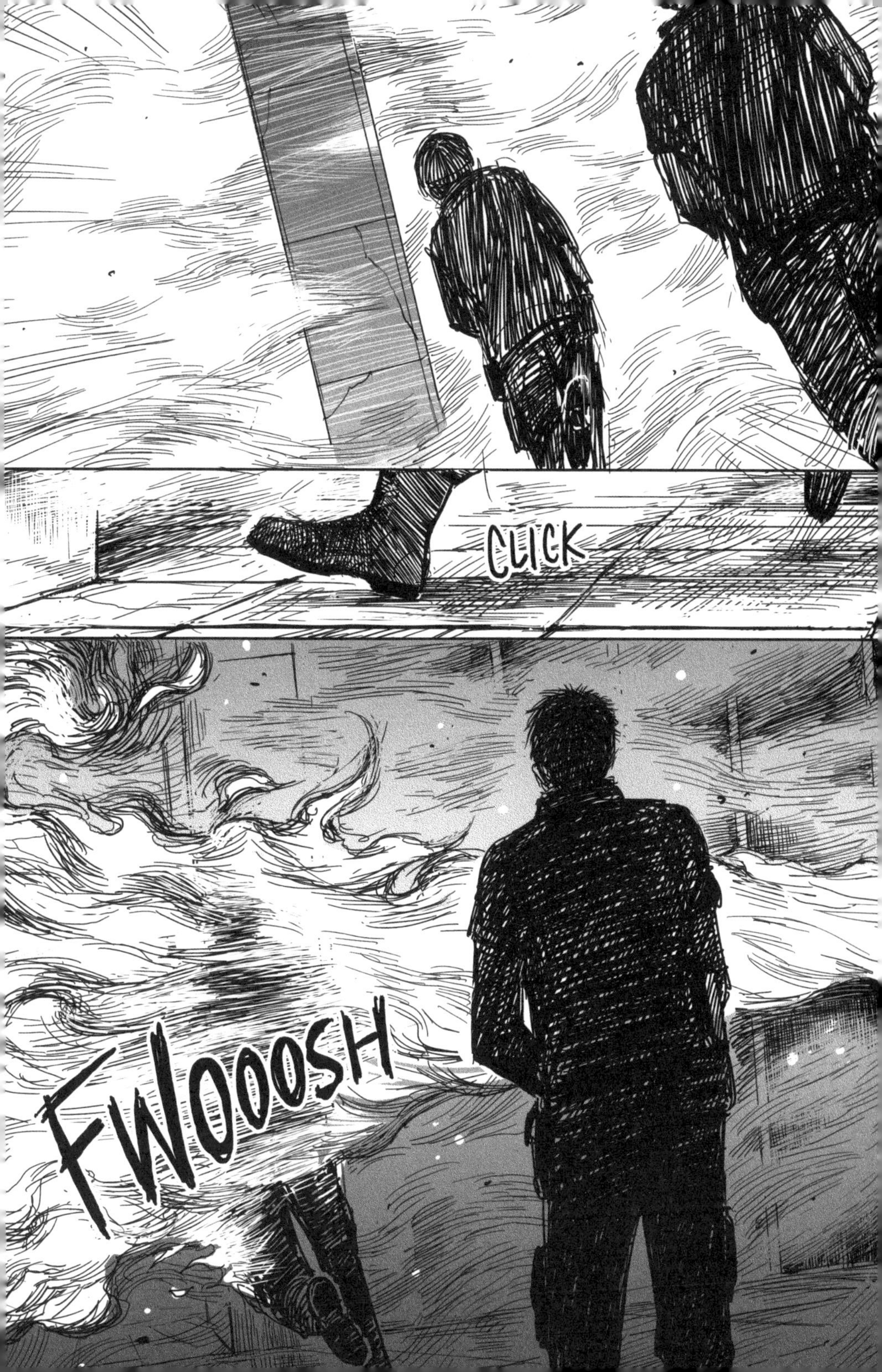
CLICK
FWOOOSH

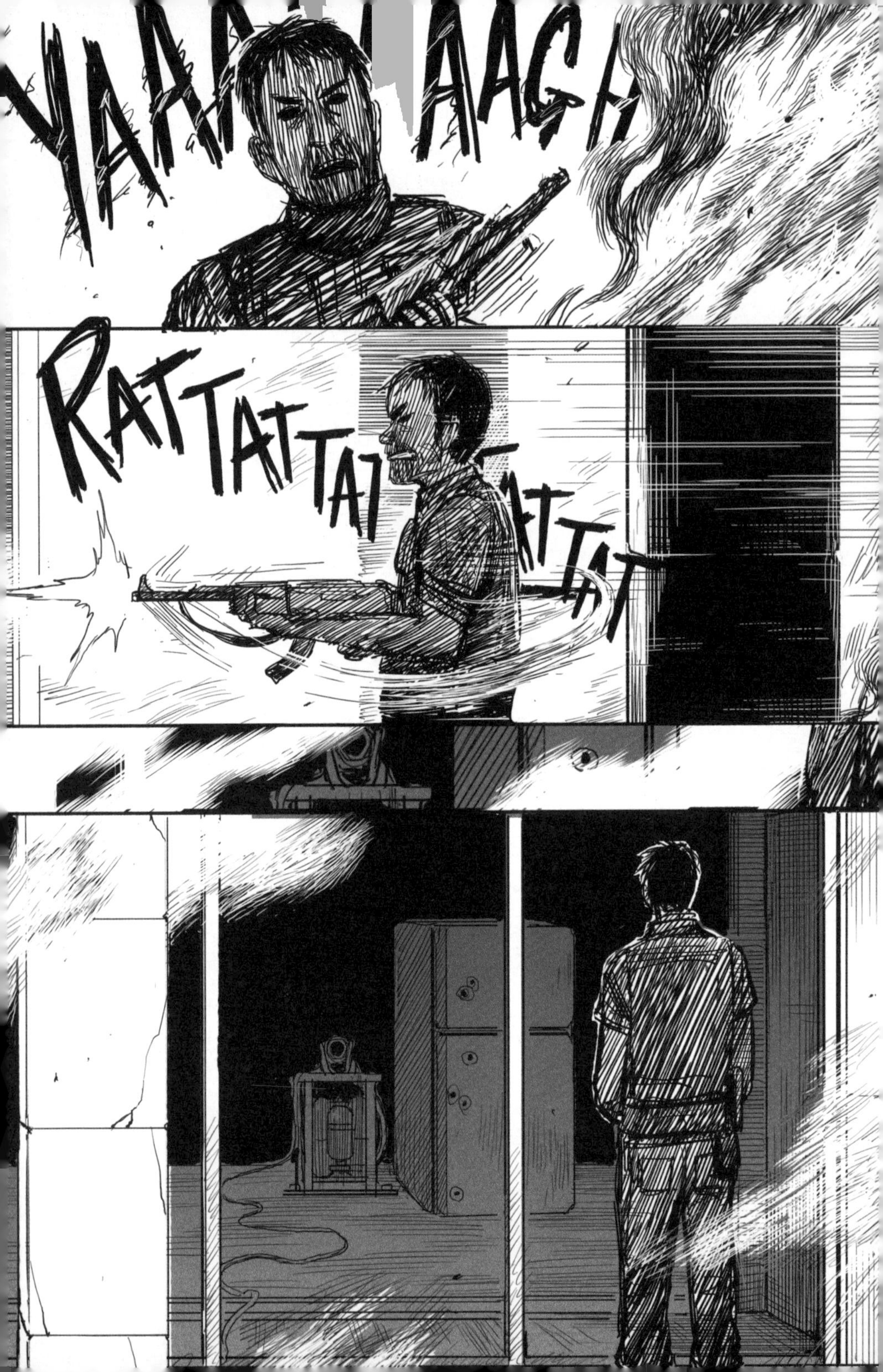
YAAAAAAGH
RATTATTATTATTAT

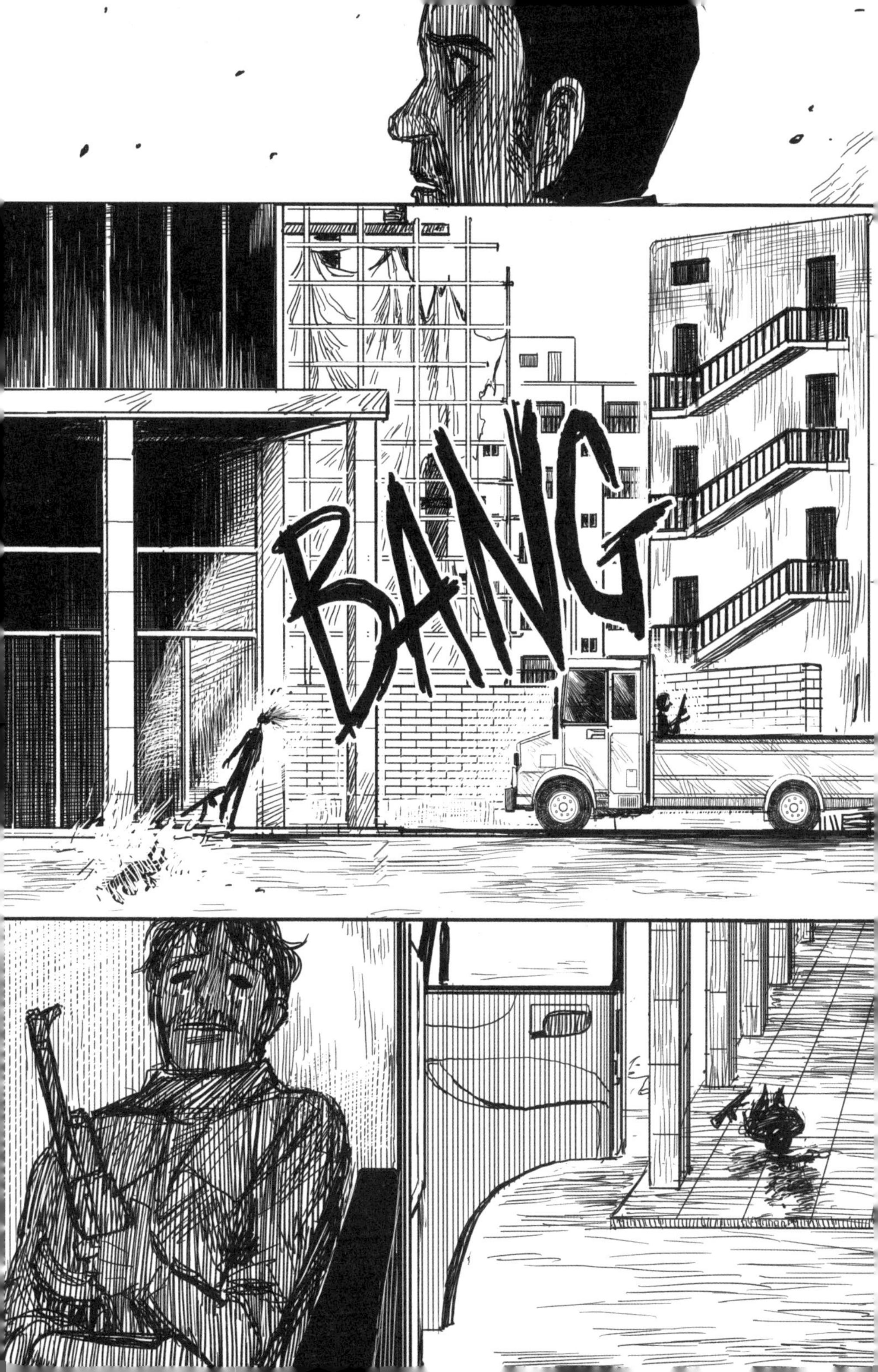
BANG

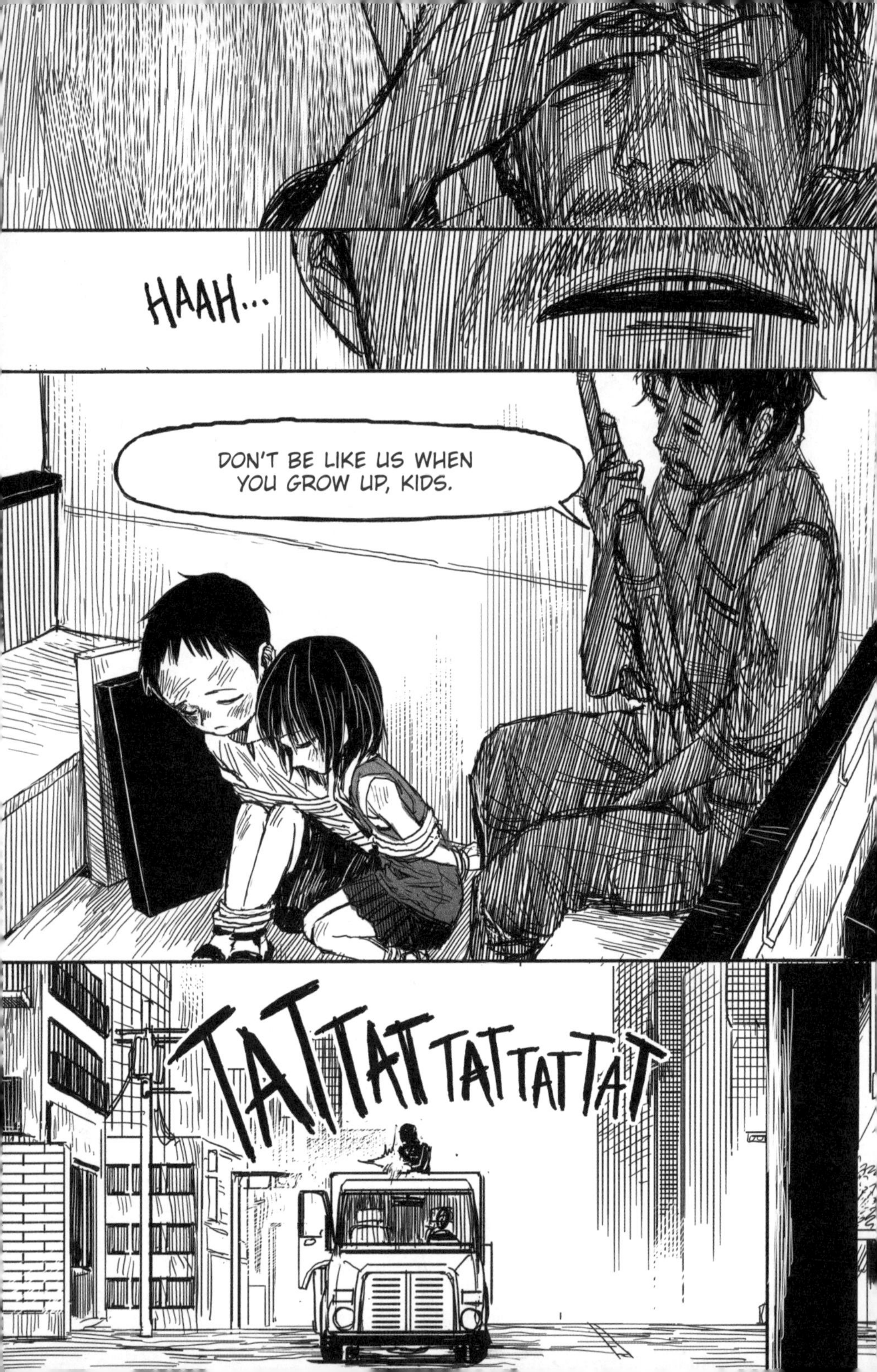
HAAH...
DON'T BE LIKE US WHEN YOU GROW UP, KIDS.
TATTATTATTATTAT

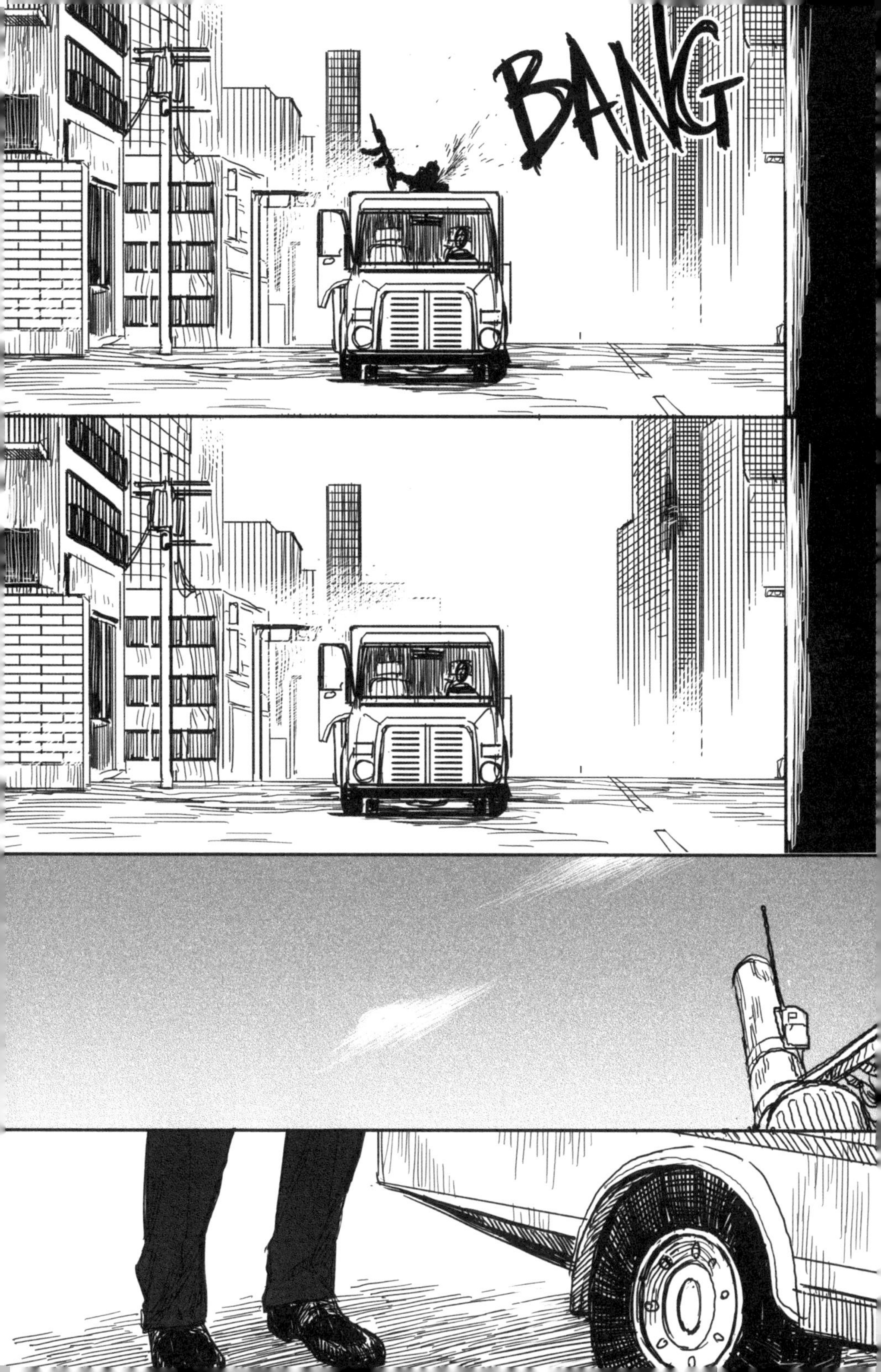
BANG

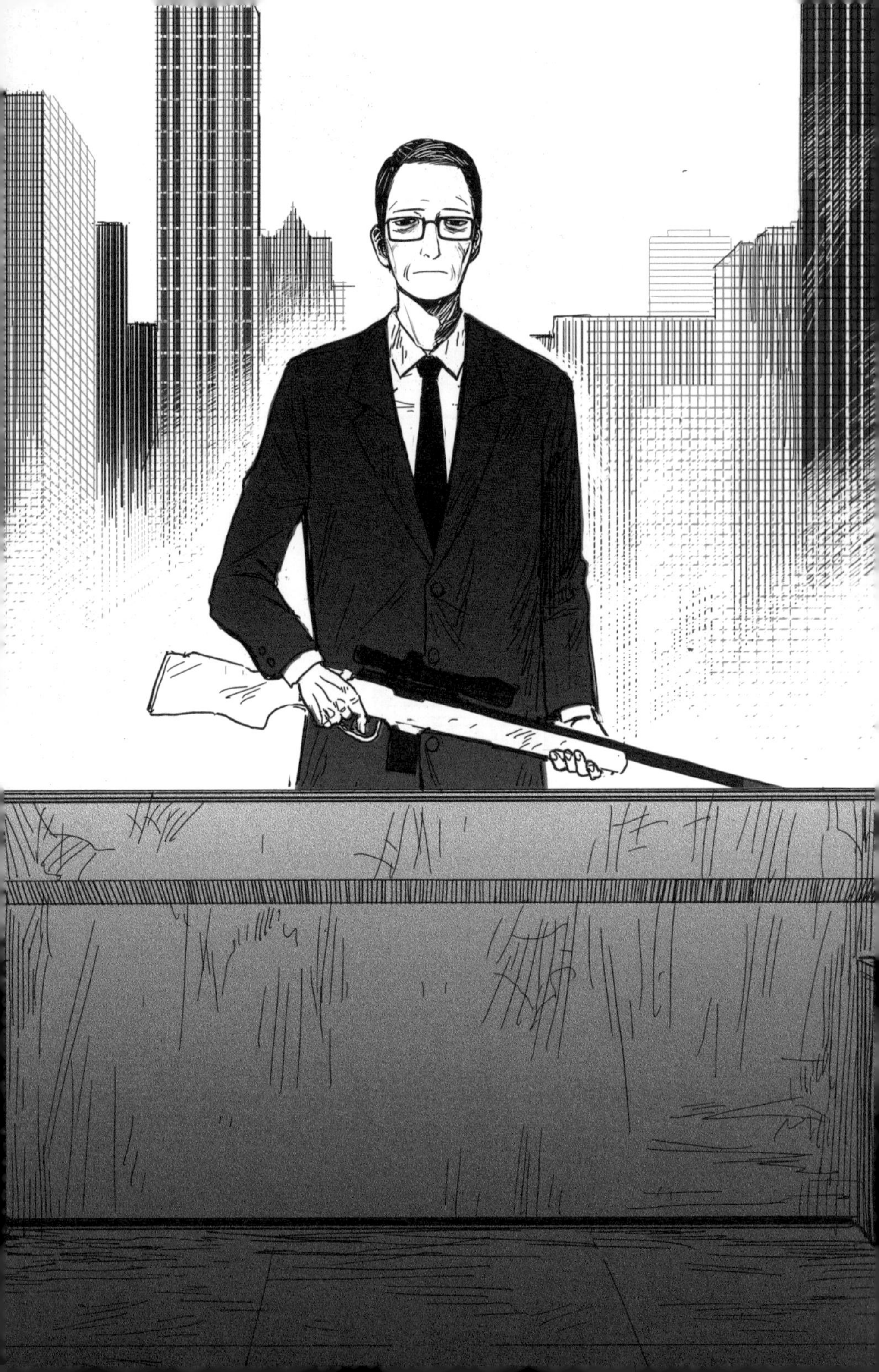

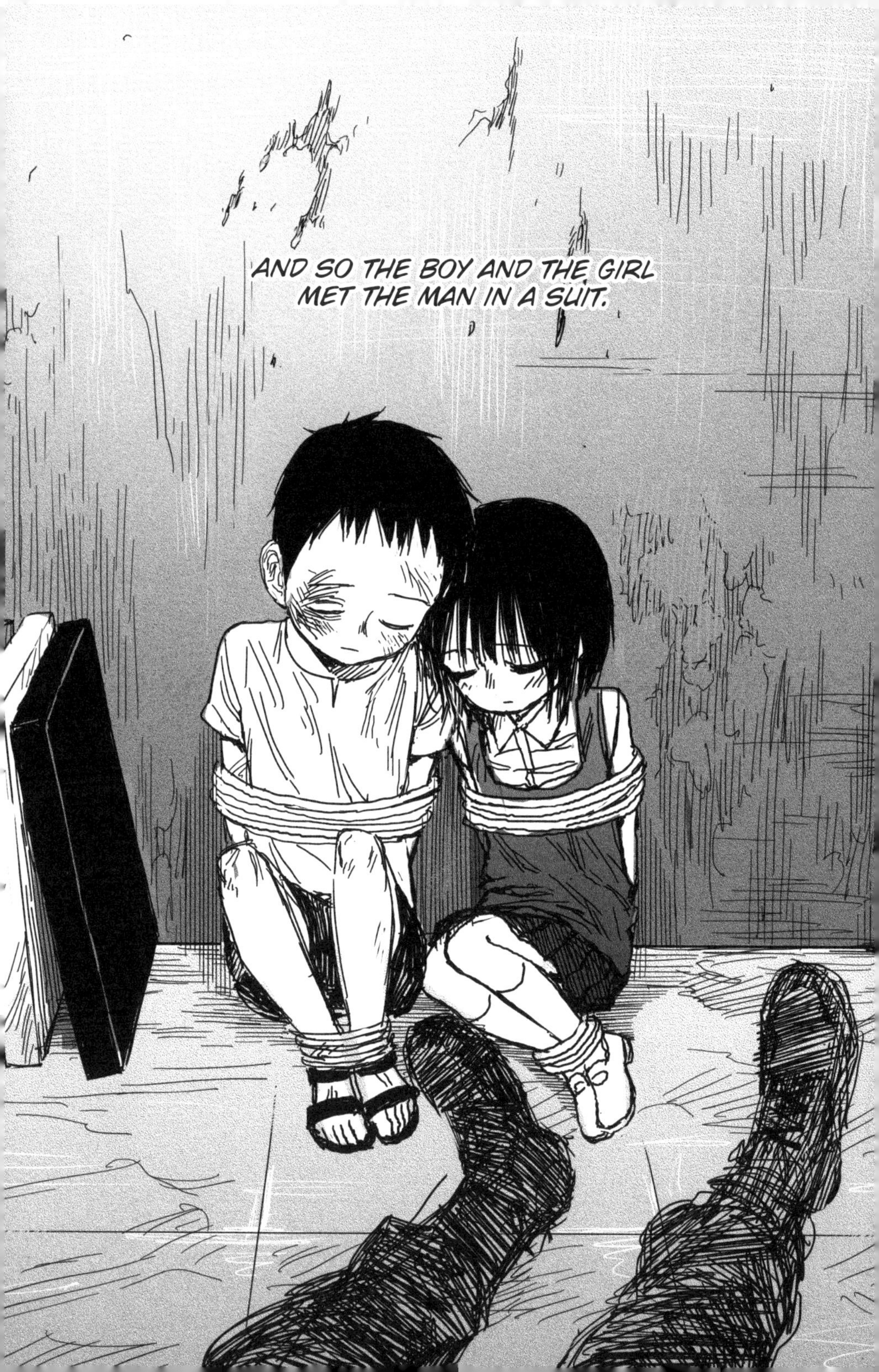
AND SO THE BOY AND THE GIRL MET THE MAN IN A SUIT.

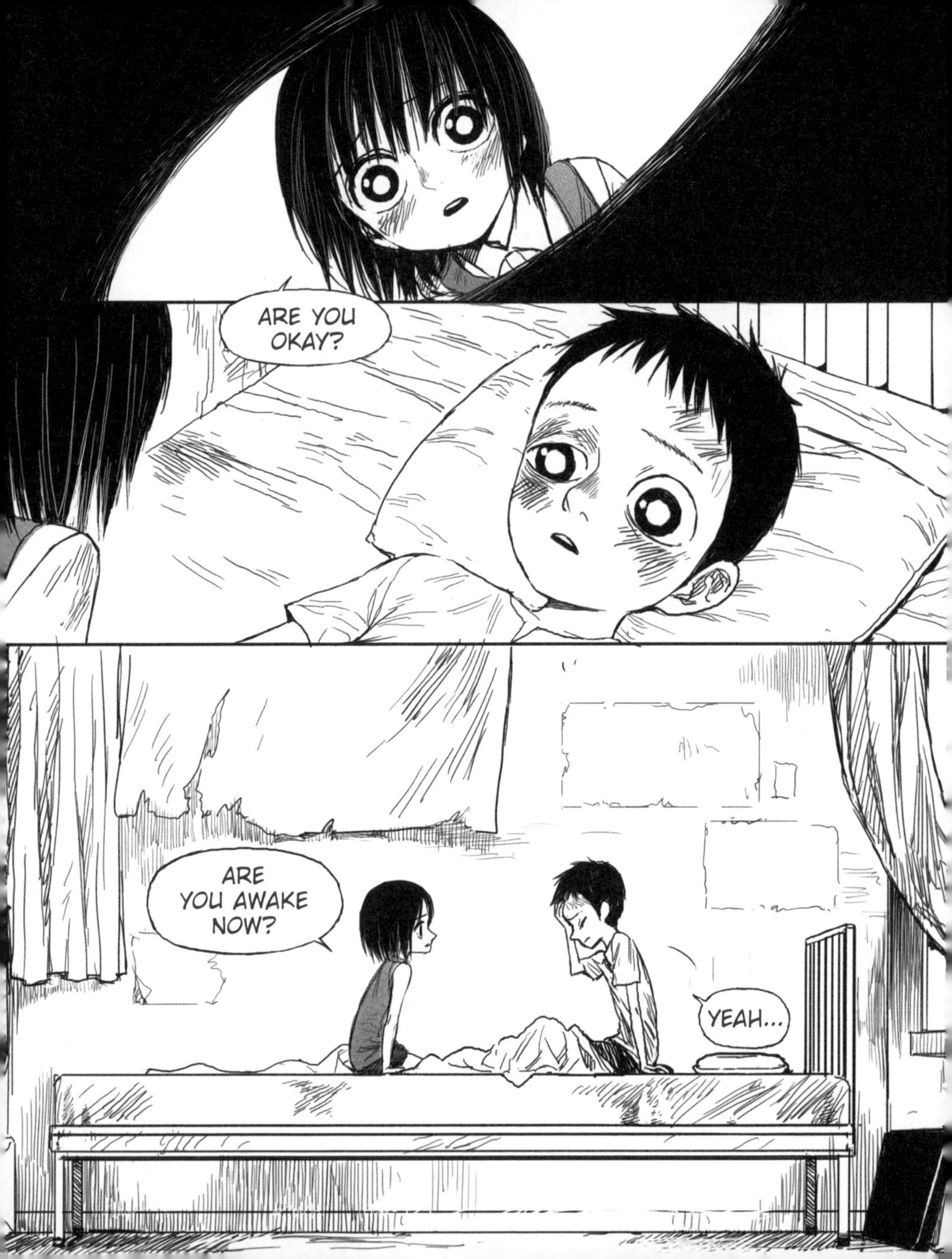
ARE YOU OKAY?
ARE YOU AWAKE NOW?
YEAH...

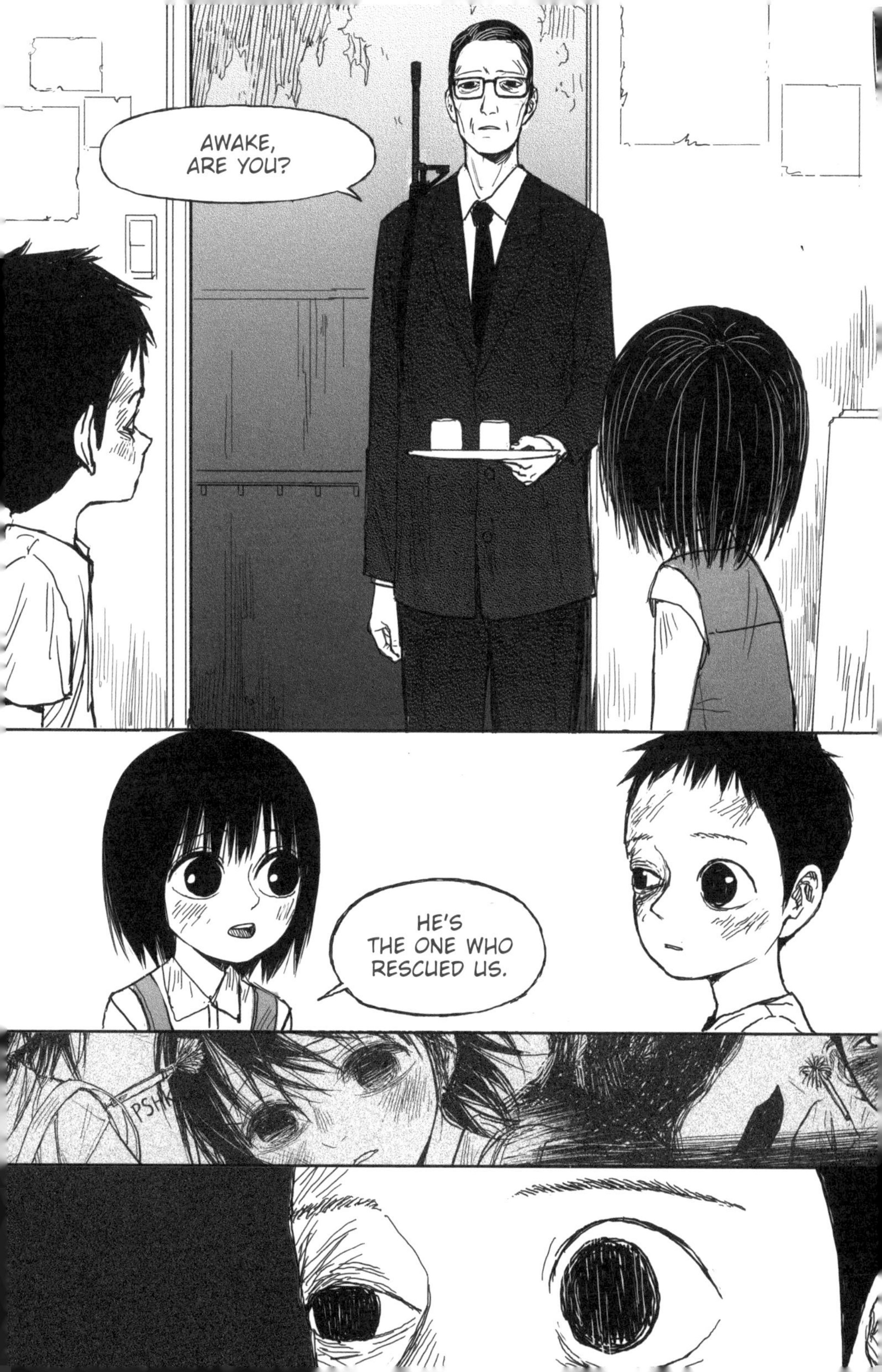
AWAKE, ARE YOU?
HE'S THE ONE WHO RESCUED US.

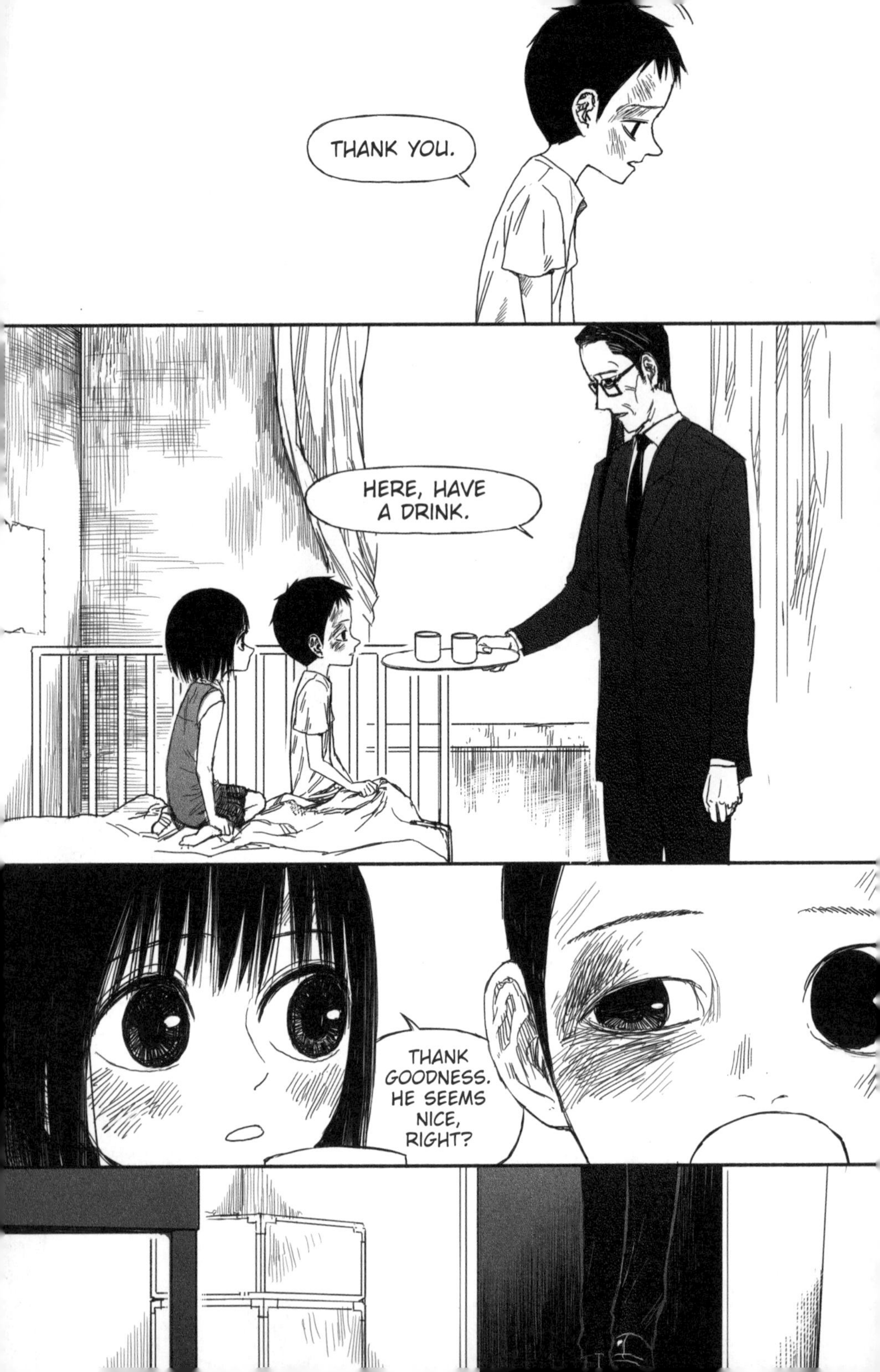
THANK YOU.
HERE, HAVE A DRINK.
THANK GOODNESS. HE SEEMS NICE, RIGHT?

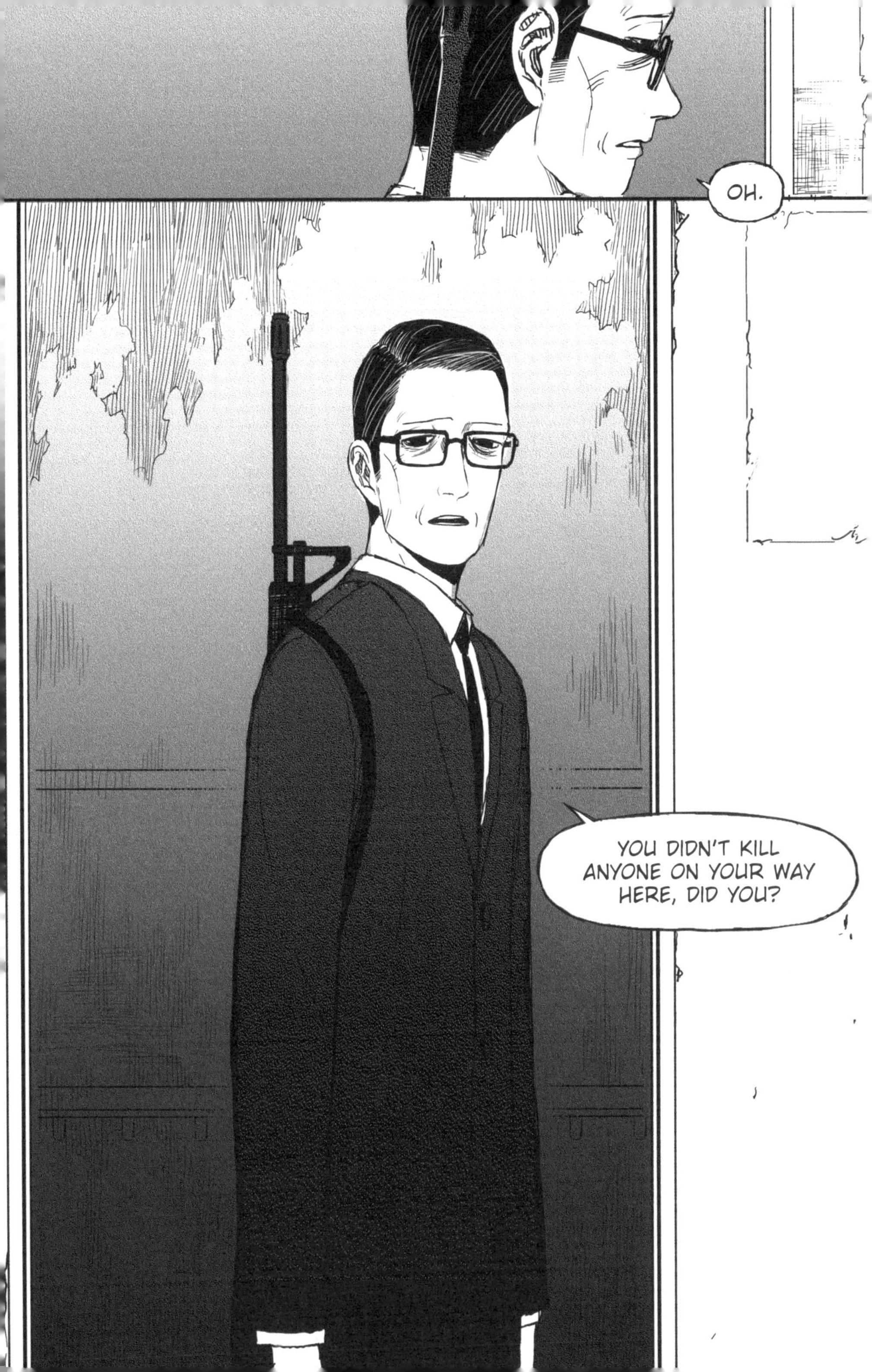
OH.
YOU DIDN'T KILL ANYONE ON YOUR WAY HERE, DID YOU?

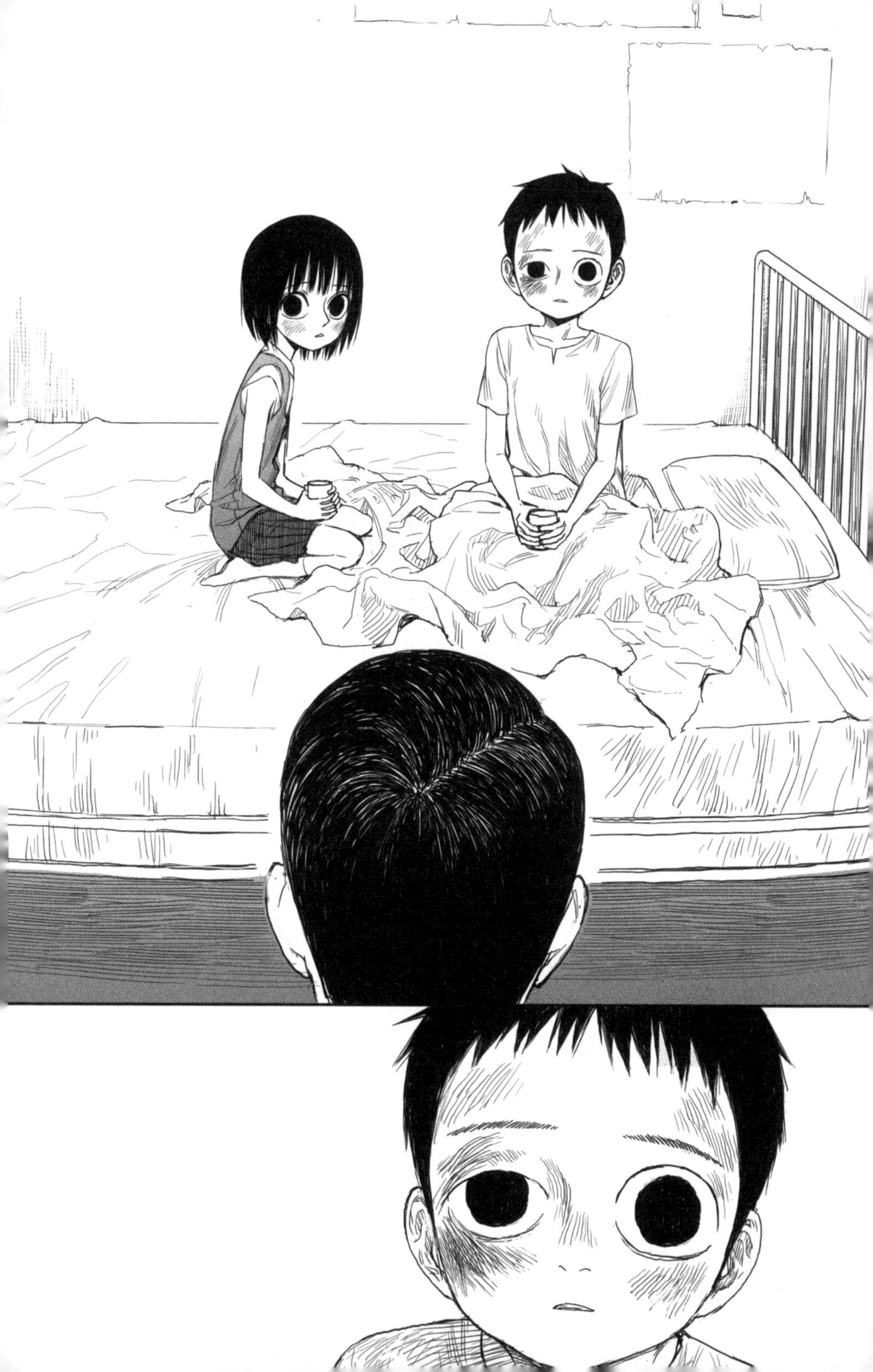

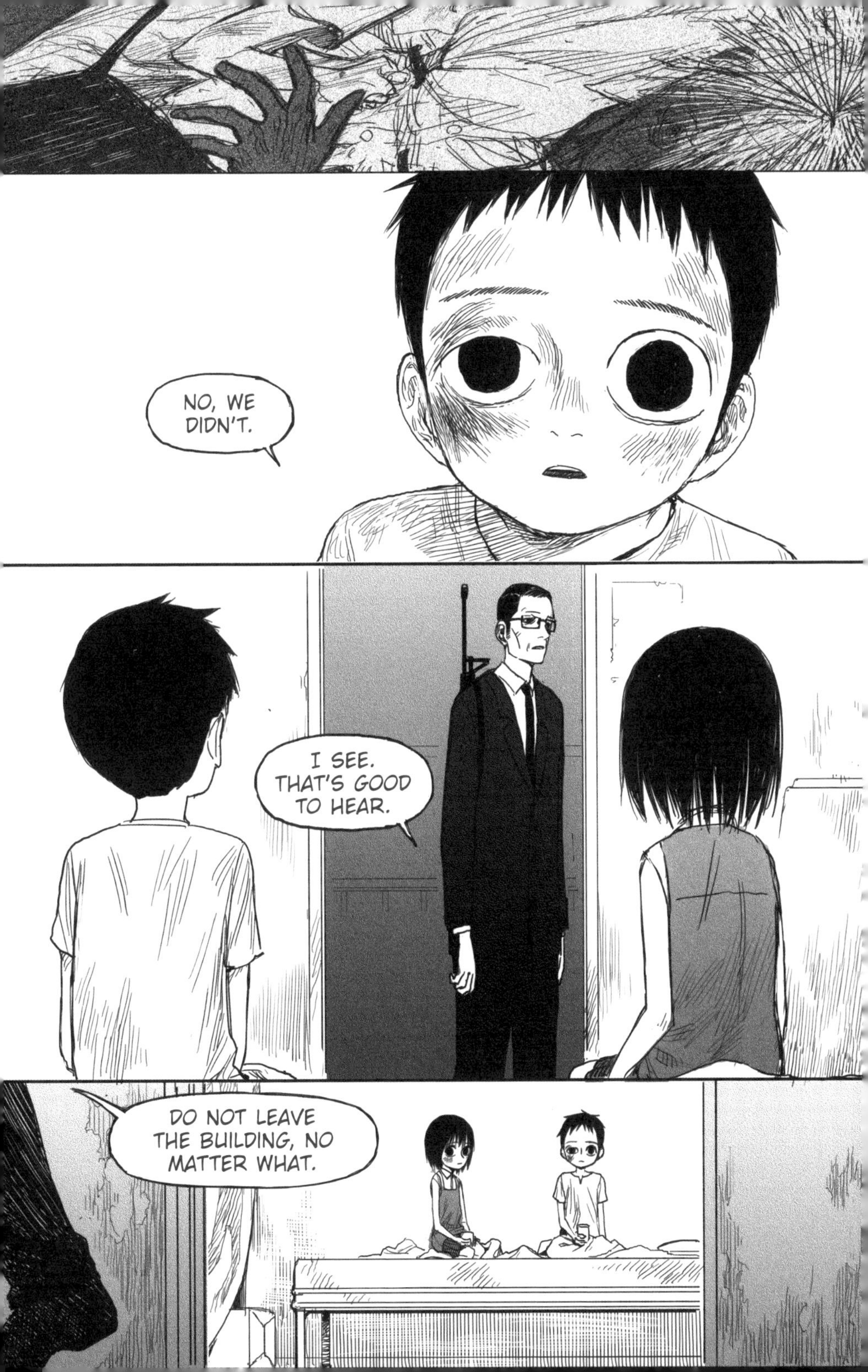
NO, WE DIDN'T.
I SEE. THAT'S GOOD TO HEAR.
DO NOT LEAVE THE BUILDING, NO MATTER WHAT.

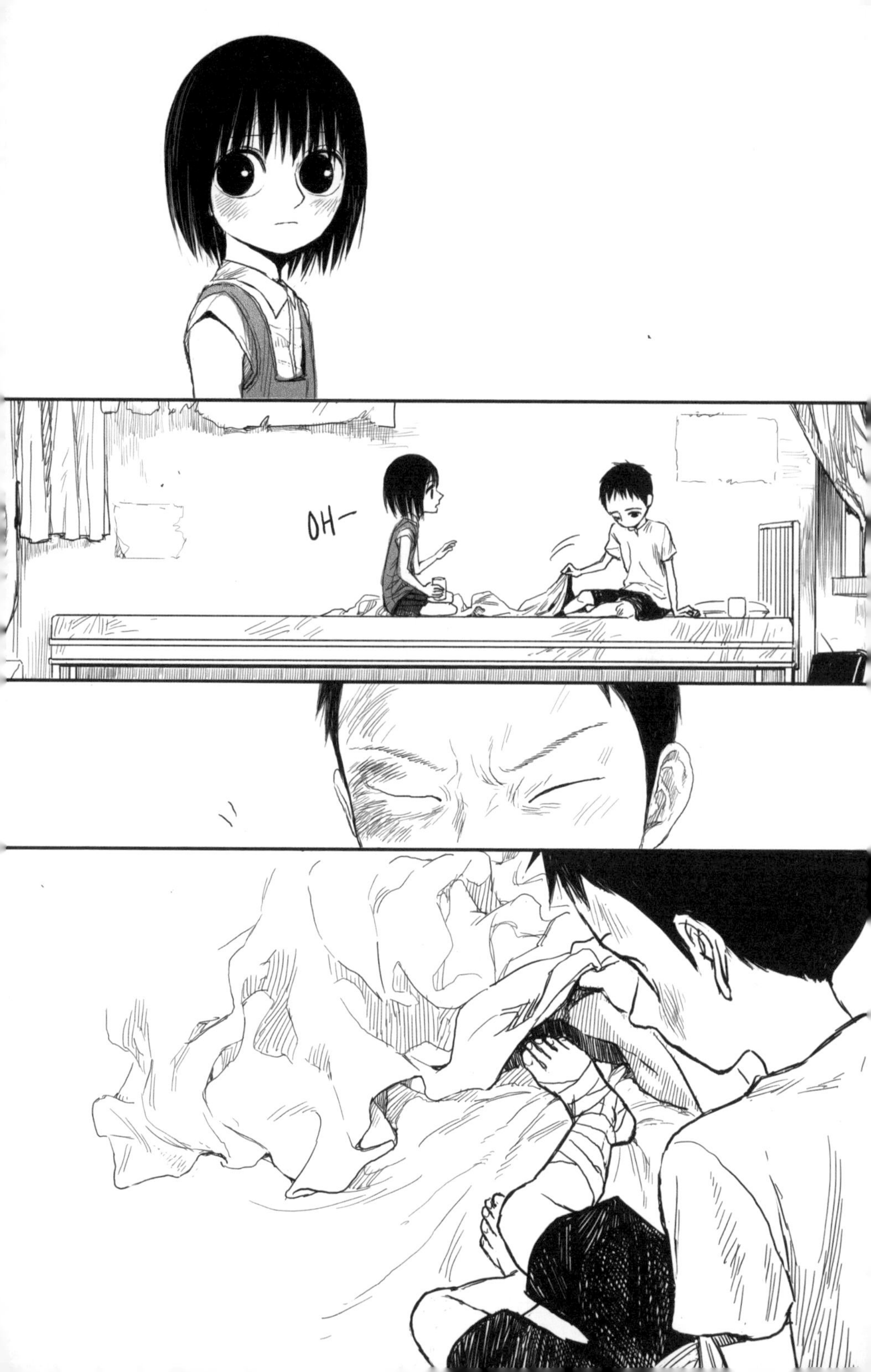
OH–

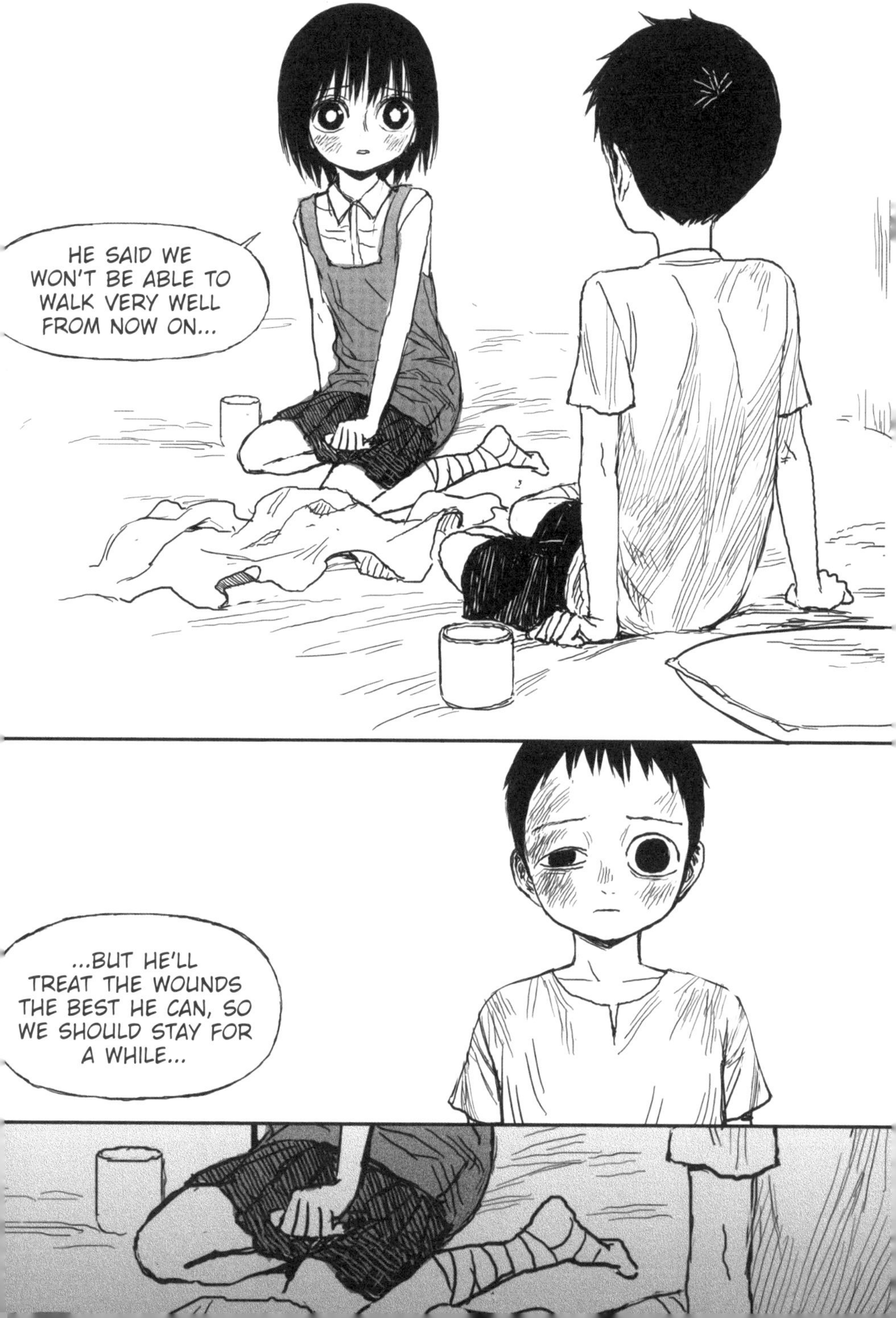
HE SAID WE WON'T BE ABLE TO WALK VERY WELL FROM NOW ON...
...BUT HE'LL TREAT THE WOUNDS THE BEST HE CAN, SO WE SHOULD STAY FOR A WHILE...

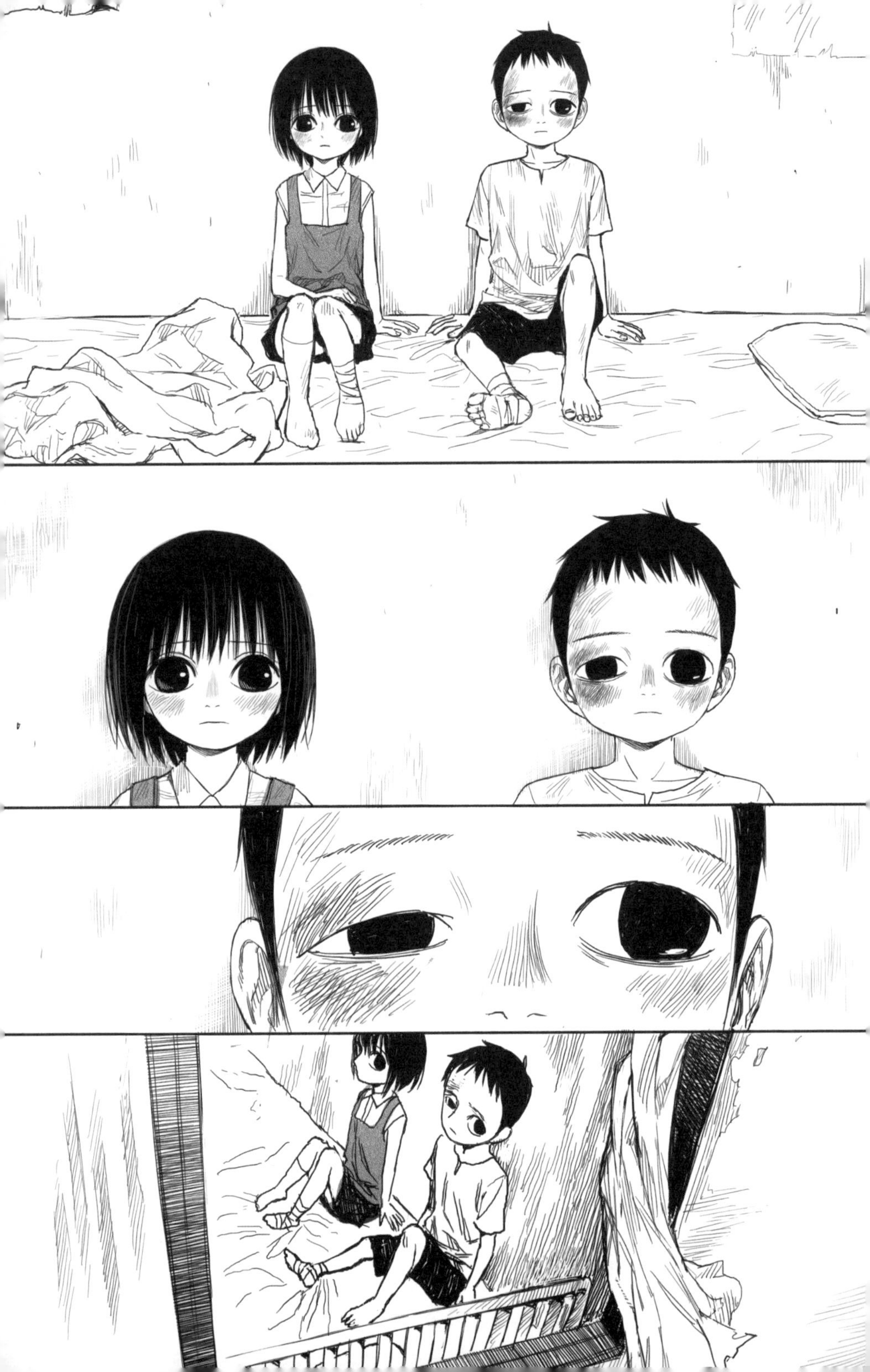

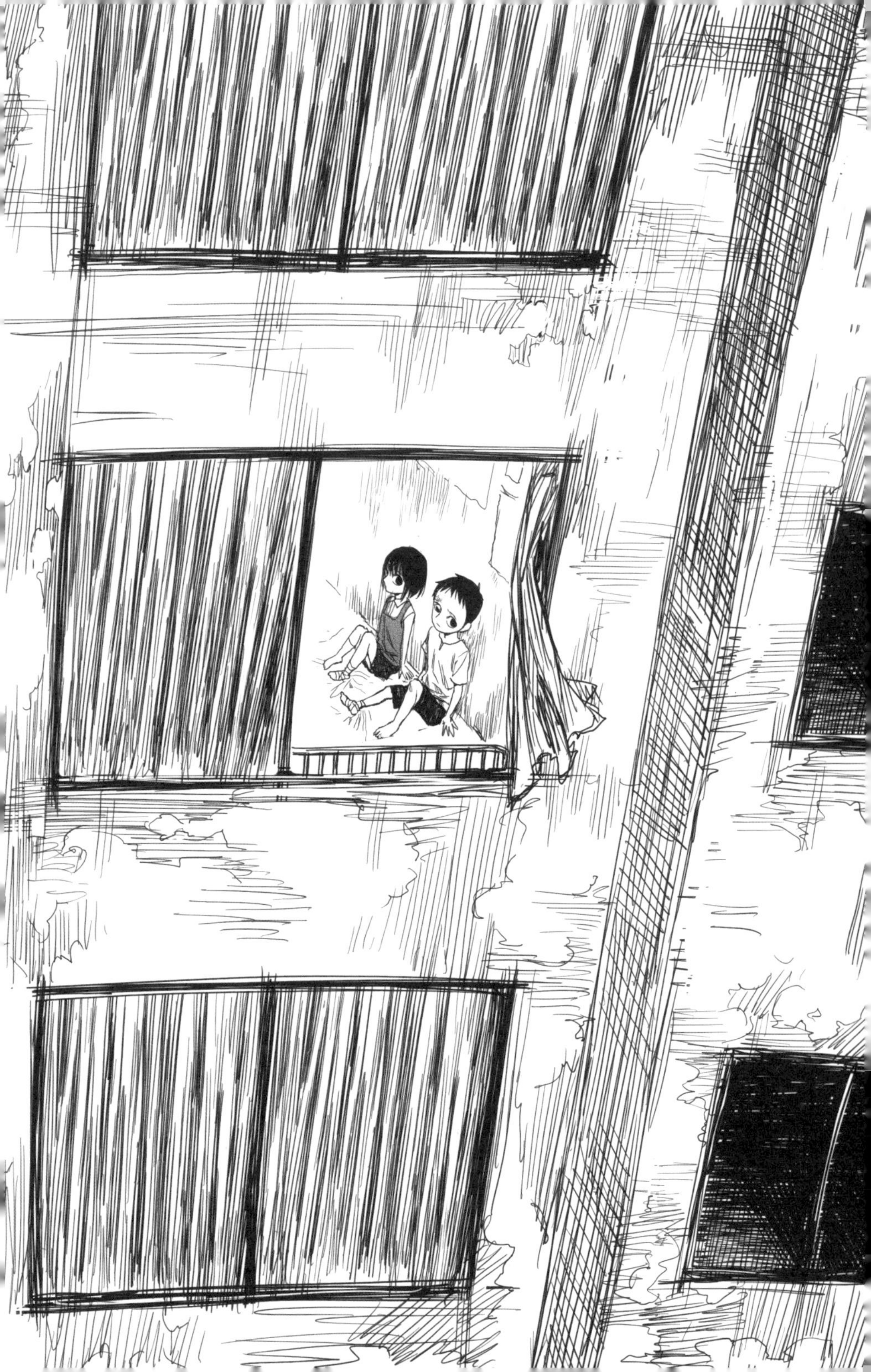

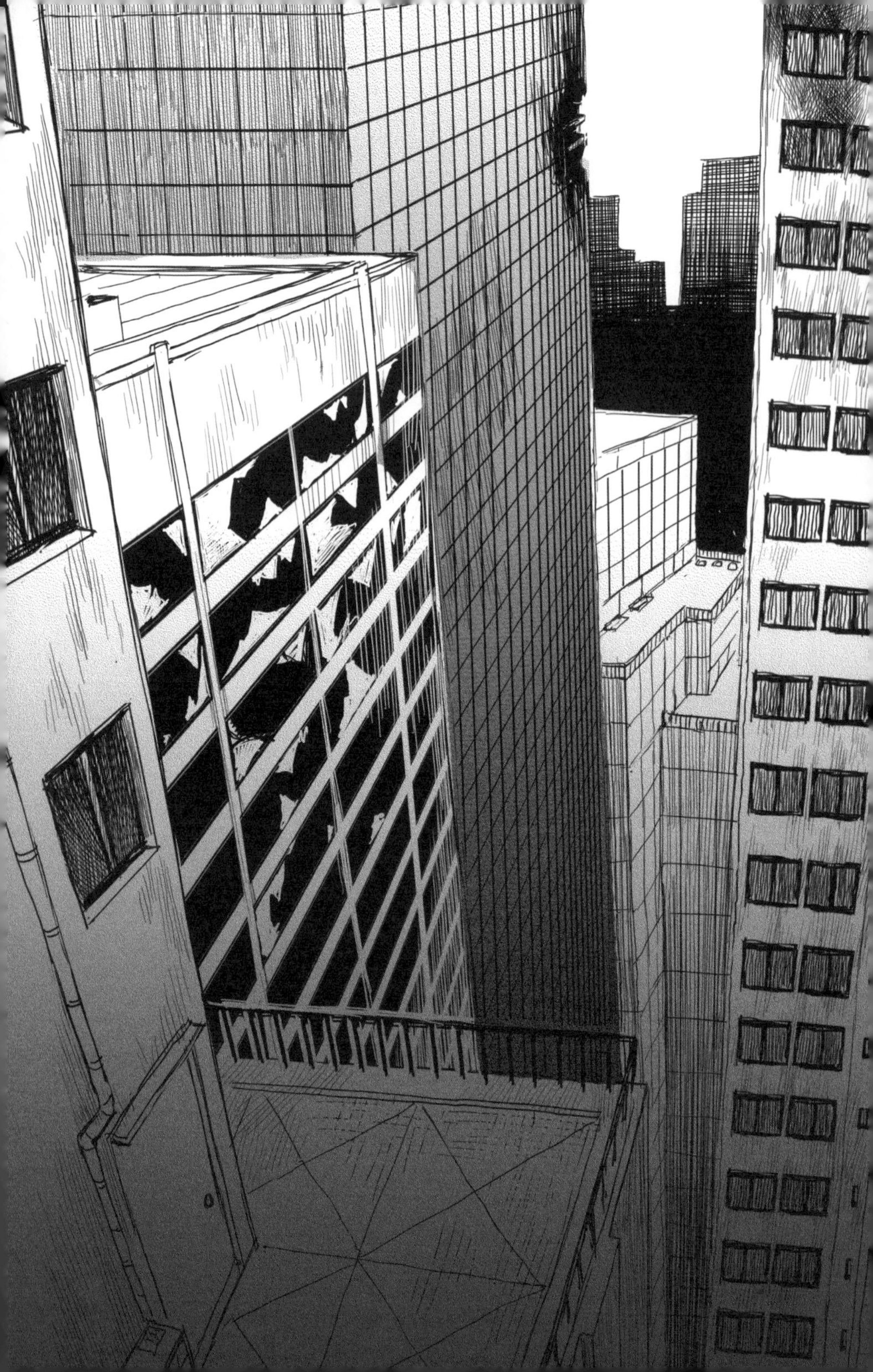

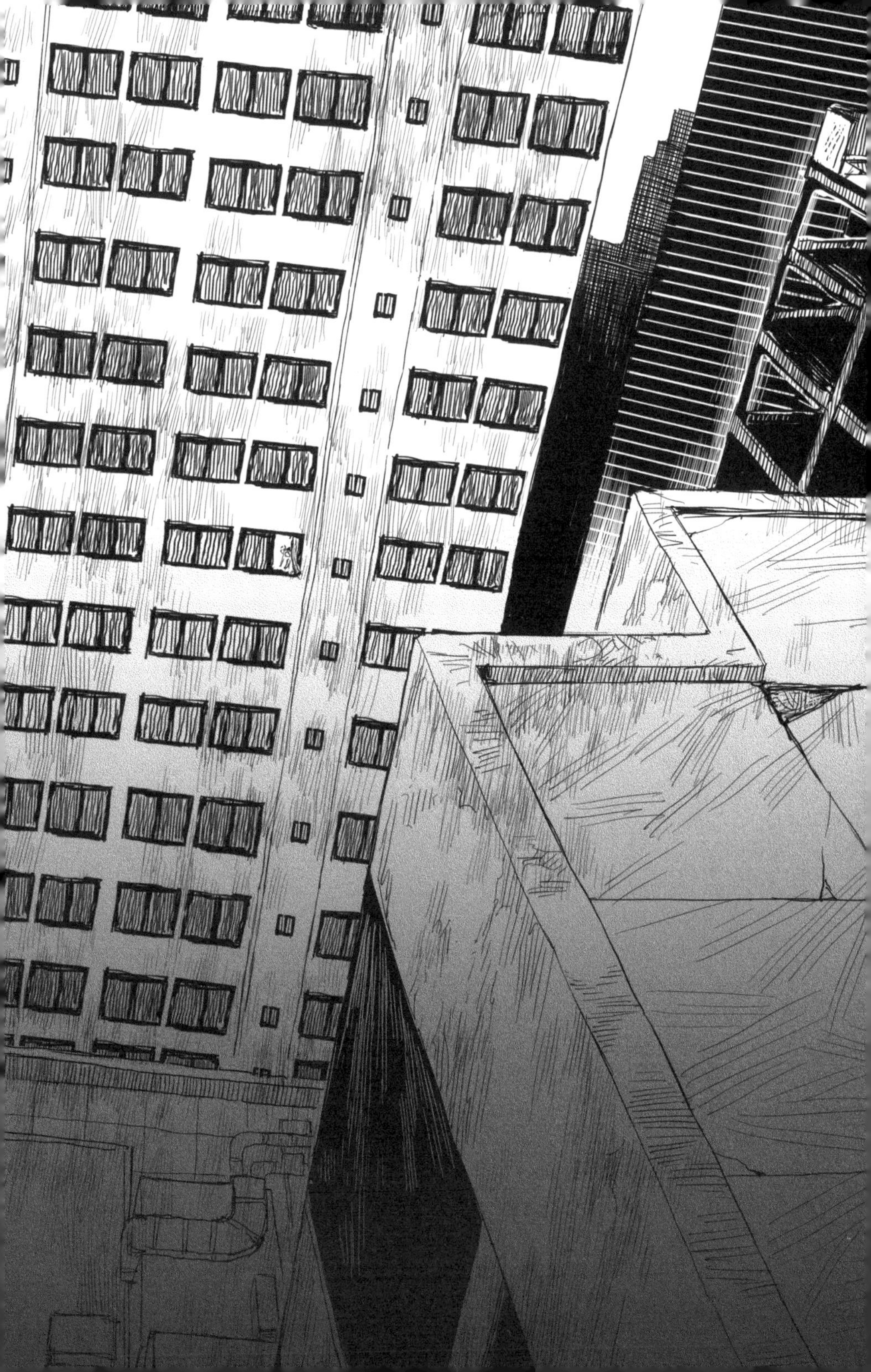

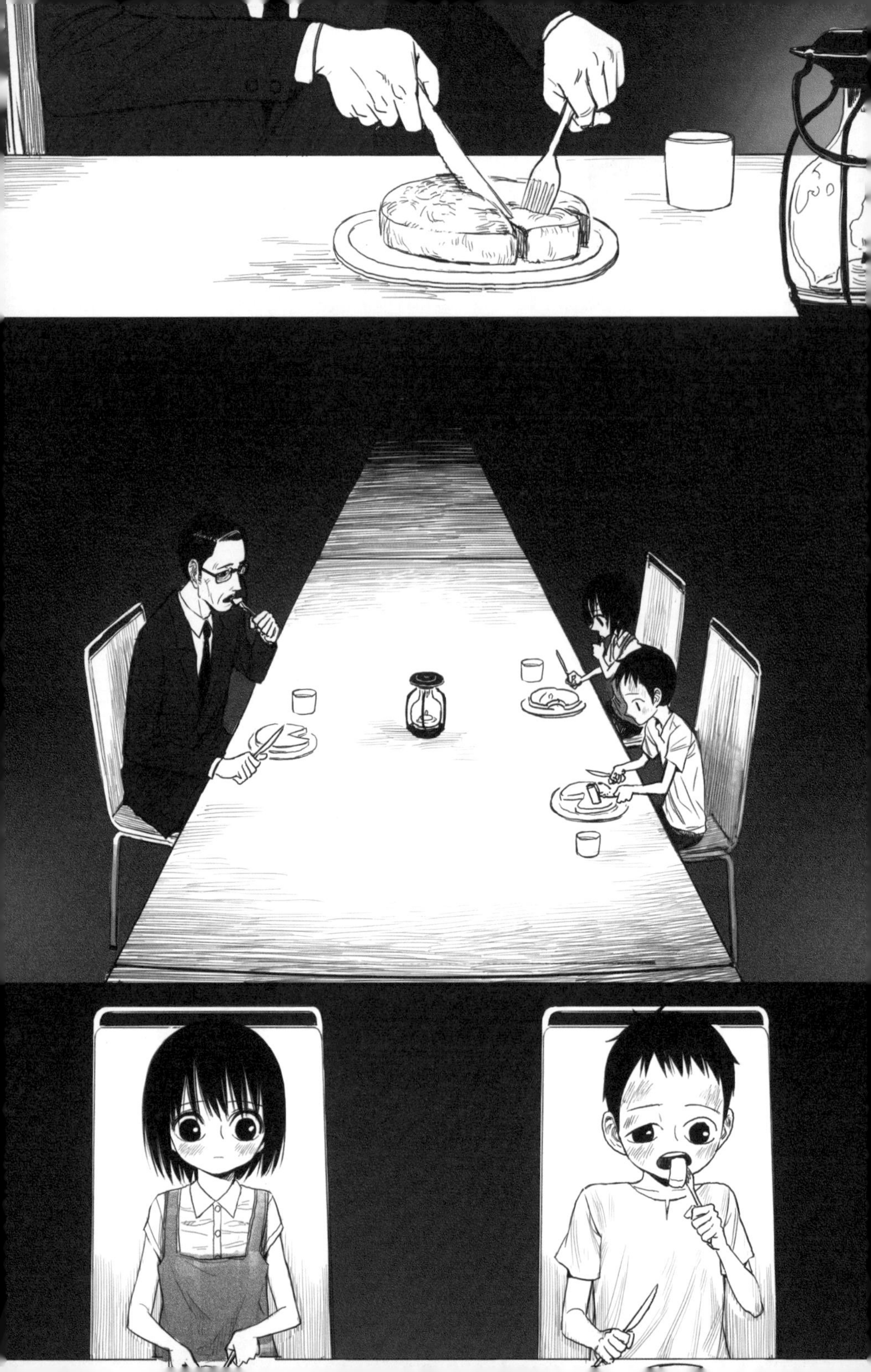

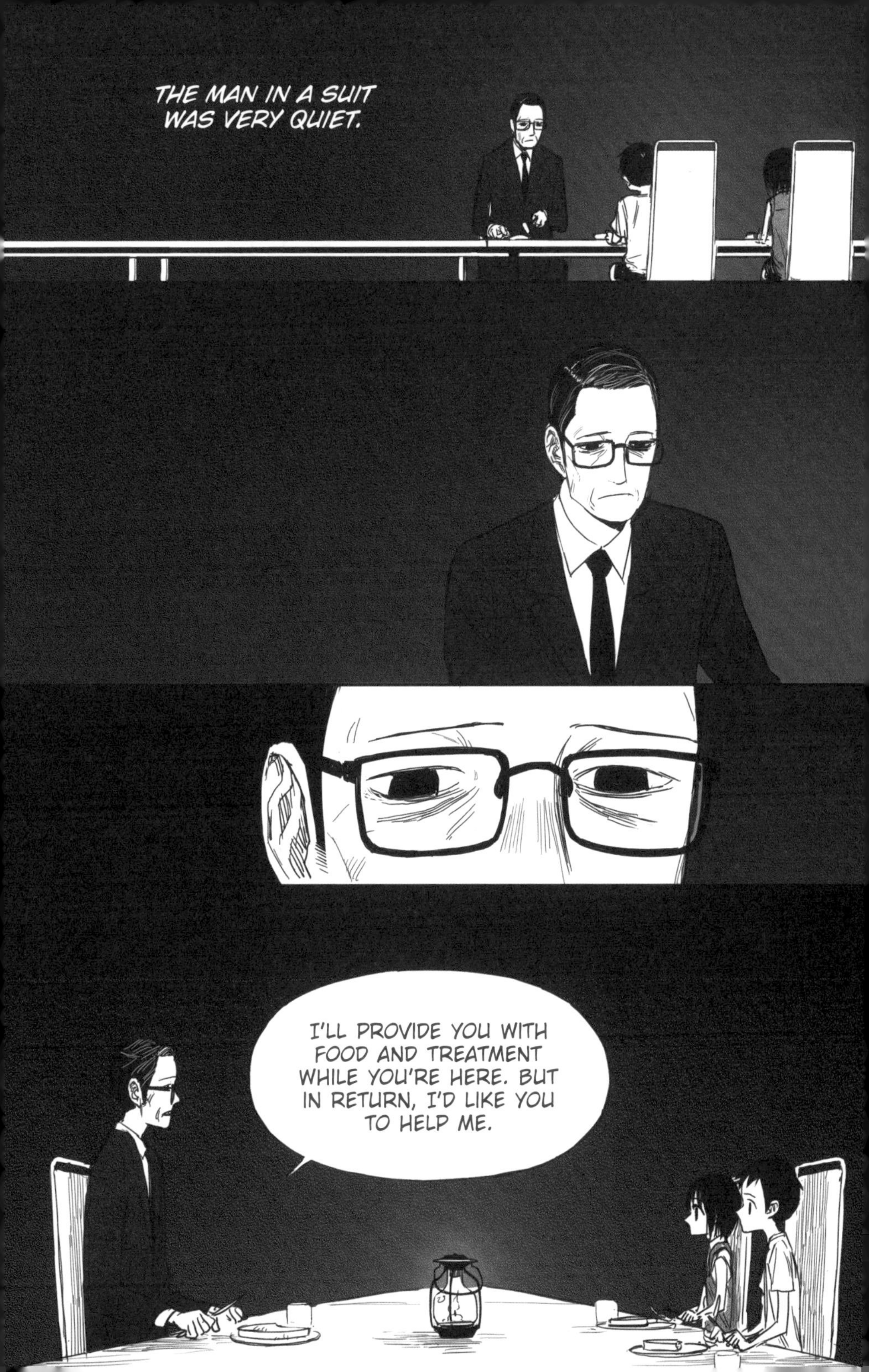
THE MAN IN A SUIT WAS VERY QUIET.
I'LL PROVIDE YOU WITH FOOD AND TREATMENT WHILE YOU'RE HERE. BUT IN RETURN, I'D LIKE YOU TO HELP ME.

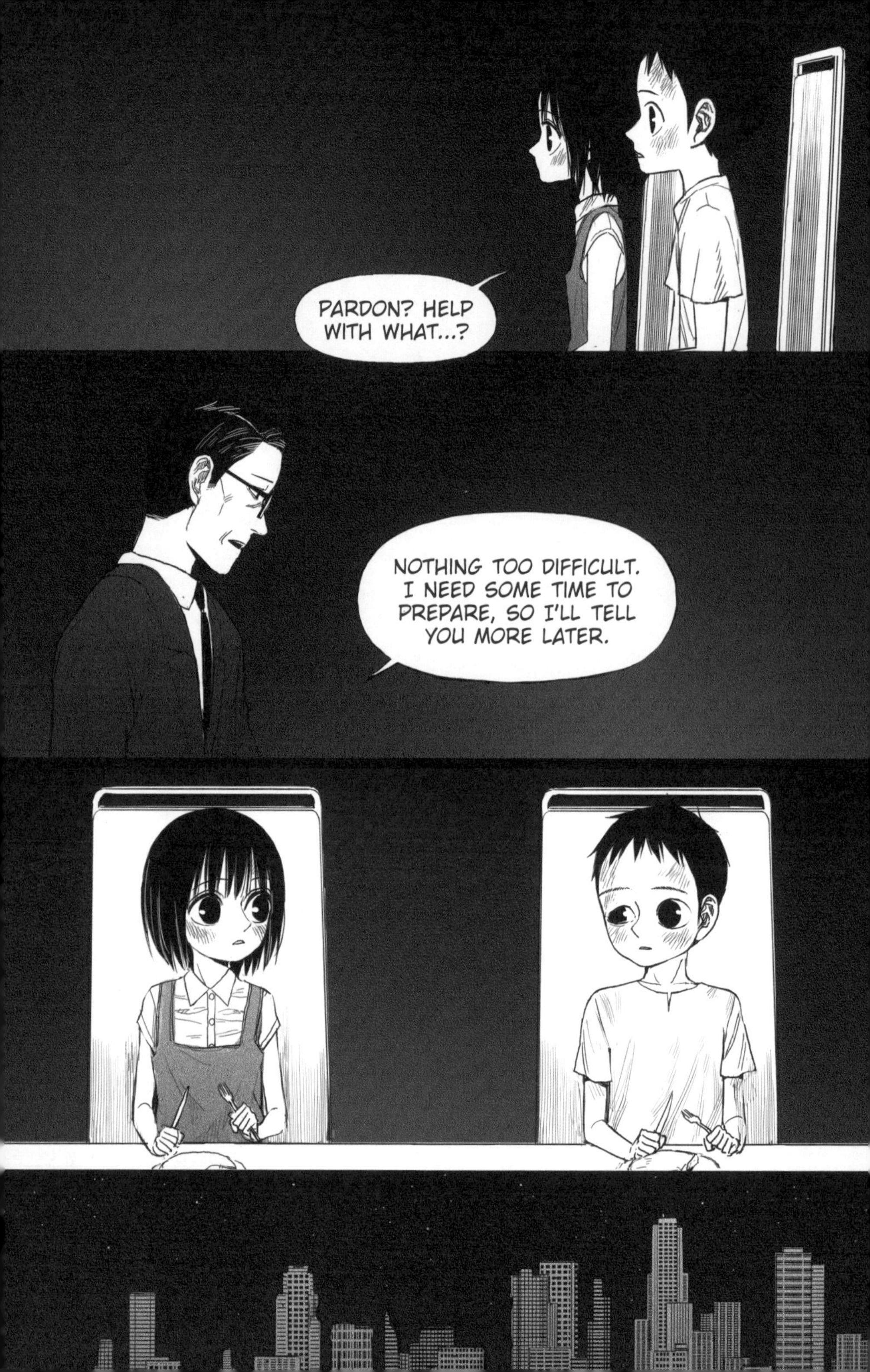
PARDON? HELP WITH WHAT...?
NOTHING TOO DIFFICULT. I NEED SOME TIME TO PREPARE, SO I'LL TELL YOU MORE LATER.

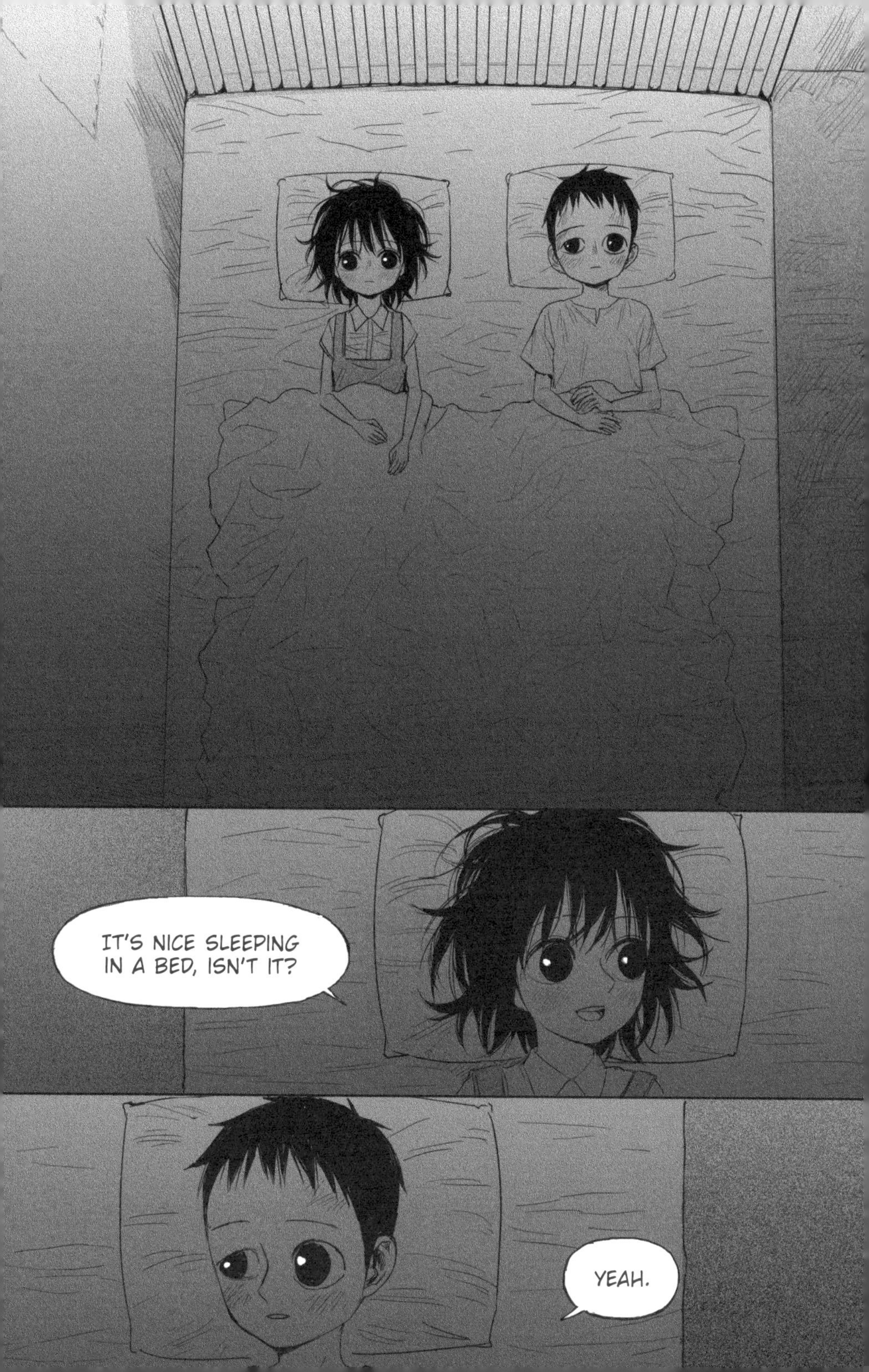
IT'S NICE SLEEPING IN A BED, ISN'T IT?
YEAH.

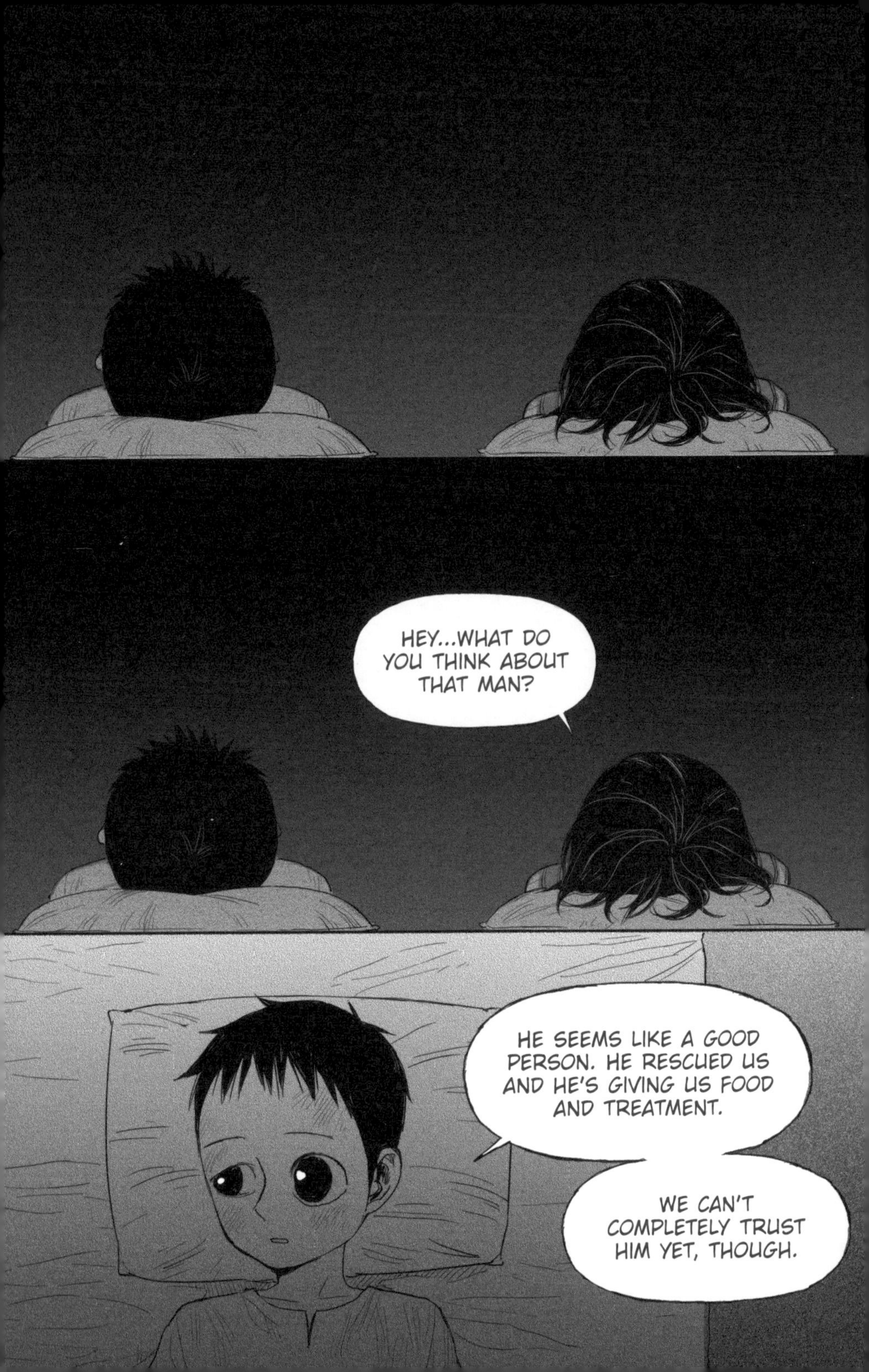
HEY...WHAT DO YOU THINK ABOUT THAT MAN?
HE SEEMS LIKE A GOOD PERSON. HE RESCUED US AND HE'S GIVING US FOOD AND TREATMENT.
WE CAN'T COMPLETELY TRUST HIM YET, THOUGH.

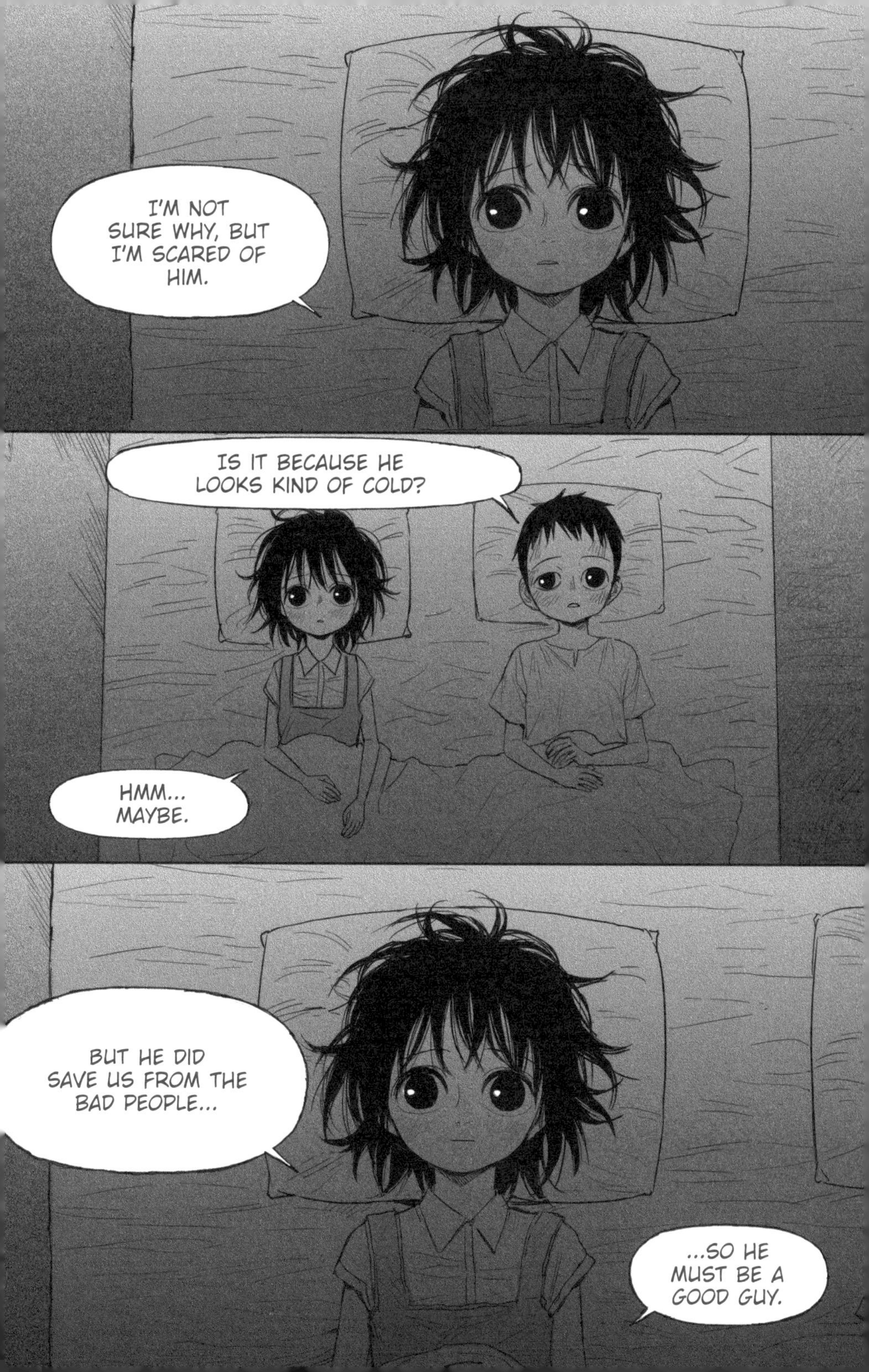
I'M NOT SURE WHY, BUT I'M SCARED OF HIM.
IS IT BECAUSE HE LOOKS KIND OF COLD?
HMM... MAYBE.
BUT HE DID SAVE US FROM THE BAD PEOPLE...
...SO HE MUST BE A GOOD GUY.

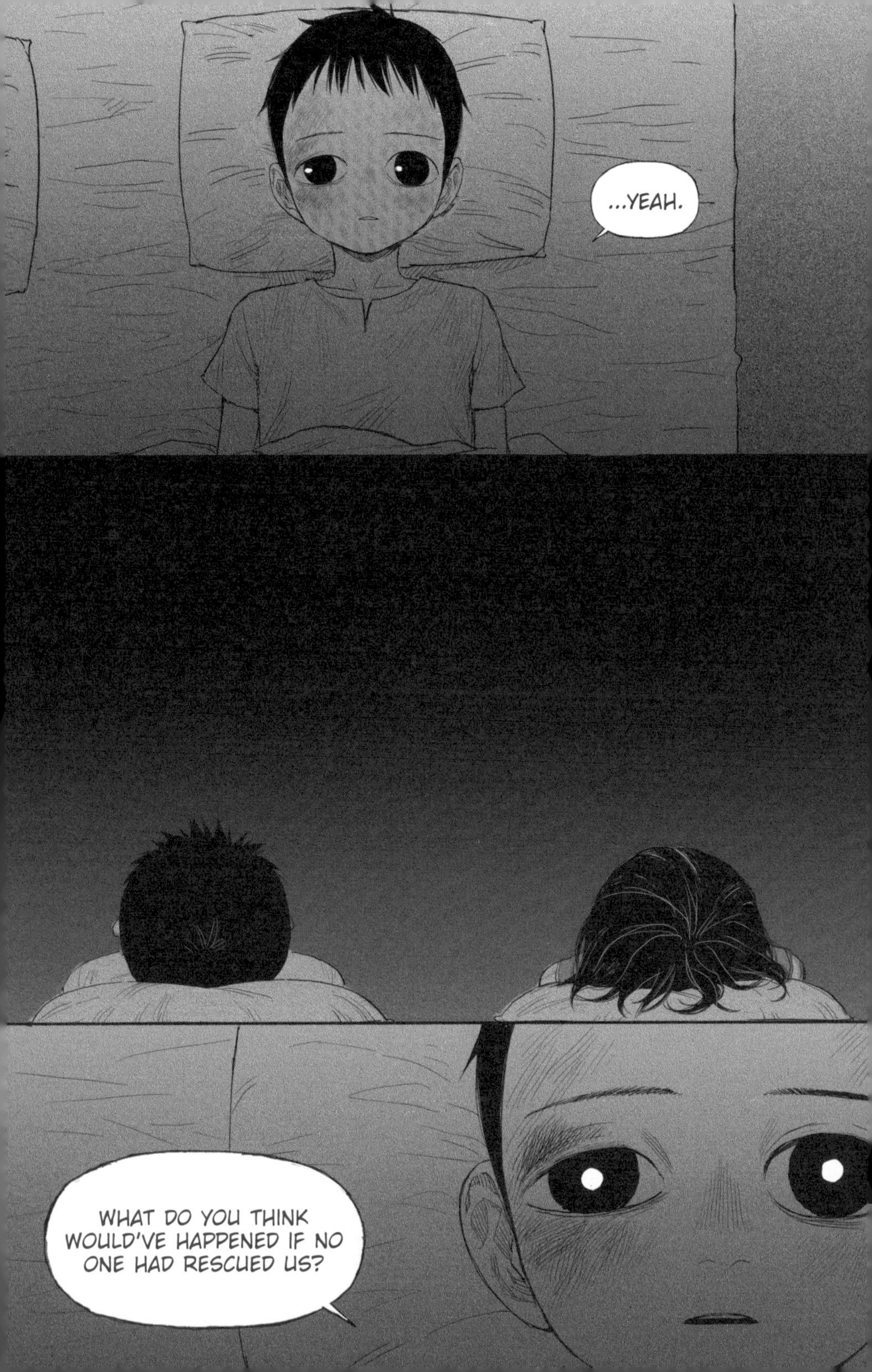
...YEAH.
WHAT DO YOU THINK WOULD'VE HAPPENED IF NO ONE HAD RESCUED US?

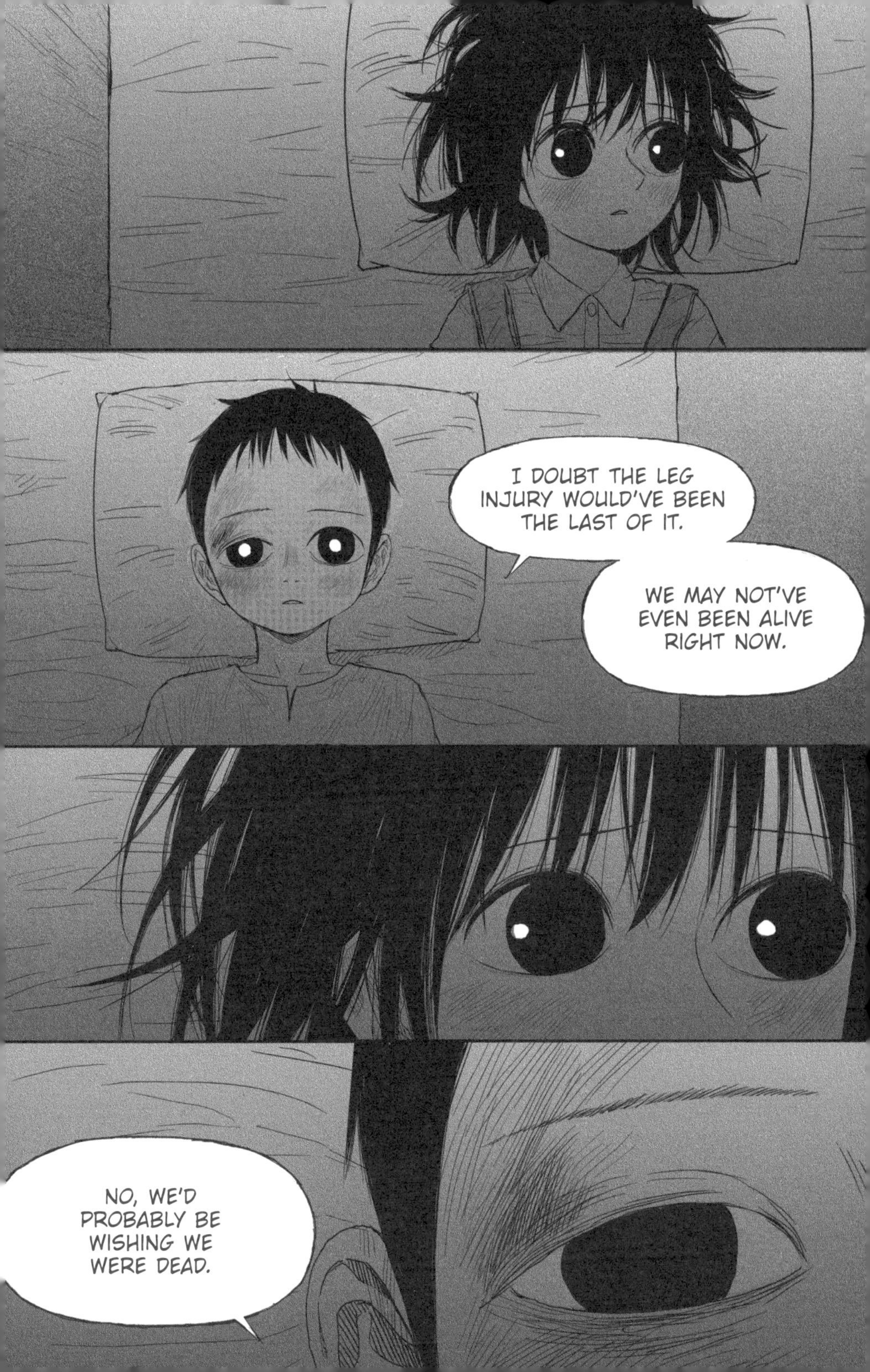
I DOUBT THE LEG INJURY WOULD'VE BEEN THE LAST OF IT.
WE MAY NOT'VE EVEN BEEN ALIVE RIGHT NOW.
NO, WE'D PROBABLY BE WISHING WE WERE DEAD.

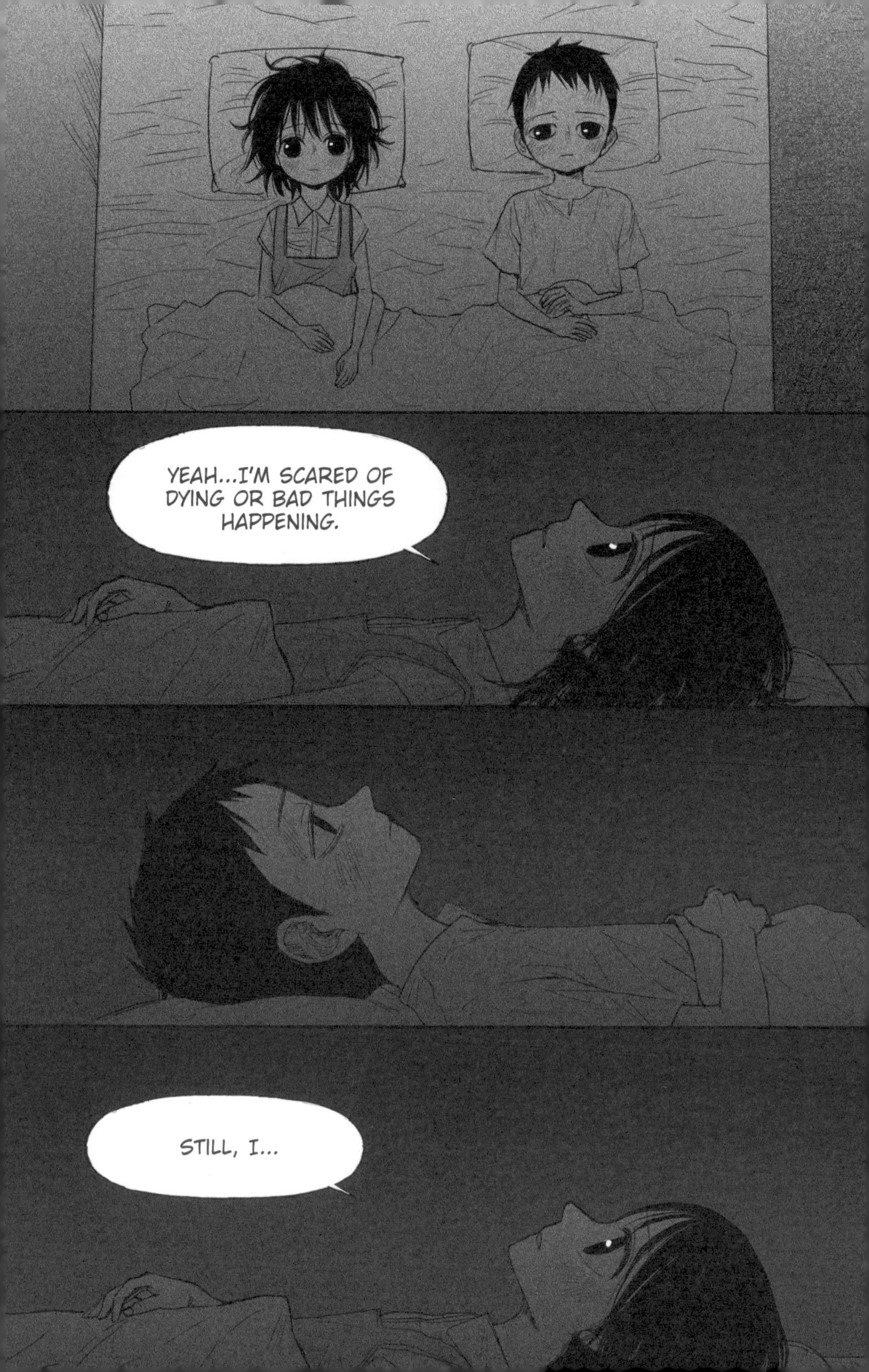
YEAH...I'M SCARED OF DYING OR BAD THINGS HAPPENING.
STILL, I...

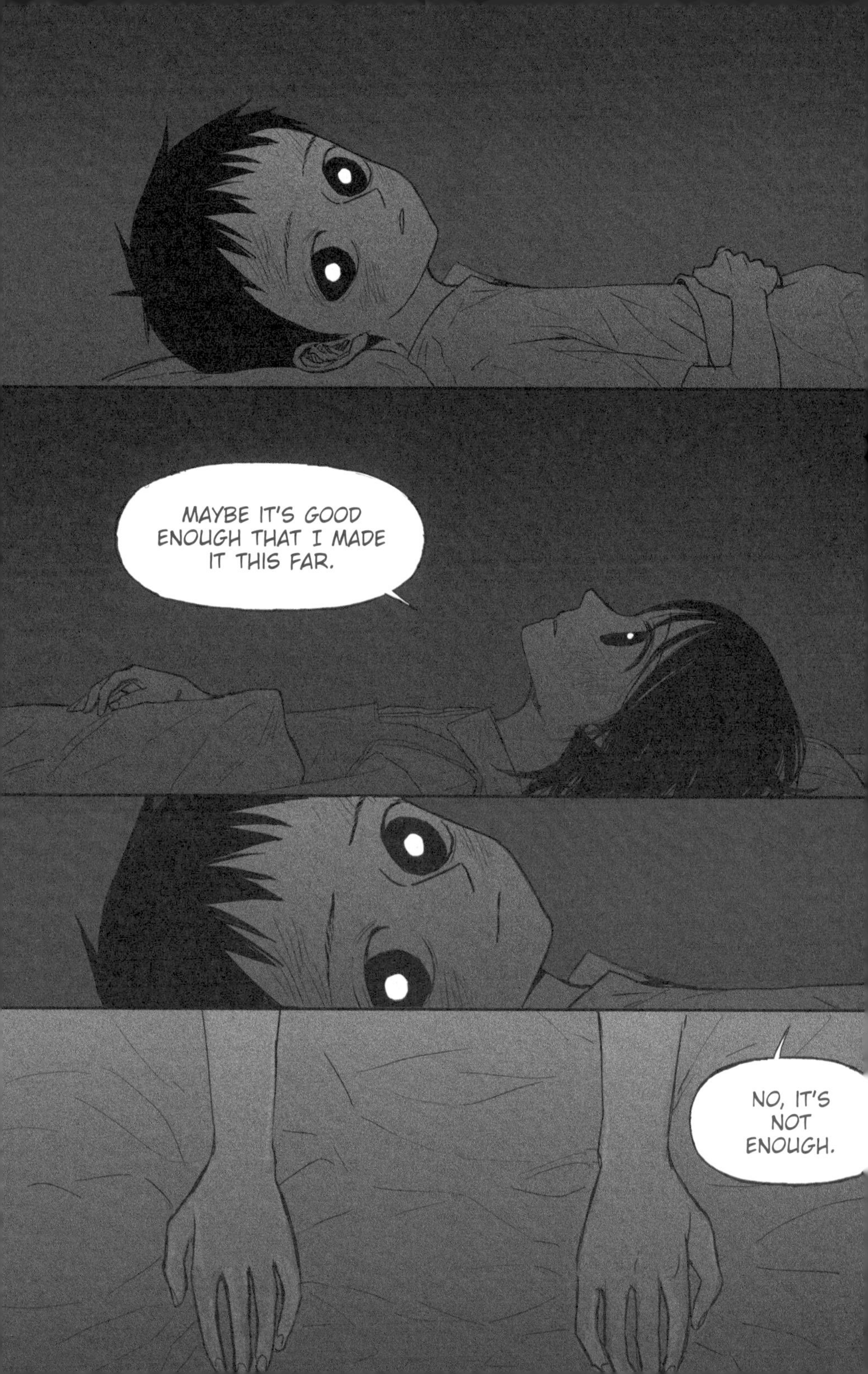
MAYBE IT'S GOOD ENOUGH THAT I MADE IT THIS FAR.
NO, IT'S NOT ENOUGH.

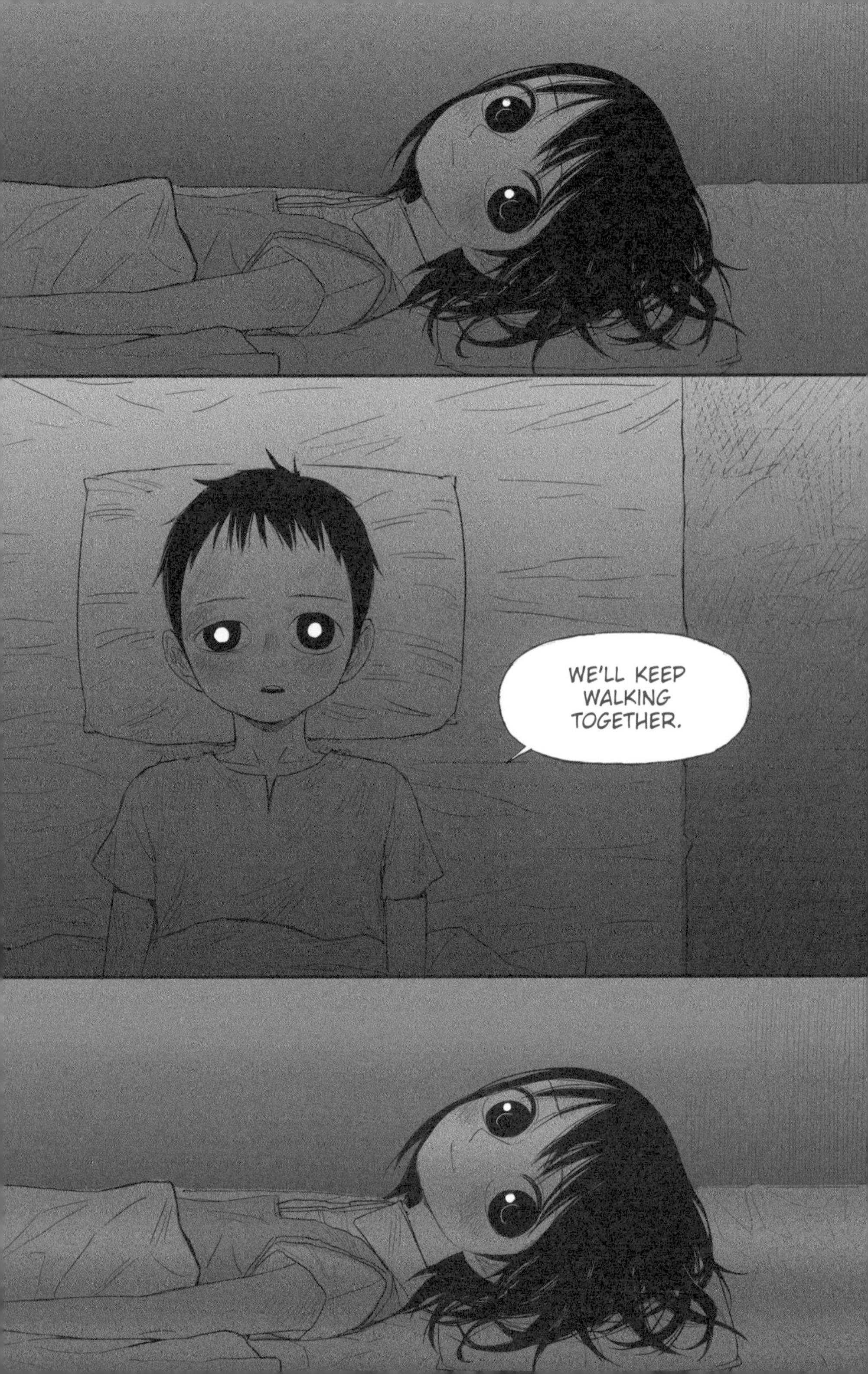
WE'LL KEEP WALKING TOGETHER.

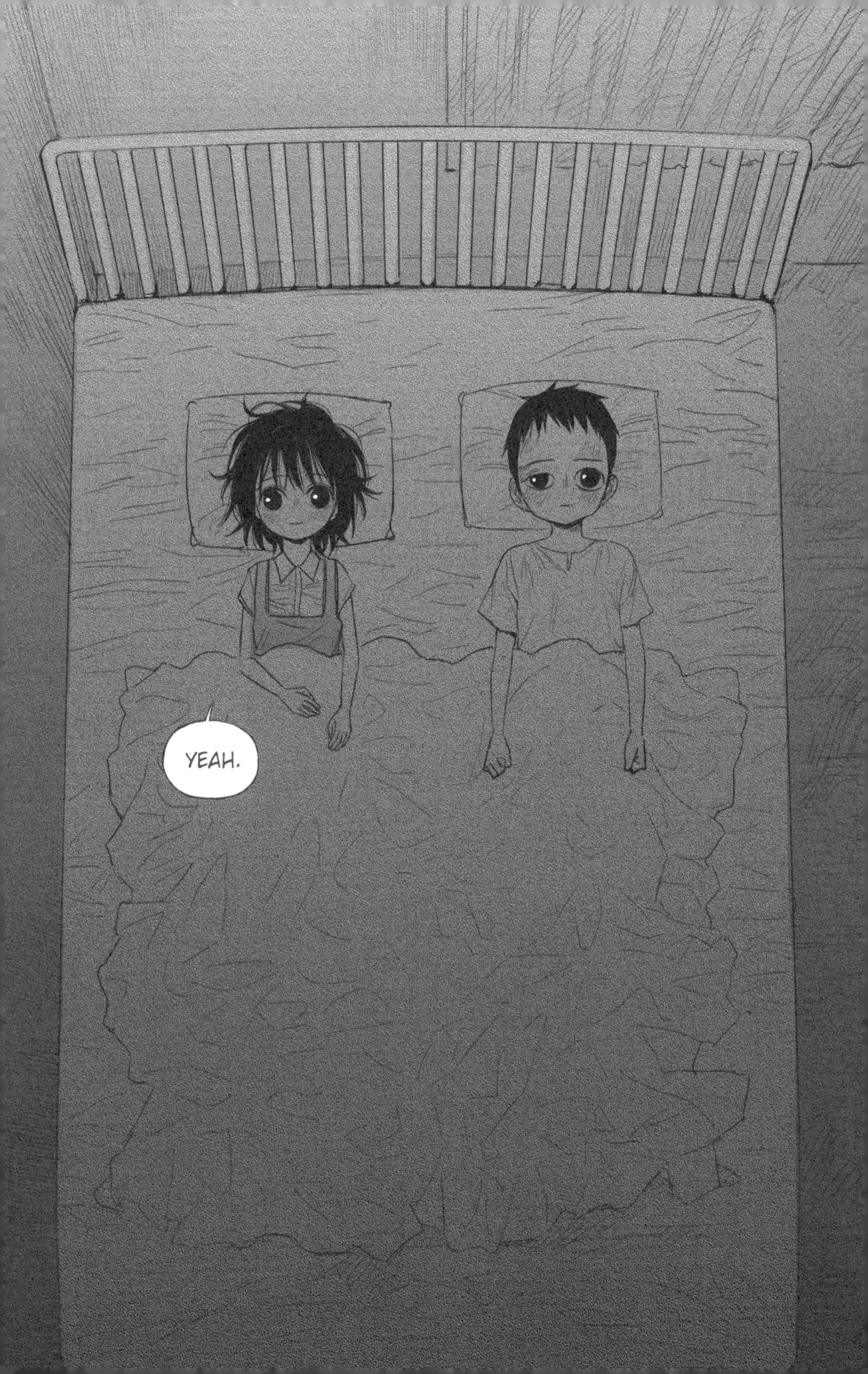
YEAH.

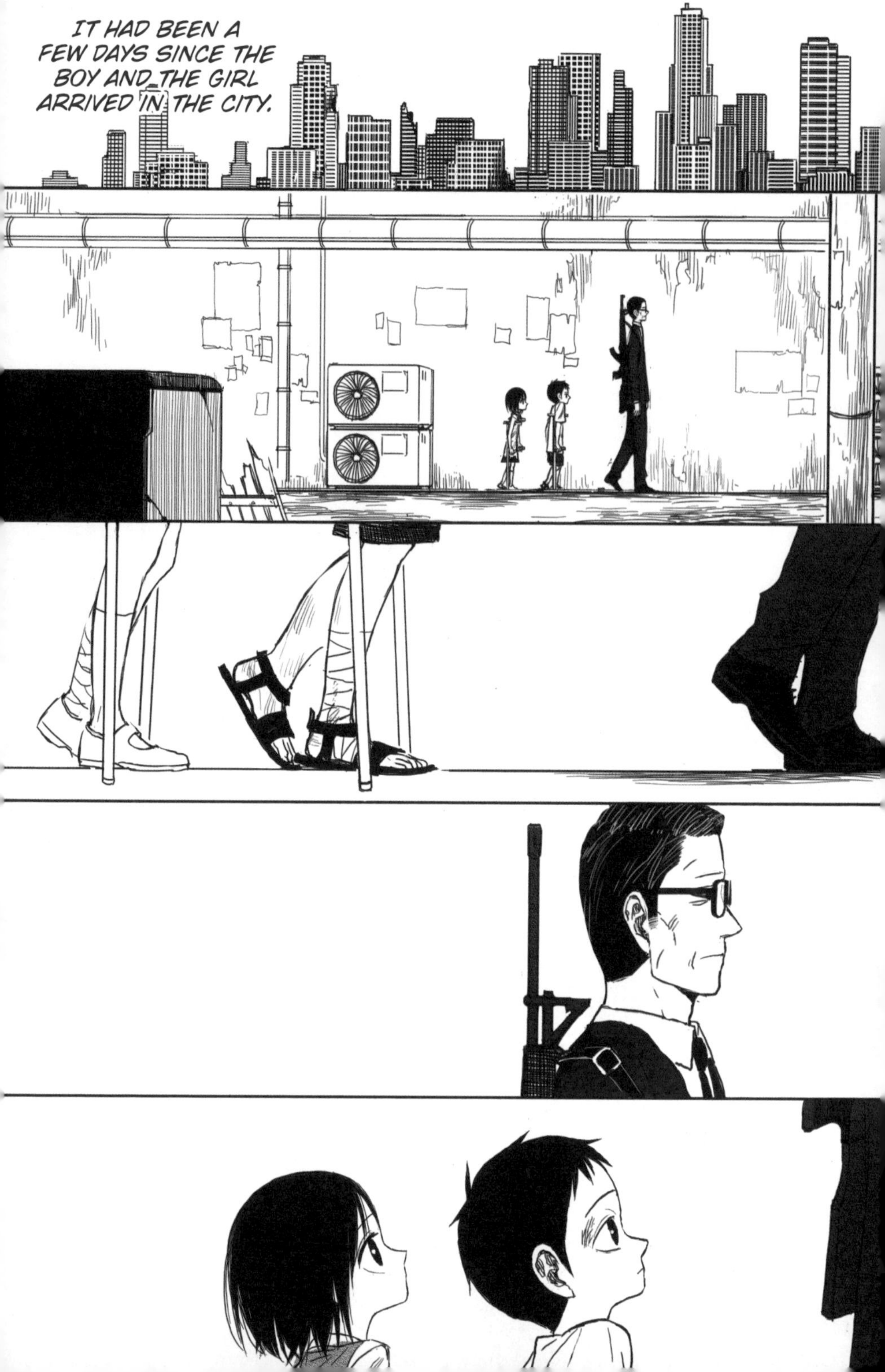
IT HAD BEEN A FEW DAYS SINCE THE BOY AND THE GIRL ARRIVED IN THE CITY.

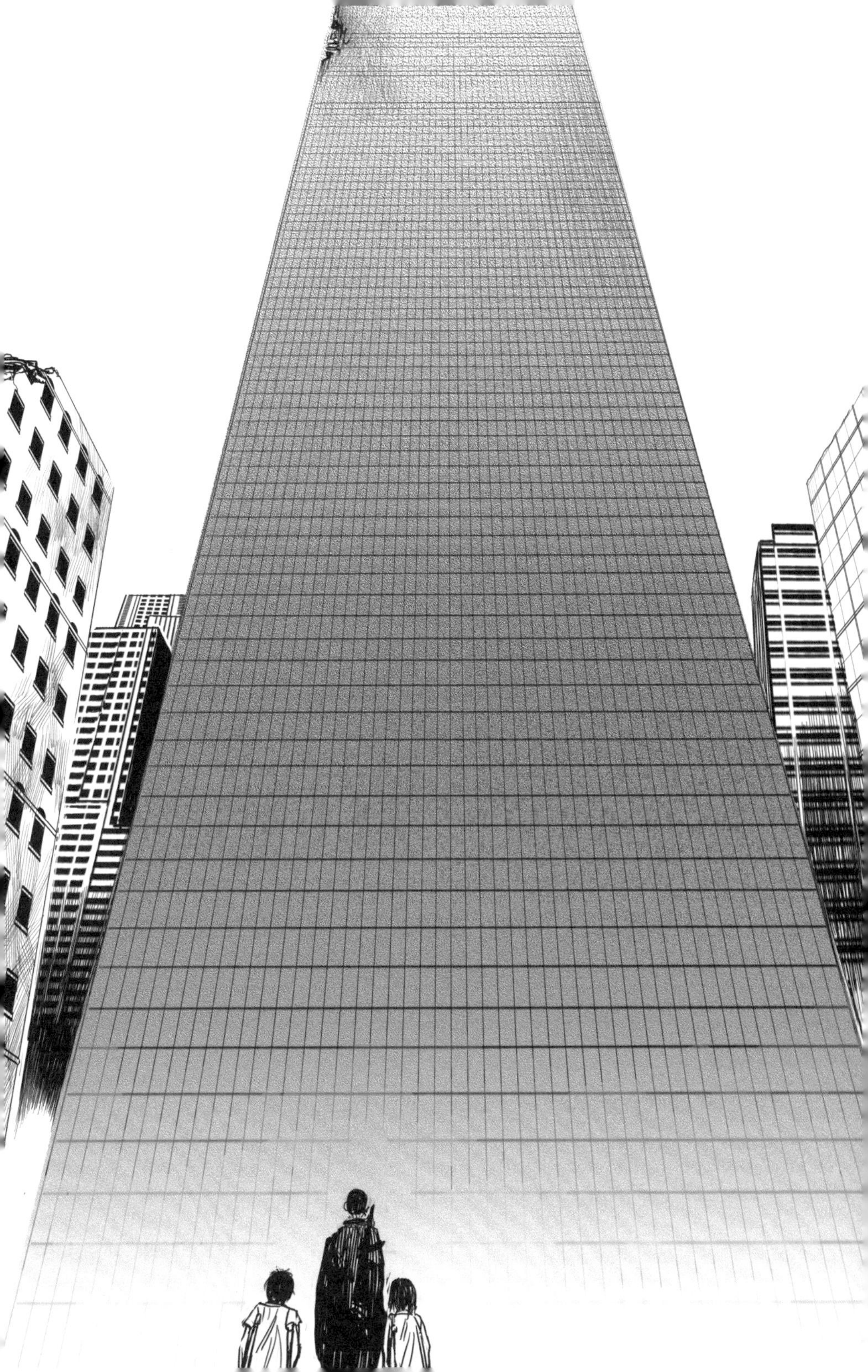

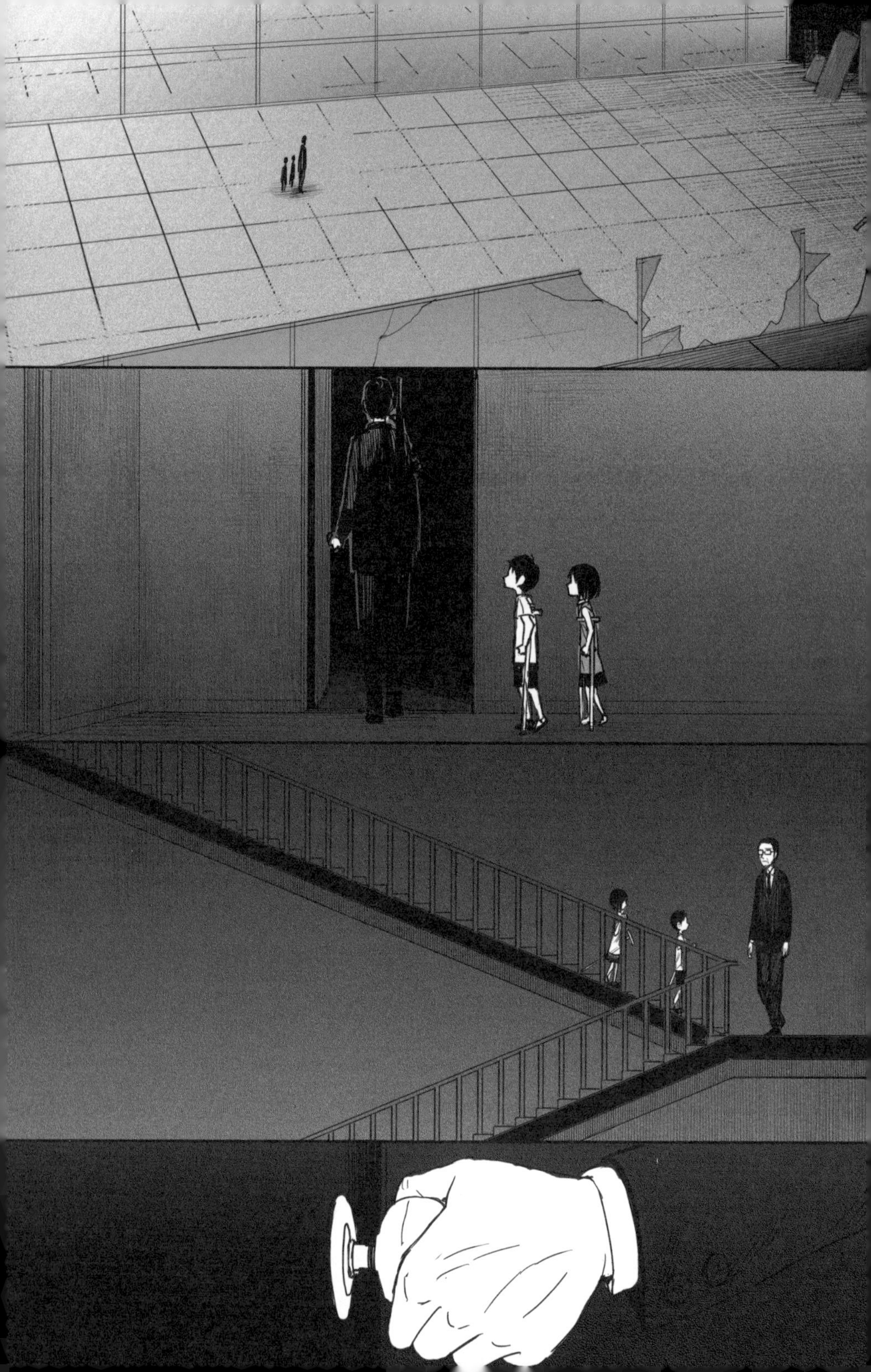

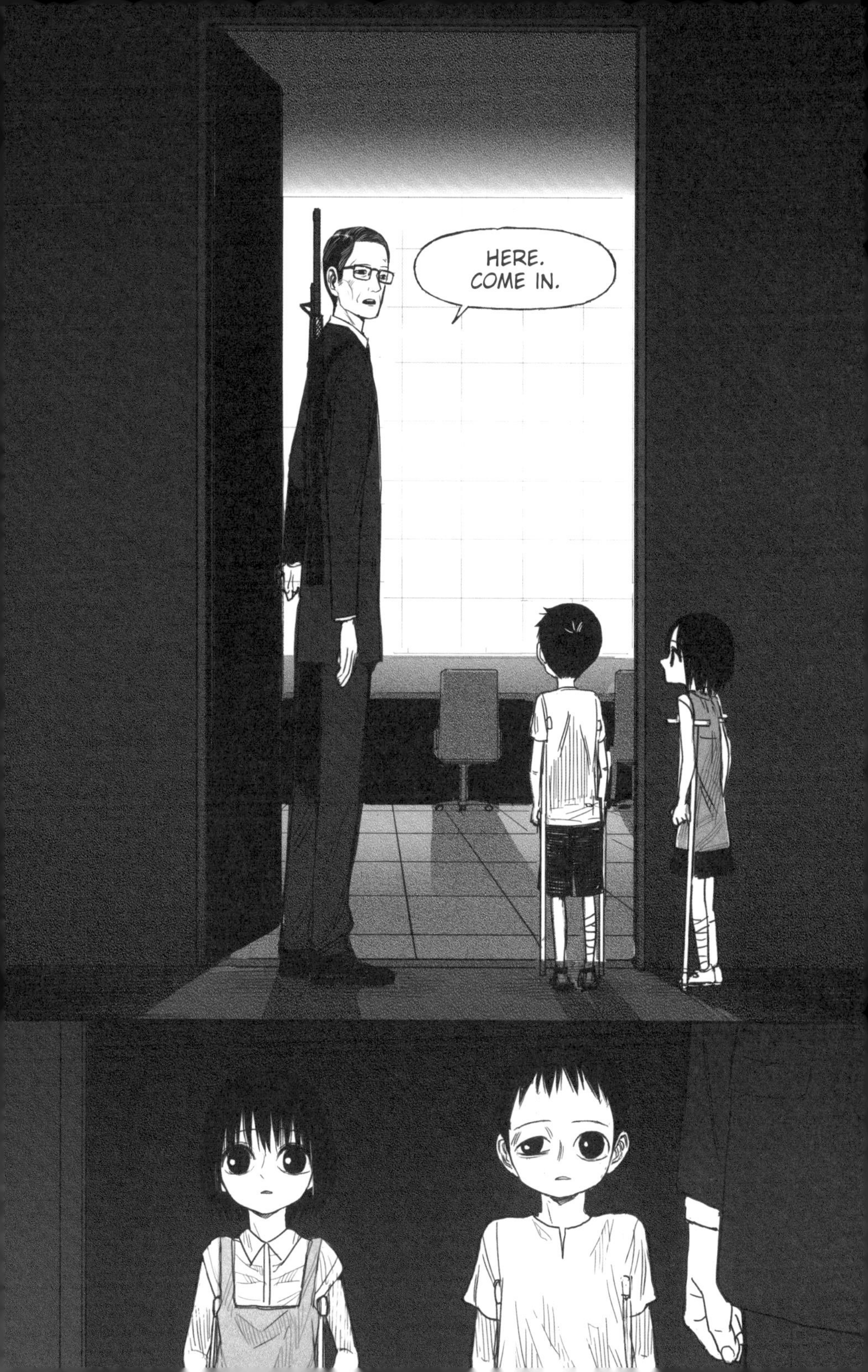
HERE.
COME IN.

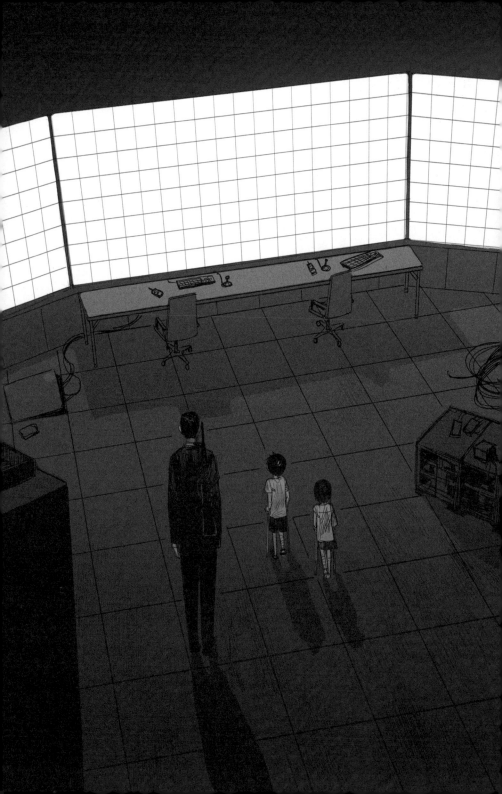

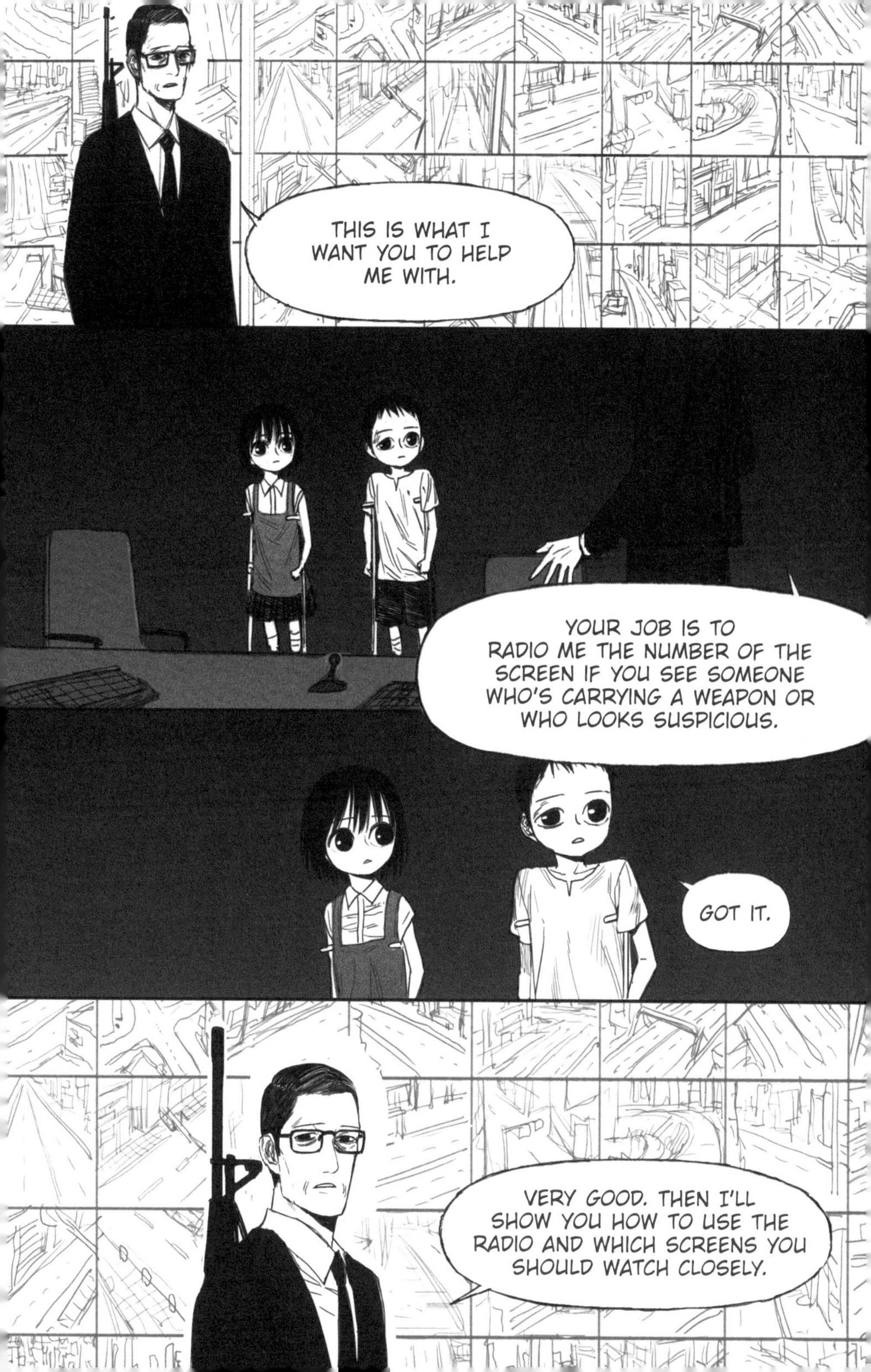
THIS IS WHAT I WANT YOU TO HELP ME WITH.
YOUR JOB IS TO RADIO ME THE NUMBER OF THE SCREEN IF YOU SEE SOMEONE WHO'S CARRYING A WEAPON OR WHO LOOKS SUSPICIOUS.
GOT IT.
VERY GOOD. THEN I'LL SHOW YOU HOW TO USE THE RADIO AND WHICH SCREENS YOU SHOULD WATCH CLOSELY.

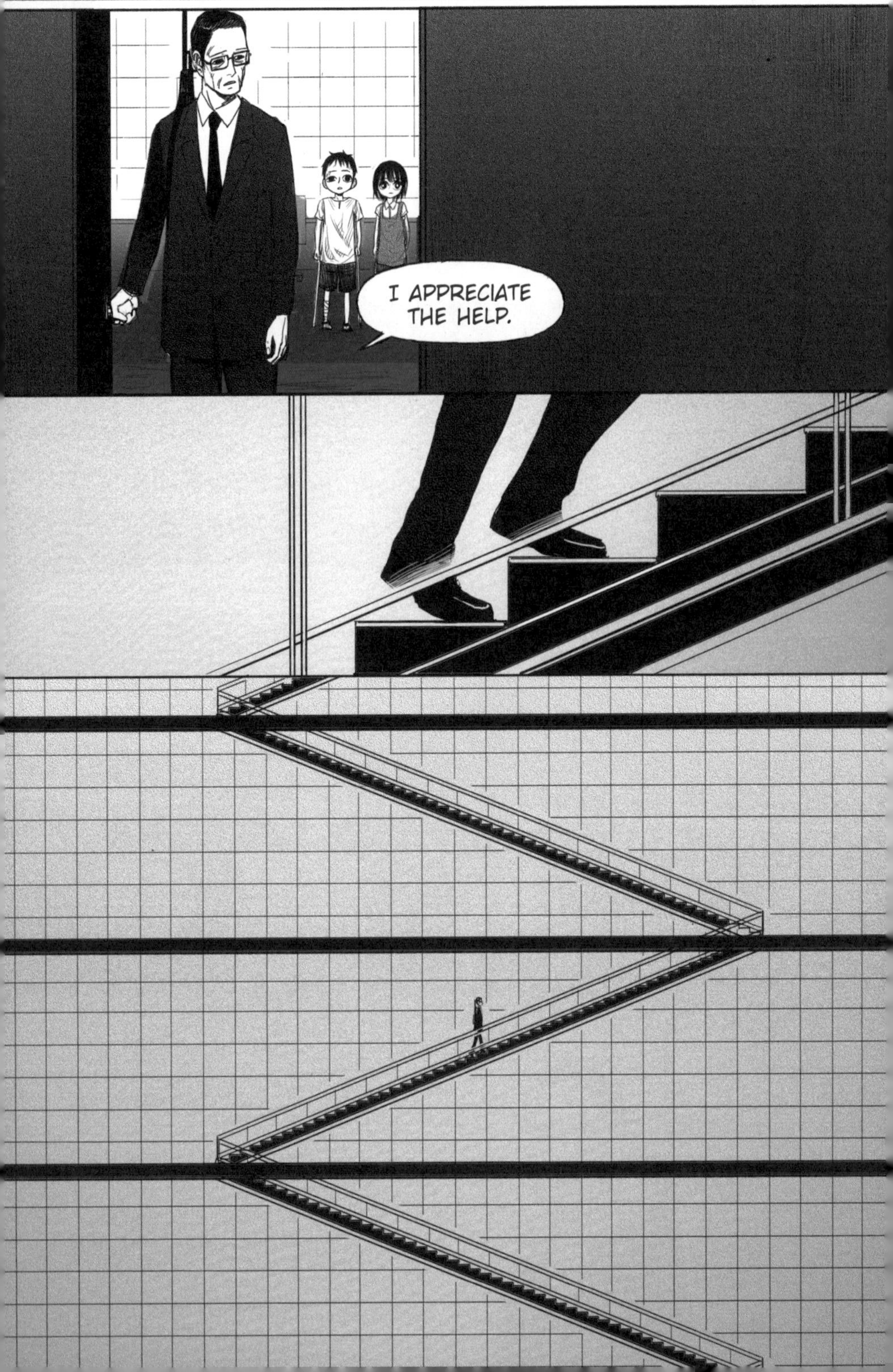
I APPRECIATE THE HELP.

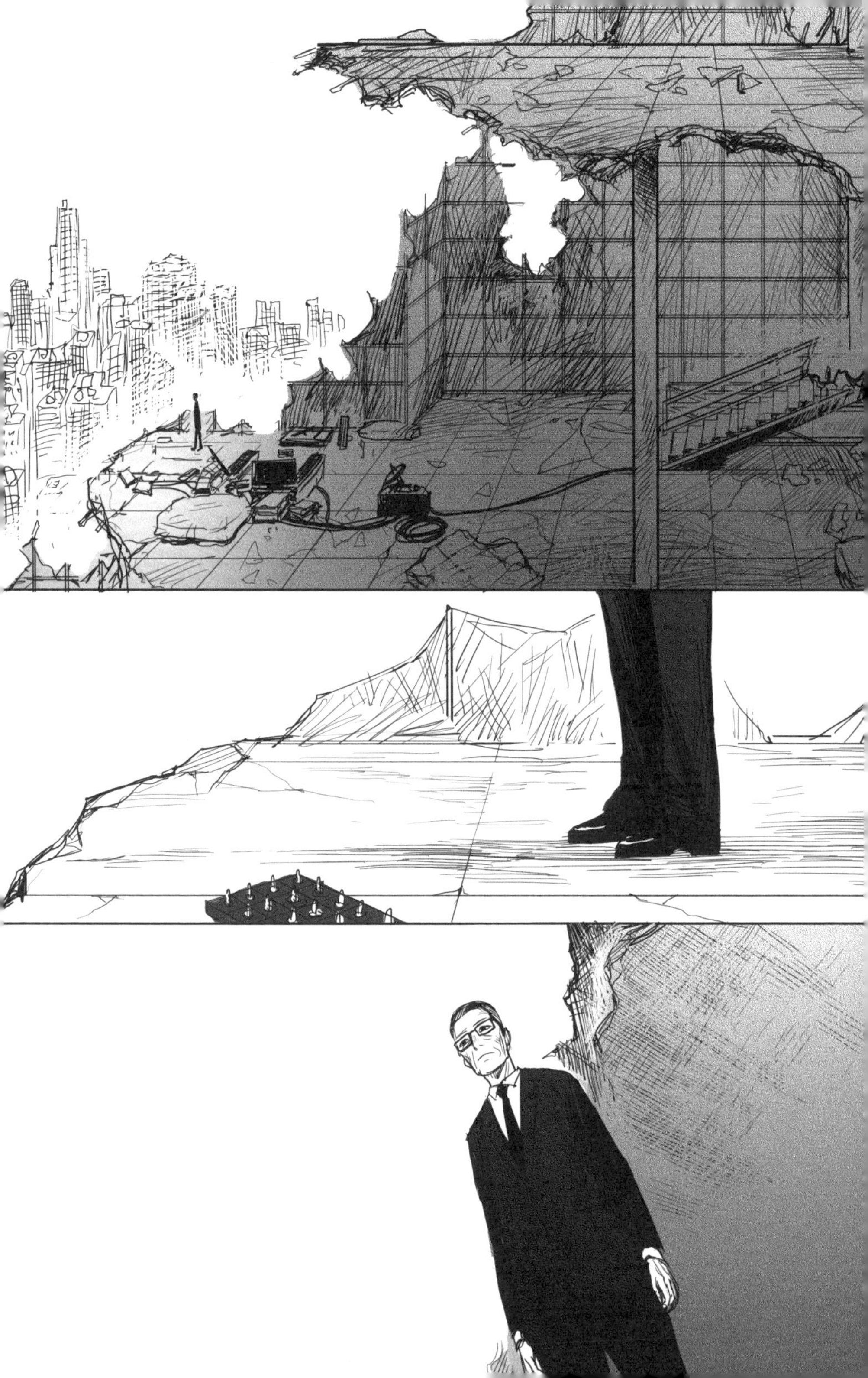

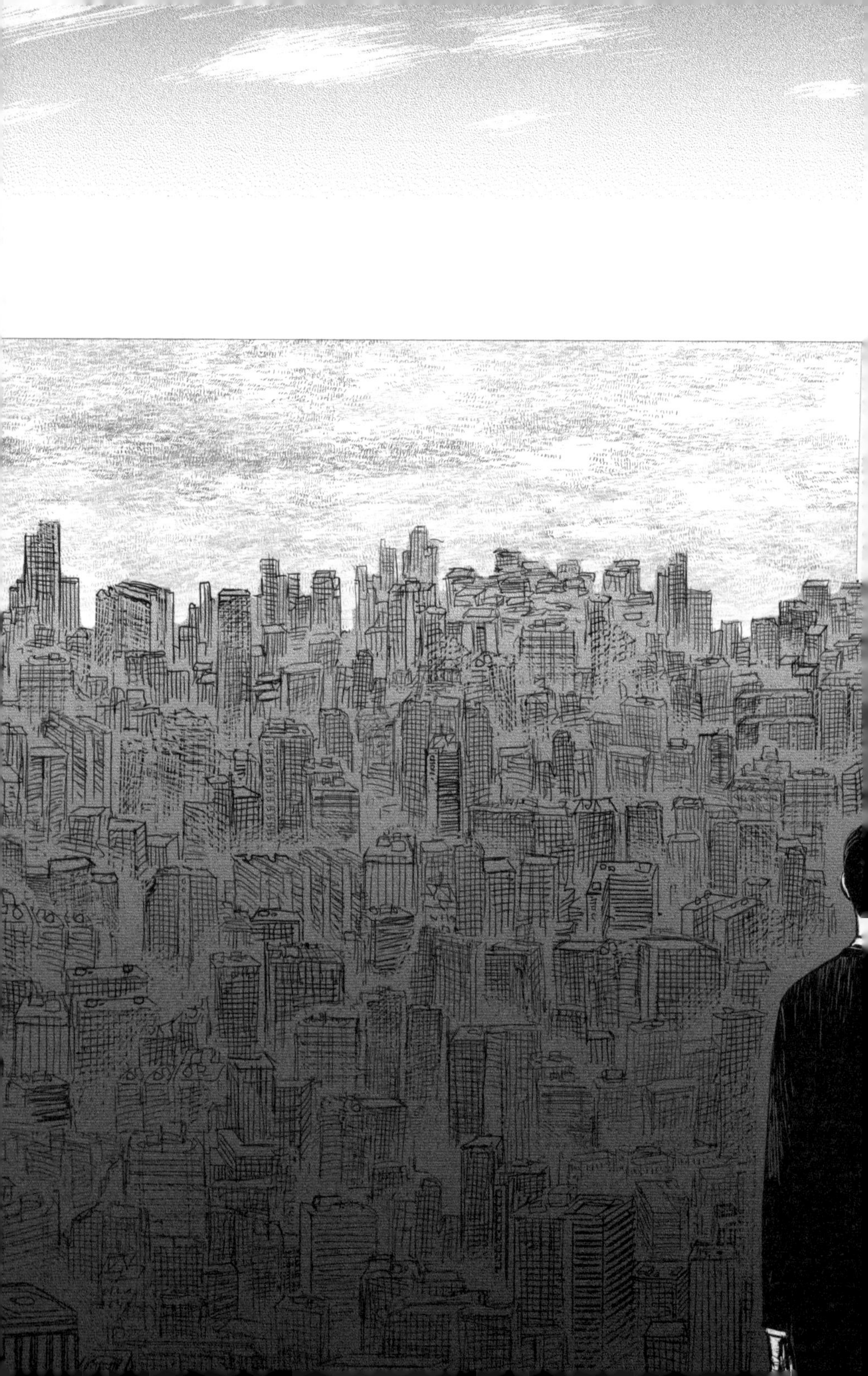

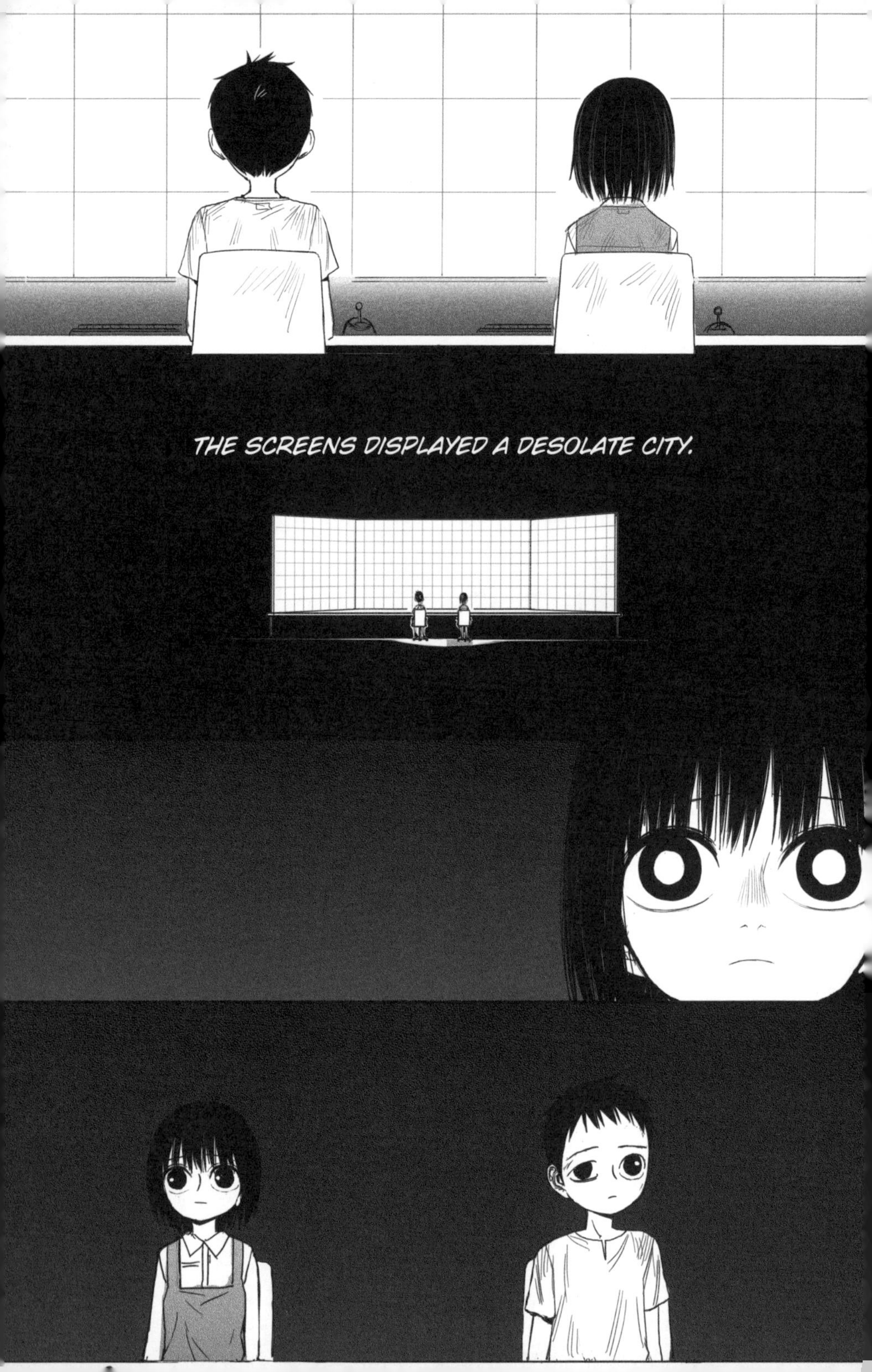
THE SCREENS DISPLAYED A DESOLATE CITY.

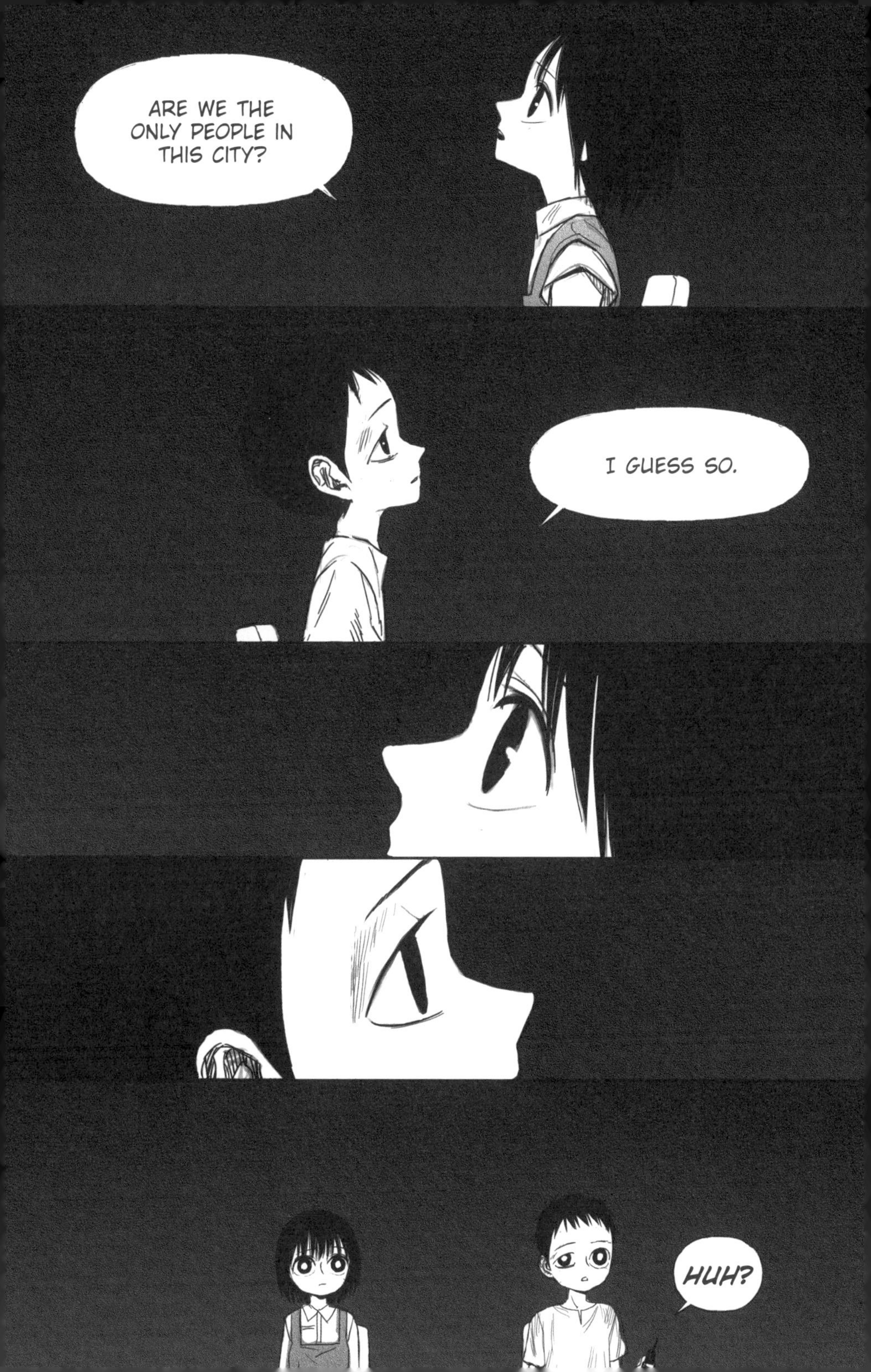
ARE WE THE ONLY PEOPLE IN THIS CITY?
I GUESS SO.
HUH?

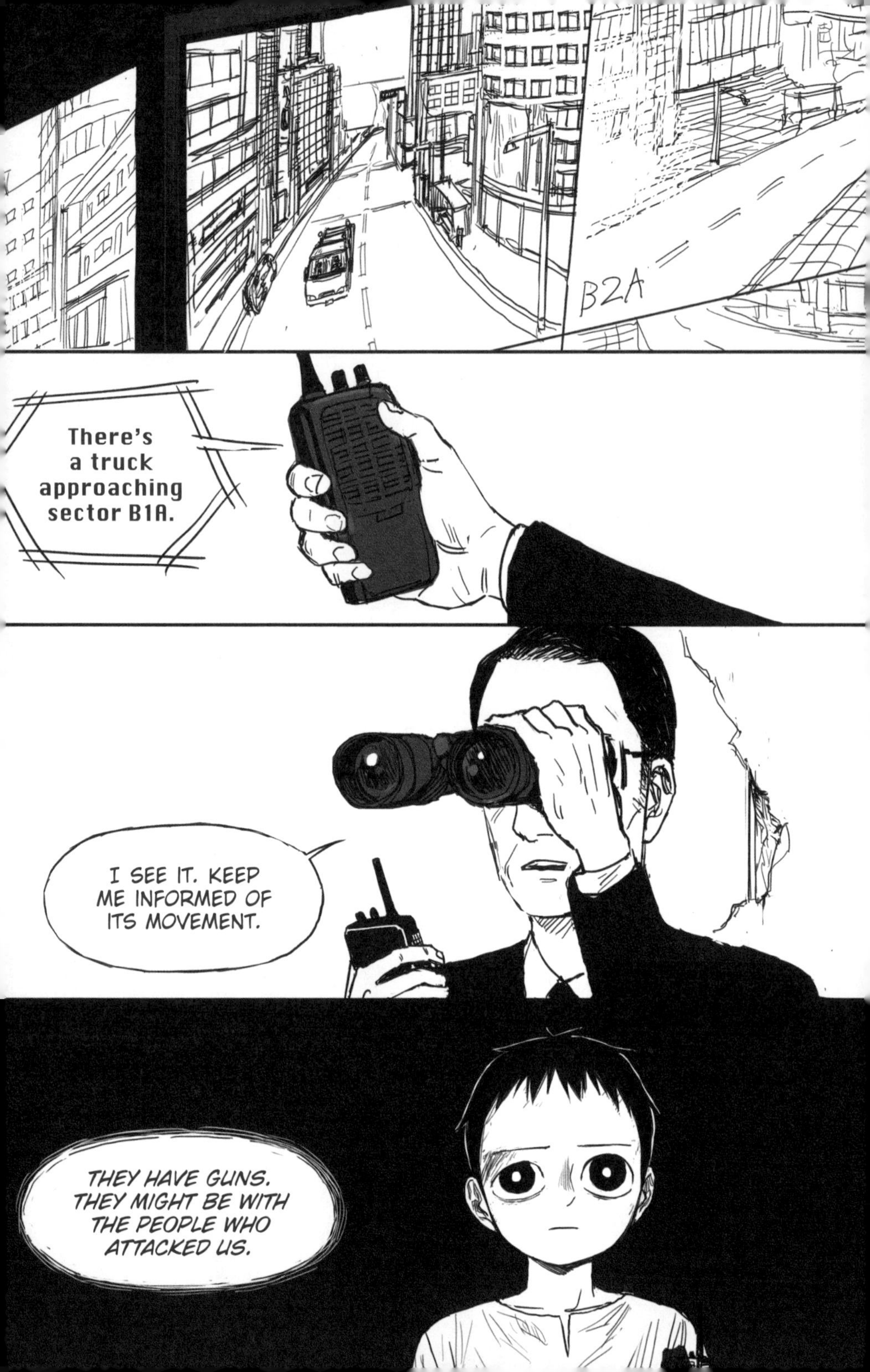
B2A
There's a truck approaching sector B1A.
I SEE IT. KEEP ME INFORMED OF ITS MOVEMENT.
THEY HAVE GUNS. THEY MIGHT BE WITH THE PEOPLE WHO ATTACKED US.

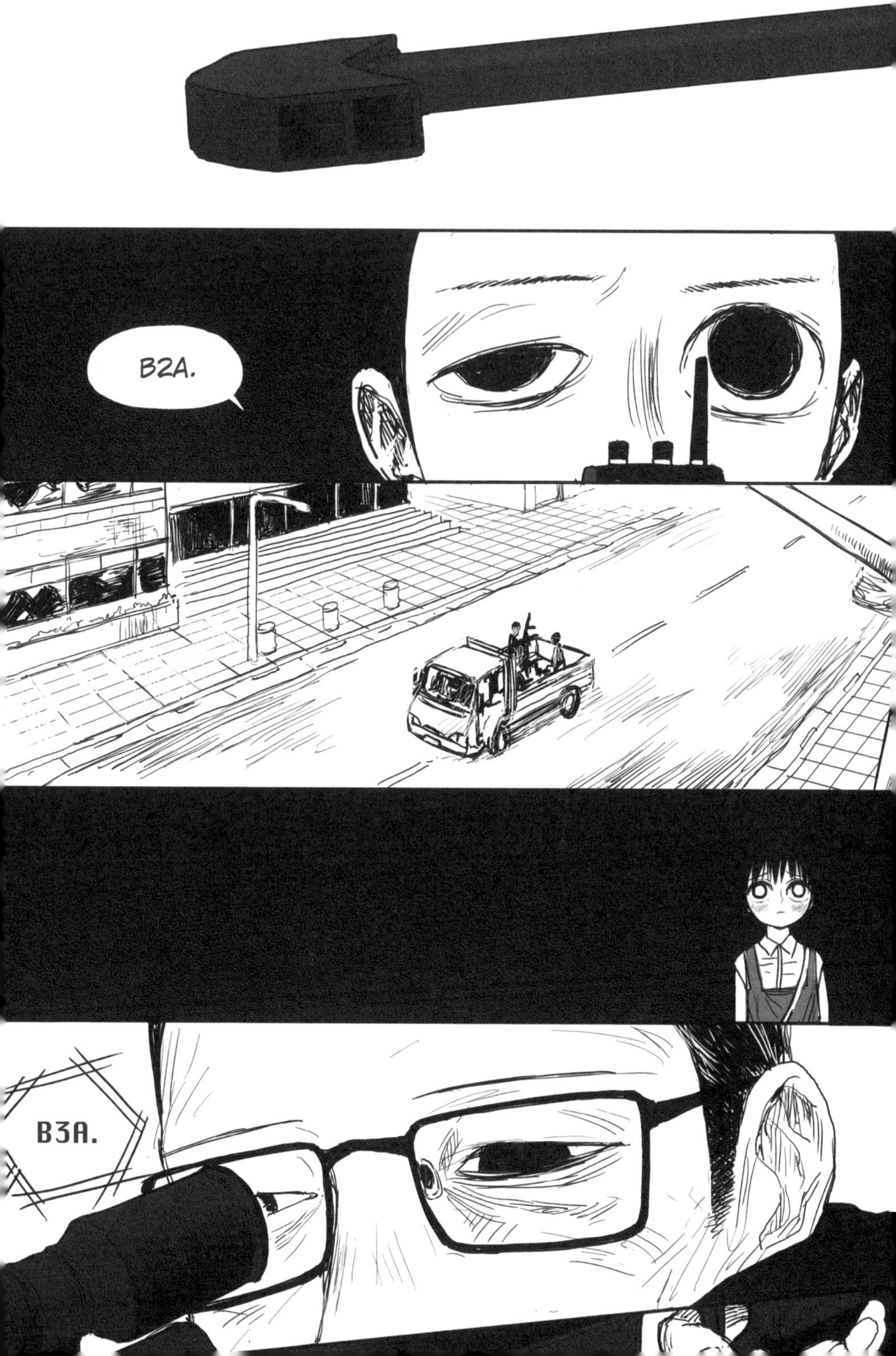

B2A.
B3A.

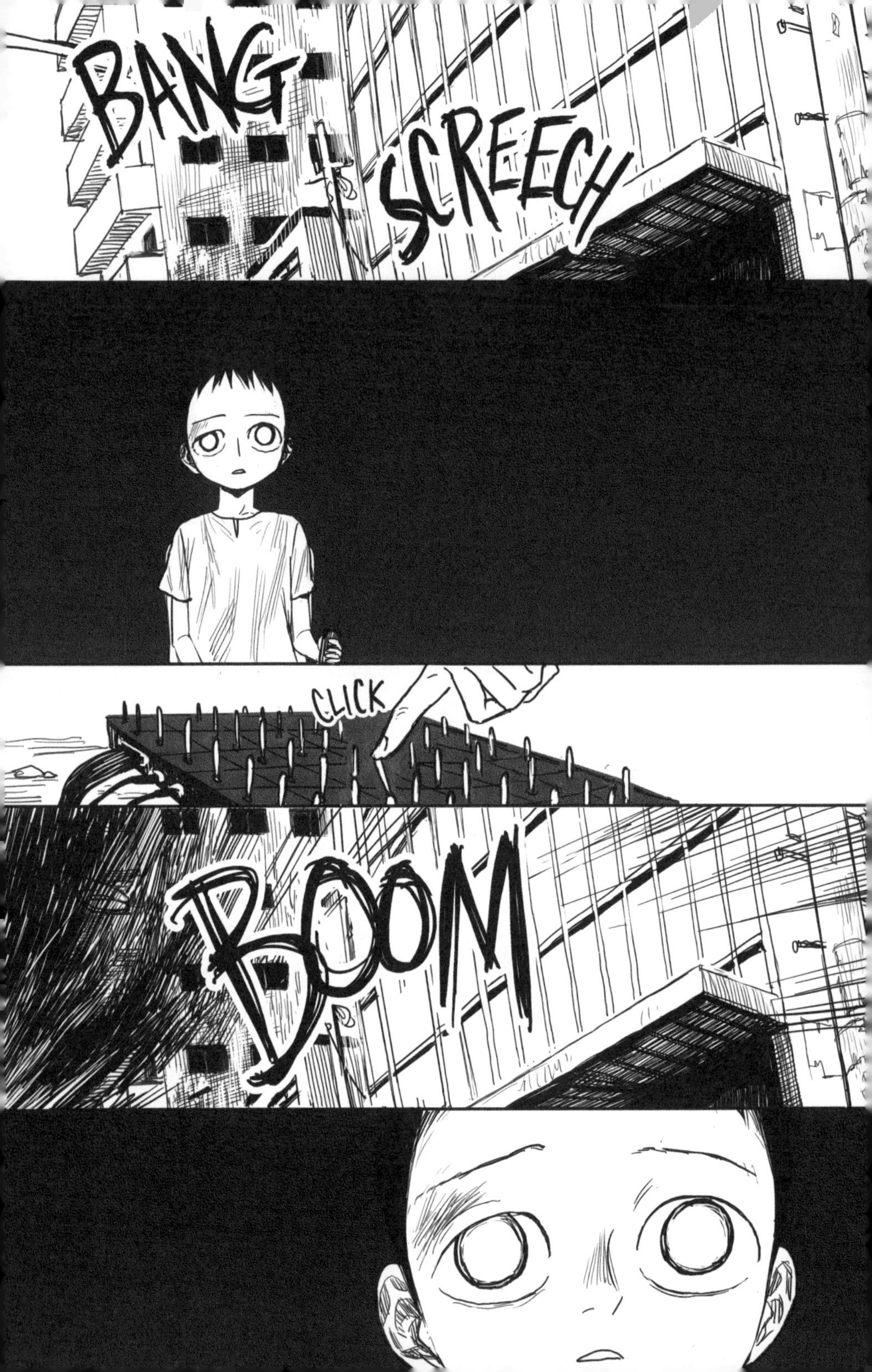
BANG
SCREECH
CLICK
BOOM

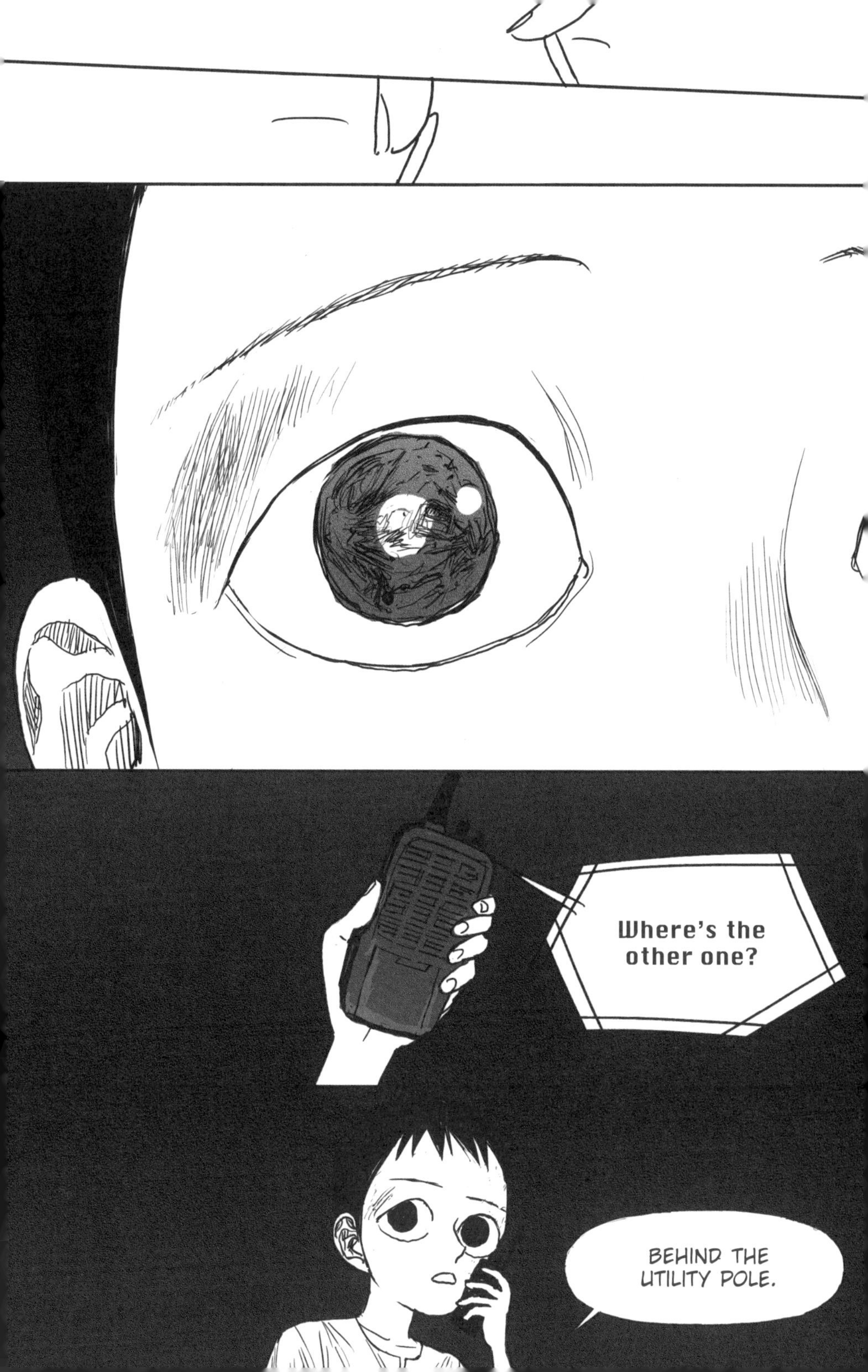
Where's the other one?
BEHIND THE UTILITY POLE.

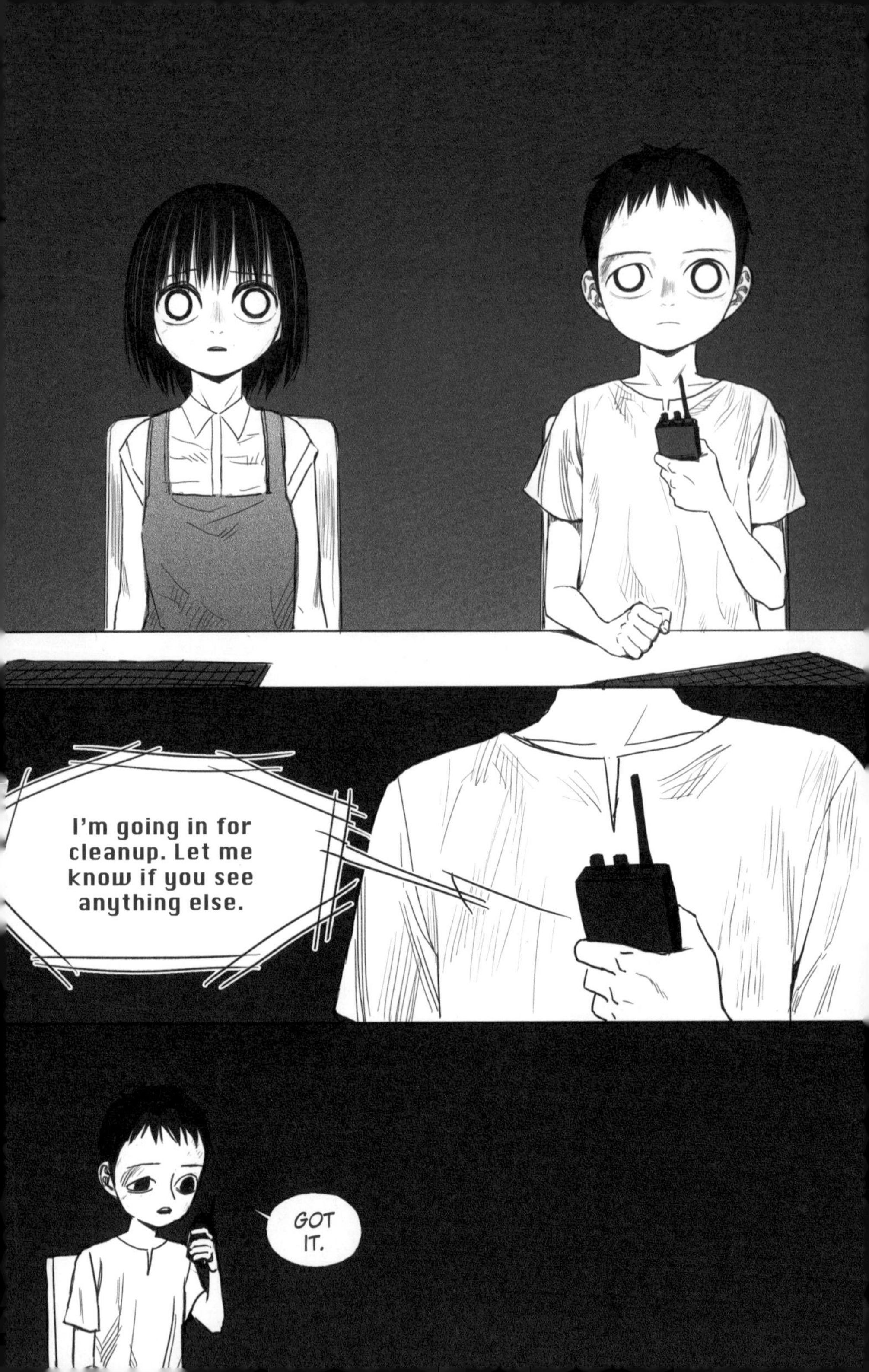
I'm going in for cleanup. Let me know if you see anything else.
GOT IT.

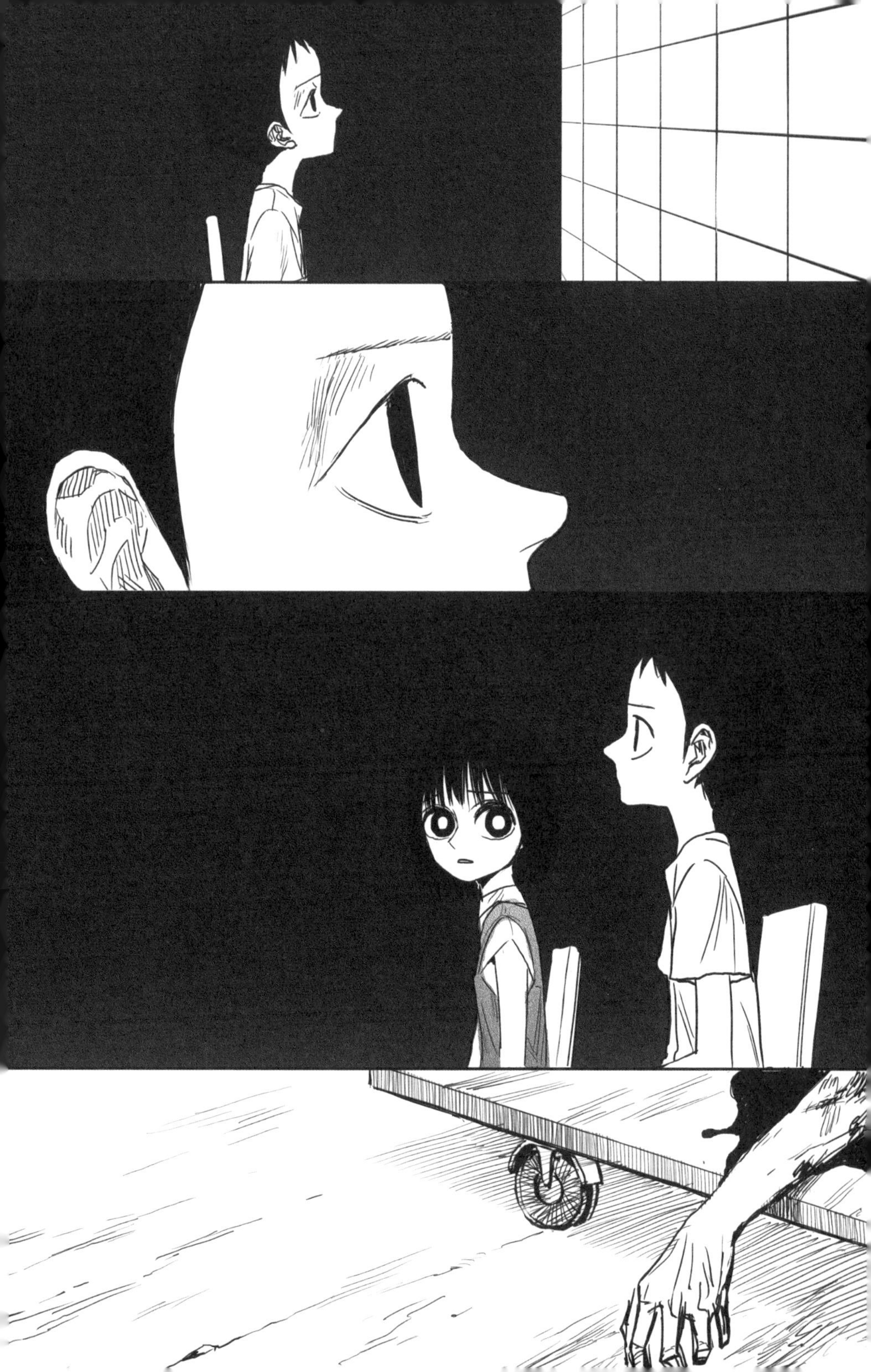

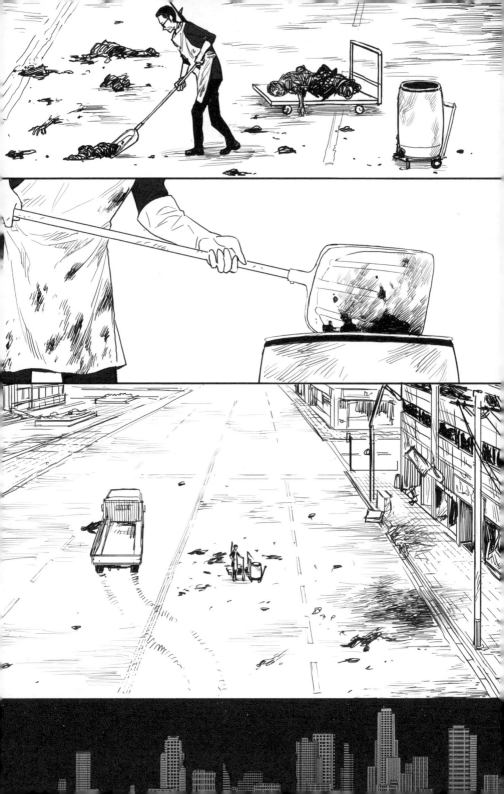

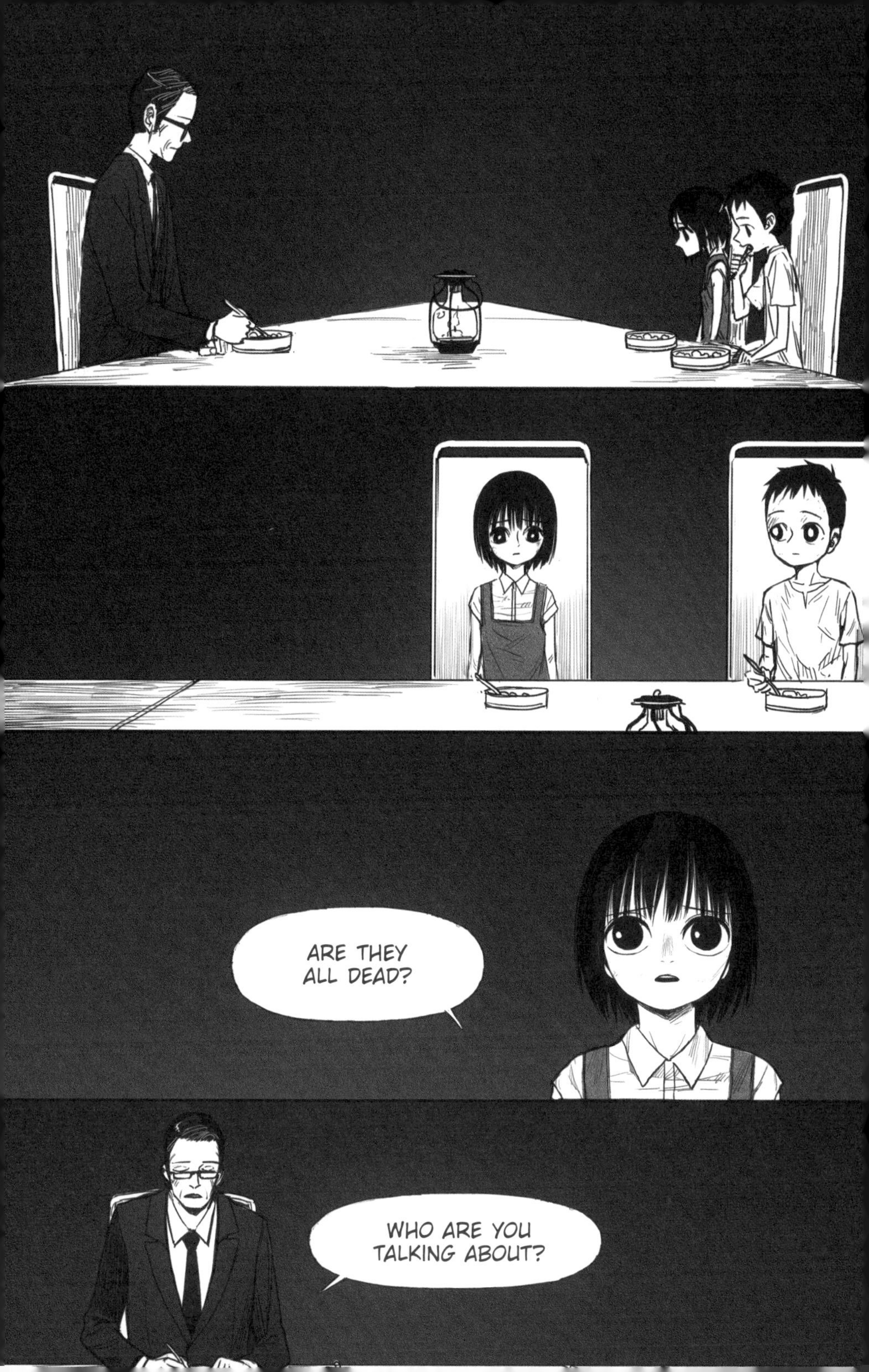
ARE THEY ALL DEAD?
WHO ARE YOU TALKING ABOUT?

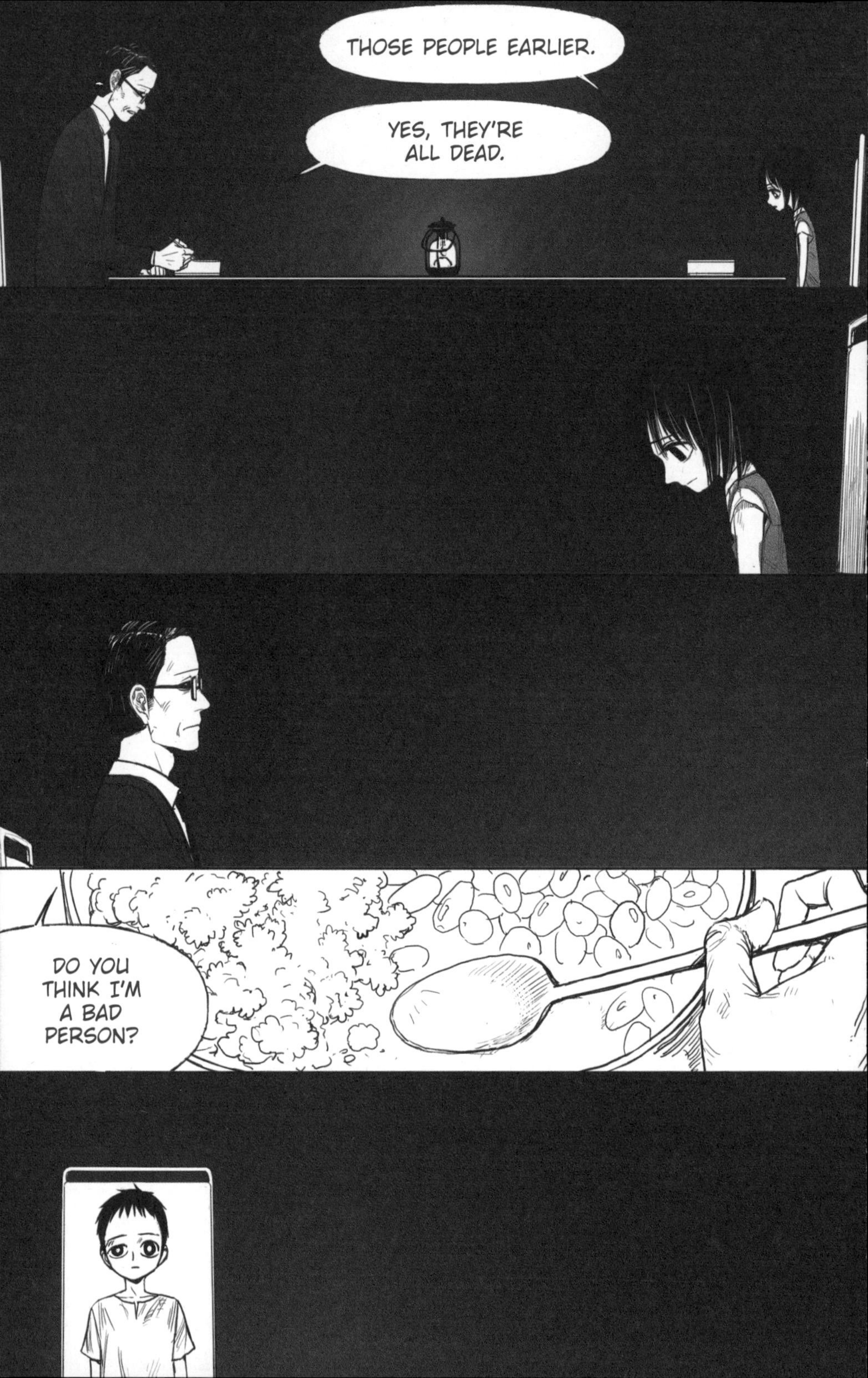
THOSE PEOPLE EARLIER.
YES, THEY'RE ALL DEAD.
DO YOU THINK I'M A BAD PERSON?

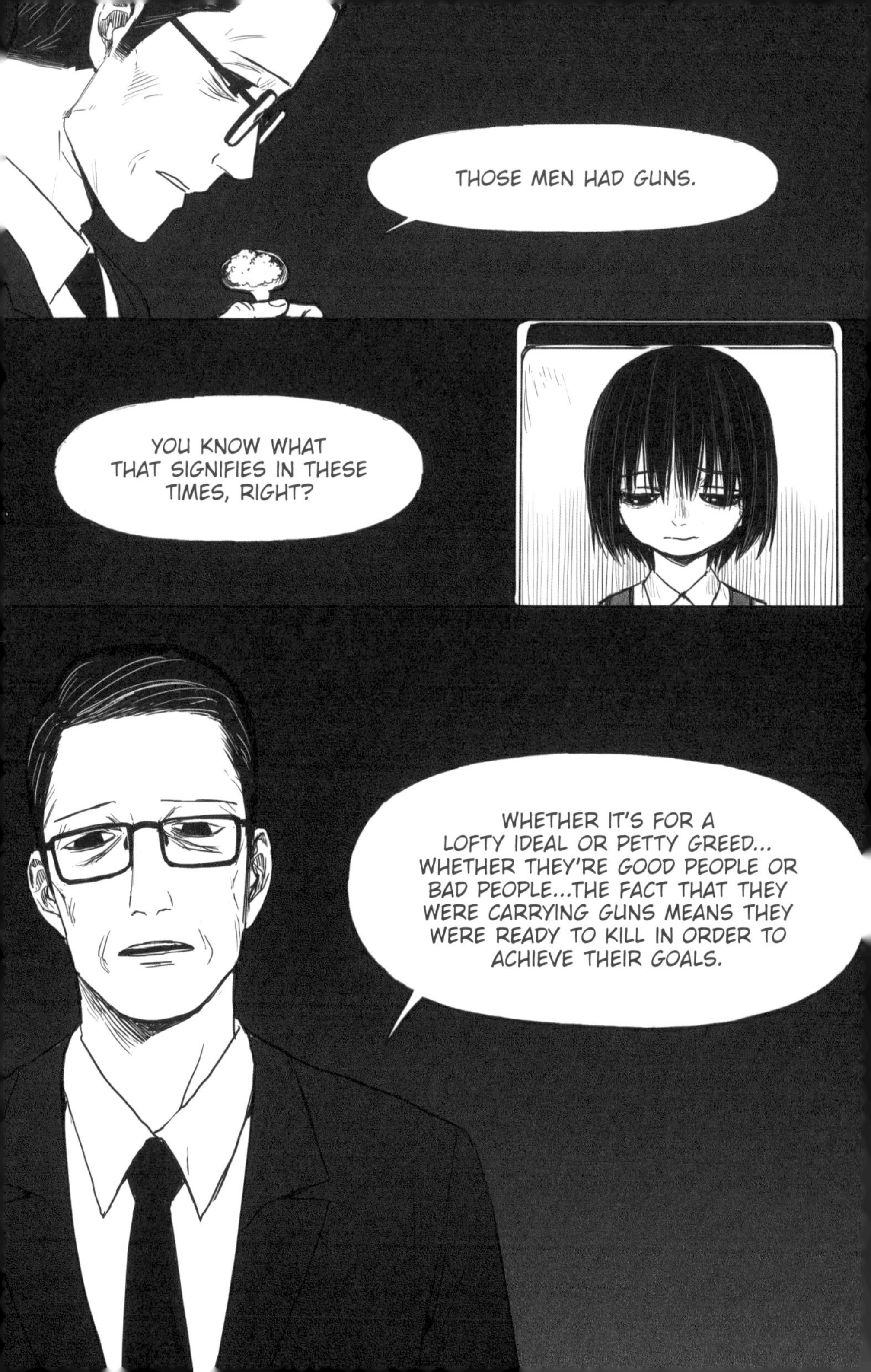
THOSE MEN HAD GUNS.
YOU KNOW WHAT THAT SIGNIFIES IN THESE TIMES, RIGHT?
WHETHER IT'S FOR A LOFTY IDEAL OR PETTY GREED... WHETHER THEY'RE GOOD PEOPLE OR BAD PEOPLE...THE FACT THAT THEY WERE CARRYING GUNS MEANS THEY WERE READY TO KILL IN ORDER TO ACHIEVE THEIR GOALS.

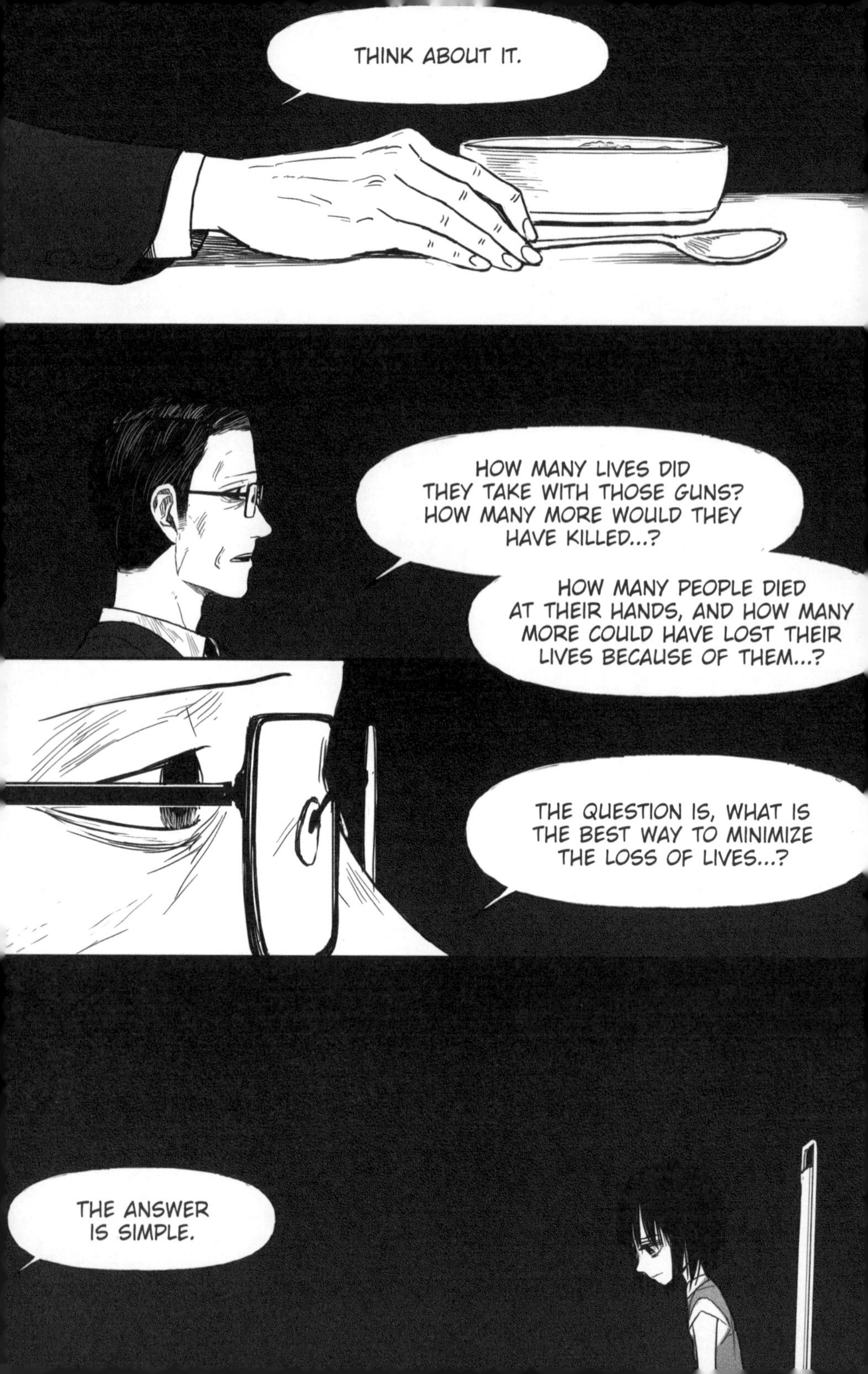
THINK ABOUT IT.
HOW MANY LIVES DID THEY TAKE WITH THOSE GUNS? HOW MANY MORE WOULD THEY HAVE KILLED...?
HOW MANY PEOPLE DIED AT THEIR HANDS, AND HOW MANY MORE COULD HAVE LOST THEIR LIVES BECAUSE OF THEM...?
THE QUESTION IS, WHAT IS THE BEST WAY TO MINIMIZE THE LOSS OF LIVES...?
THE ANSWER IS SIMPLE.

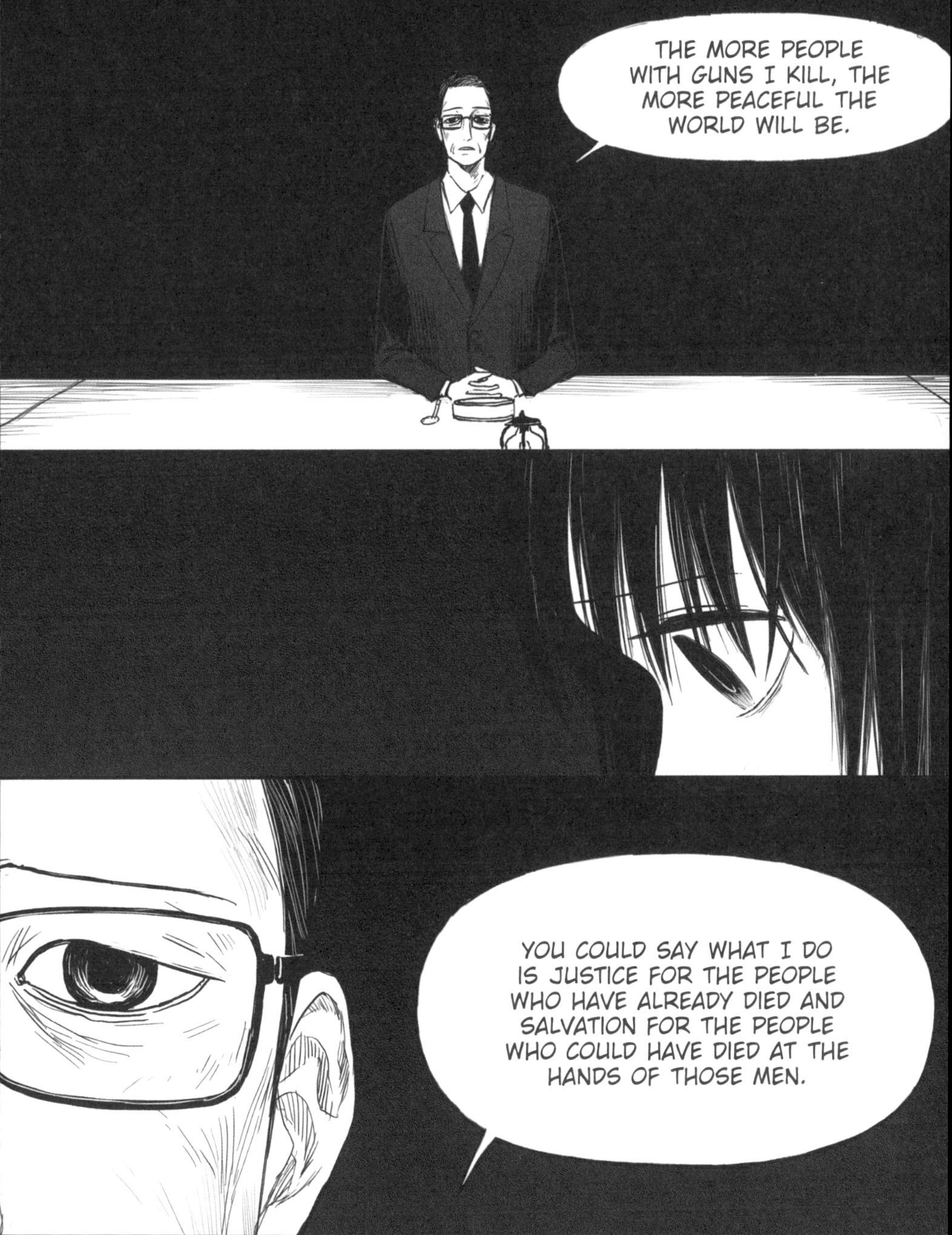
THE MORE PEOPLE WITH GUNS I KILL, THE MORE PEACEFUL THE WORLD WILL BE.
YOU COULD SAY WHAT I DO IS JUSTICE FOR THE PEOPLE WHO HAVE ALREADY DIED AND SALVATION FOR THE PEOPLE WHO COULD HAVE DIED AT THE HANDS OF THOSE MEN.

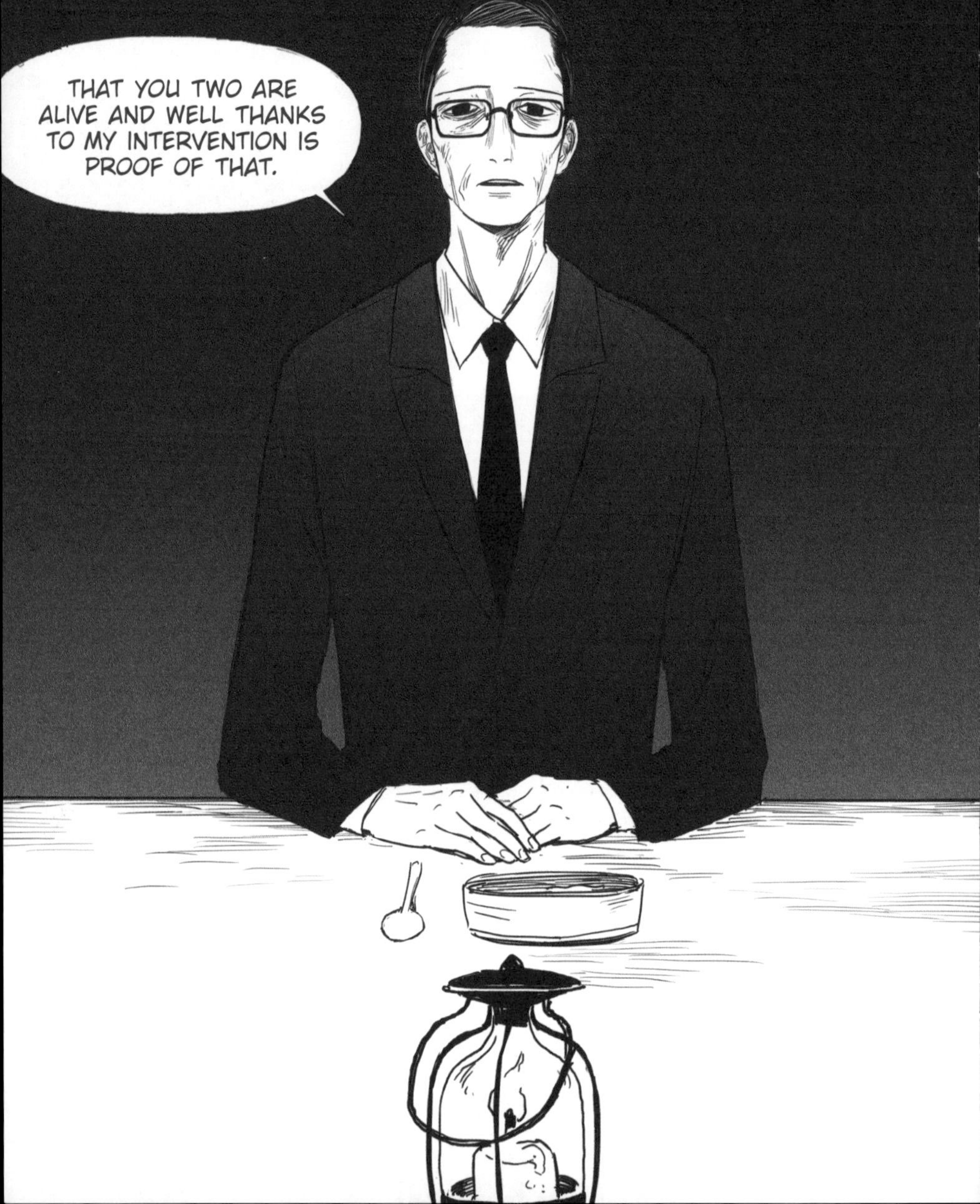
THAT YOU TWO ARE ALIVE AND WELL THANKS TO MY INTERVENTION IS PROOF OF THAT.

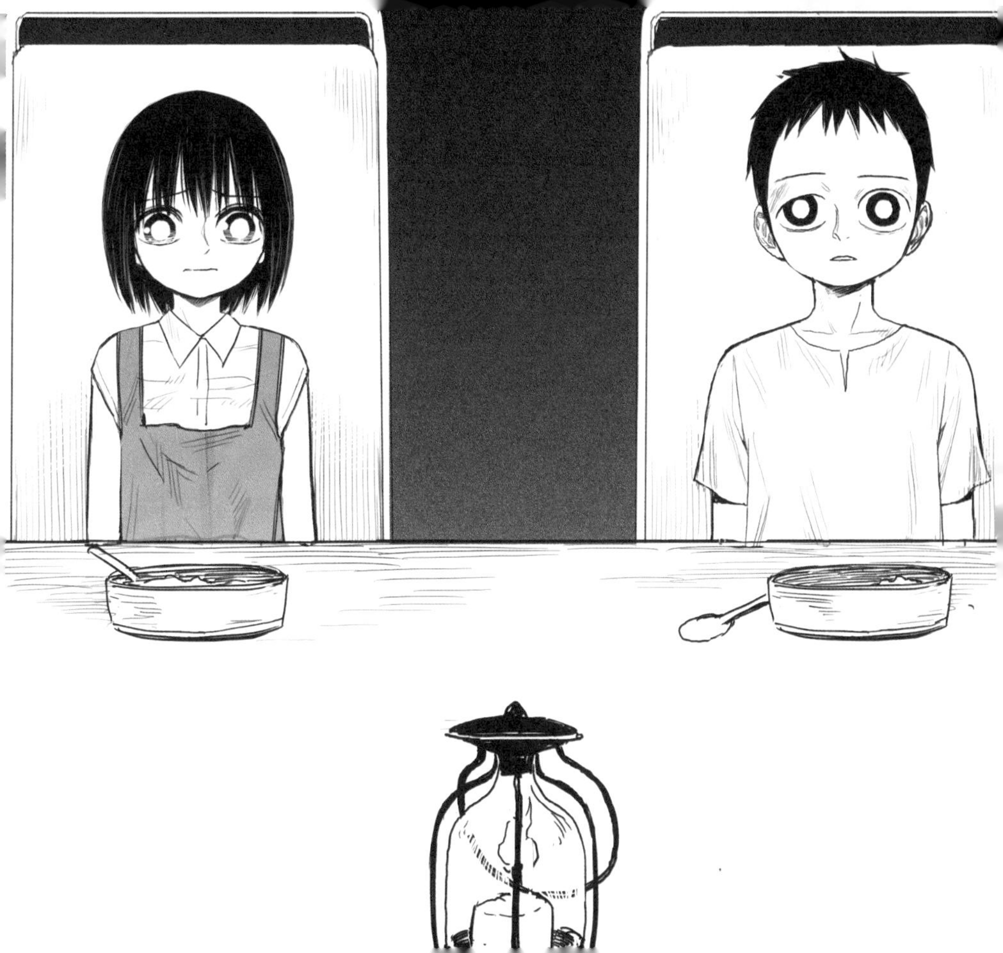

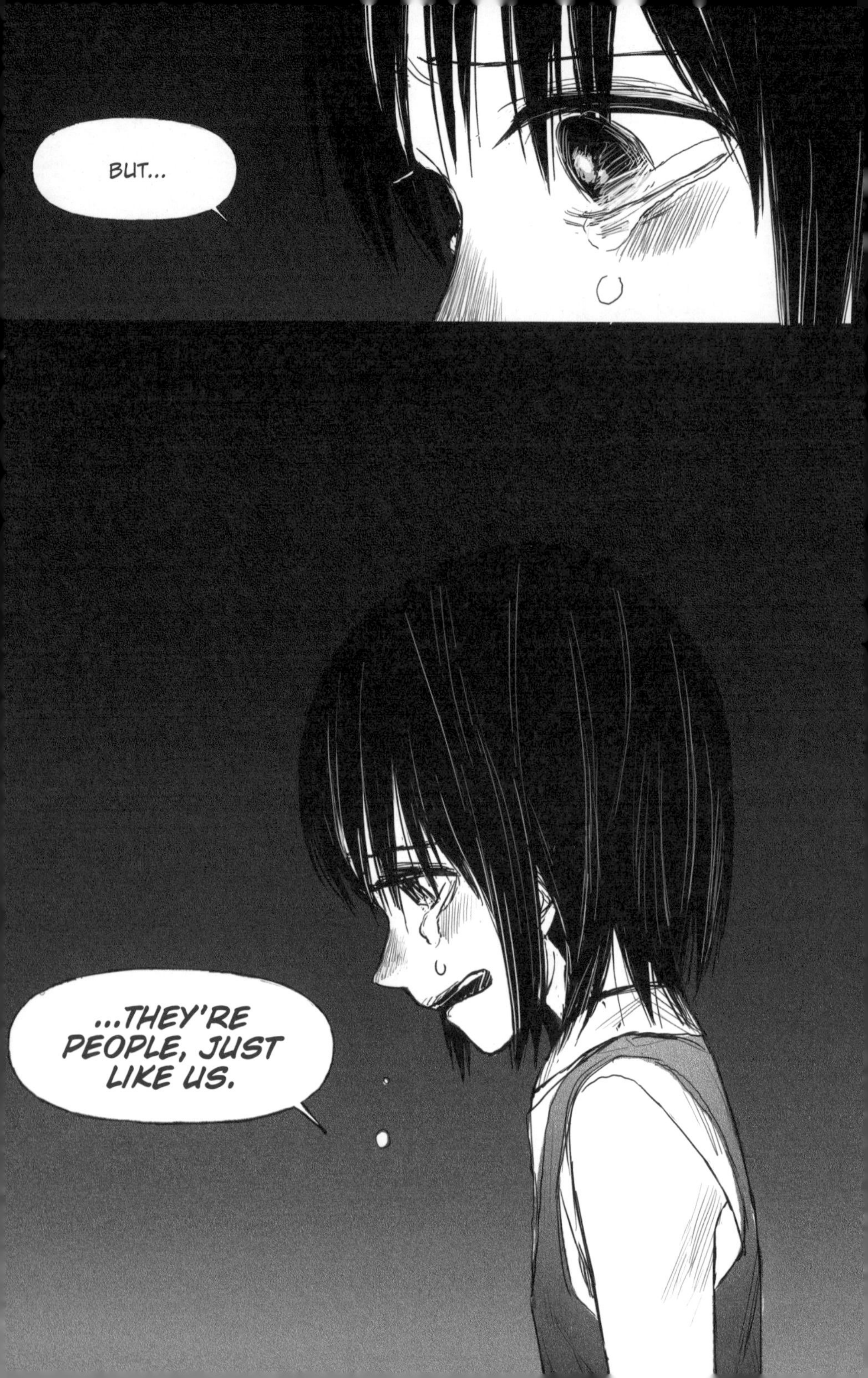
BUT...
...THEY'RE PEOPLE, JUST LIKE US.

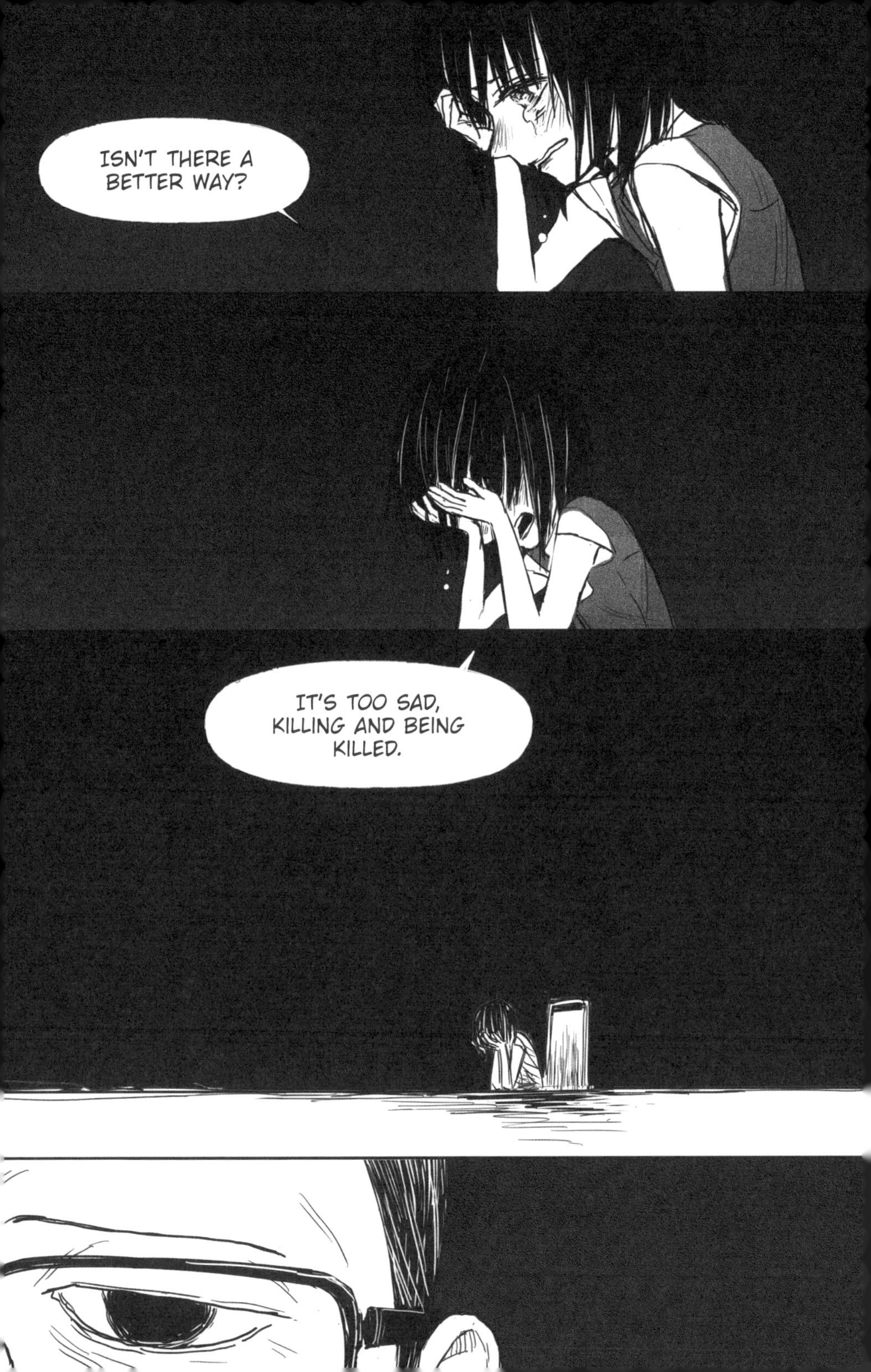
ISN'T THERE A BETTER WAY?
IT'S TOO SAD, KILLING AND BEING KILLED.

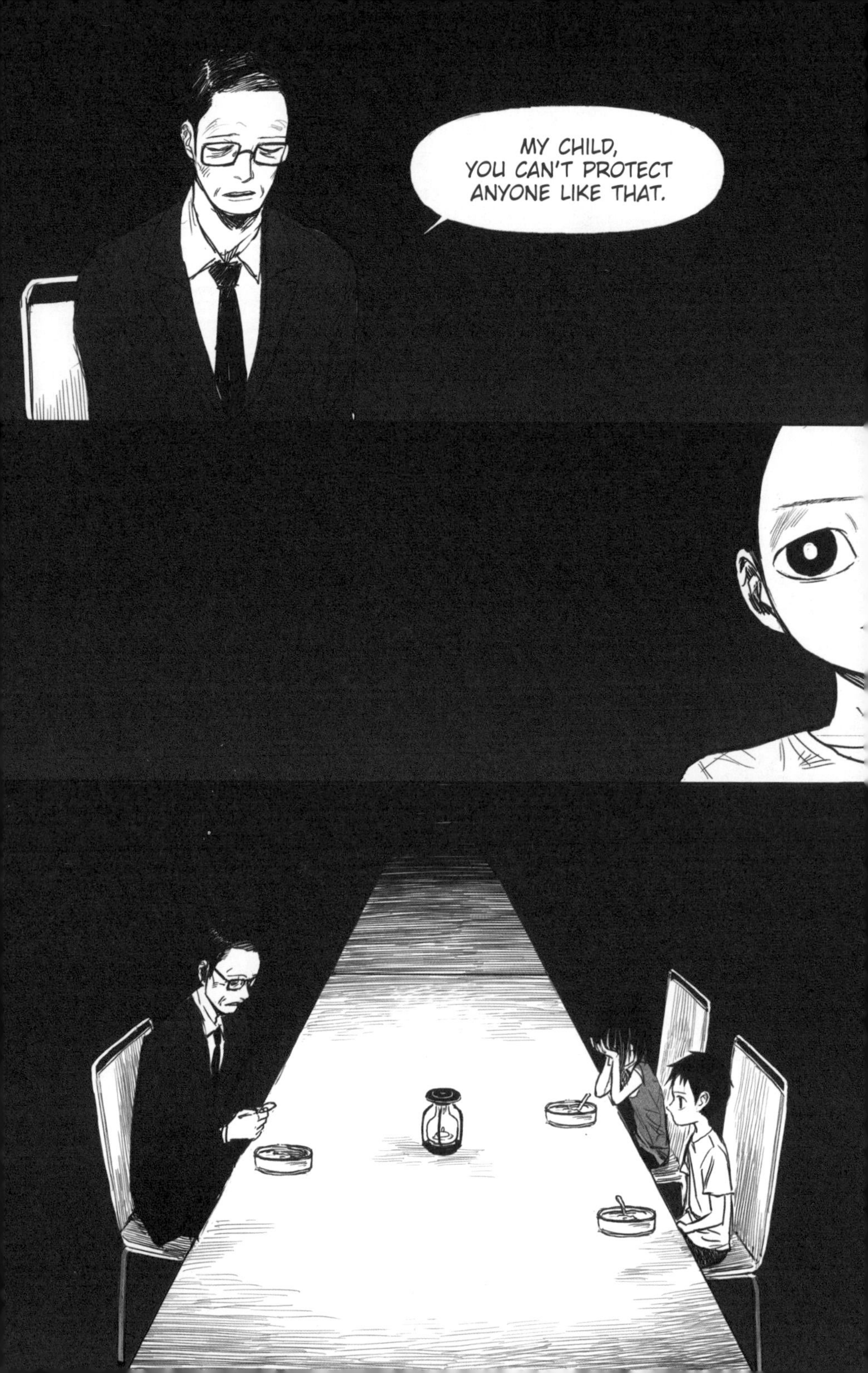
MY CHILD, YOU CAN'T PROTECT ANYONE LIKE THAT.

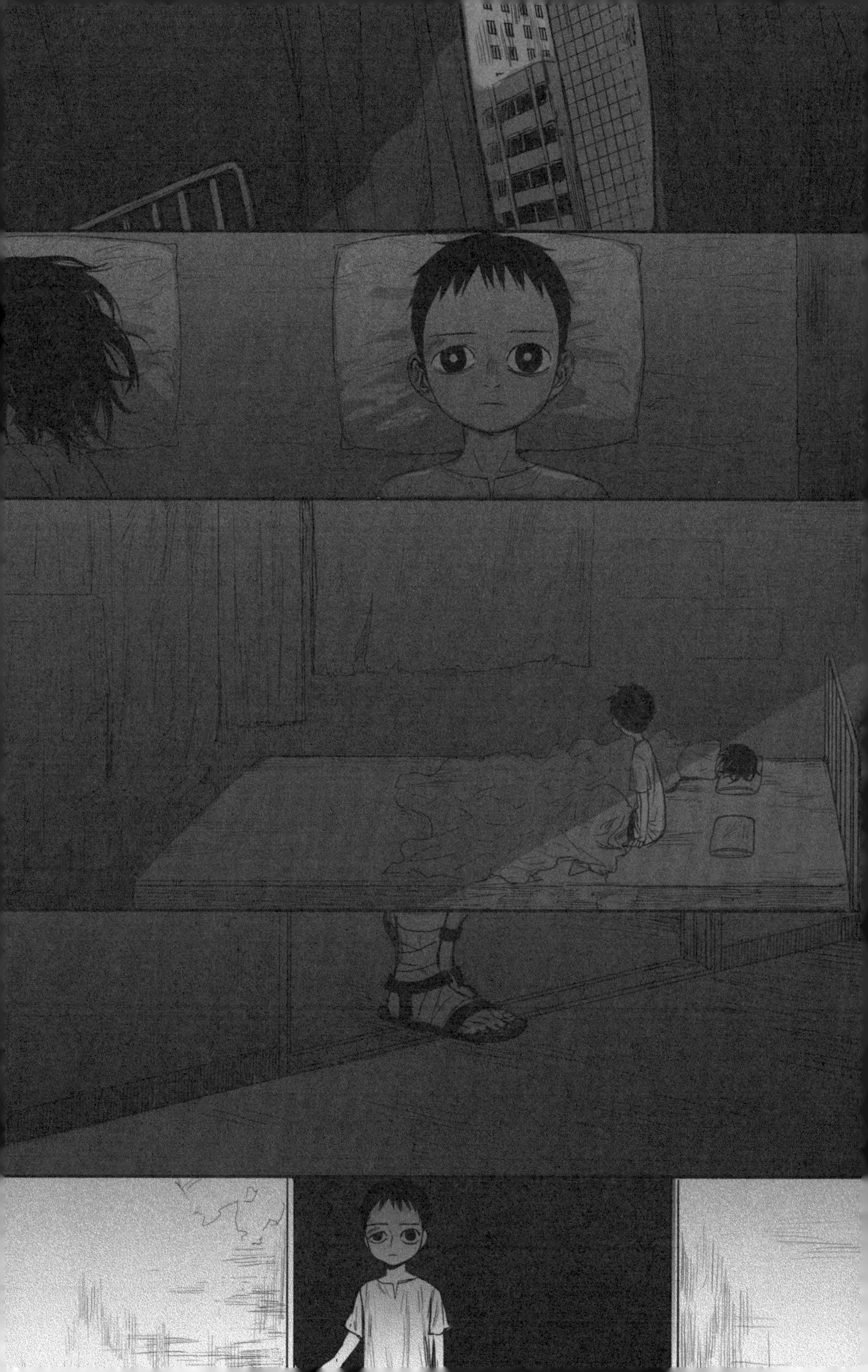

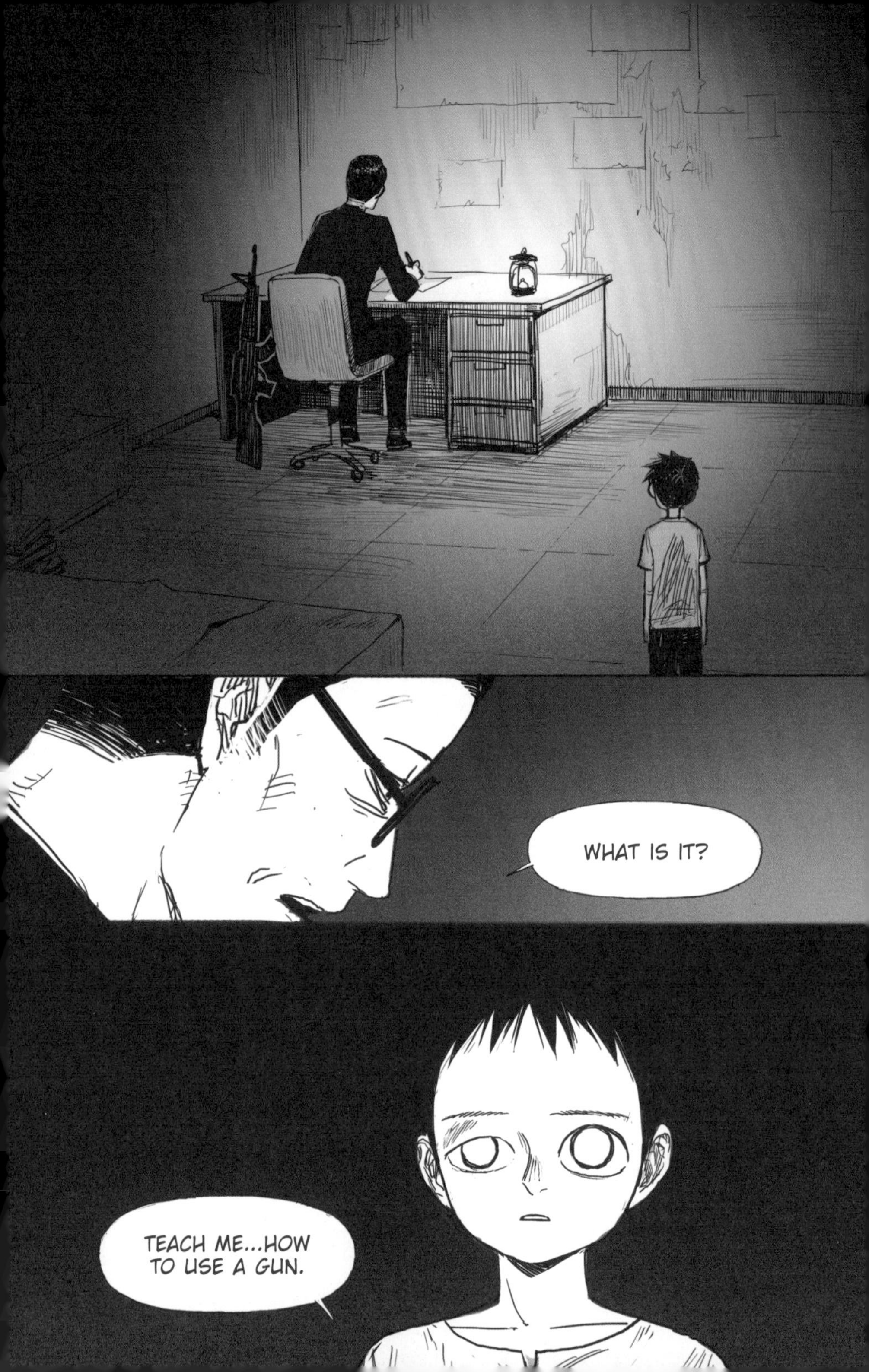
WHAT IS IT?
TEACH ME...HOW TO USE A GUN.

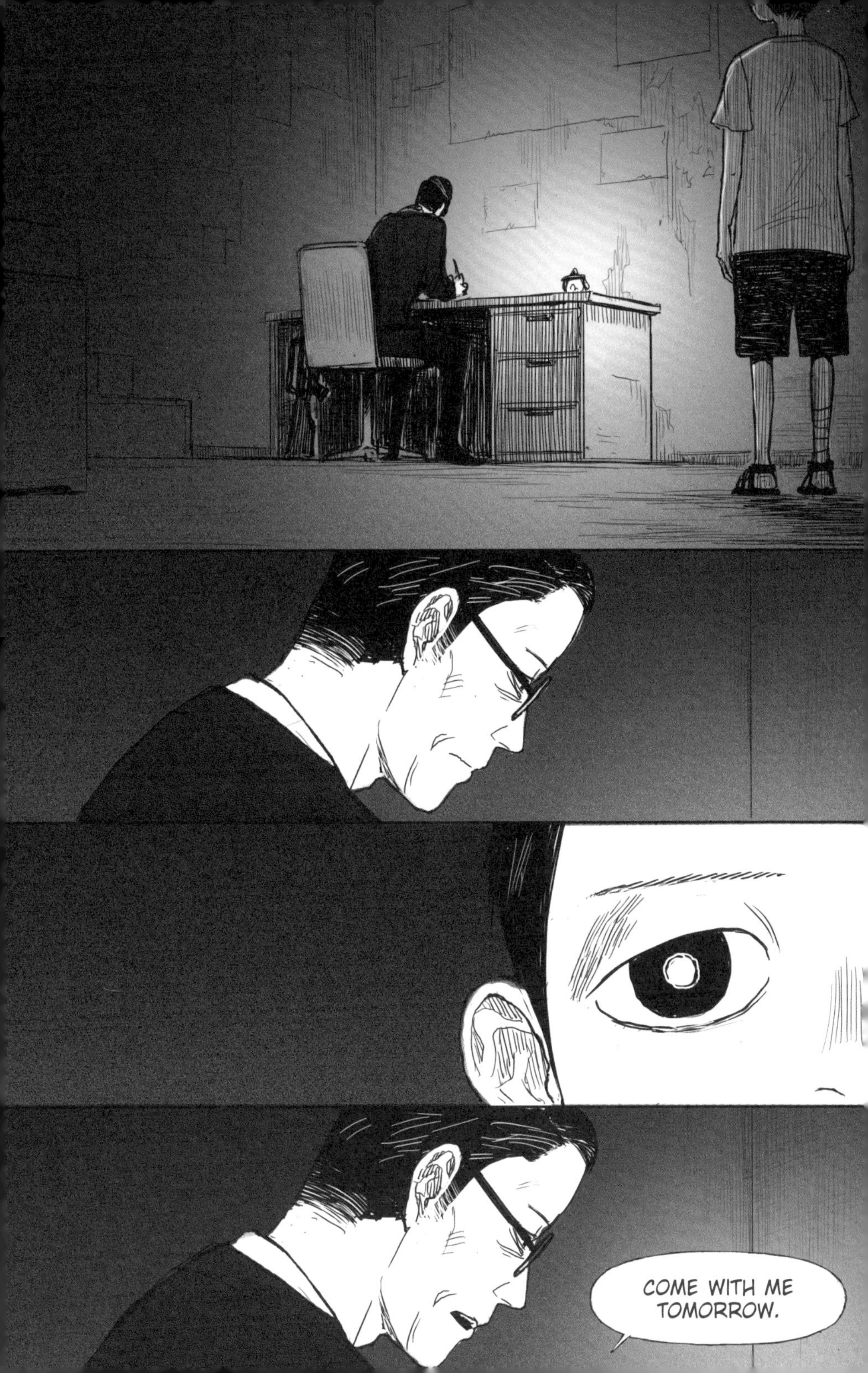
COME WITH ME
TOMORROW.

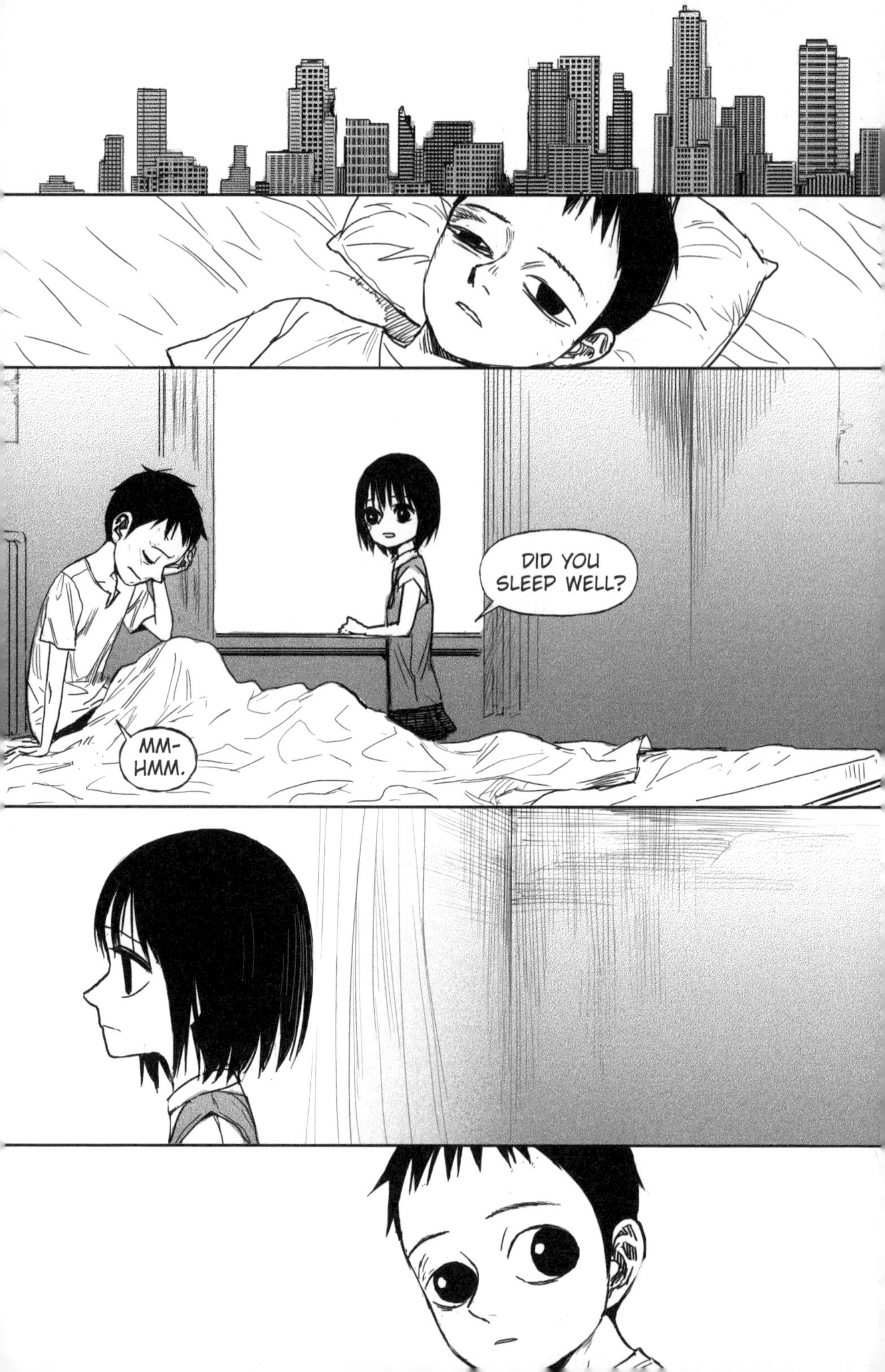
DID YOU SLEEP WELL?
MM-HMM.

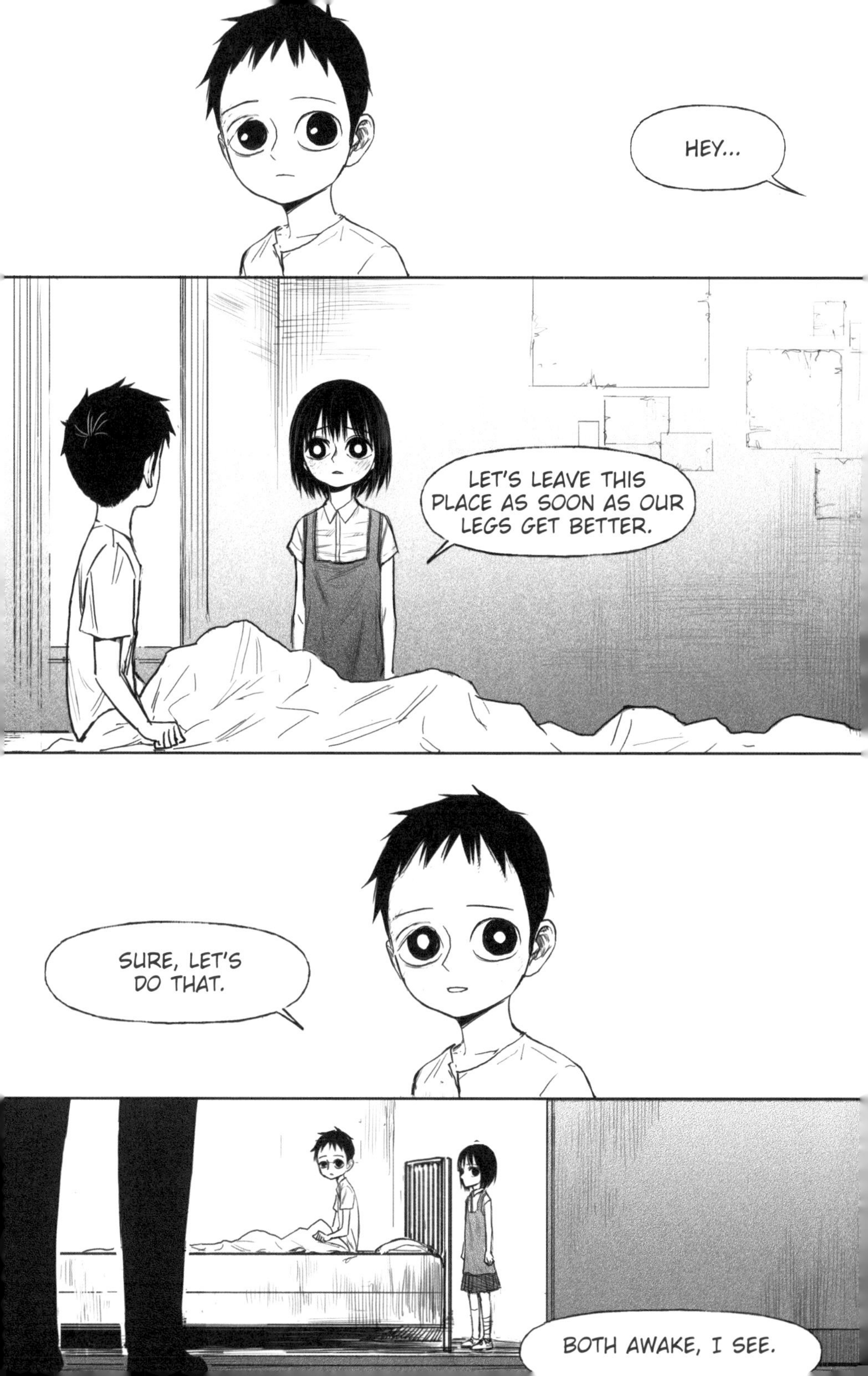
HEY...
LET'S LEAVE THIS PLACE AS SOON AS OUR LEGS GET BETTER.
SURE, LET'S DO THAT.
BOTH AWAKE, I SEE.

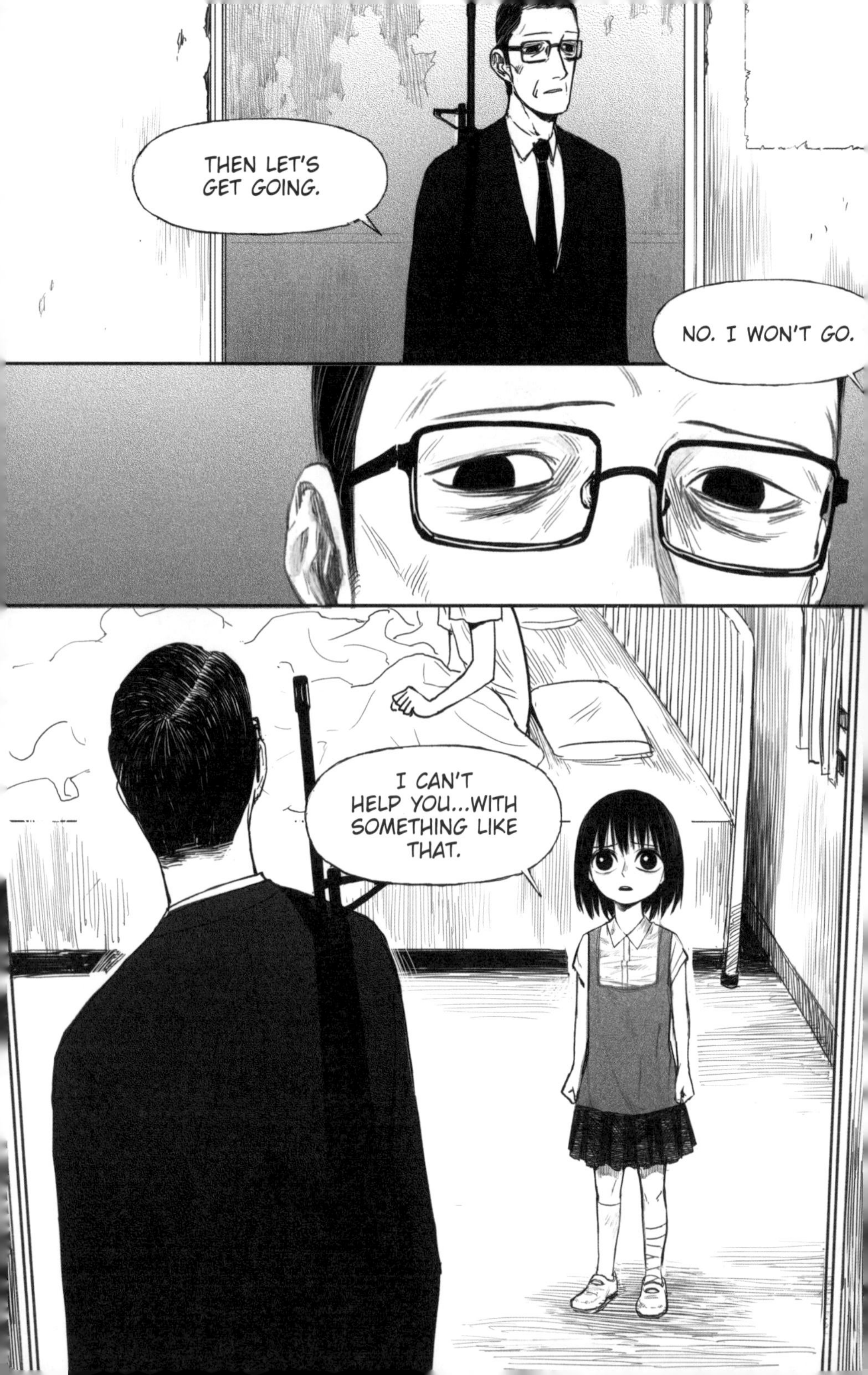
THEN LET'S GET GOING.
NO. I WON'T GO.
I CAN'T HELP YOU...WITH SOMETHING LIKE THAT.

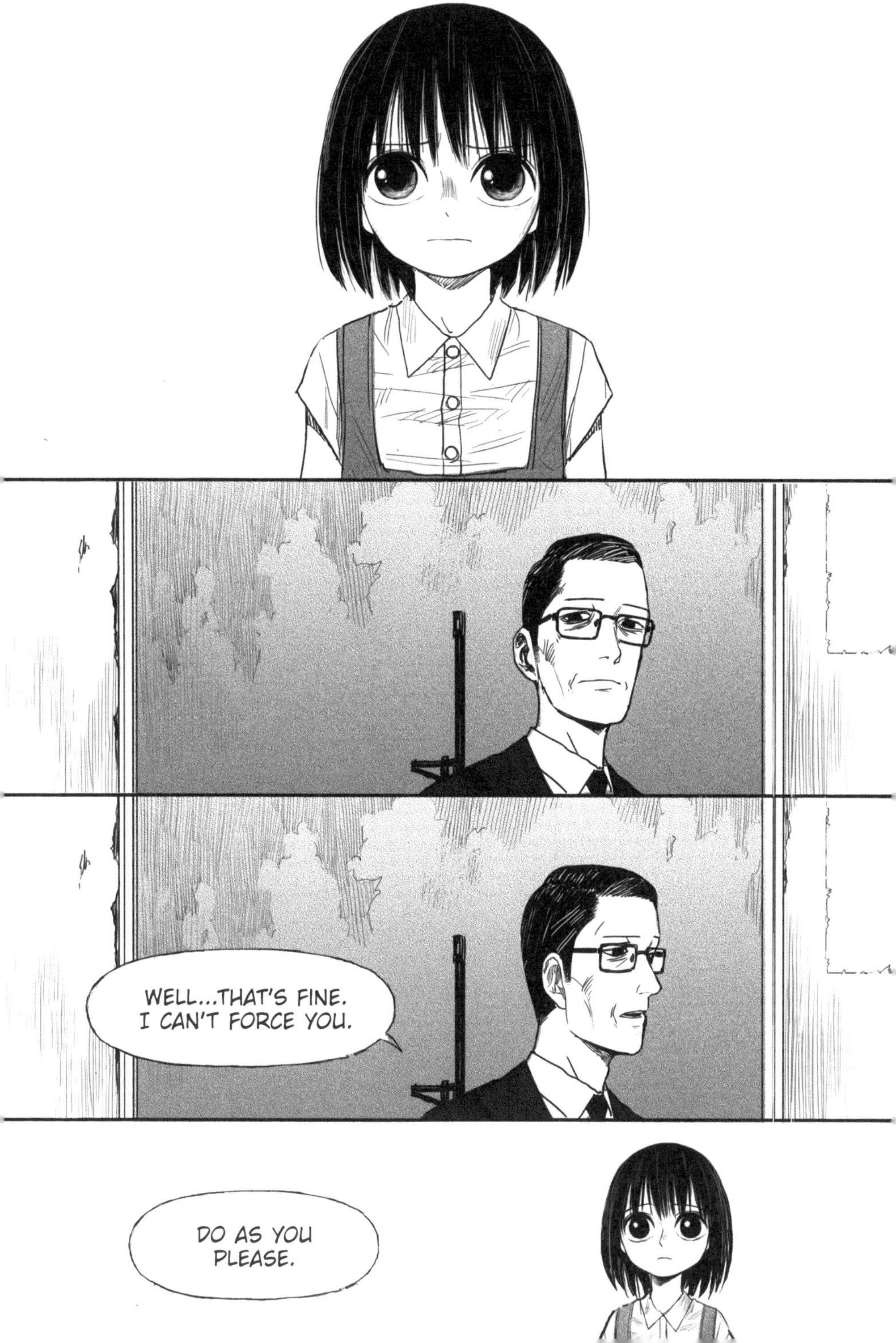
WELL...THAT'S FINE.
I CAN'T FORCE YOU.
DO AS YOU PLEASE.

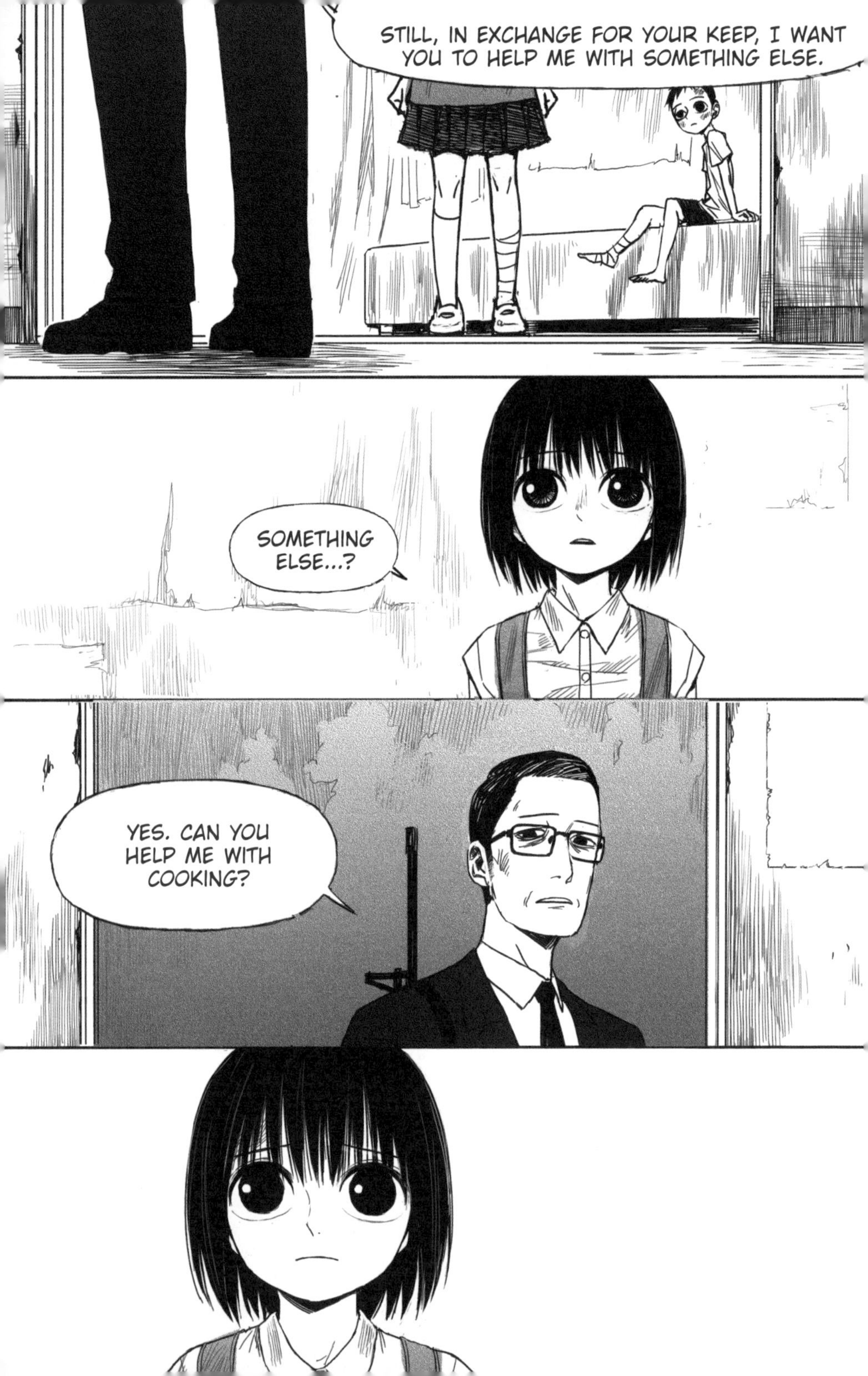
STILL, IN EXCHANGE FOR YOUR KEEP, I WANT YOU TO HELP ME WITH SOMETHING ELSE.
SOMETHING ELSE...?
YES. CAN YOU HELP ME WITH COOKING?

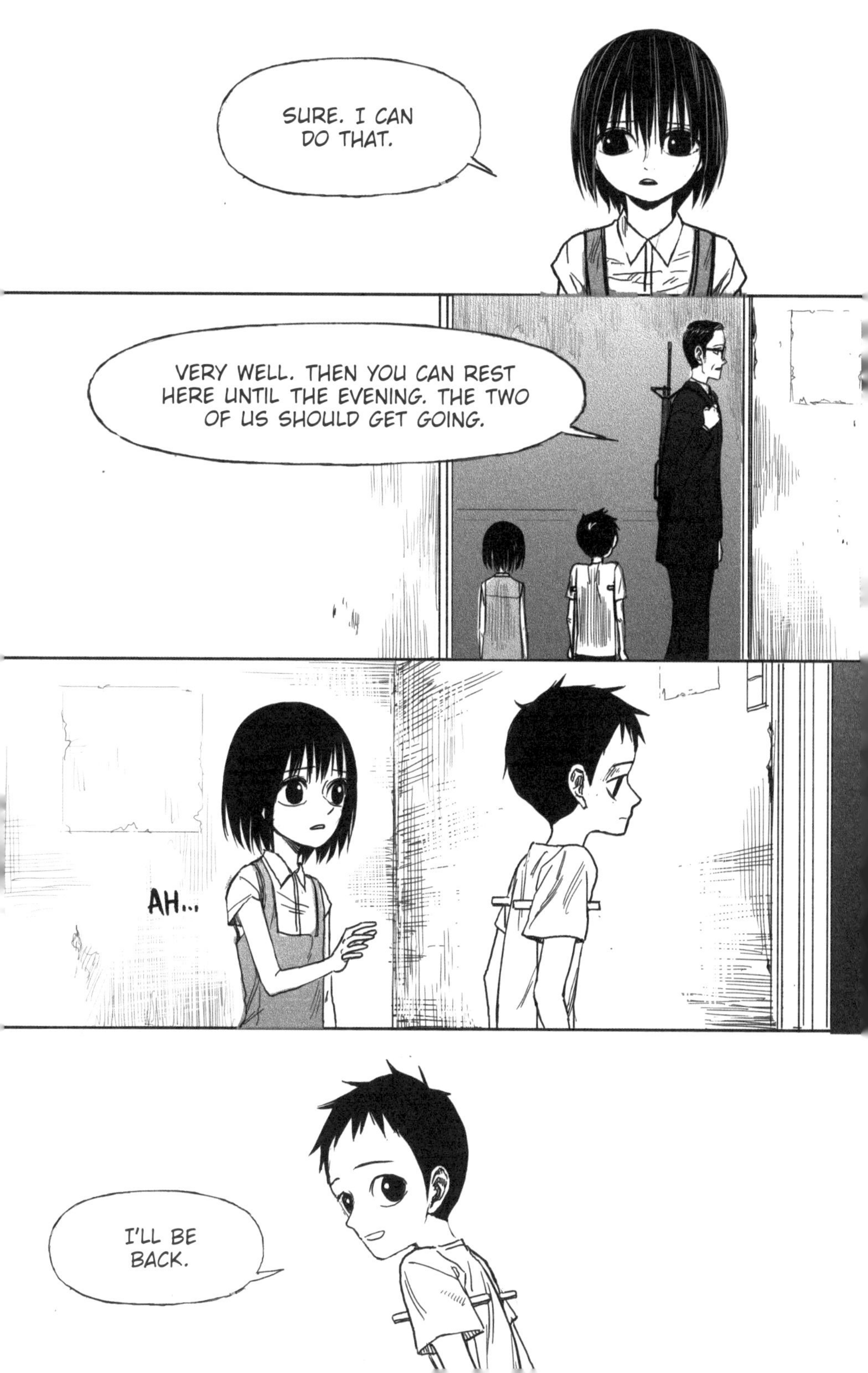
SURE. I CAN DO THAT.
VERY WELL. THEN YOU CAN REST HERE UNTIL THE EVENING. THE TWO OF US SHOULD GET GOING.
AH...
I'LL BE BACK.

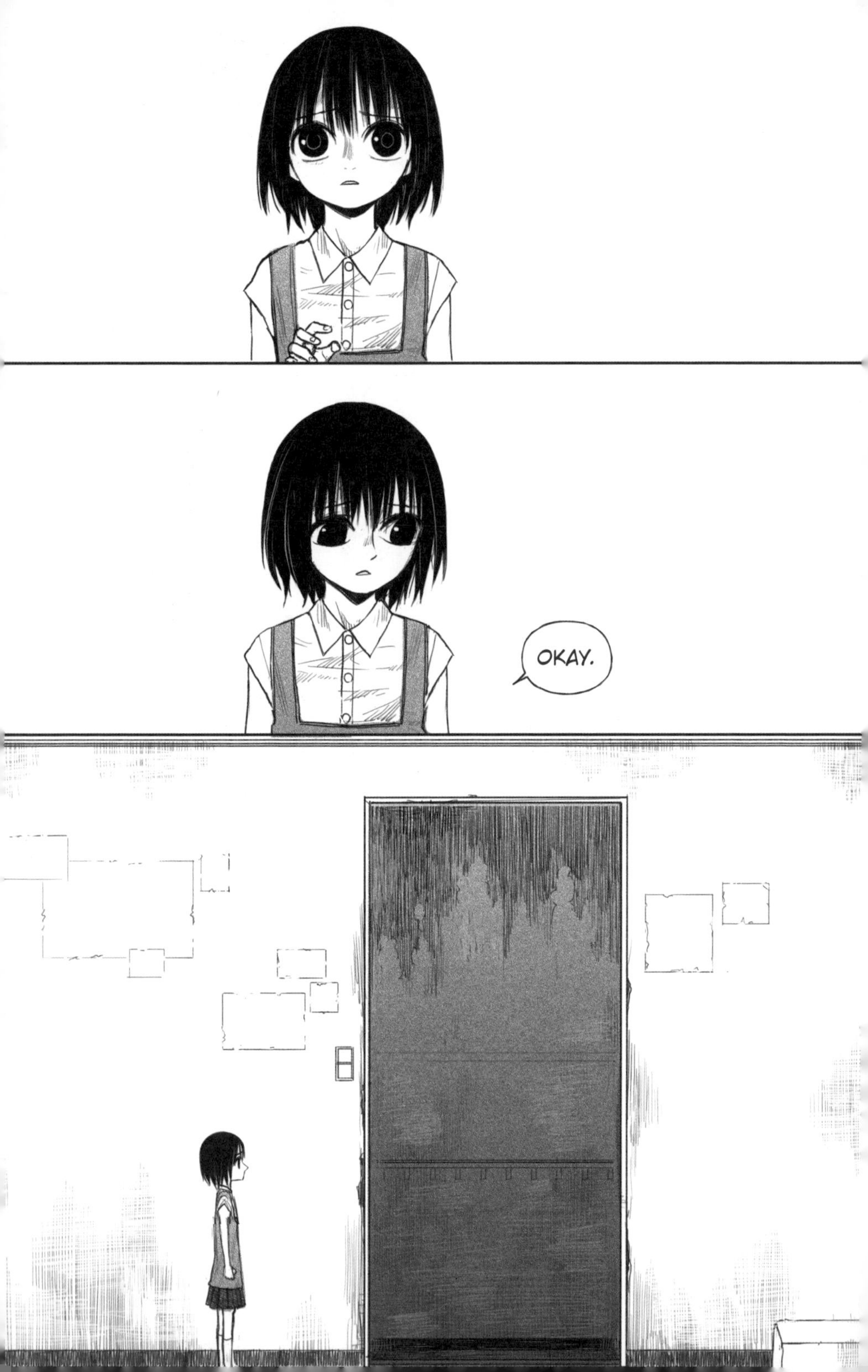
OKAY.

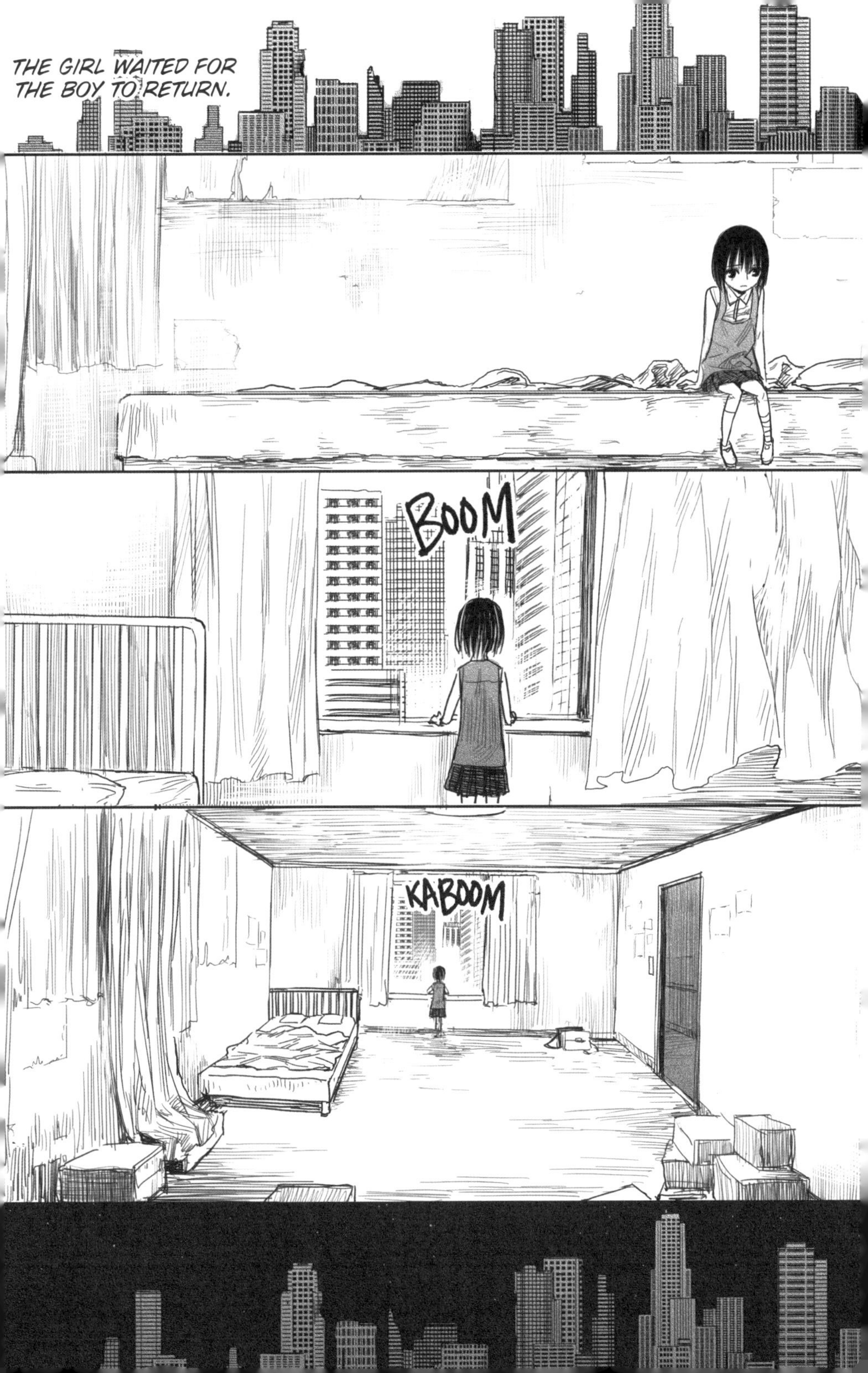
THE GIRL WAITED FOR THE BOY TO RETURN.
BOOM
KABOOM

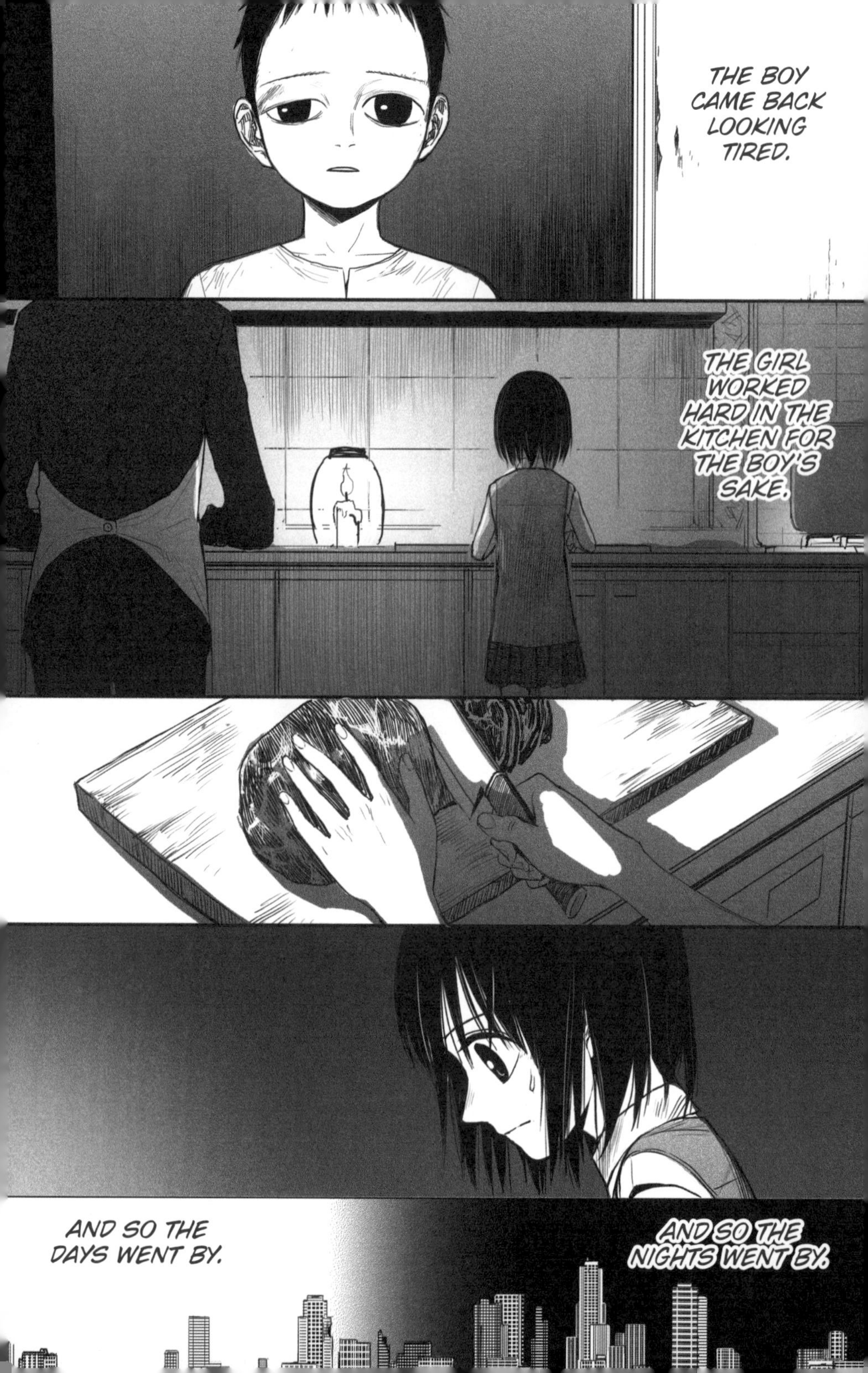
THE BOY CAME BACK LOOKING TIRED.
THE GIRL WORKED HARD IN THE KITCHEN FOR THE BOY'S SAKE.
AND SO THE NIGHTS WENT BY.
AND SO THE DAYS WENT BY.

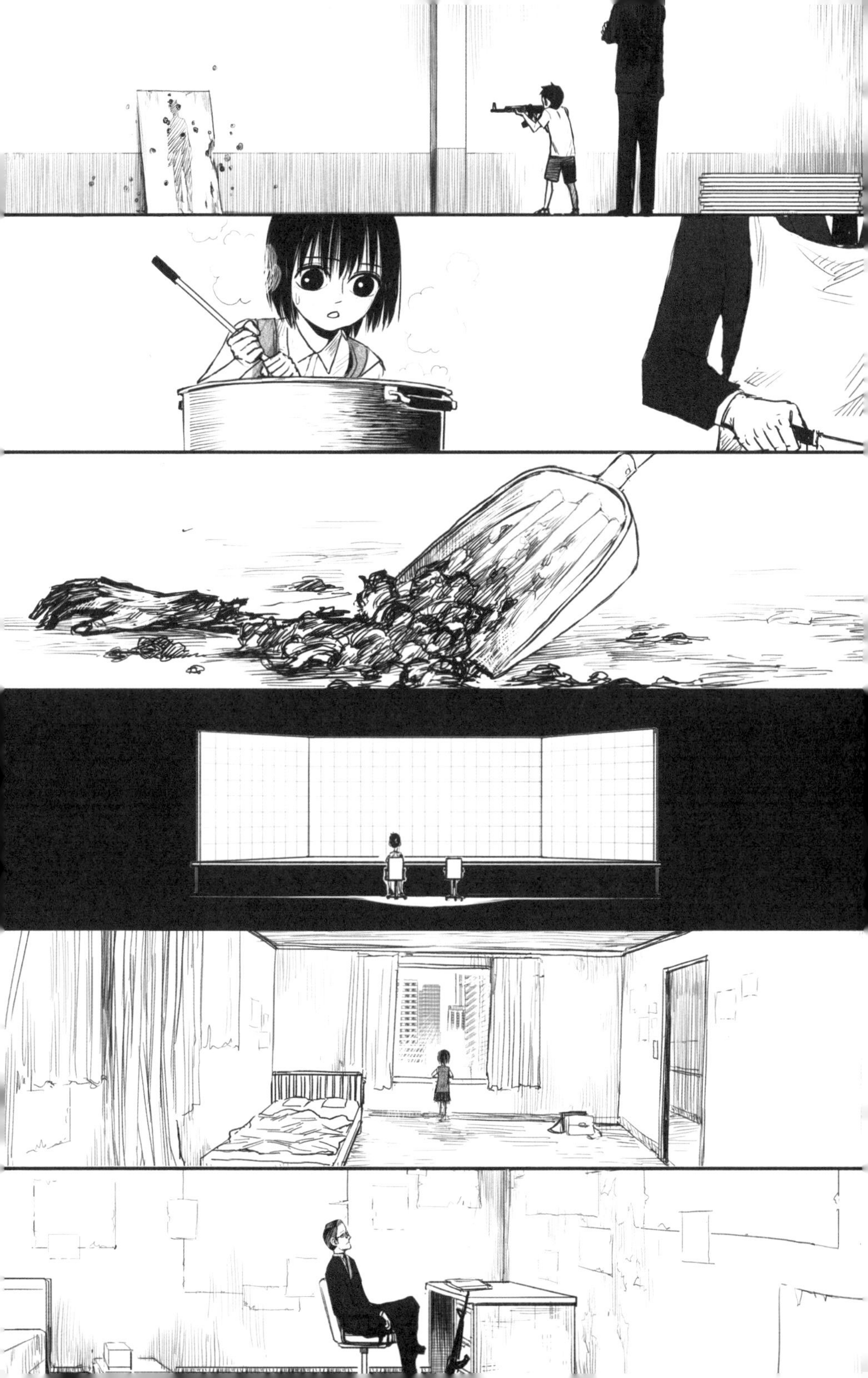

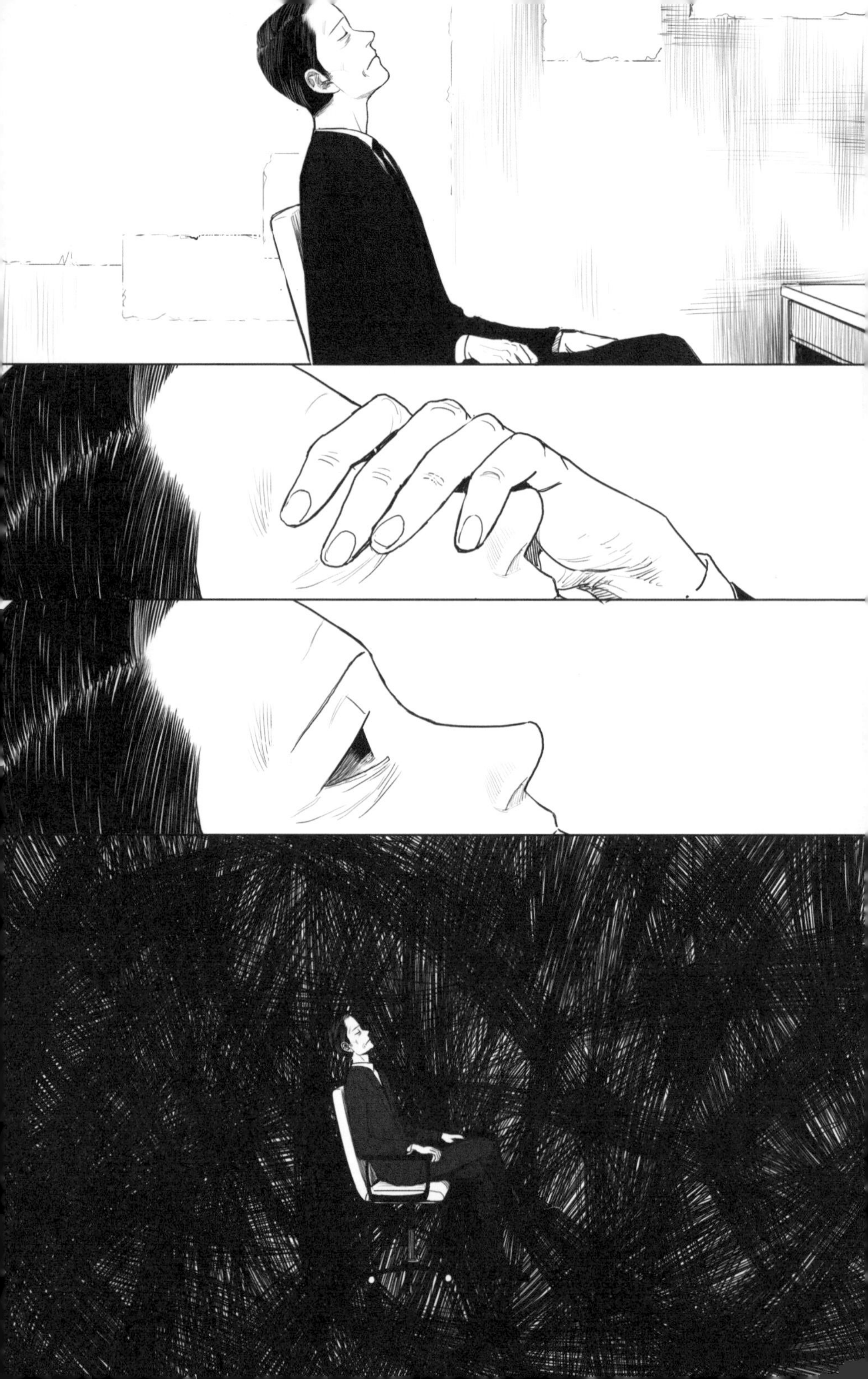

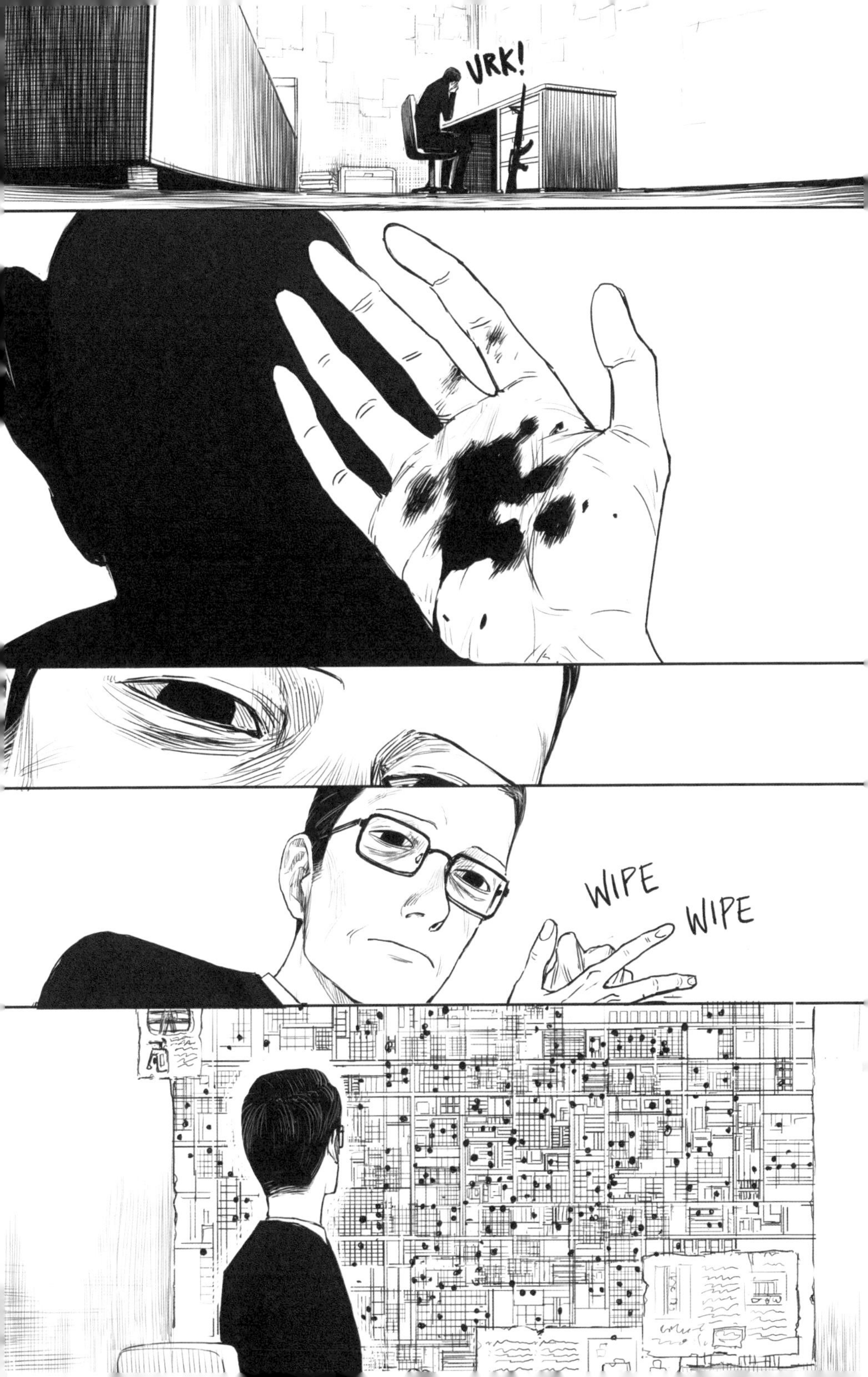
URK!
WIPE
WIPE

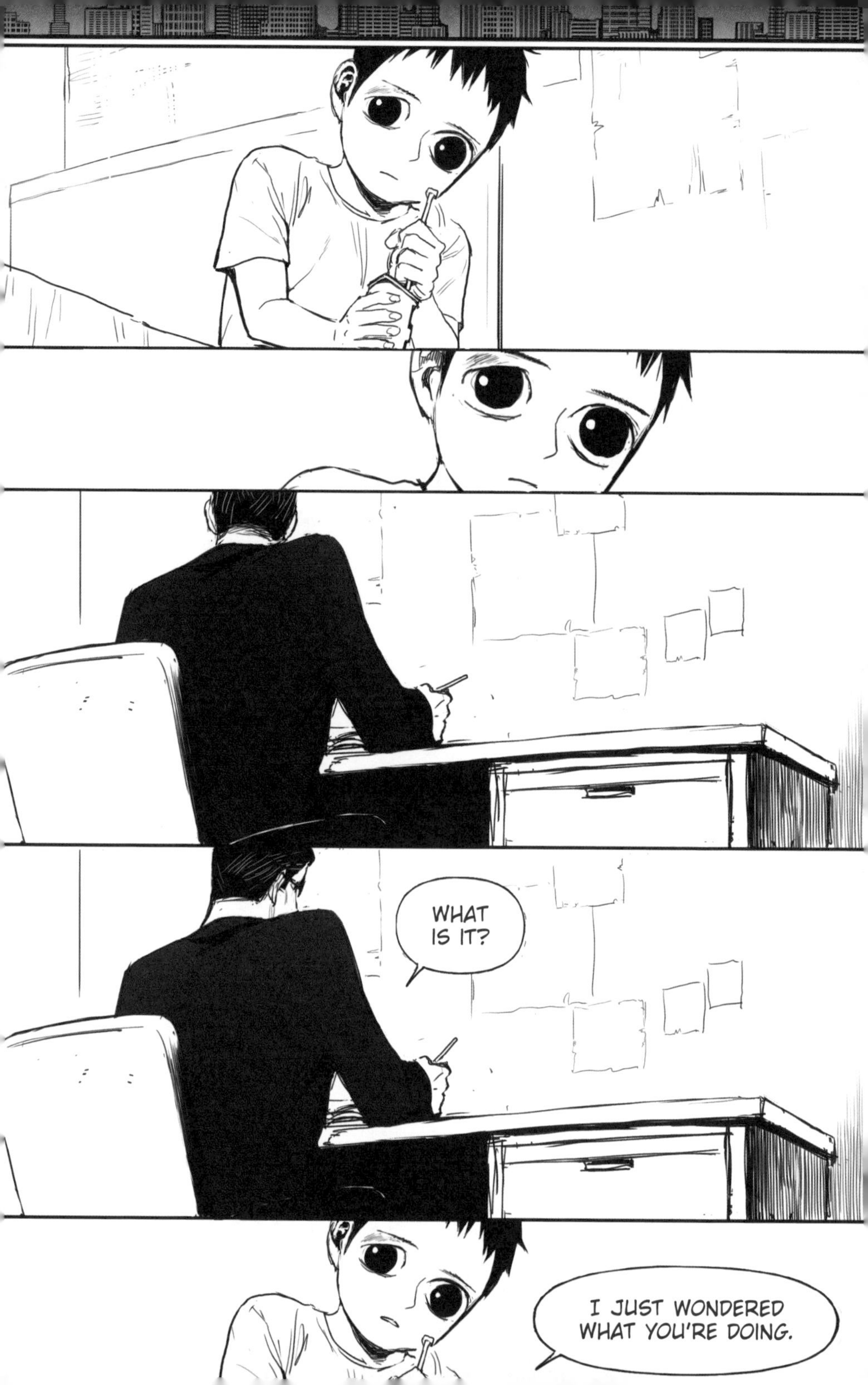
WHAT IS IT?
I JUST WONDERED WHAT YOU'RE DOING.

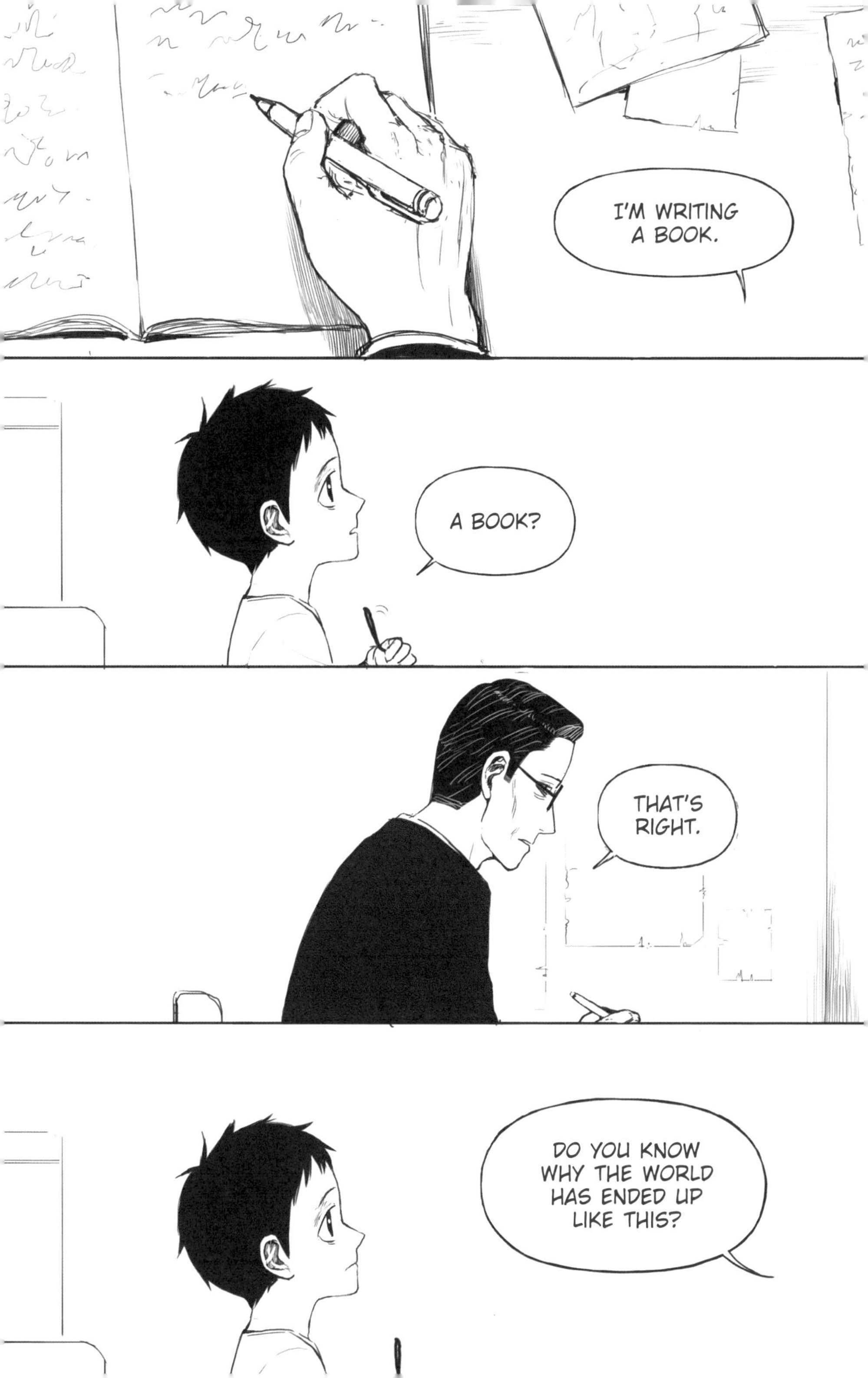
I'M WRITING A BOOK.
A BOOK?
THAT'S RIGHT.
DO YOU KNOW WHY THE WORLD HAS ENDED UP LIKE THIS?

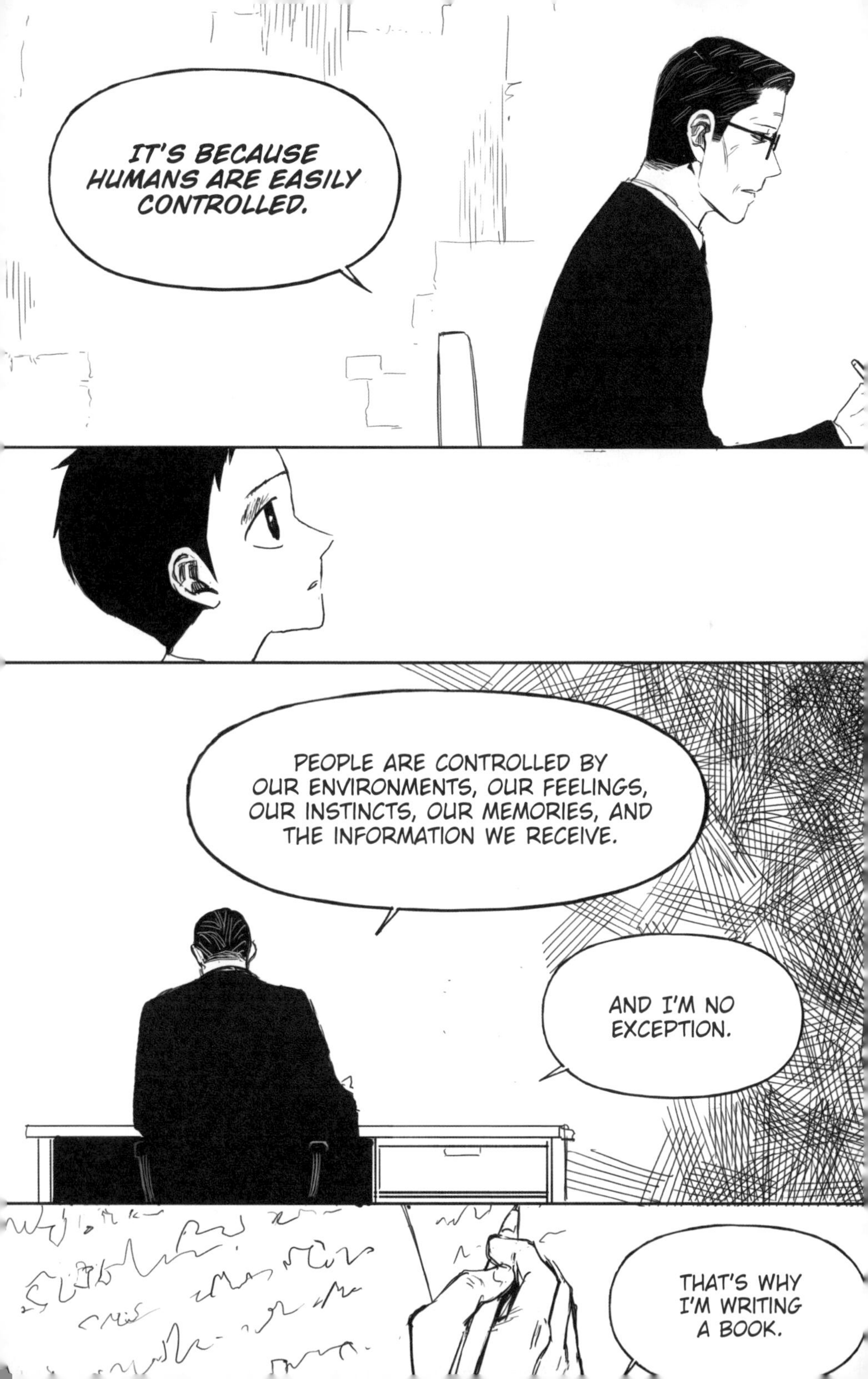
IT'S BECAUSE HUMANS ARE EASILY CONTROLLED.
PEOPLE ARE CONTROLLED BY OUR ENVIRONMENTS, OUR FEELINGS, OUR INSTINCTS, OUR MEMORIES, AND THE INFORMATION WE RECEIVE.
AND I'M NO EXCEPTION.
THAT'S WHY I'M WRITING A BOOK.

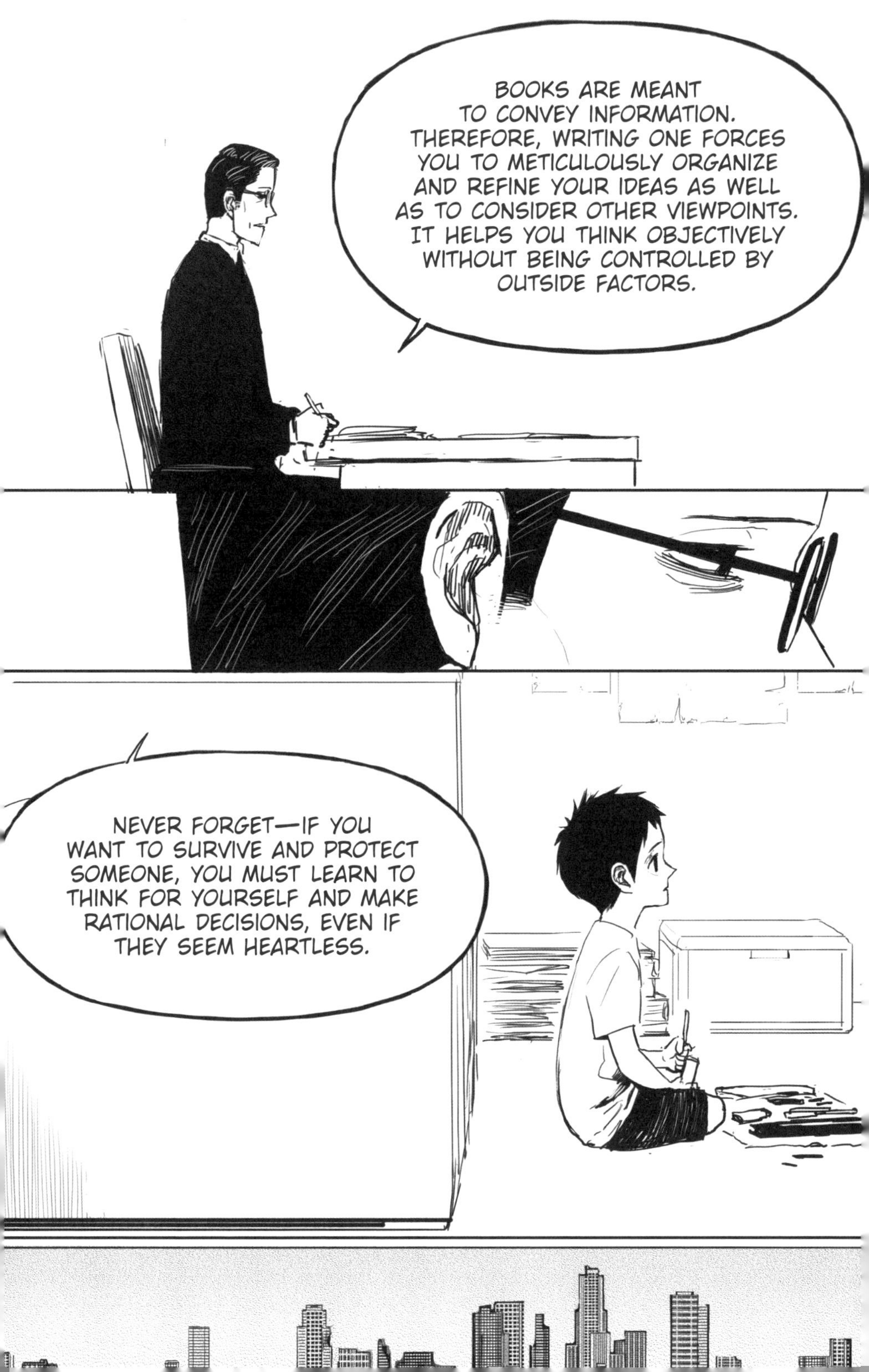
BOOKS ARE MEANT TO CONVEY INFORMATION. THEREFORE, WRITING ONE FORCES YOU TO METICULOUSLY ORGANIZE AND REFINE YOUR IDEAS AS WELL AS TO CONSIDER OTHER VIEWPOINTS. IT HELPS YOU THINK OBJECTIVELY WITHOUT BEING CONTROLLED BY OUTSIDE FACTORS.
NEVER FORGET—IF YOU WANT TO SURVIVE AND PROTECT SOMEONE, YOU MUST LEARN TO THINK FOR YOURSELF AND MAKE RATIONAL DECISIONS, EVEN IF THEY SEEM HEARTLESS.

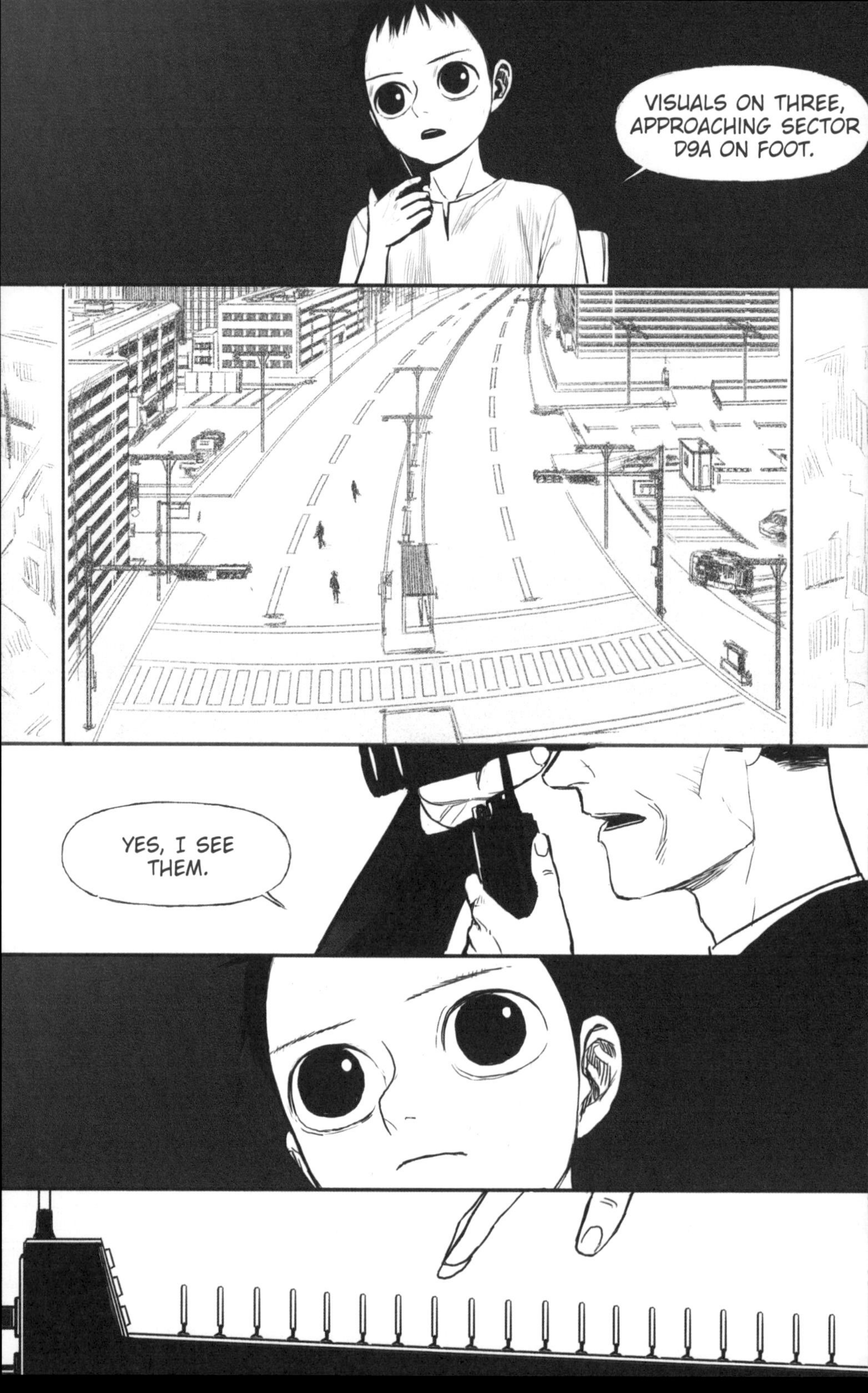
VISUALS ON THREE, APPROACHING SECTOR D9A ON FOOT.
YES, I SEE THEM.

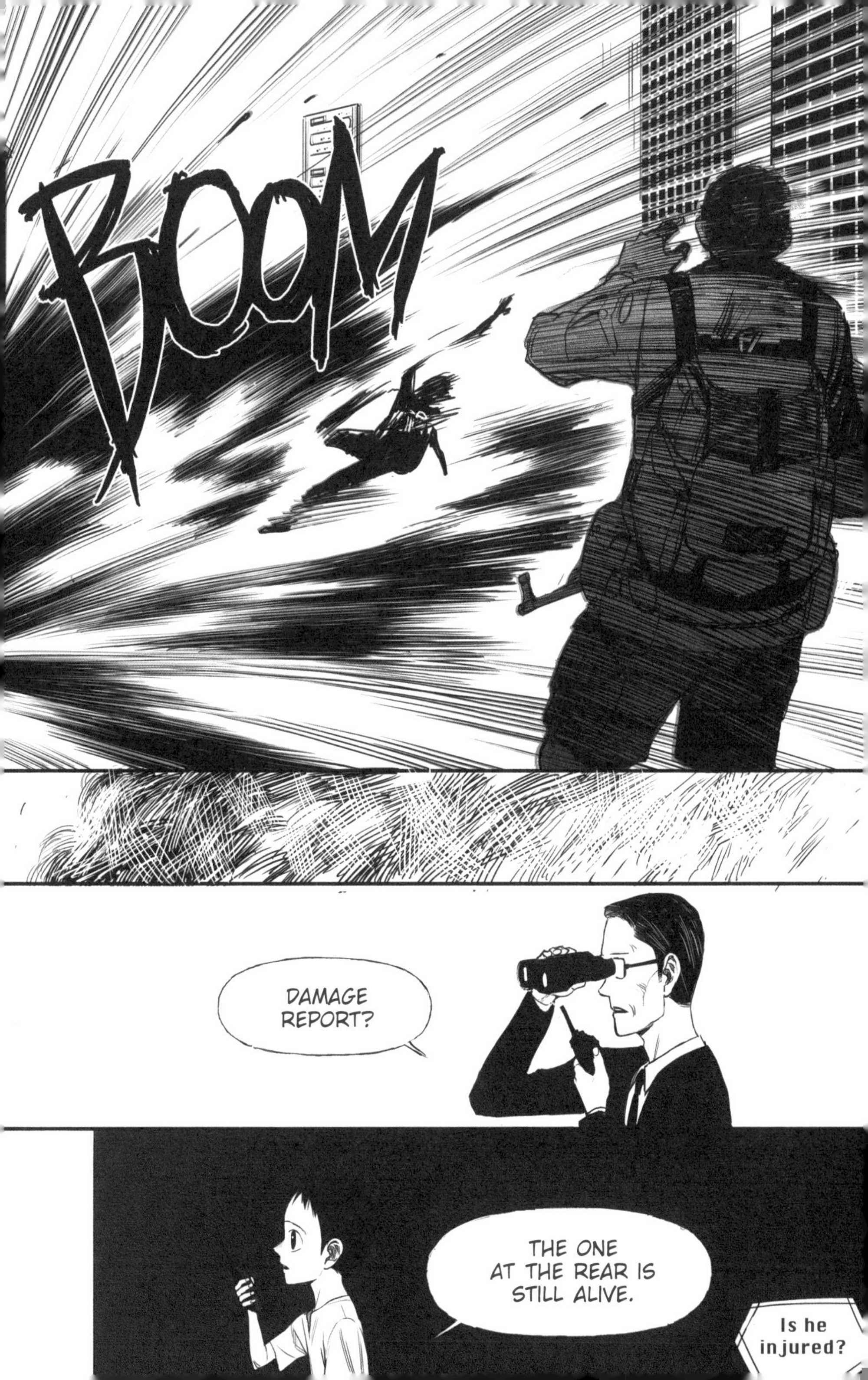
BOOM
DAMAGE REPORT?
THE ONE AT THE REAR IS STILL ALIVE.
Is he injured?

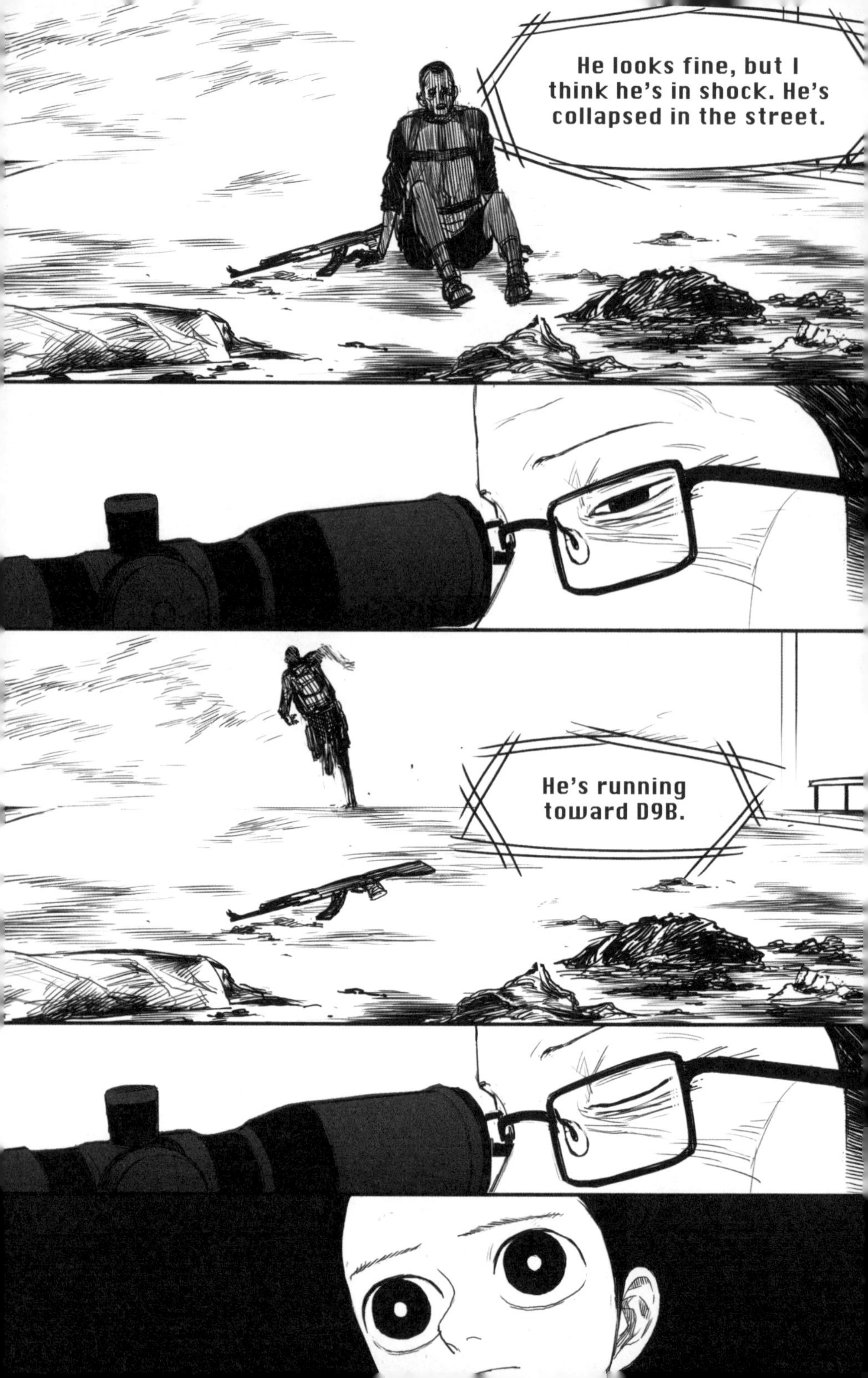
He looks fine, but I think he's in shock. He's collapsed in the street.
He's running toward D9B.

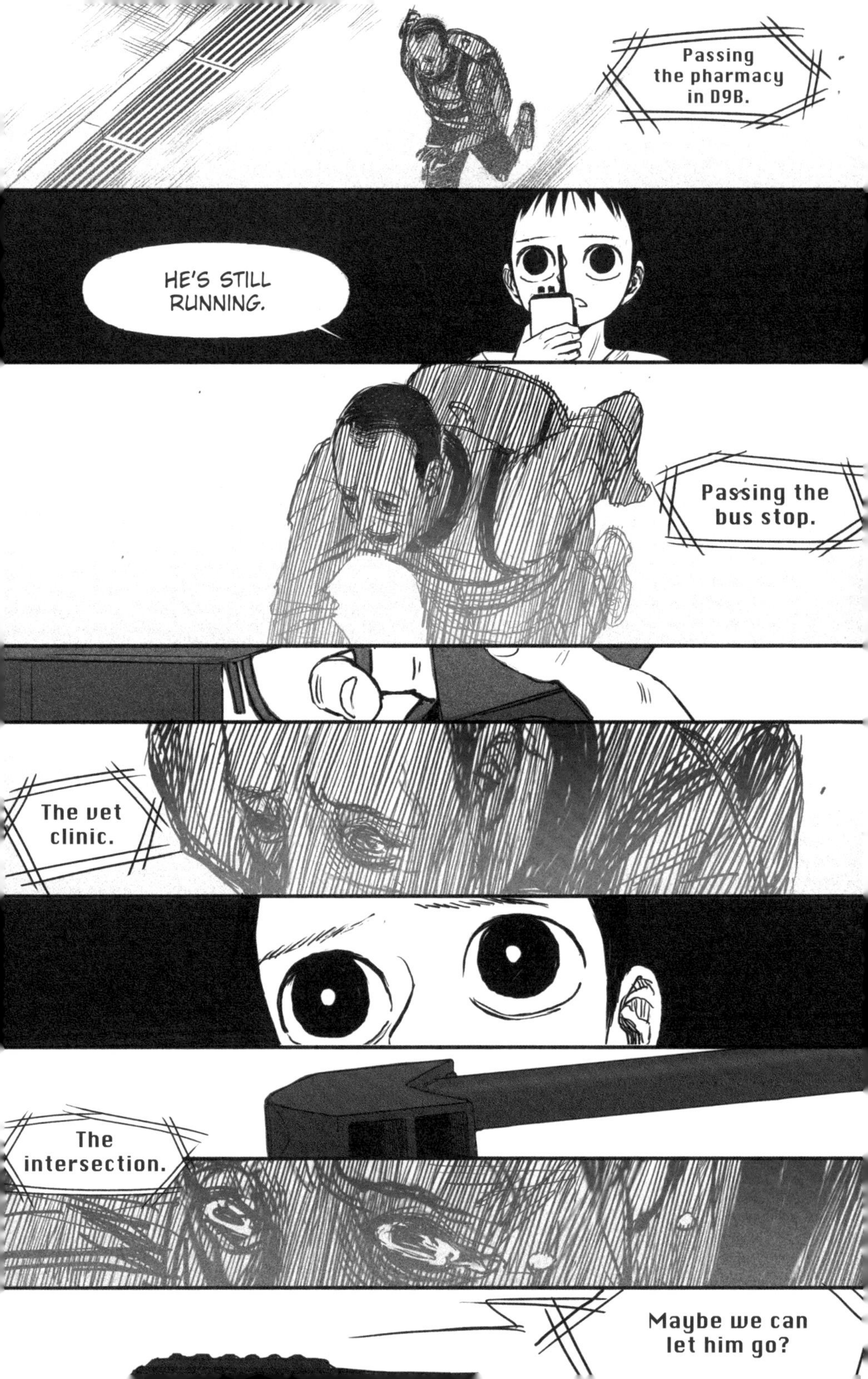
Passing the pharmacy in D9B.
HE'S STILL RUNNING.
Passing the bus stop.
The vet clinic.
The intersection.
Maybe we can let him go?

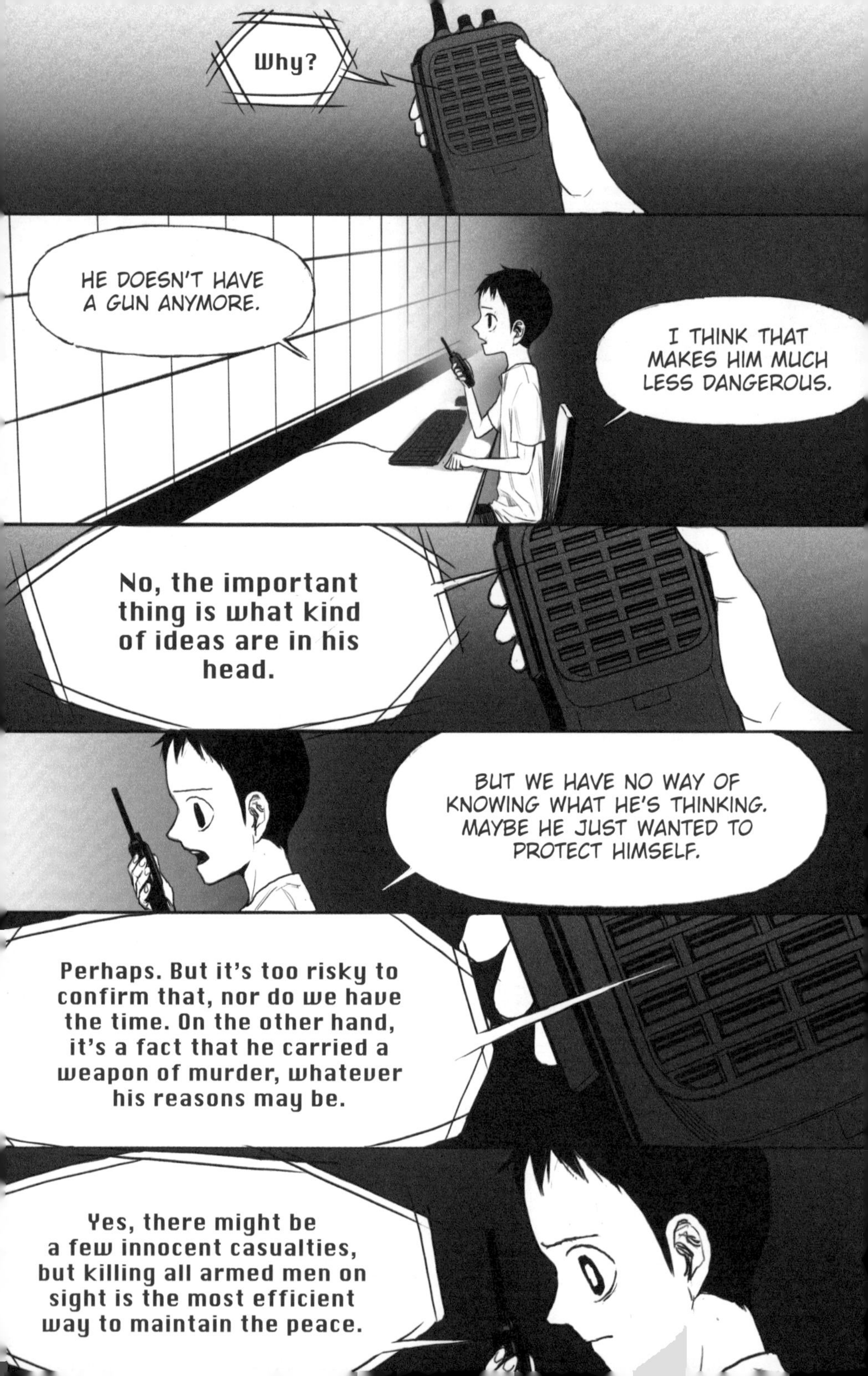
Why?
HE DOESN'T HAVE A GUN ANYMORE.
I THINK THAT MAKES HIM MUCH LESS DANGEROUS.
No, the important thing is what kind of ideas are in his head.
BUT WE HAVE NO WAY OF KNOWING WHAT HE'S THINKING. MAYBE HE JUST WANTED TO PROTECT HIMSELF.
Perhaps. But it's too risky to confirm that, nor do we have the time. On the other hand, it's a fact that he carried a weapon of murder, whatever his reasons may be.
Yes, there might be a few innocent casualties, but killing all armed men on sight is the most efficient way to maintain the peace.

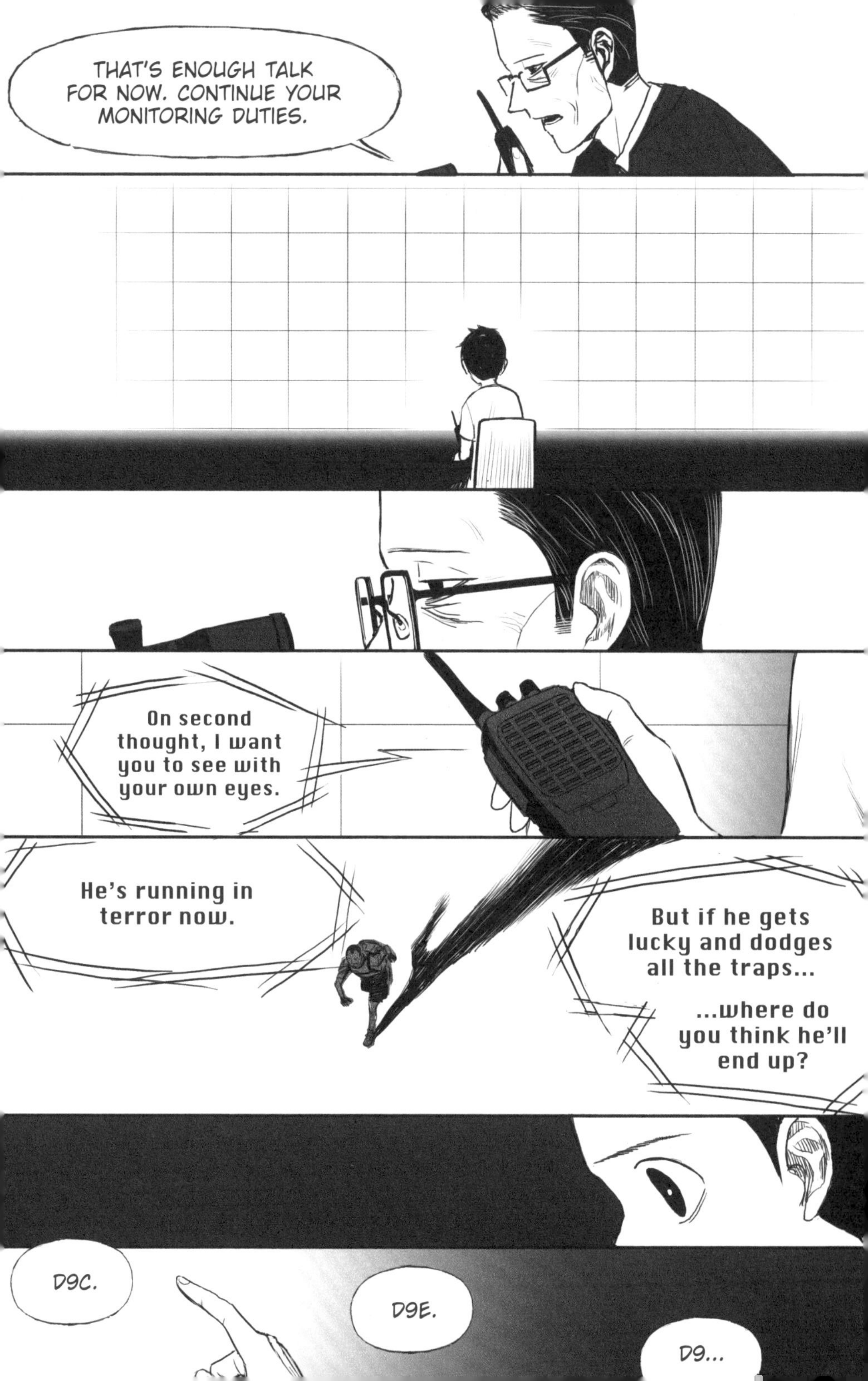
THAT'S ENOUGH TALK FOR NOW. CONTINUE YOUR MONITORING DUTIES.
On second thought, I want you to see with your own eyes.
He's running in terror now.
But if he gets lucky and dodges all the traps...
...where do you think he'll end up?
D9C.
D9E.
D9...

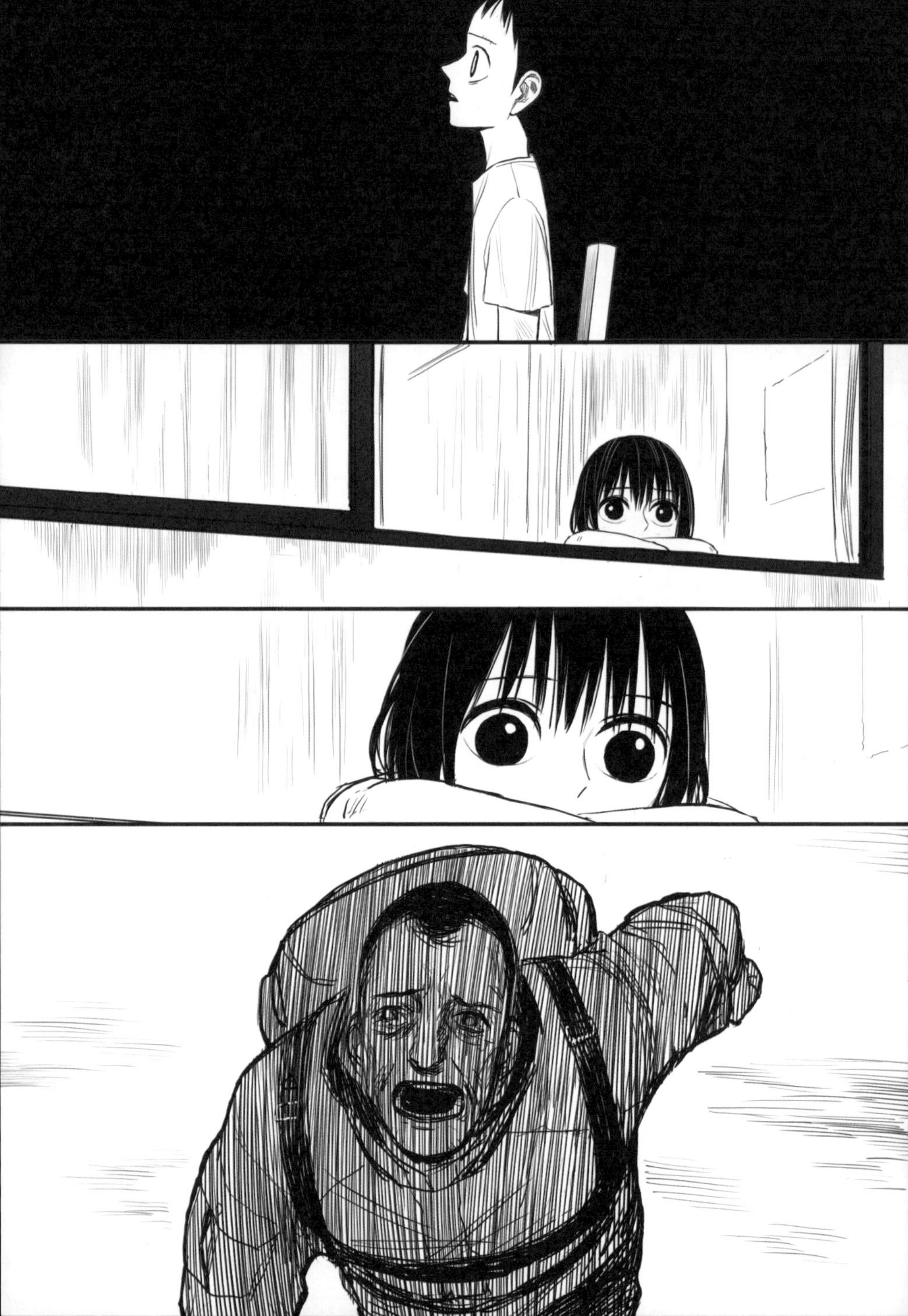

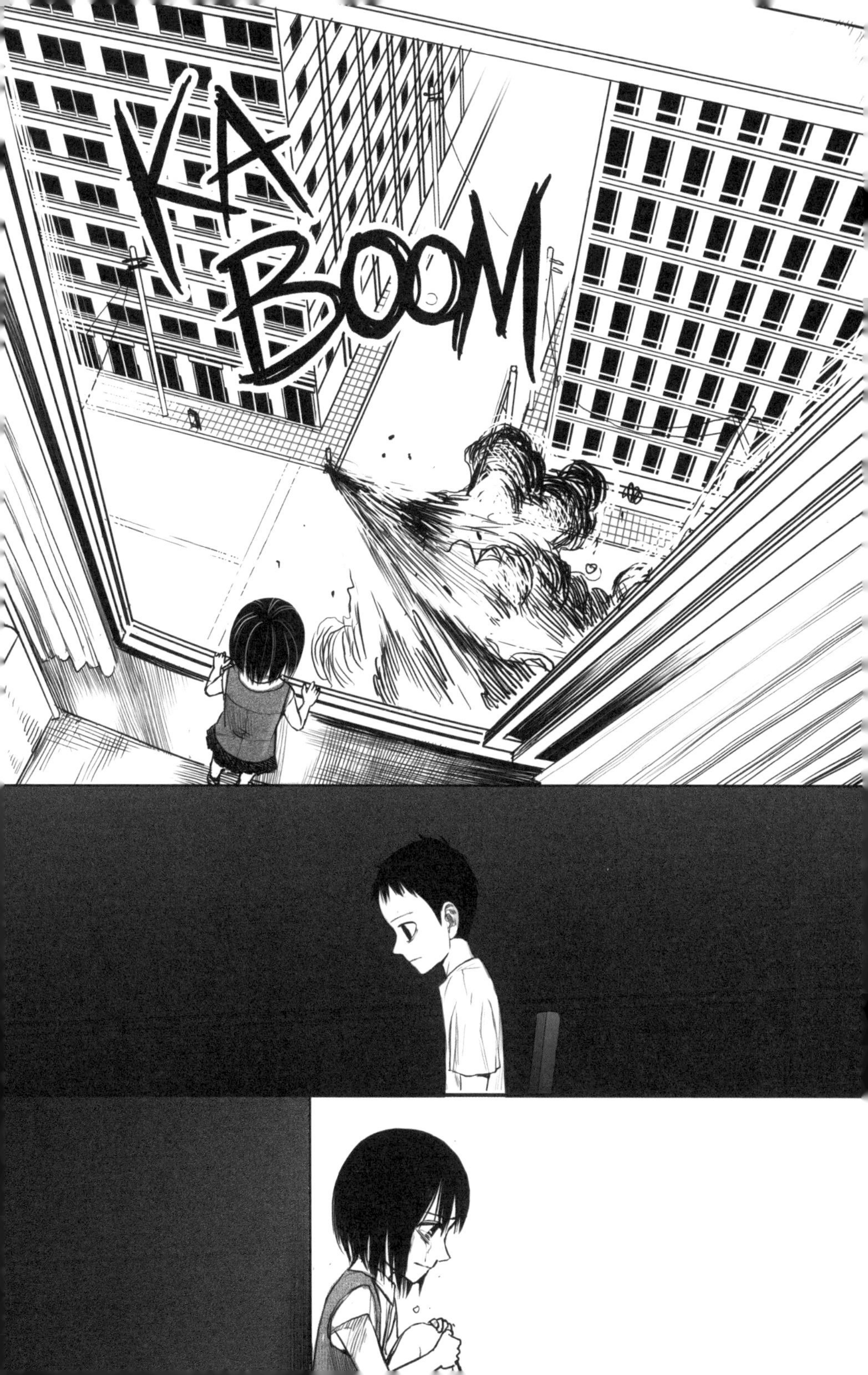
KA
BOOM

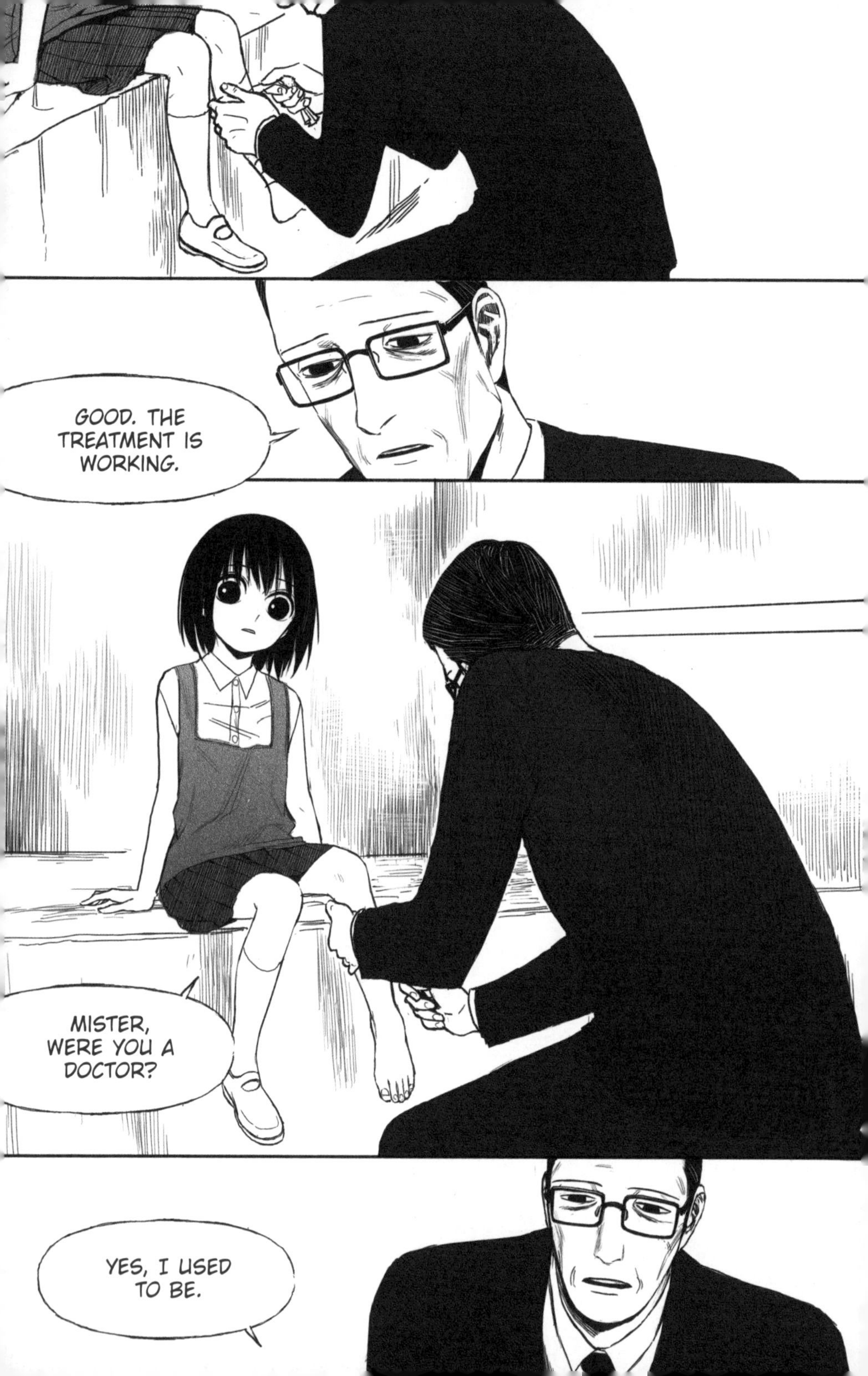
GOOD. THE TREATMENT IS WORKING.
MISTER, WERE YOU A DOCTOR?
YES, I USED TO BE.

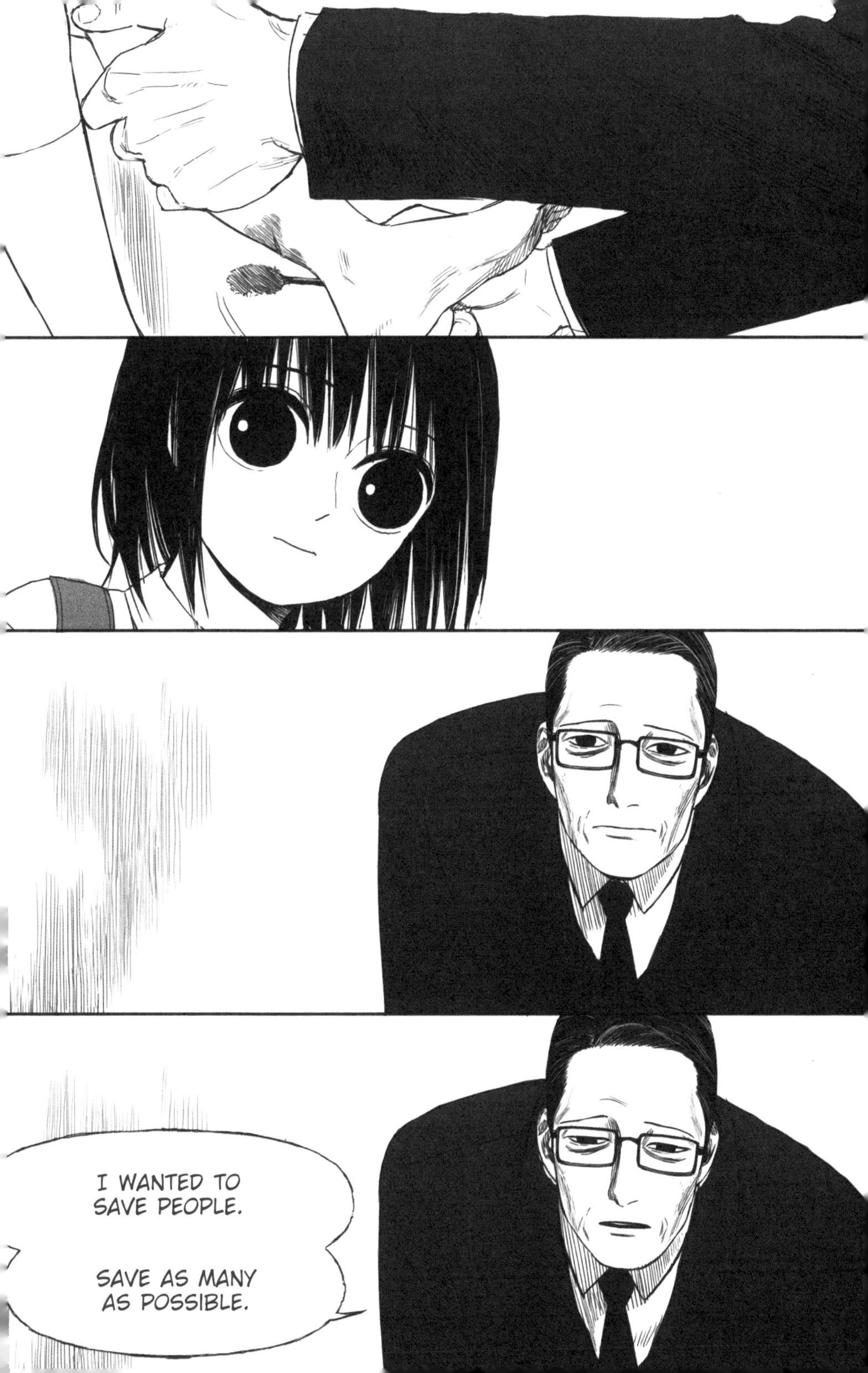
I WANTED TO SAVE PEOPLE.
SAVE AS MANY AS POSSIBLE.

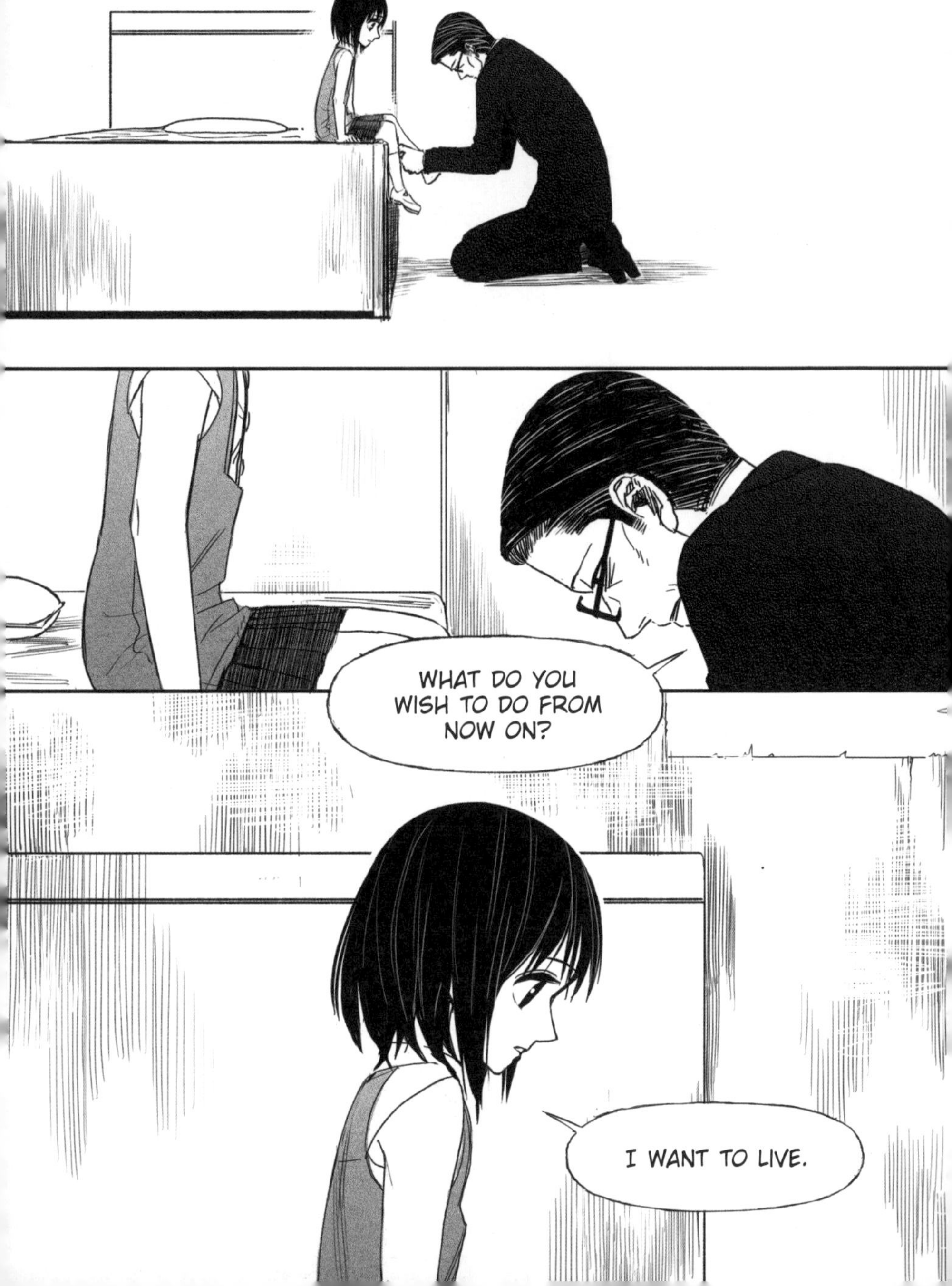
WHAT DO YOU WISH TO DO FROM NOW ON?
I WANT TO LIVE.

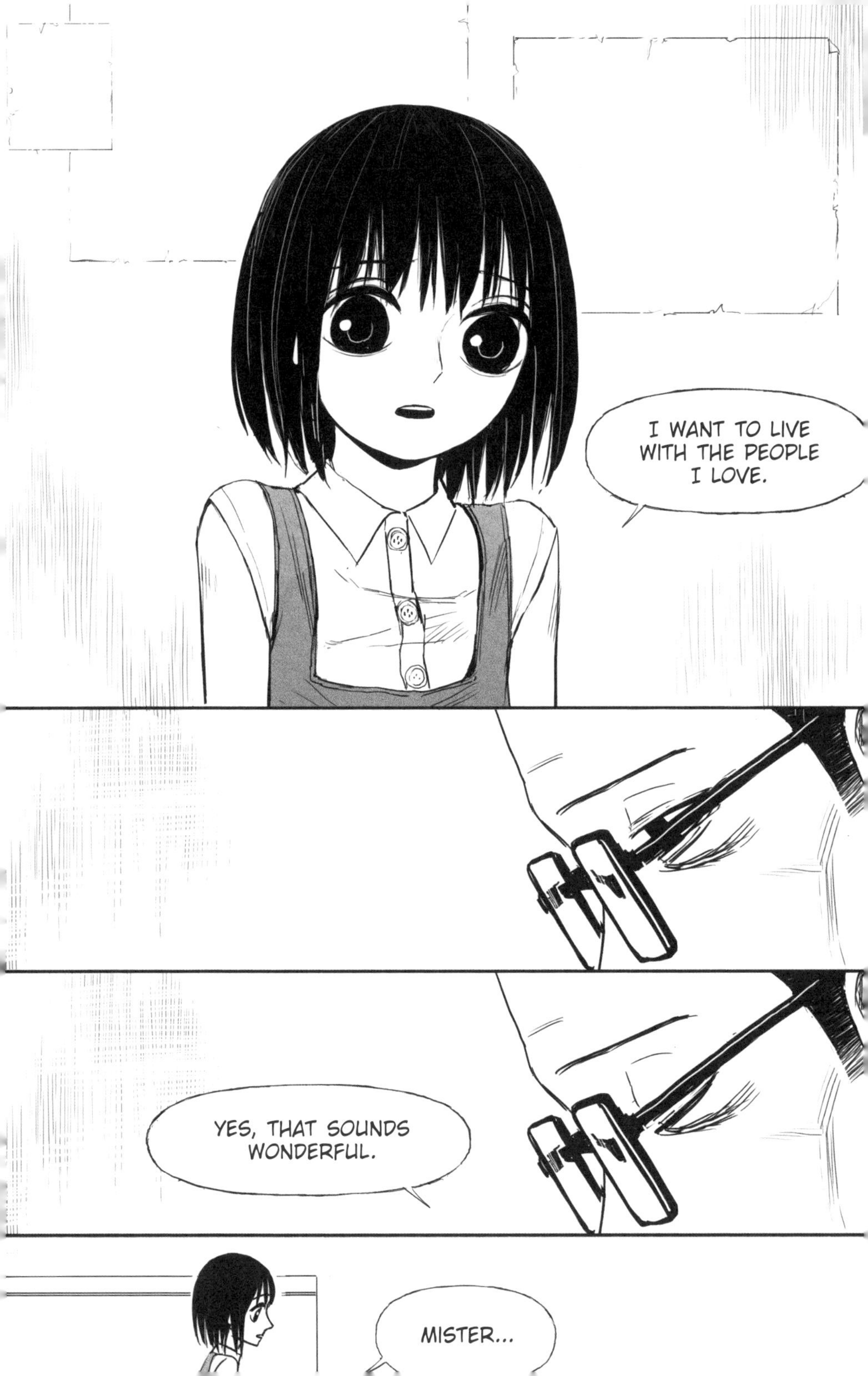
I WANT TO LIVE WITH THE PEOPLE I LOVE.
YES, THAT SOUNDS WONDERFUL.
MISTER...

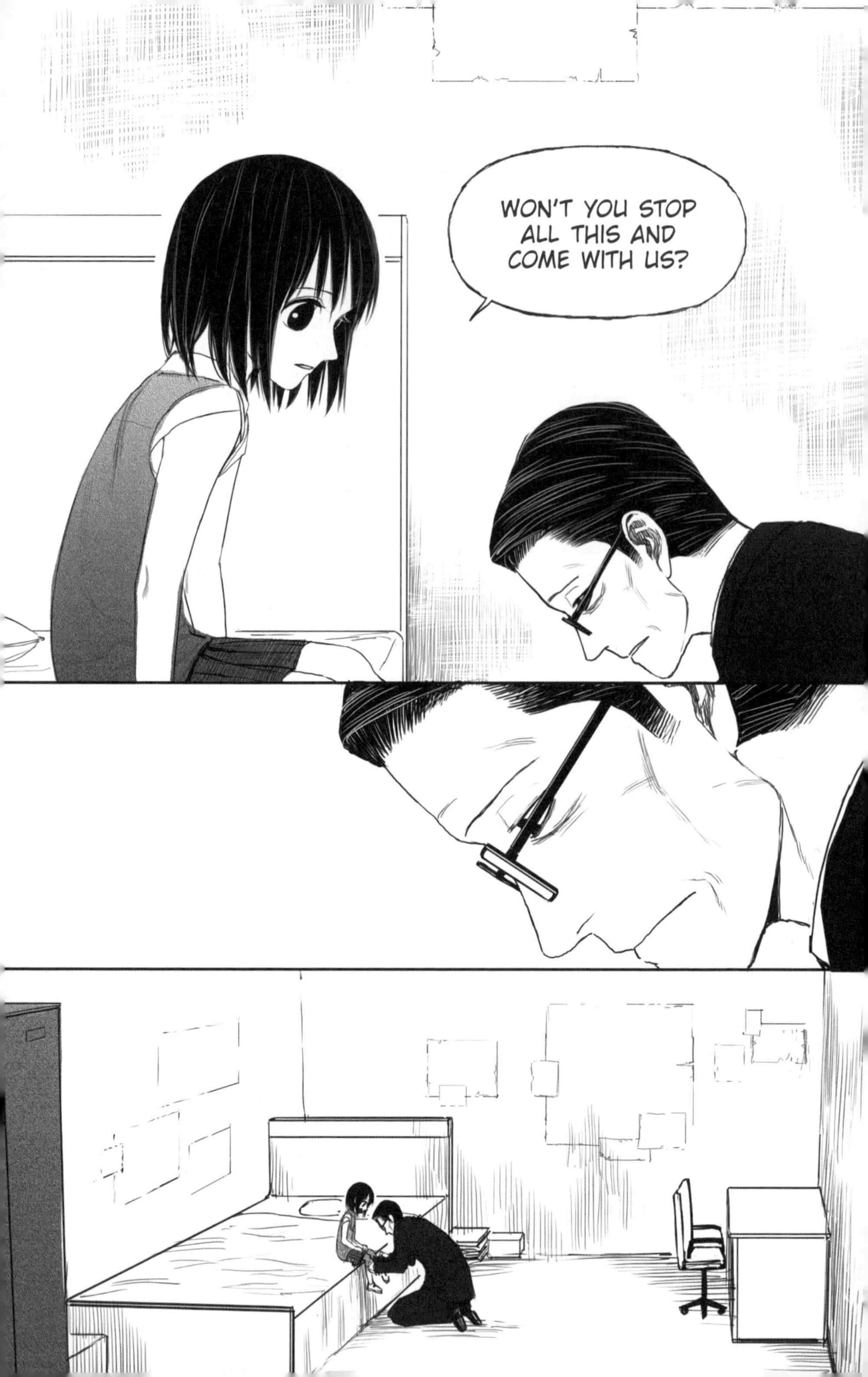
WON'T YOU STOP ALL THIS AND COME WITH US?

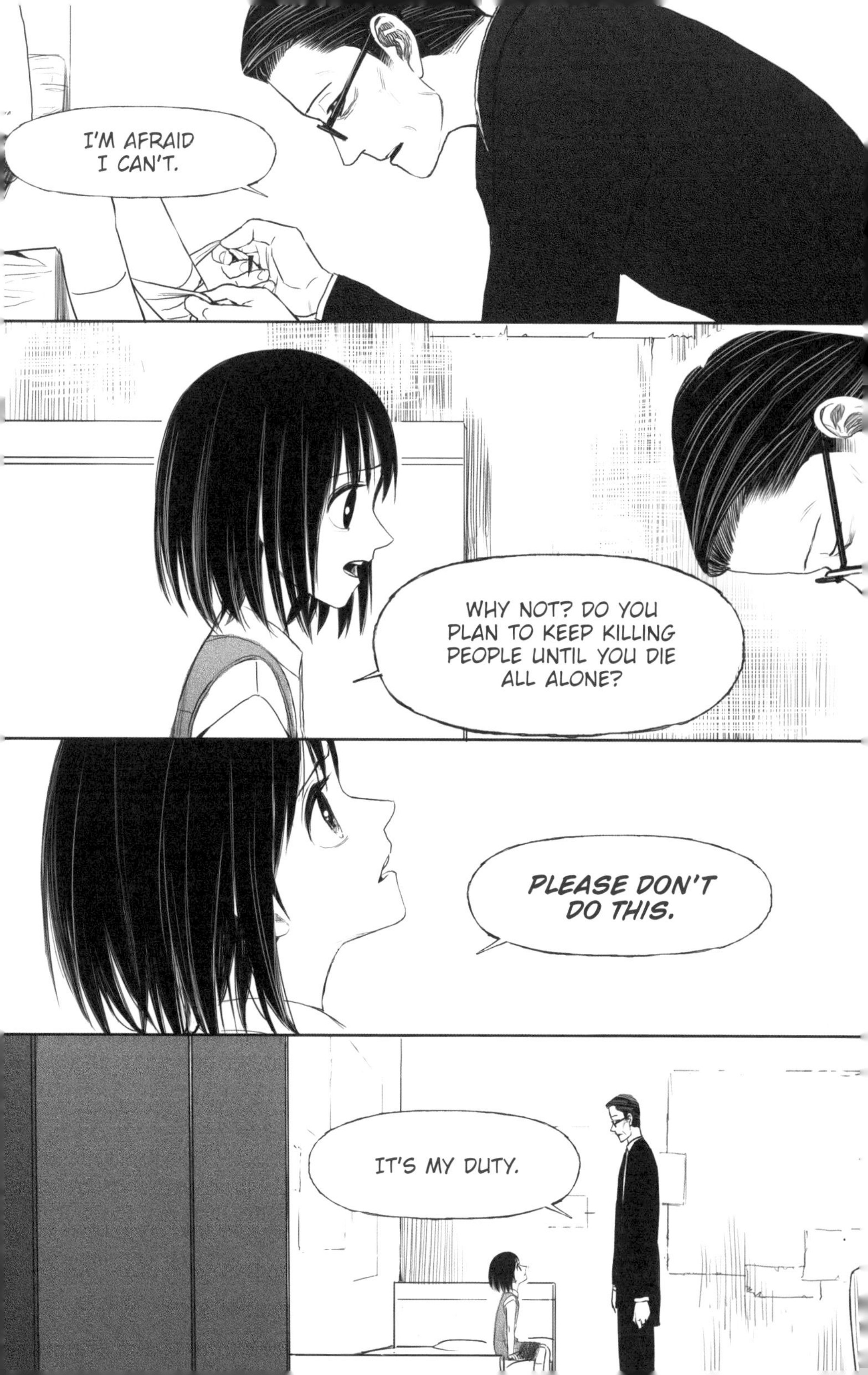
I'M AFRAID I CAN'T.
WHY NOT? DO YOU PLAN TO KEEP KILLING PEOPLE UNTIL YOU DIE ALL ALONE?
PLEASE DON'T DO THIS.
IT'S MY DUTY.

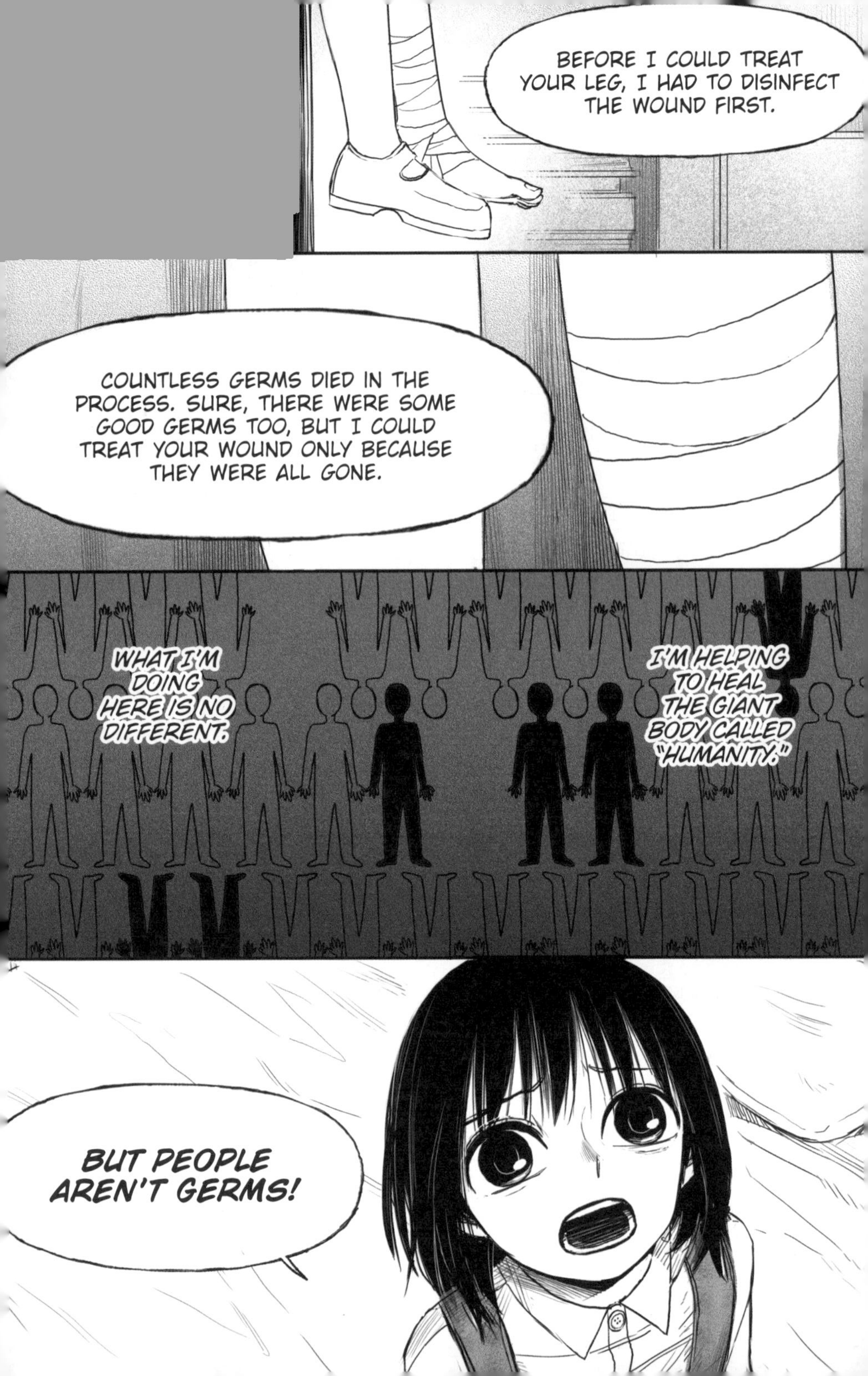
BEFORE I COULD TREAT YOUR LEG, I HAD TO DISINFECT THE WOUND FIRST.
COUNTLESS GERMS DIED IN THE PROCESS. SURE, THERE WERE SOME GOOD GERMS TOO, BUT I COULD TREAT YOUR WOUND ONLY BECAUSE THEY WERE ALL GONE.
WHAT I'M DOING HERE IS NO DIFFERENT.
I'M HELPING TO HEAL THE GIANT BODY CALLED "HUMANITY."
BUT PEOPLE AREN'T GERMS!

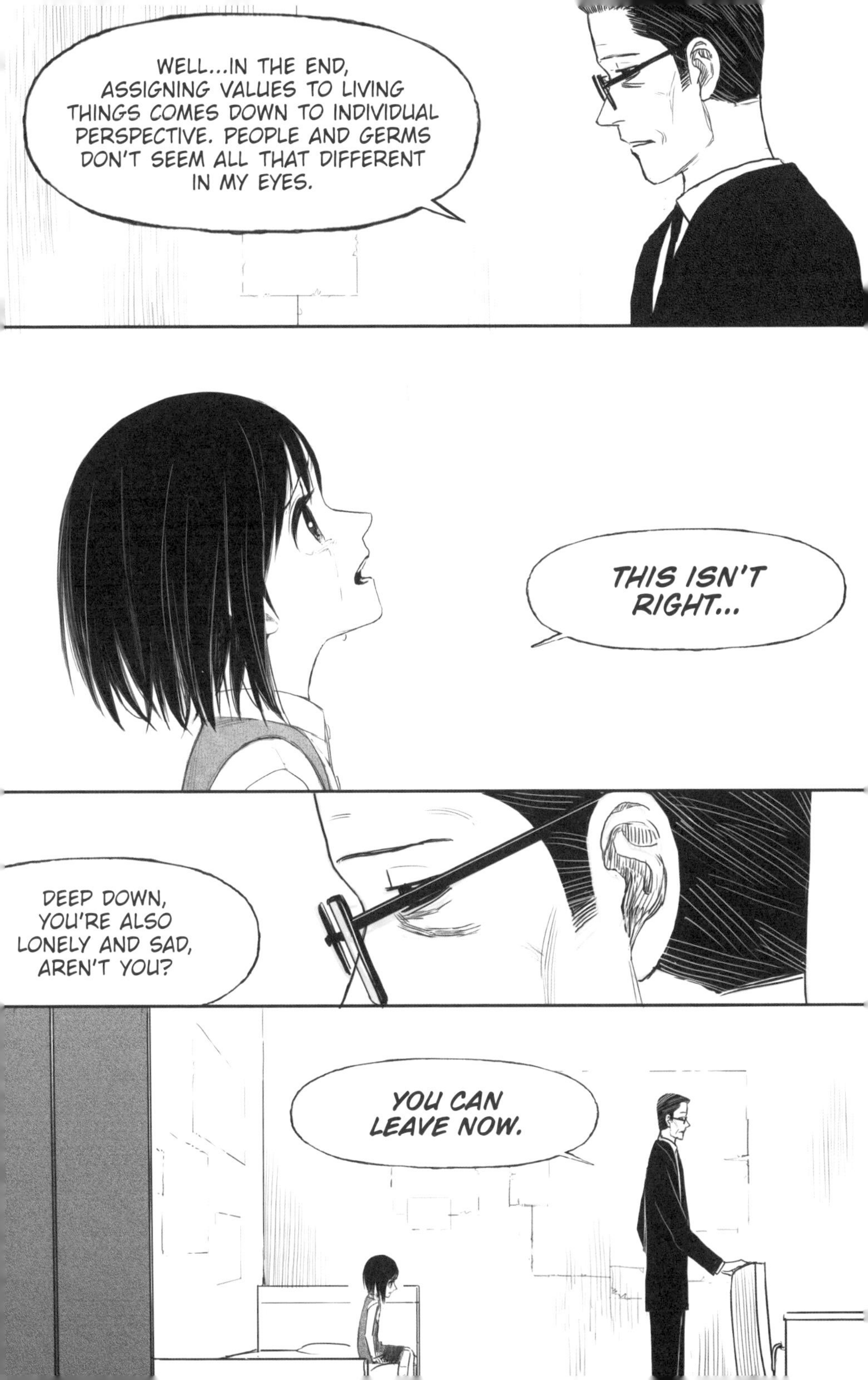
WELL...IN THE END, ASSIGNING VALUES TO LIVING THINGS COMES DOWN TO INDIVIDUAL PERSPECTIVE. PEOPLE AND GERMS DON'T SEEM ALL THAT DIFFERENT IN MY EYES.
THIS ISN'T RIGHT...
DEEP DOWN, YOU'RE ALSO LONELY AND SAD, AREN'T YOU?
YOU CAN LEAVE NOW.

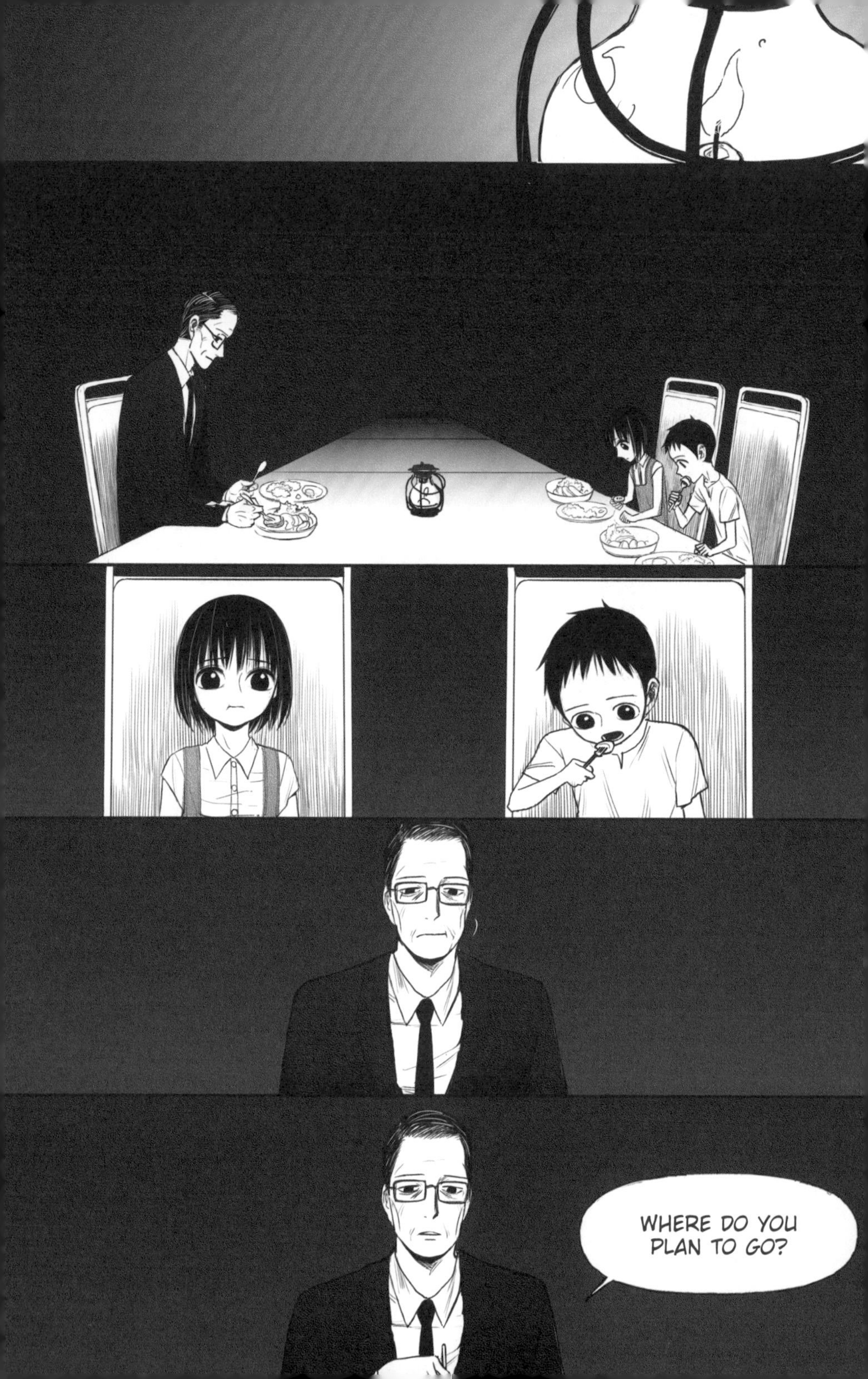
WHERE DO YOU PLAN TO GO?

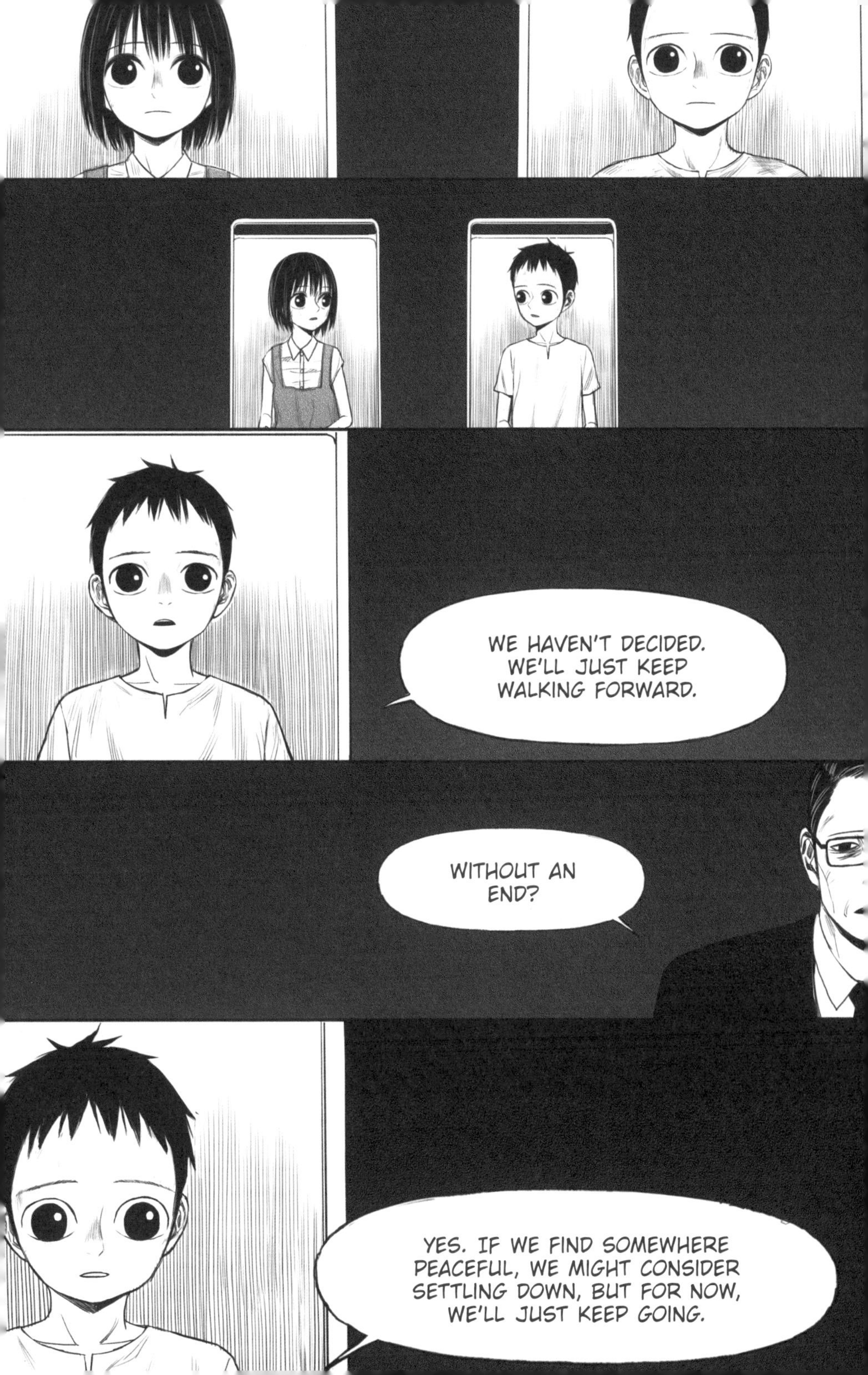
WE HAVEN'T DECIDED. WE'LL JUST KEEP WALKING FORWARD.
WITHOUT AN END?
YES. IF WE FIND SOMEWHERE PEACEFUL, WE MIGHT CONSIDER SETTLING DOWN, BUT FOR NOW, WE'LL JUST KEEP GOING.

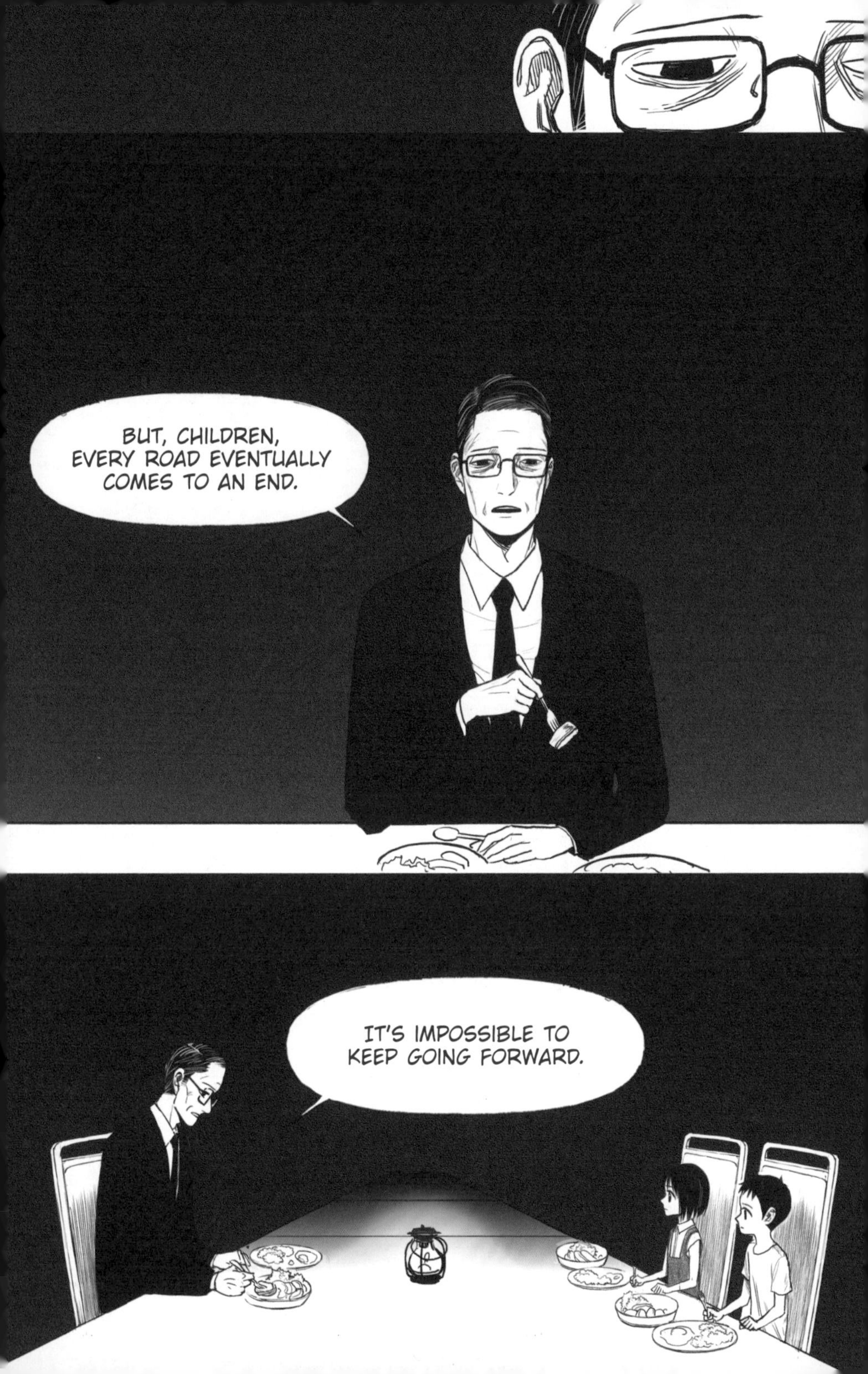
BUT, CHILDREN,
EVERY ROAD EVENTUALLY
COMES TO AN END.
IT'S IMPOSSIBLE TO
KEEP GOING FORWARD.

NO, IT'S NOT IMPOSSIBLE!

I'M SORRY, MY CHILD, BUT THAT'S SIMPLY NOT TRUE.

NO ONE CAN ENDLESSLY KEEP WALKING FORWARD.

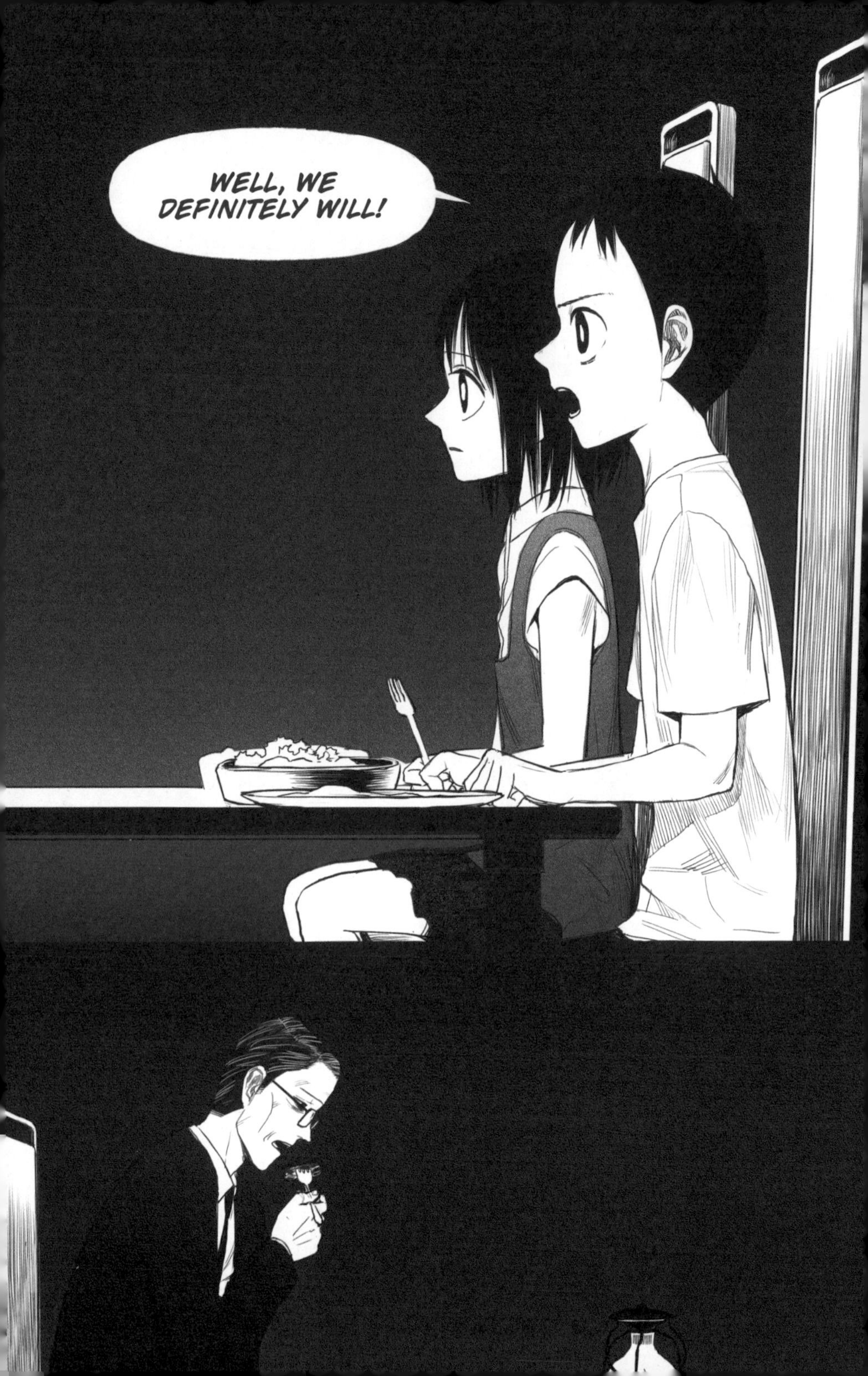
WELL, WE DEFINITELY WILL!

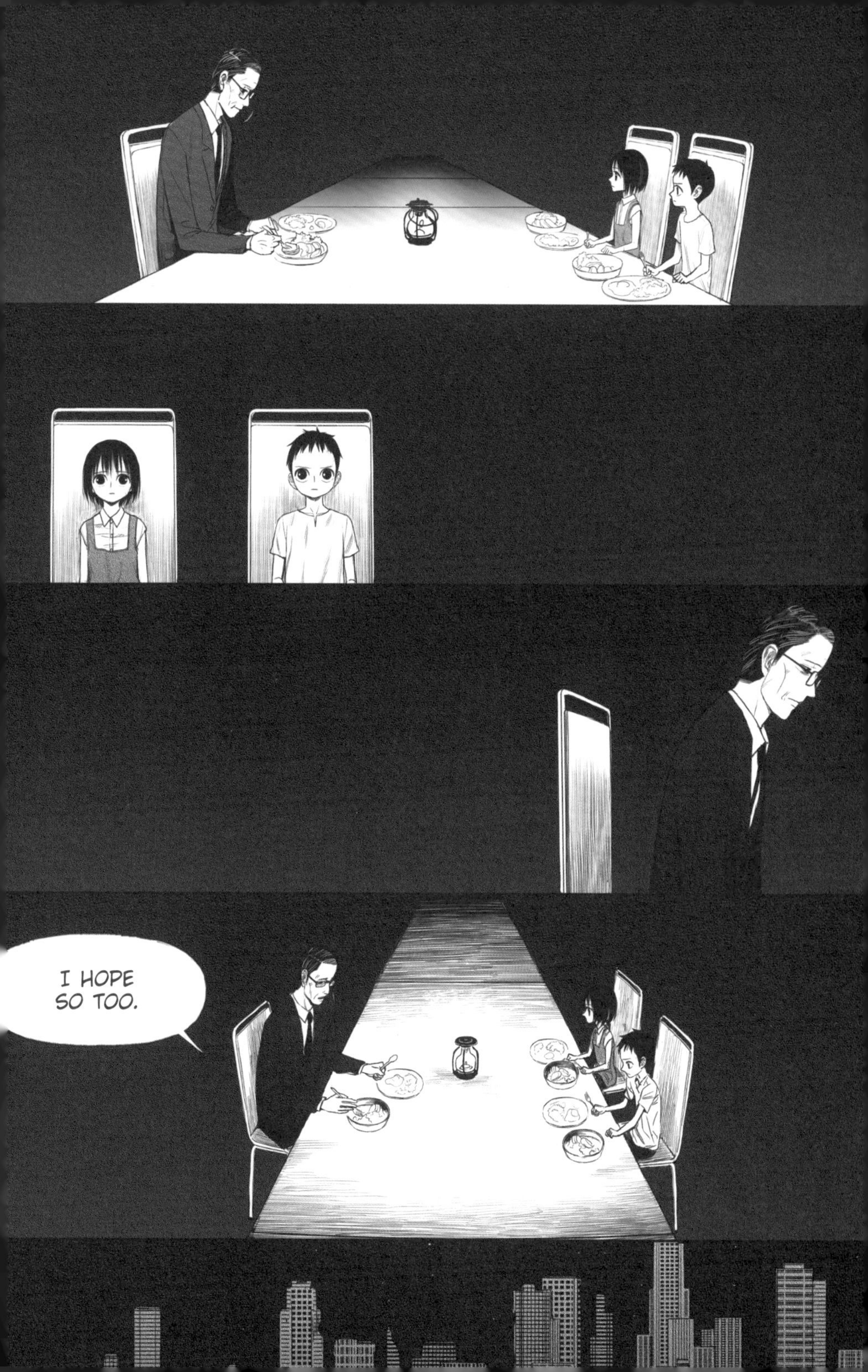
I HOPE SO TOO.

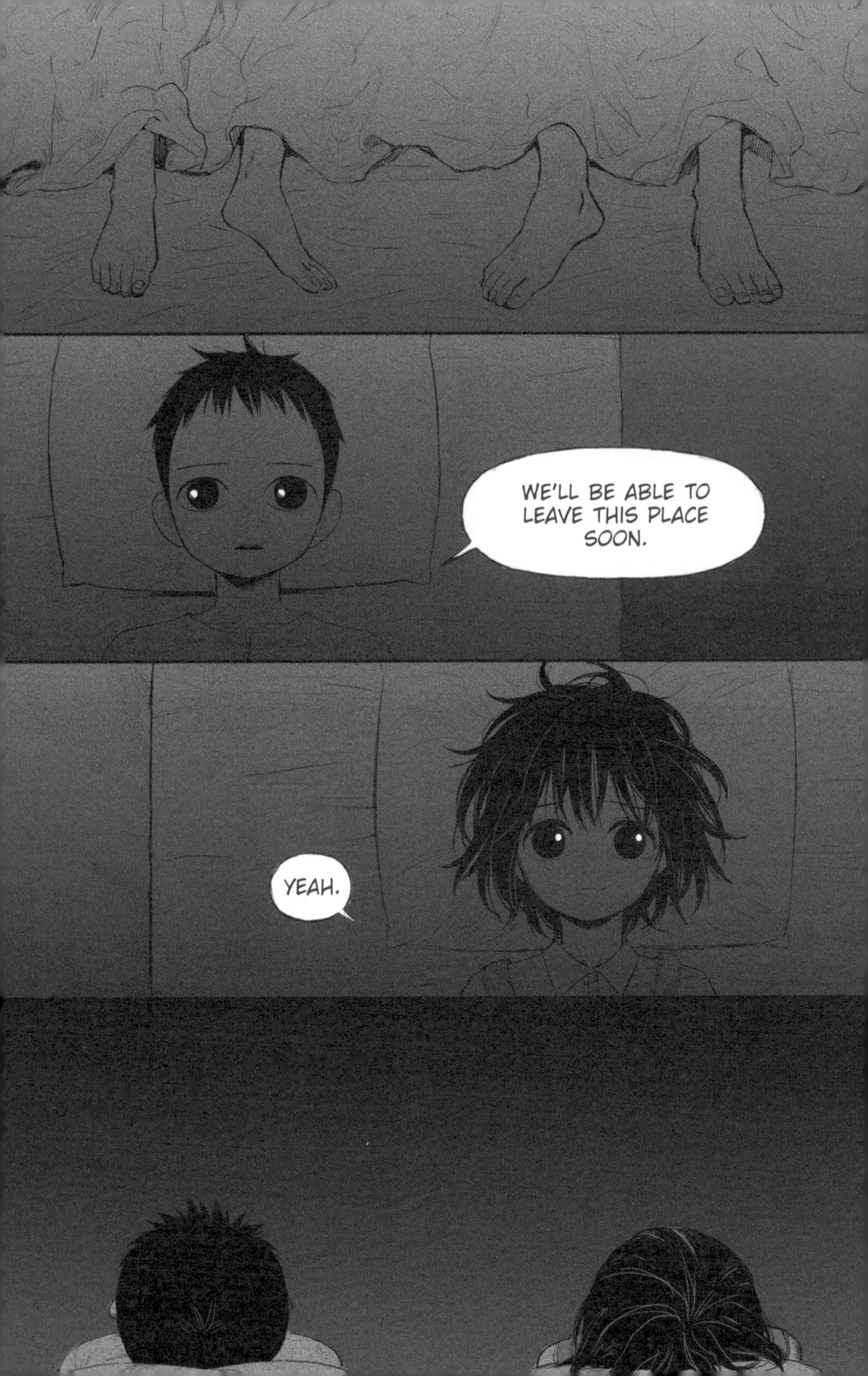
WE'LL BE ABLE TO LEAVE THIS PLACE SOON.
YEAH.

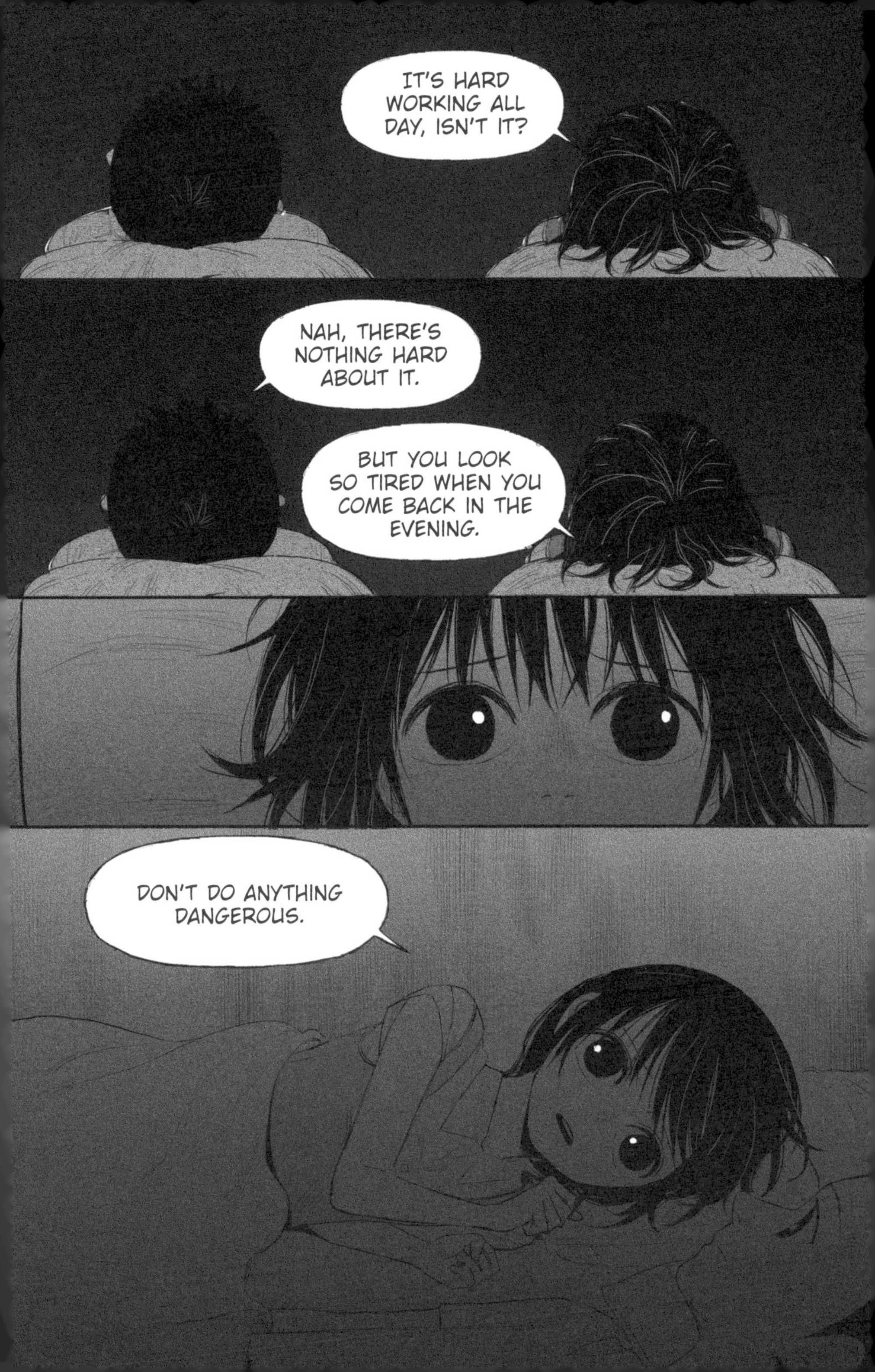
IT'S HARD WORKING ALL DAY, ISN'T IT?
NAH, THERE'S NOTHING HARD ABOUT IT.
BUT YOU LOOK SO TIRED WHEN YOU COME BACK IN THE EVENING.
DON'T DO ANYTHING DANGEROUS.

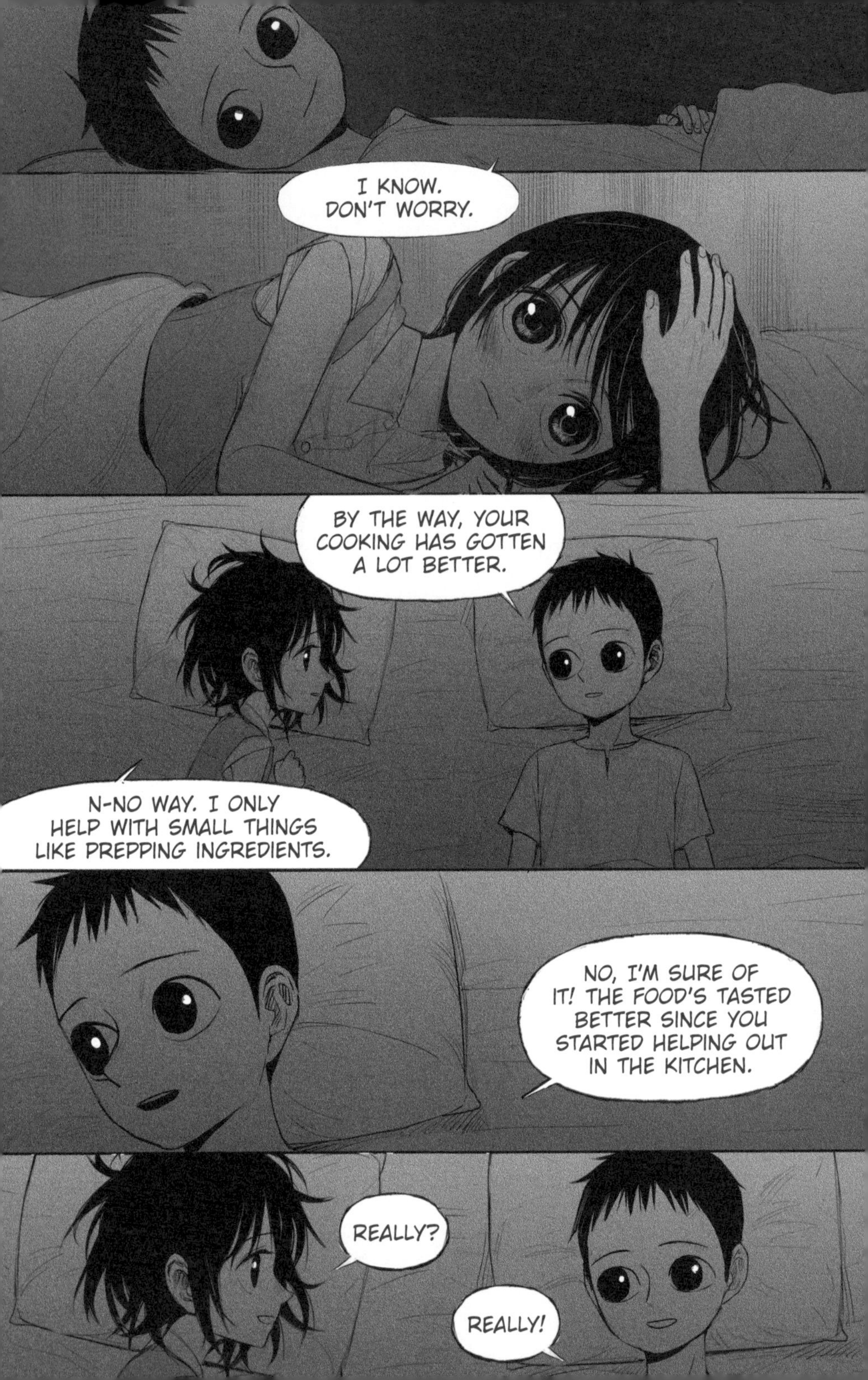
I KNOW. DON'T WORRY.
BY THE WAY, YOUR COOKING HAS GOTTEN A LOT BETTER.
N-NO WAY. I ONLY HELP WITH SMALL THINGS LIKE PREPPING INGREDIENTS.
NO, I'M SURE OF IT! THE FOOD'S TASTED BETTER SINCE YOU STARTED HELPING OUT IN THE KITCHEN.
REALLY?
REALLY!

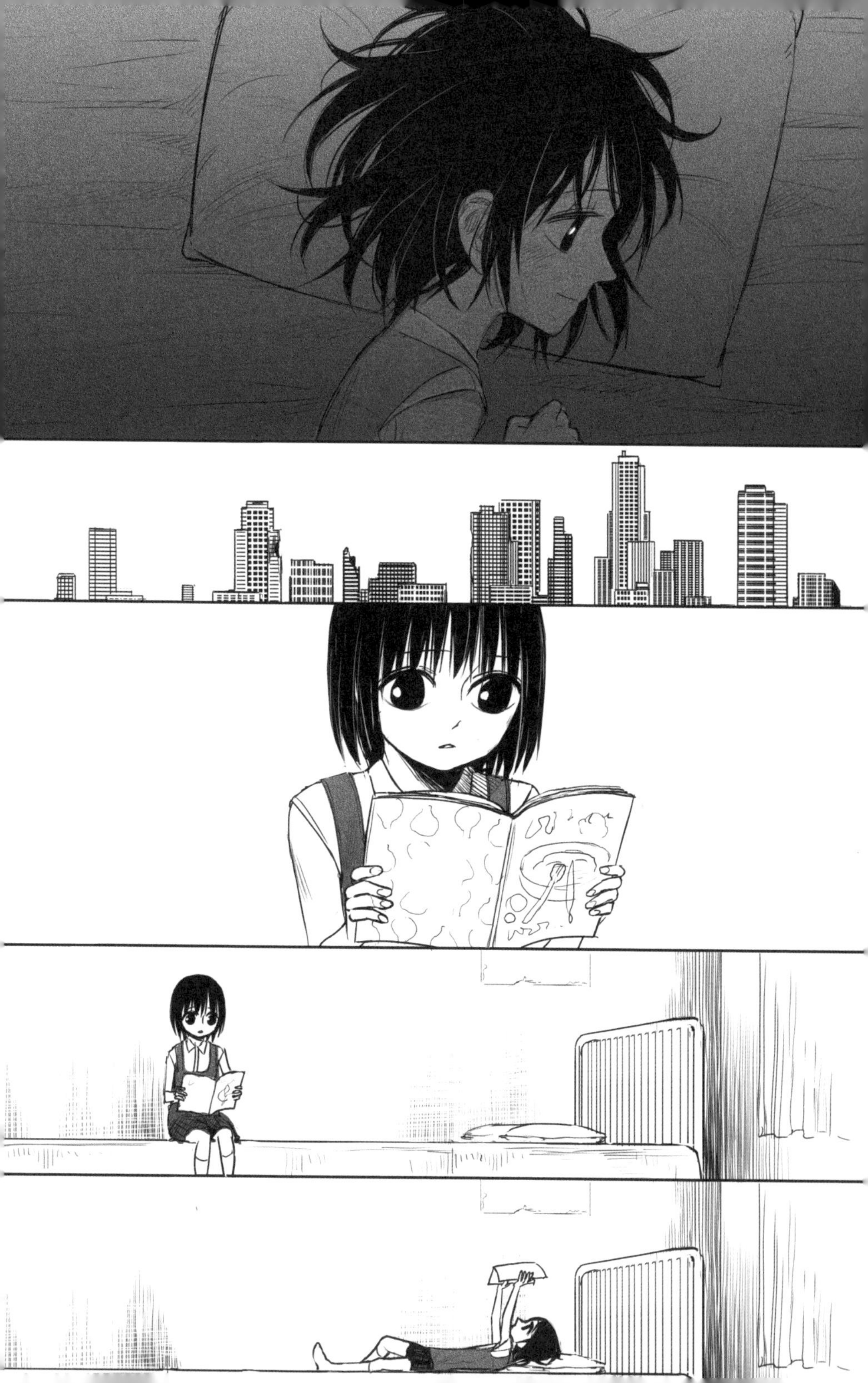

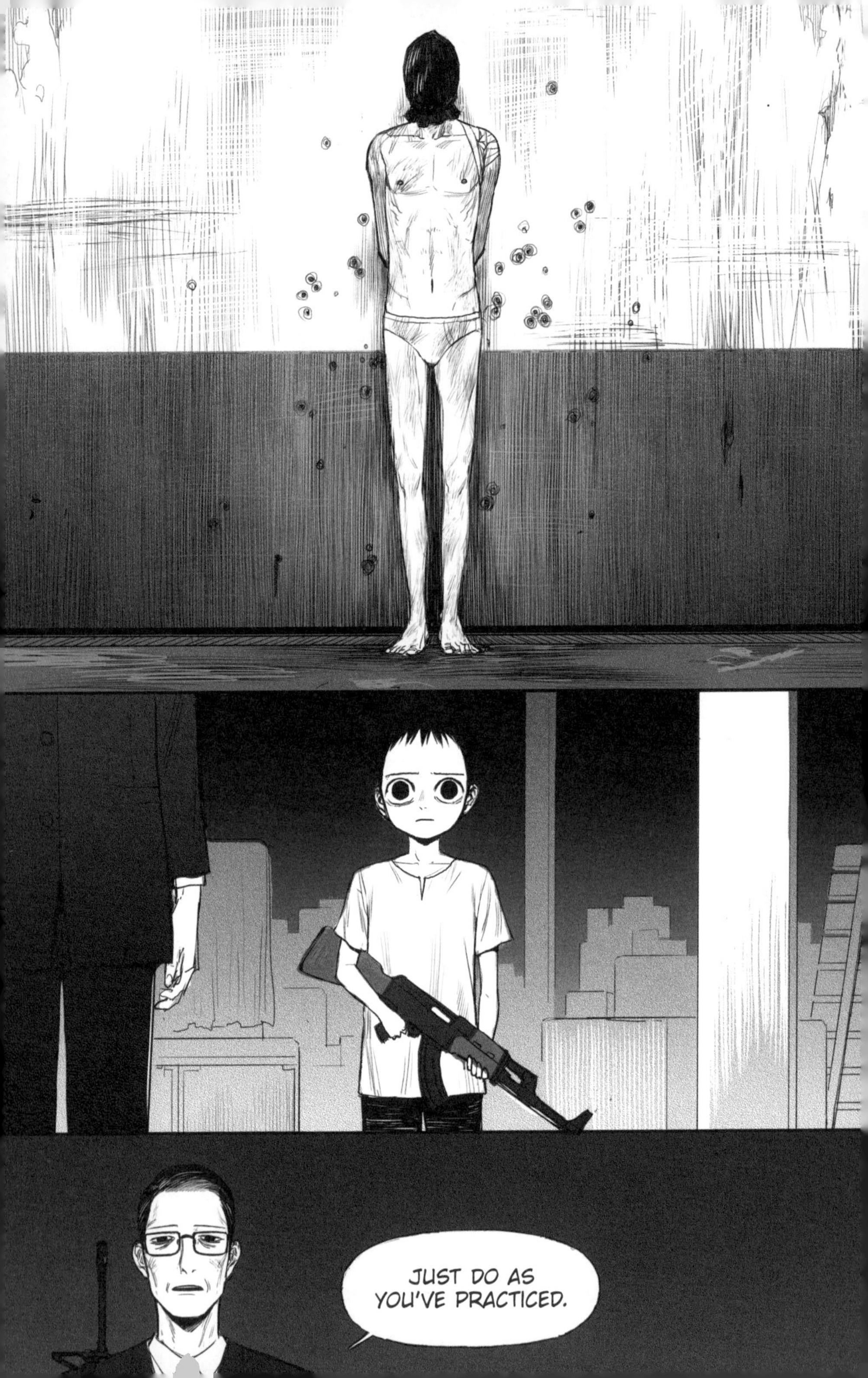
JUST DO AS YOU'VE PRACTICED.

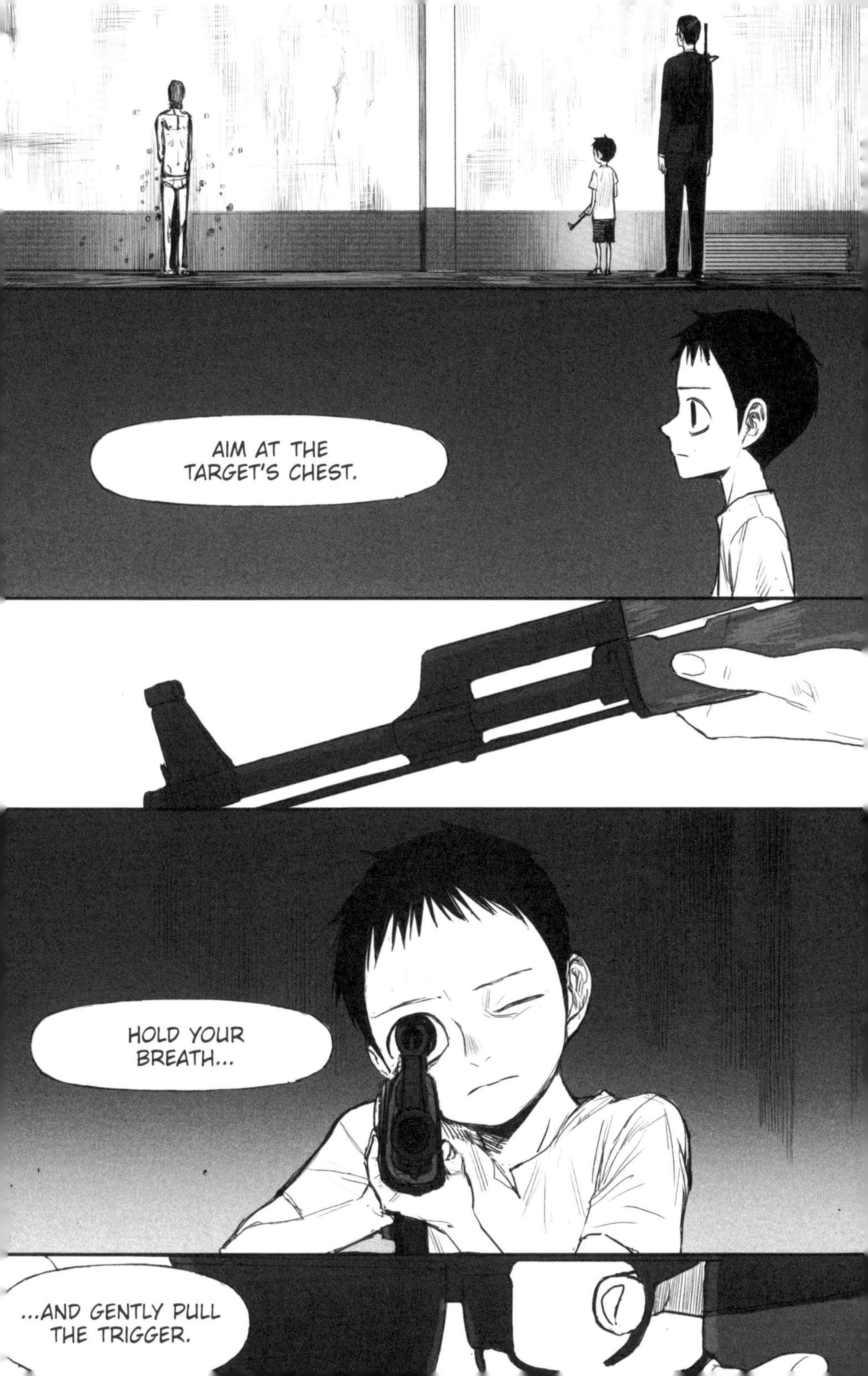
AIM AT THE TARGET'S CHEST.
HOLD YOUR BREATH...
...AND GENTLY PULL THE TRIGGER.

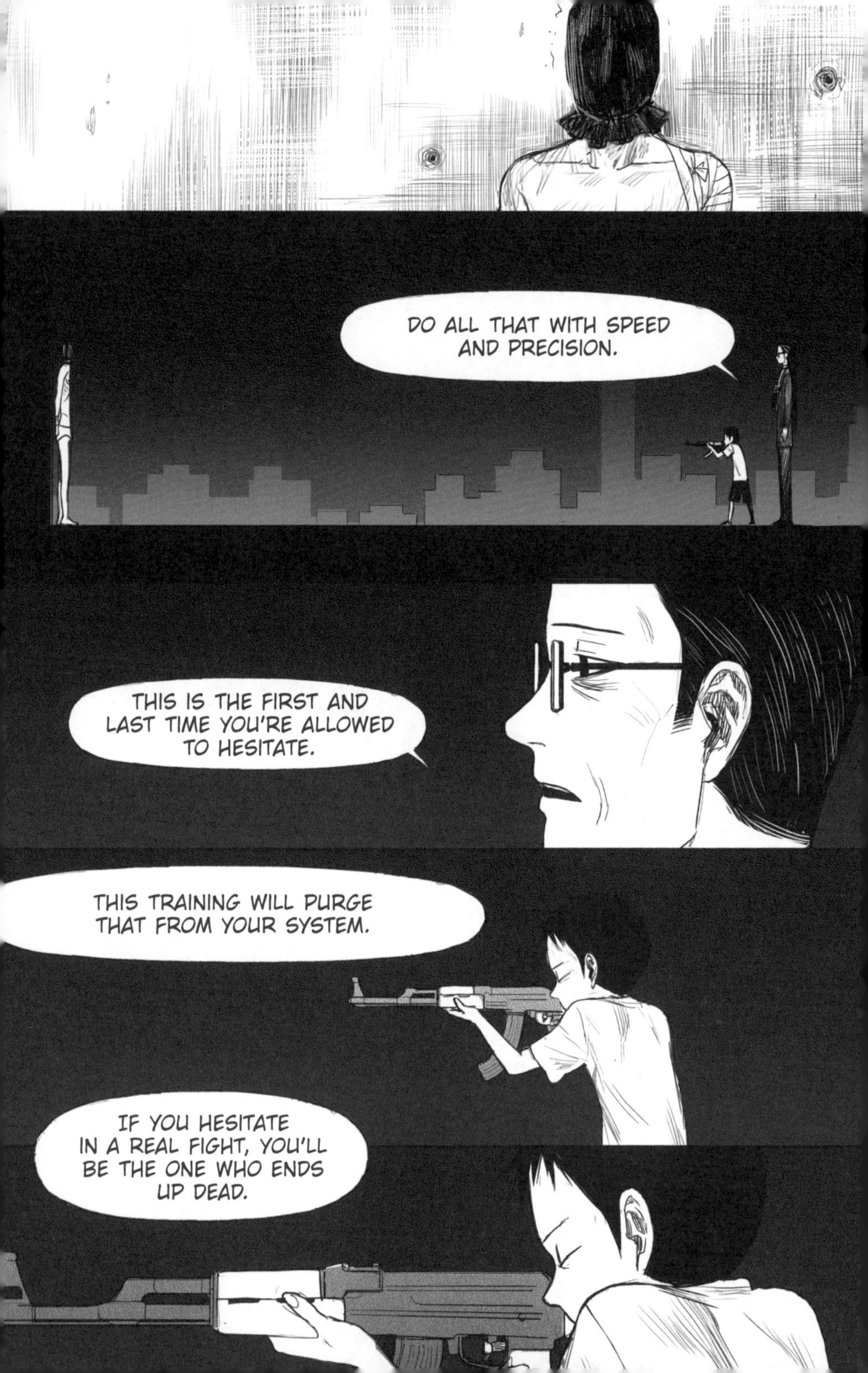
DO ALL THAT WITH SPEED AND PRECISION.
THIS IS THE FIRST AND LAST TIME YOU'RE ALLOWED TO HESITATE.
THIS TRAINING WILL PURGE THAT FROM YOUR SYSTEM.
IF YOU HESITATE IN A REAL FIGHT, YOU'LL BE THE ONE WHO ENDS UP DEAD.

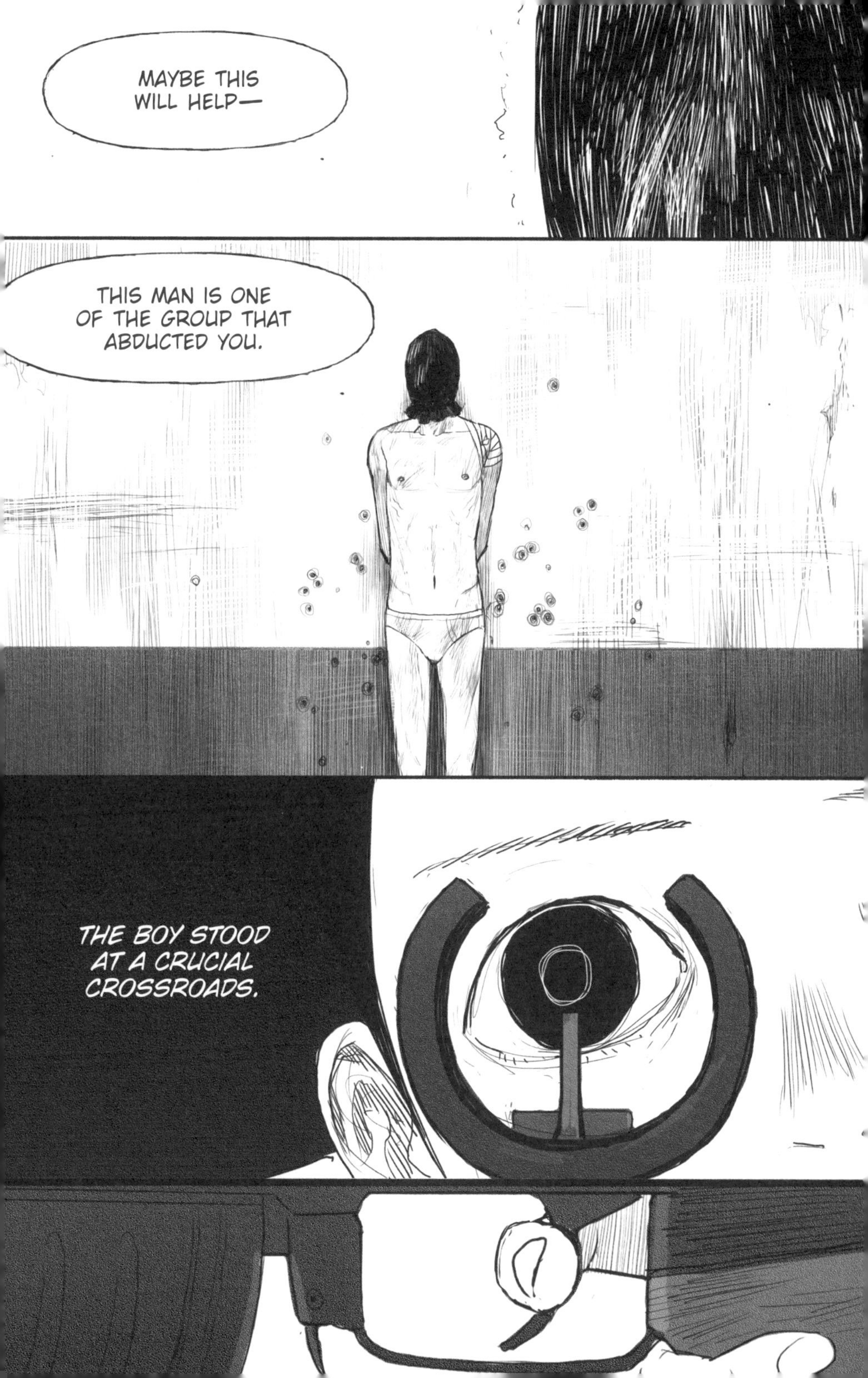
MAYBE THIS WILL HELP—
THIS MAN IS ONE OF THE GROUP THAT ABDUCTED YOU.
THE BOY STOOD AT A CRUCIAL CROSSROADS.

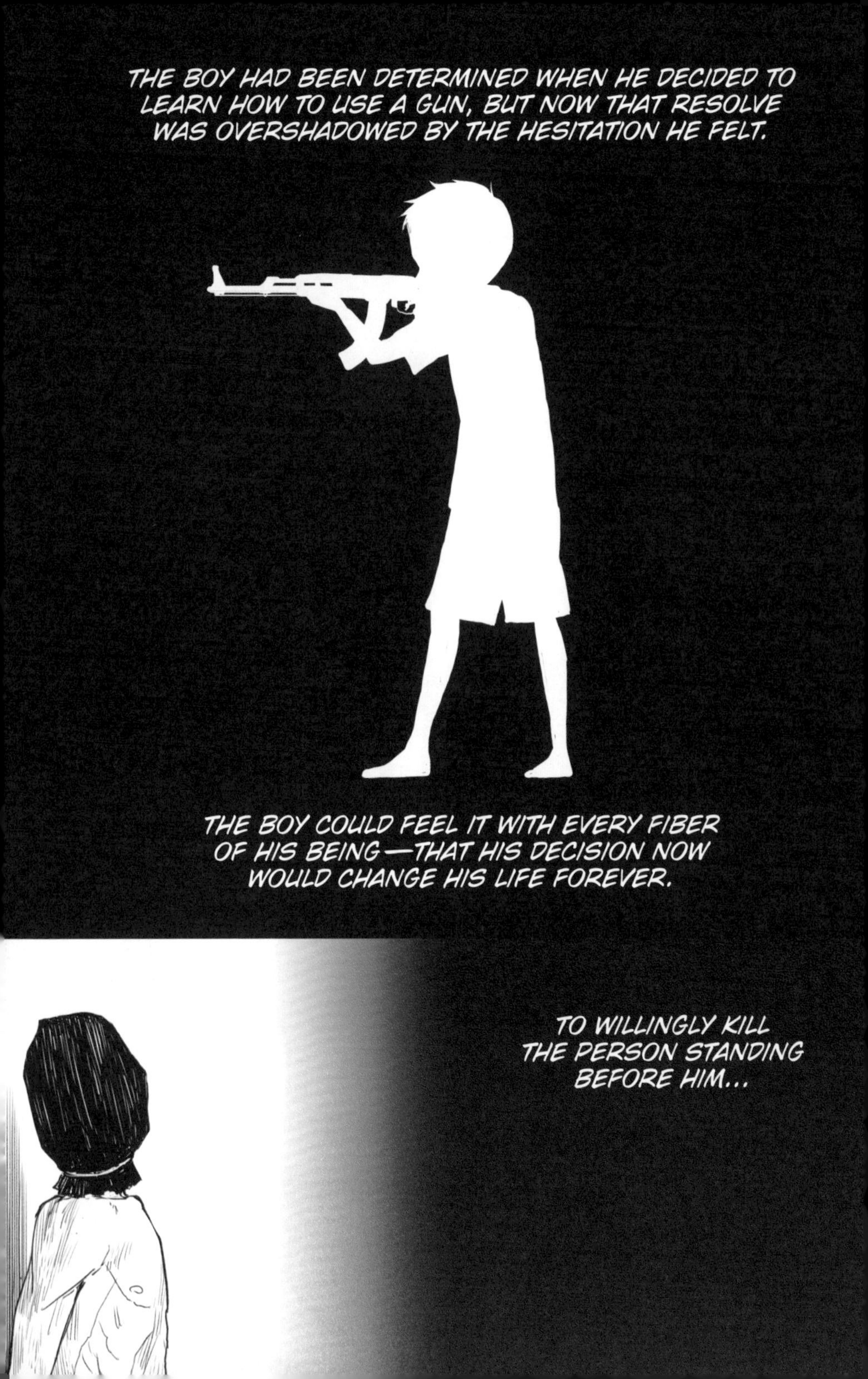
THE BOY HAD BEEN DETERMINED WHEN HE DECIDED TO LEARN HOW TO USE A GUN, BUT NOW THAT RESOLVE WAS OVERSHADOWED BY THE HESITATION HE FELT.
THE BOY COULD FEEL IT WITH EVERY FIBER OF HIS BEING—THAT HIS DECISION NOW WOULD CHANGE HIS LIFE FOREVER.
TO WILLINGLY KILL THE PERSON STANDING BEFORE HIM...

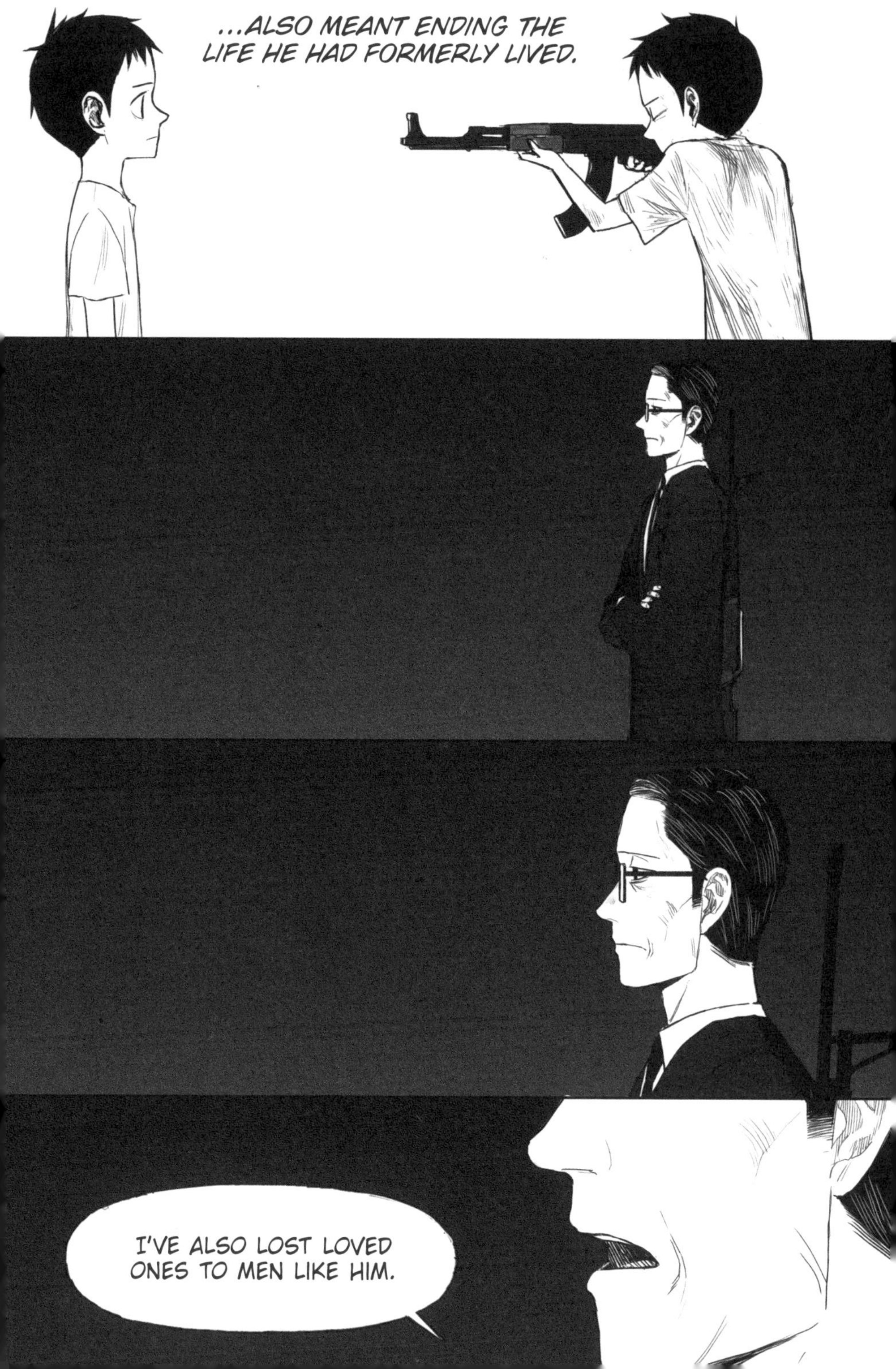
...ALSO MEANT ENDING THE LIFE HE HAD FORMERLY LIVED.
I'VE ALSO LOST LOVED ONES TO MEN LIKE HIM.

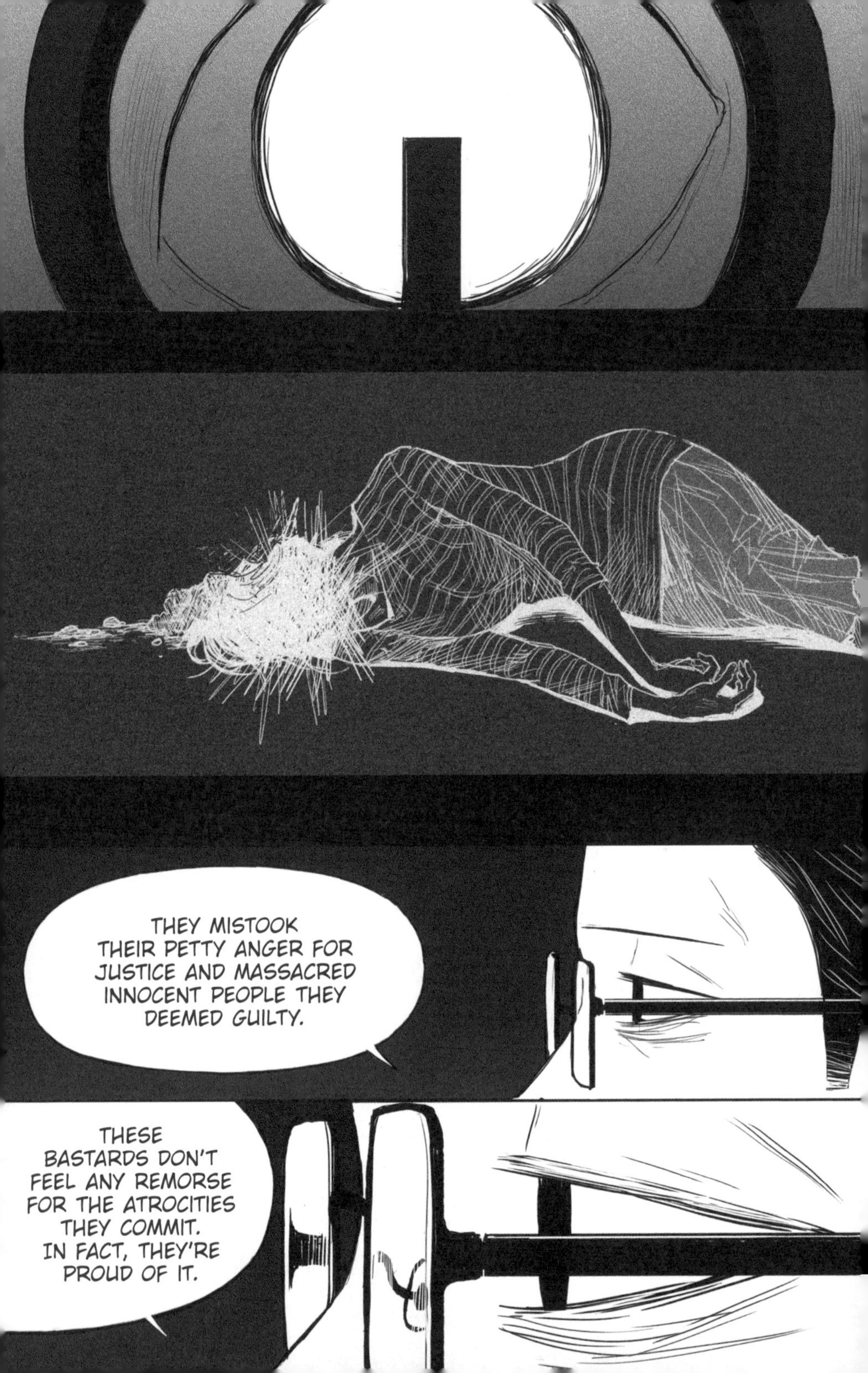
THEY MISTOOK THEIR PETTY ANGER FOR JUSTICE AND MASSACRED INNOCENT PEOPLE THEY DEEMED GUILTY.
THESE BASTARDS DON'T FEEL ANY REMORSE FOR THE ATROCITIES THEY COMMIT. IN FACT, THEY'RE PROUD OF IT.

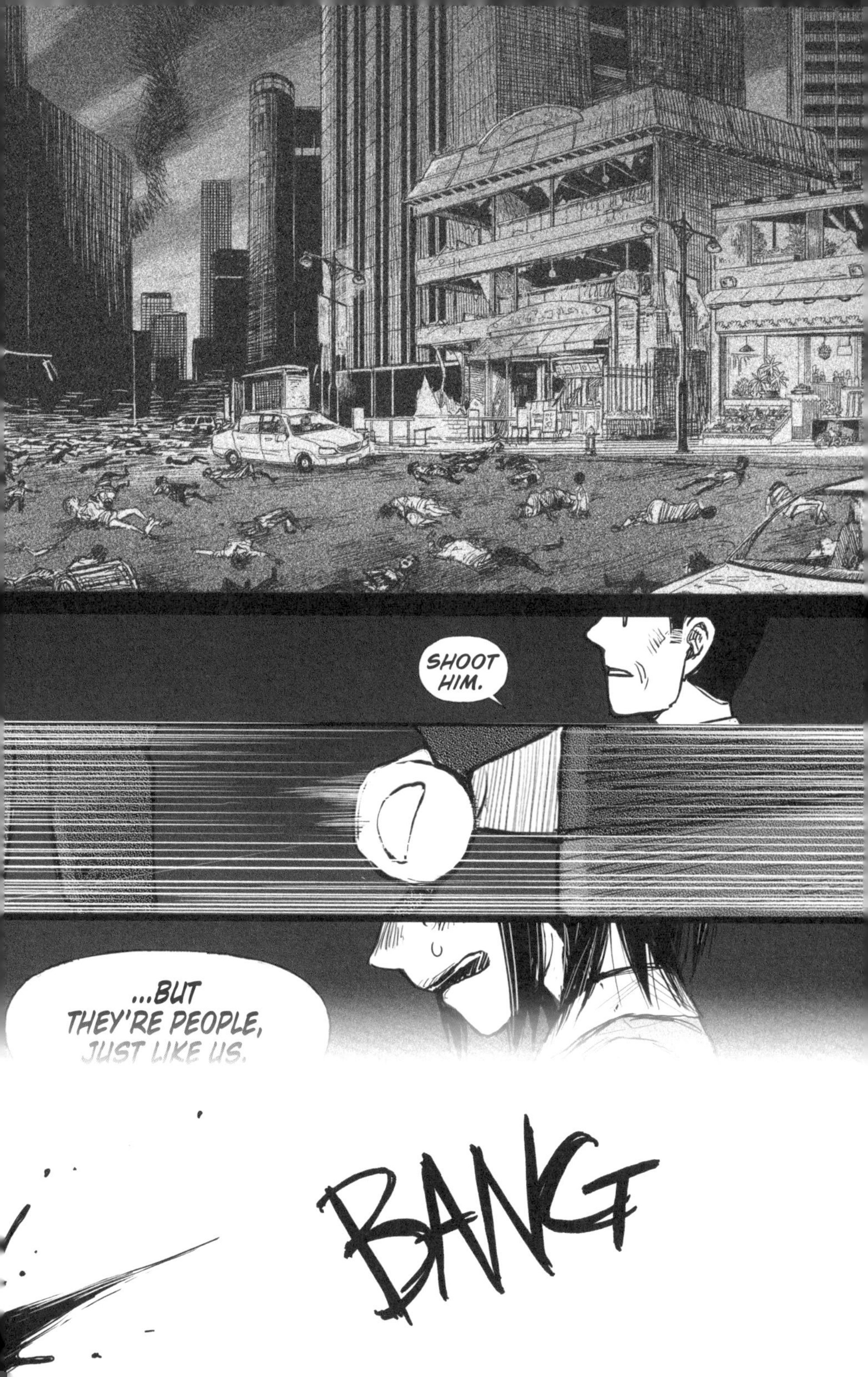
SHOOT HIM.
...BUT THEY'RE PEOPLE, JUST LIKE US.
BANG

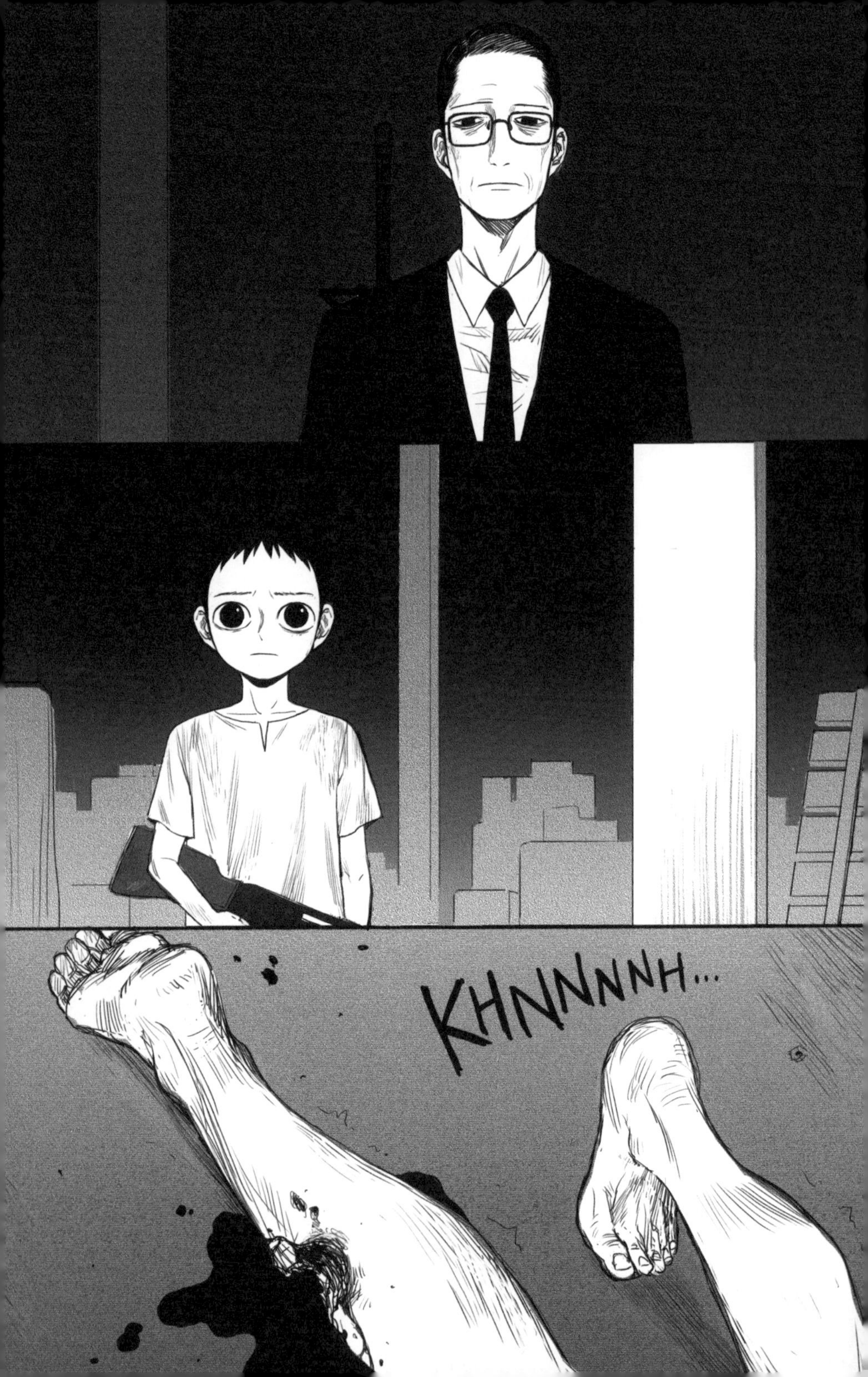
KHNNNNH...

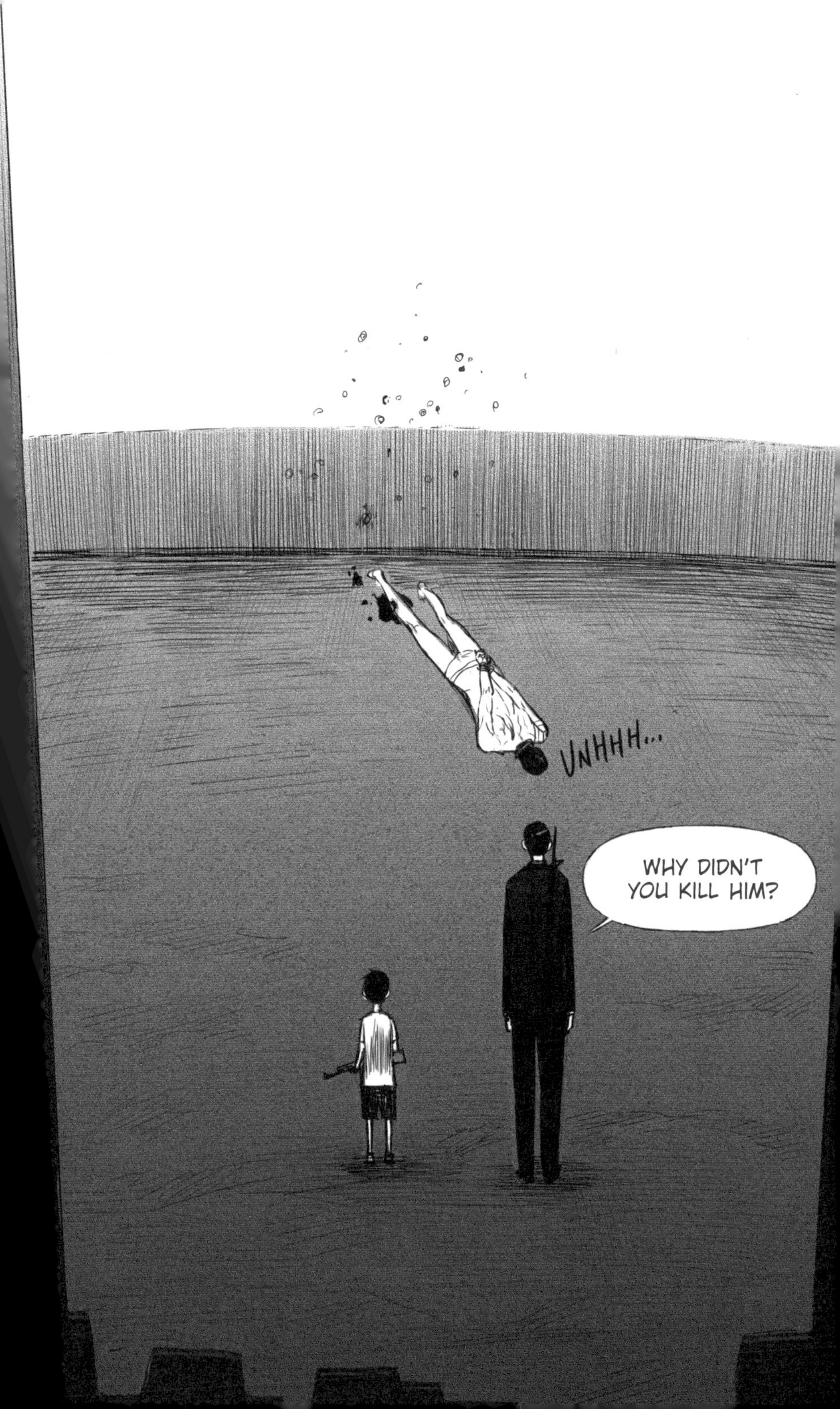
UNHHH...
WHY DIDN'T YOU KILL HIM?

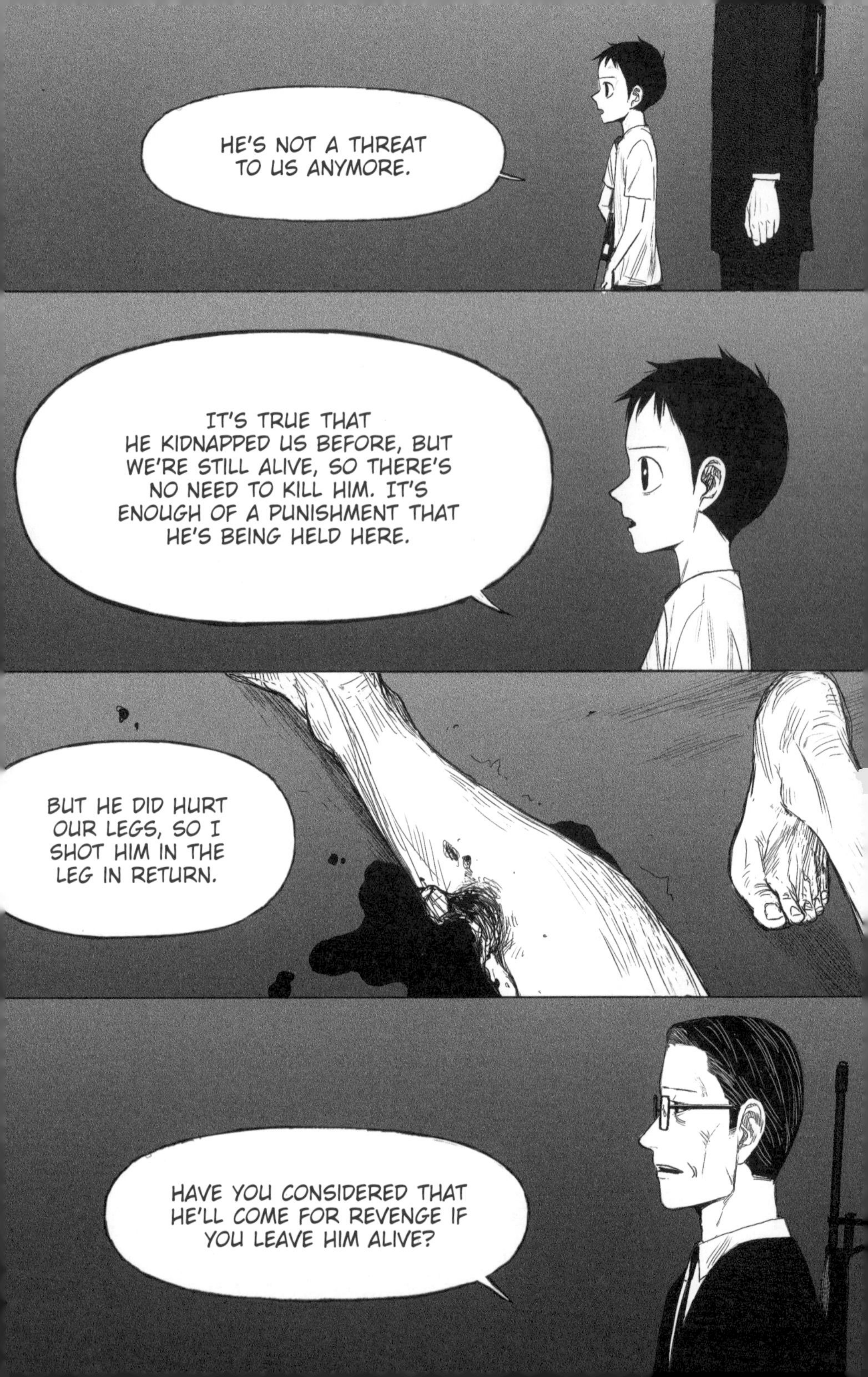
HE'S NOT A THREAT TO US ANYMORE.
IT'S TRUE THAT HE KIDNAPPED US BEFORE, BUT WE'RE STILL ALIVE, SO THERE'S NO NEED TO KILL HIM. IT'S ENOUGH OF A PUNISHMENT THAT HE'S BEING HELD HERE.
BUT HE DID HURT OUR LEGS, SO I SHOT HIM IN THE LEG IN RETURN.
HAVE YOU CONSIDERED THAT HE'LL COME FOR REVENGE IF YOU LEAVE HIM ALIVE?

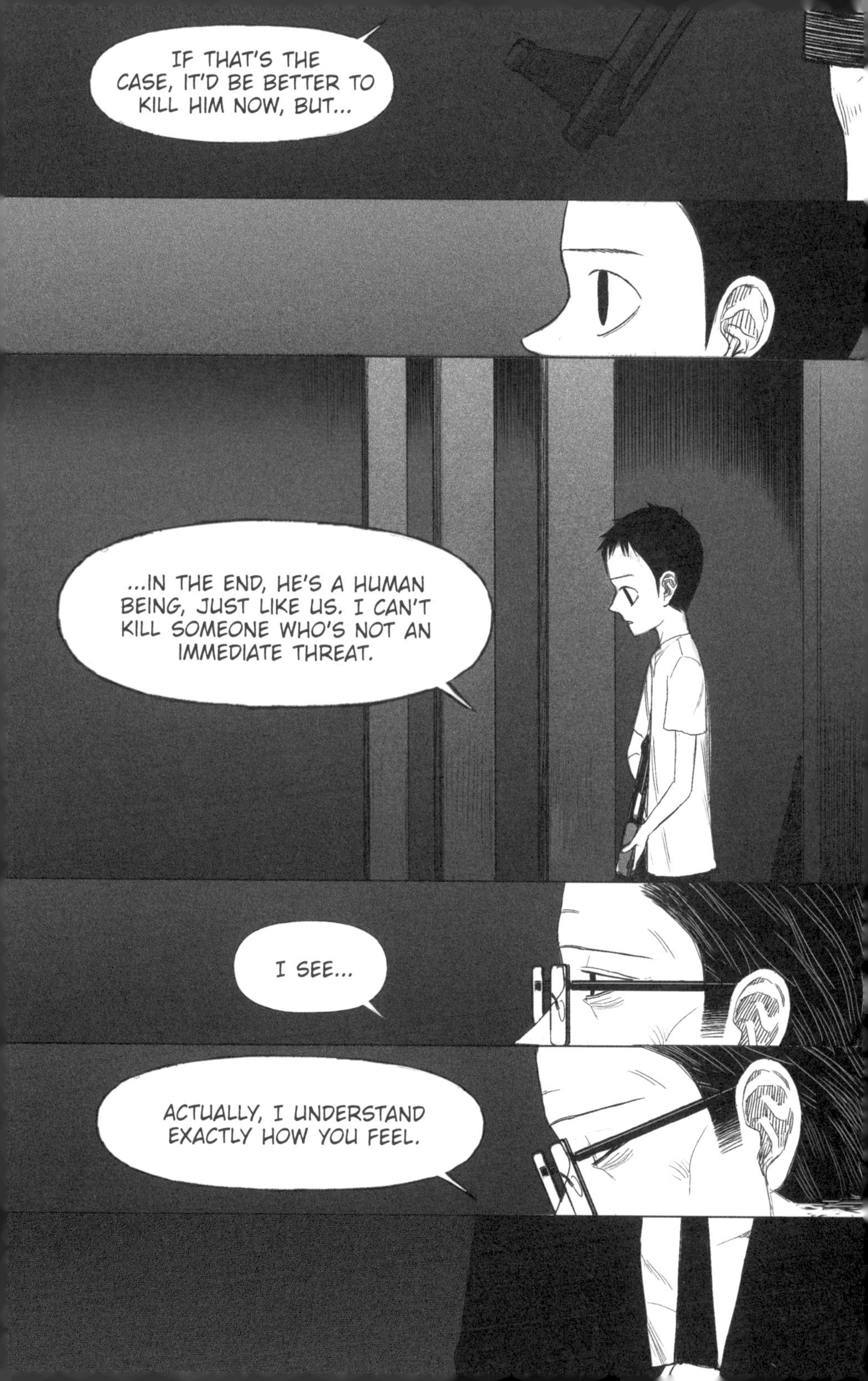
IF THAT'S THE CASE, IT'D BE BETTER TO KILL HIM NOW, BUT...
...IN THE END, HE'S A HUMAN BEING, JUST LIKE US. I CAN'T KILL SOMEONE WHO'S NOT AN IMMEDIATE THREAT.
I SEE...
ACTUALLY, I UNDERSTAND EXACTLY HOW YOU FEEL.

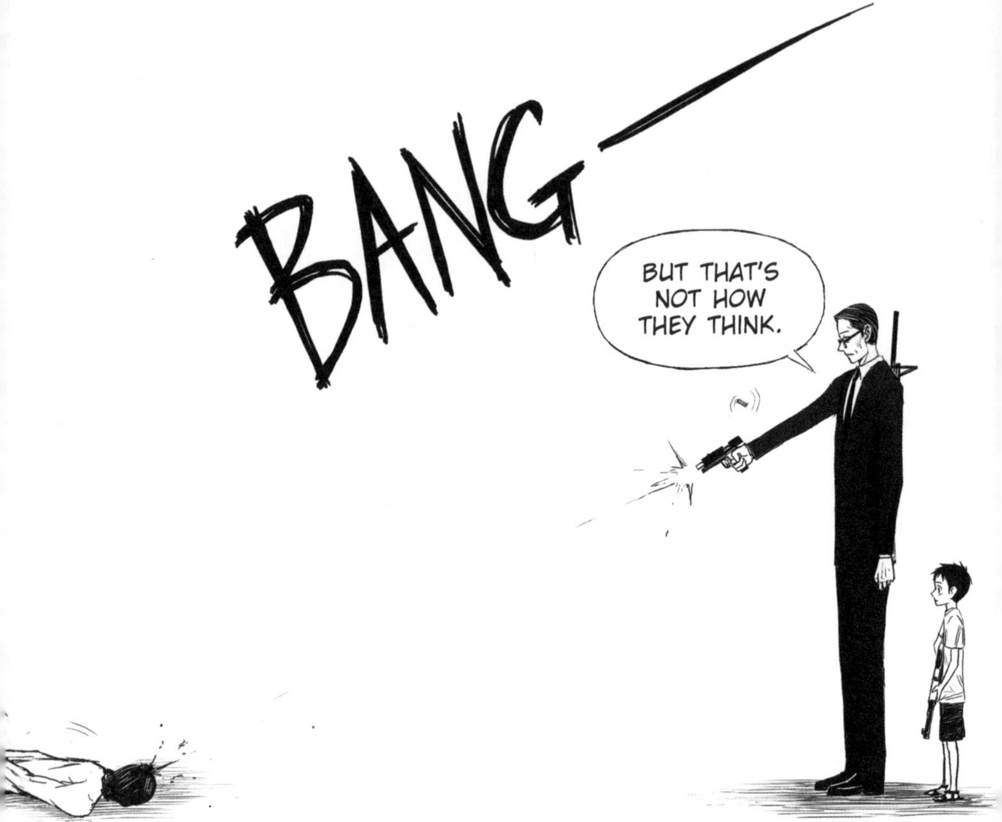
BANG
BUT THAT'S NOT HOW THEY THINK.

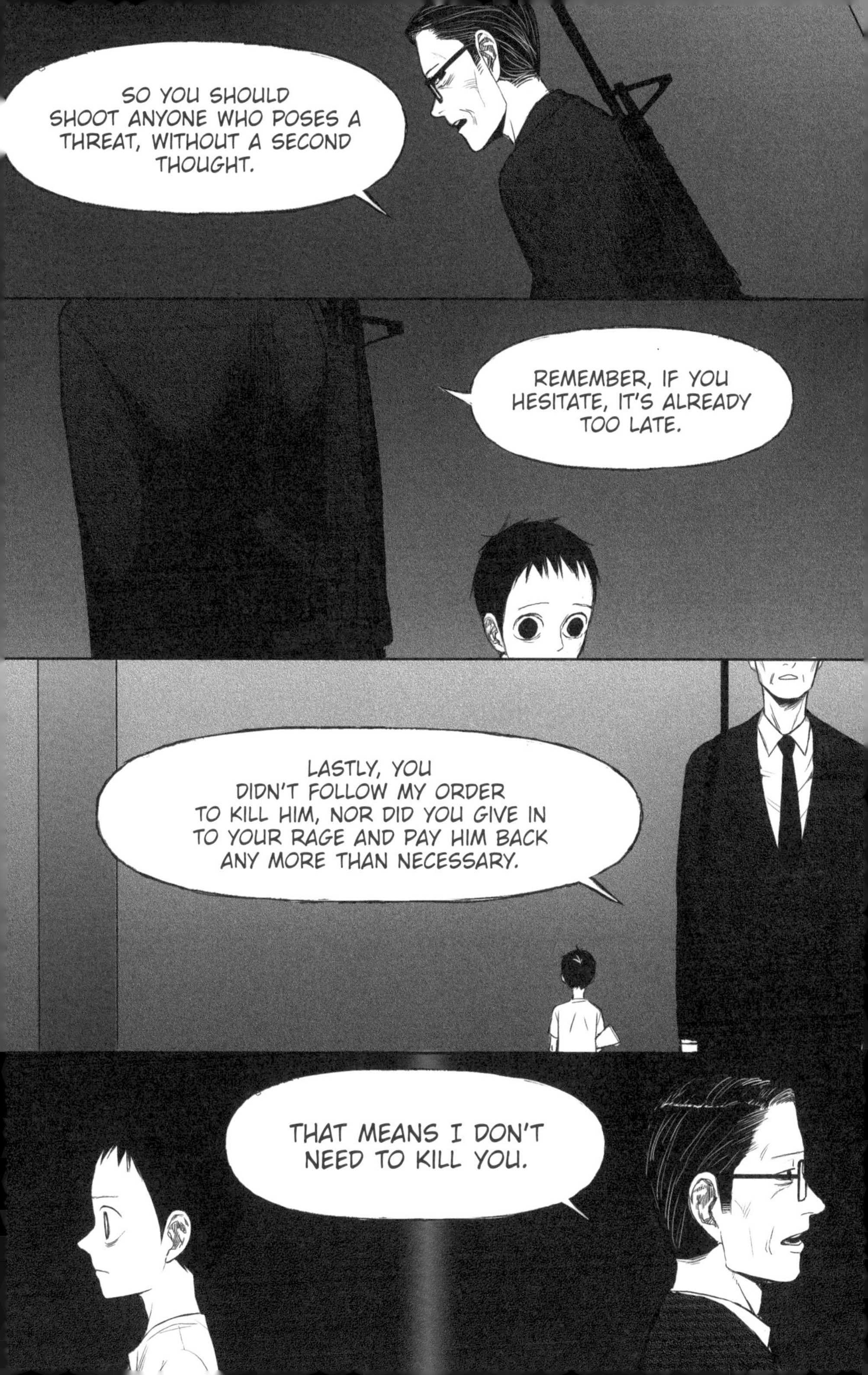
SO YOU SHOULD SHOOT ANYONE WHO POSES A THREAT, WITHOUT A SECOND THOUGHT.
REMEMBER, IF YOU HESITATE, IT'S ALREADY TOO LATE.
LASTLY, YOU DIDN'T FOLLOW MY ORDER TO KILL HIM, NOR DID YOU GIVE IN TO YOUR RAGE AND PAY HIM BACK ANY MORE THAN NECESSARY.
THAT MEANS I DON'T NEED TO KILL YOU.

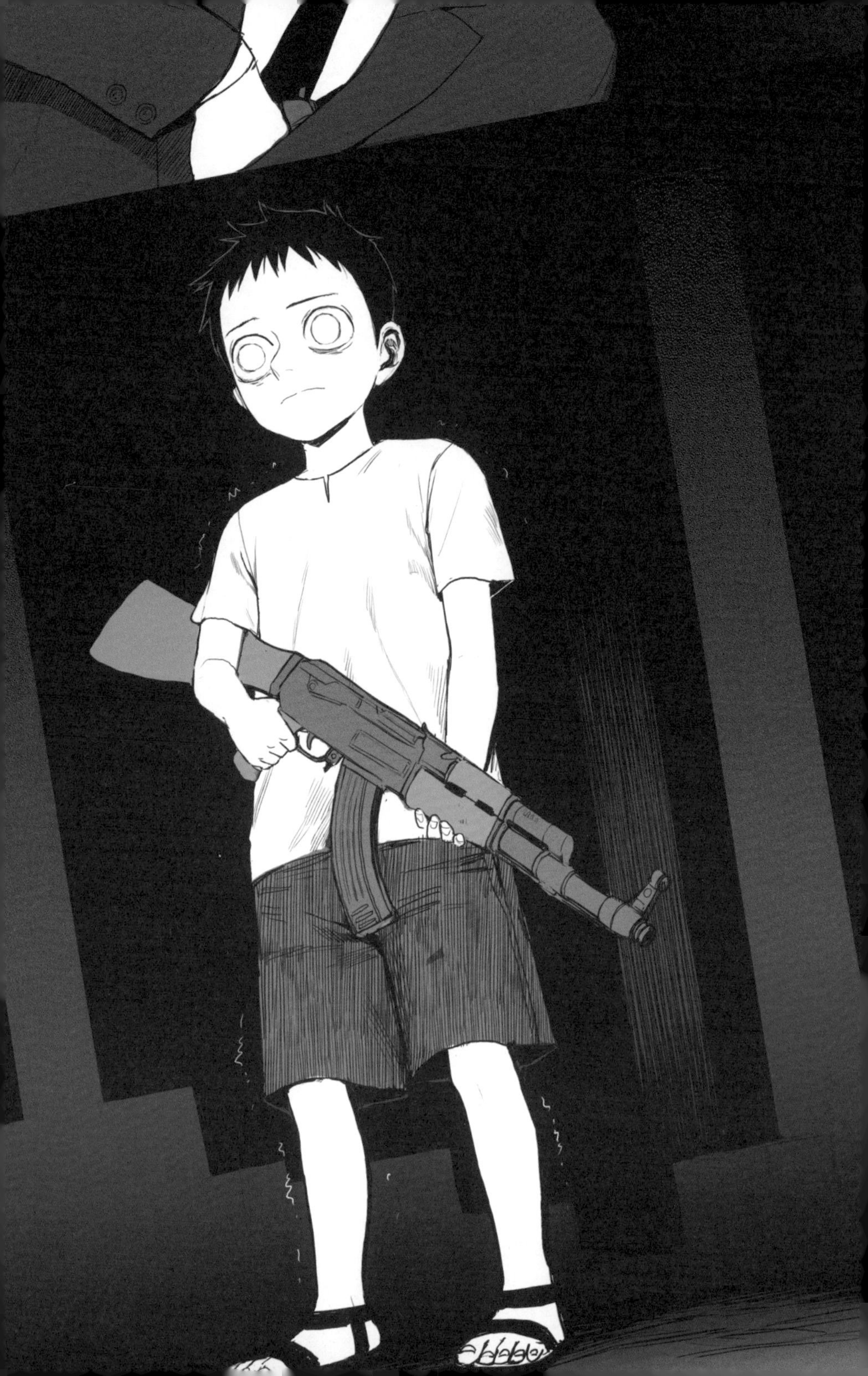

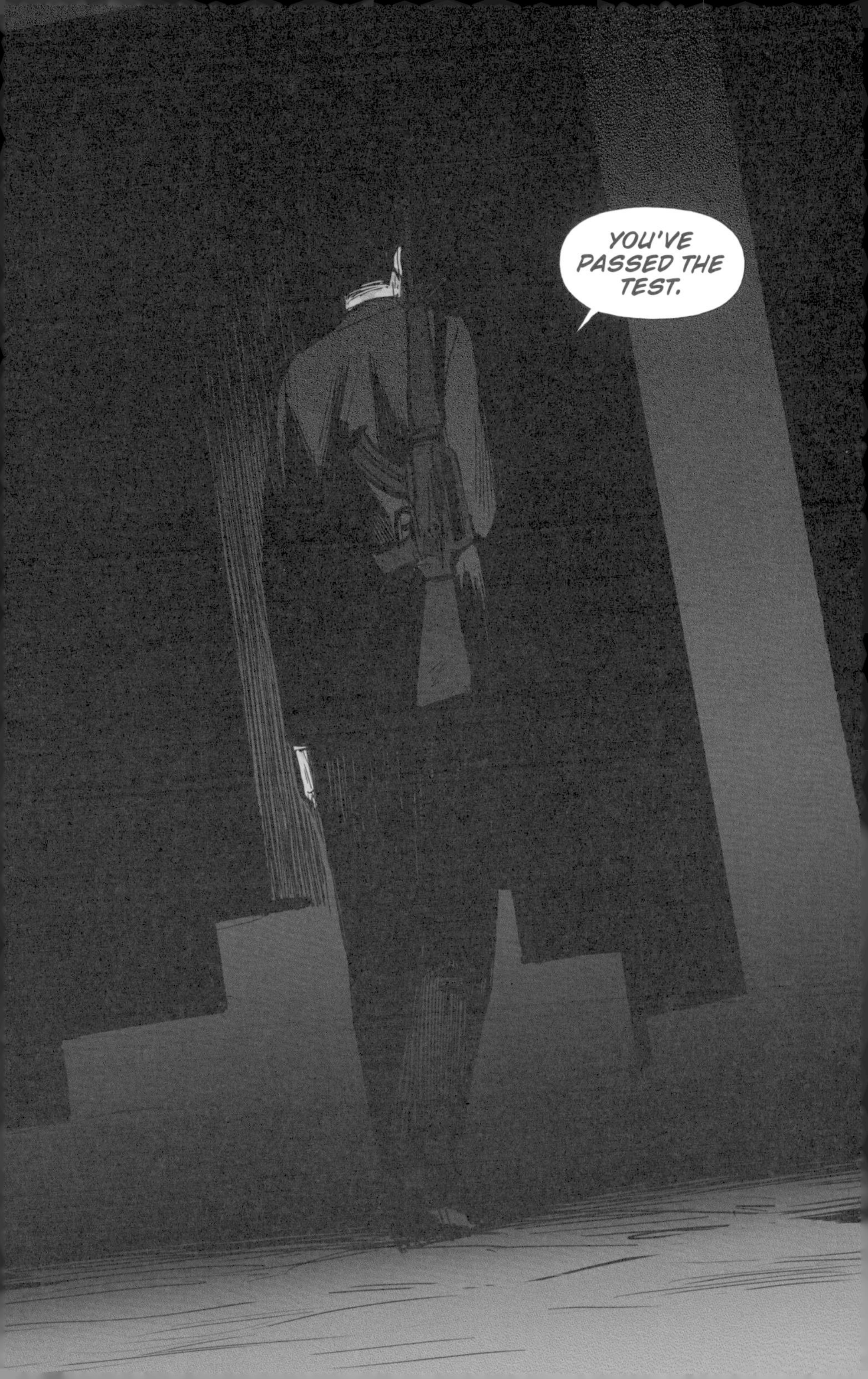
YOU'VE PASSED THE TEST.

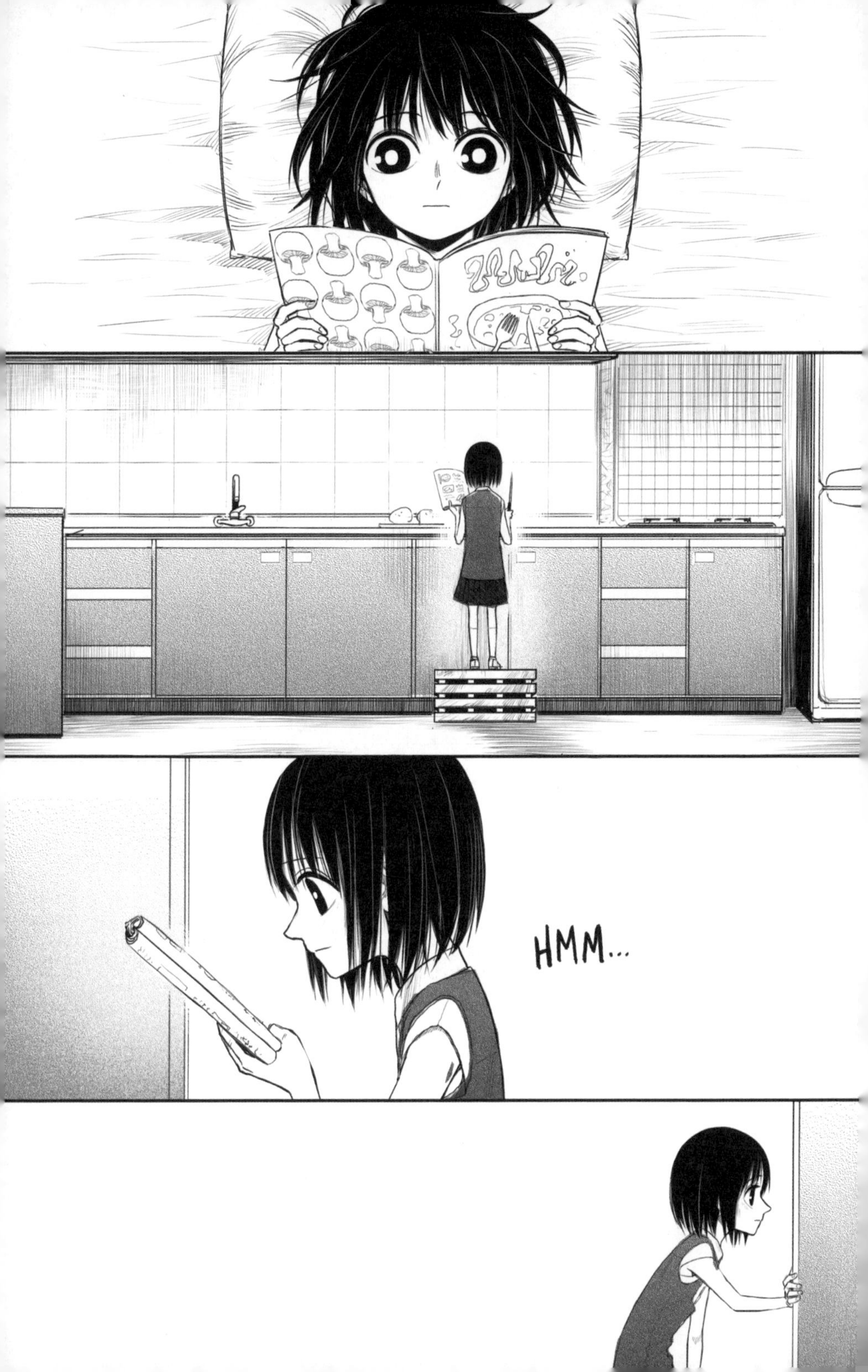
HMM...

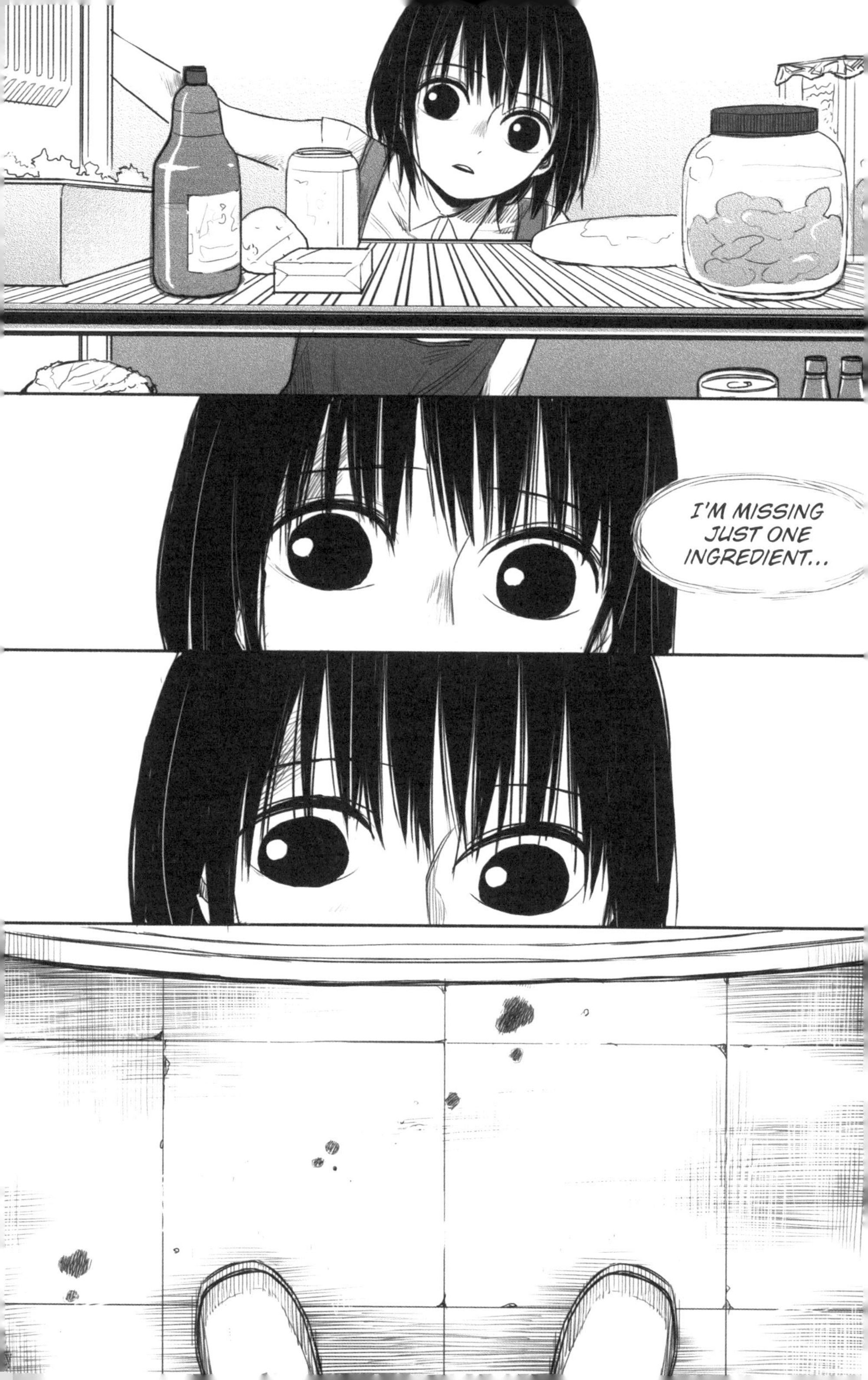
I'M MISSING JUST ONE INGREDIENT...

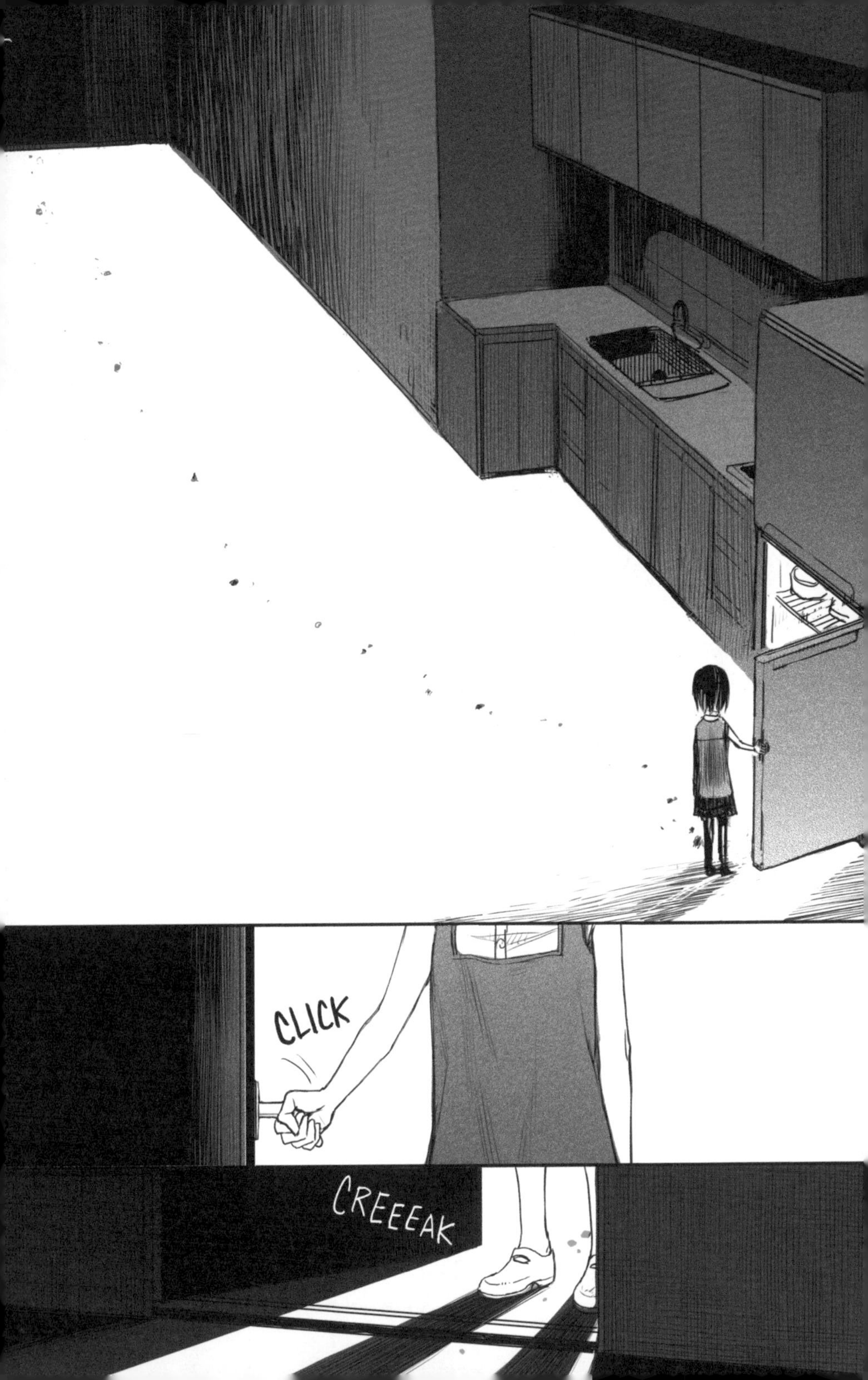
CLICK
CREEEAK

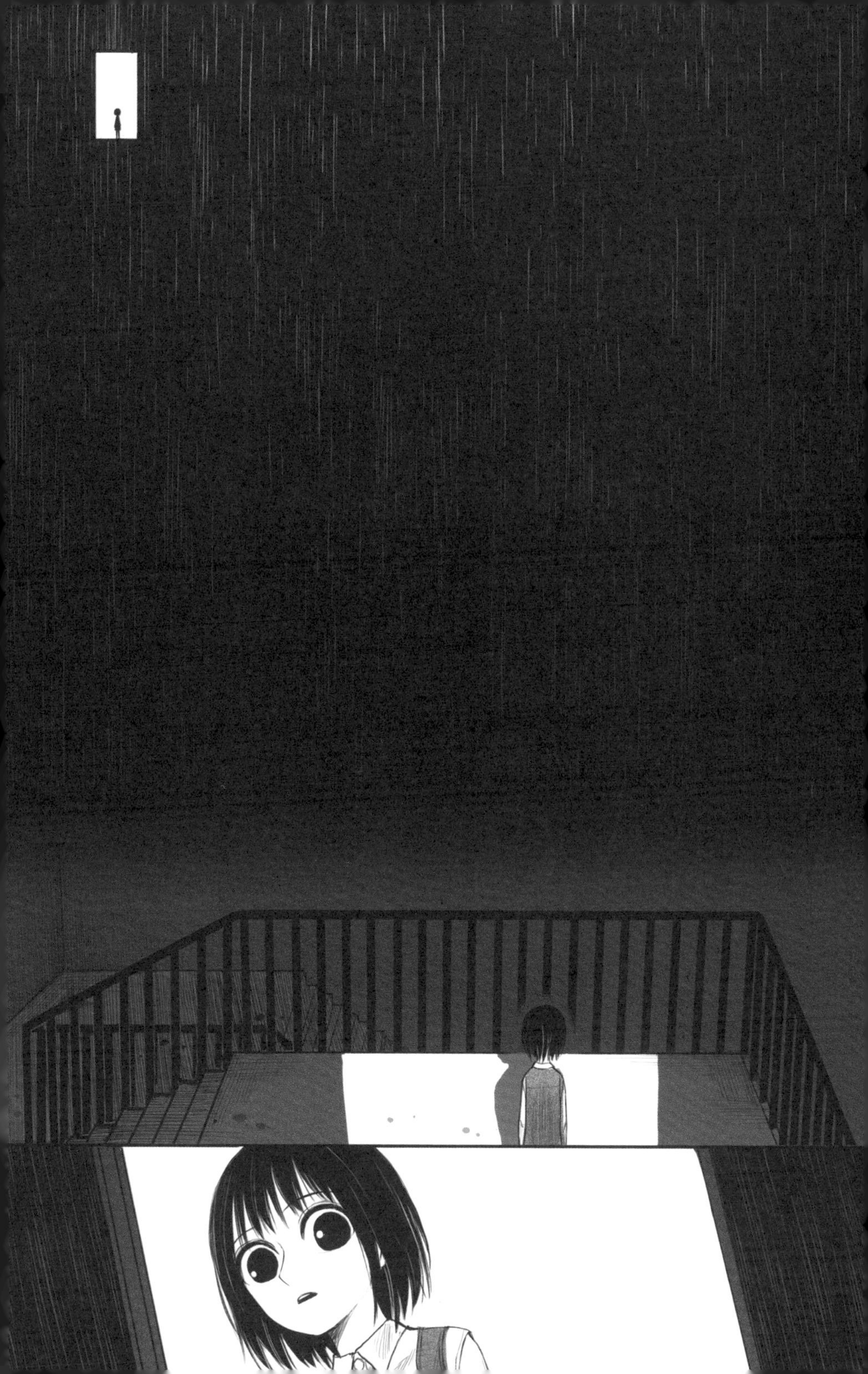

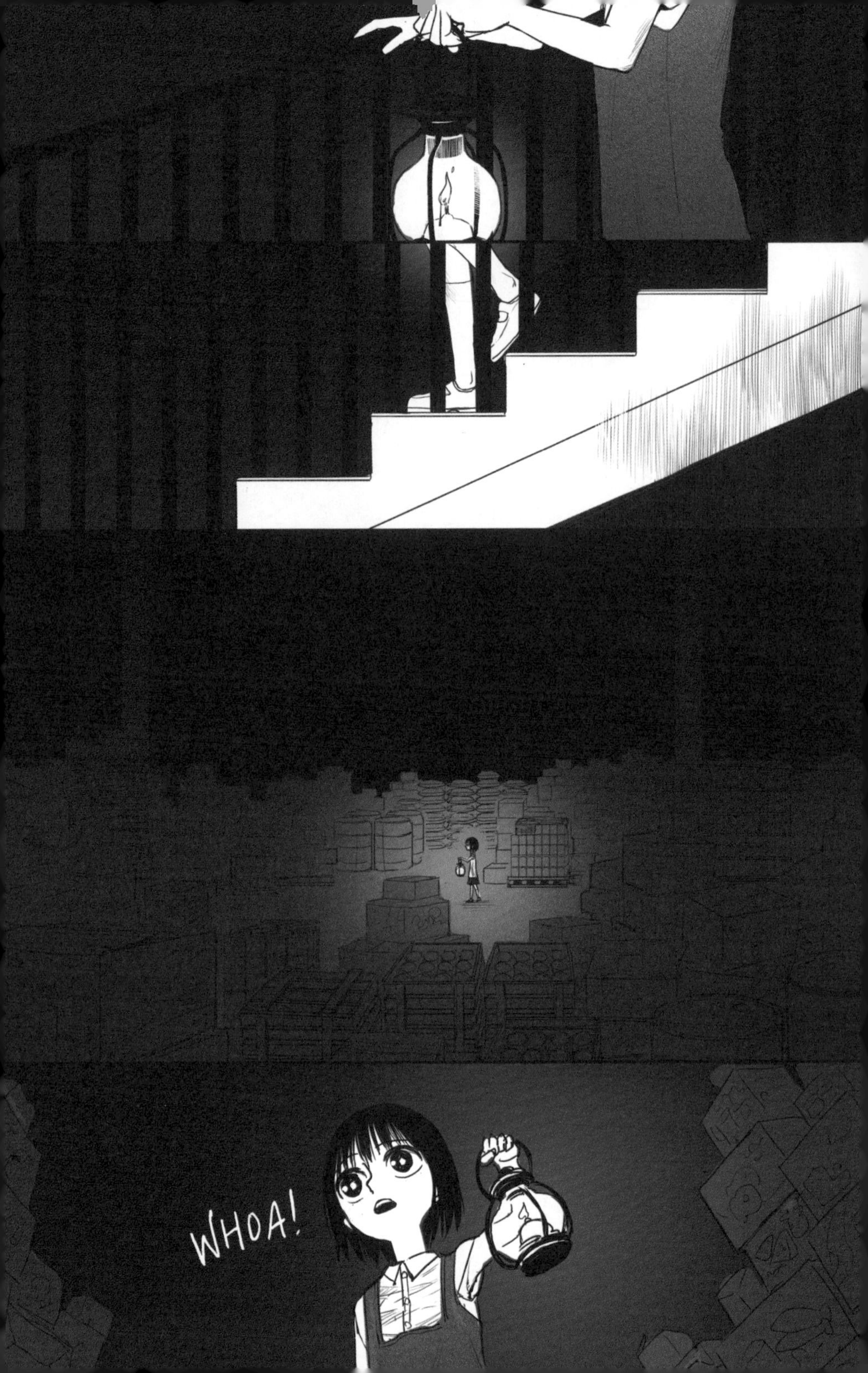
WHOA!

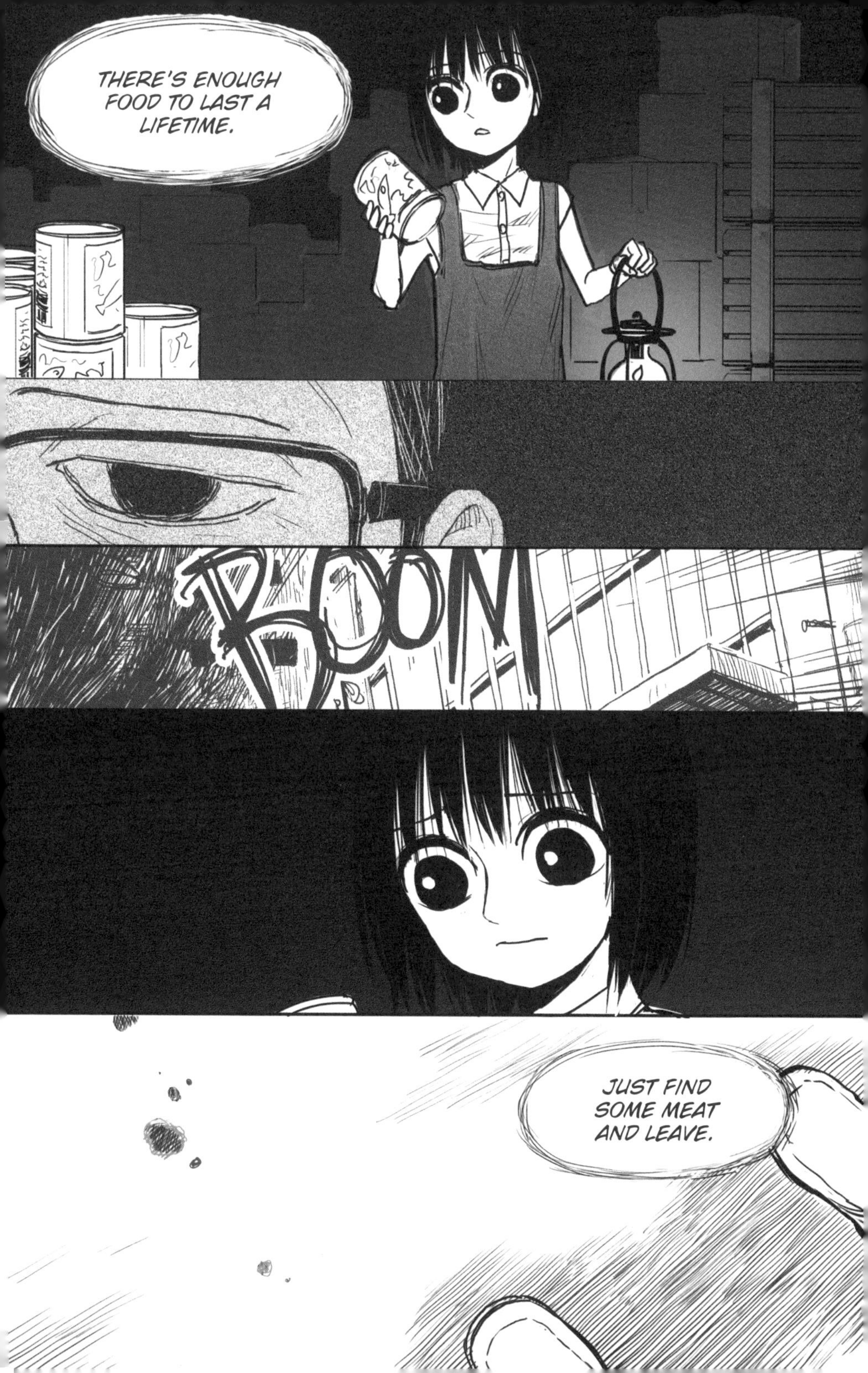
THERE'S ENOUGH FOOD TO LAST A LIFETIME.
BOOM
JUST FIND SOME MEAT AND LEAVE.

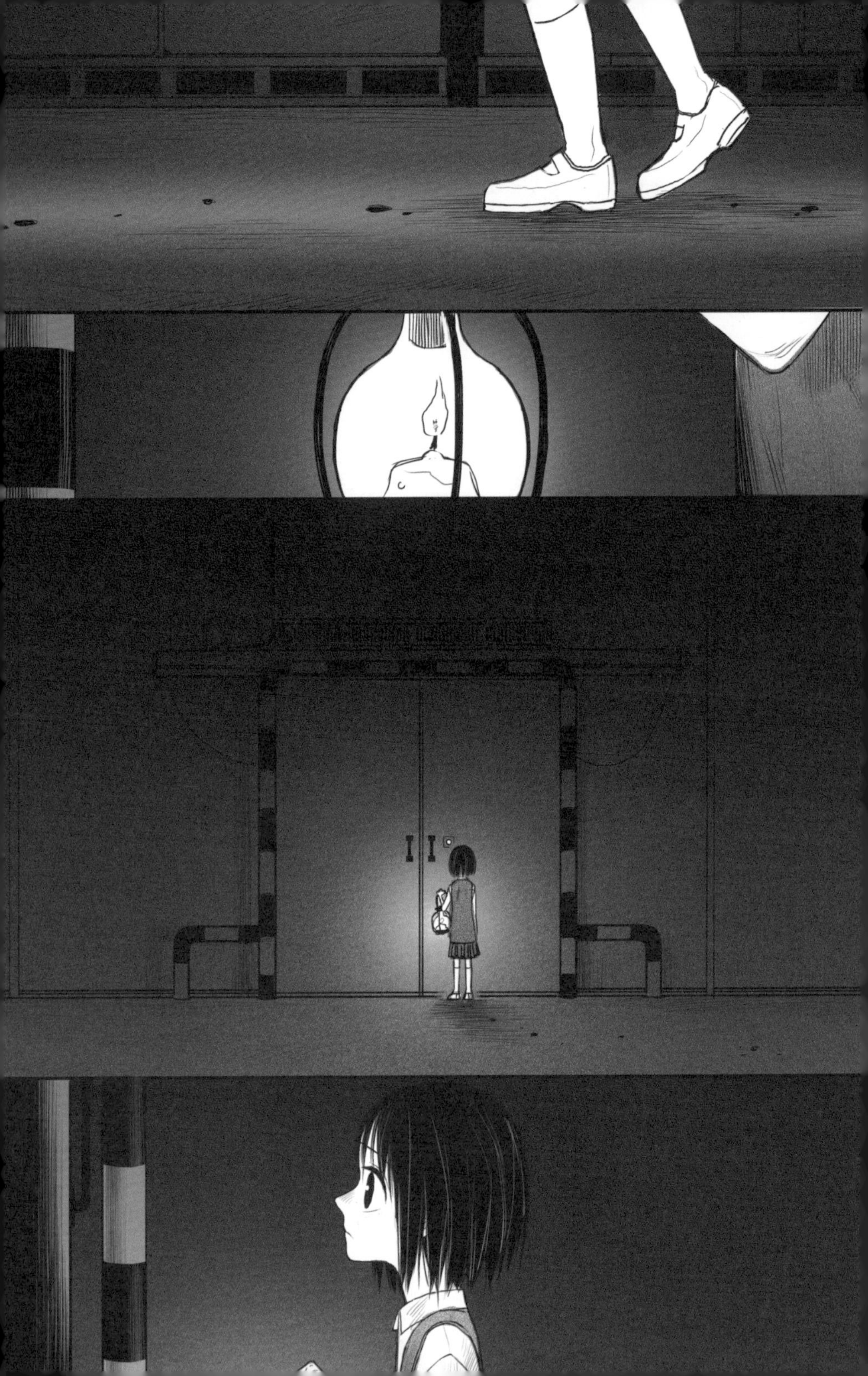

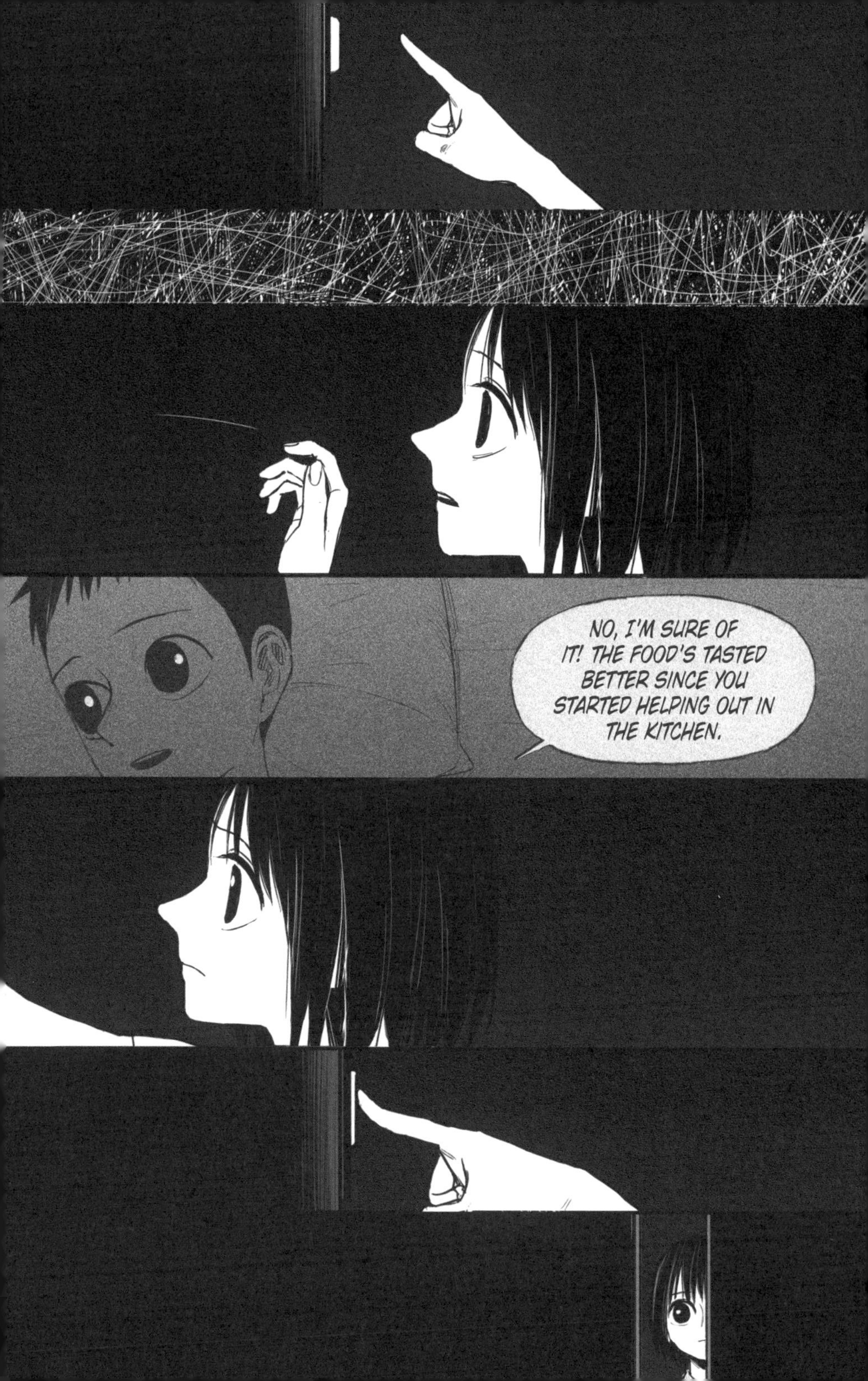
NO, I'M SURE OF IT! THE FOOD'S TASTED BETTER SINCE YOU STARTED HELPING OUT IN THE KITCHEN.

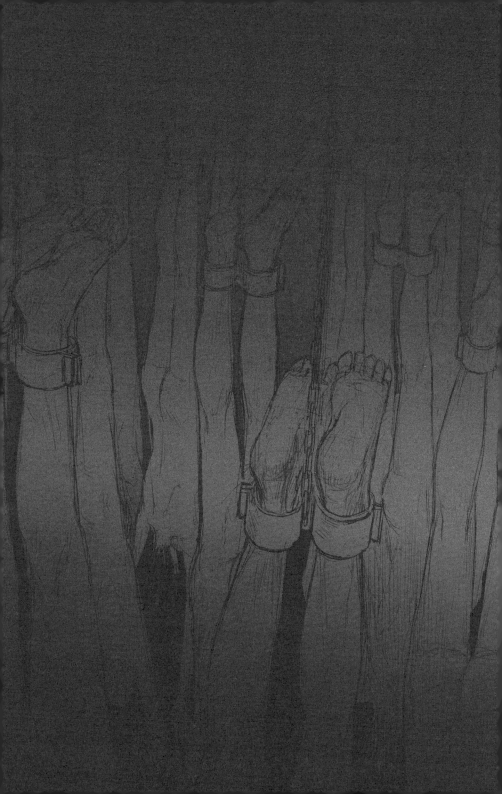

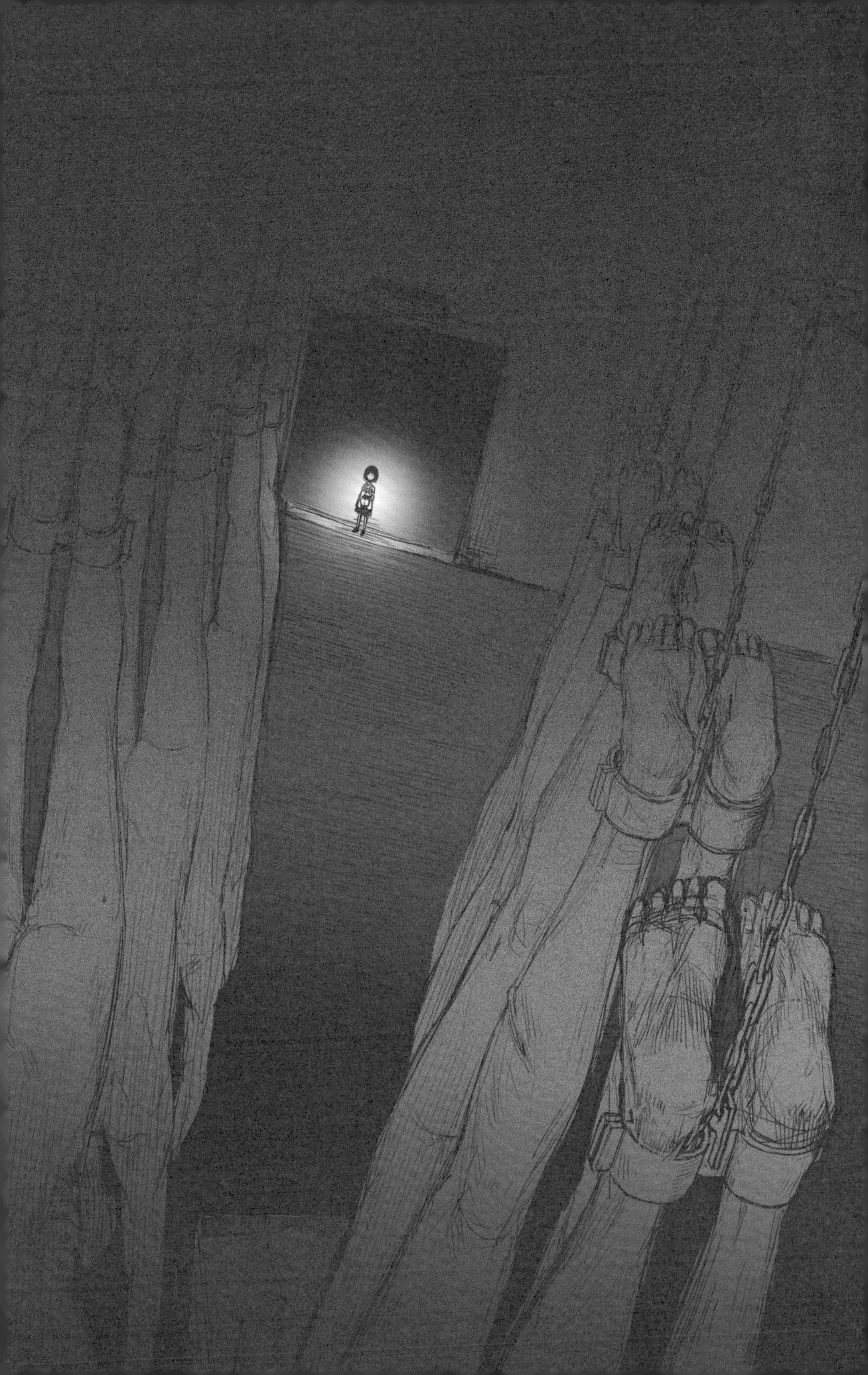

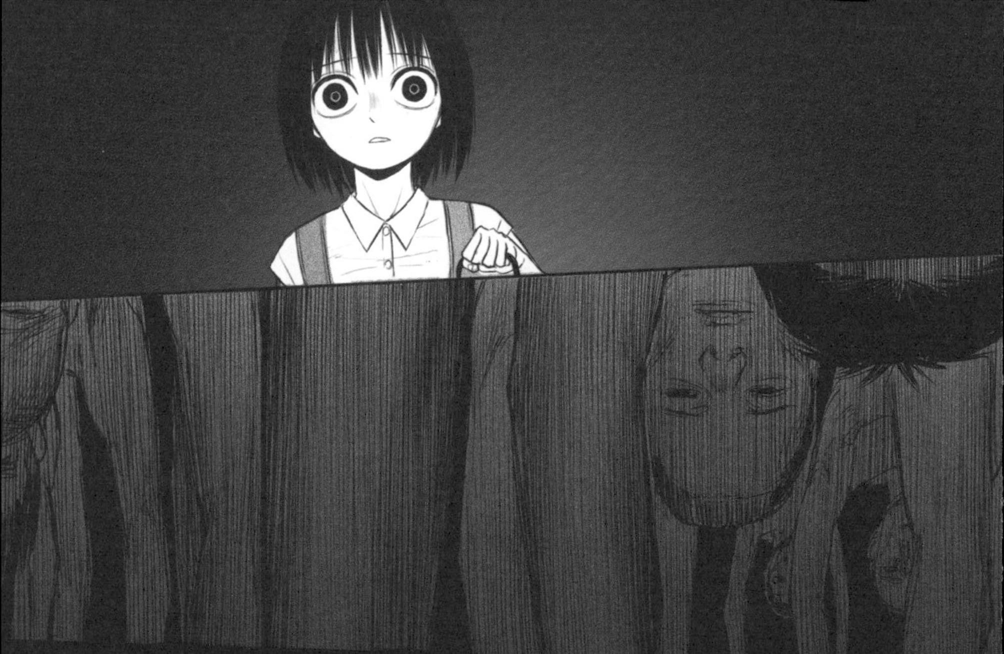

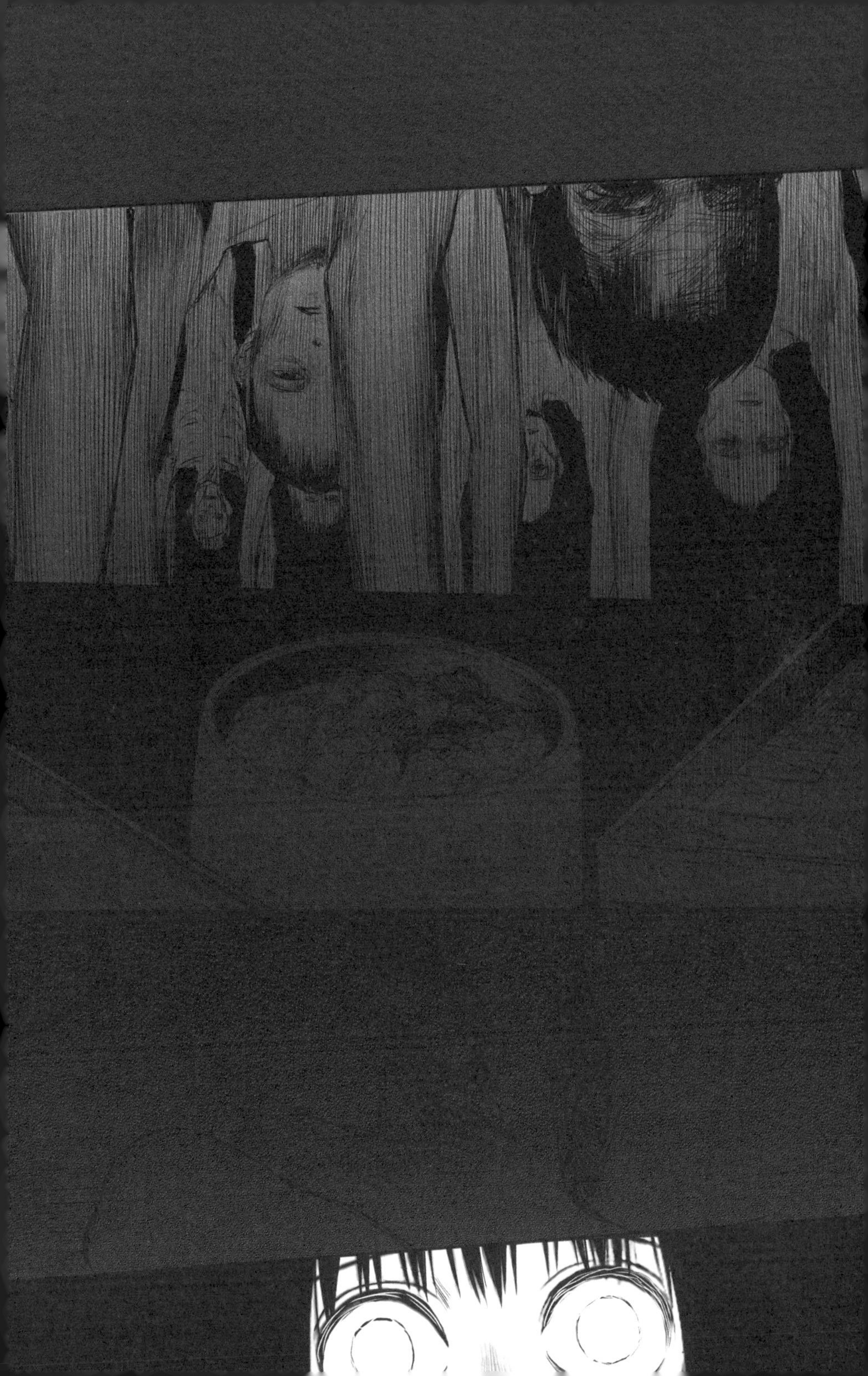

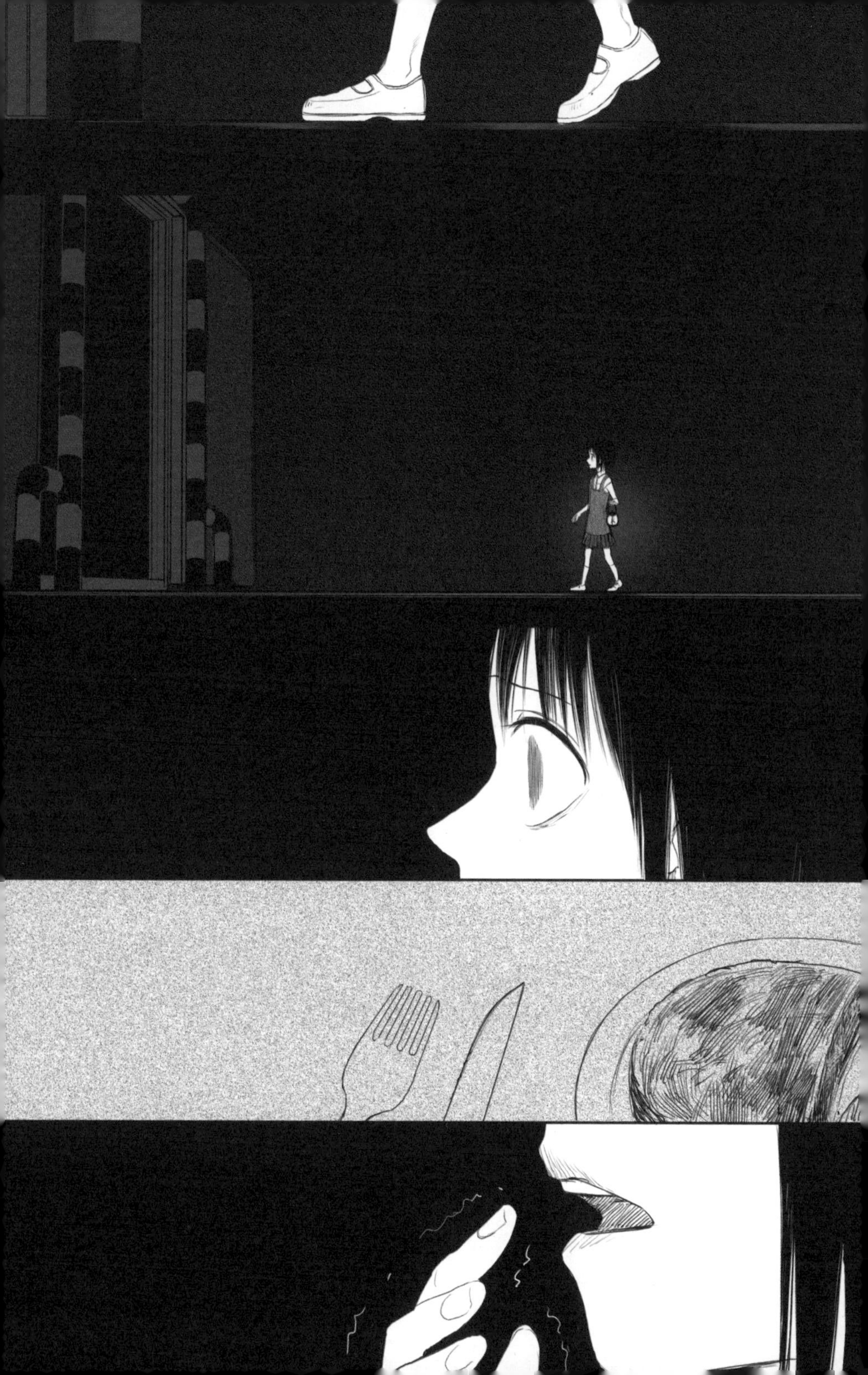

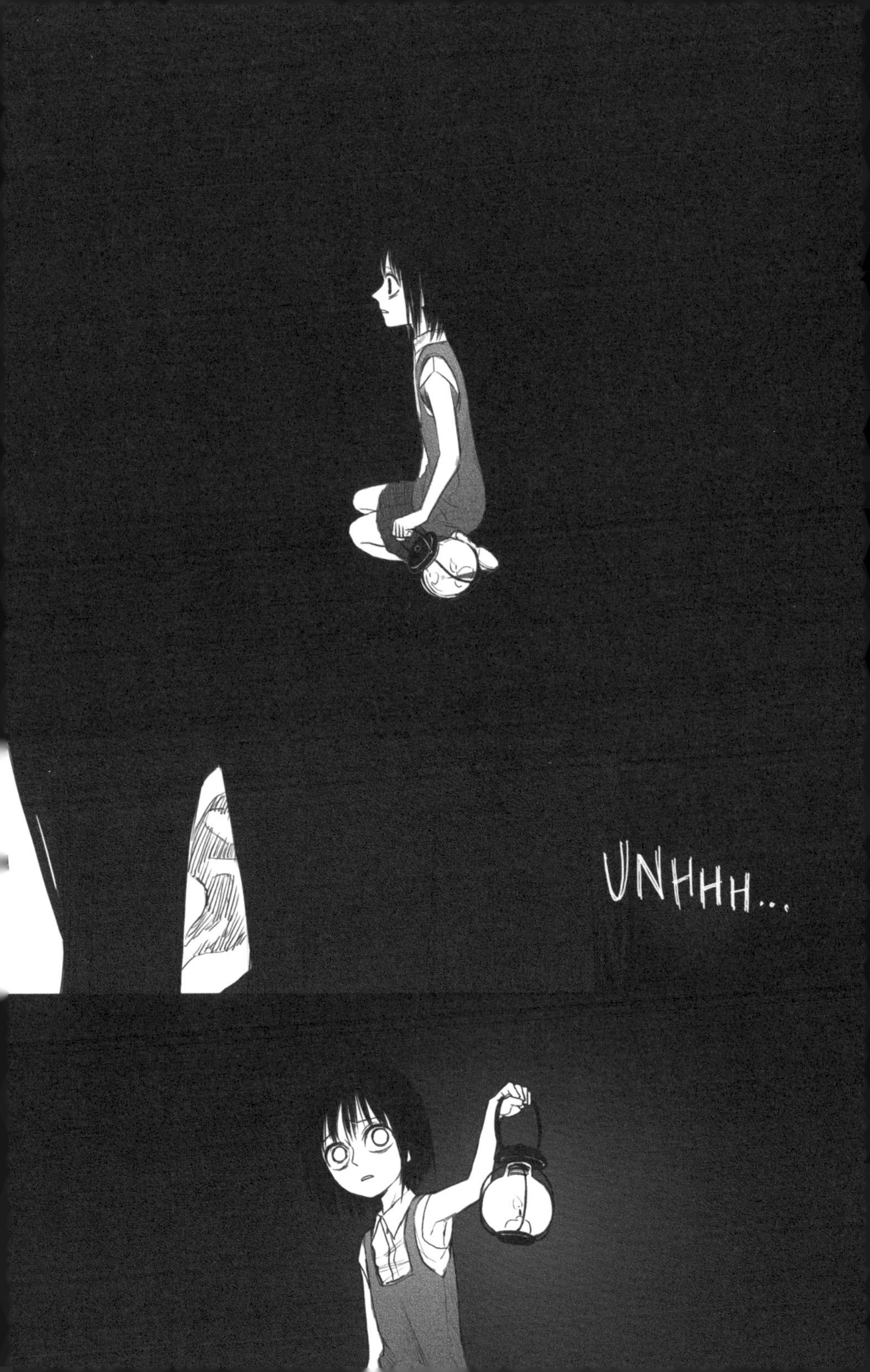
UNHHH...

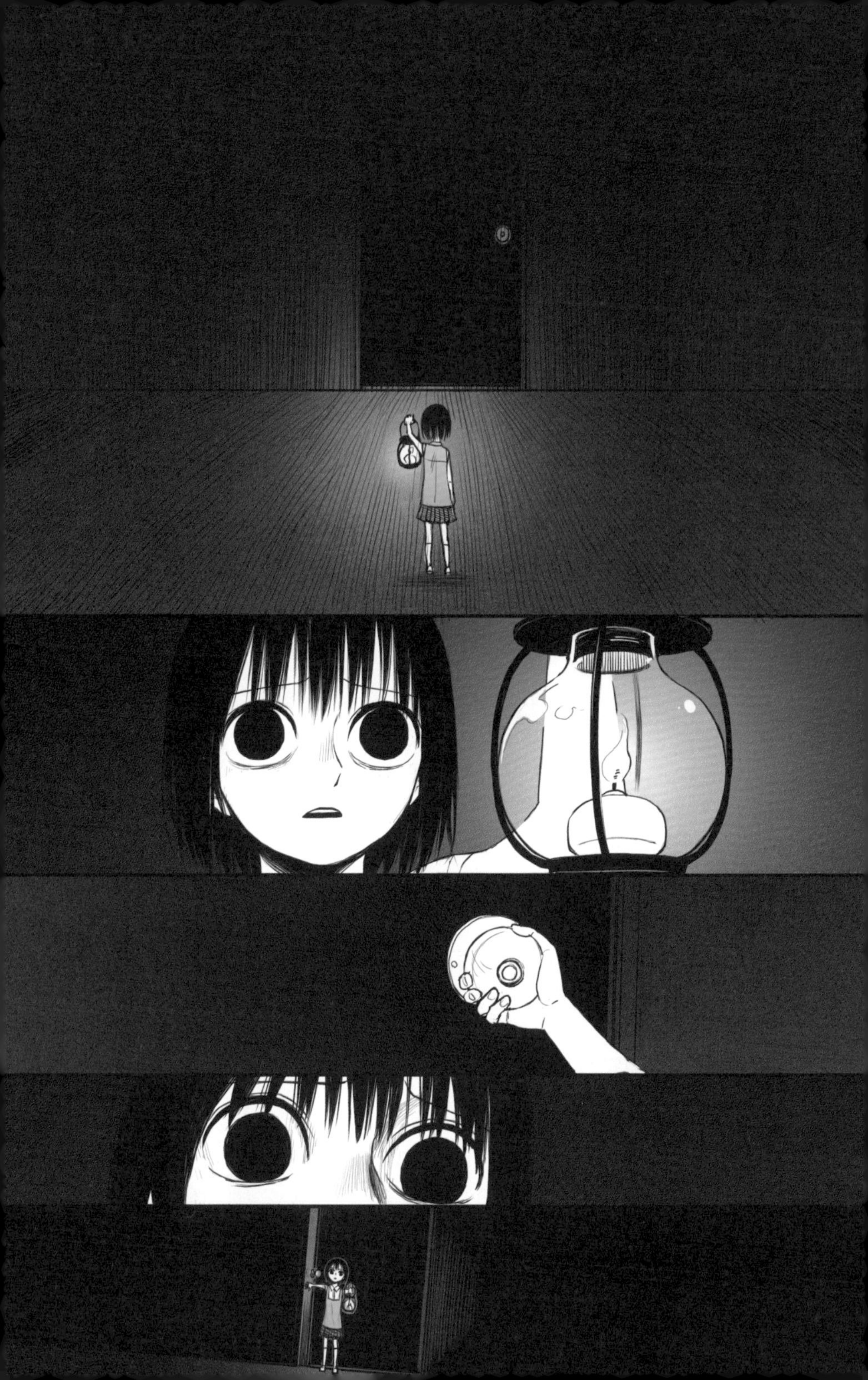

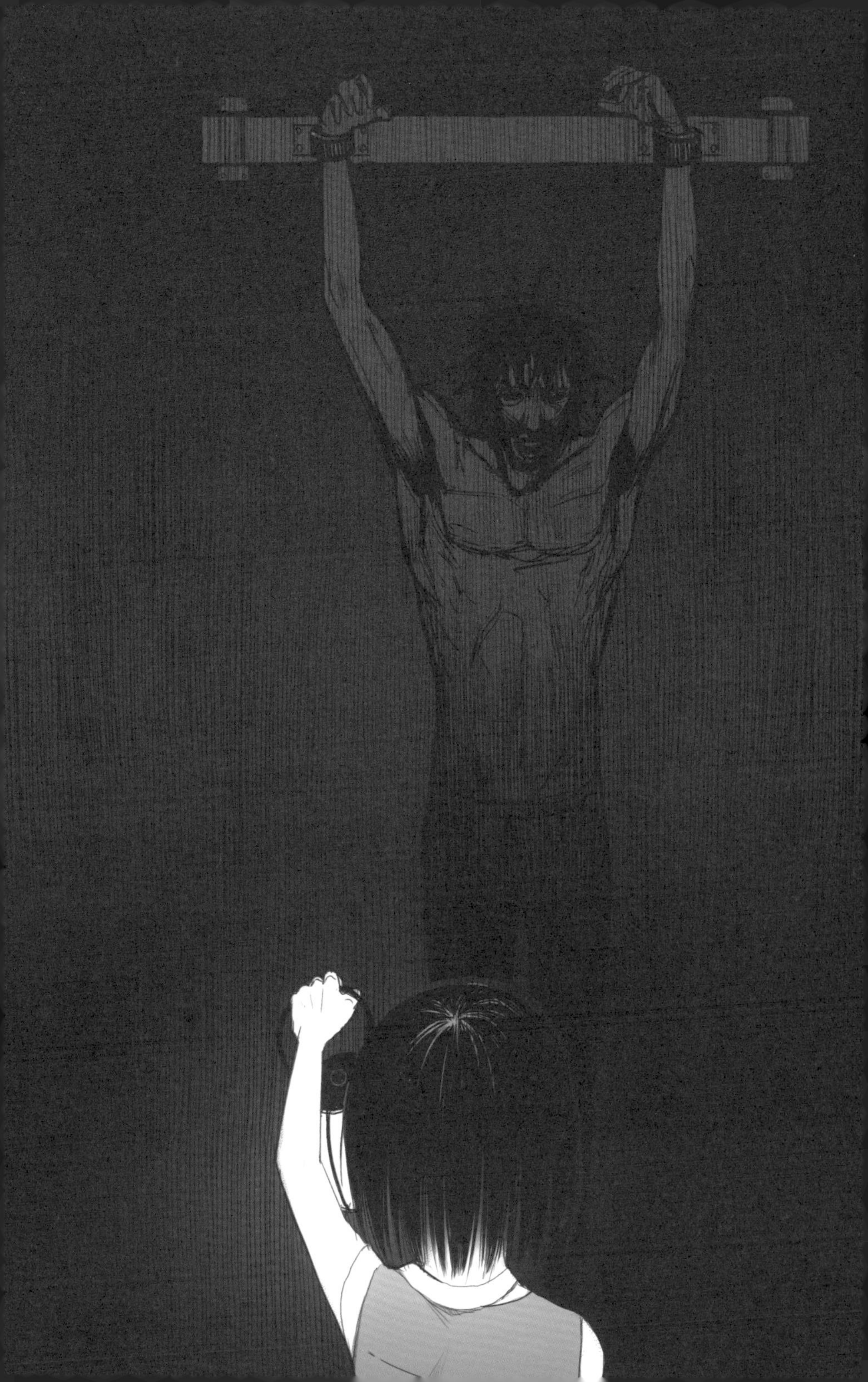

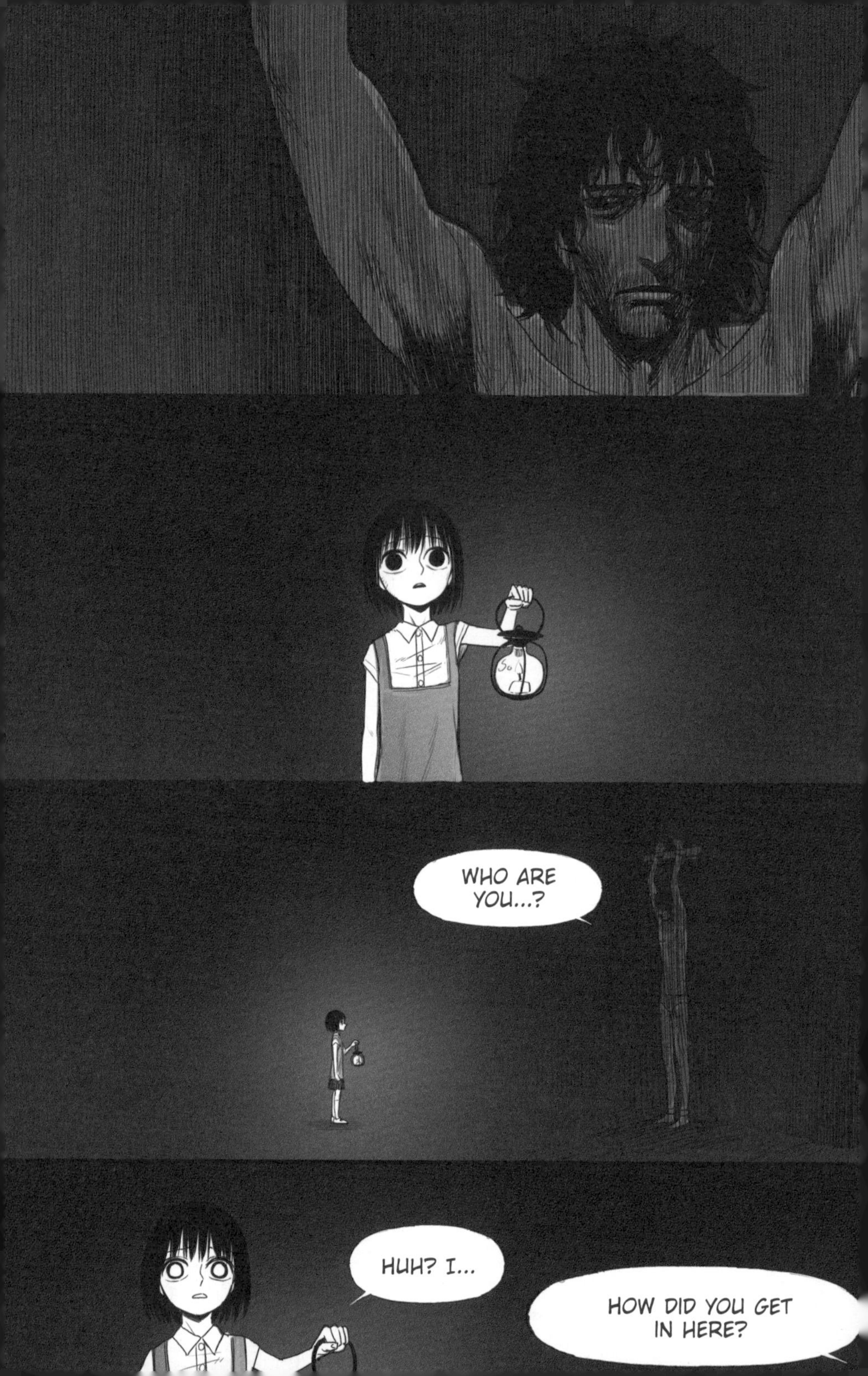
WHO ARE YOU...?
HUH? I...
HOW DID YOU GET IN HERE?

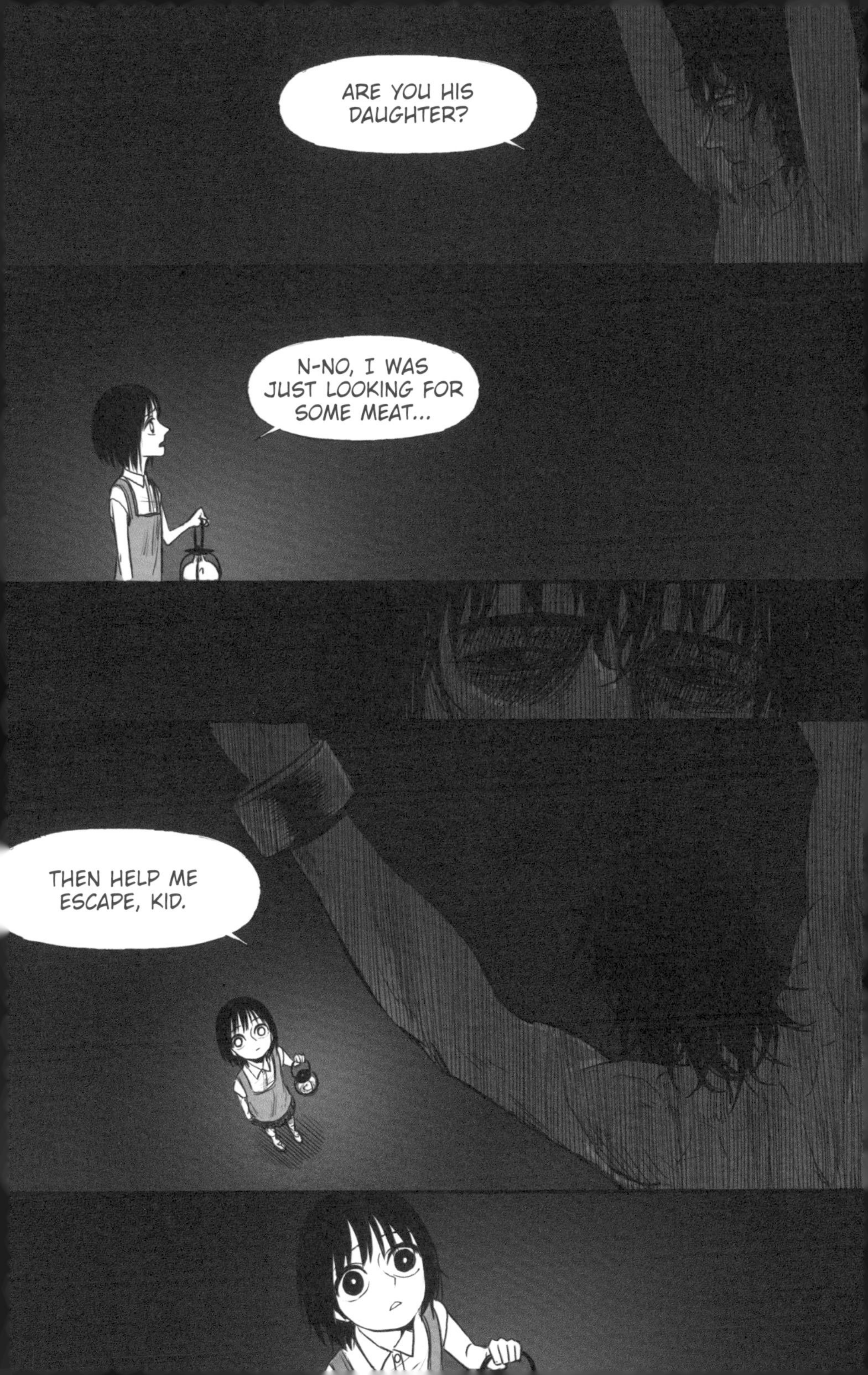
ARE YOU HIS DAUGHTER?
N-NO, I WAS JUST LOOKING FOR SOME MEAT...
THEN HELP ME ESCAPE, KID.

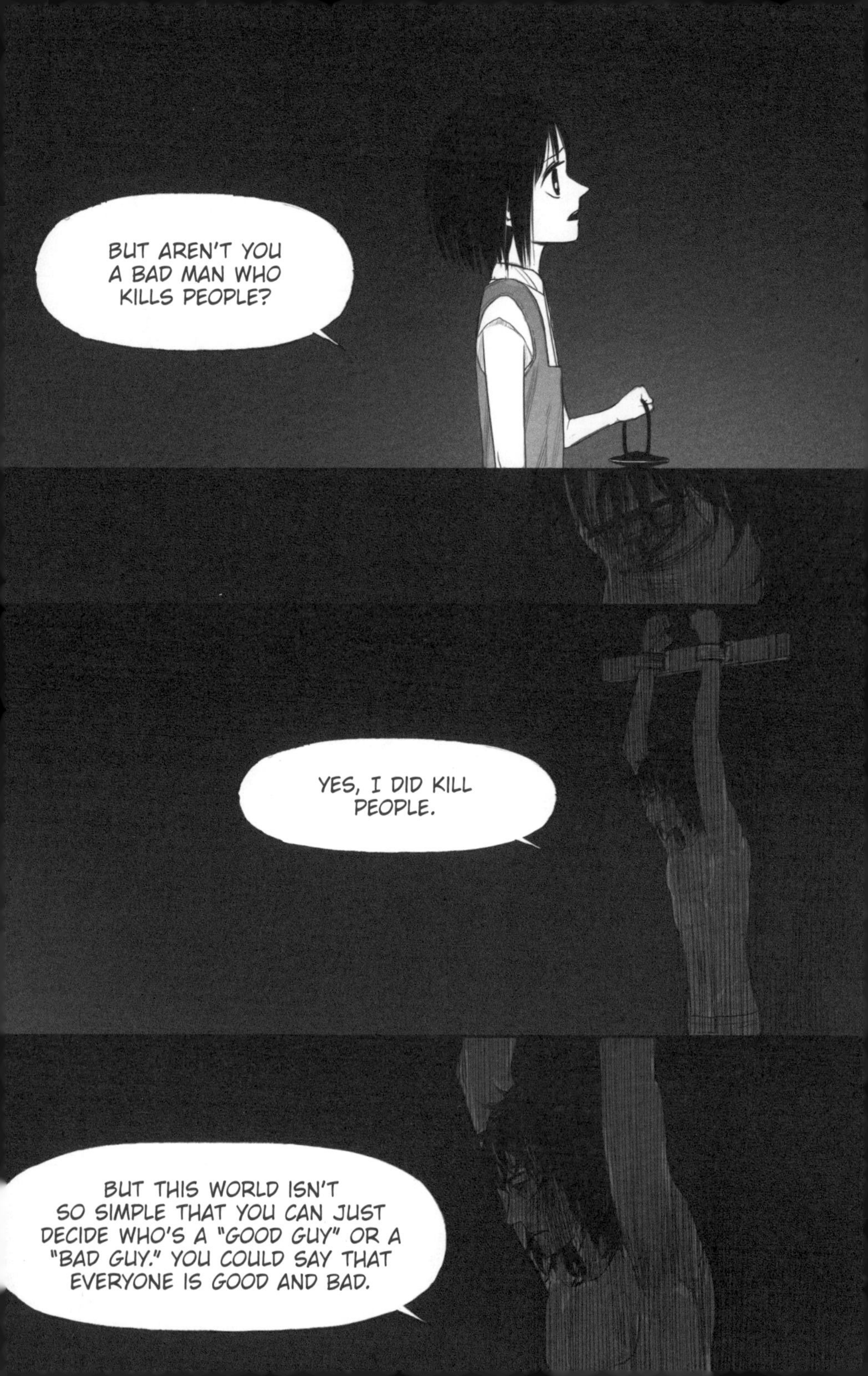
BUT AREN'T YOU A BAD MAN WHO KILLS PEOPLE?
YES, I DID KILL PEOPLE.
BUT THIS WORLD ISN'T SO SIMPLE THAT YOU CAN JUST DECIDE WHO'S A "GOOD GUY" OR A "BAD GUY." YOU COULD SAY THAT EVERYONE IS GOOD AND BAD.

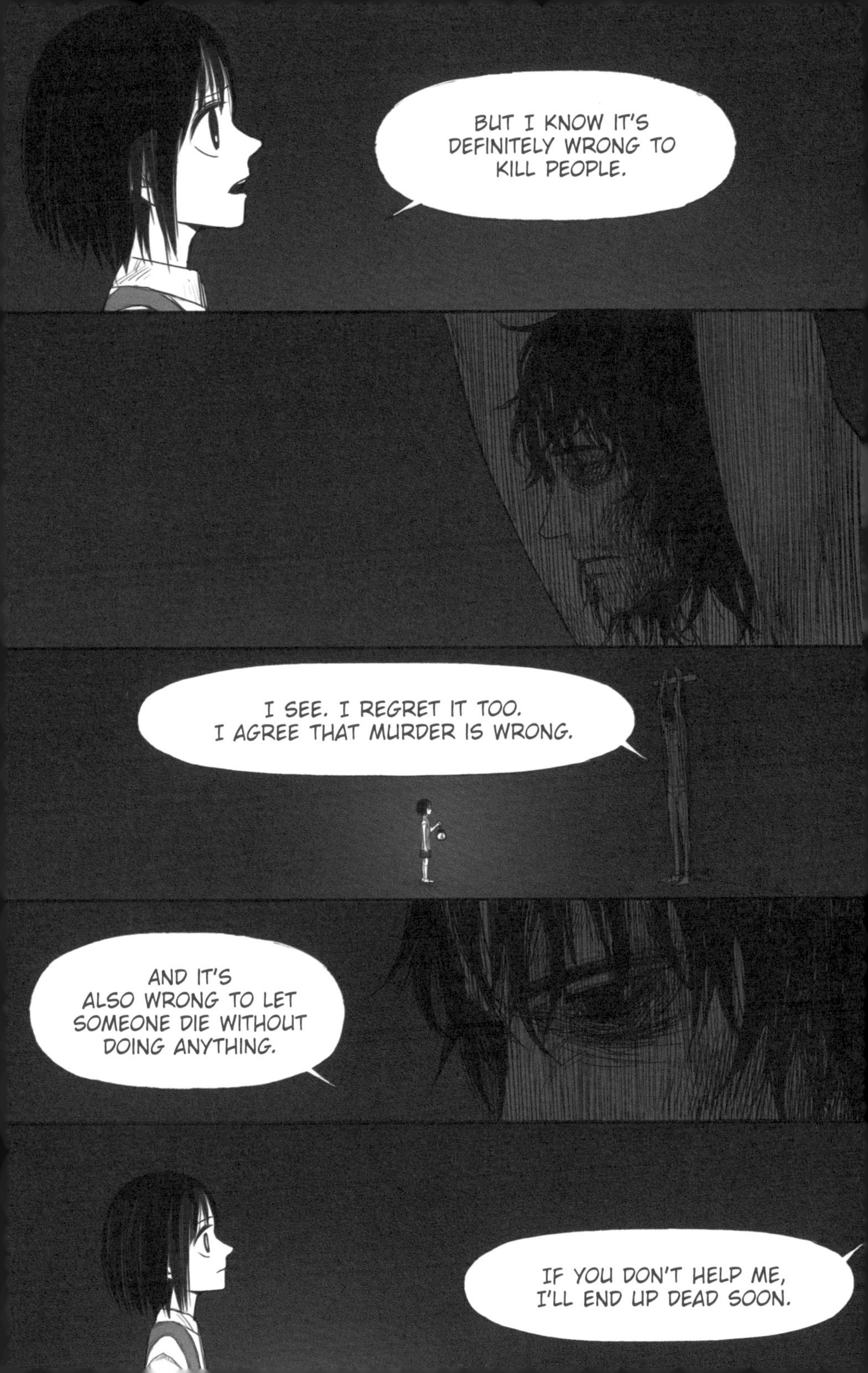
BUT I KNOW IT'S DEFINITELY WRONG TO KILL PEOPLE.
I SEE. I REGRET IT TOO. I AGREE THAT MURDER IS WRONG.
AND IT'S ALSO WRONG TO LET SOMEONE DIE WITHOUT DOING ANYTHING.
IF YOU DON'T HELP ME, I'LL END UP DEAD SOON.

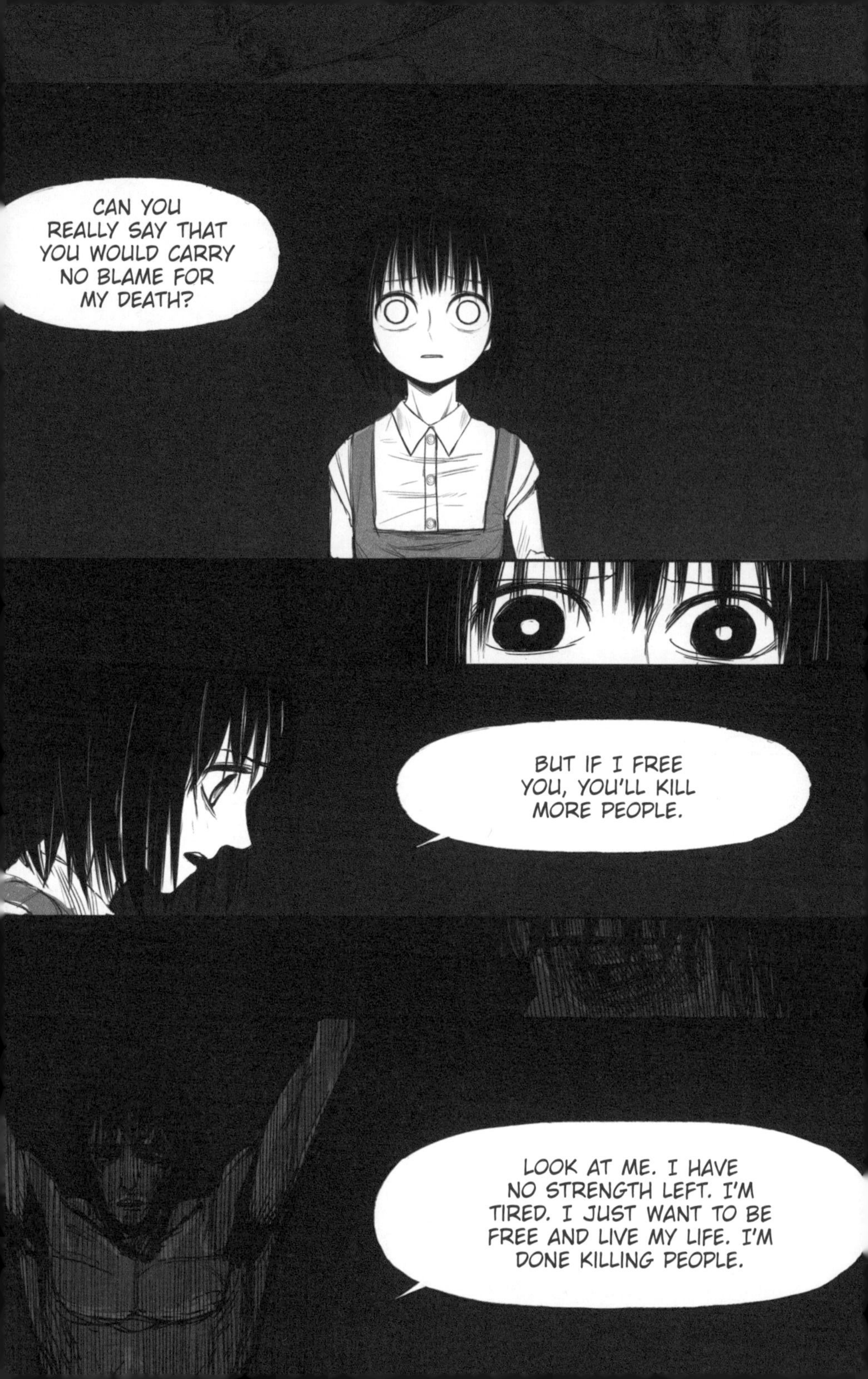
CAN YOU REALLY SAY THAT YOU WOULD CARRY NO BLAME FOR MY DEATH?
BUT IF I FREE YOU, YOU'LL KILL MORE PEOPLE.
LOOK AT ME. I HAVE NO STRENGTH LEFT. I'M TIRED. I JUST WANT TO BE FREE AND LIVE MY LIFE. I'M DONE KILLING PEOPLE.

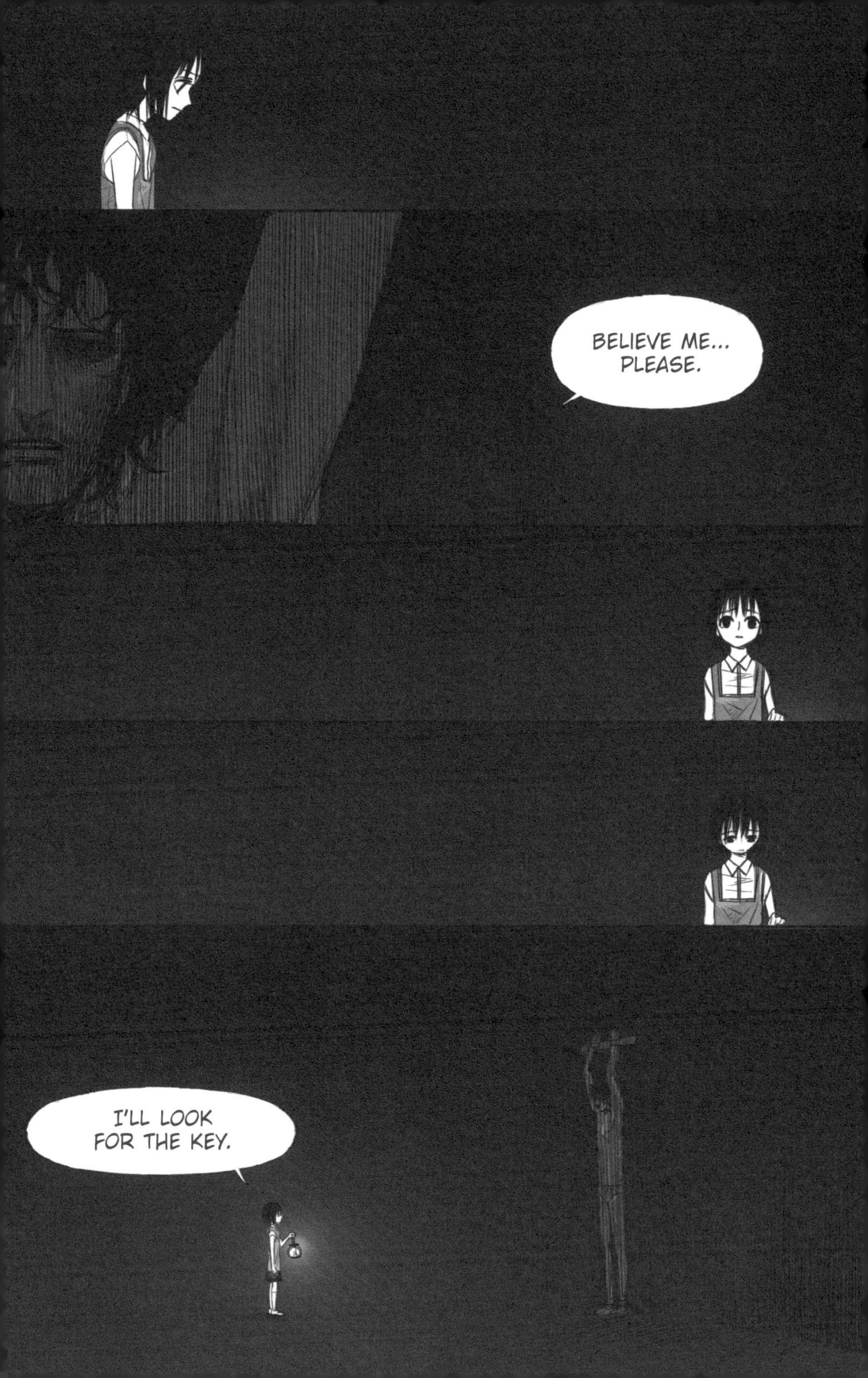
BELIEVE ME... PLEASE.
I'LL LOOK FOR THE KEY.

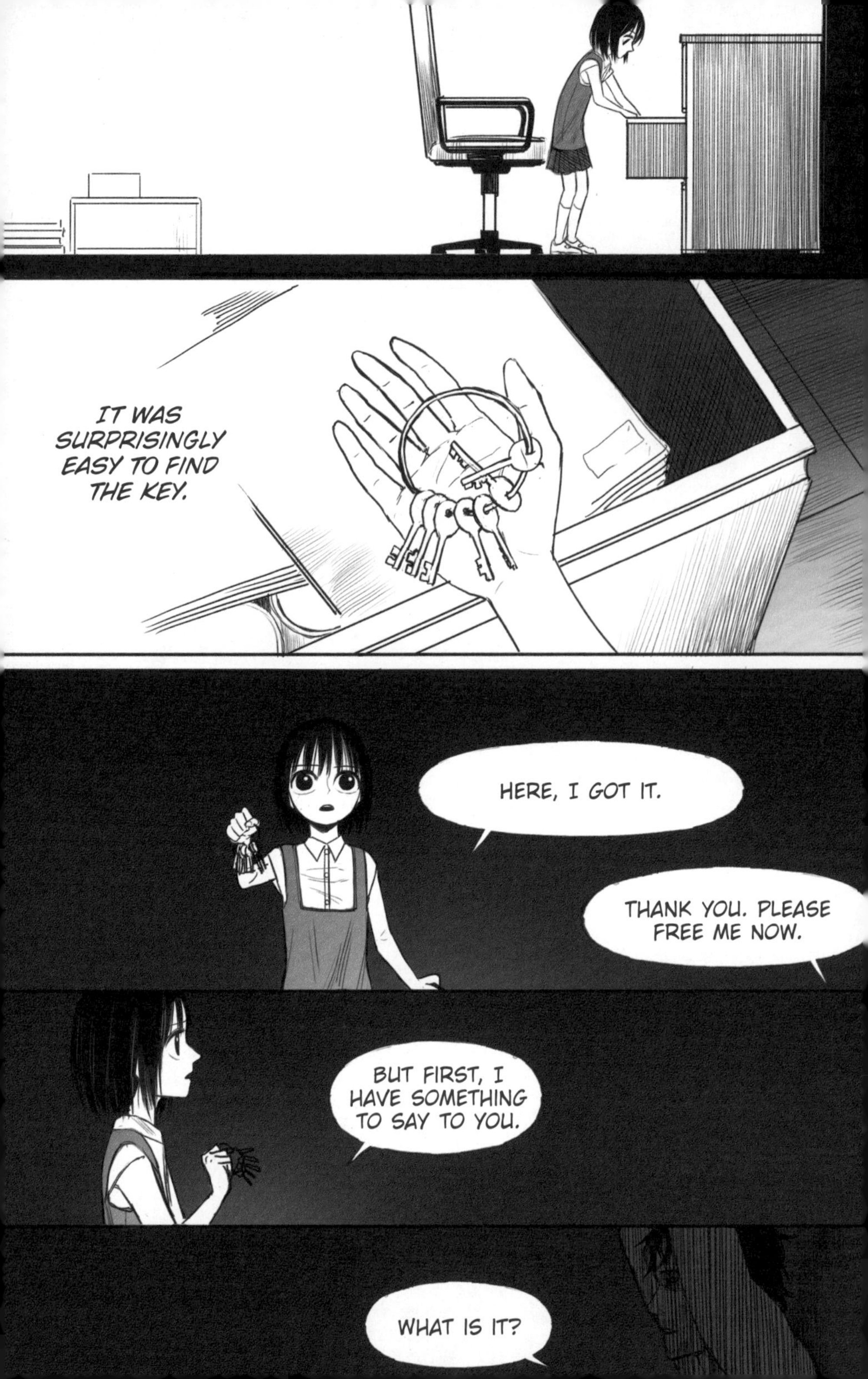
IT WAS SURPRISINGLY EASY TO FIND THE KEY.
HERE, I GOT IT.
THANK YOU. PLEASE FREE ME NOW.
BUT FIRST, I HAVE SOMETHING TO SAY TO YOU.
WHAT IS IT?

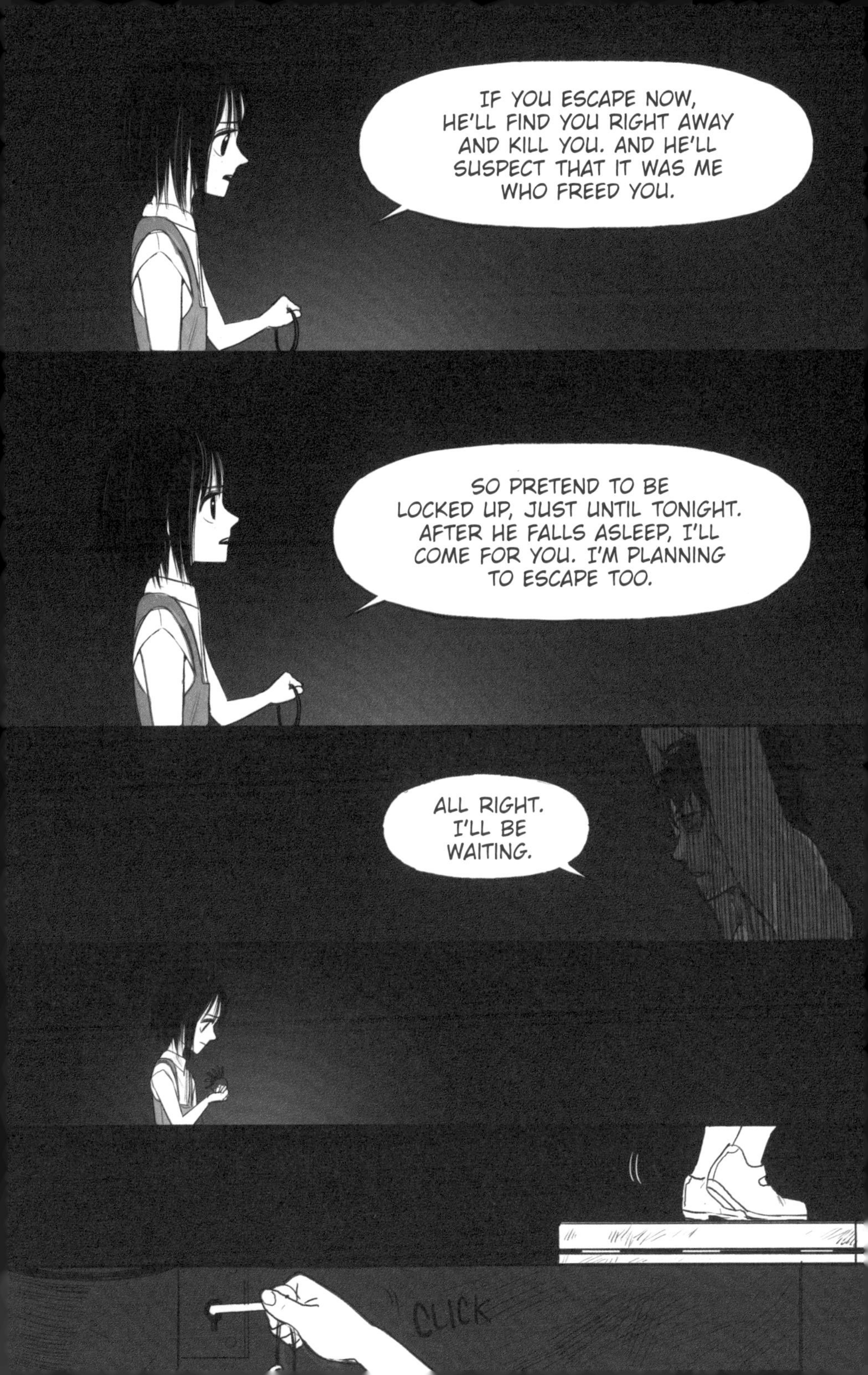
IF YOU ESCAPE NOW, HE'LL FIND YOU RIGHT AWAY AND KILL YOU. AND HE'LL SUSPECT THAT IT WAS ME WHO FREED YOU.
SO PRETEND TO BE LOCKED UP, JUST UNTIL TONIGHT. AFTER HE FALLS ASLEEP, I'LL COME FOR YOU. I'M PLANNING TO ESCAPE TOO.
ALL RIGHT. I'LL BE WAITING.
CLICK

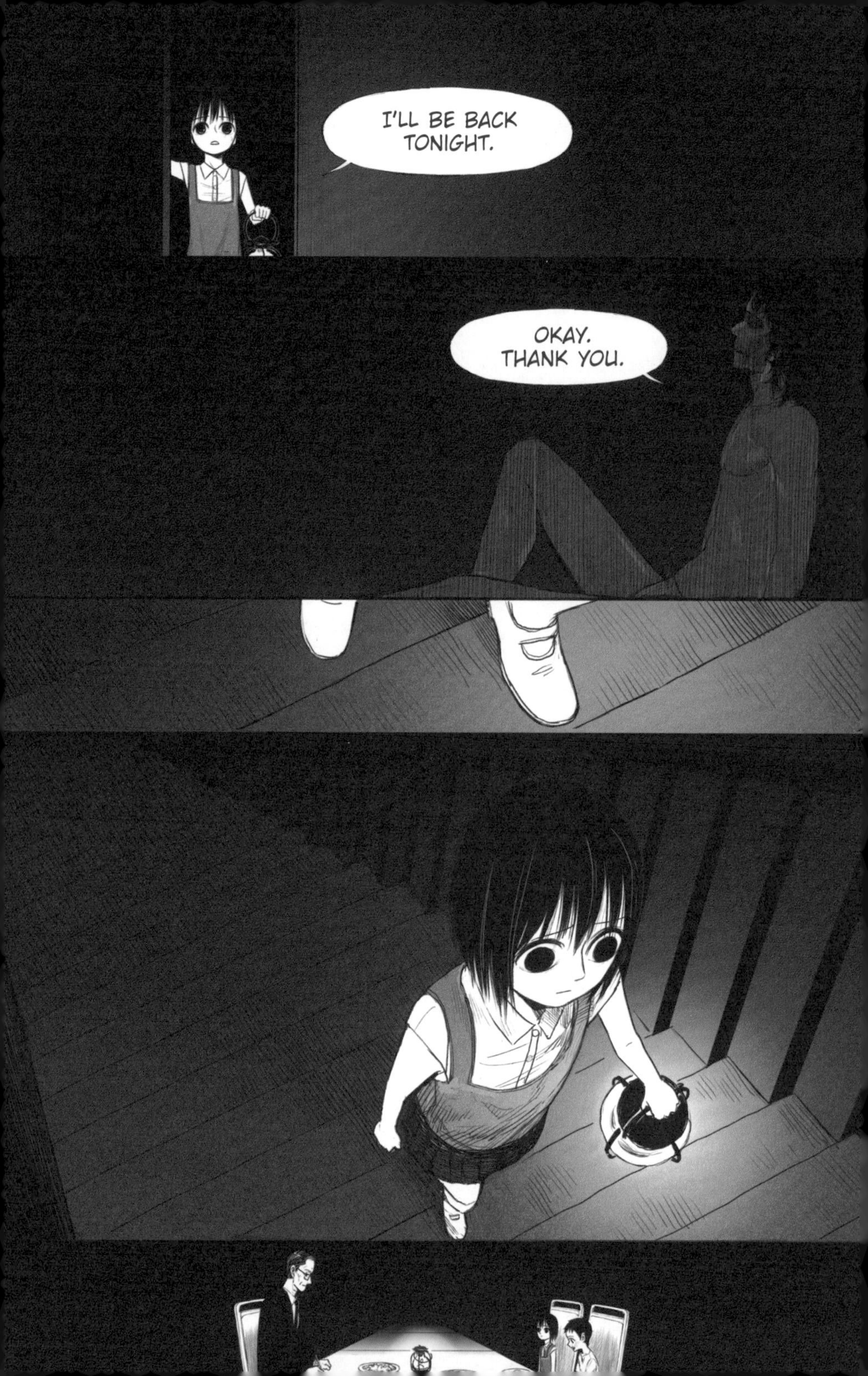
I'LL BE BACK TONIGHT.
OKAY. THANK YOU.

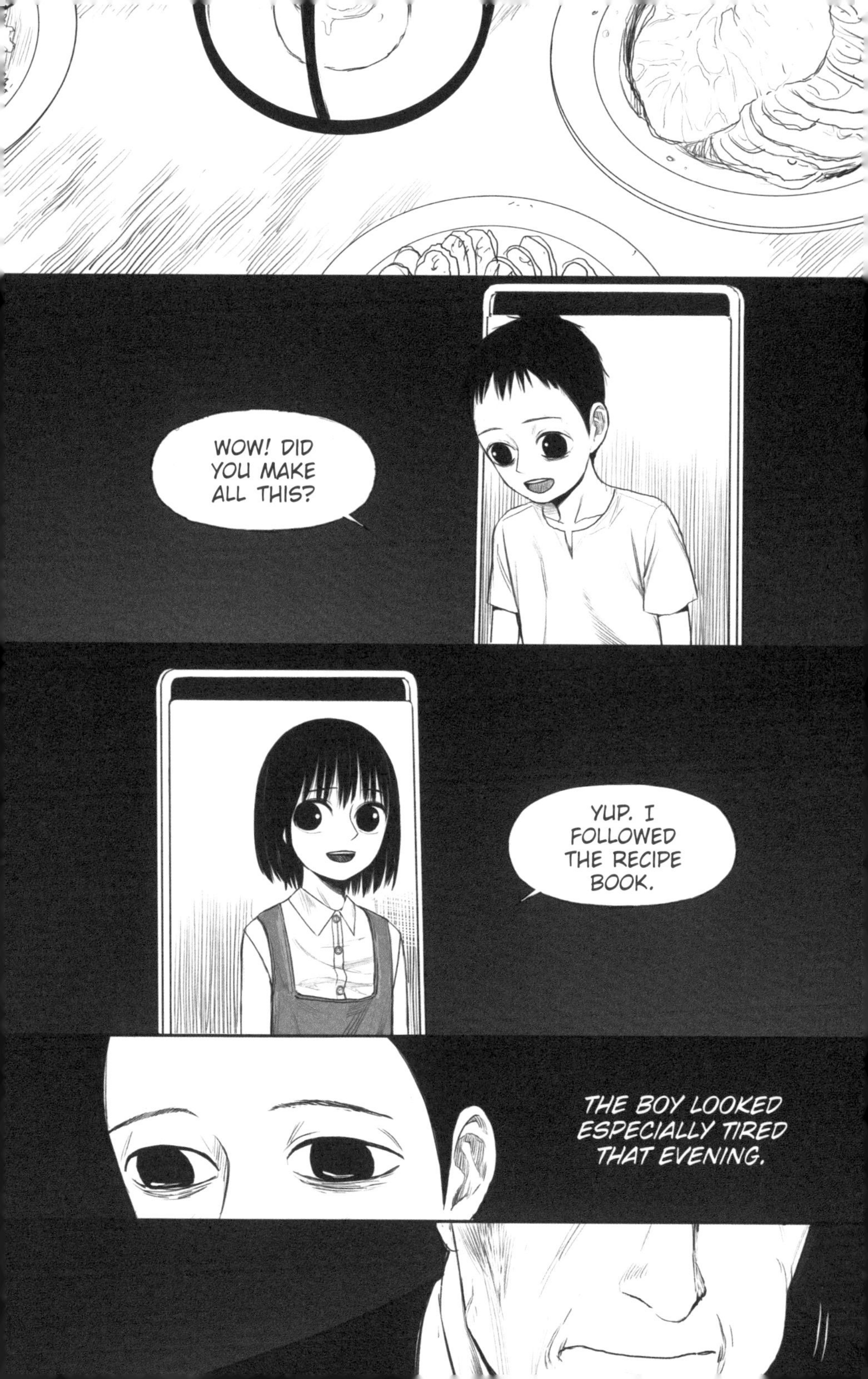
WOW! DID YOU MAKE ALL THIS?
YUP. I FOLLOWED THE RECIPE BOOK.
THE BOY LOOKED ESPECIALLY TIRED THAT EVENING.

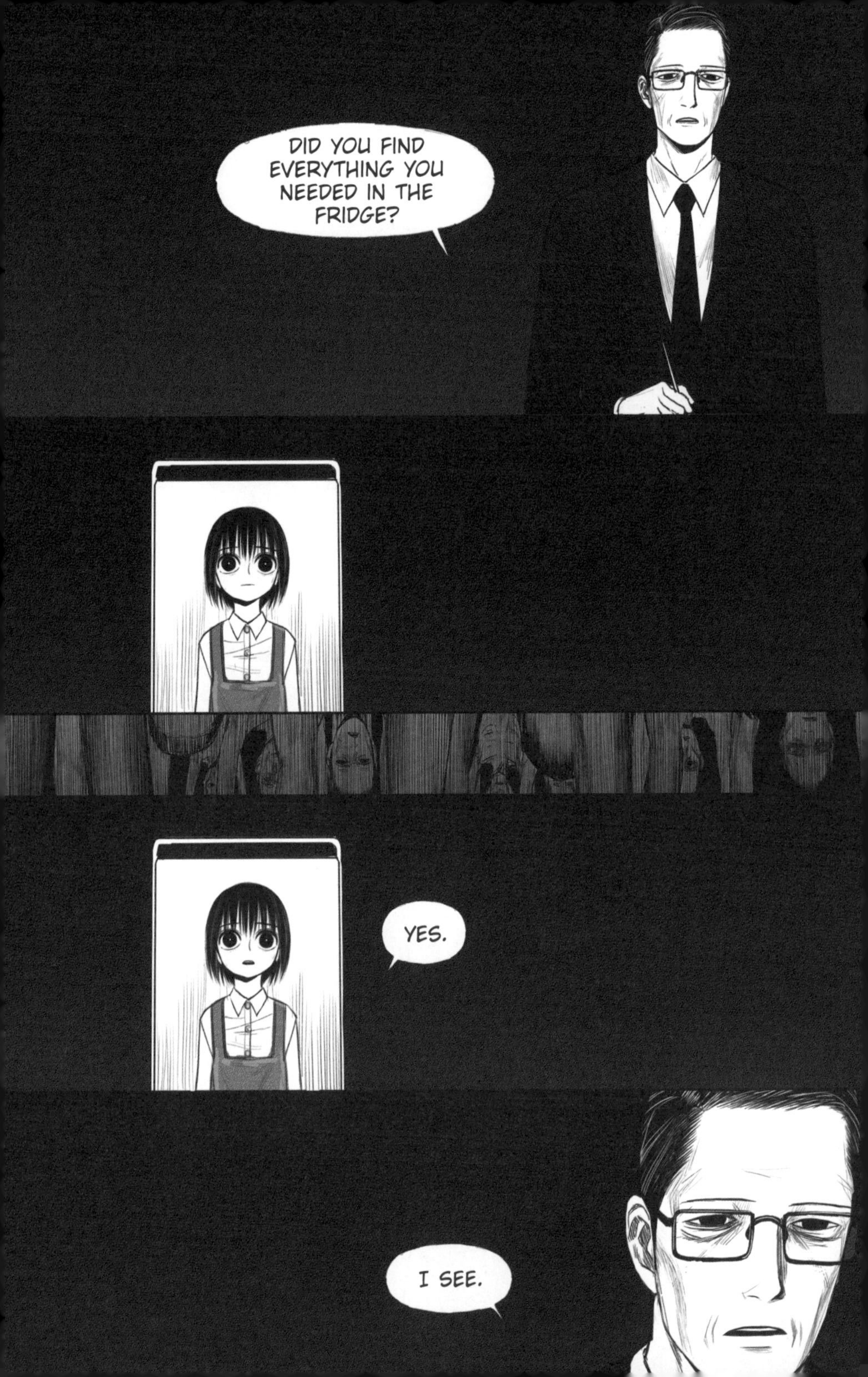
DID YOU FIND EVERYTHING YOU NEEDED IN THE FRIDGE?
YES.
I SEE.

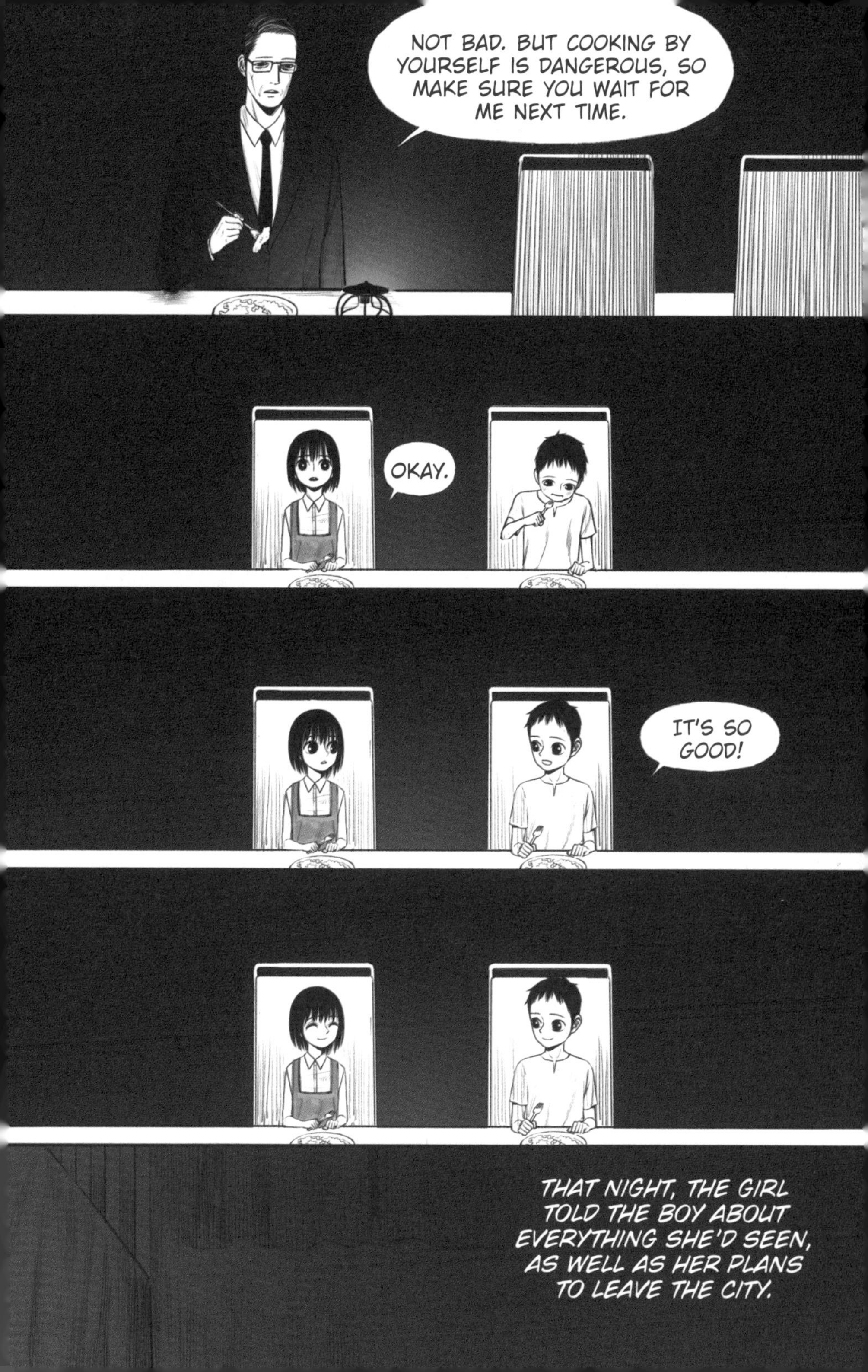
NOT BAD. BUT COOKING BY YOURSELF IS DANGEROUS, SO MAKE SURE YOU WAIT FOR ME NEXT TIME.
OKAY.
IT'S SO GOOD!
THAT NIGHT, THE GIRL TOLD THE BOY ABOUT EVERYTHING SHE'D SEEN, AS WELL AS HER PLANS TO LEAVE THE CITY.

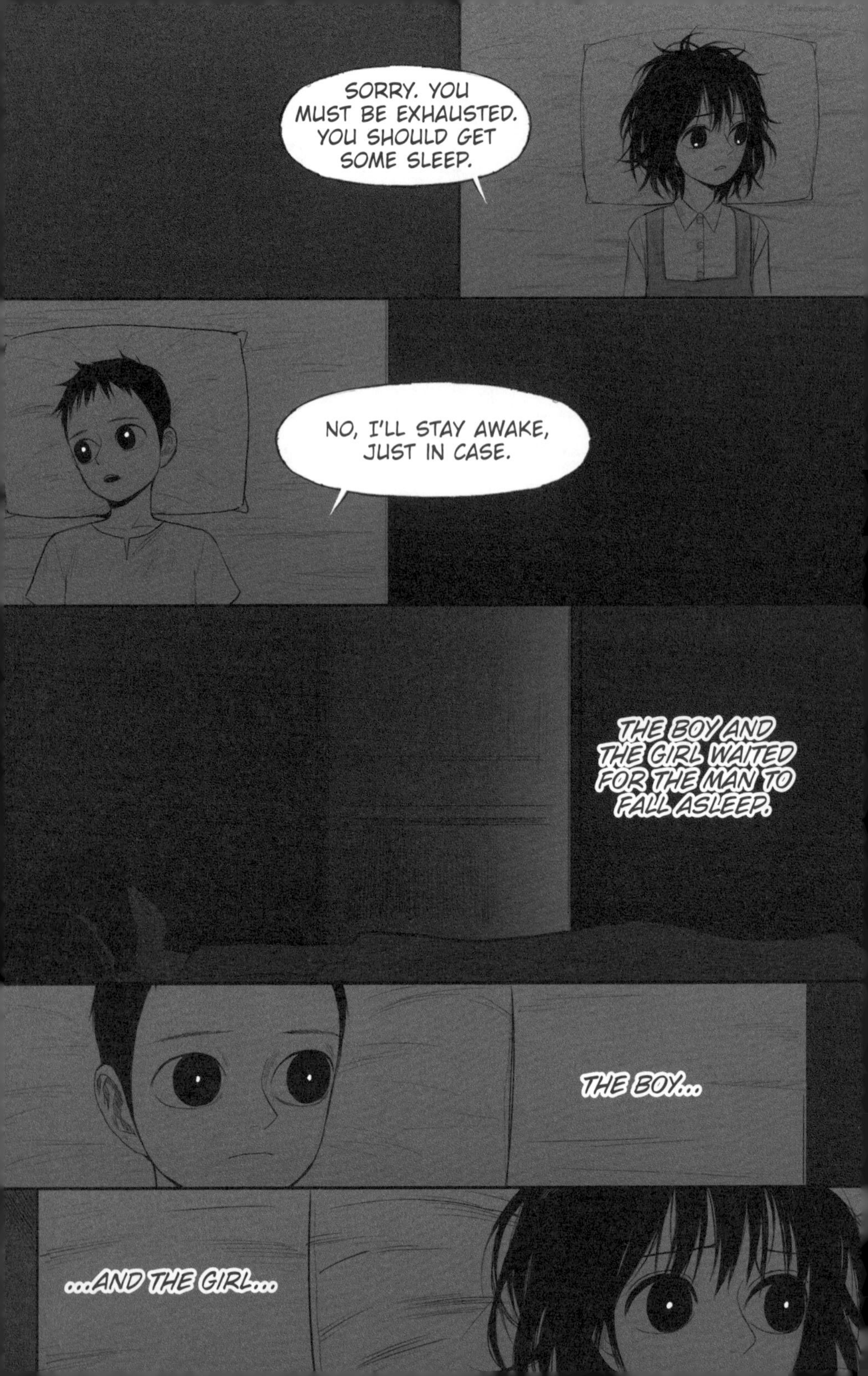
SORRY. YOU MUST BE EXHAUSTED. YOU SHOULD GET SOME SLEEP.
NO, I'LL STAY AWAKE, JUST IN CASE.
THE BOY AND THE GIRL WAITED FOR THE MAN TO FALL ASLEEP.
THE BOY...
...AND THE GIRL...

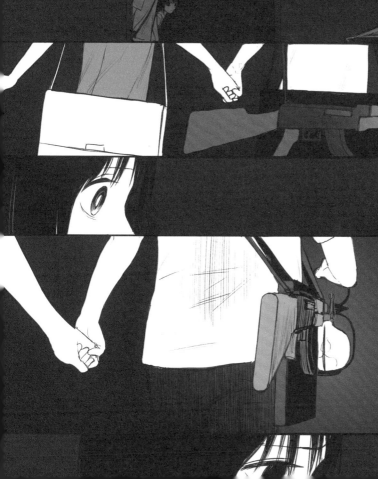

...WERE NERVOUS ABOUT THE FUTURE.

THE MAN FINALLY WENT TO SLEEP VERY LATE INTO THE NIGHT.

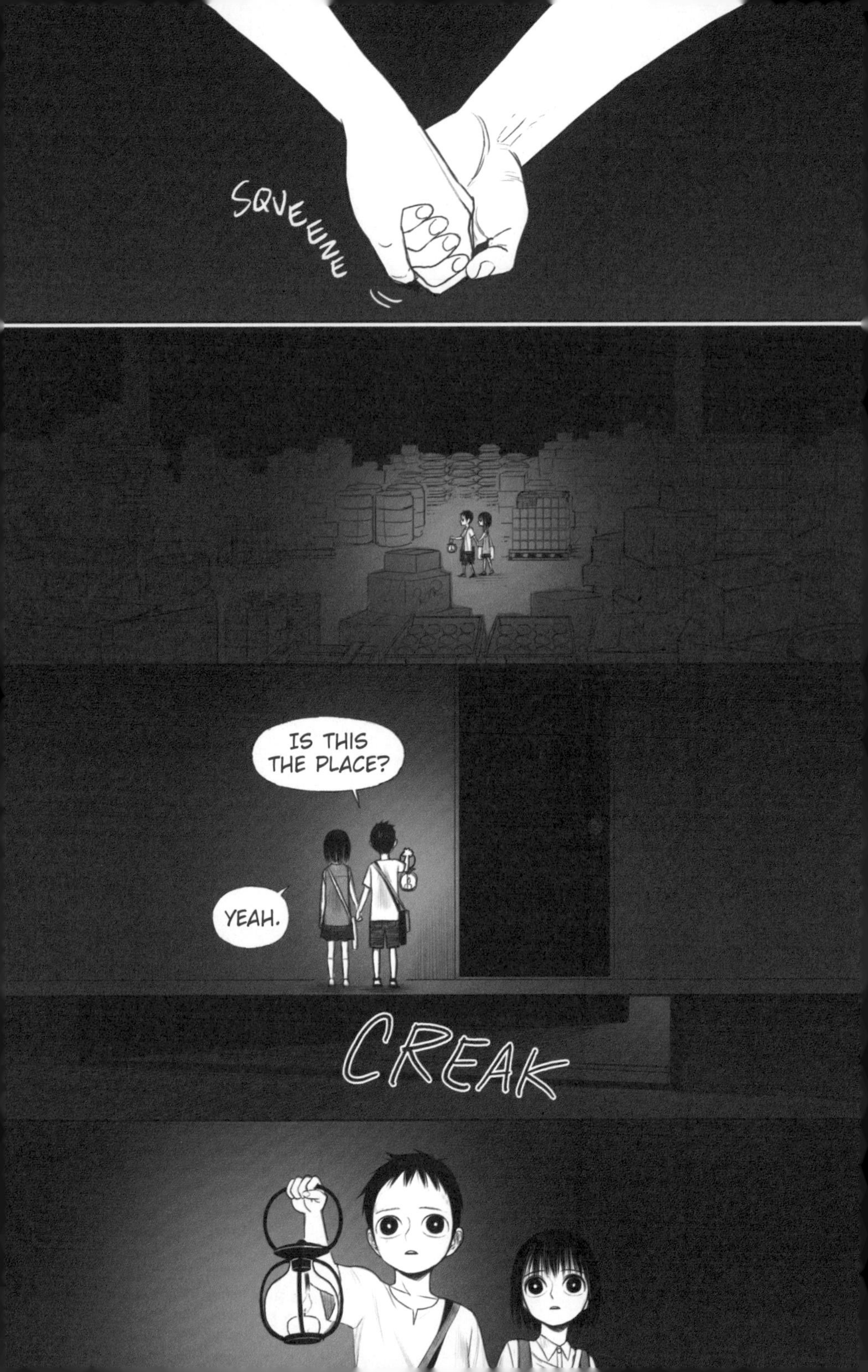
SQUEEZE
IS THIS THE PLACE?
YEAH.
CREAK

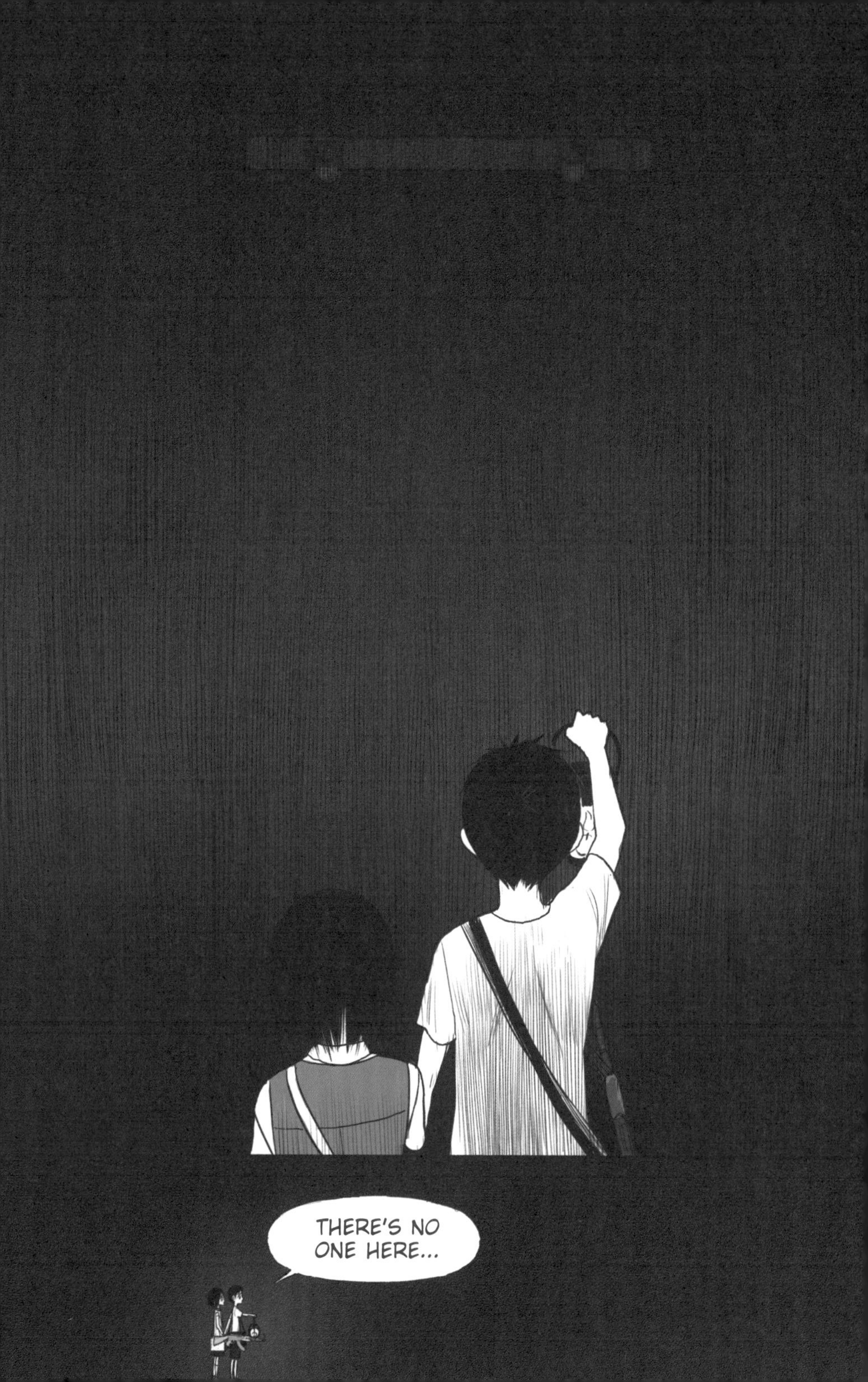
THERE'S NO ONE HERE...

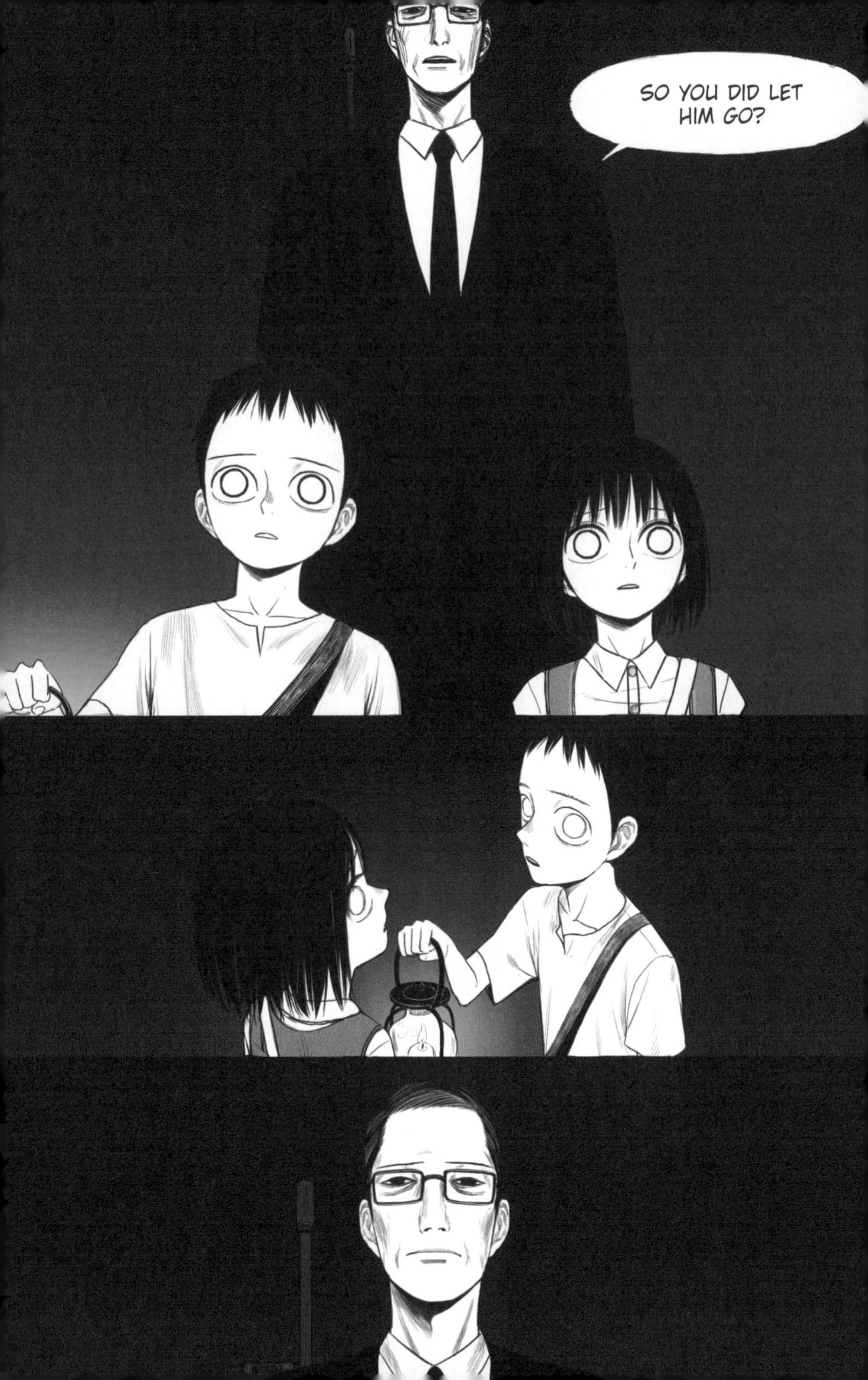
SO YOU DID LET
HIM GO?

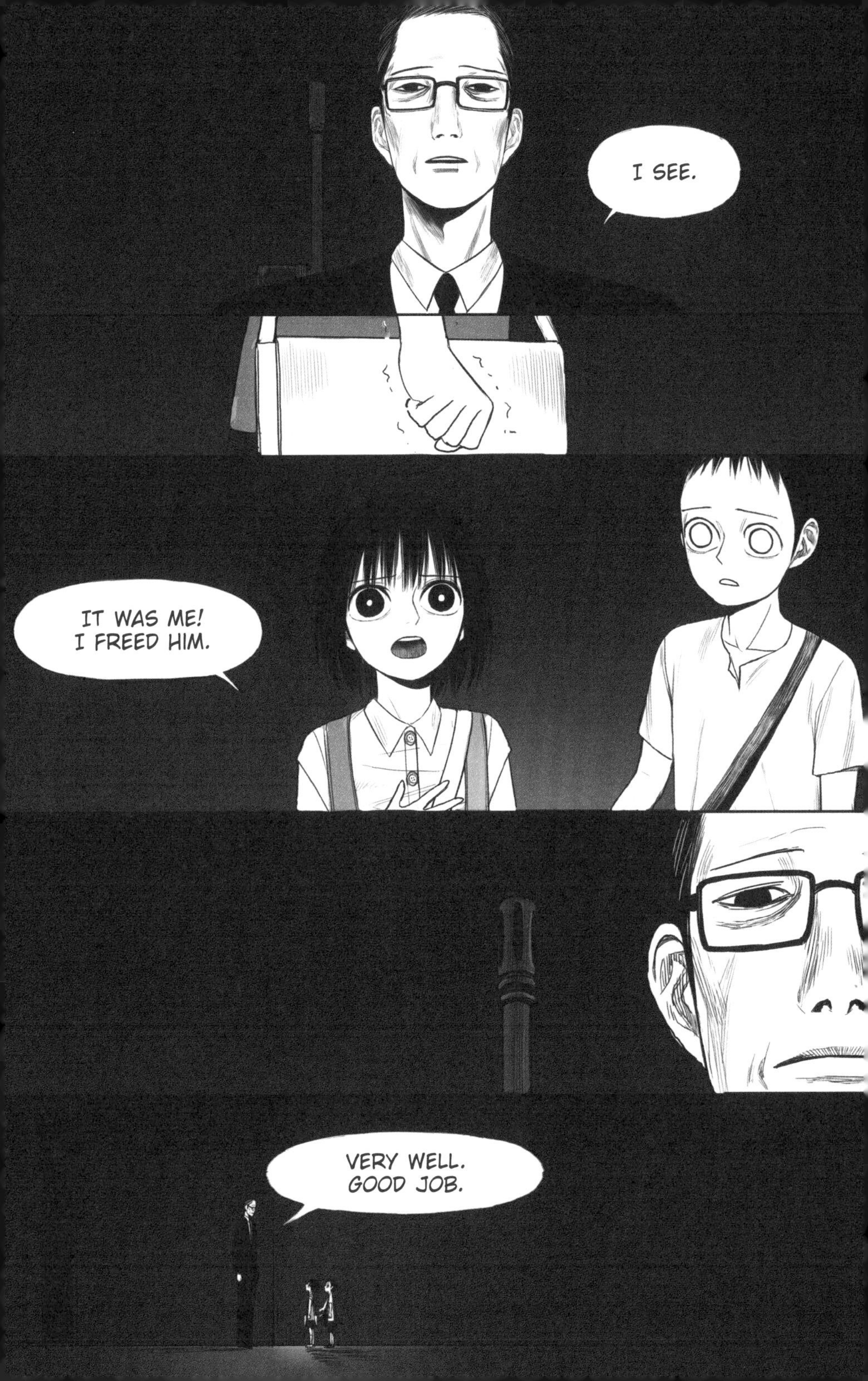
I SEE.
IT WAS ME! I FREED HIM.
VERY WELL. GOOD JOB.

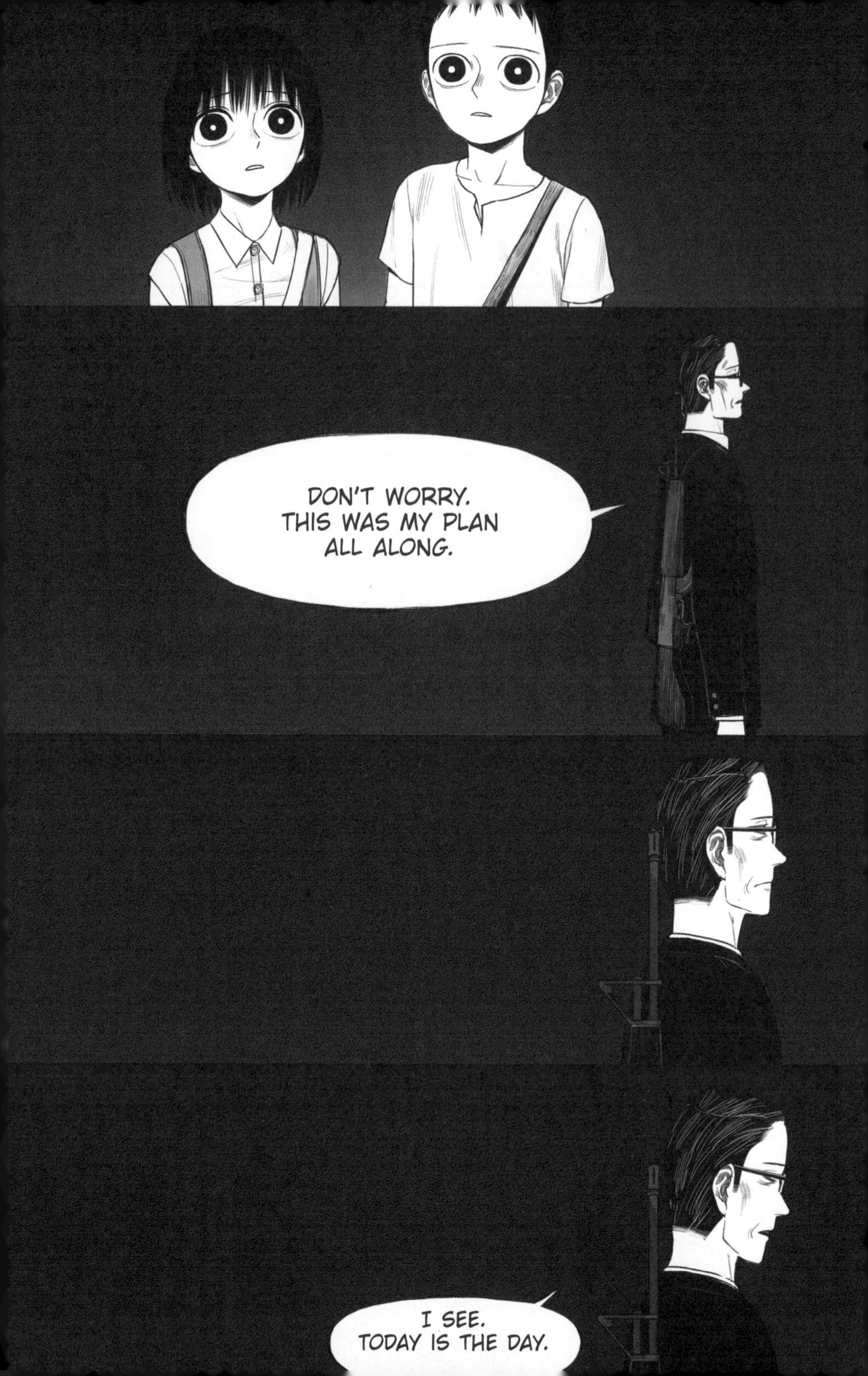
DON'T WORRY. THIS WAS MY PLAN ALL ALONG.
I SEE. TODAY IS THE DAY.

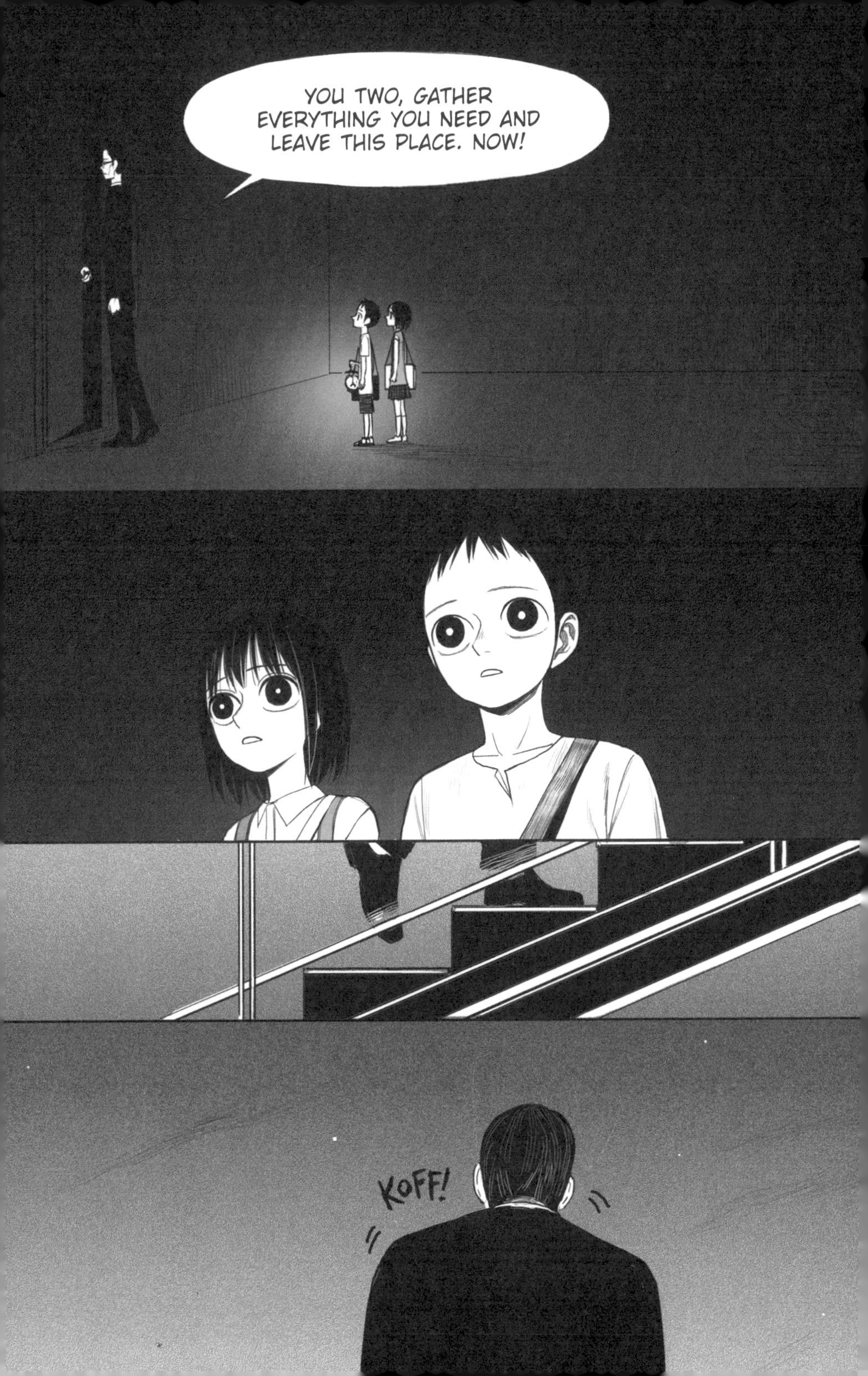
YOU TWO, GATHER EVERYTHING YOU NEED AND LEAVE THIS PLACE. NOW!
KOFF!

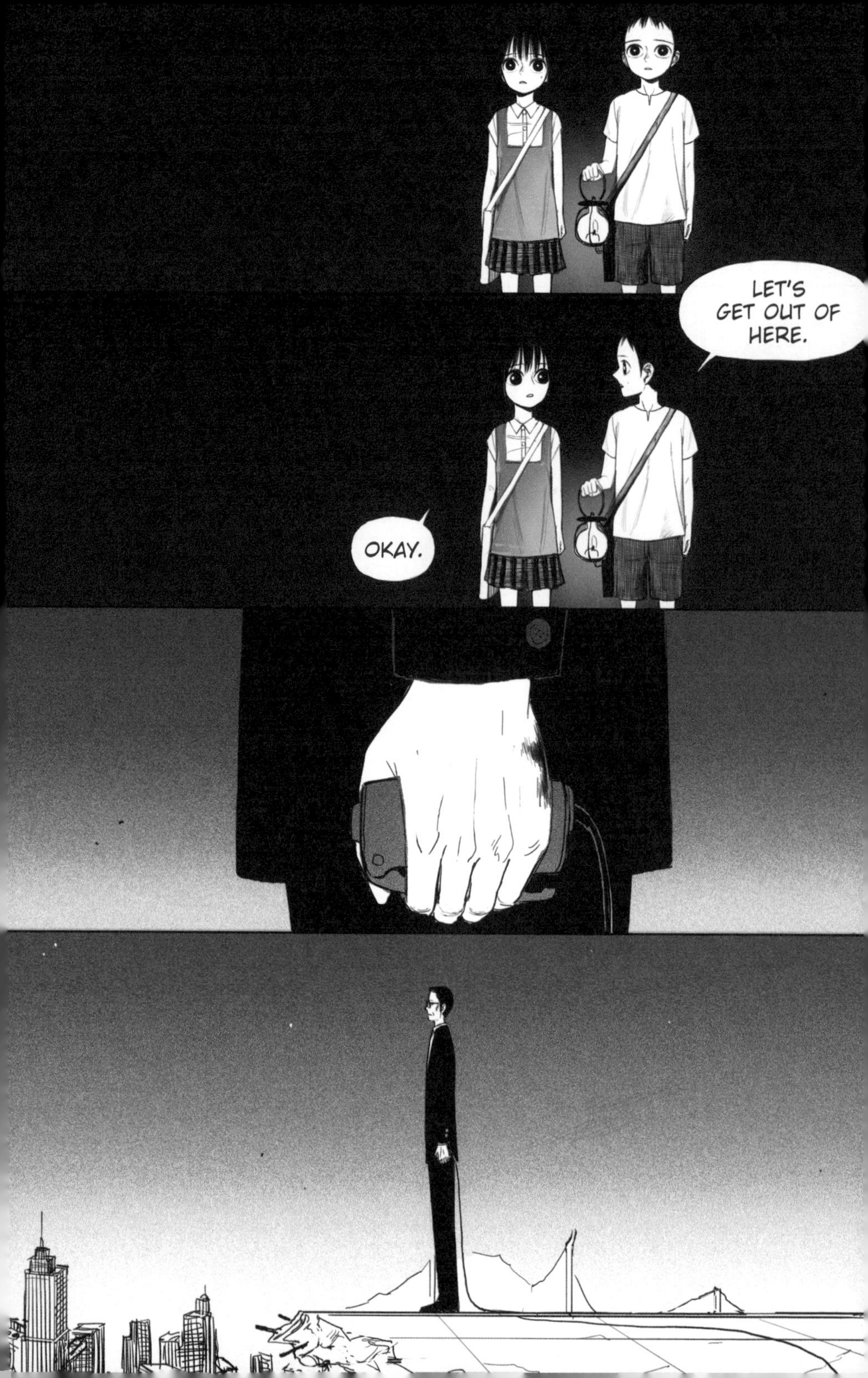
LET'S GET OUT OF HERE.
OKAY.

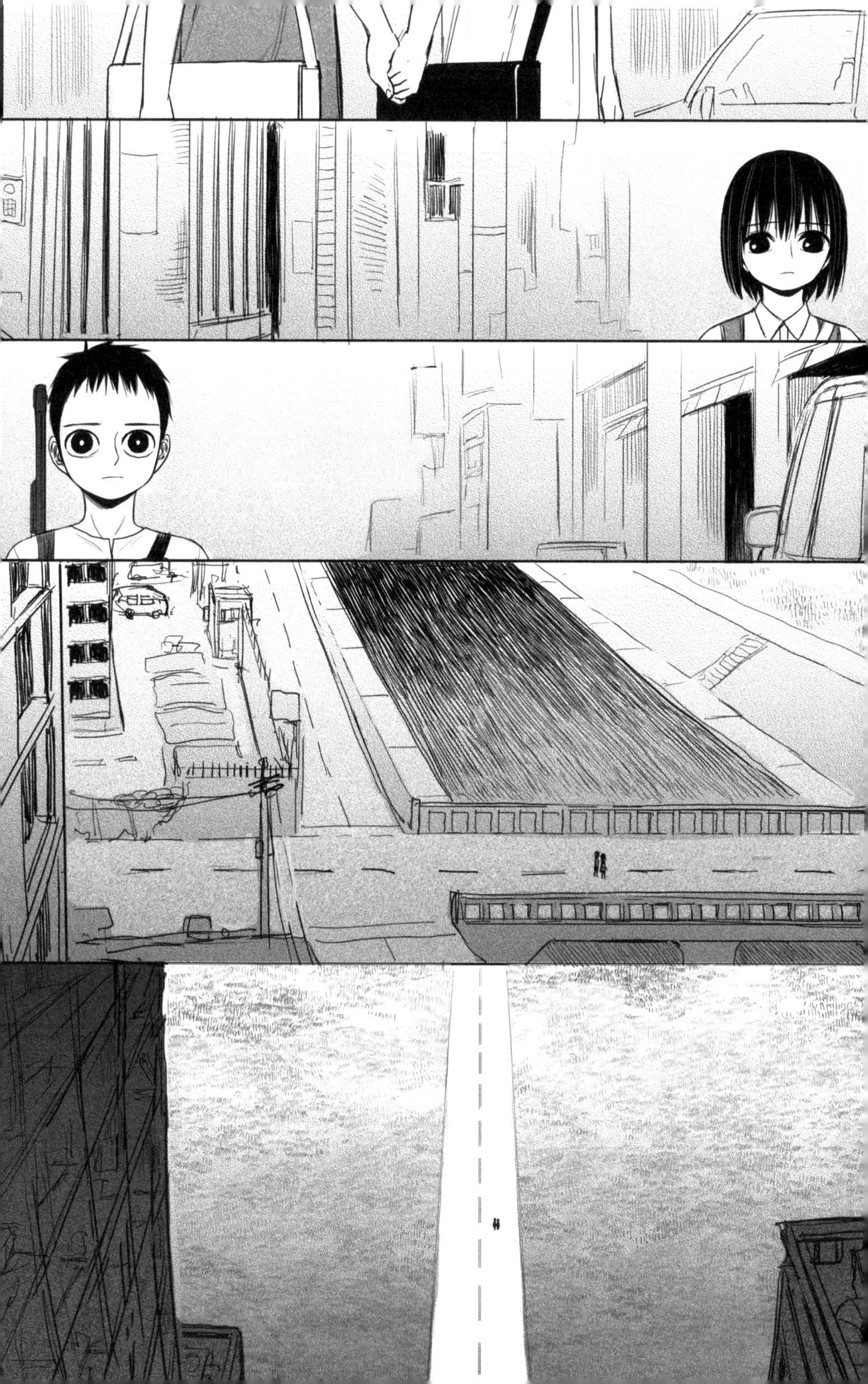

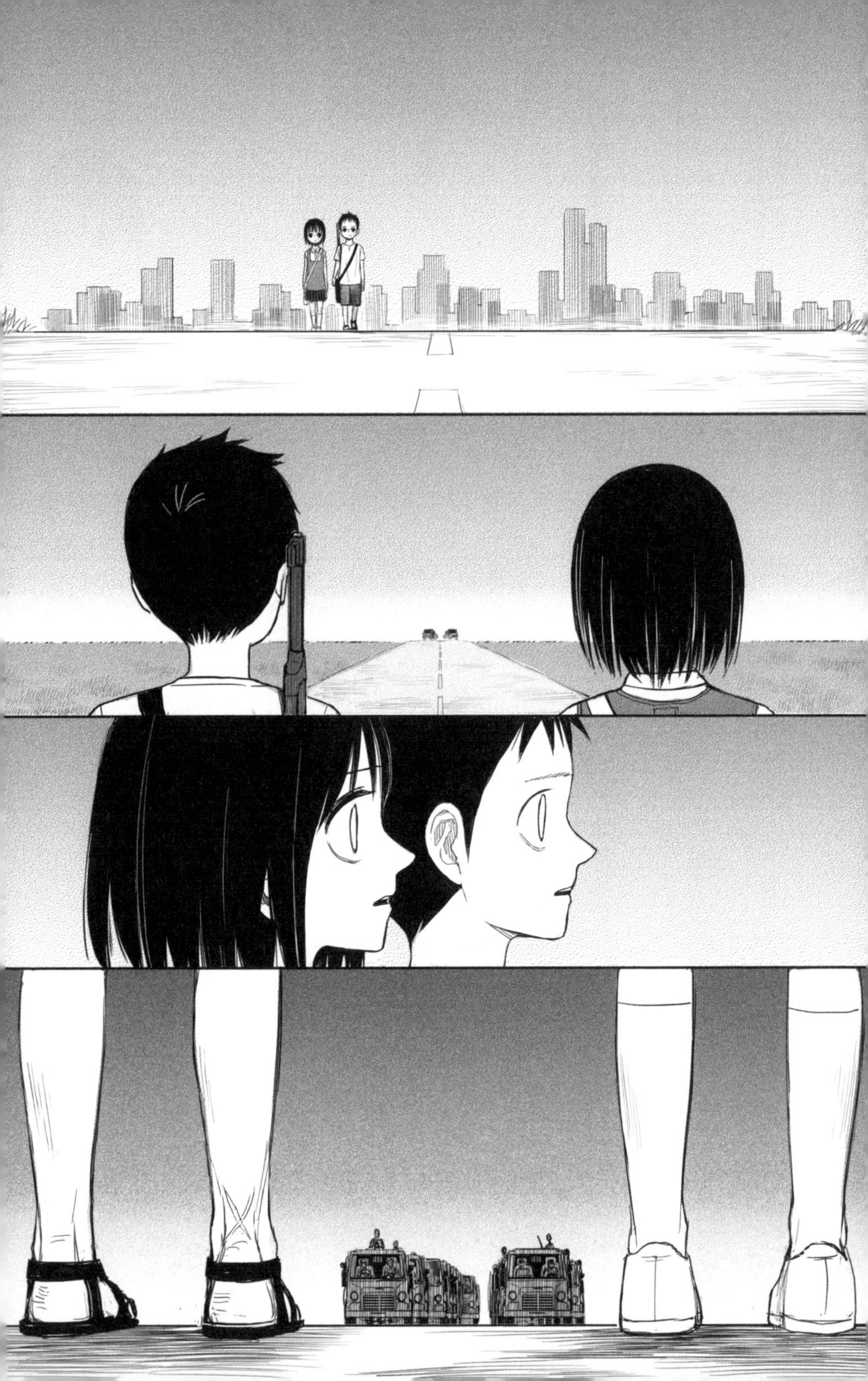

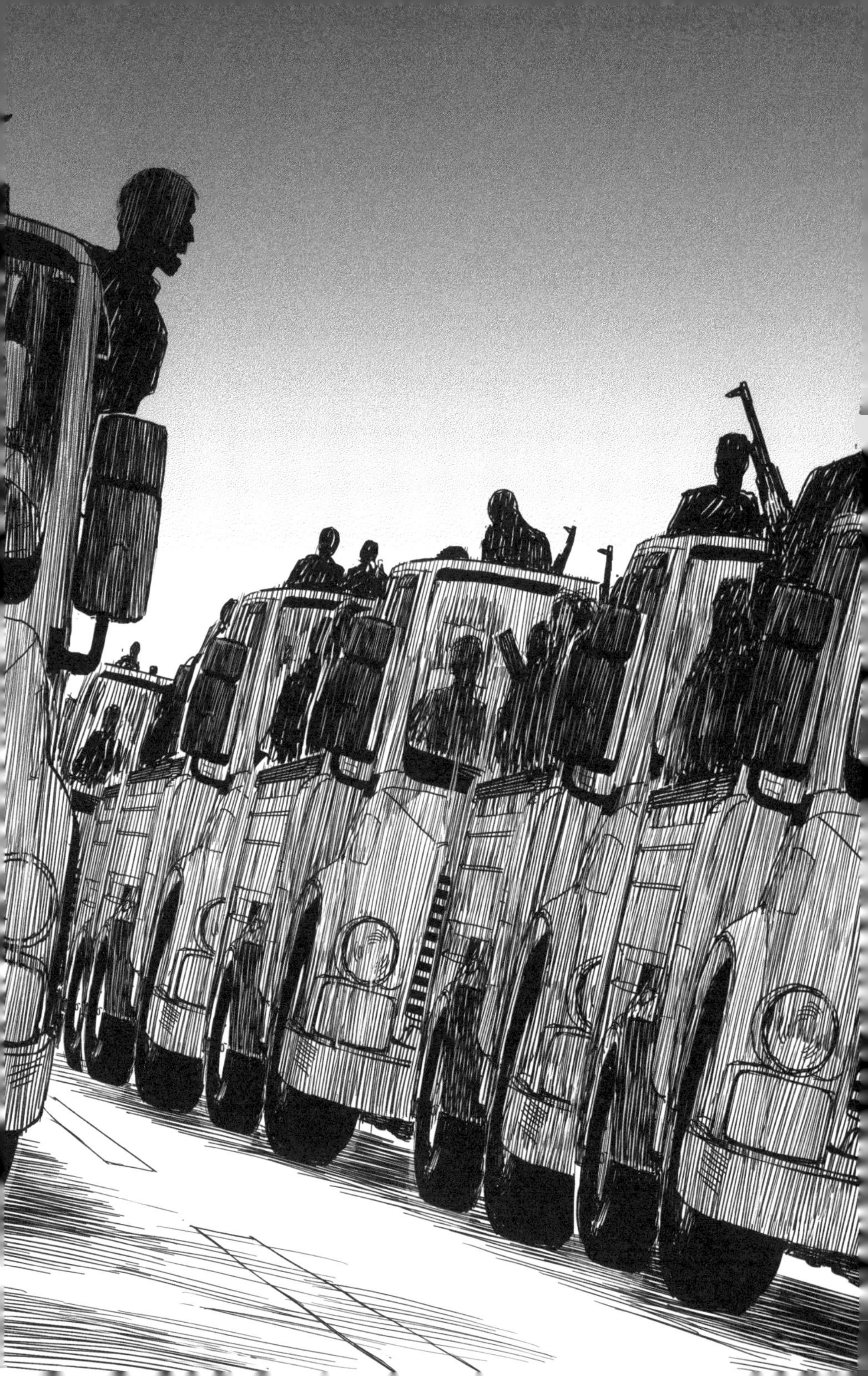

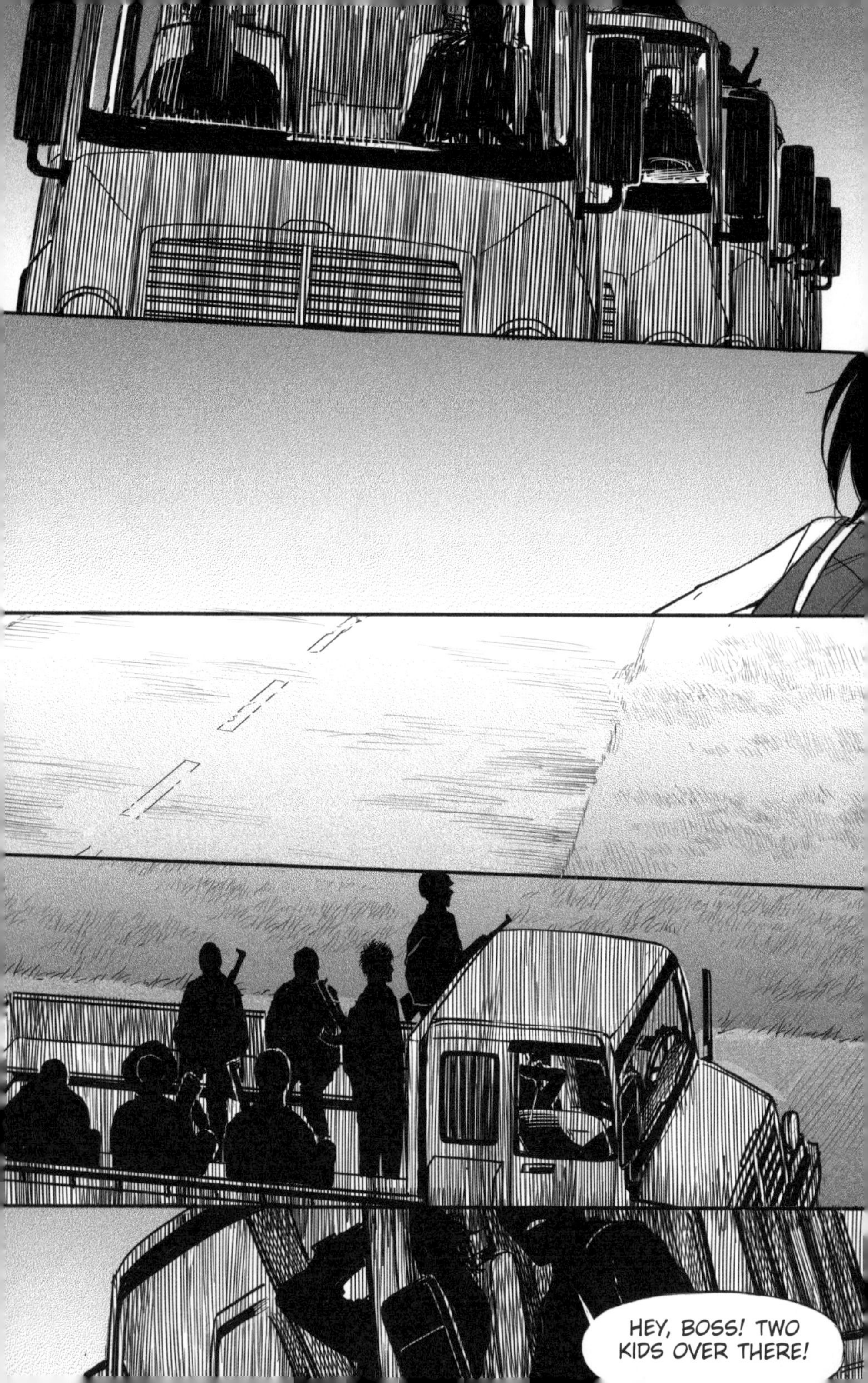
HEY, BOSS! TWO KIDS OVER THERE!

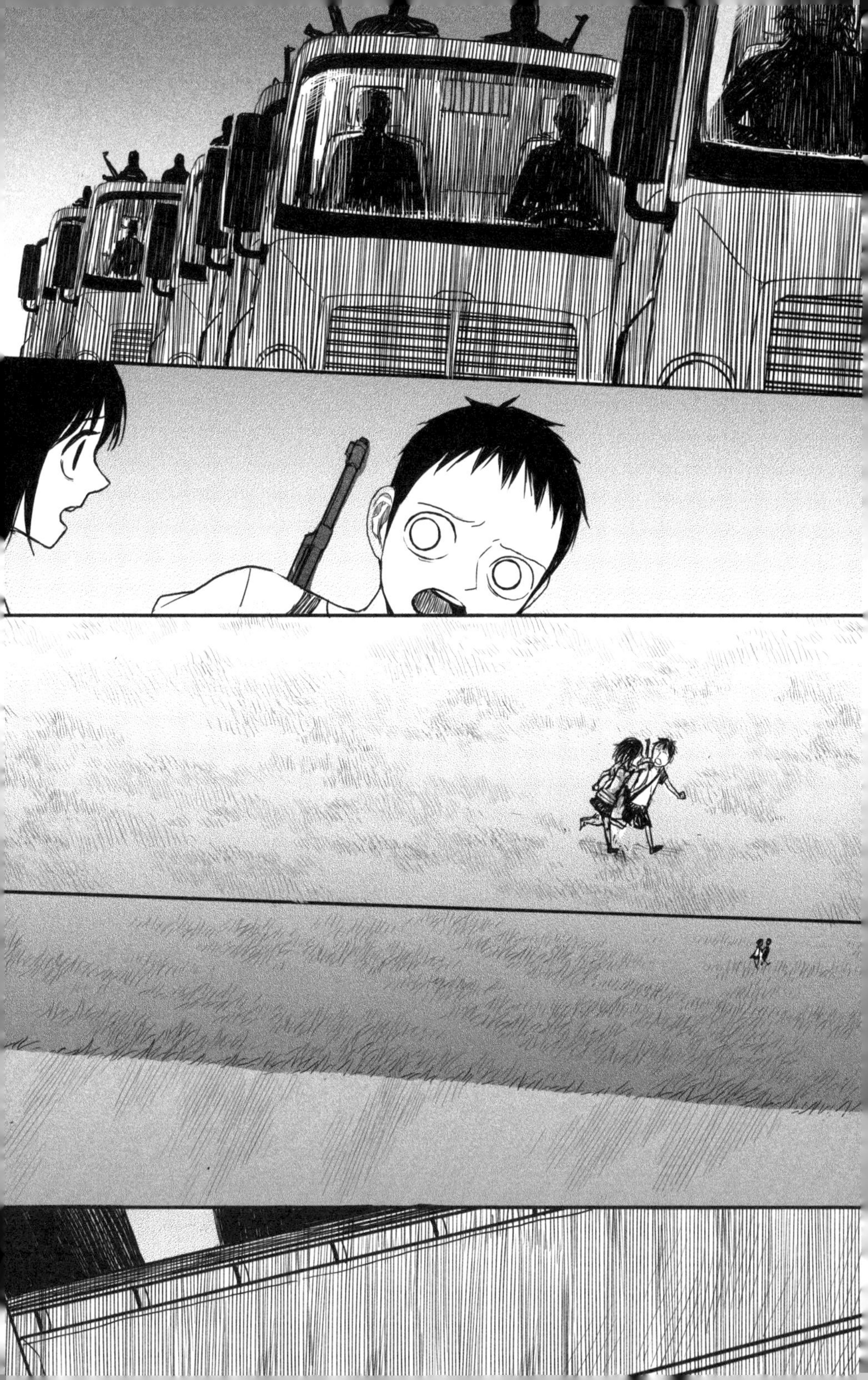

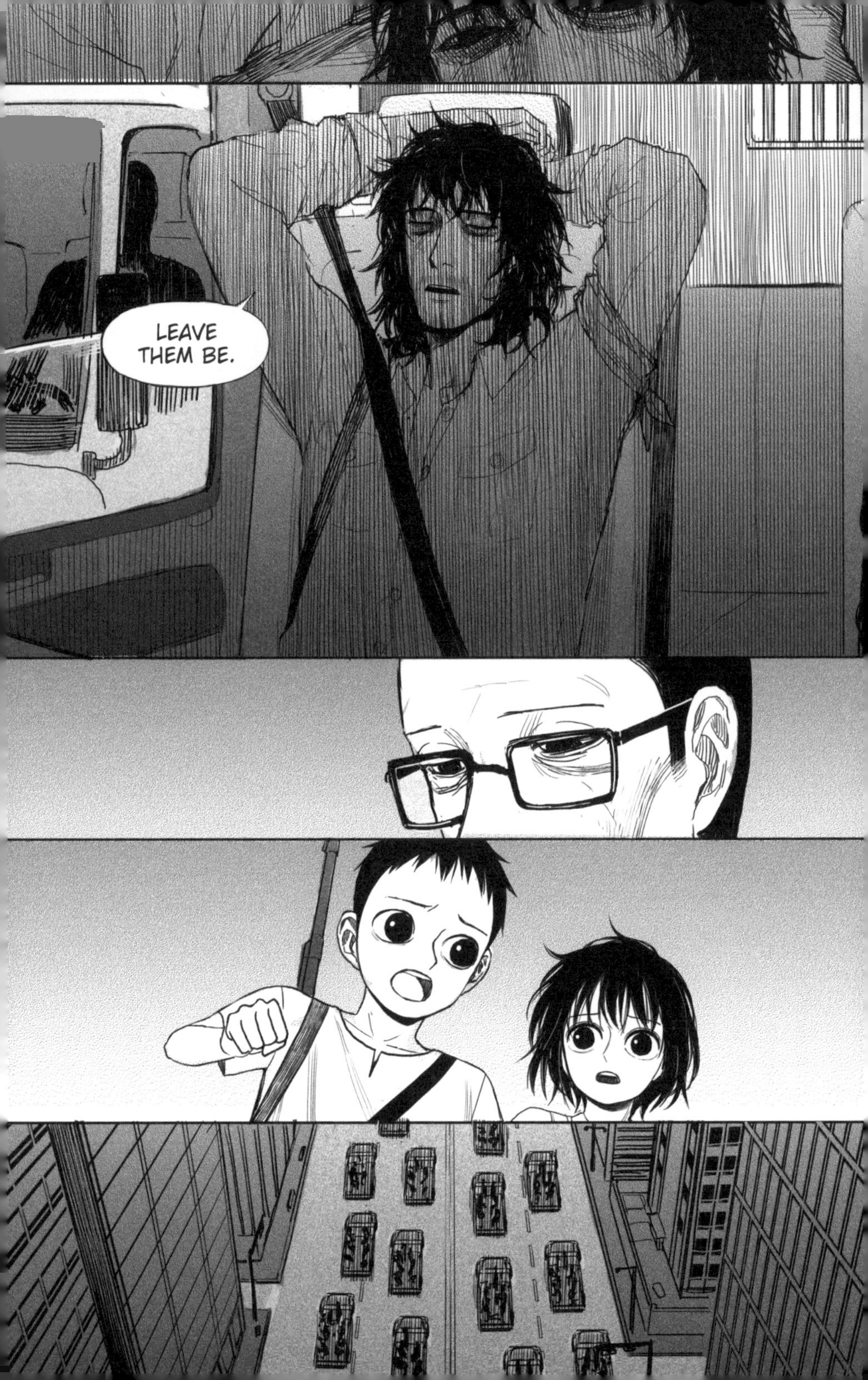
LEAVE THEM BE.

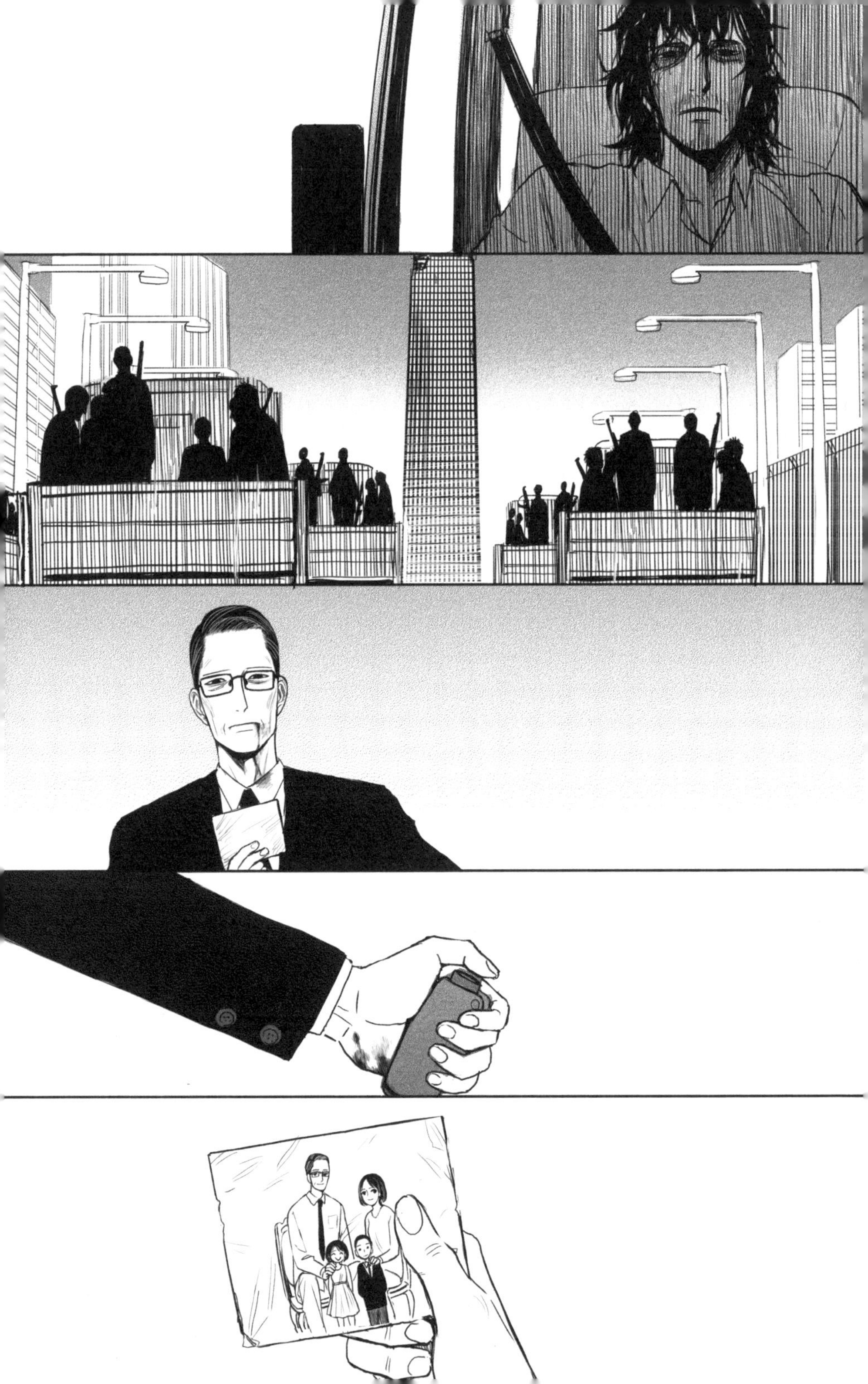

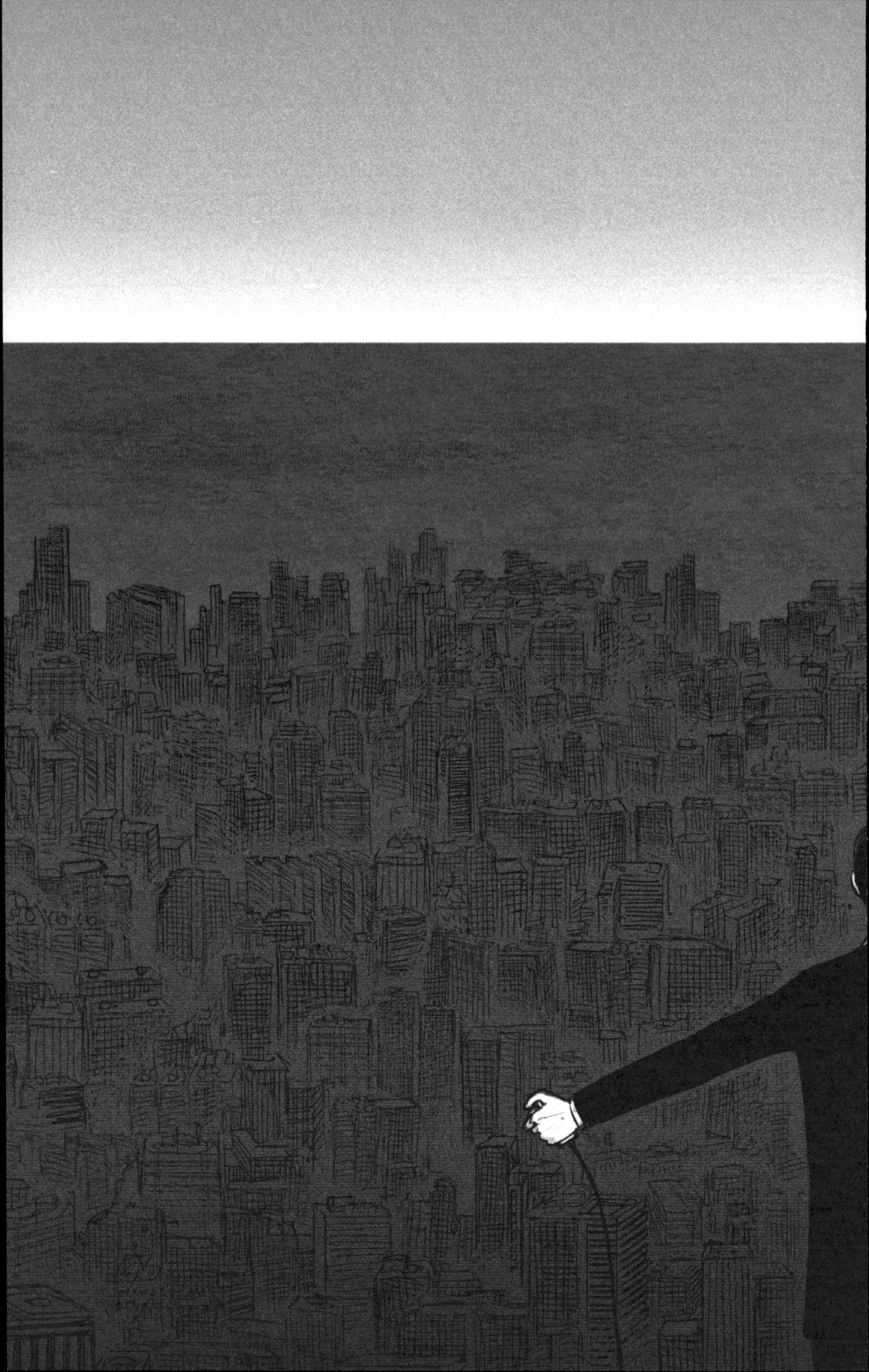

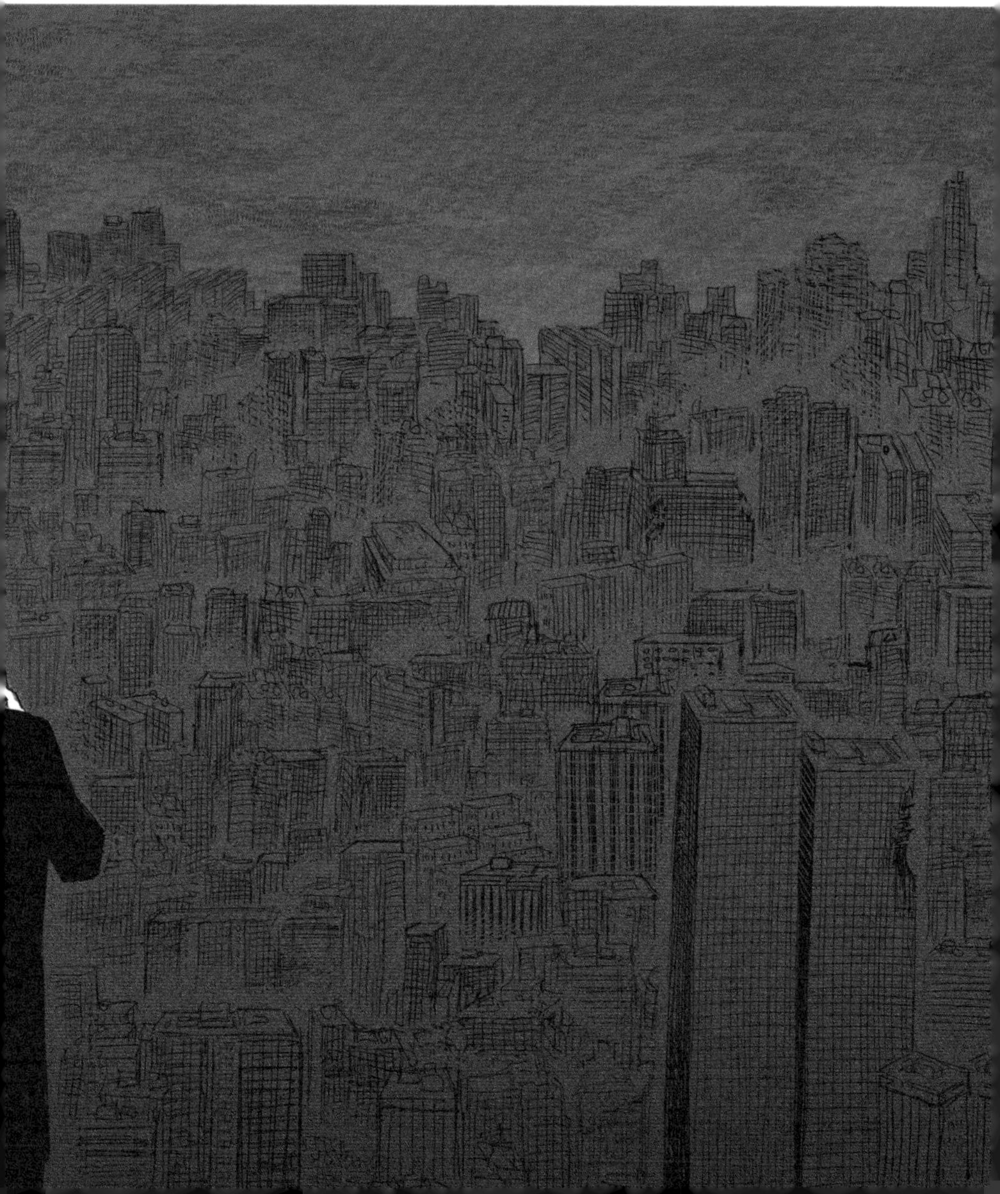

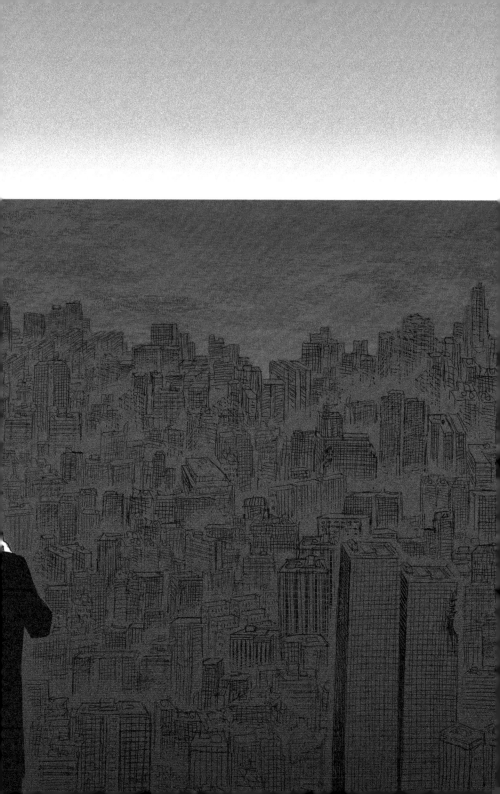

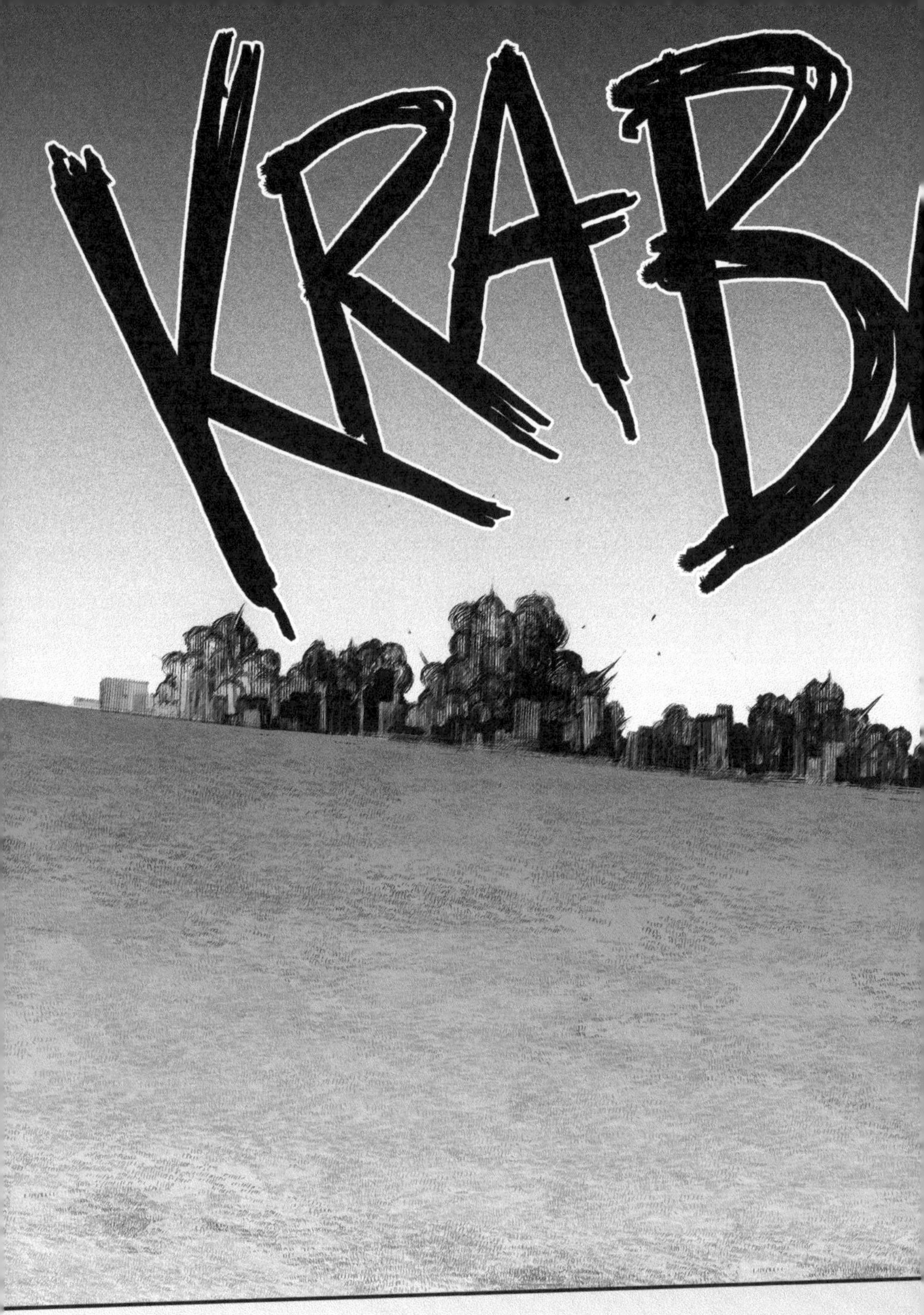
KRAB

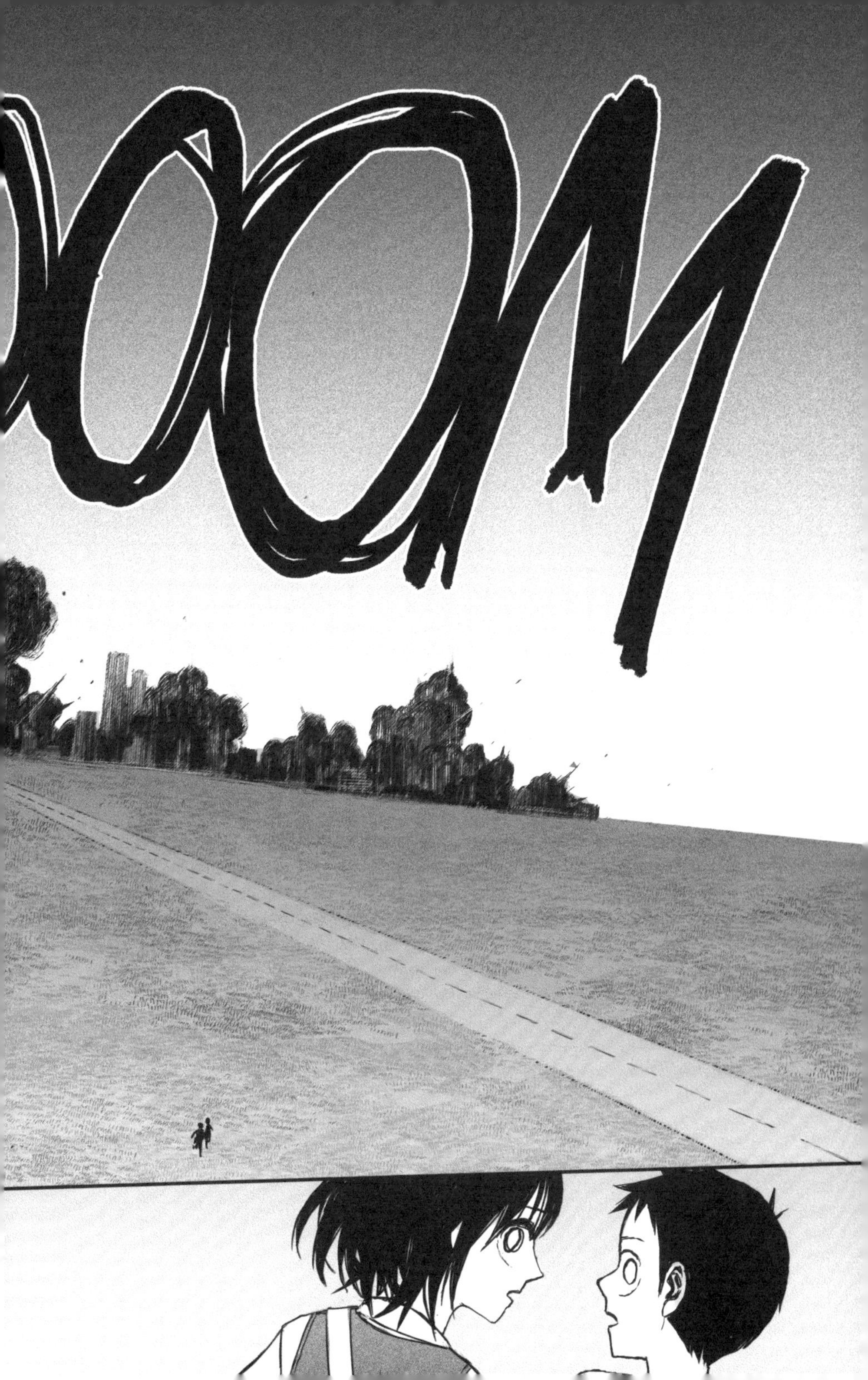
OOM

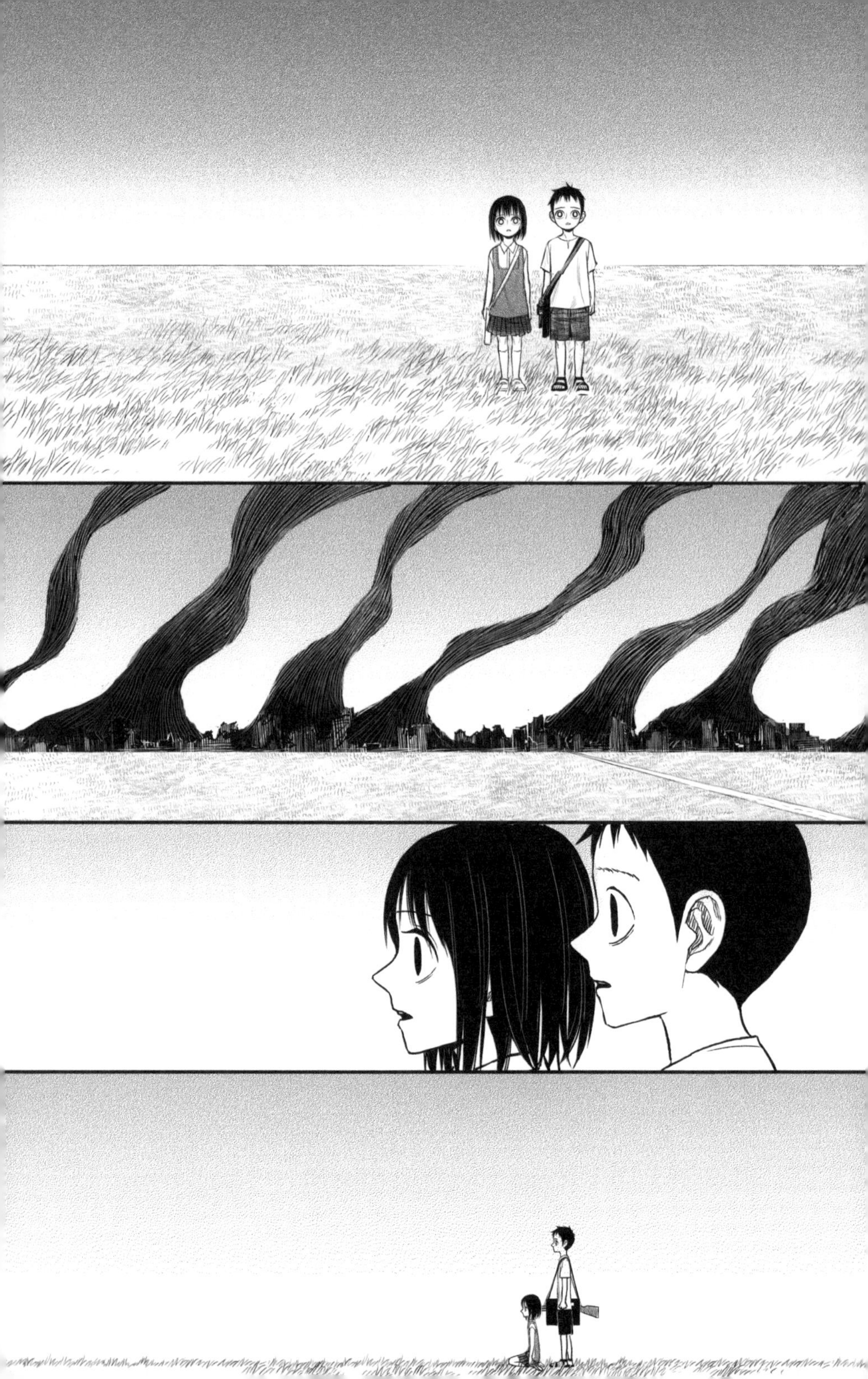

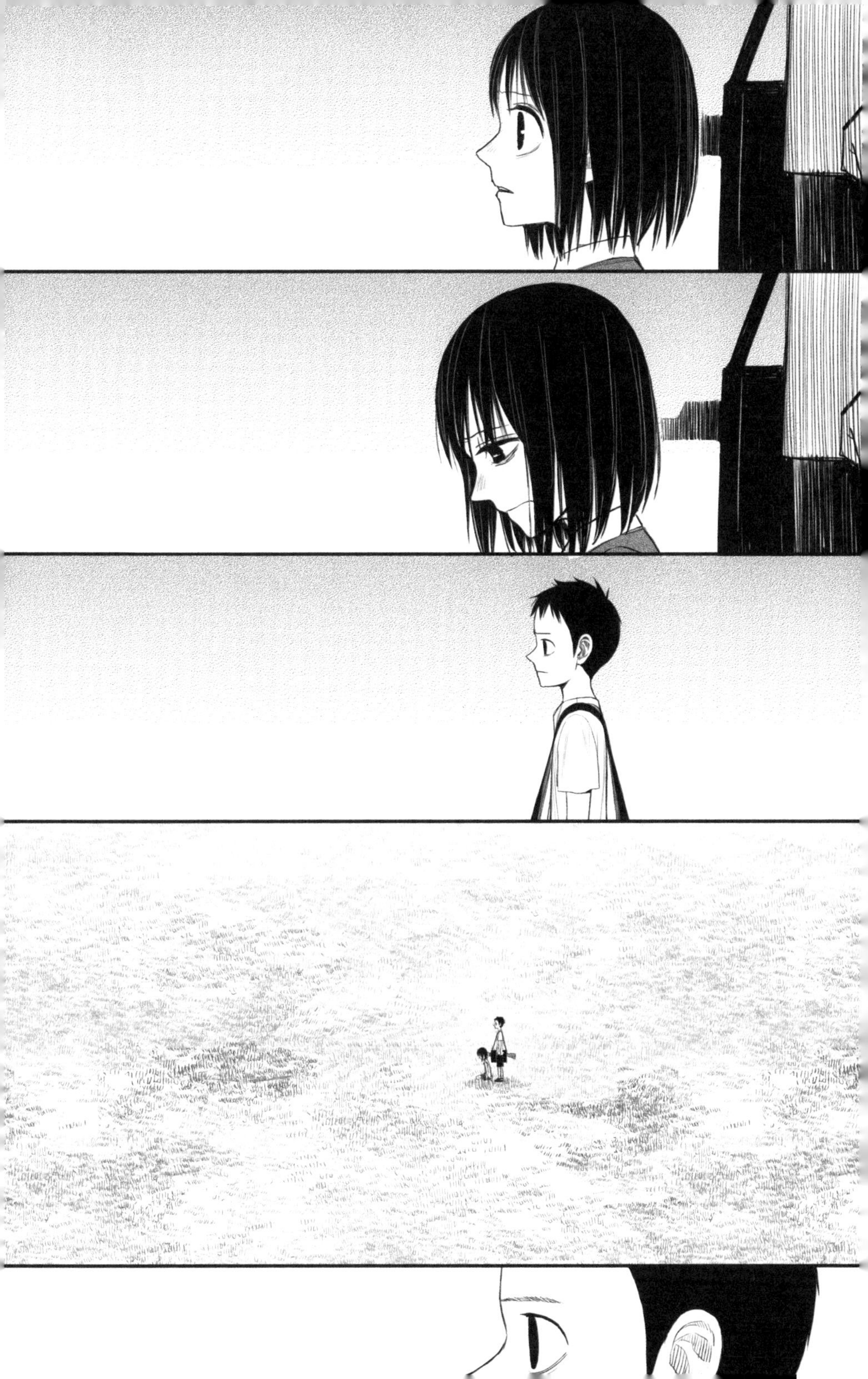

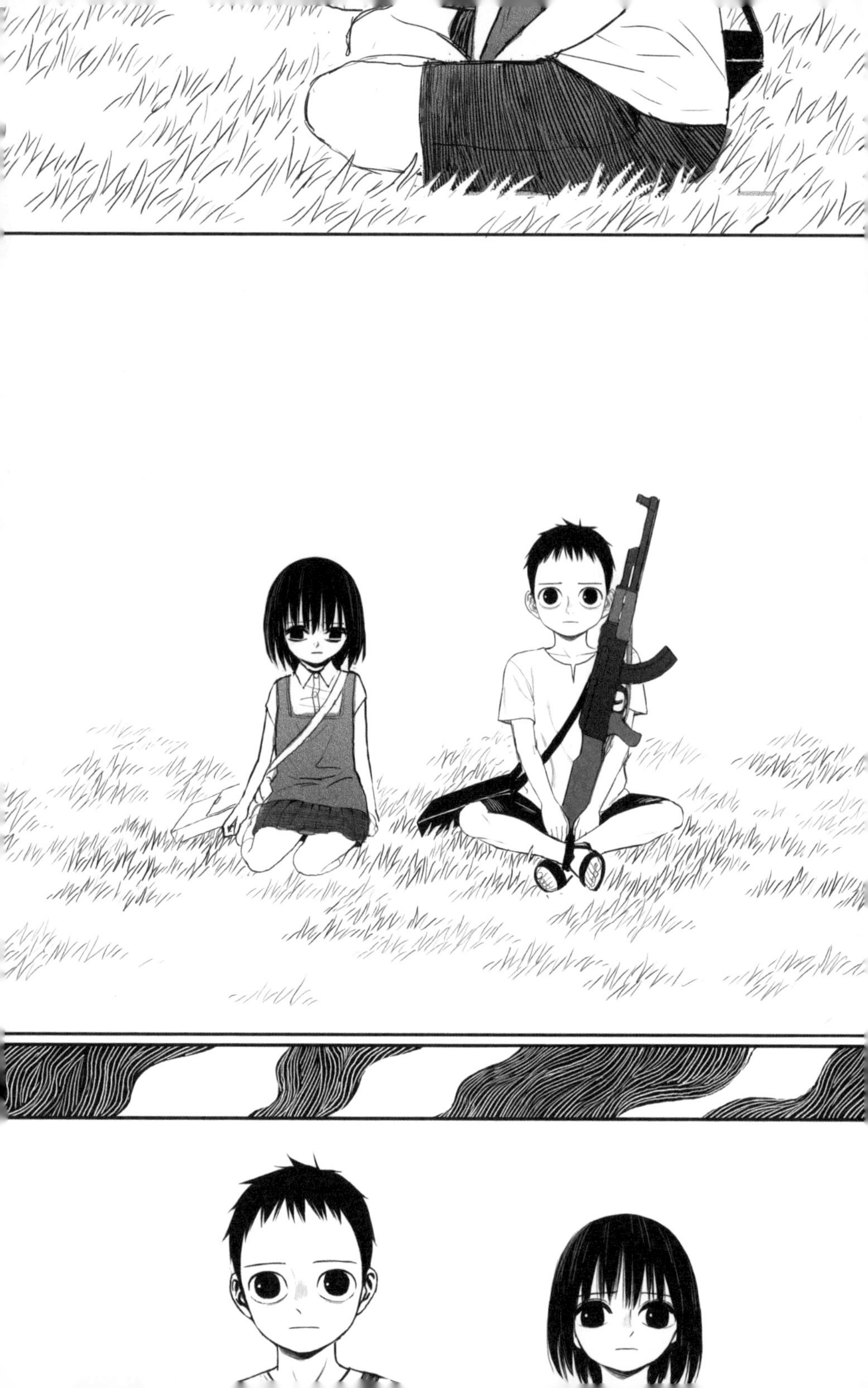

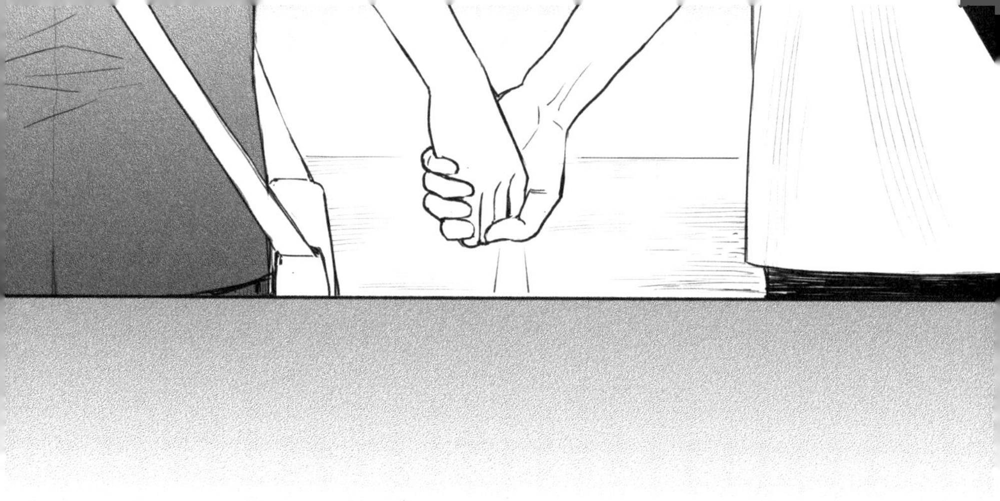

AND SO, THE BOY AND THE GIRL
CONTINUED ON THEIR JOURNEY.

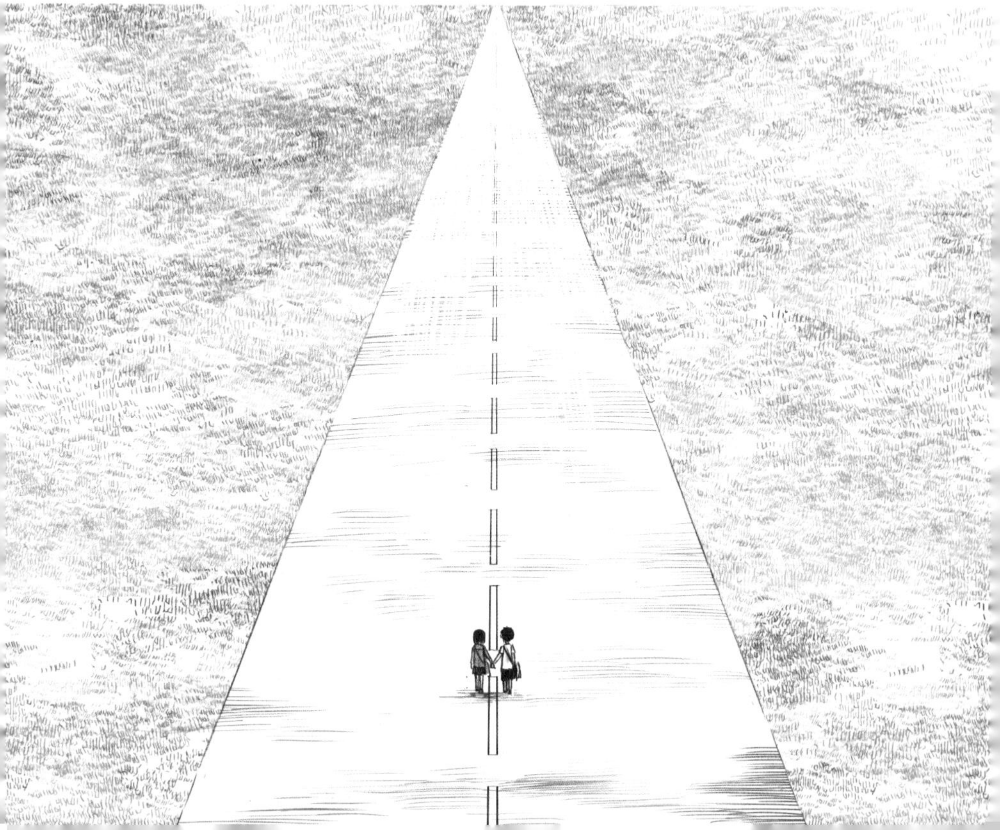

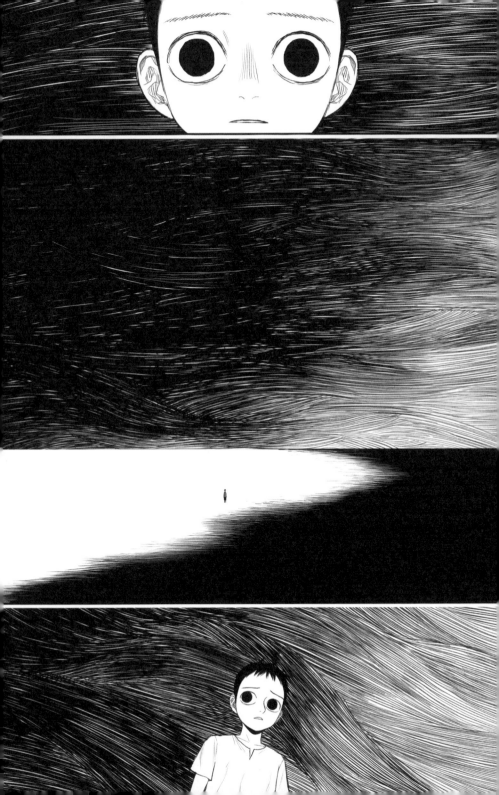

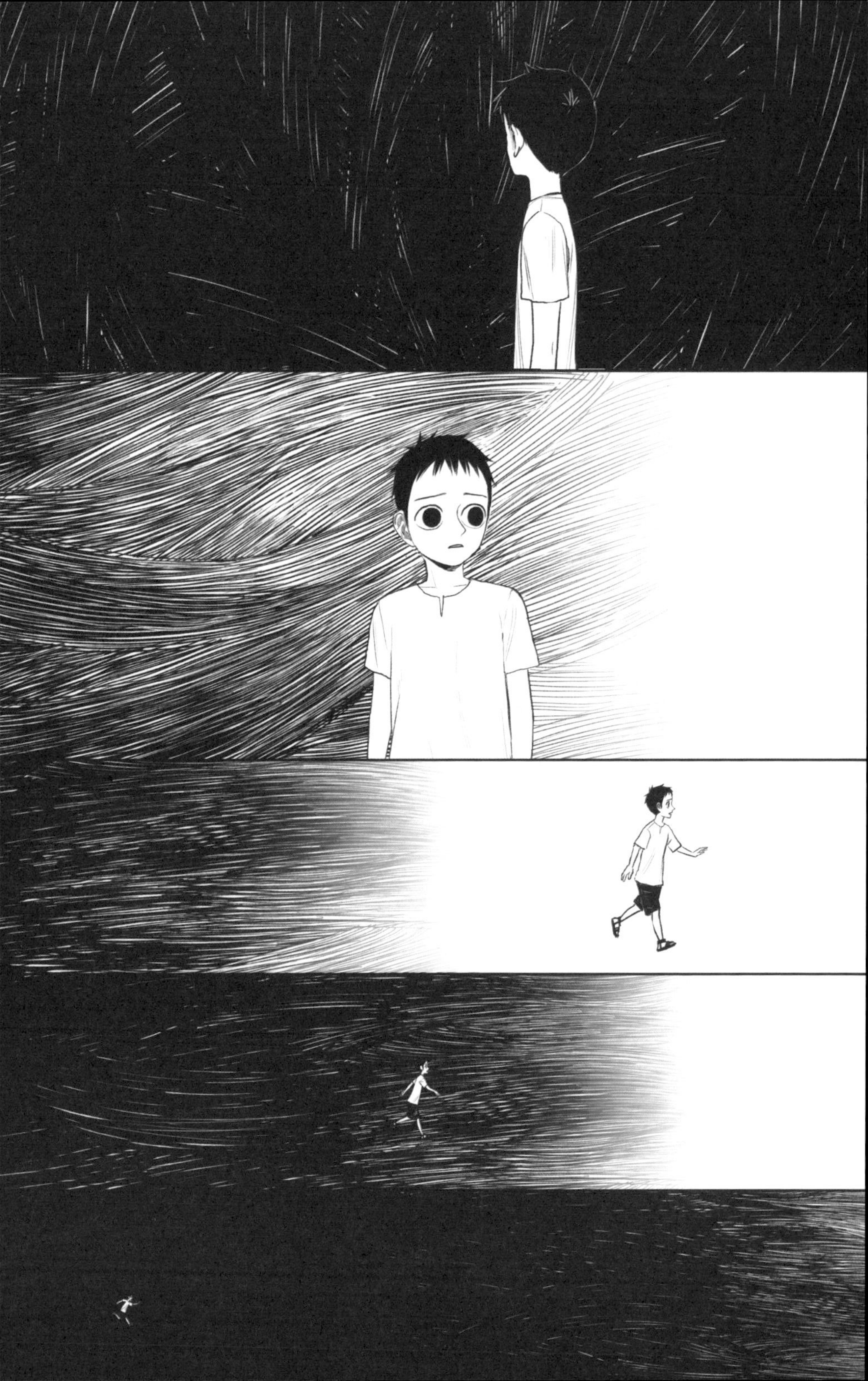

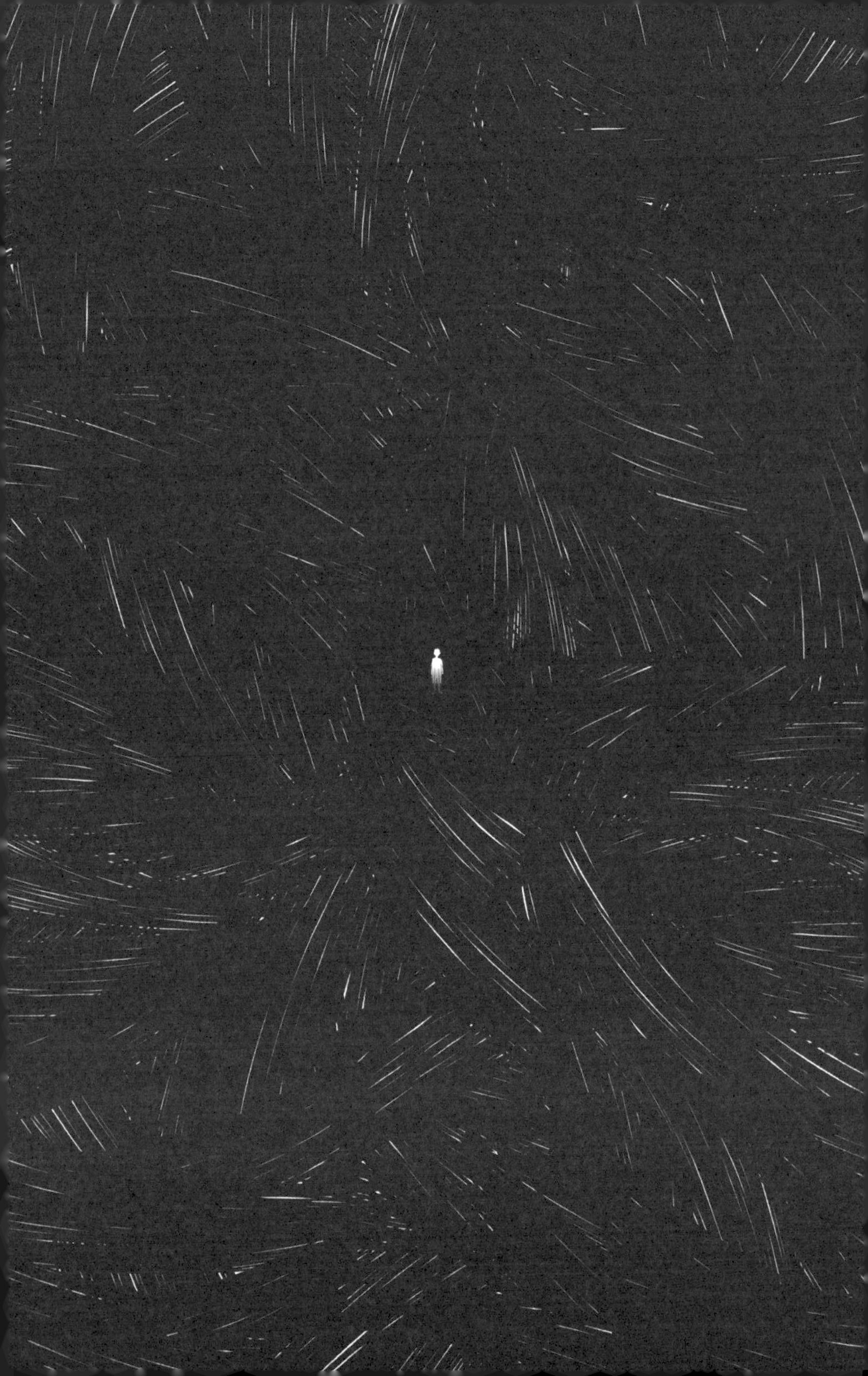

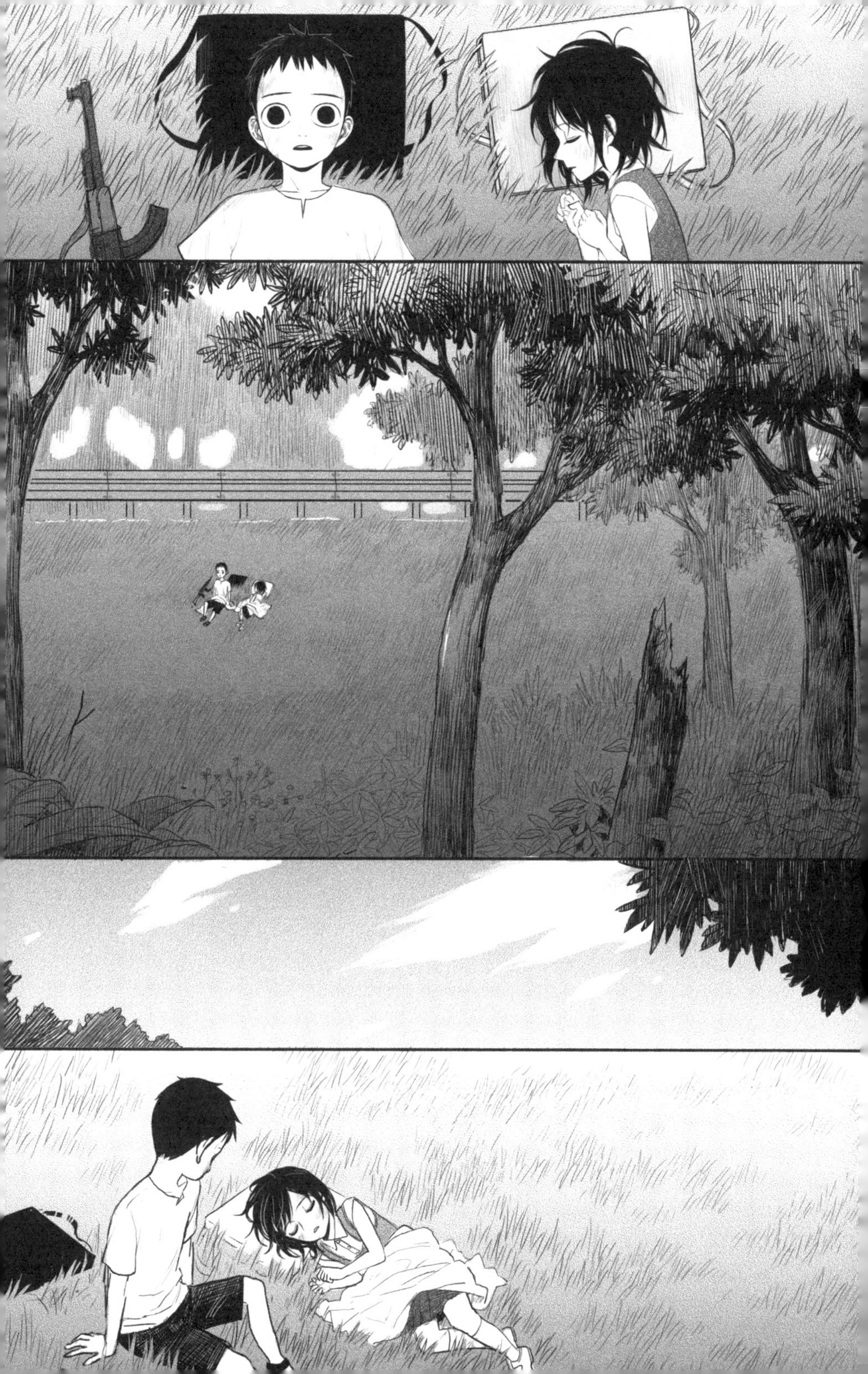

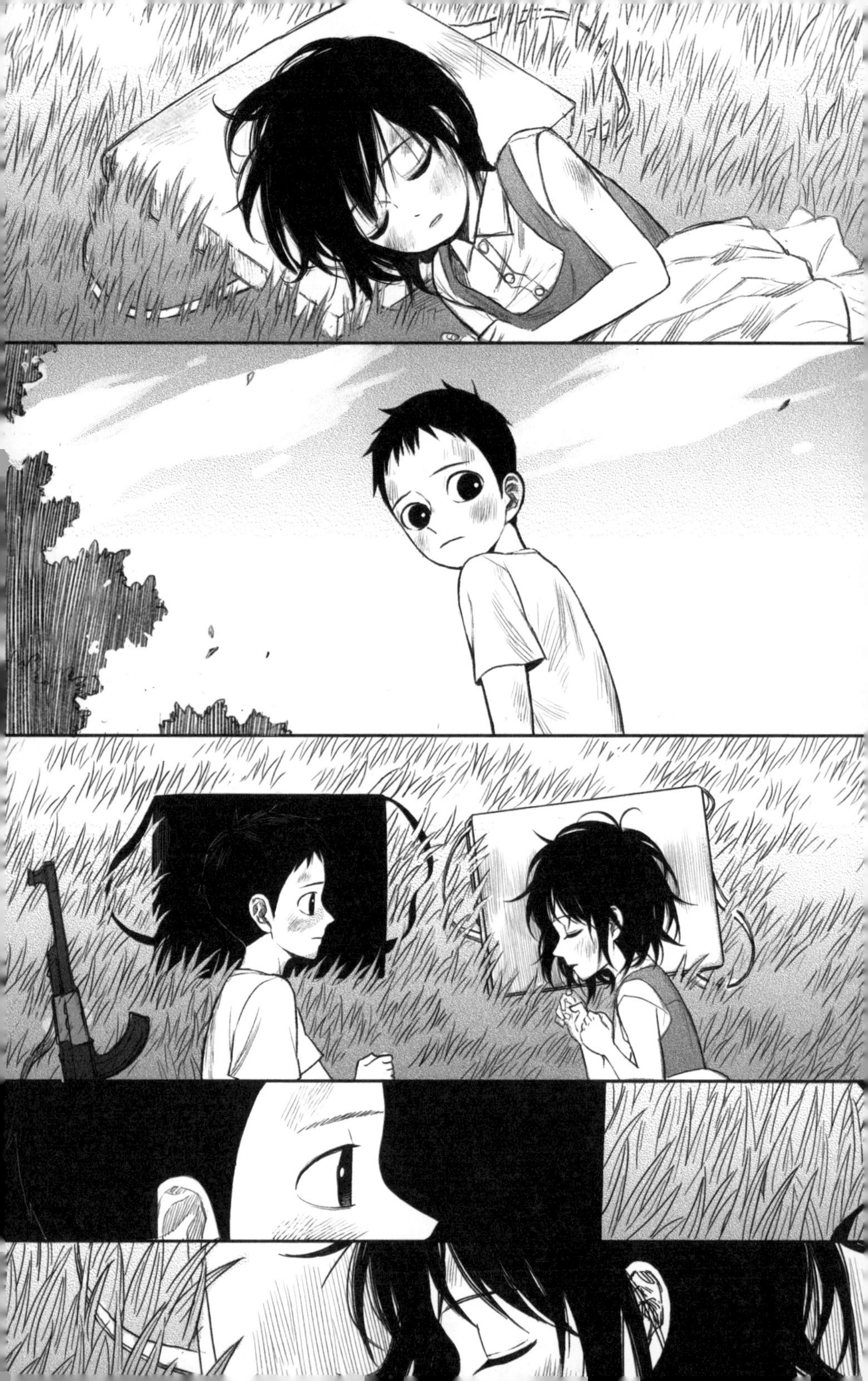

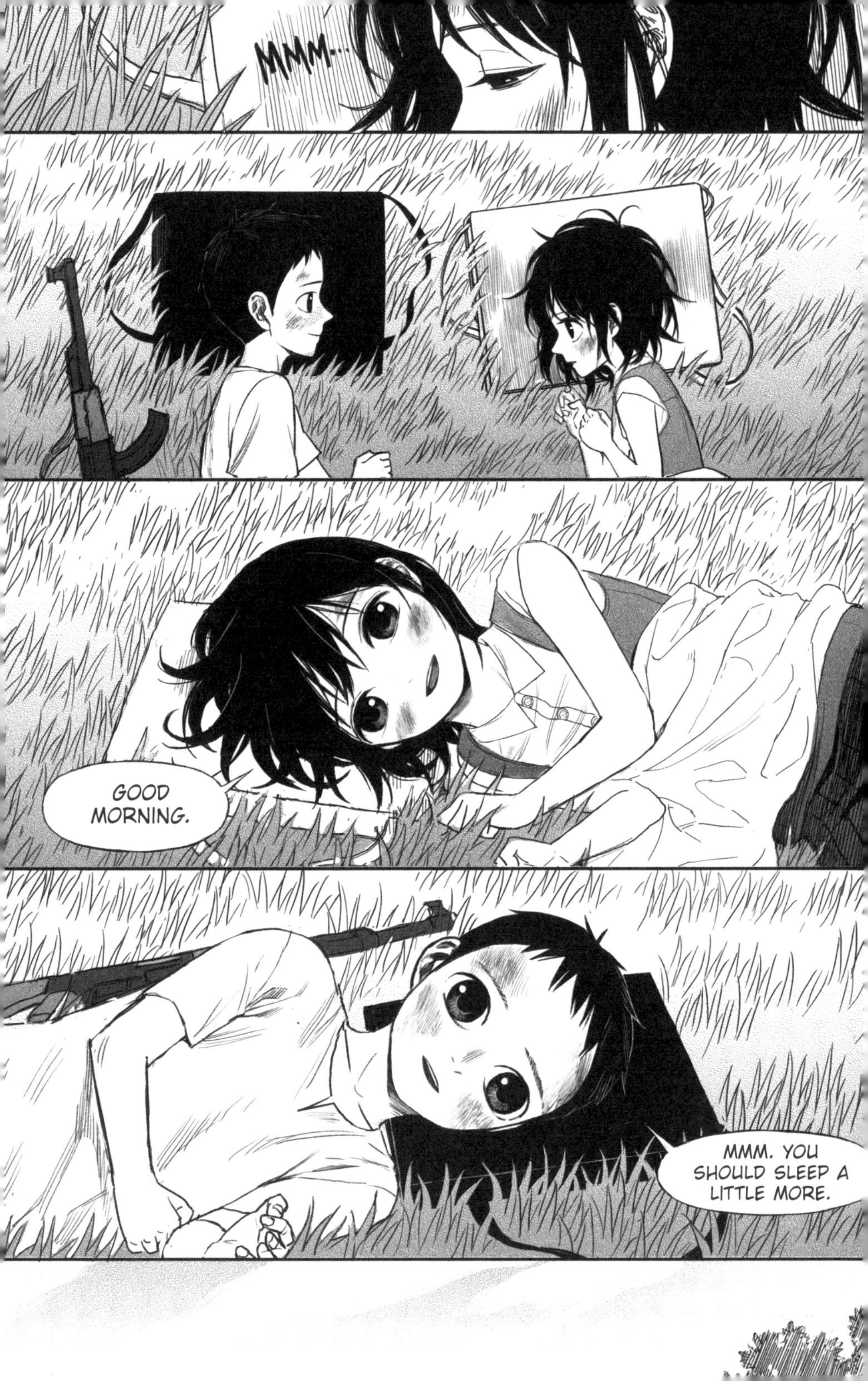
MMM...
GOOD MORNING.
MMM. YOU SHOULD SLEEP A LITTLE MORE.

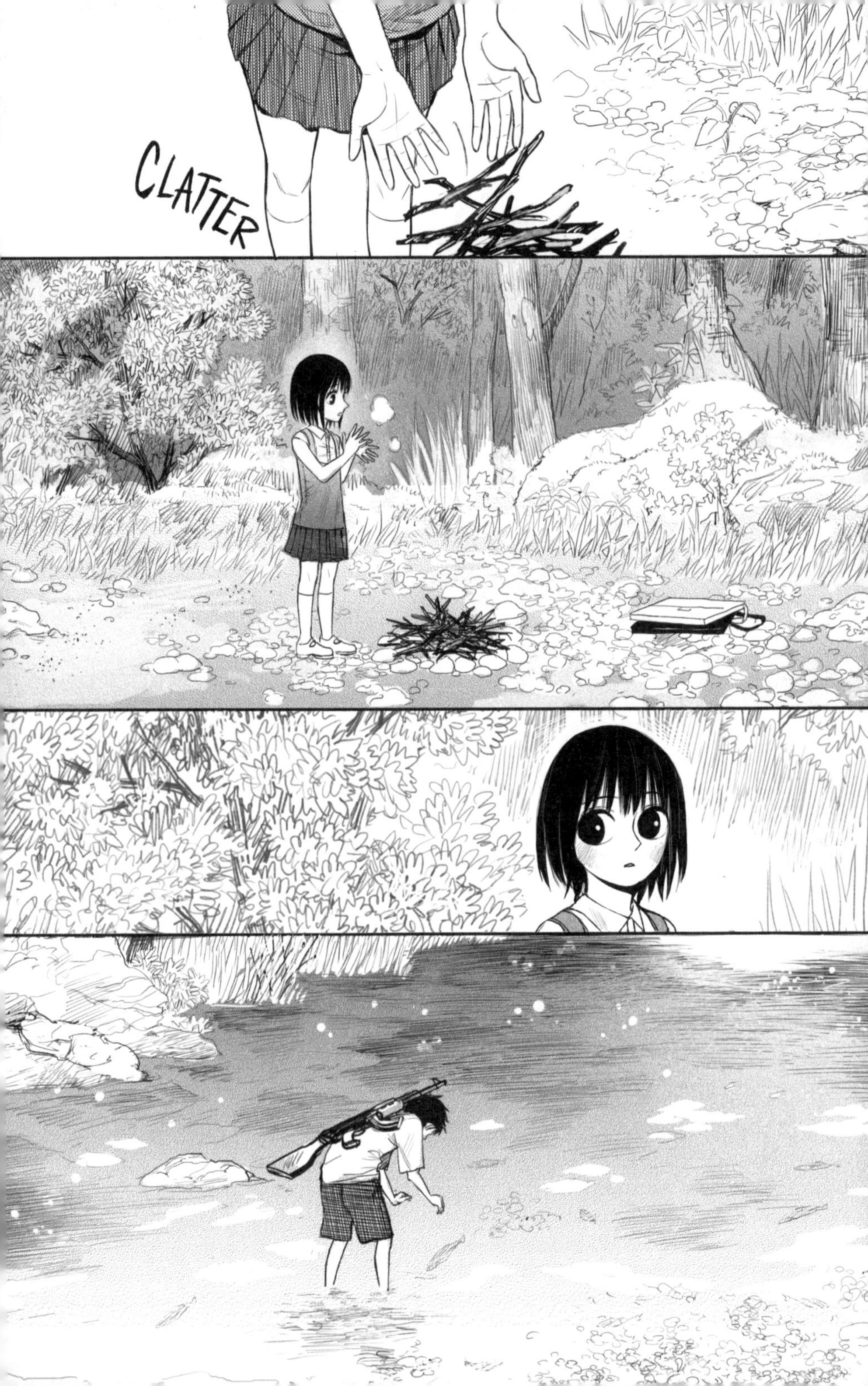
CLATTER

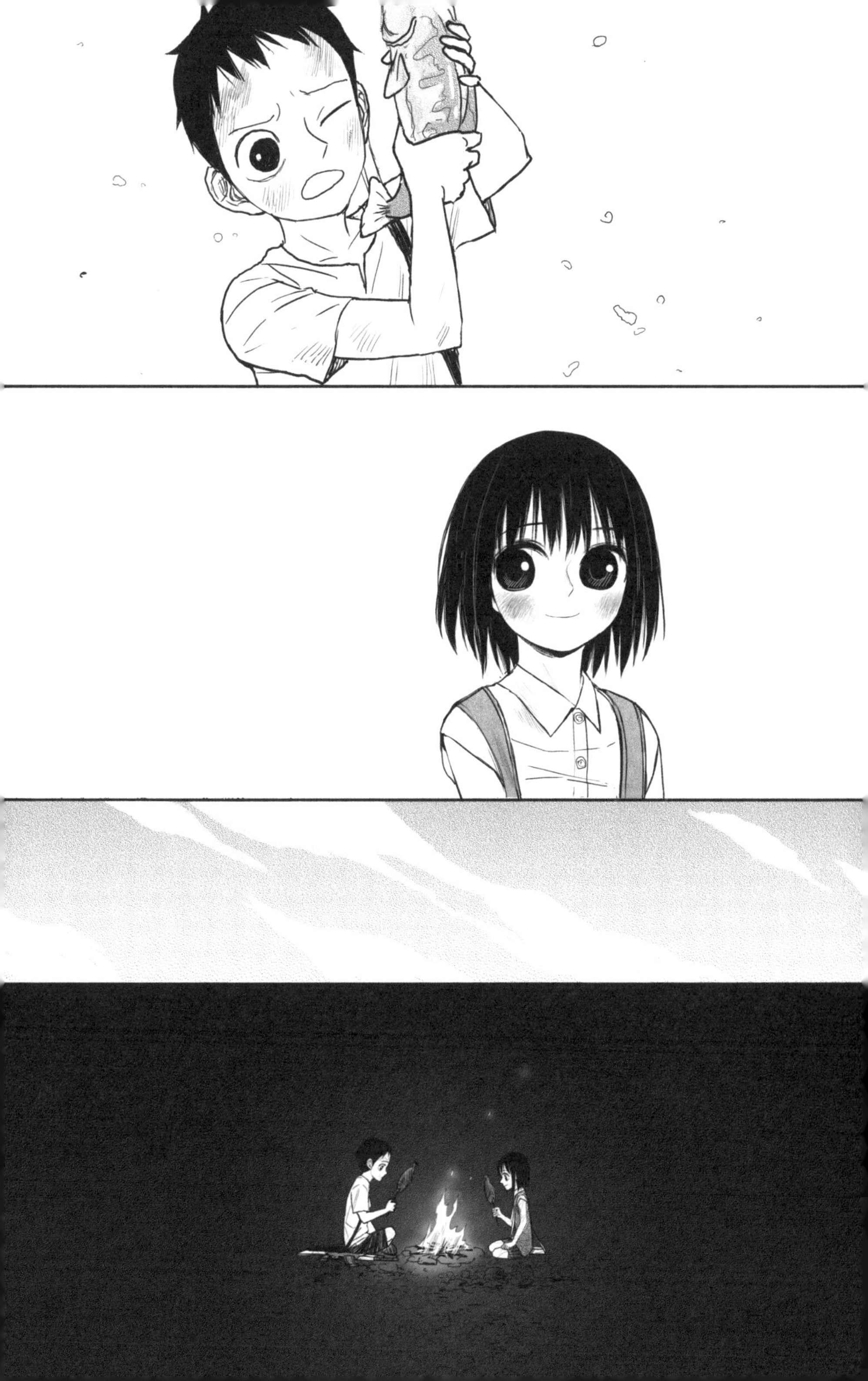

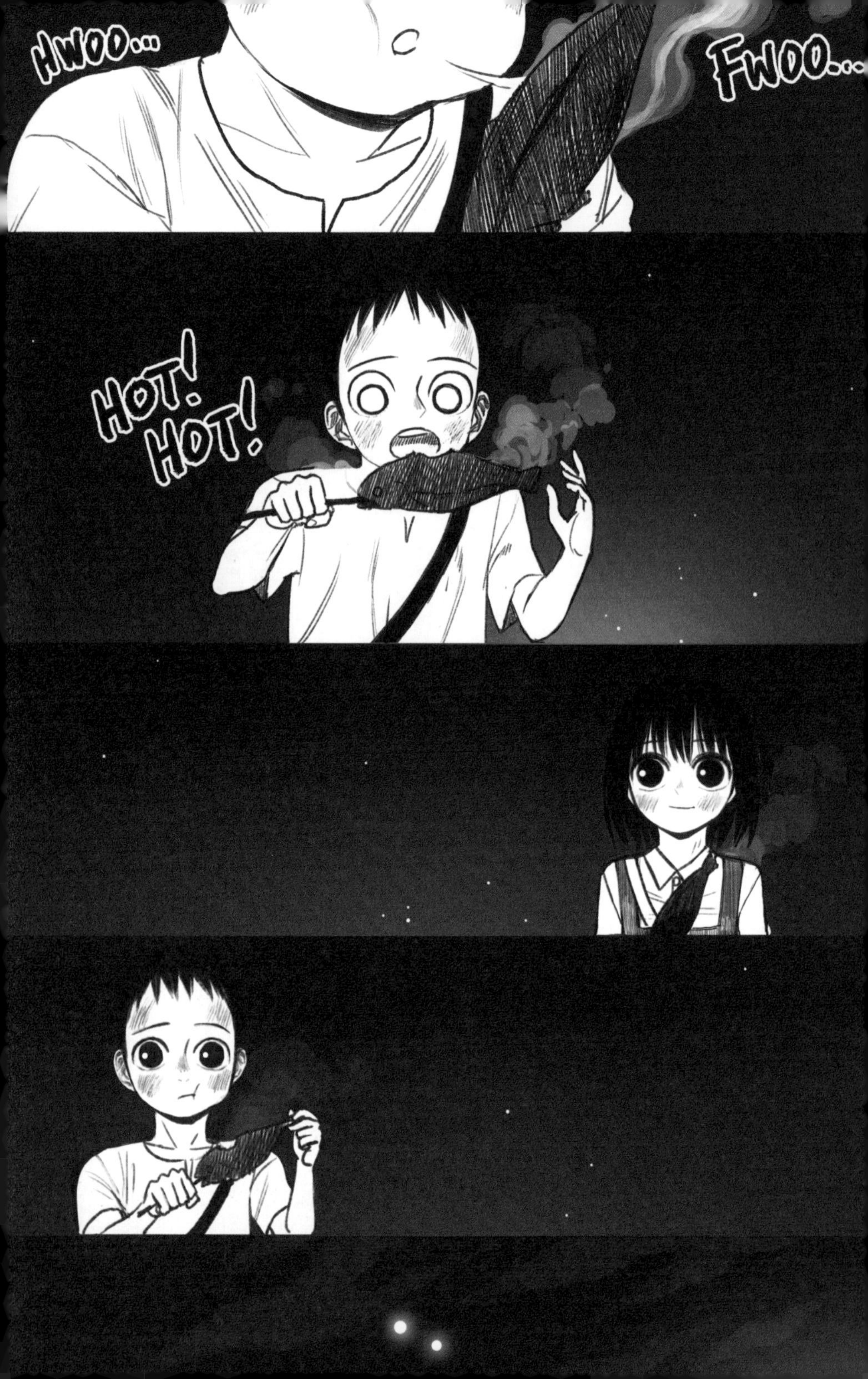
HWOO...
FWOO...
HOT! HOT!

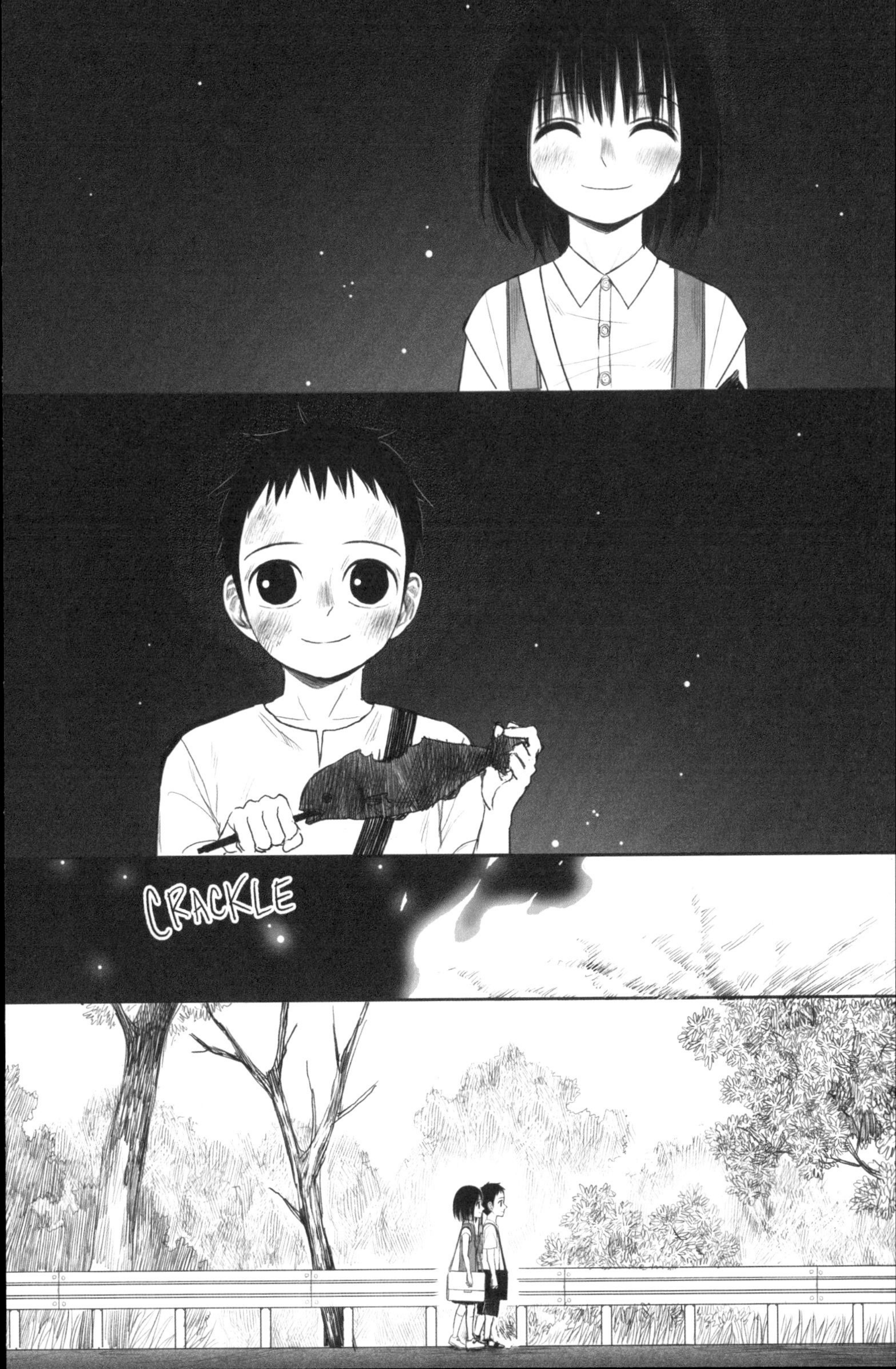
CRACKLE

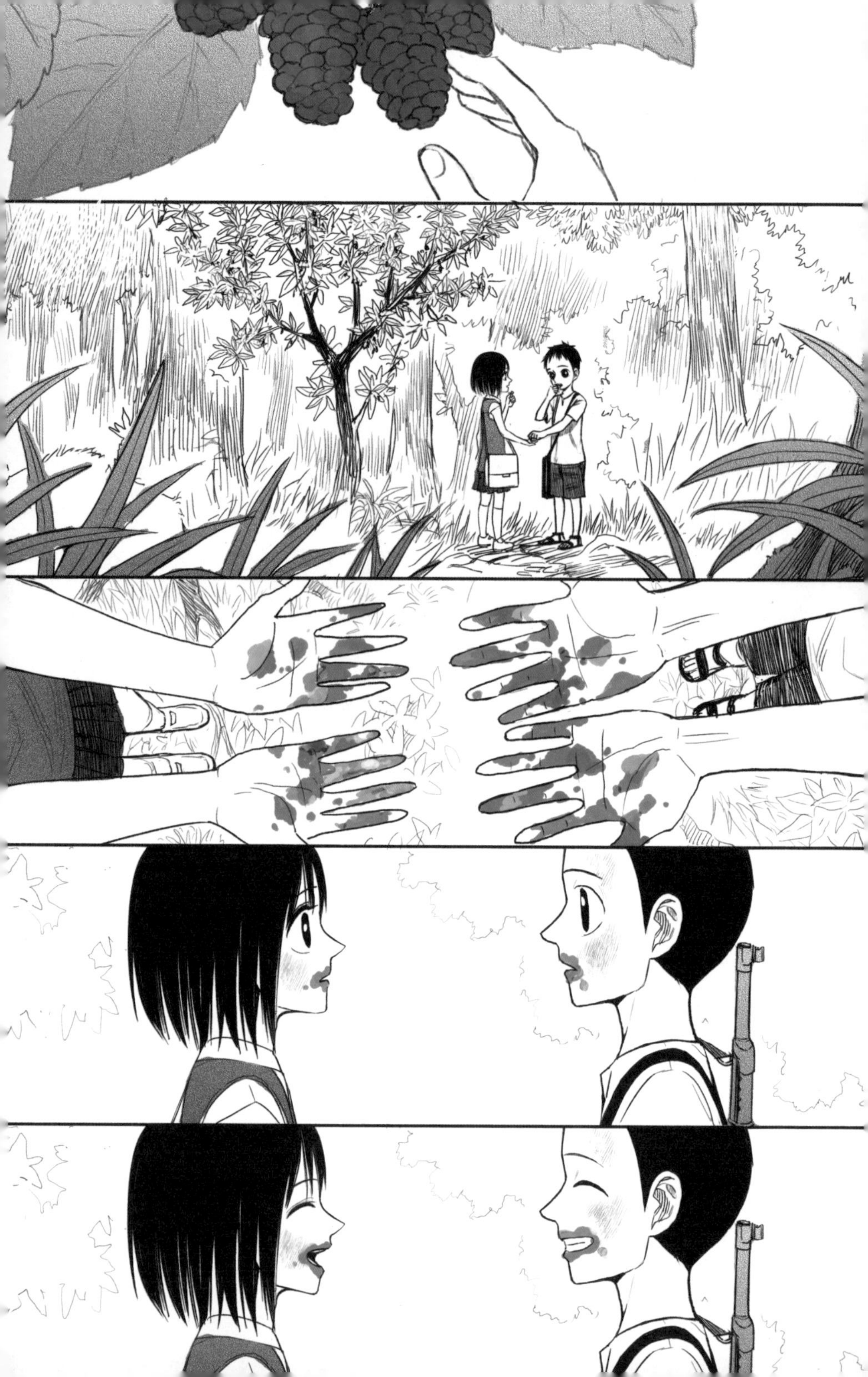

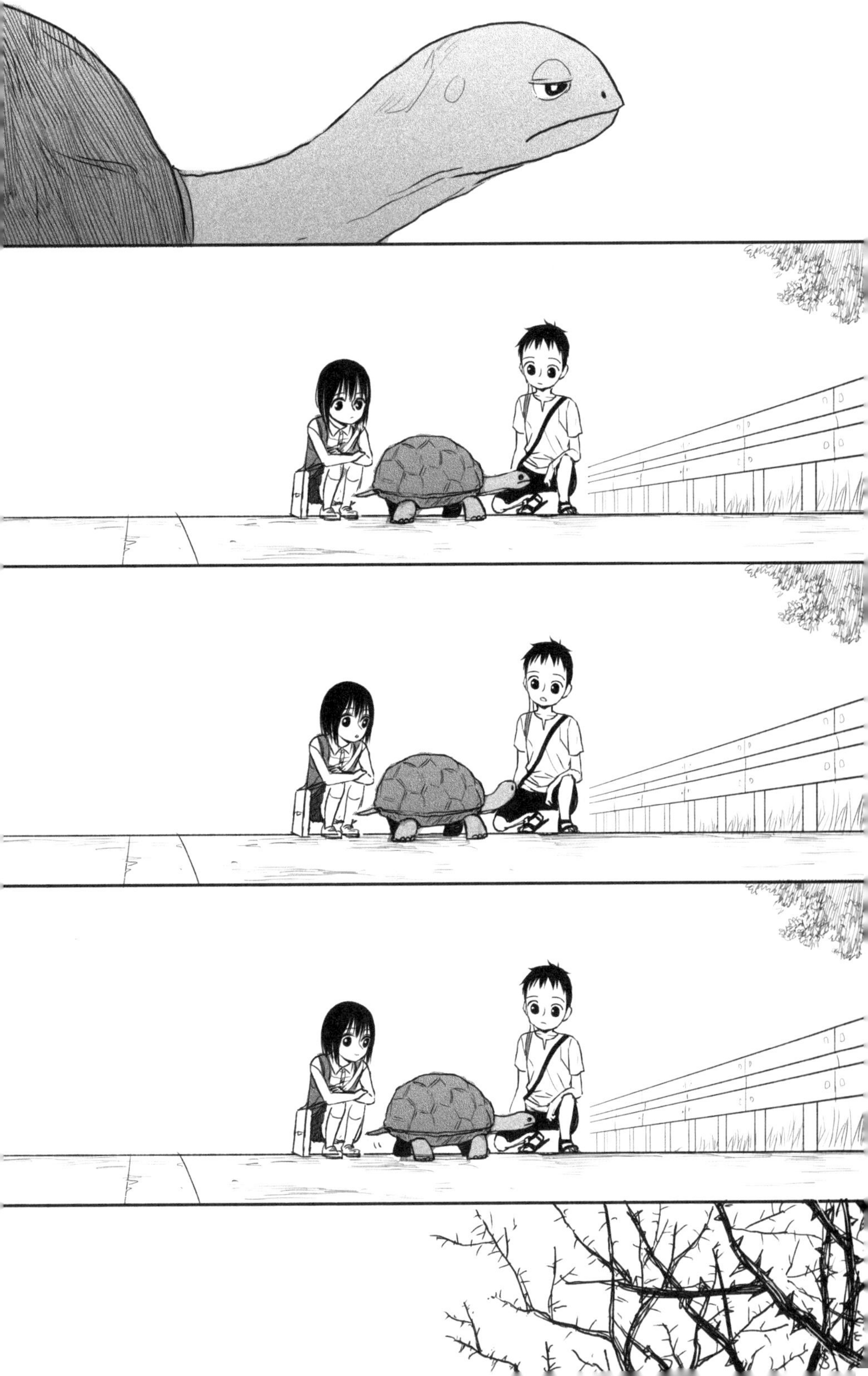

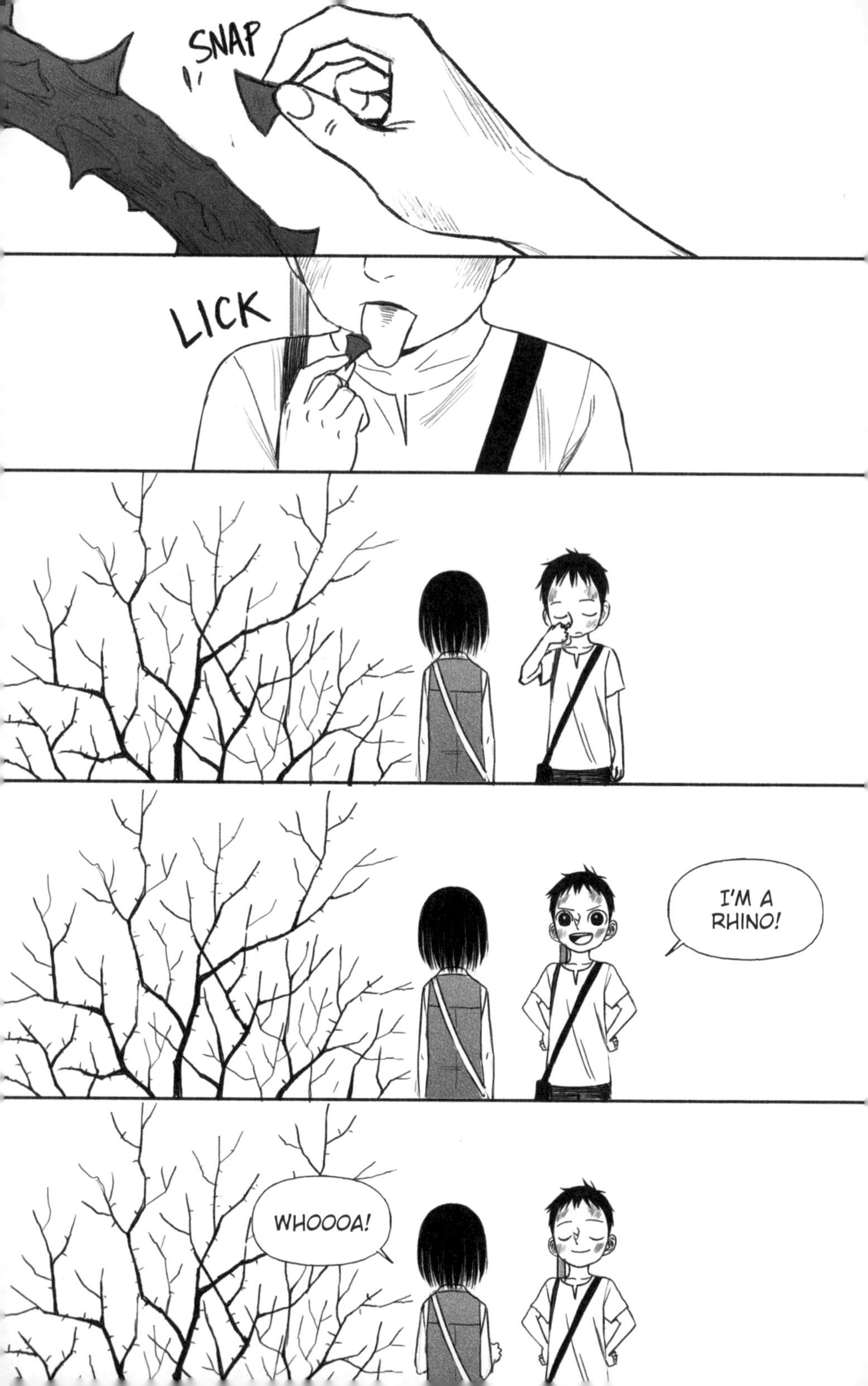
SNAP
LICK
I'M A RHINO!
WHOOOA!

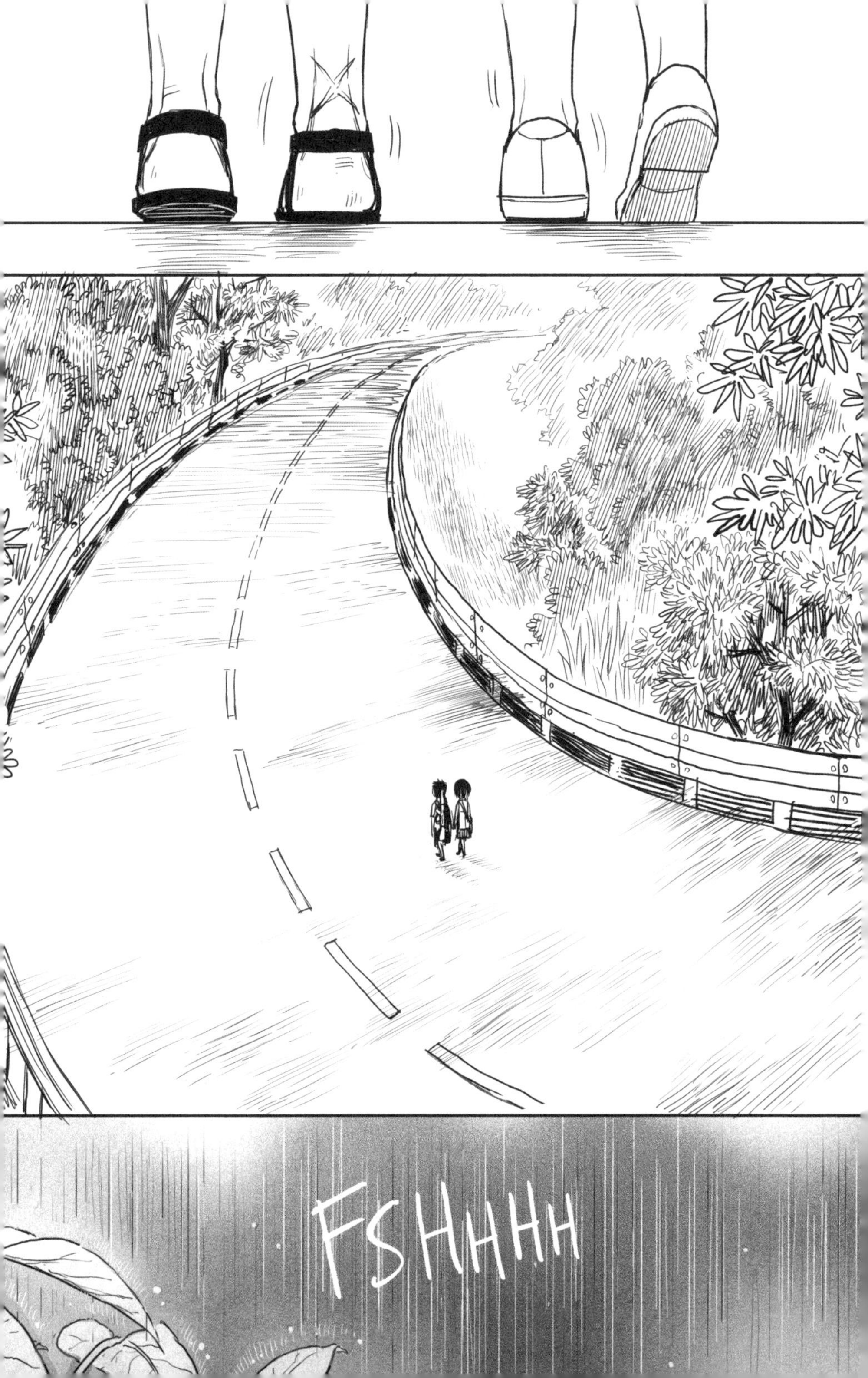
FSHHHH

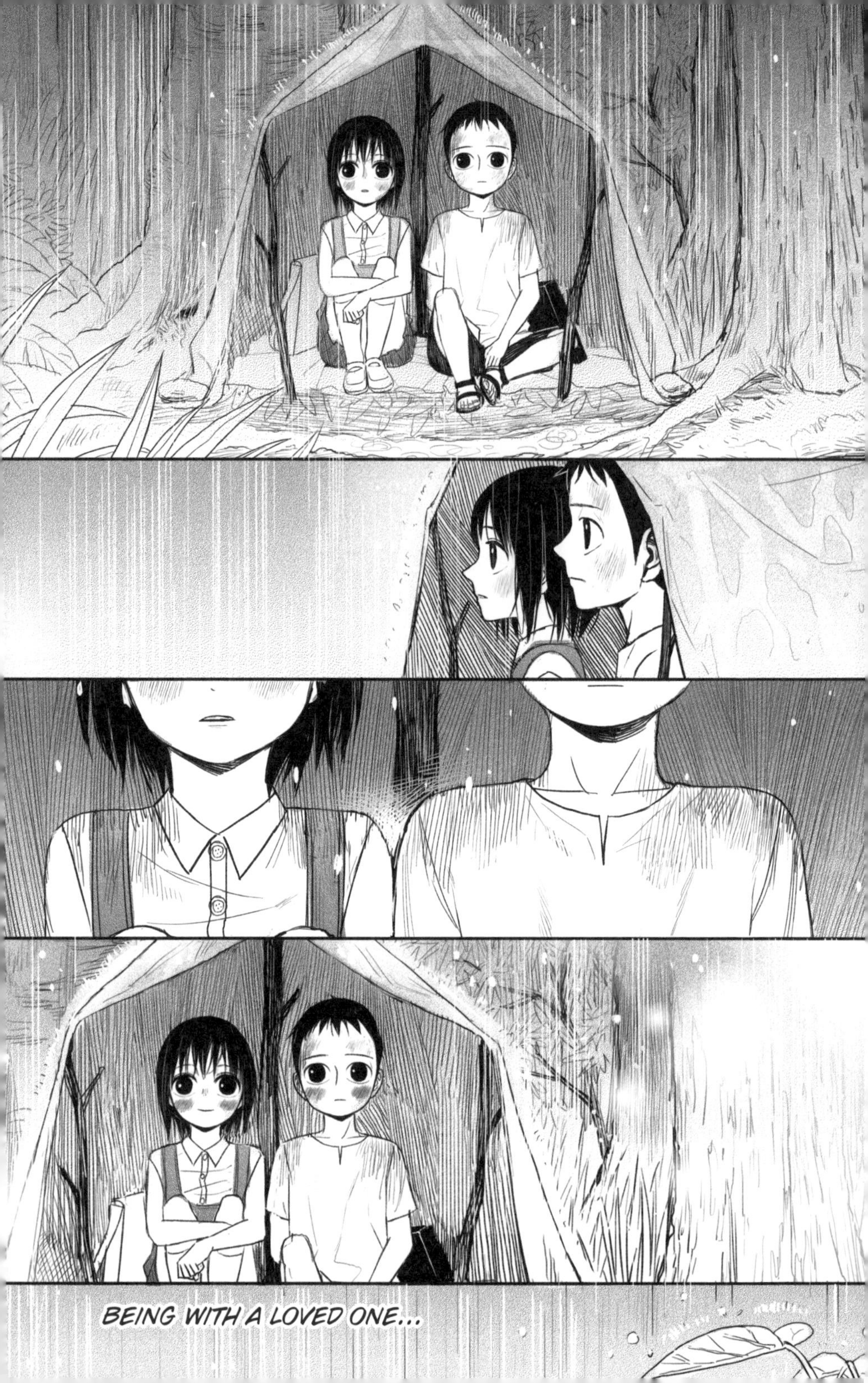
BEING WITH A LOVED ONE...

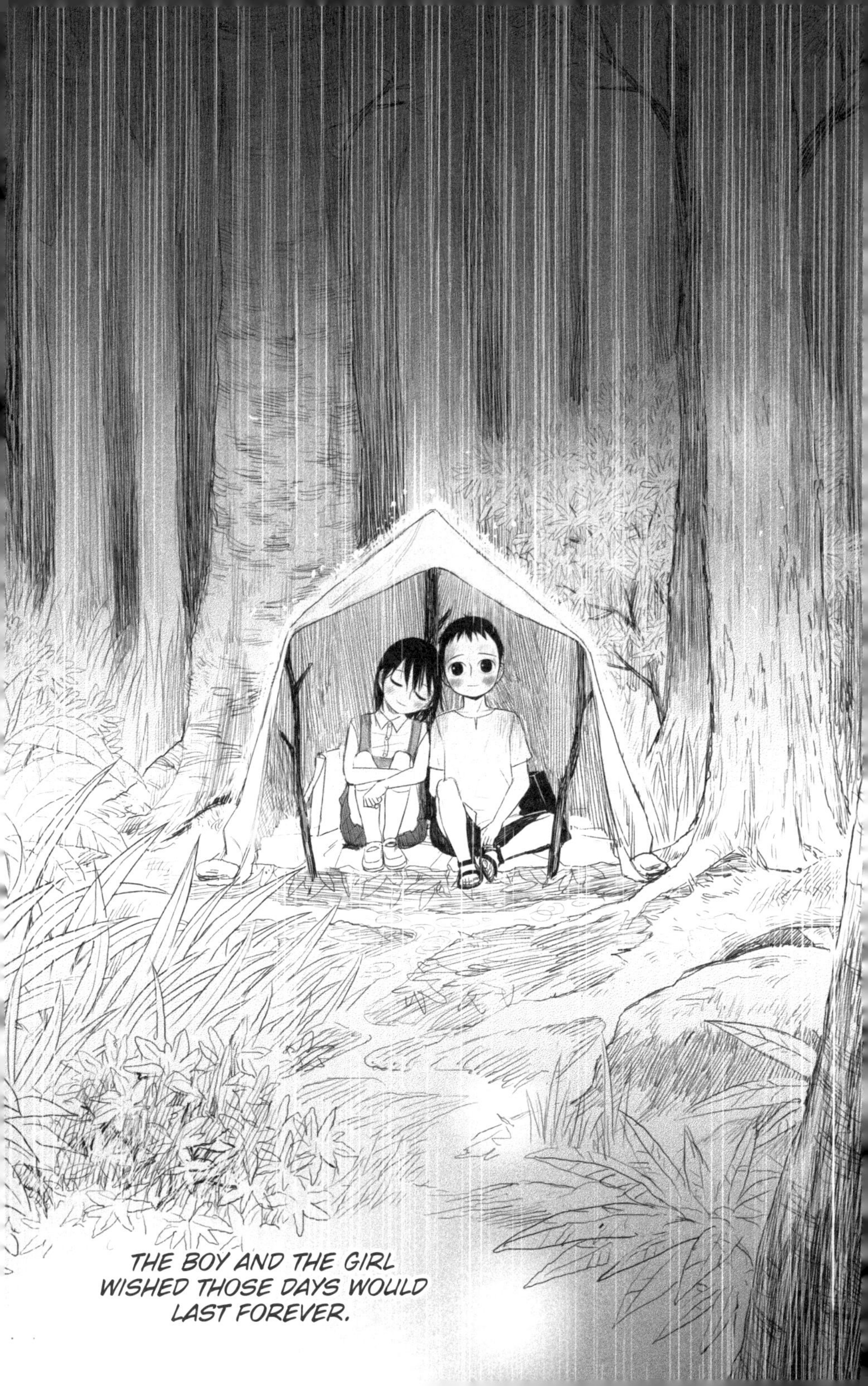
THE BOY AND THE GIRL
WISHED THOSE DAYS WOULD
LAST FOREVER.

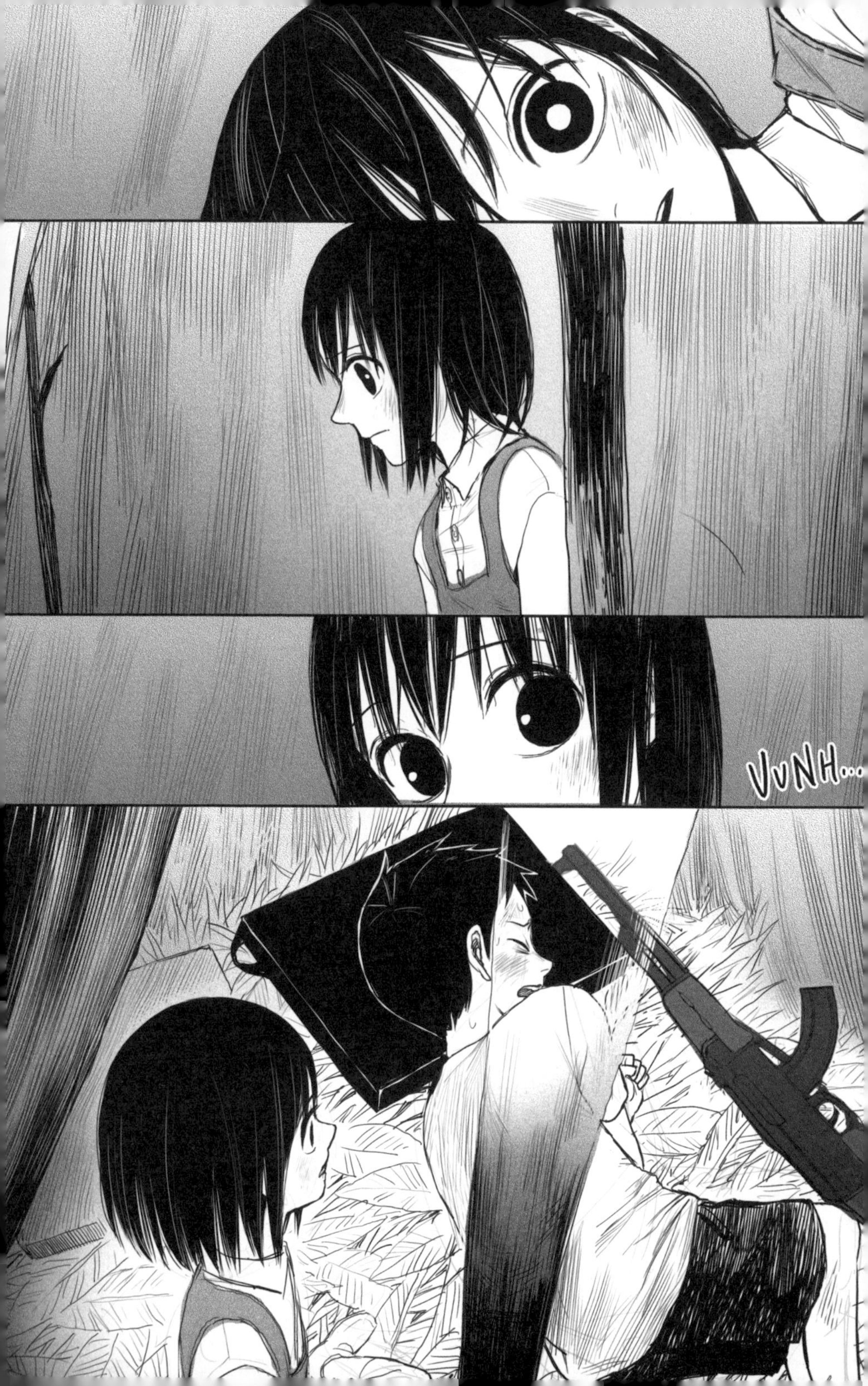
VVNH...

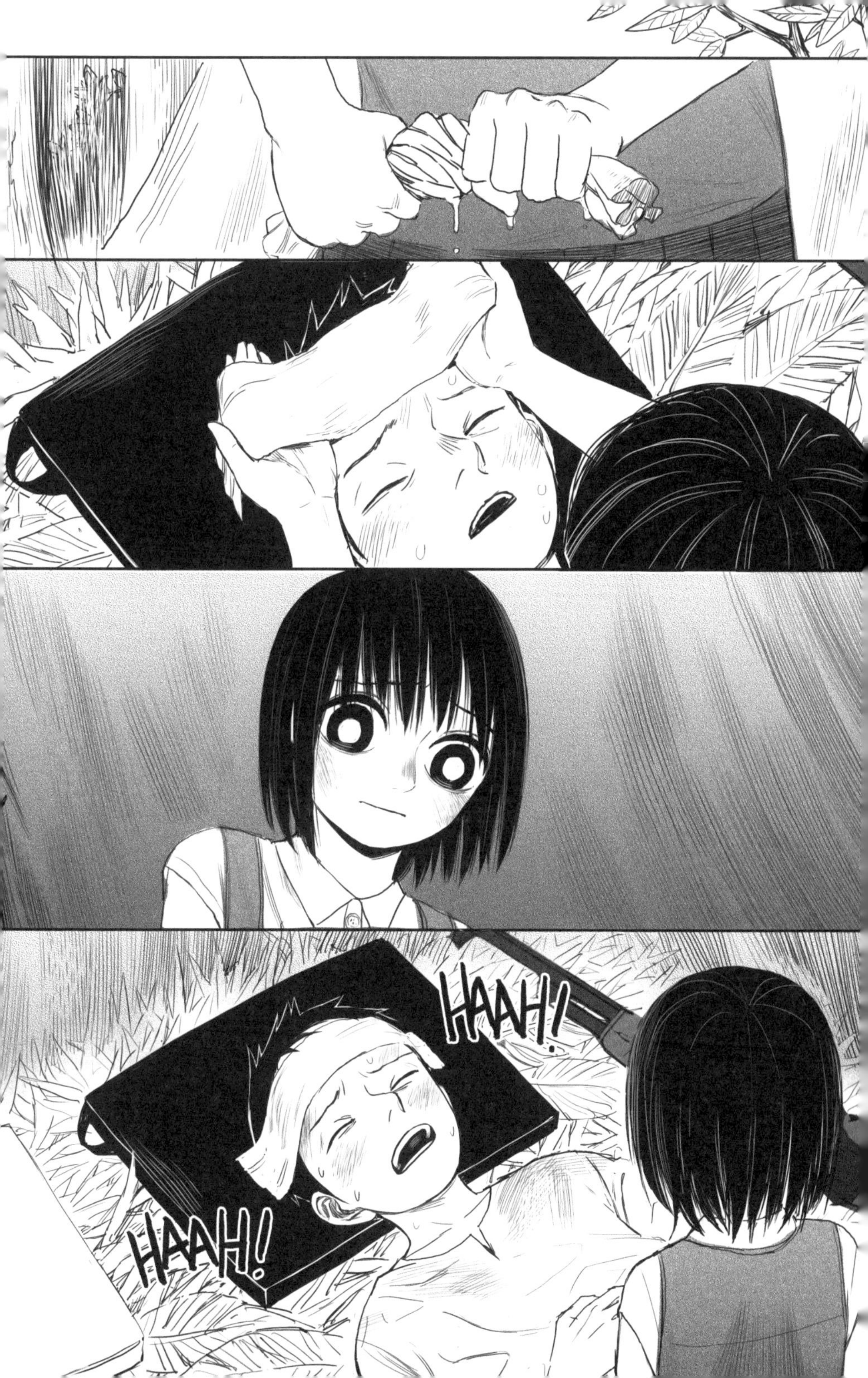

HAAH!
HAAH!

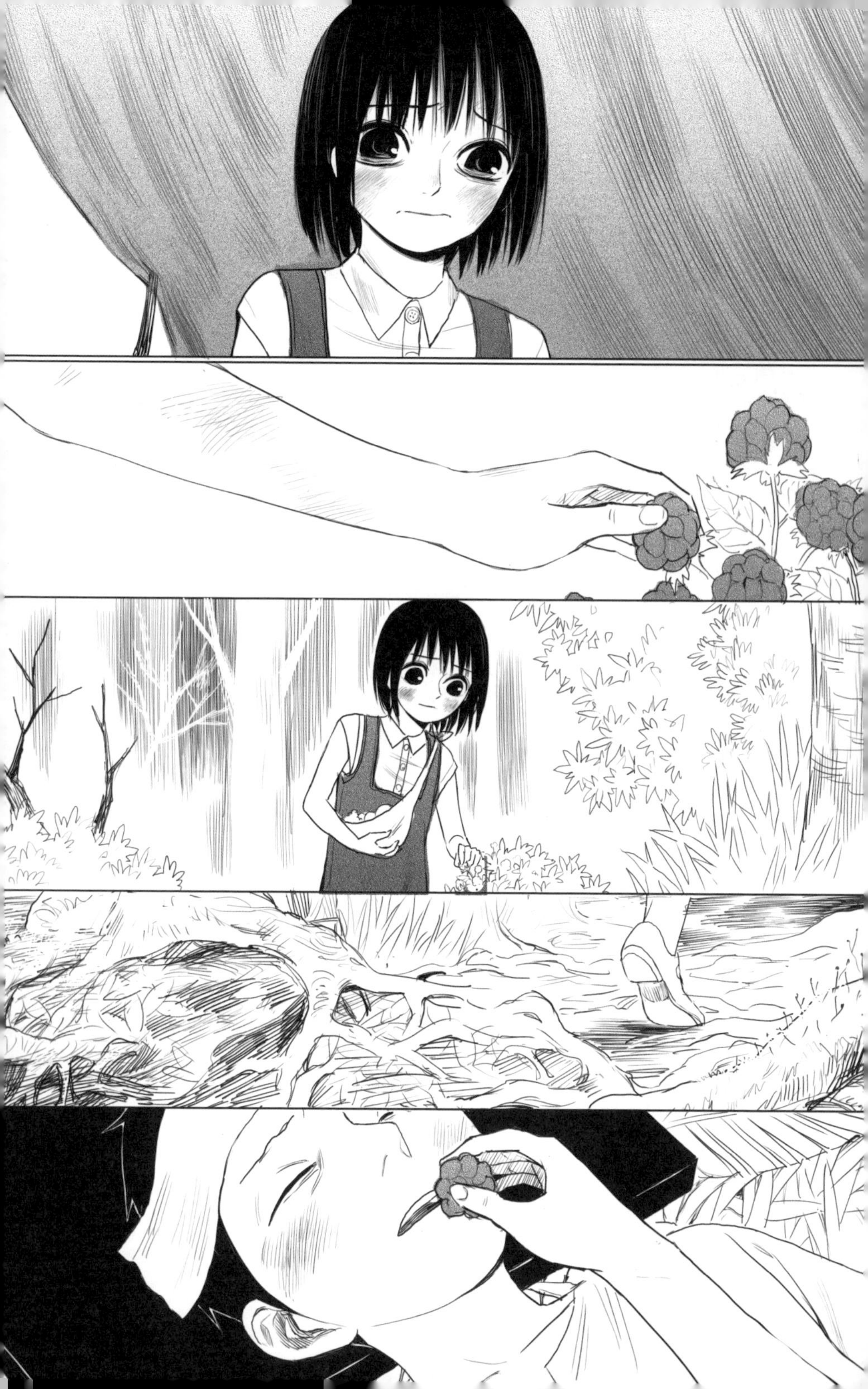

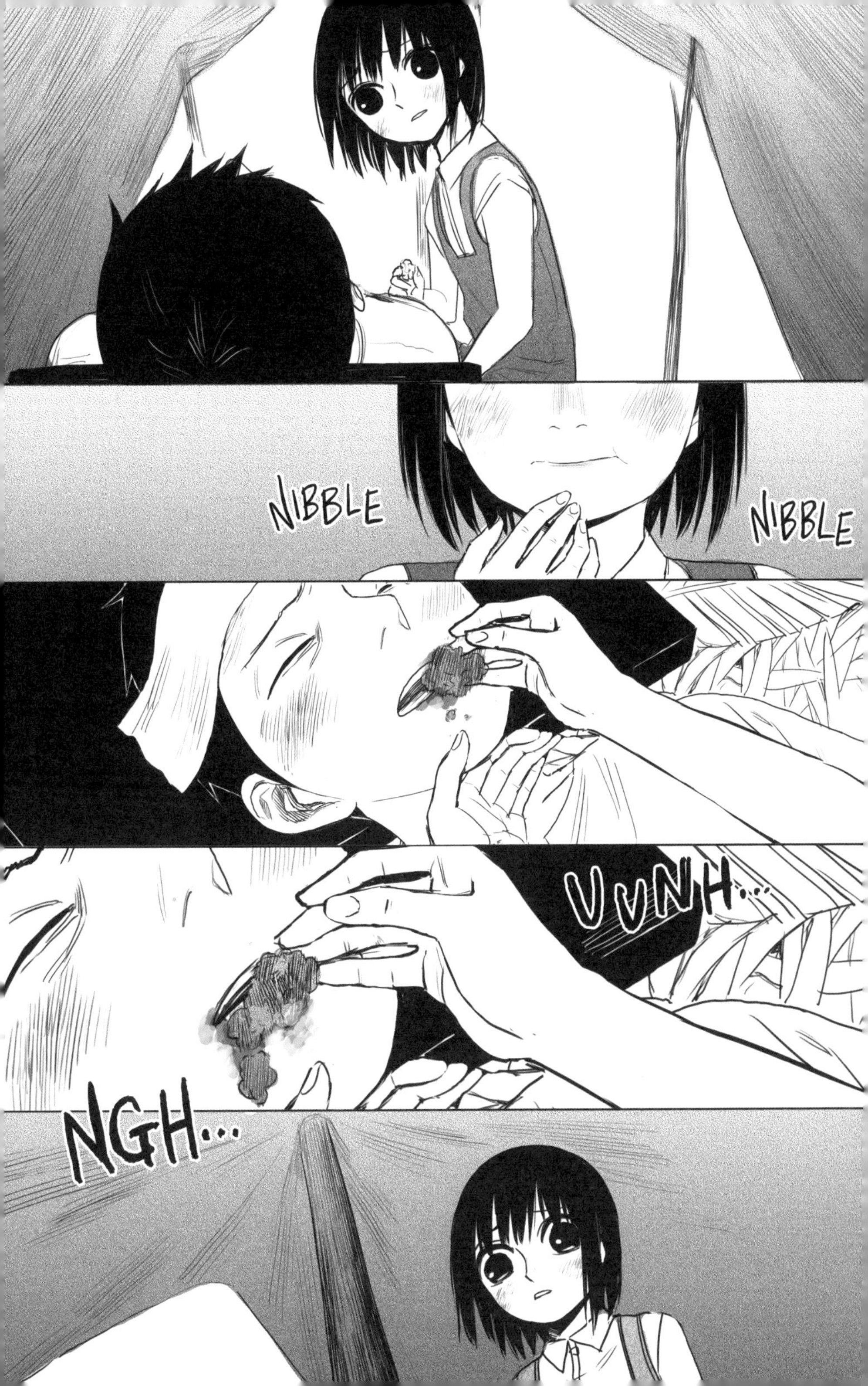
NIBBLE
NIBBLE
UUNH...
NGH...

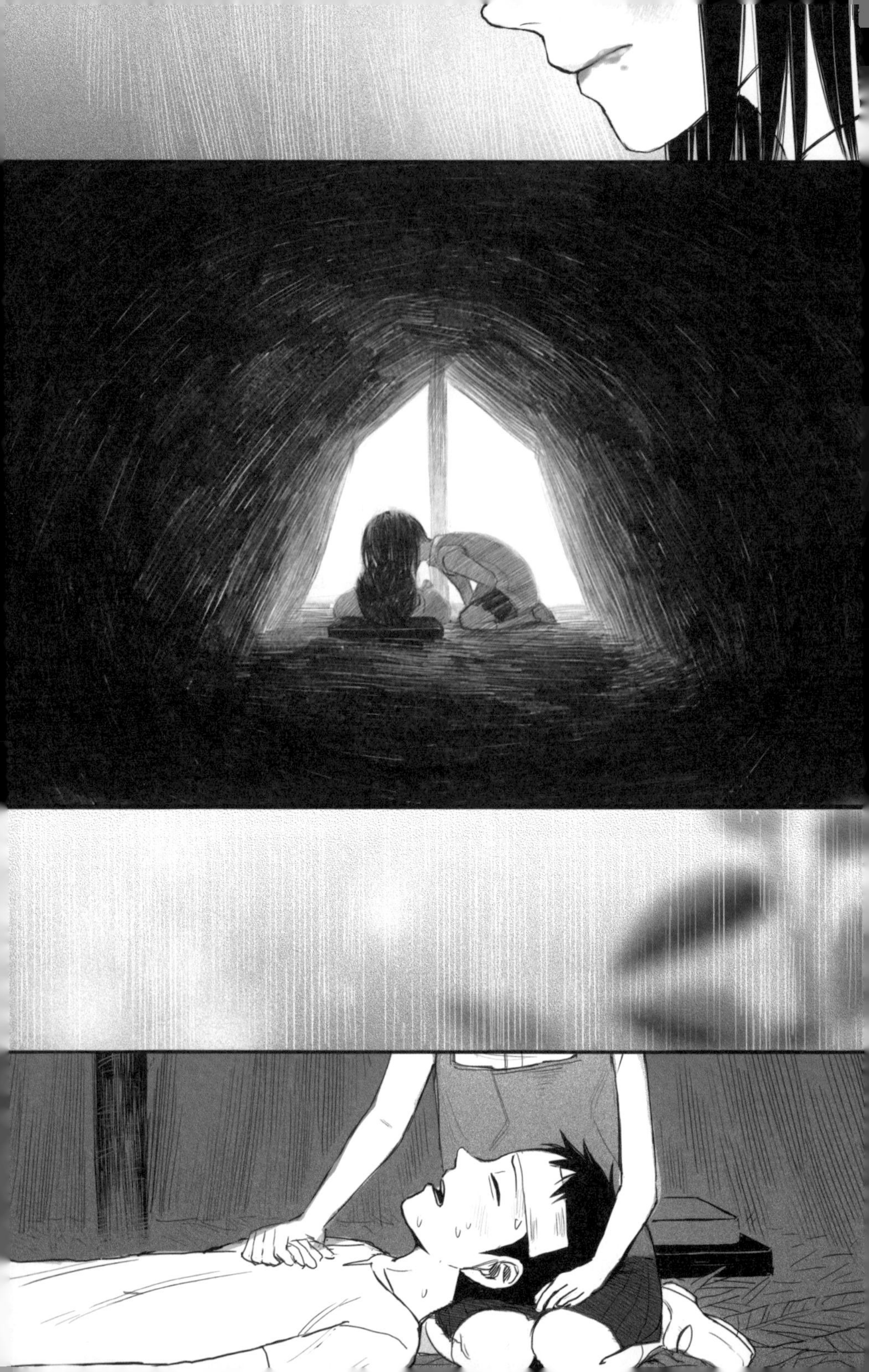

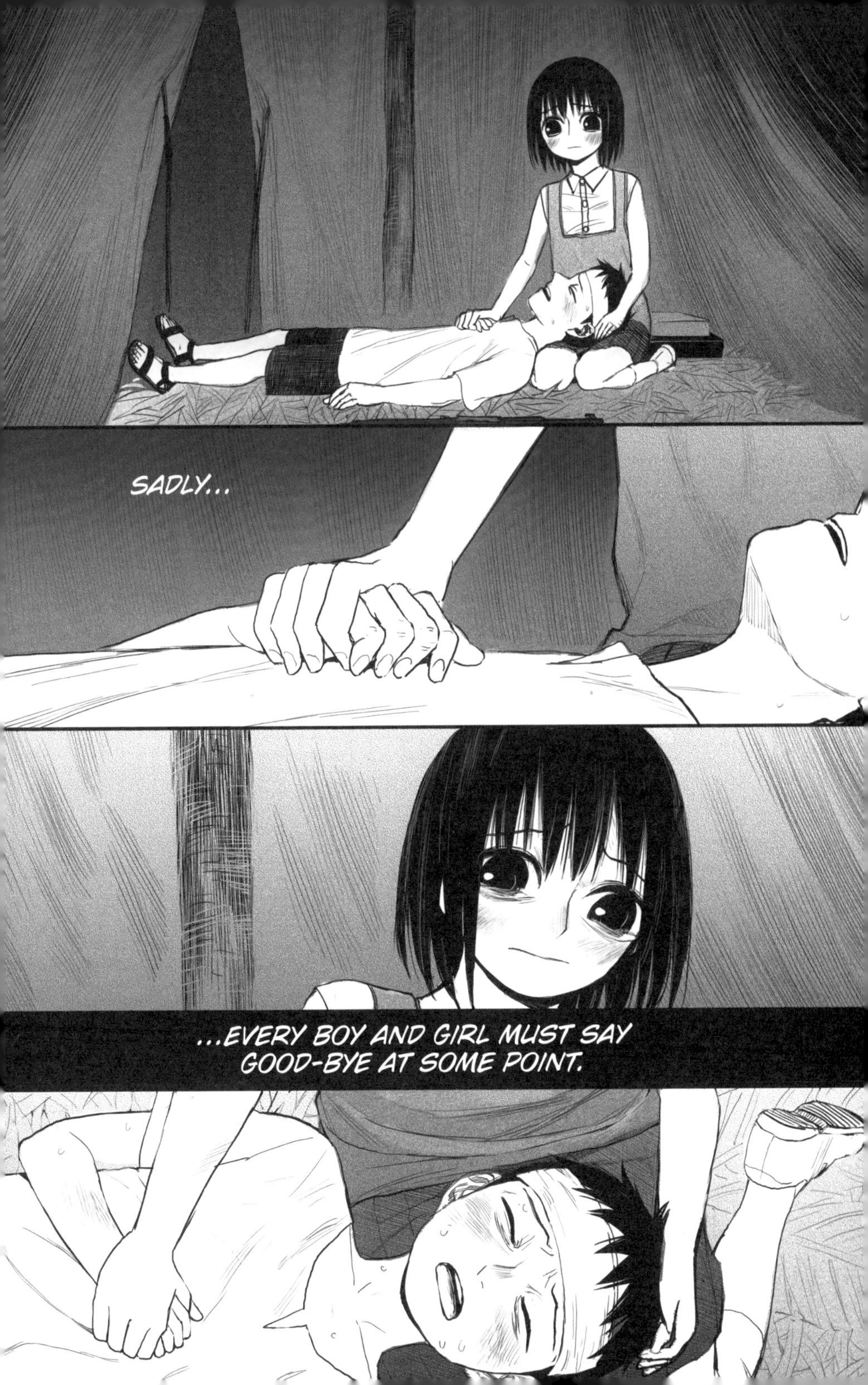
SADLY...
...EVERY BOY AND GIRL MUST SAY GOOD-BYE AT SOME POINT.

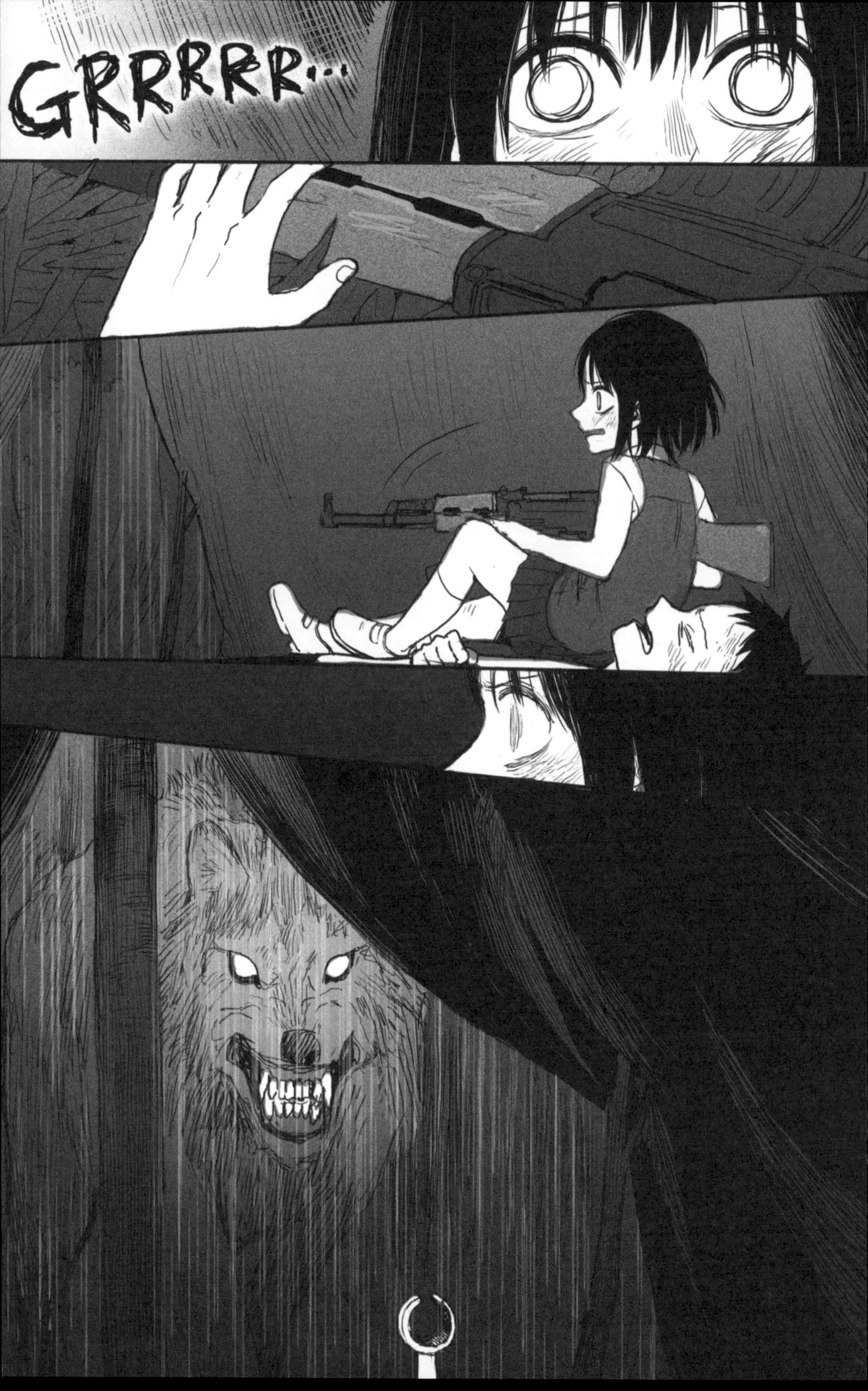
GRRRRR...

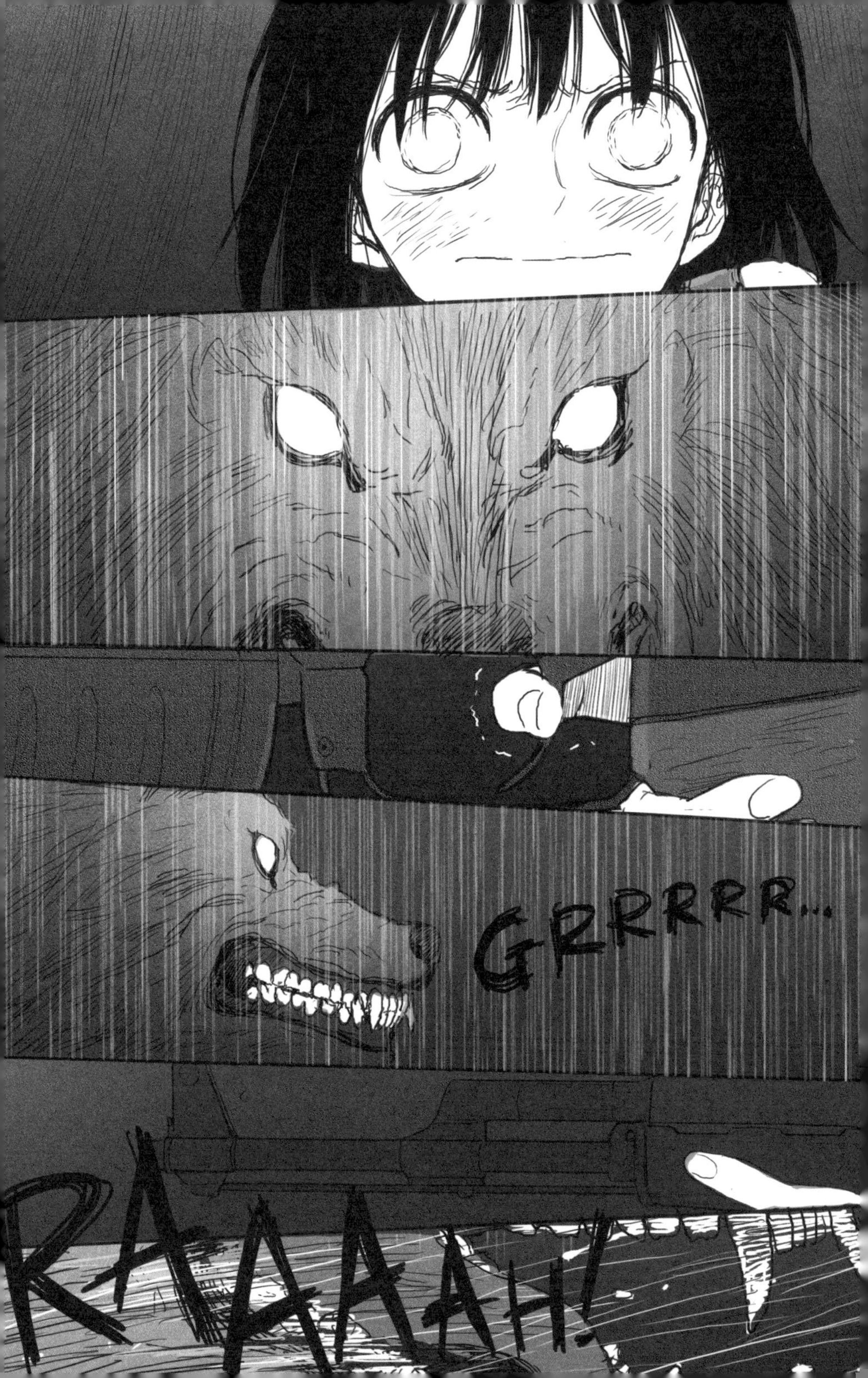
GRRRRR...
RAAAAH!

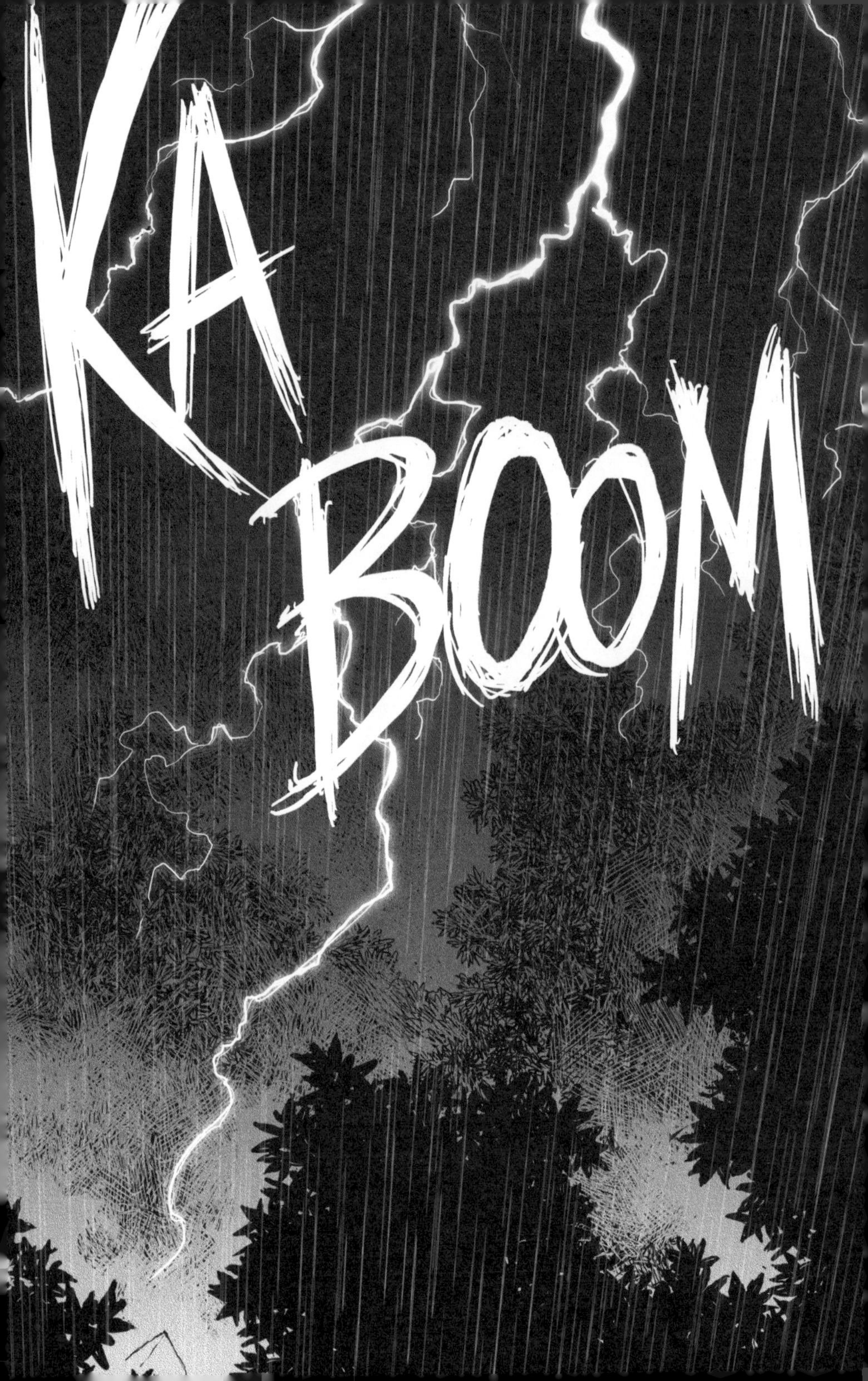
KA
BOOM

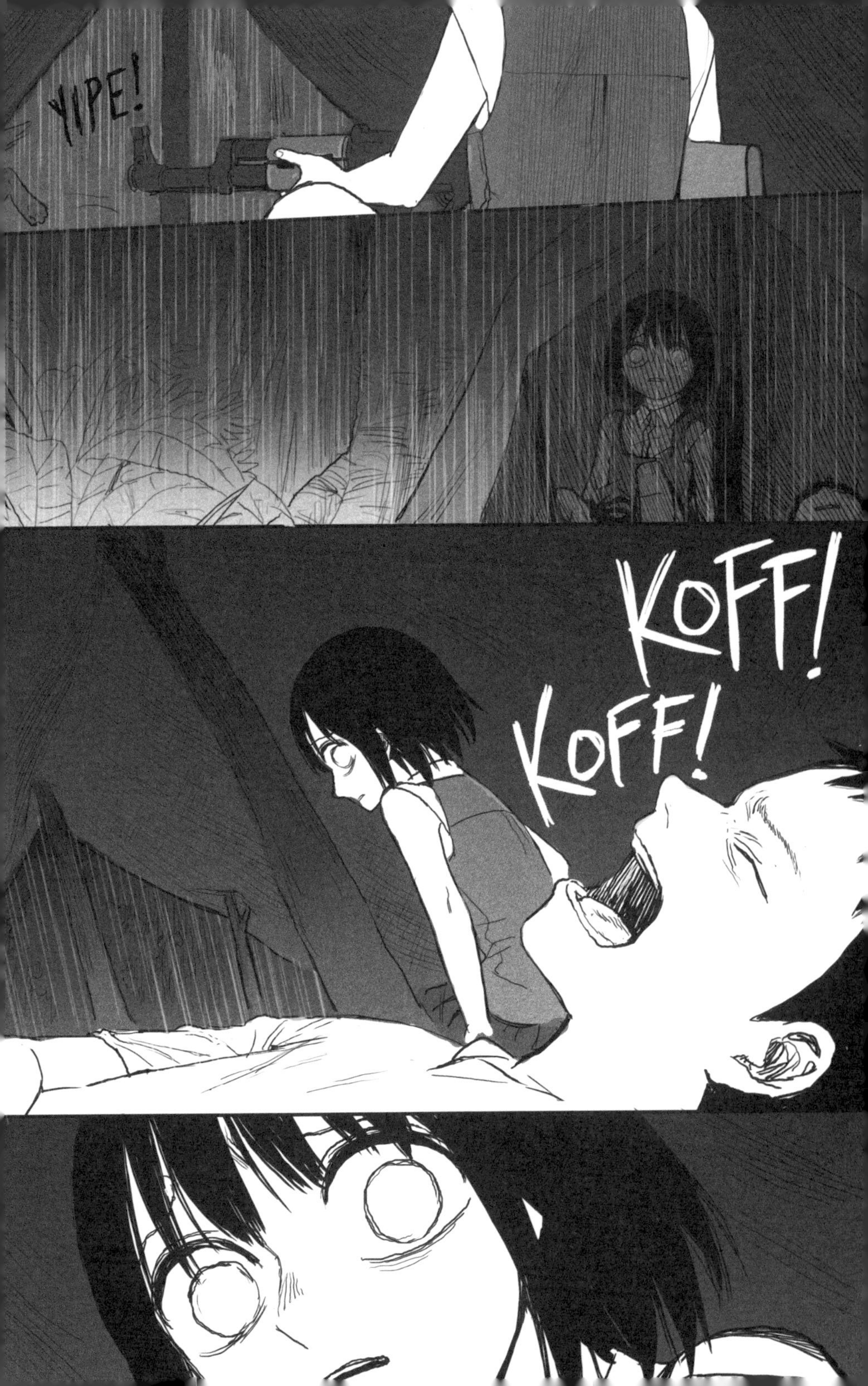
YIPE!
KOFF!
KOFF!

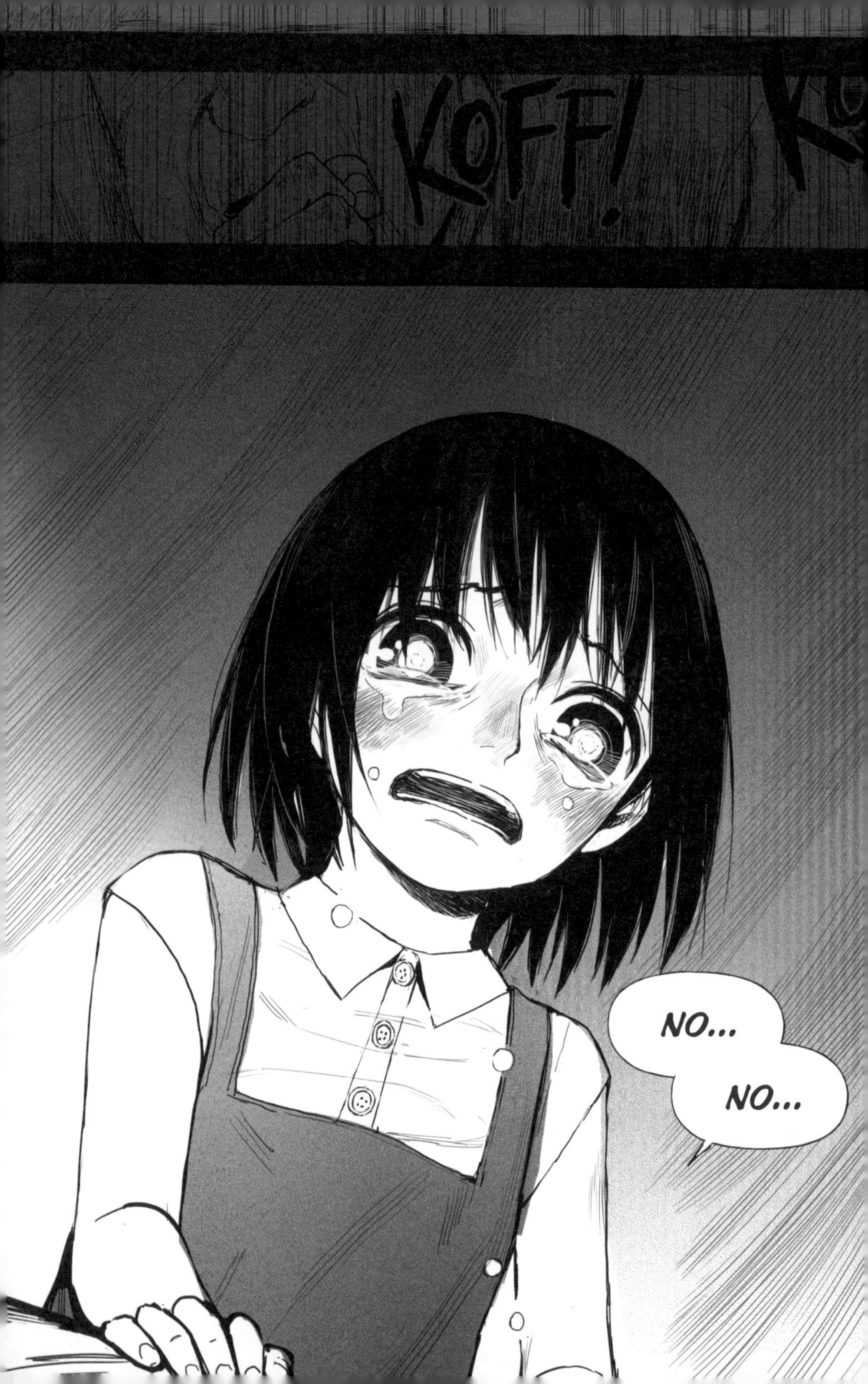
KOFF!
NO...
NO...

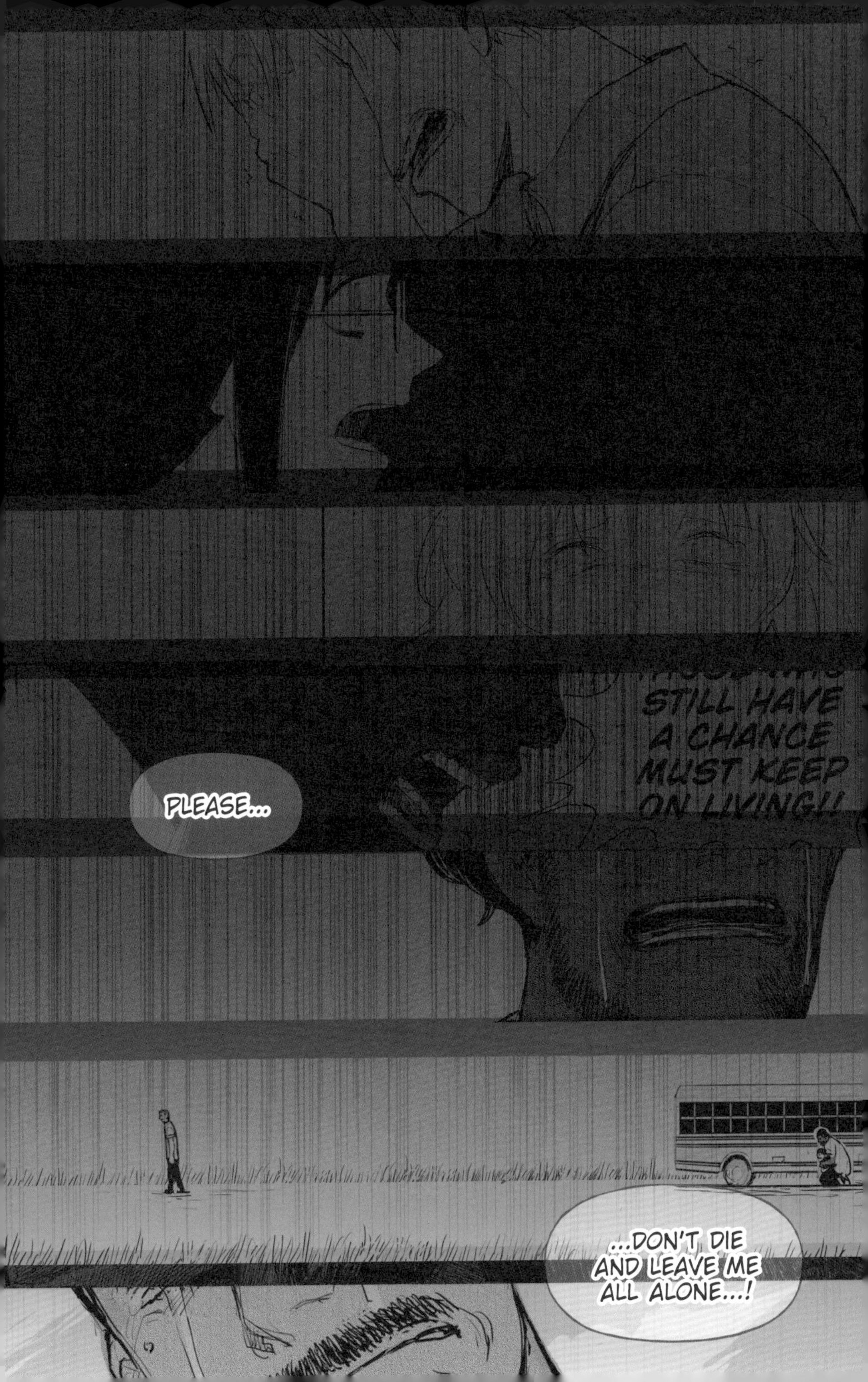
STILL HAVE A CHANCE MUST KEEP ON LIVING!!
PLEASE...
...DON'T DIE AND LEAVE ME ALL ALONE...!

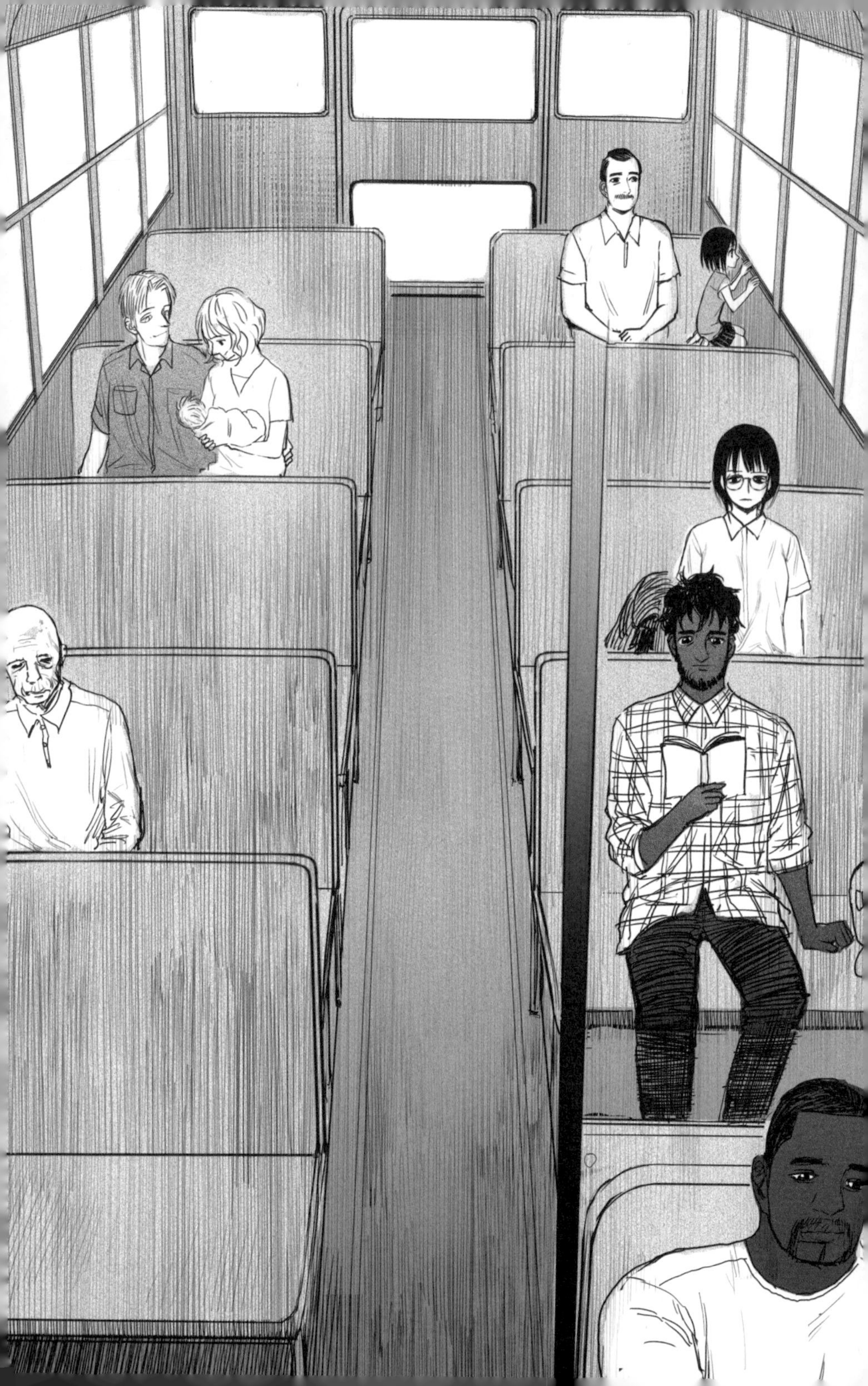

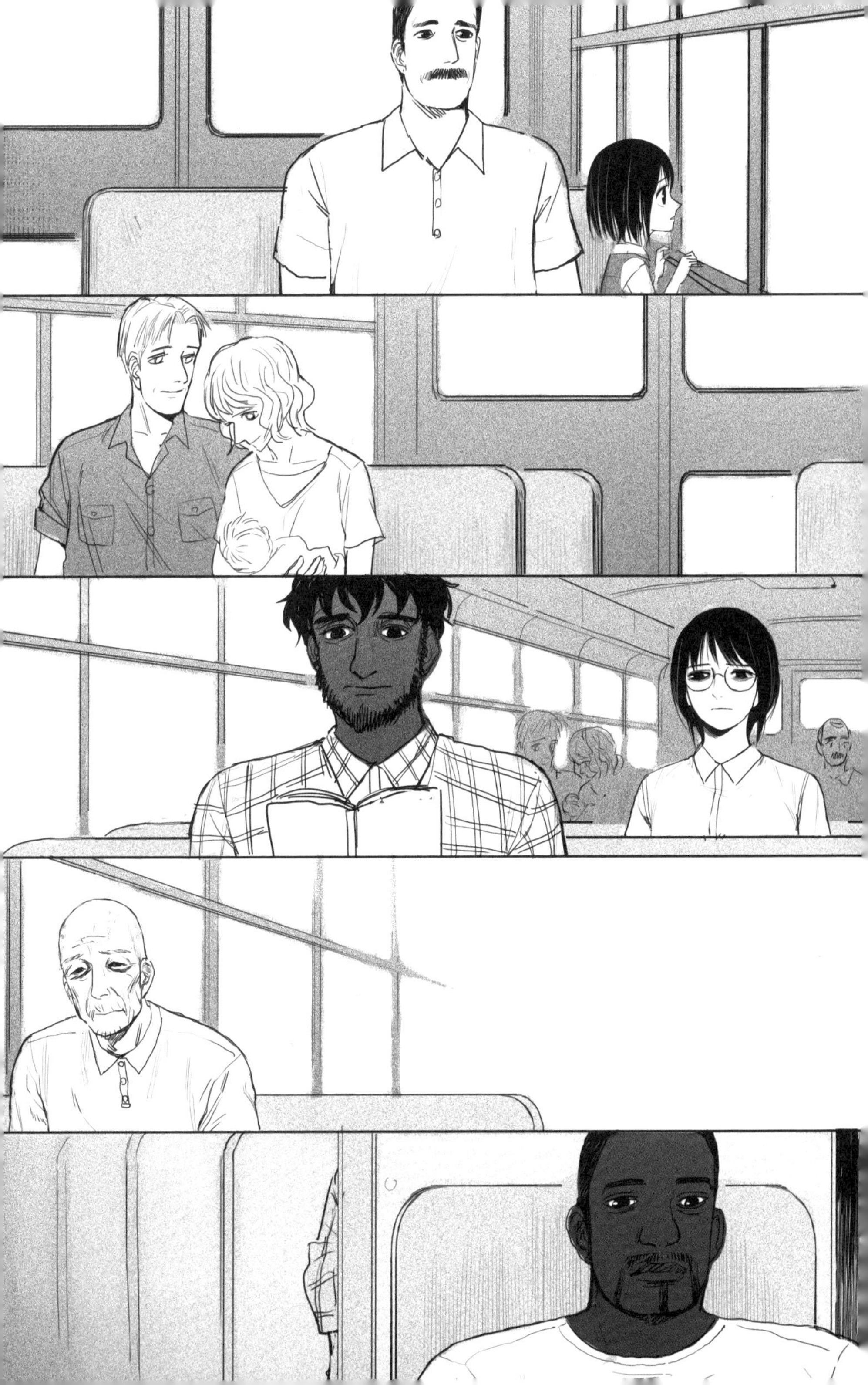

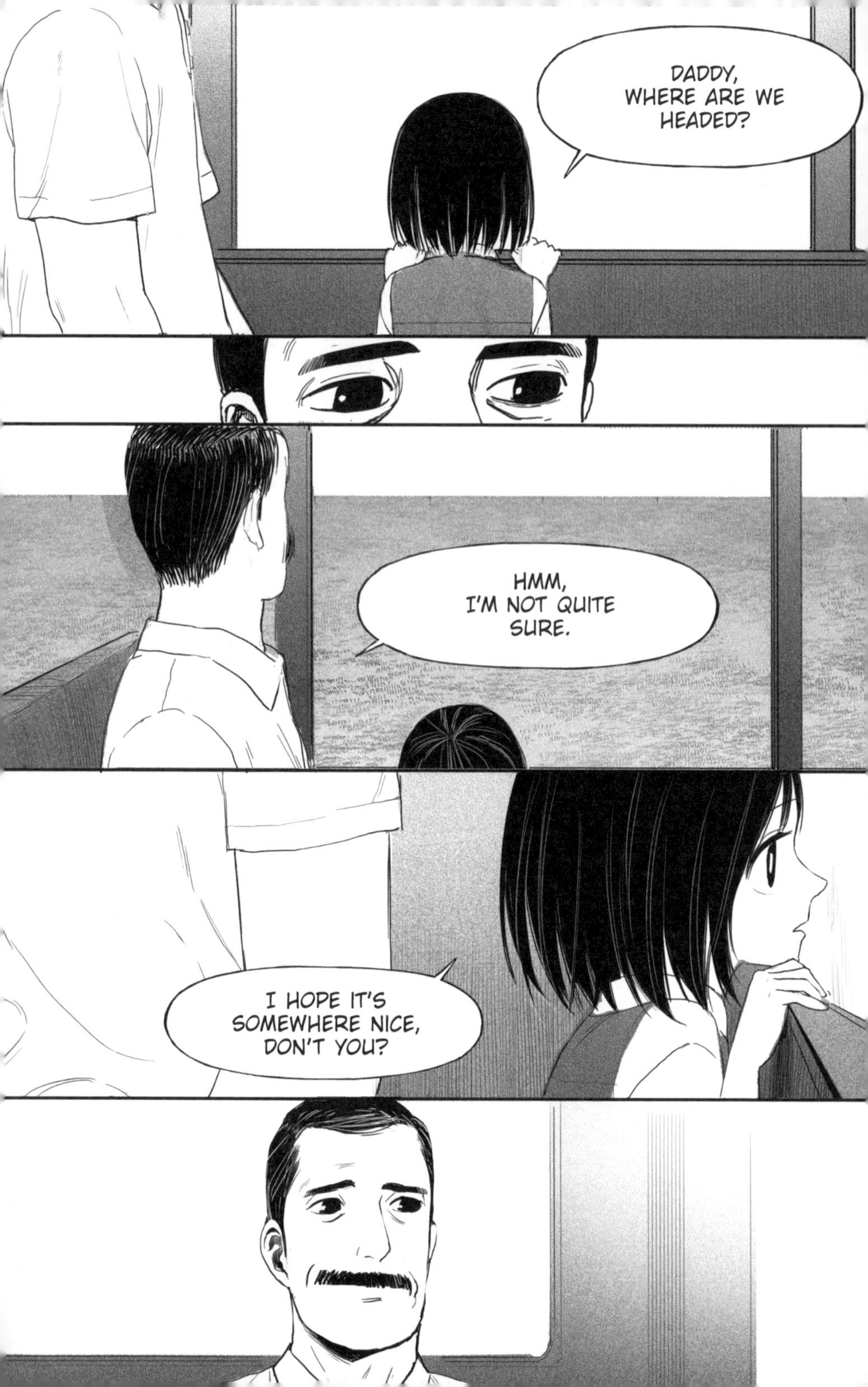
DADDY, WHERE ARE WE HEADED?
HMM, I'M NOT QUITE SURE.
I HOPE IT'S SOMEWHERE NICE, DON'T YOU?

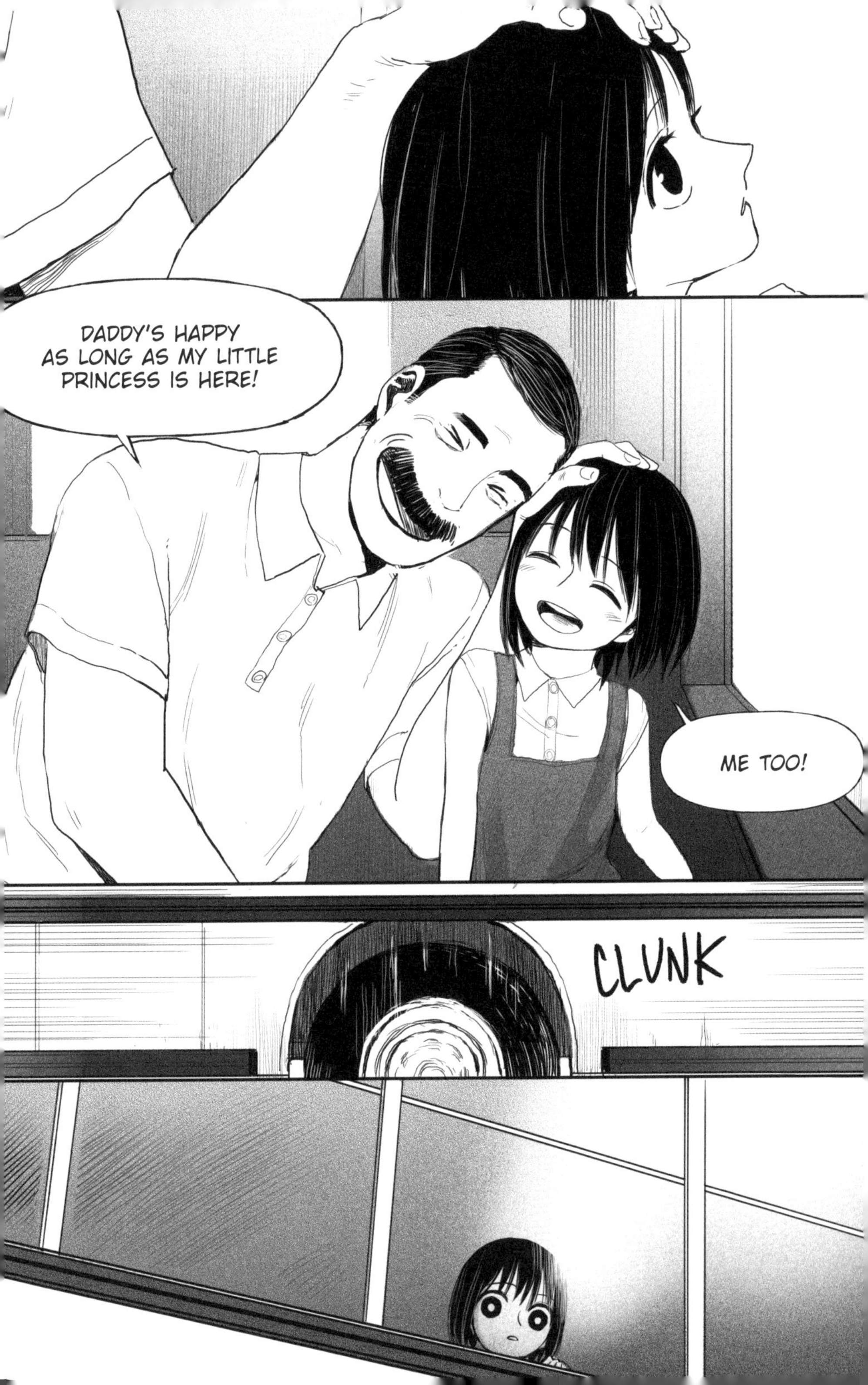
DADDY'S HAPPY AS LONG AS MY LITTLE PRINCESS IS HERE!
ME TOO!
CLUNK

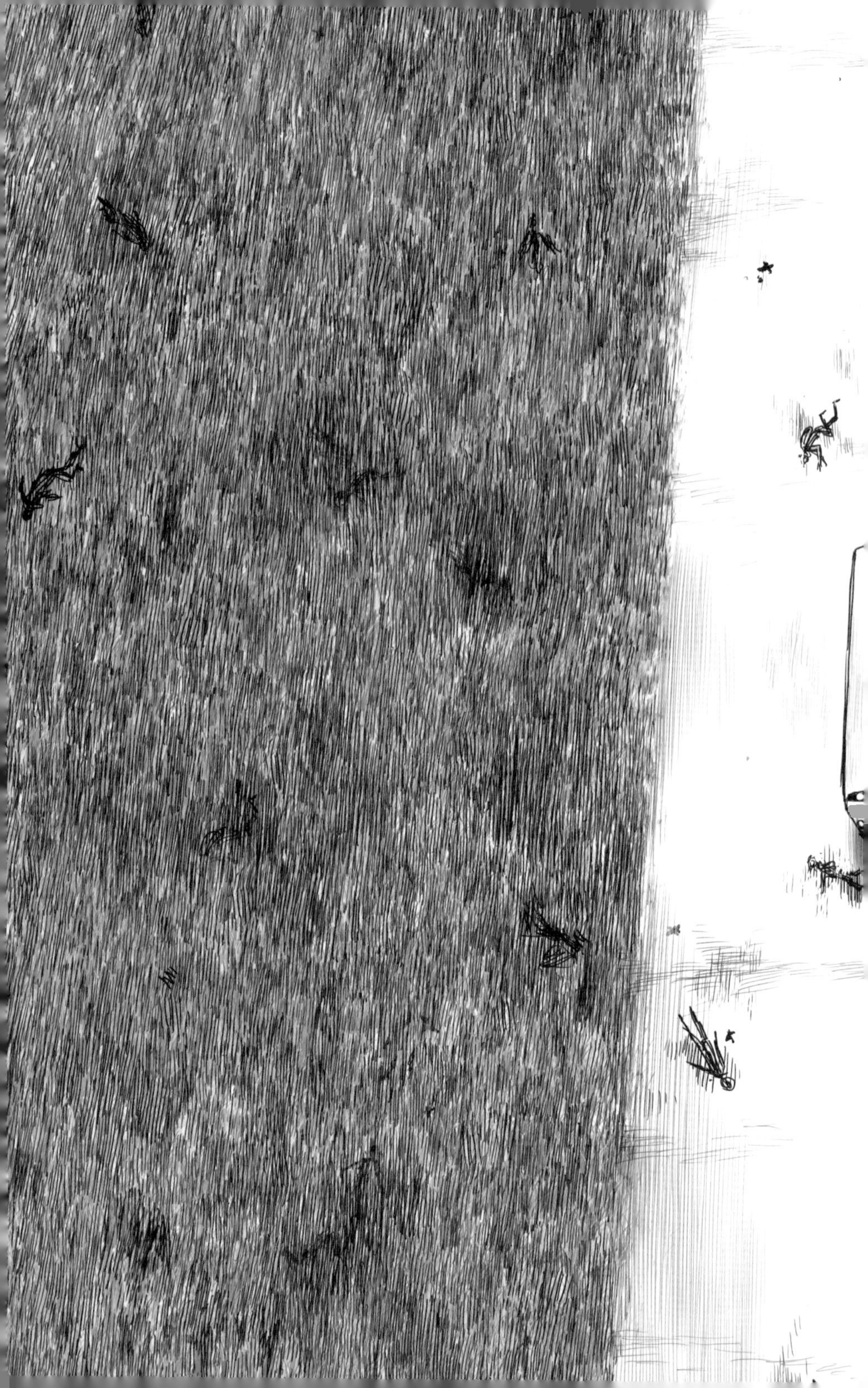

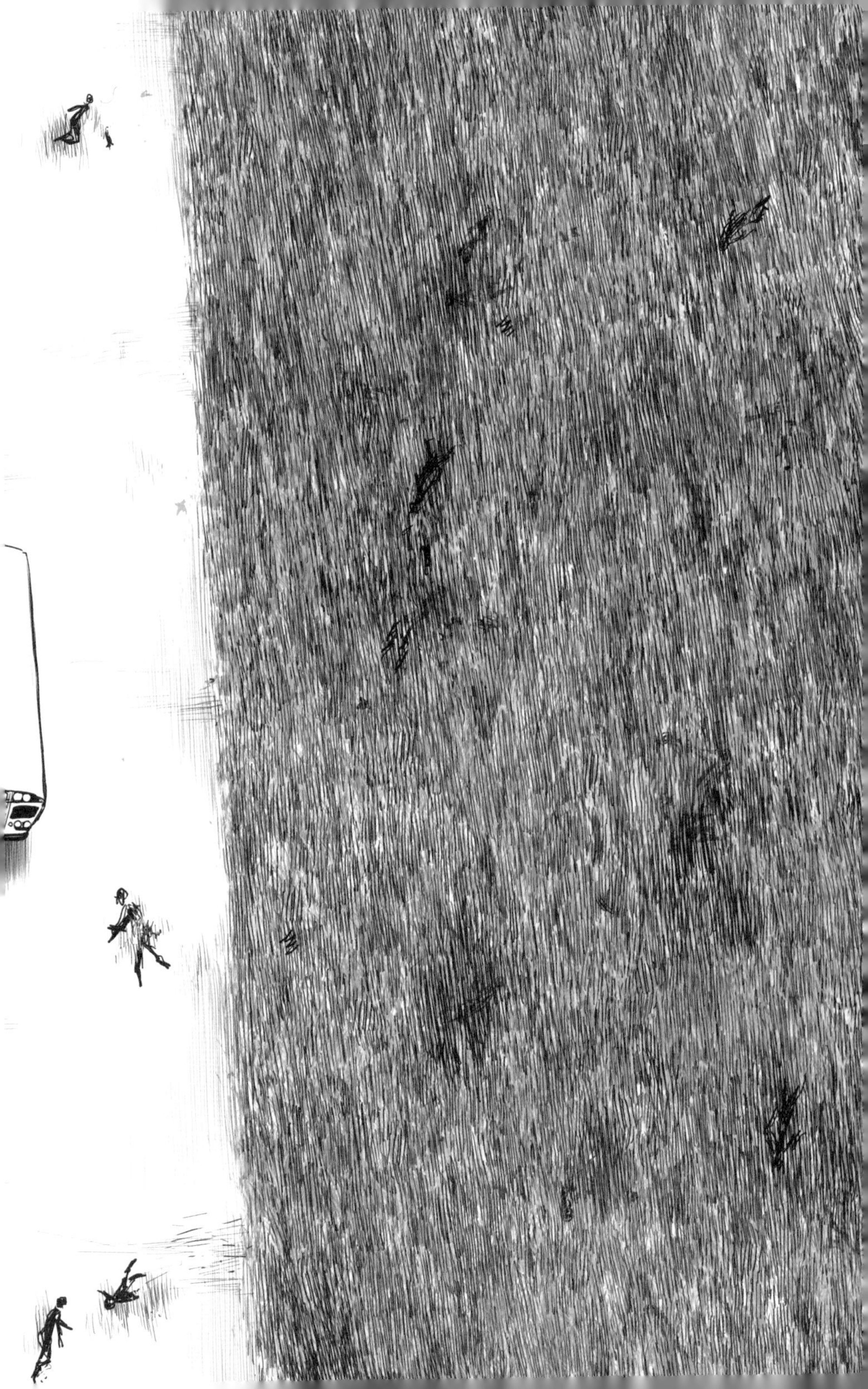

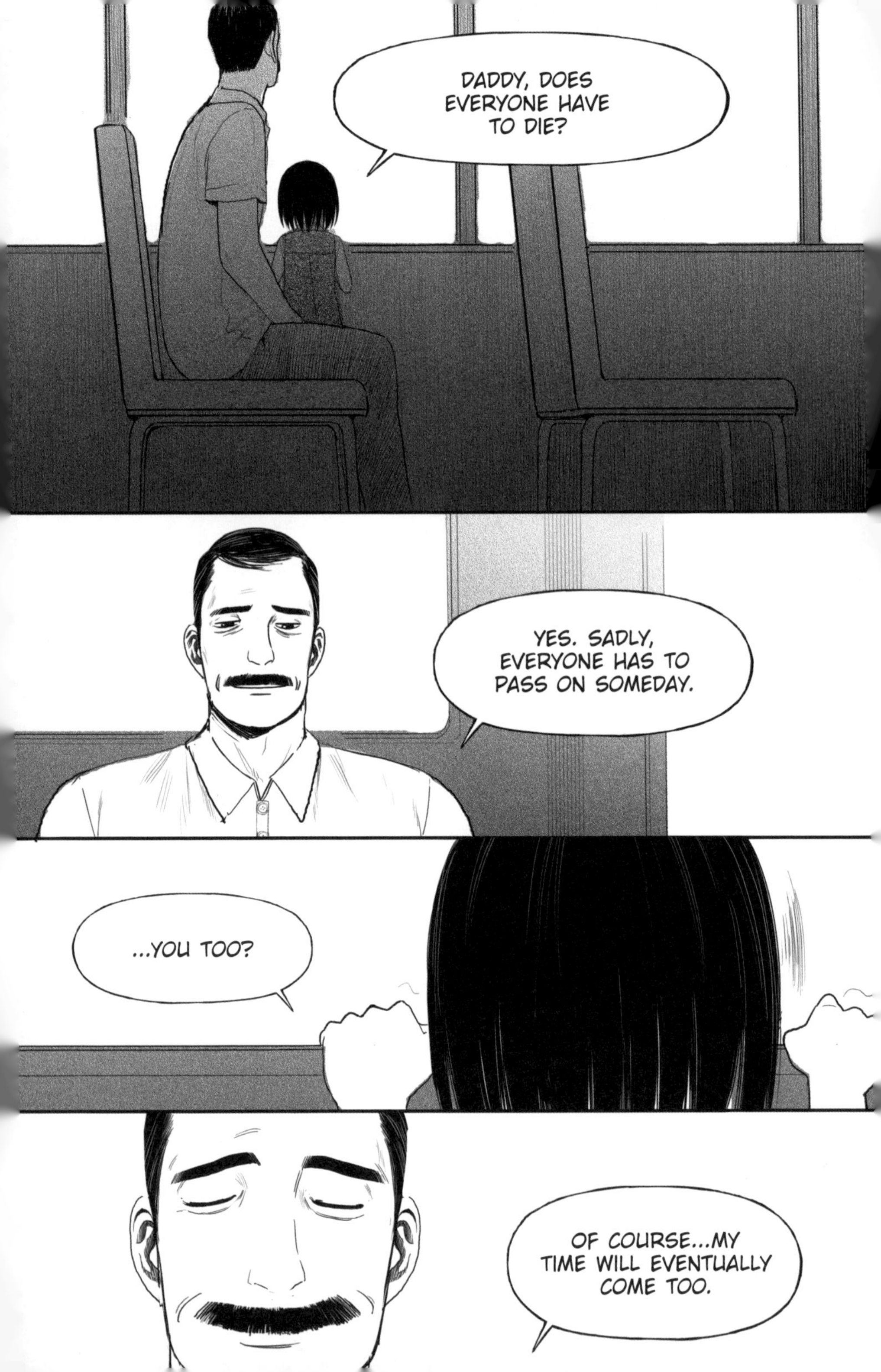
DADDY, DOES EVERYONE HAVE TO DIE?
YES. SADLY, EVERYONE HAS TO PASS ON SOMEDAY.
...YOU TOO?
OF COURSE...MY TIME WILL EVENTUALLY COME TOO.

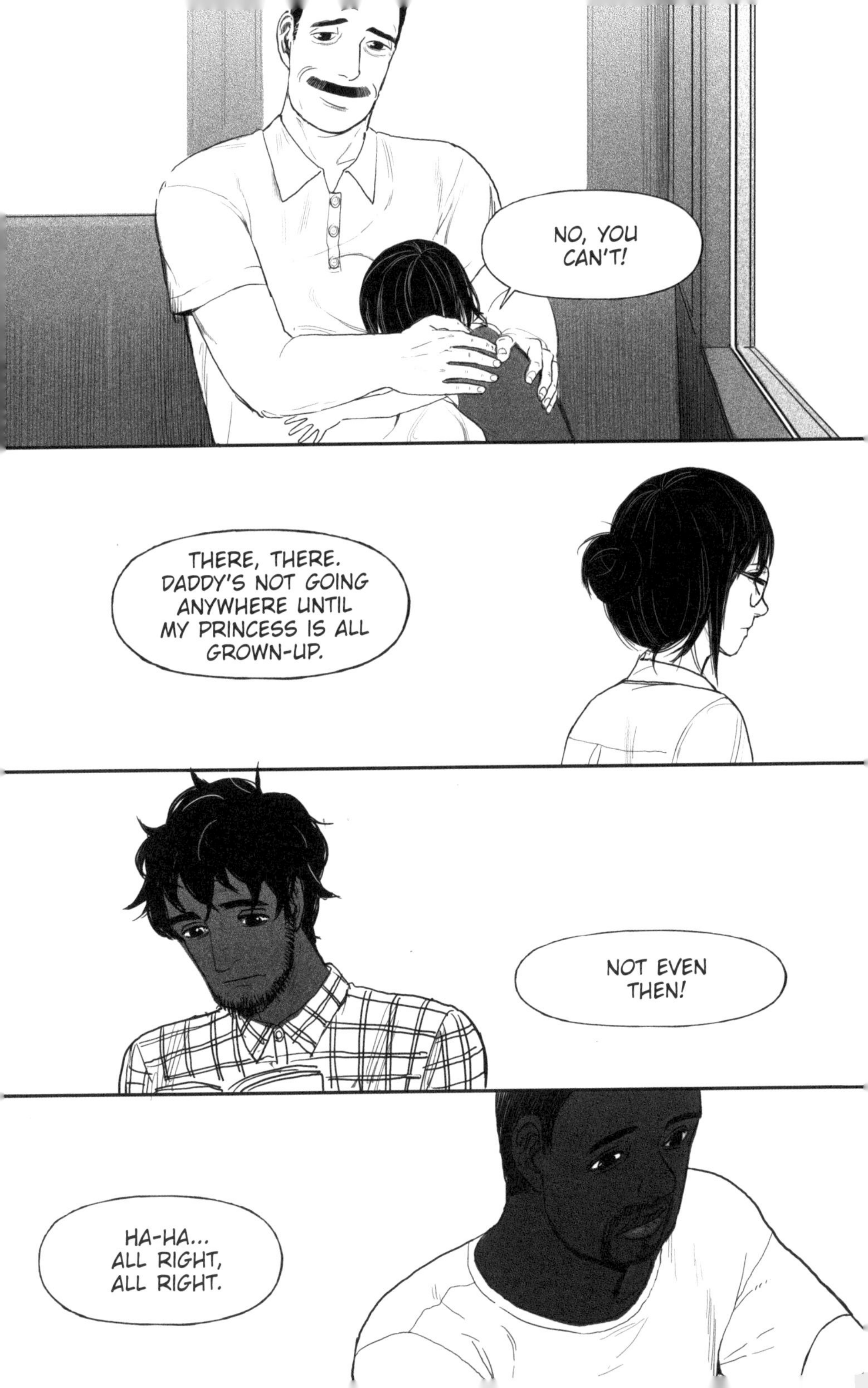
NO, YOU CAN'T!
THERE, THERE. DADDY'S NOT GOING ANYWHERE UNTIL MY PRINCESS IS ALL GROWN-UP.
NOT EVEN THEN!
HA-HA... ALL RIGHT, ALL RIGHT.

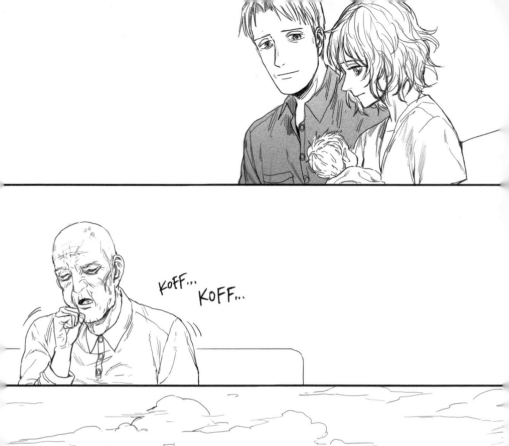

KOFF... KOFF...

WHERE ARE WE HEADED?

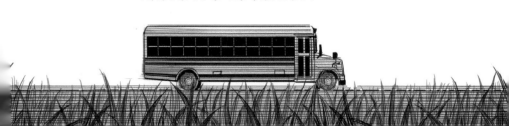

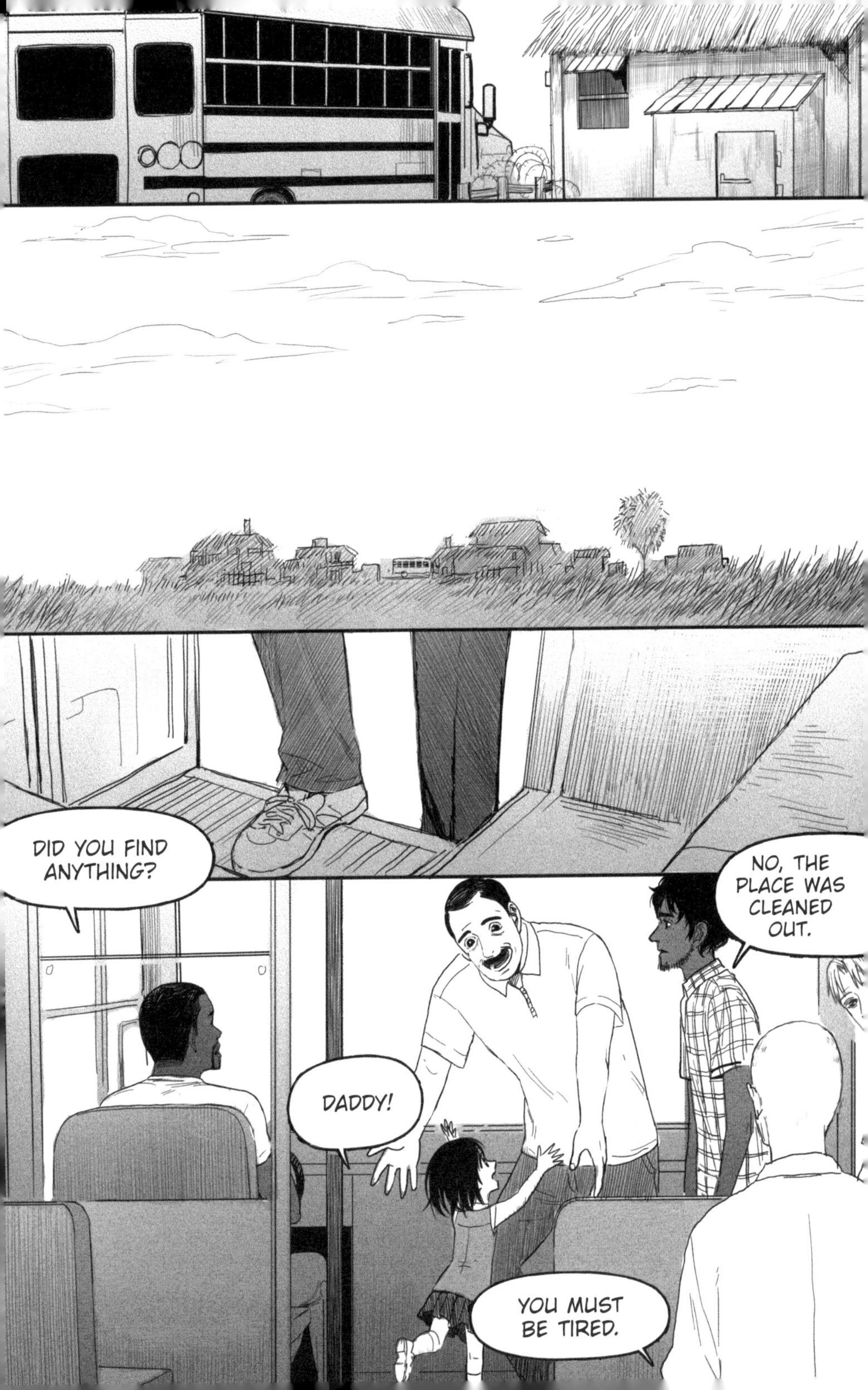
DID YOU FIND ANYTHING?
NO, THE PLACE WAS CLEANED OUT.
DADDY!
YOU MUST BE TIRED.

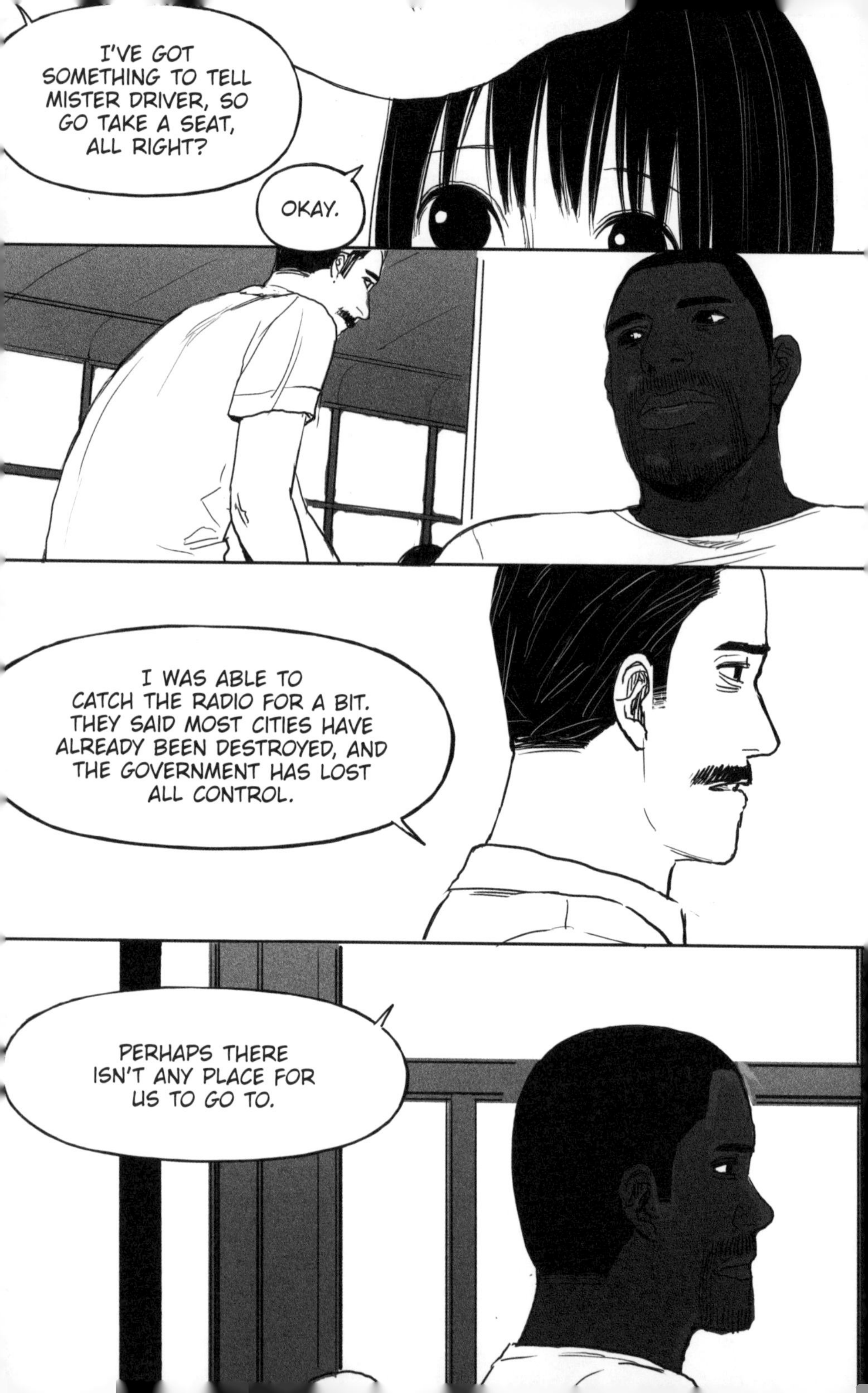
I'VE GOT SOMETHING TO TELL MISTER DRIVER, SO GO TAKE A SEAT, ALL RIGHT?
OKAY.
I WAS ABLE TO CATCH THE RADIO FOR A BIT. THEY SAID MOST CITIES HAVE ALREADY BEEN DESTROYED, AND THE GOVERNMENT HAS LOST ALL CONTROL.
PERHAPS THERE ISN'T ANY PLACE FOR US TO GO TO.

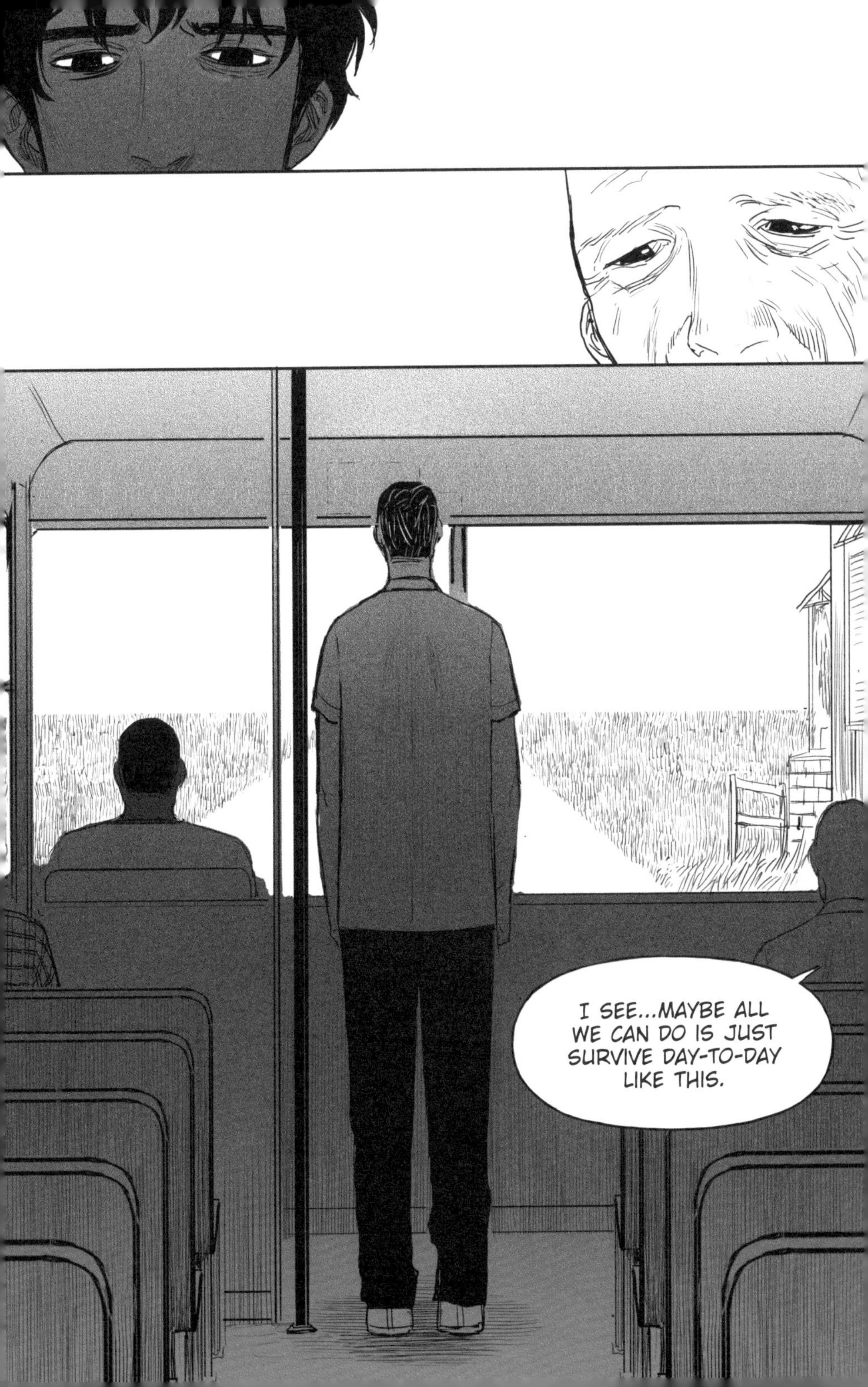
I SEE...MAYBE ALL WE CAN DO IS JUST SURVIVE DAY-TO-DAY LIKE THIS.

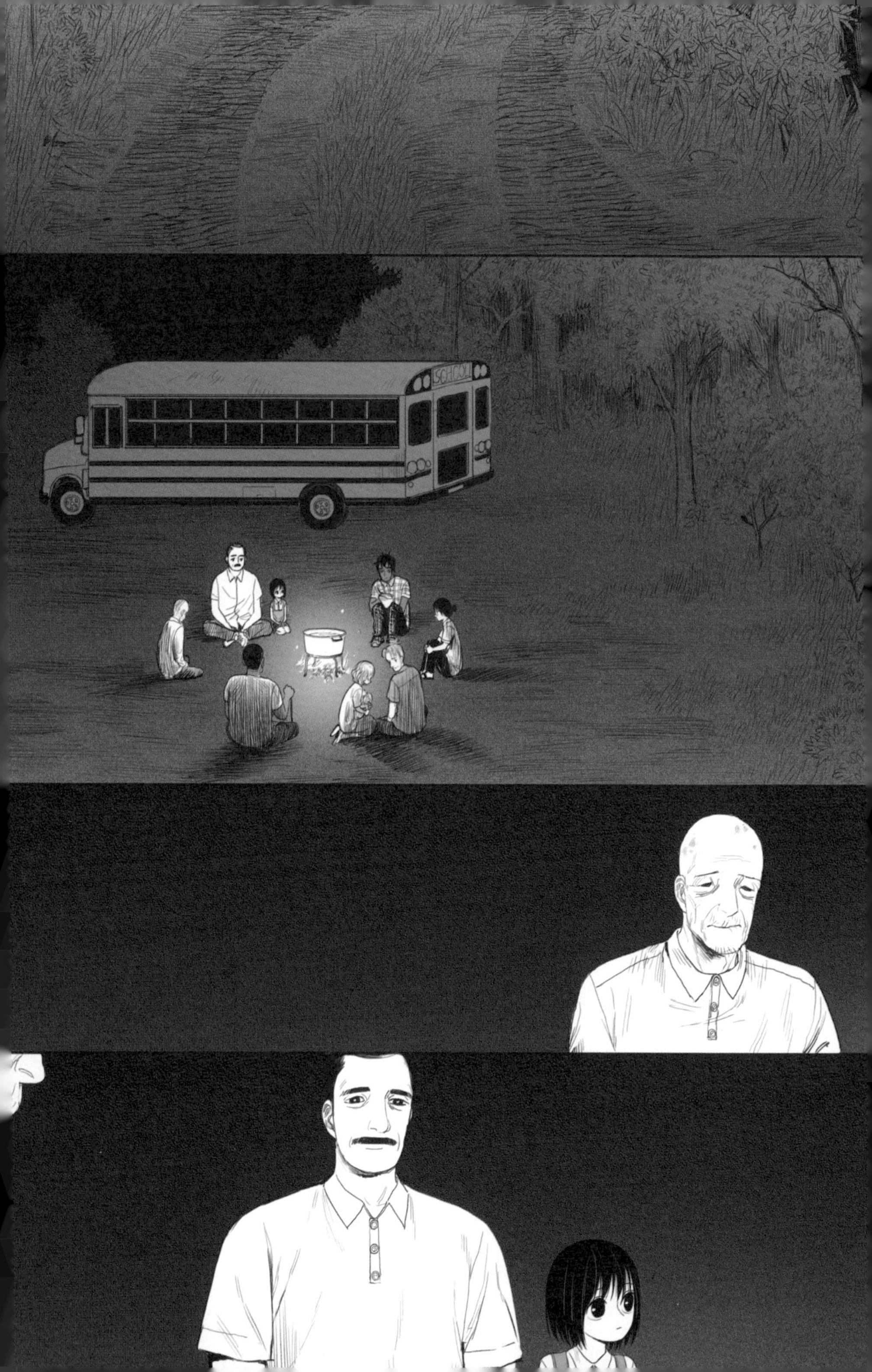
SCHOOL

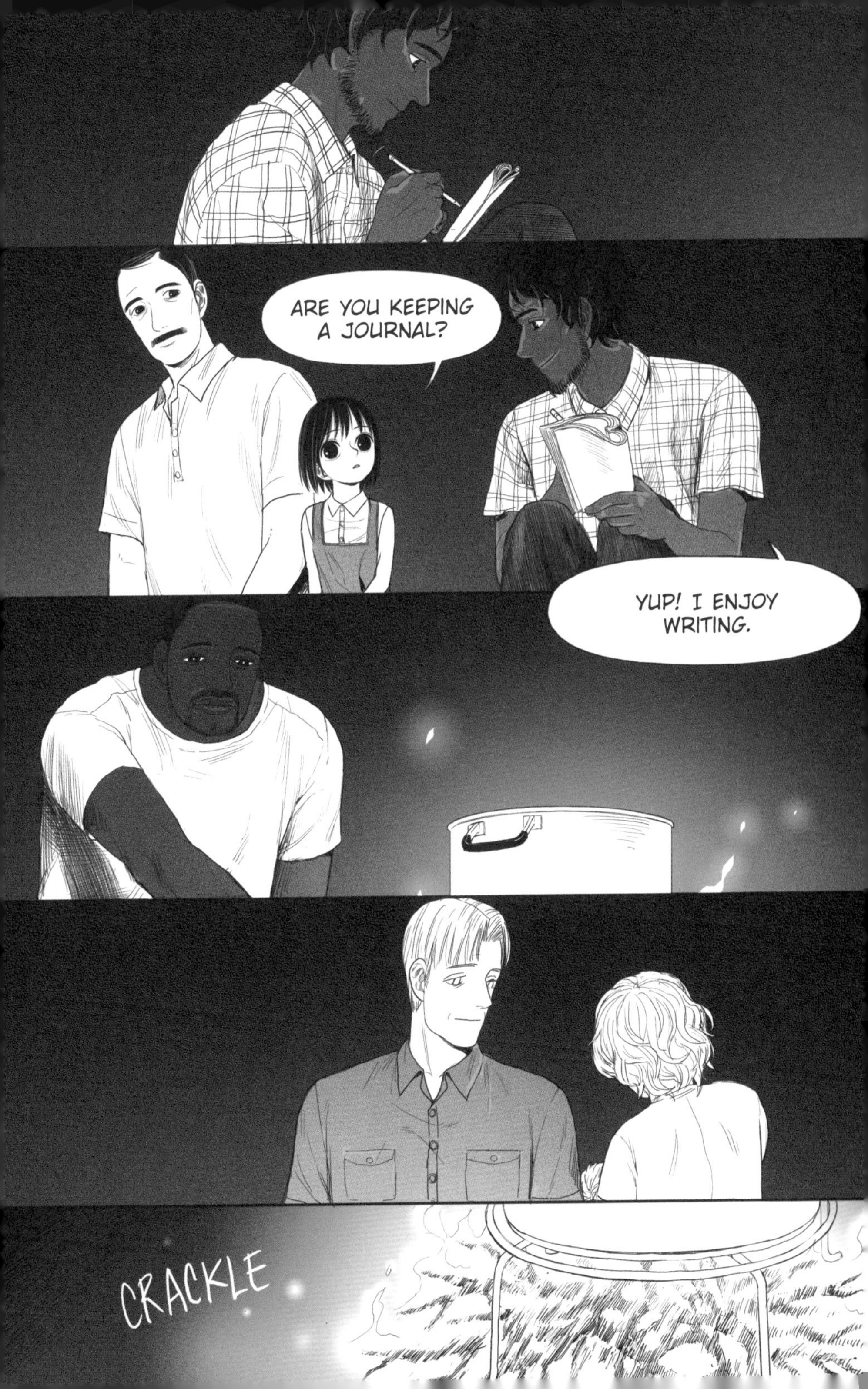
ARE YOU KEEPING A JOURNAL?
YUP! I ENJOY WRITING.
CRACKLE

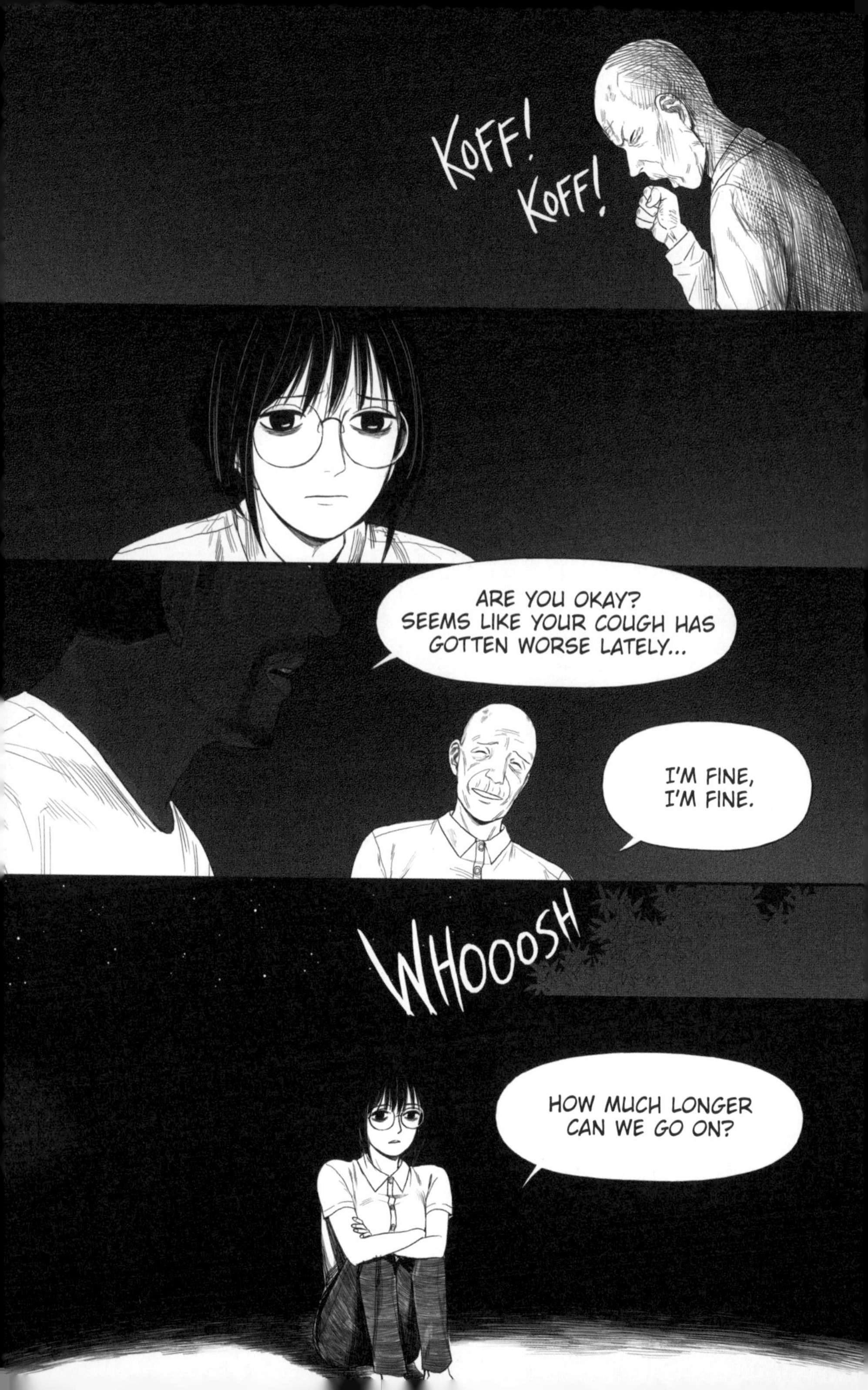
KOFF! KOFF!
ARE YOU OKAY? SEEMS LIKE YOUR COUGH HAS GOTTEN WORSE LATELY...
I'M FINE, I'M FINE.
WHOOOSH
HOW MUCH LONGER CAN WE GO ON?

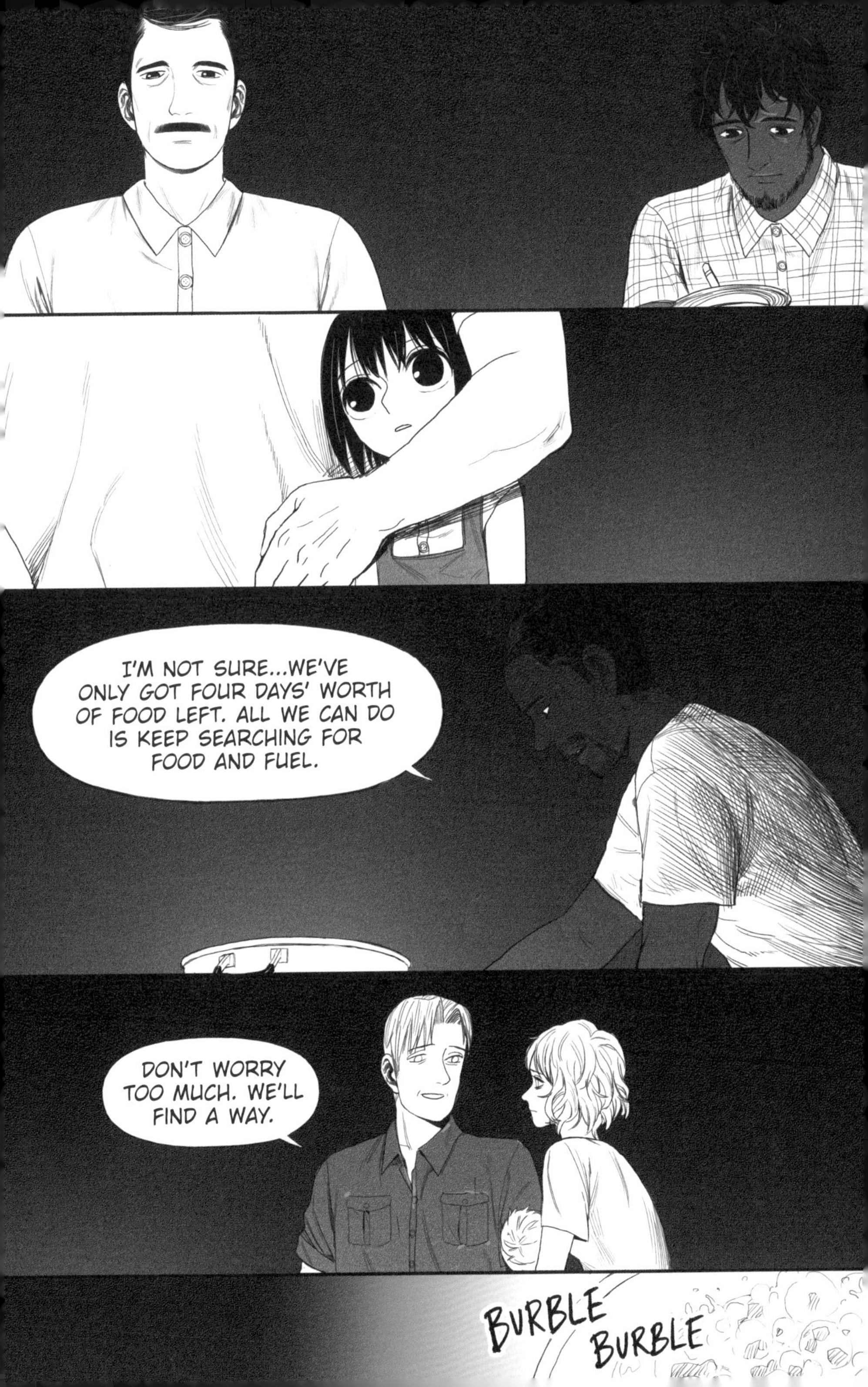
I'M NOT SURE...WE'VE ONLY GOT FOUR DAYS' WORTH OF FOOD LEFT. ALL WE CAN DO IS KEEP SEARCHING FOR FOOD AND FUEL.
DON'T WORRY TOO MUCH. WE'LL FIND A WAY.
BURBLE BURBLE

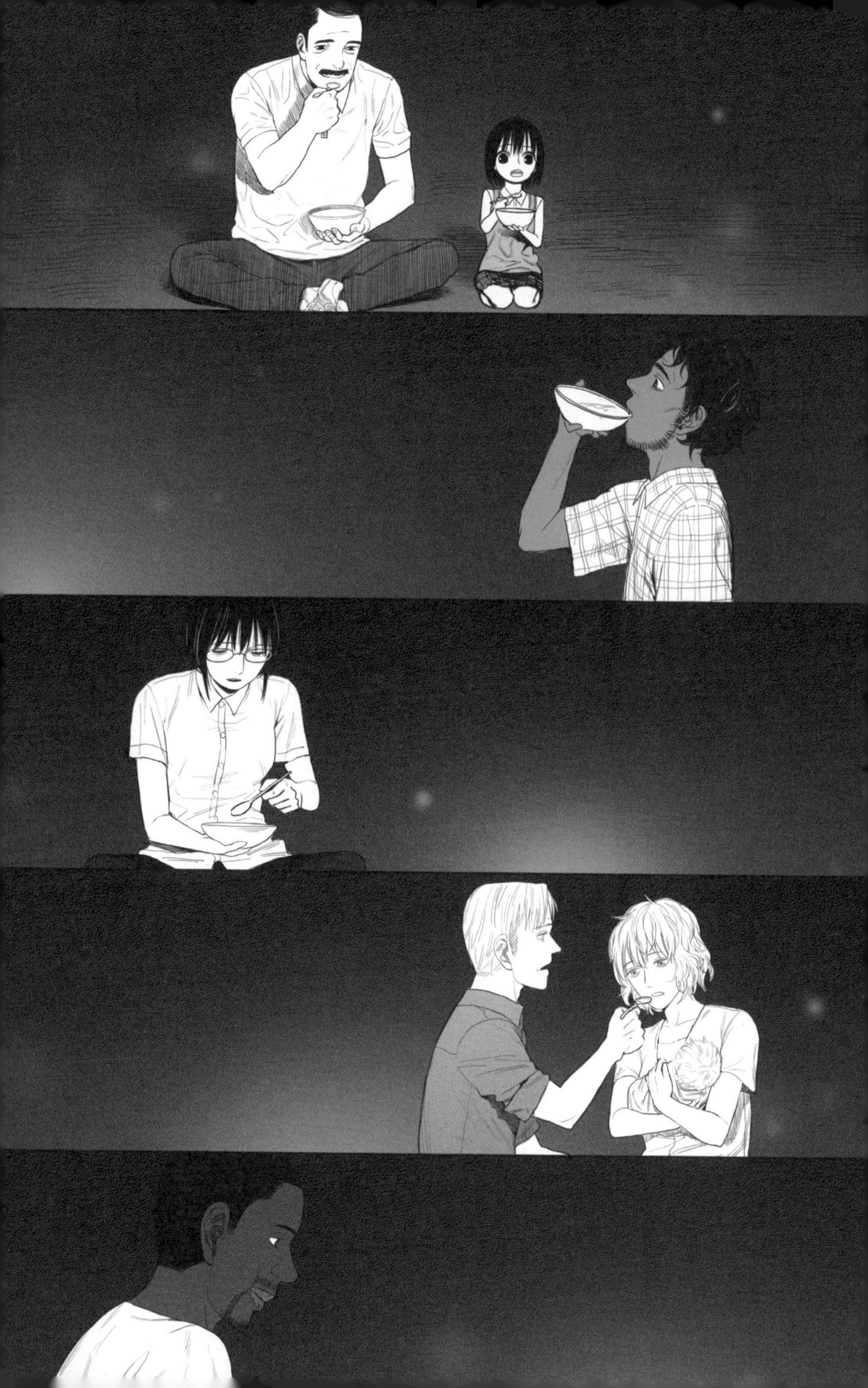

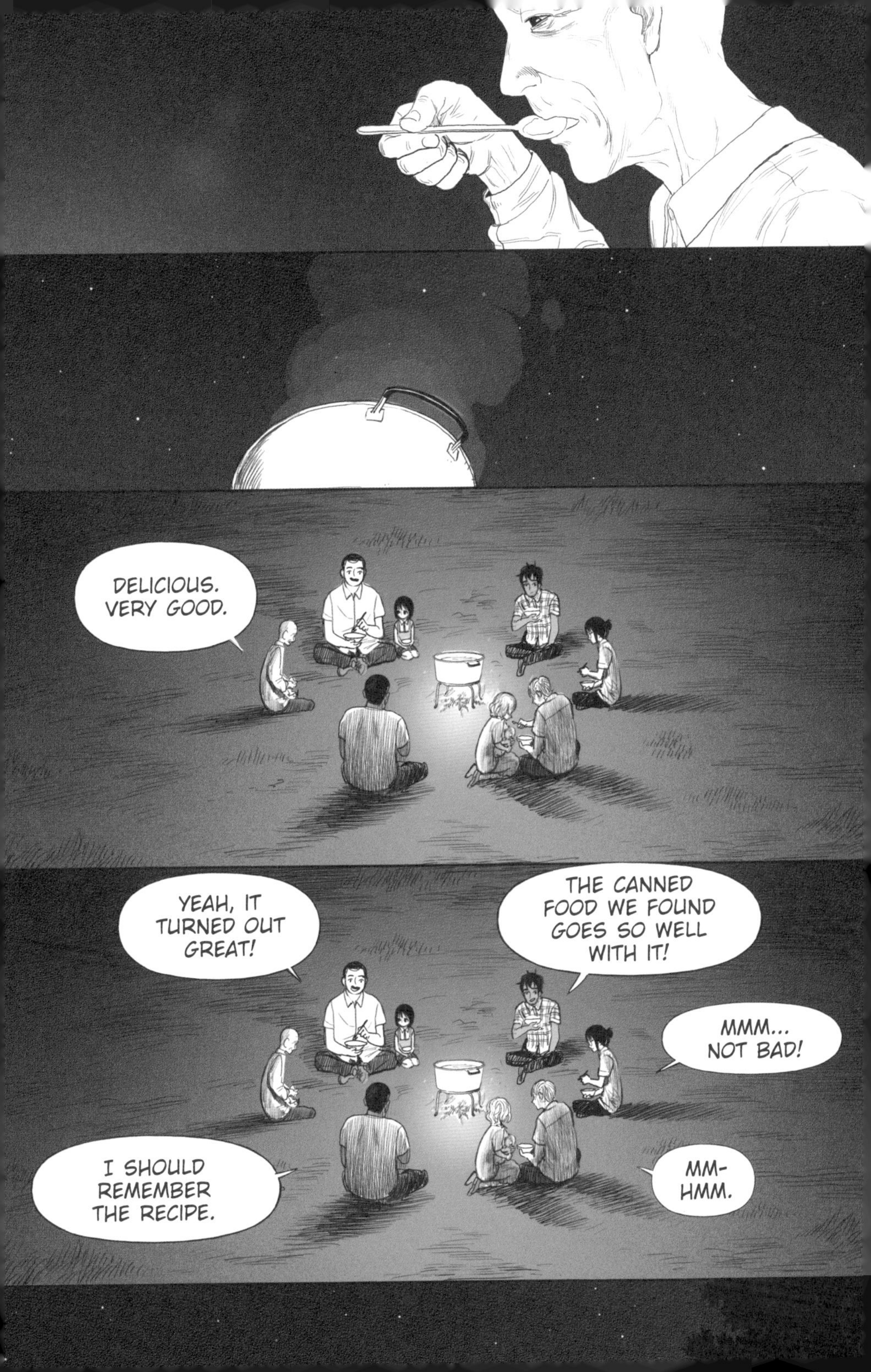
DELICIOUS. VERY GOOD.
YEAH, IT TURNED OUT GREAT!
THE CANNED FOOD WE FOUND GOES SO WELL WITH IT!
MMM... NOT BAD!
I SHOULD REMEMBER THE RECIPE.
MM-HMM.

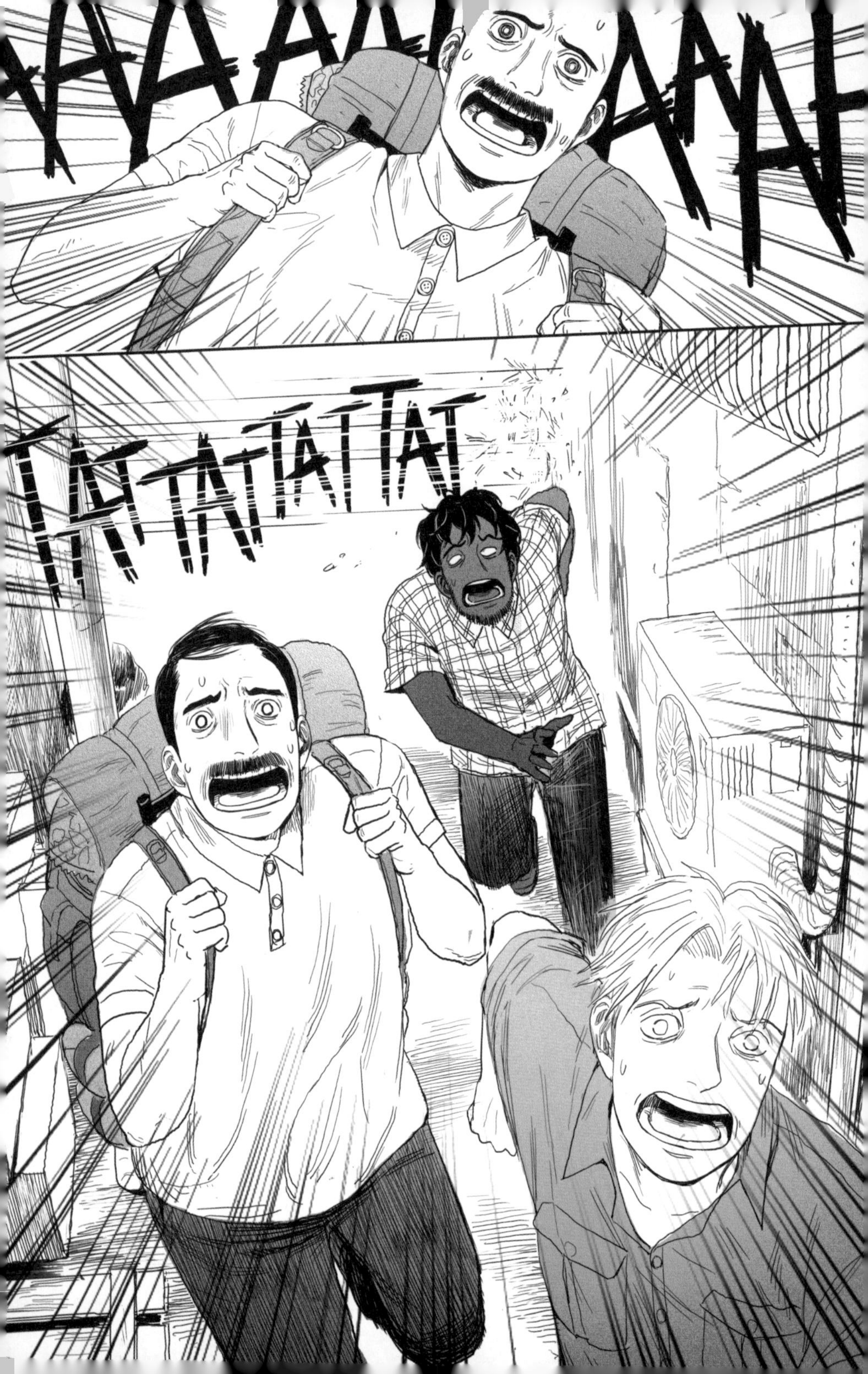

AAAAAAAAAAH
TAT TAT TAT TAT

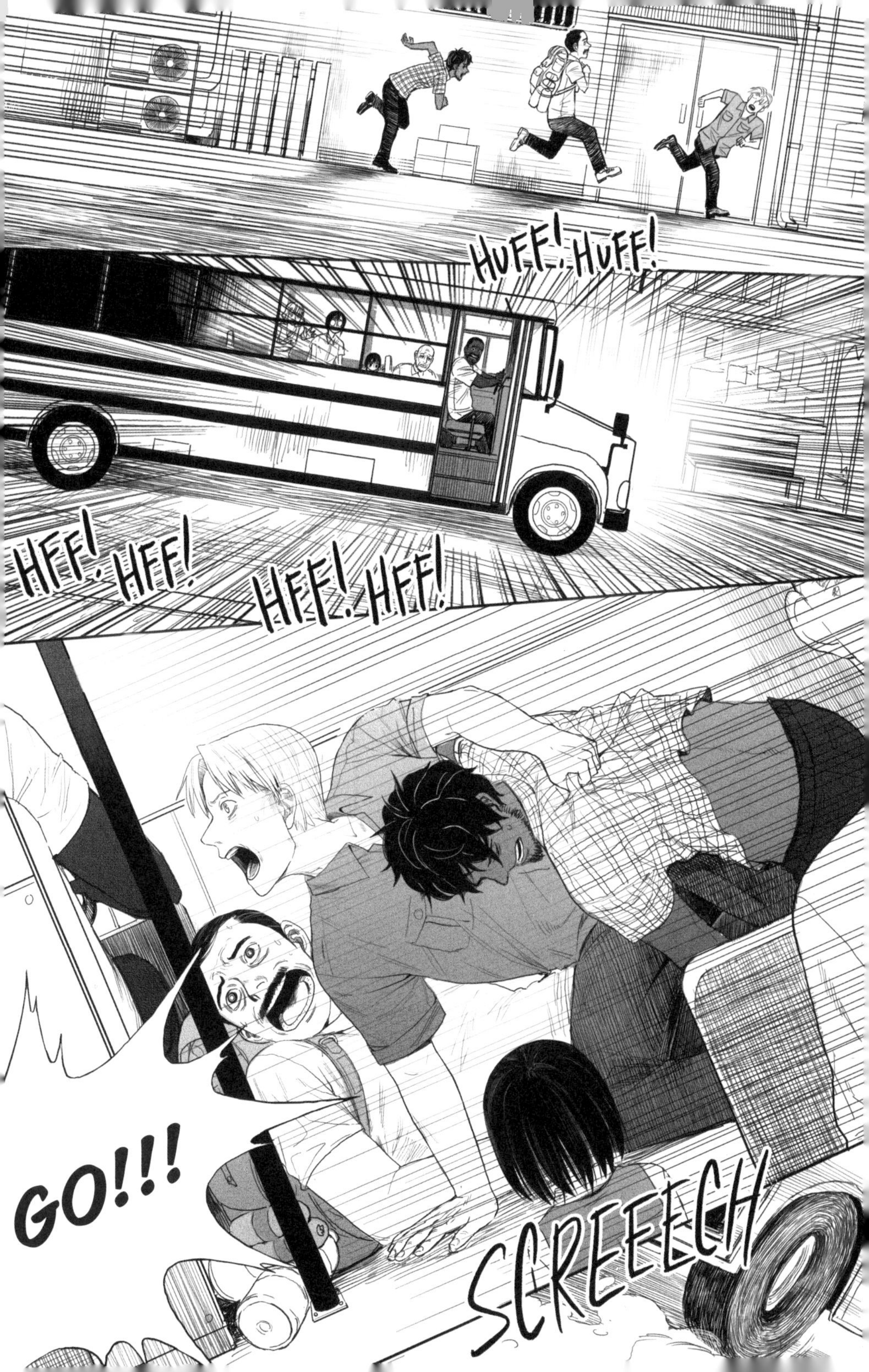
HUFF! HUFF!
HFF! HFF!
HFF! HFF!
GO!!!
SCREEECH

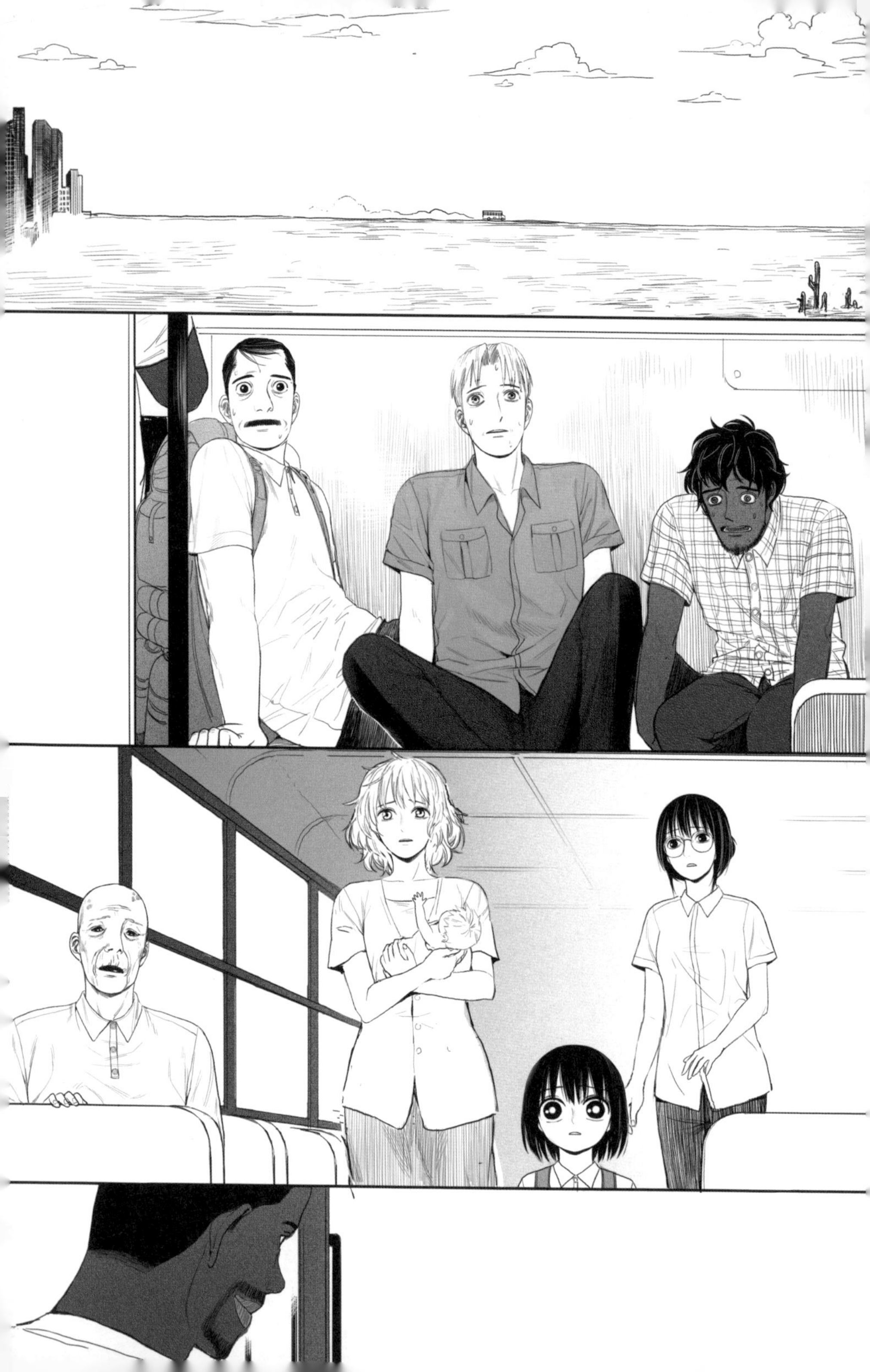

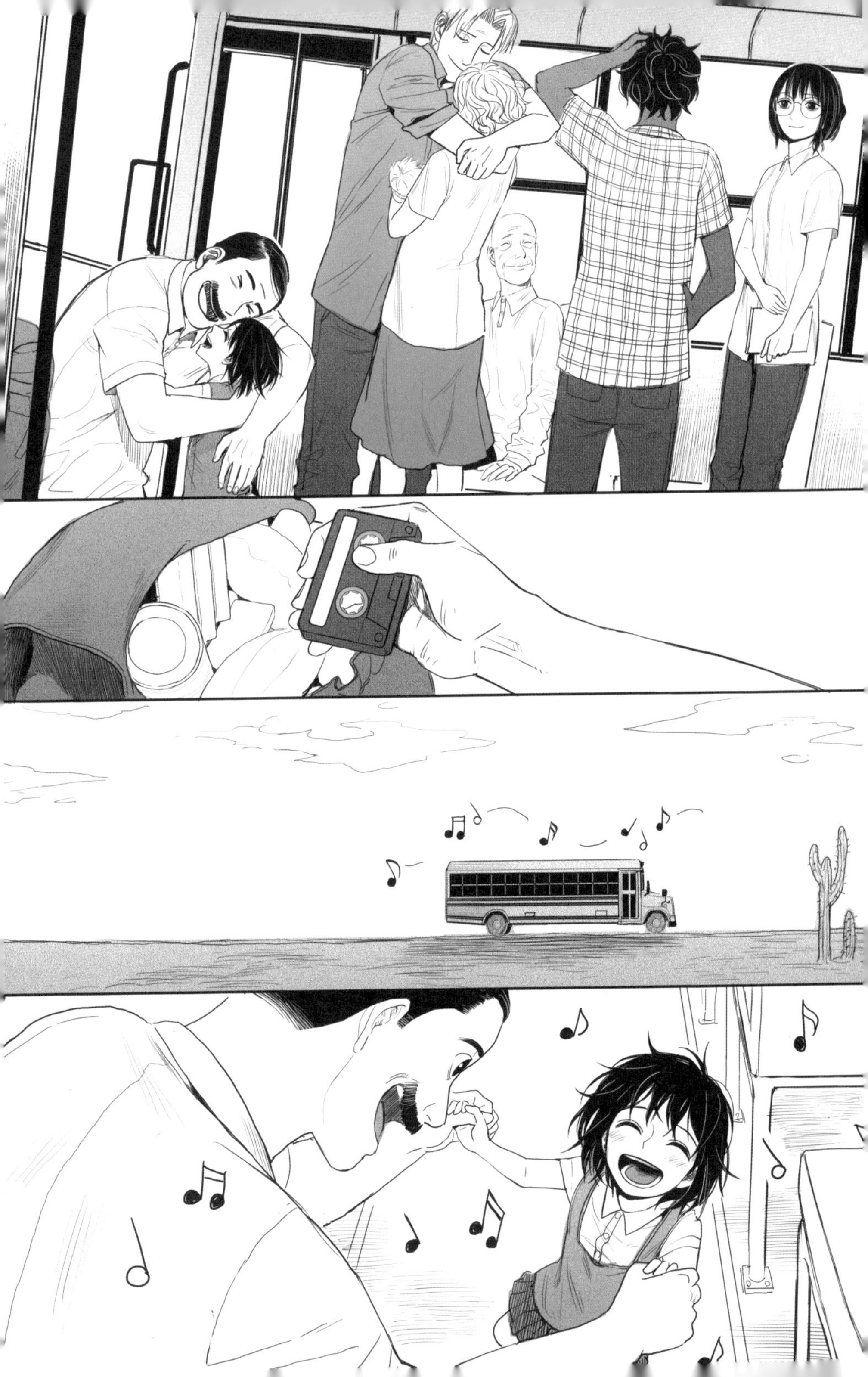

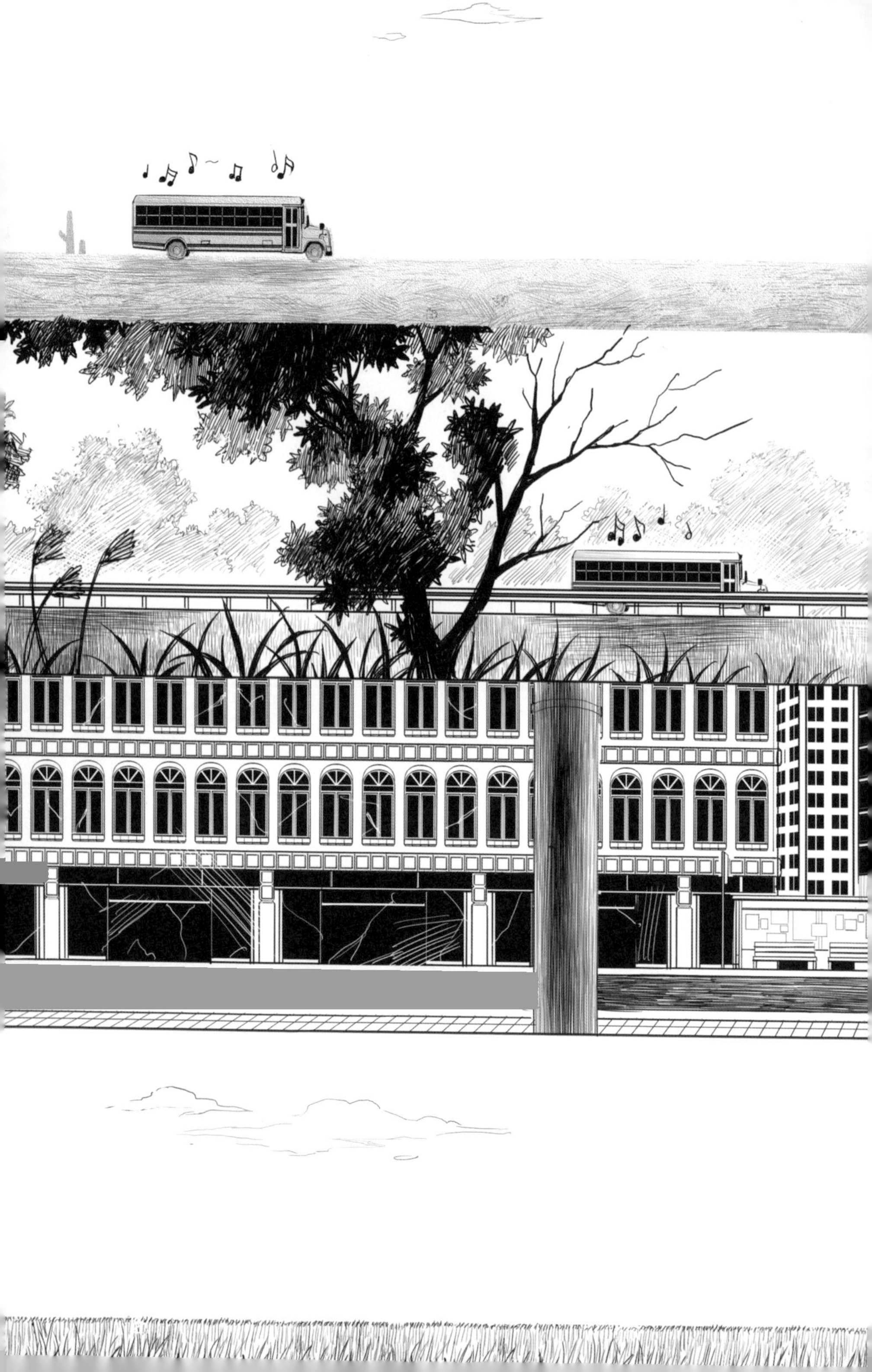

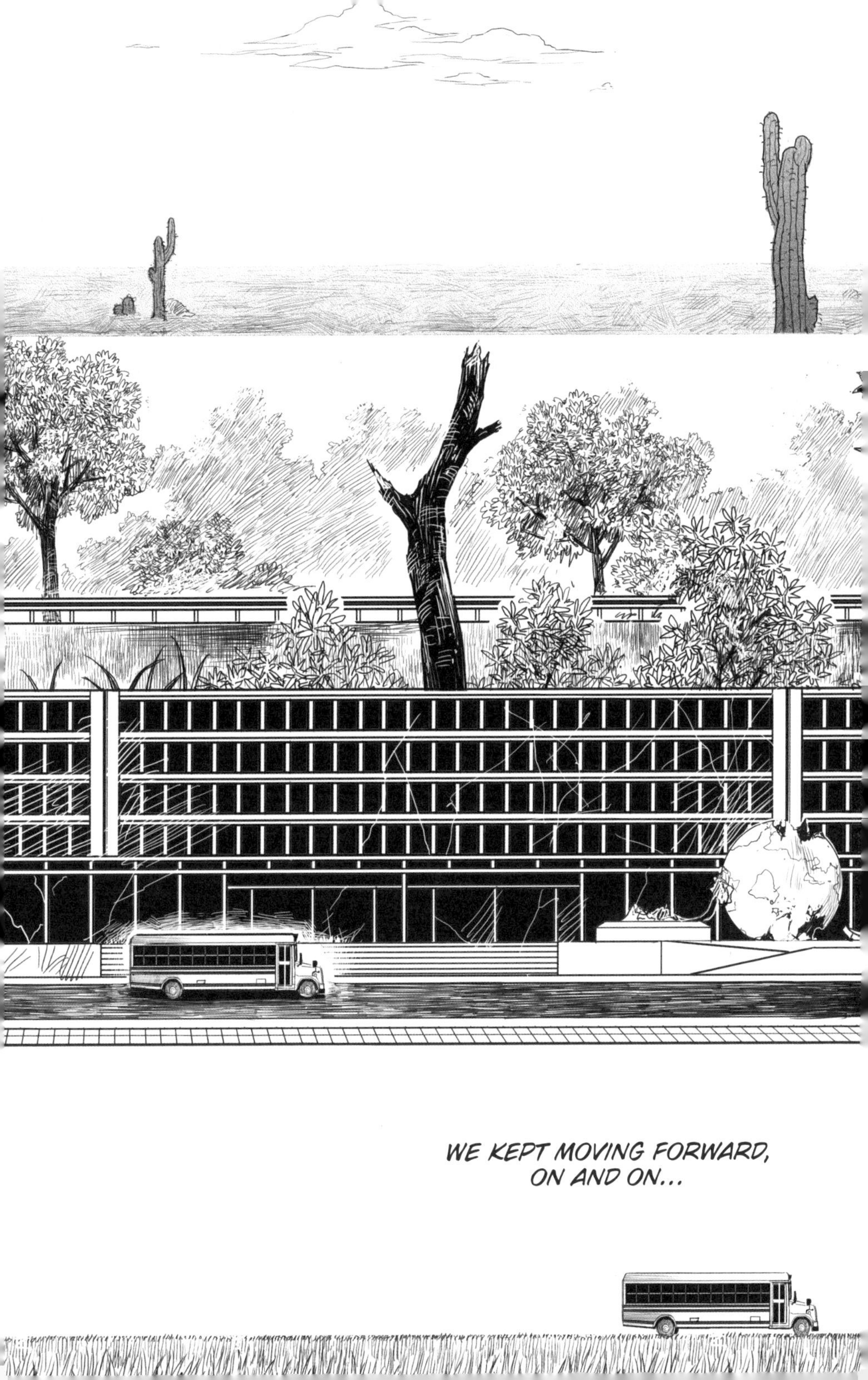
WE KEPT MOVING FORWARD,
ON AND ON...

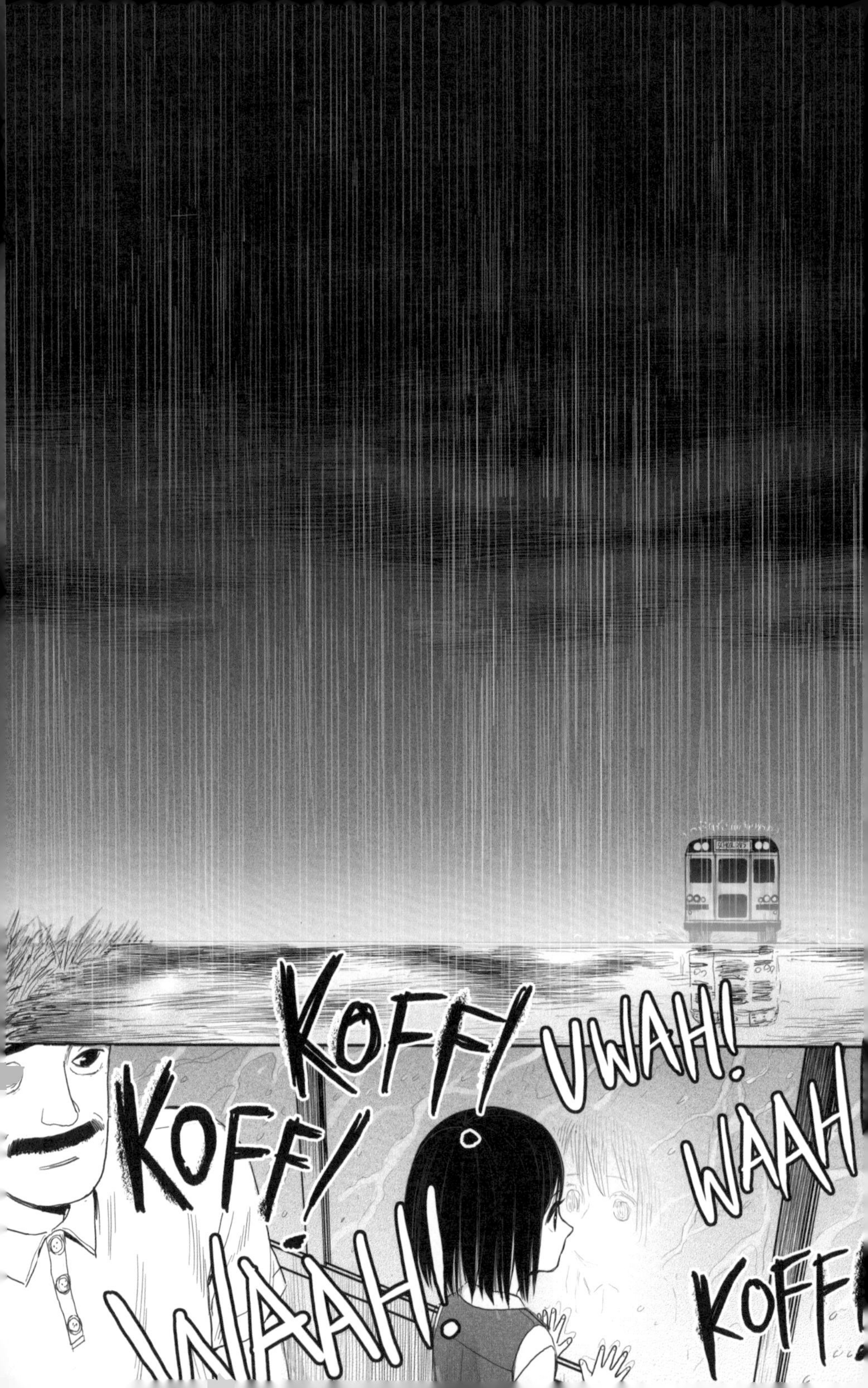
UWAH!
WAAH
KOFF!
KOFF!
KOFF!
WAAH!

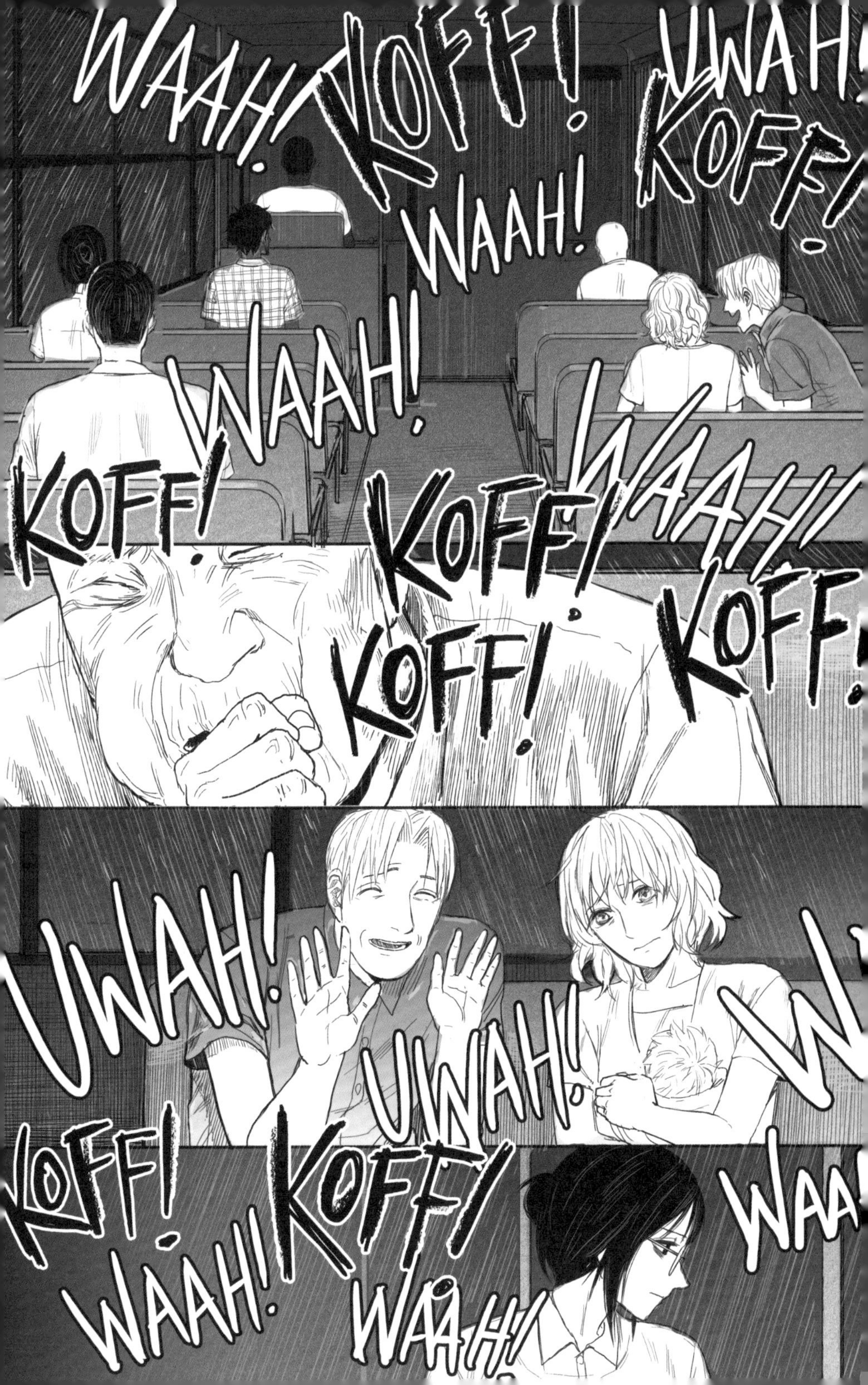
UWAH!
KOFF!
KOFF!
WAAH!
WAAH!
WAAH!
WAAH!
KOFF!
KOFF!
KOFF!
KOFF!
KOFF!
UWAH!
UWAH!
KOFF!
KOFF!
WAAH!
WAAH!

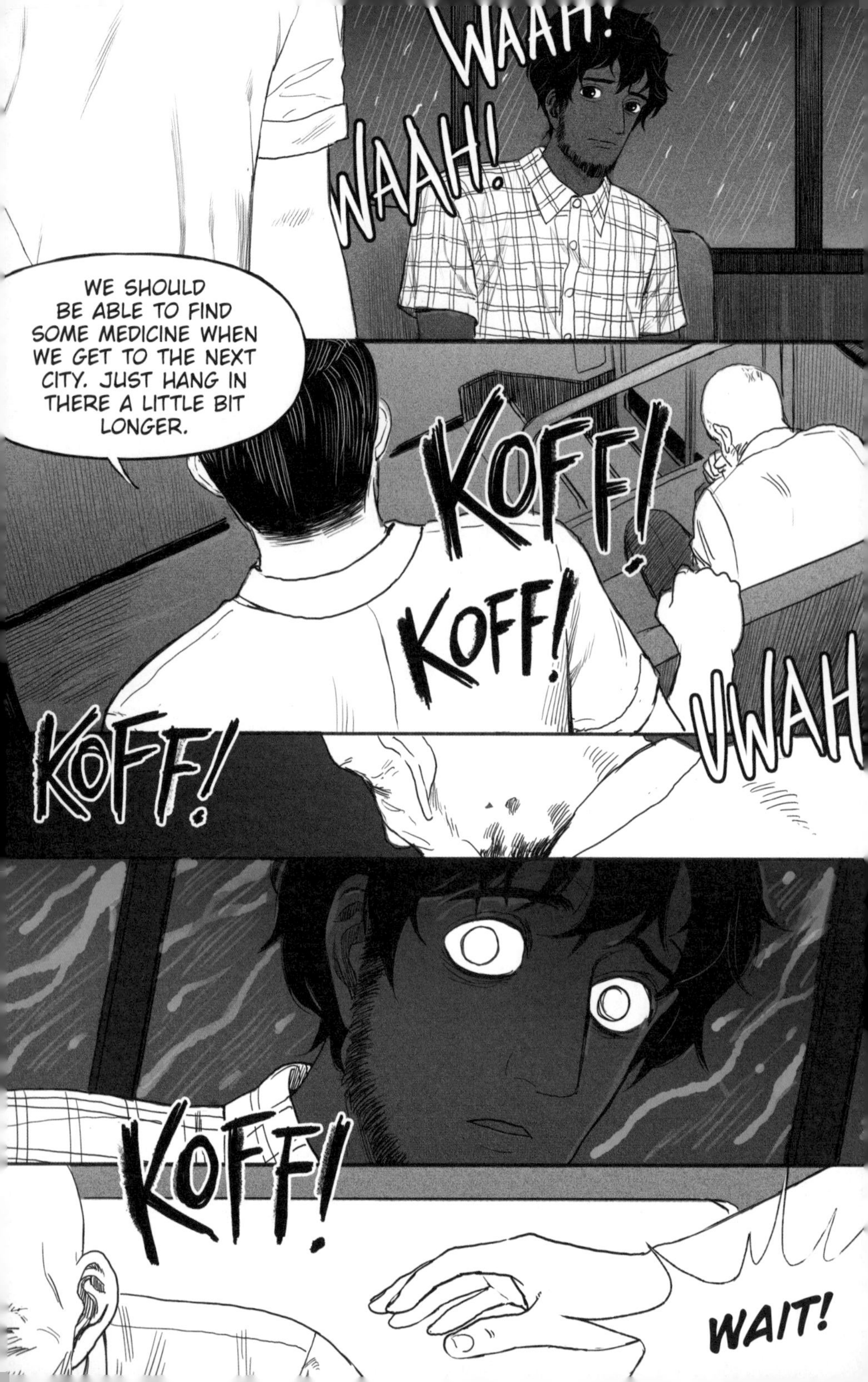
WAAH!
WAAH!
WE SHOULD BE ABLE TO FIND SOME MEDICINE WHEN WE GET TO THE NEXT CITY. JUST HANG IN THERE A LITTLE BIT LONGER.
KOFF!
KOFF!
KOFF!
WAH
KOFF!
WAIT!

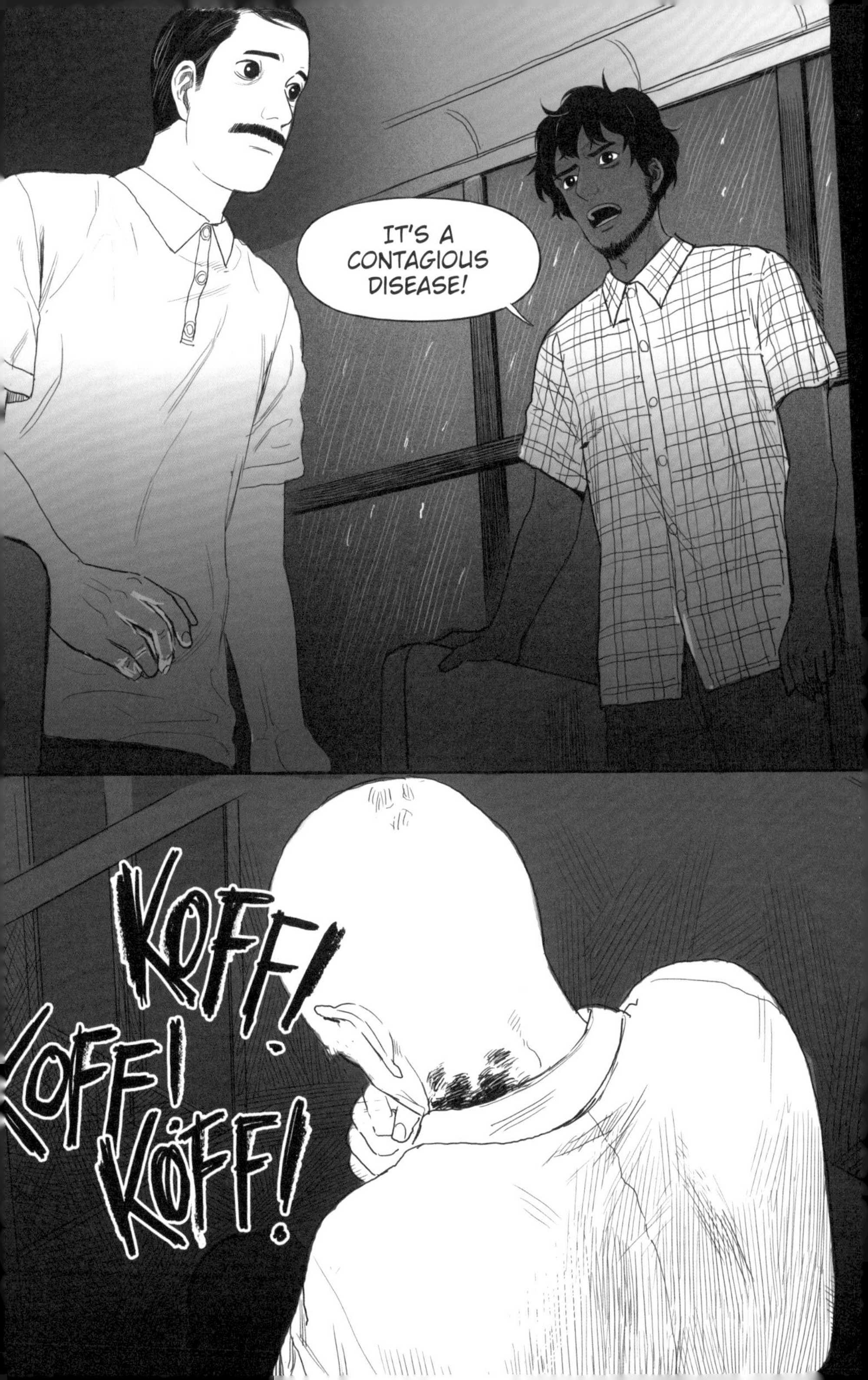
IT'S A CONTAGIOUS DISEASE!
KOFF!
KOFF!
KOFF!

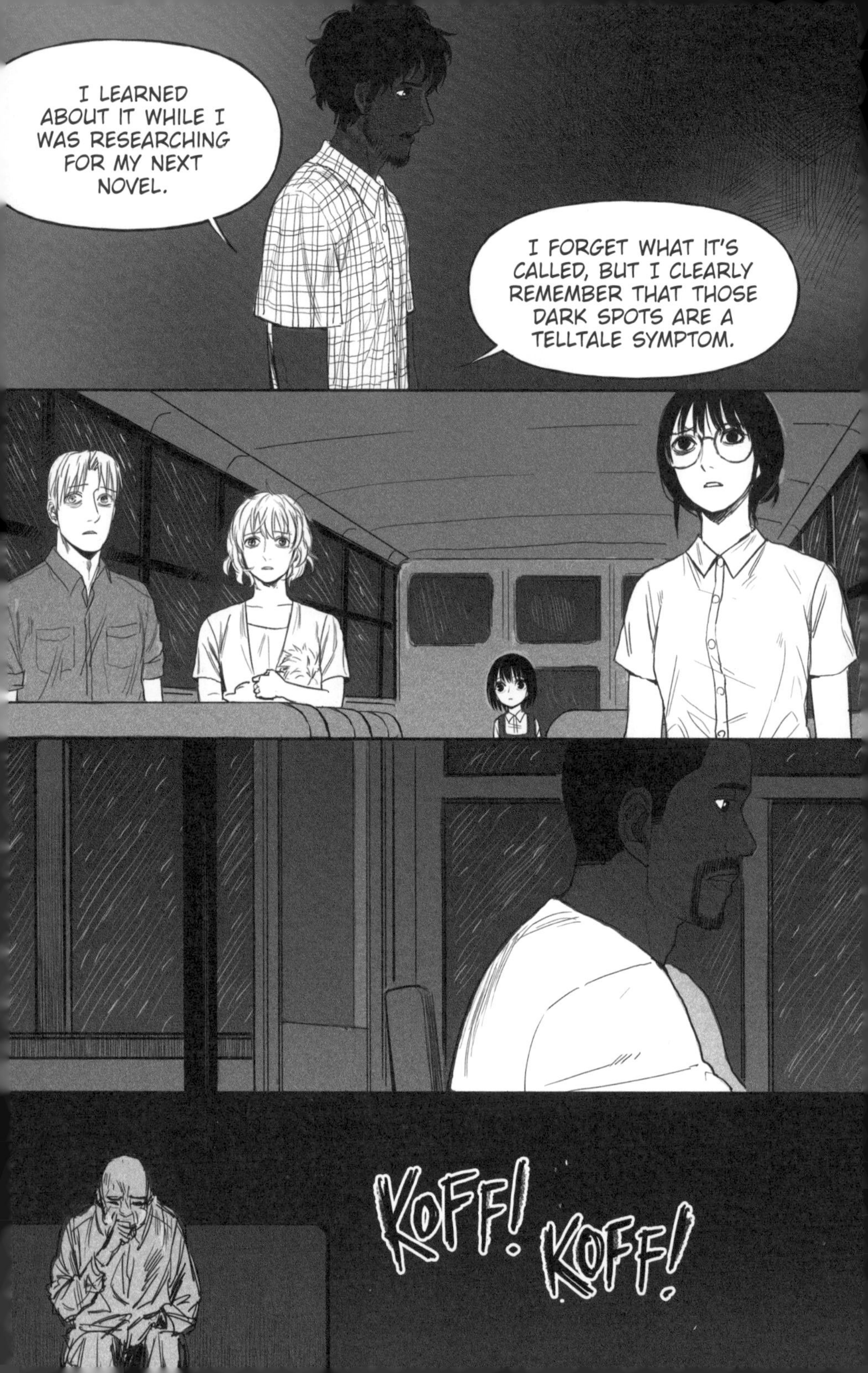
I LEARNED ABOUT IT WHILE I WAS RESEARCHING FOR MY NEXT NOVEL.
I FORGET WHAT IT'S CALLED, BUT I CLEARLY REMEMBER THAT THOSE DARK SPOTS ARE A TELLTALE SYMPTOM.
KOFF! KOFF!

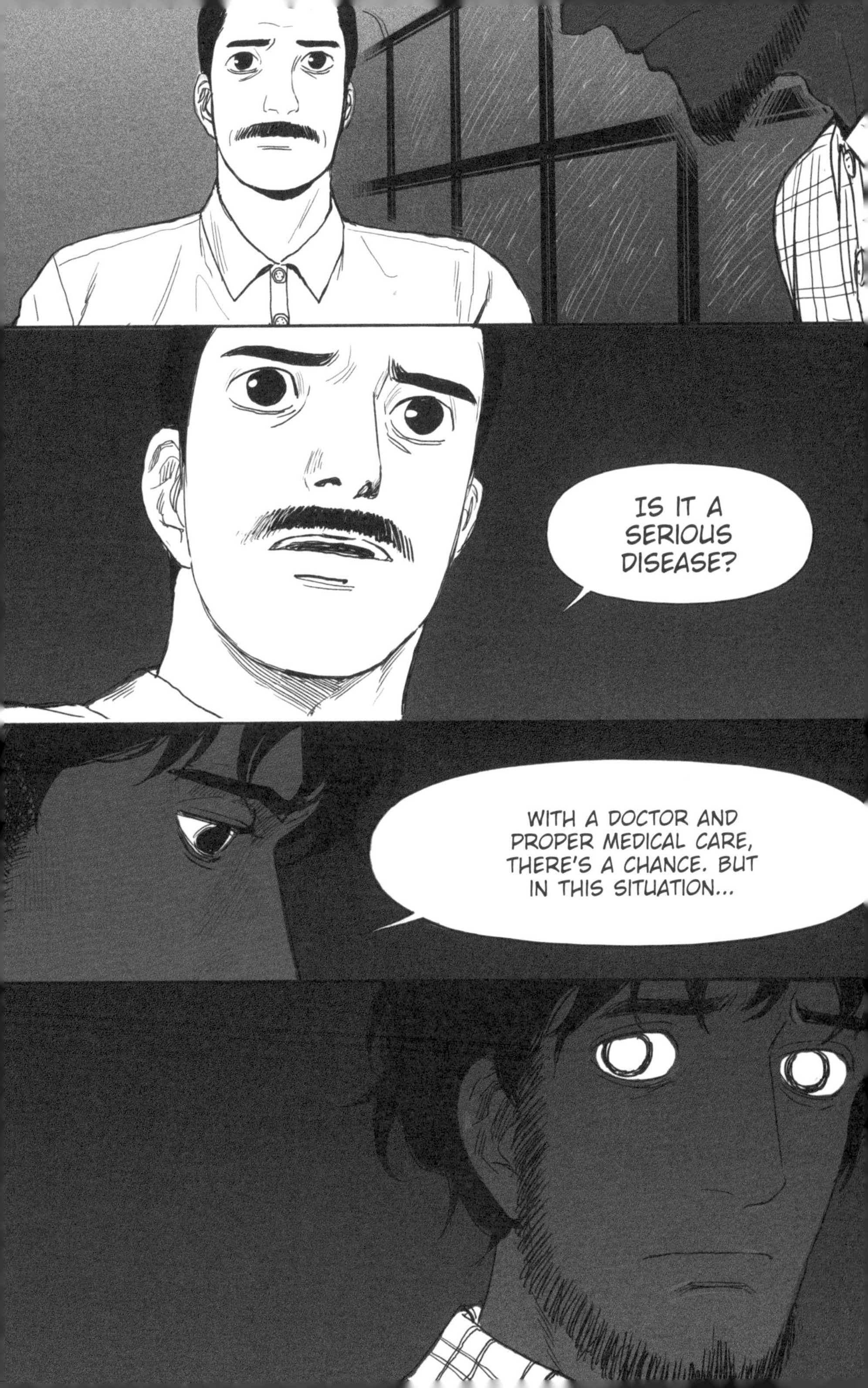
IS IT A SERIOUS DISEASE?
WITH A DOCTOR AND PROPER MEDICAL CARE, THERE'S A CHANCE. BUT IN THIS SITUATION...

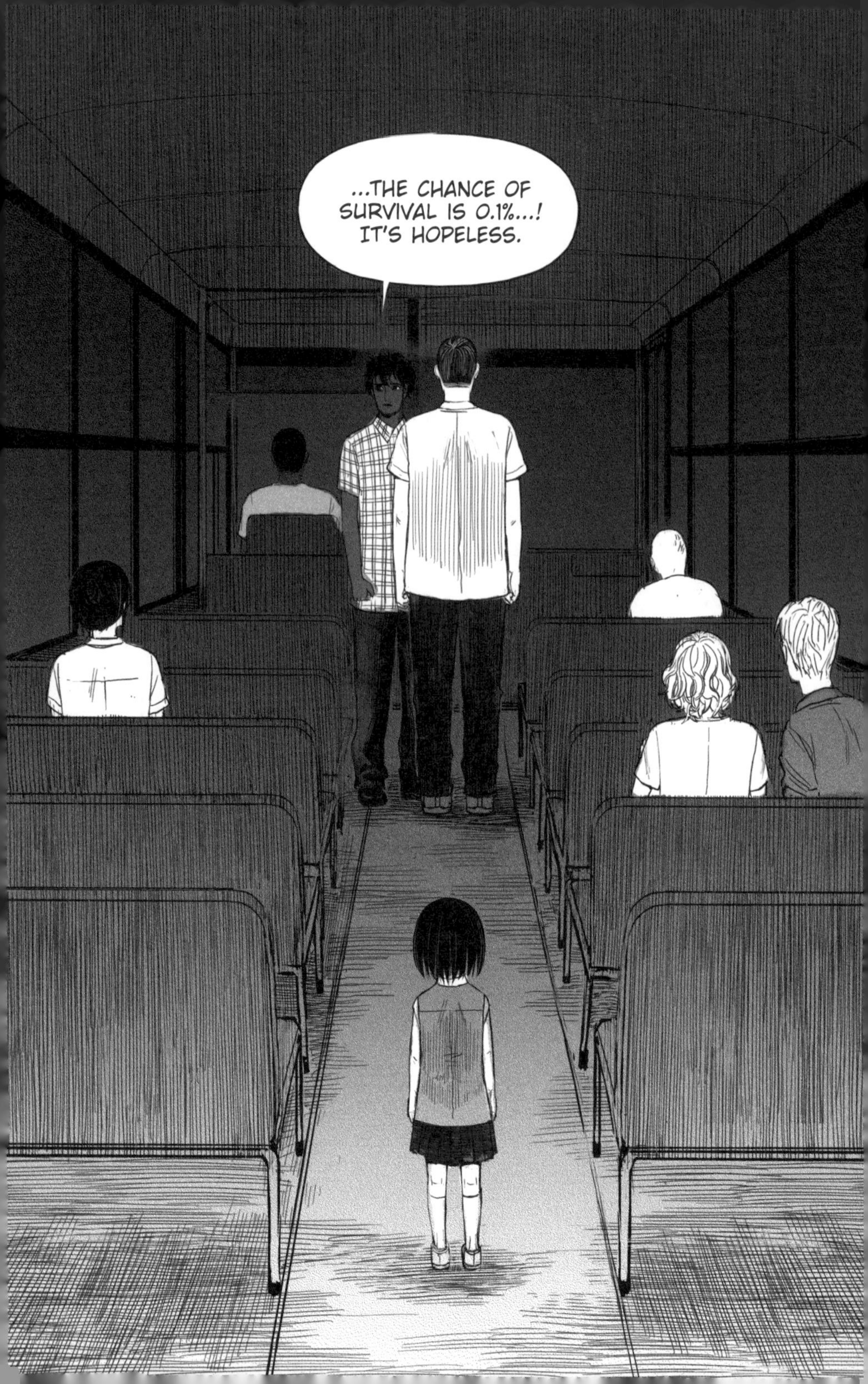
...THE CHANCE OF SURVIVAL IS 0.1%...! IT'S HOPELESS.

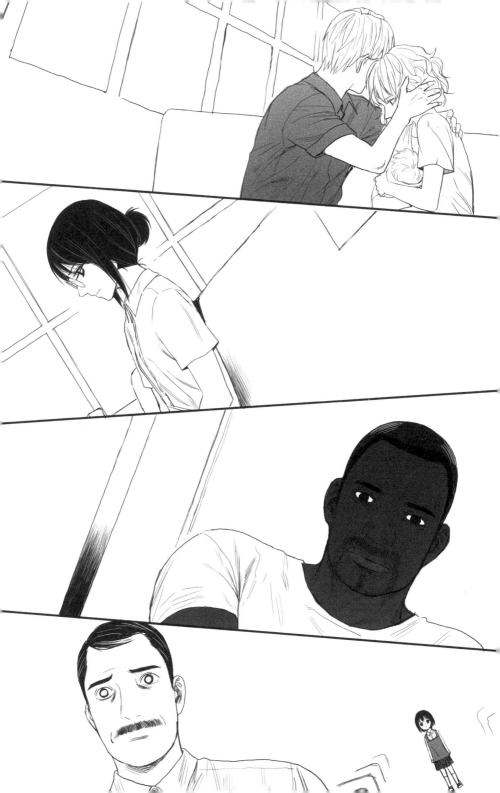

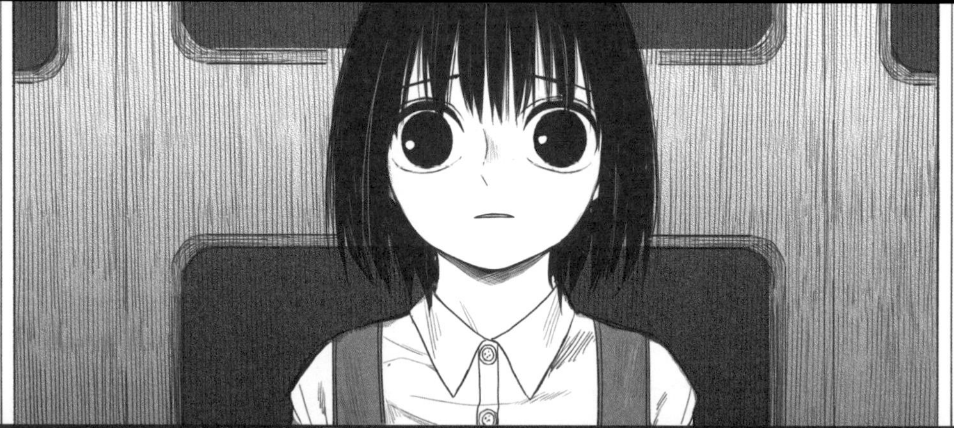
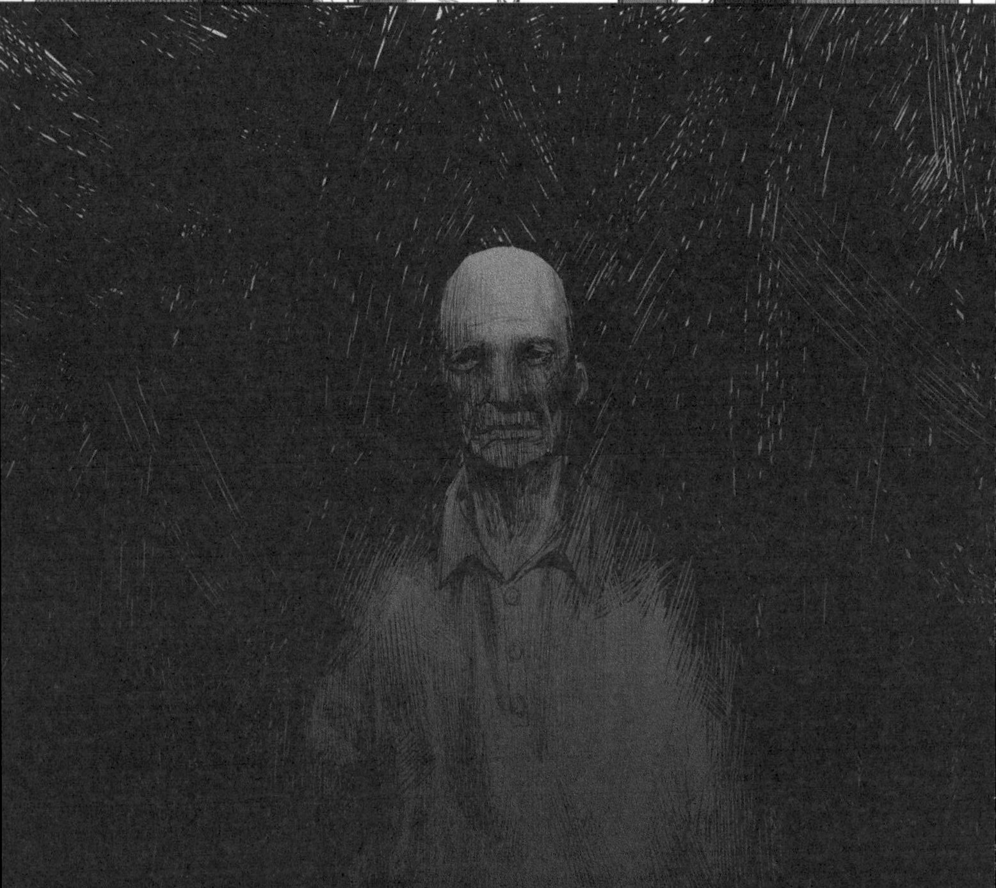

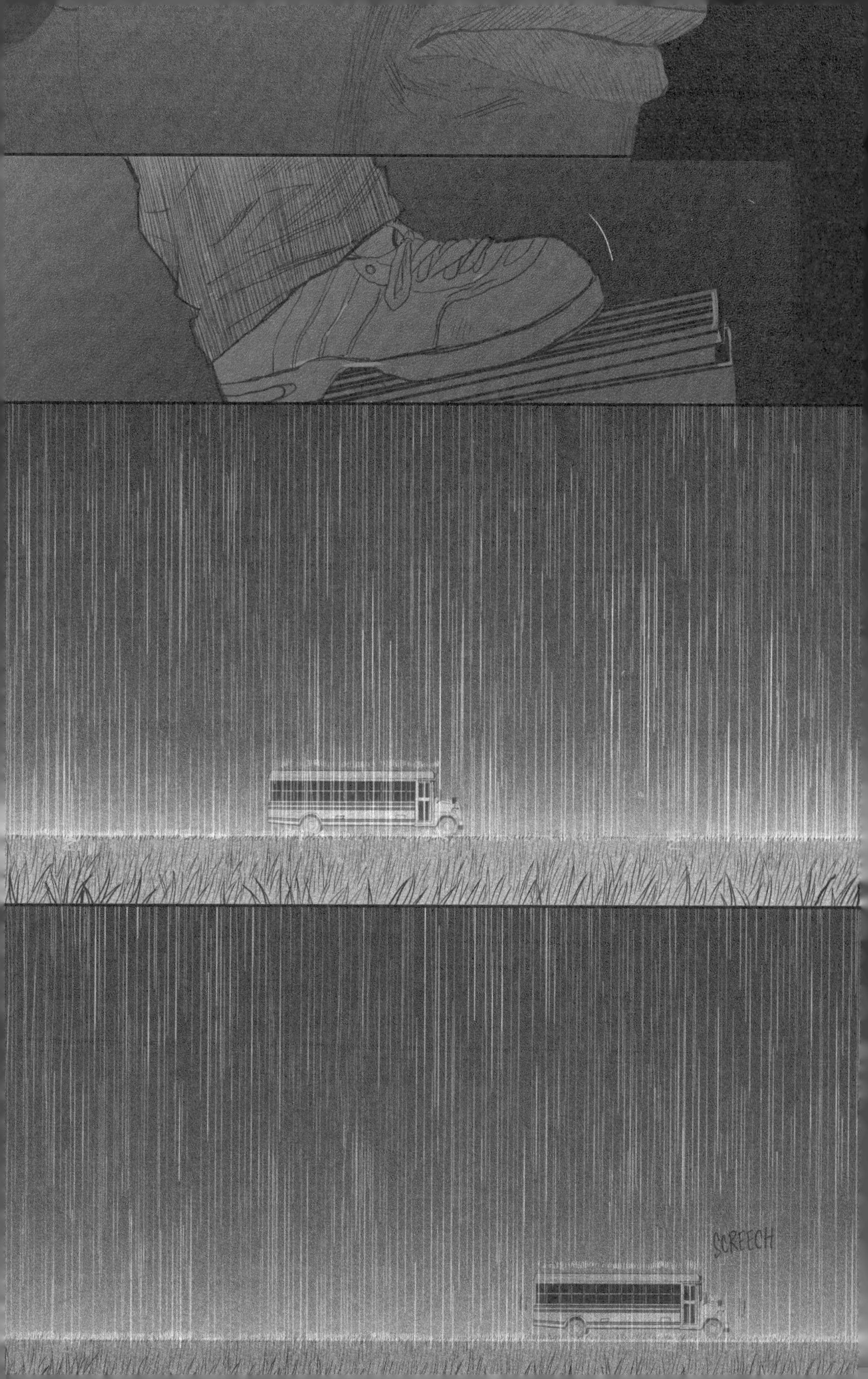
SCREECH

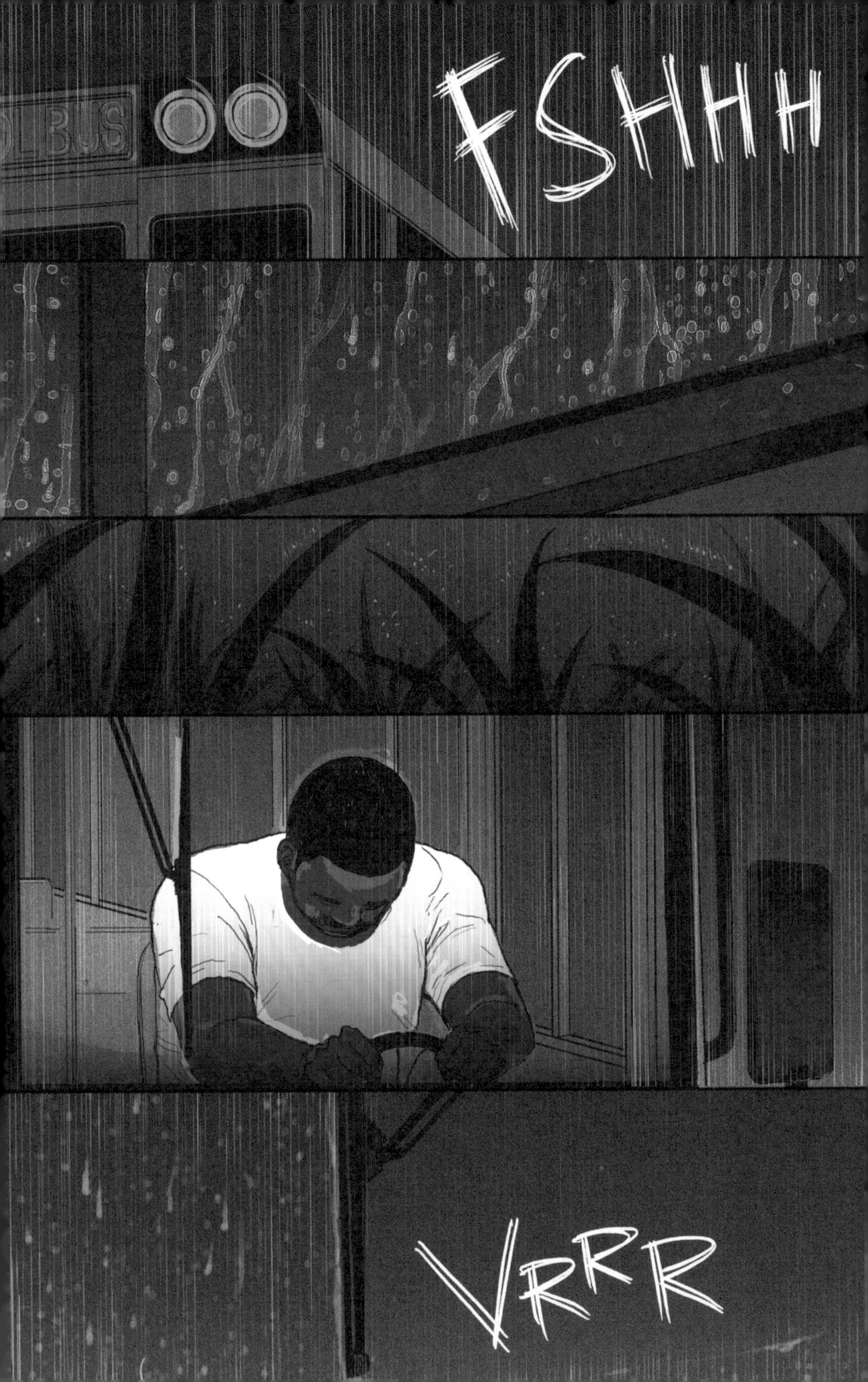

OL BUS
FSHHH
VRRR

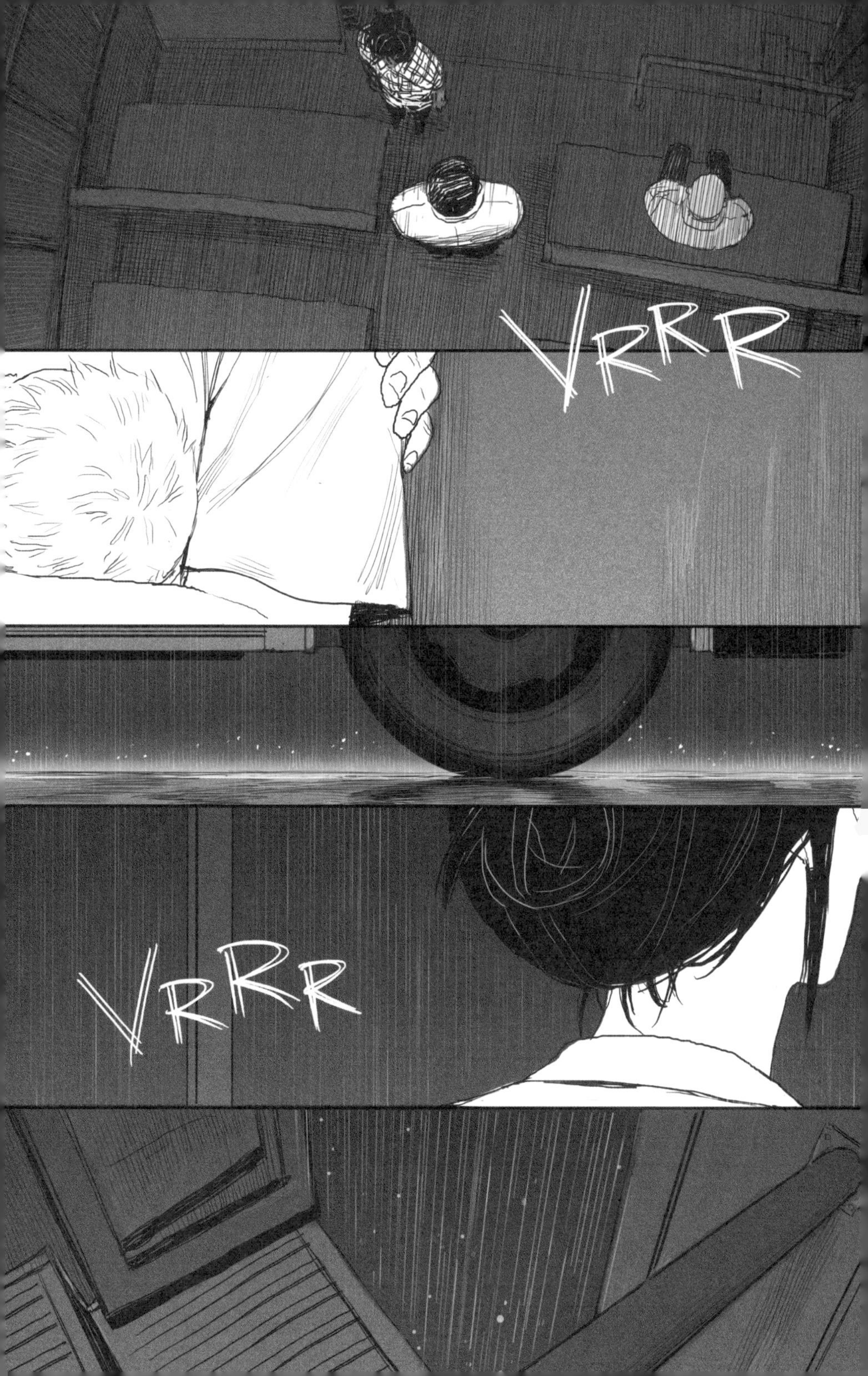
VRRR
VRRR

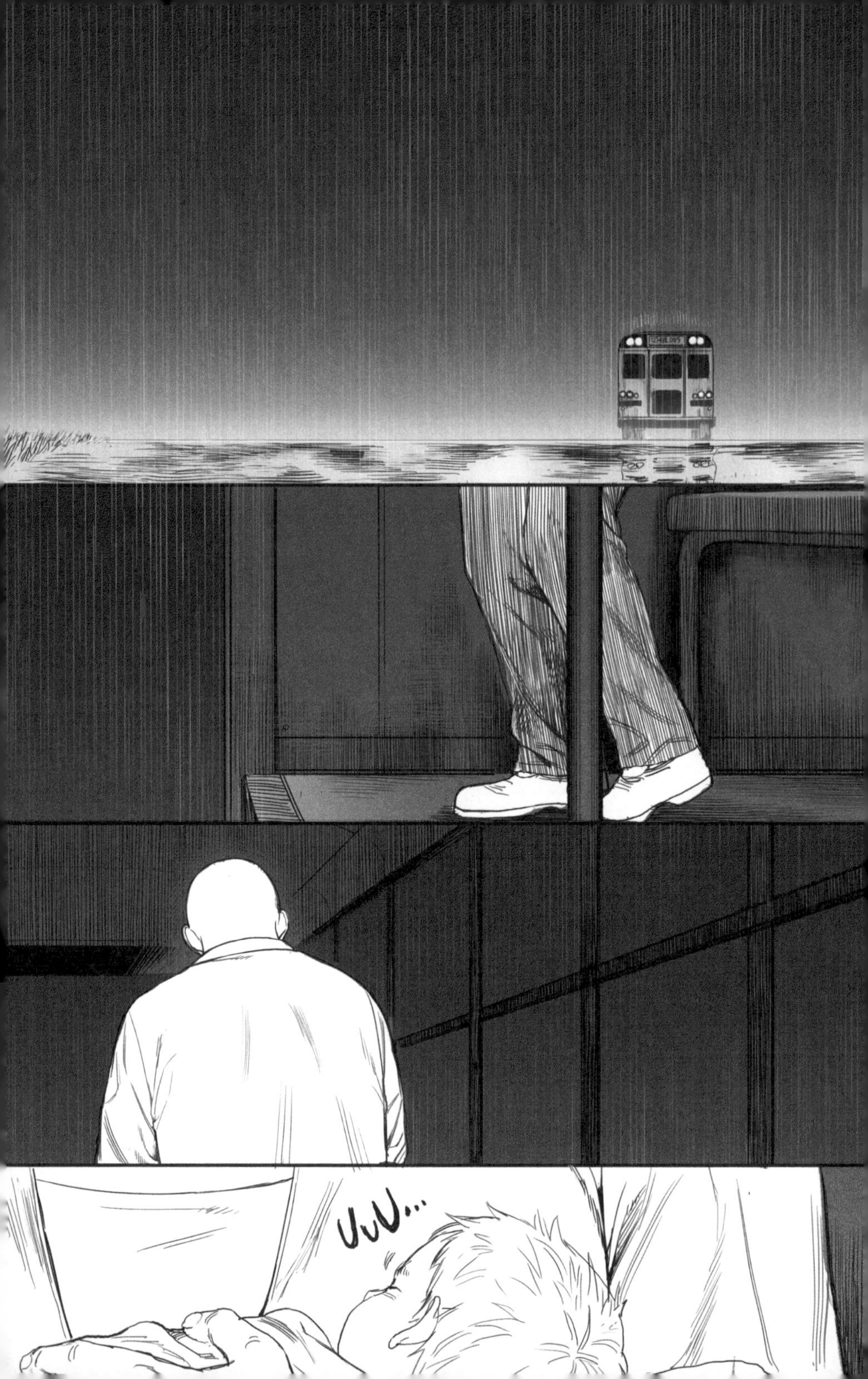
UUU...

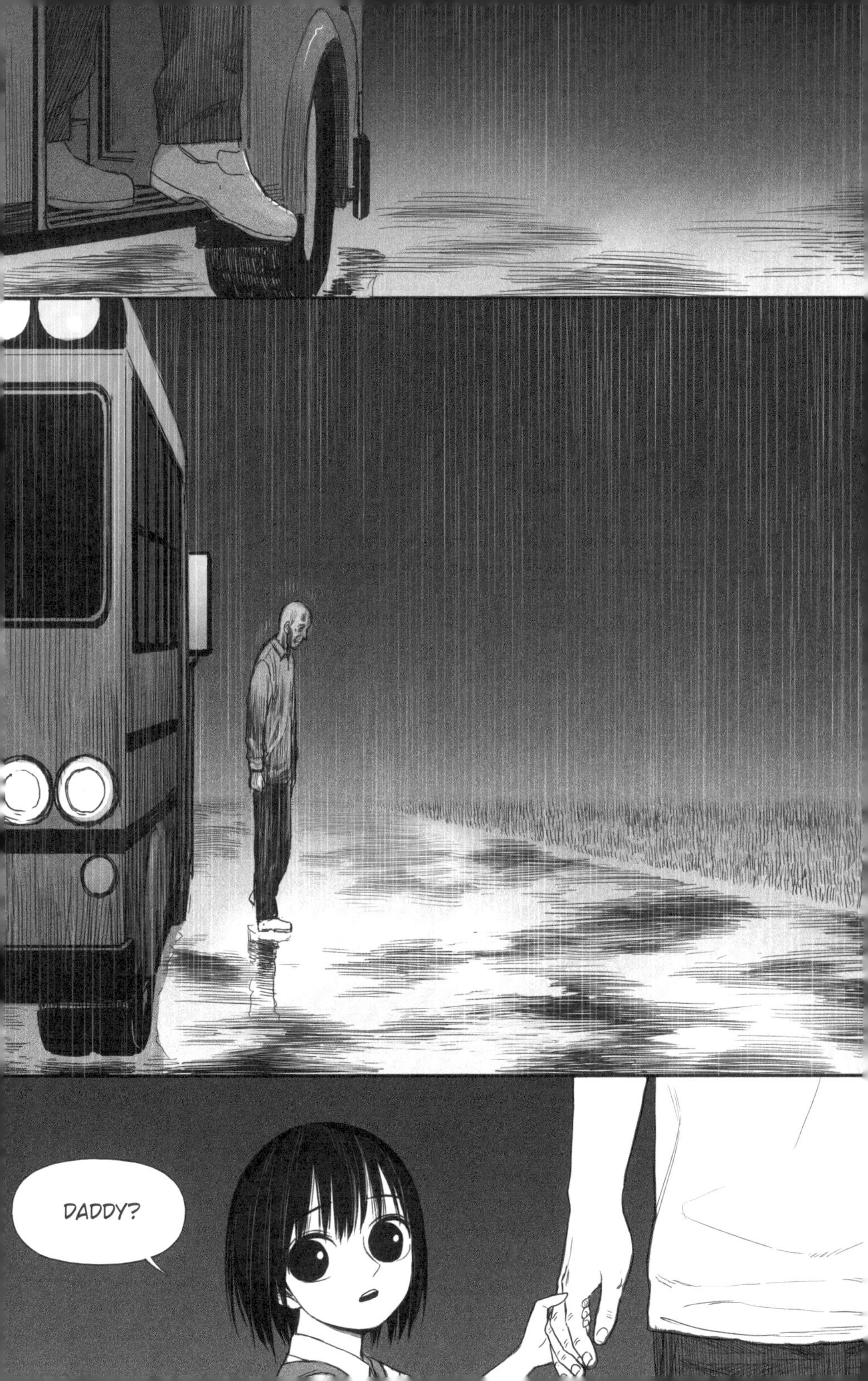
DADDY?

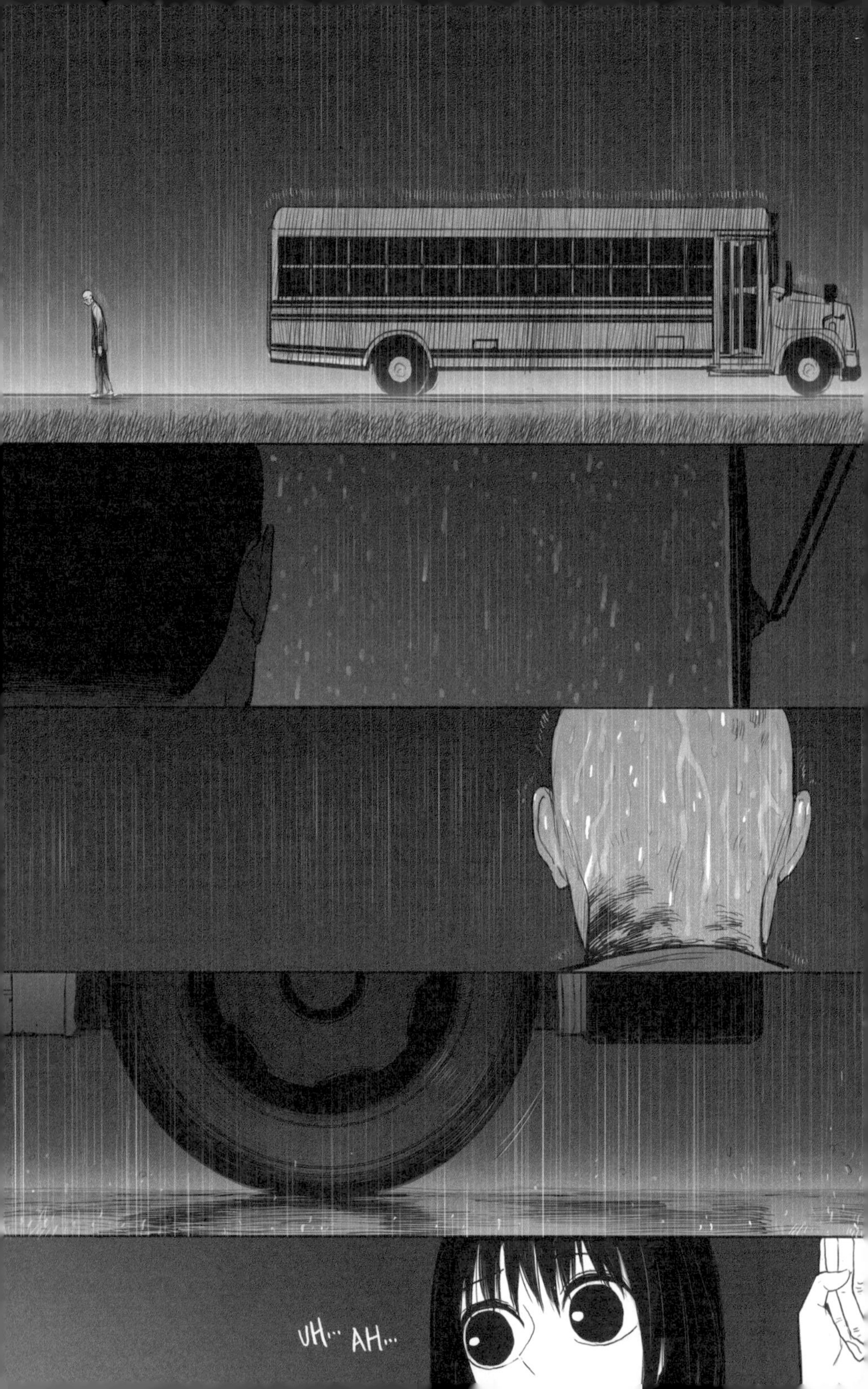
UH... AH...

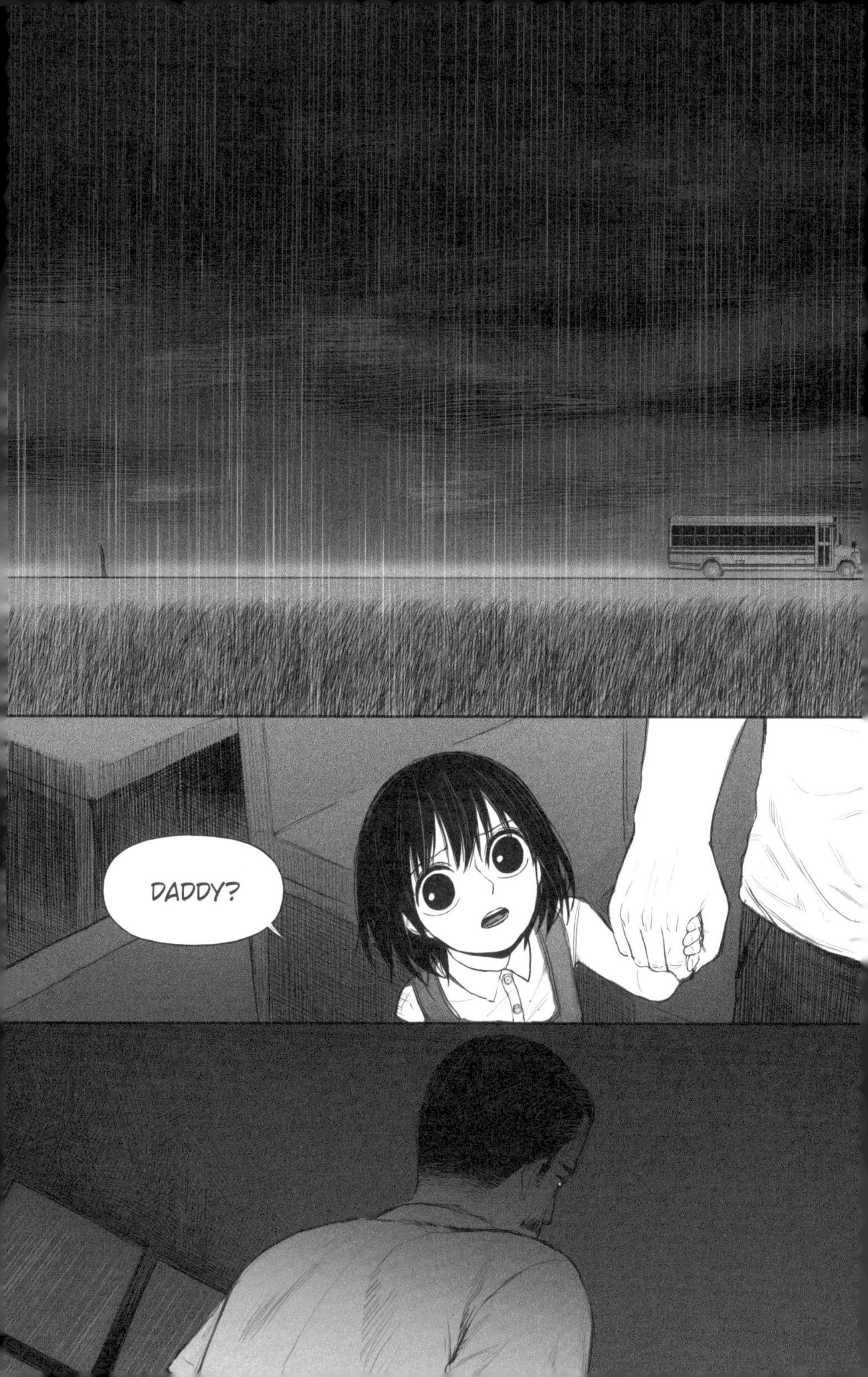
DADDY?

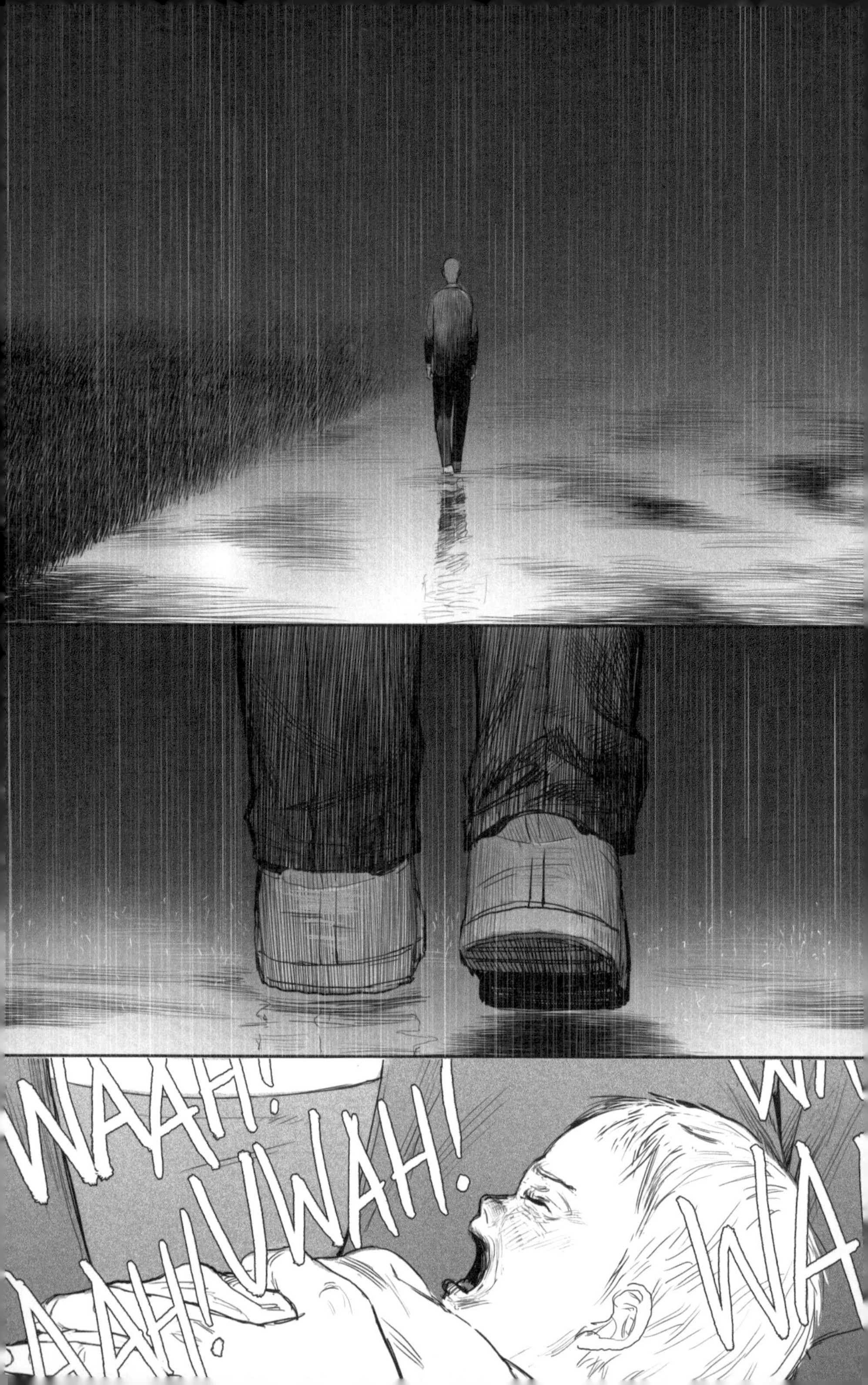
WAAH!
WAH!

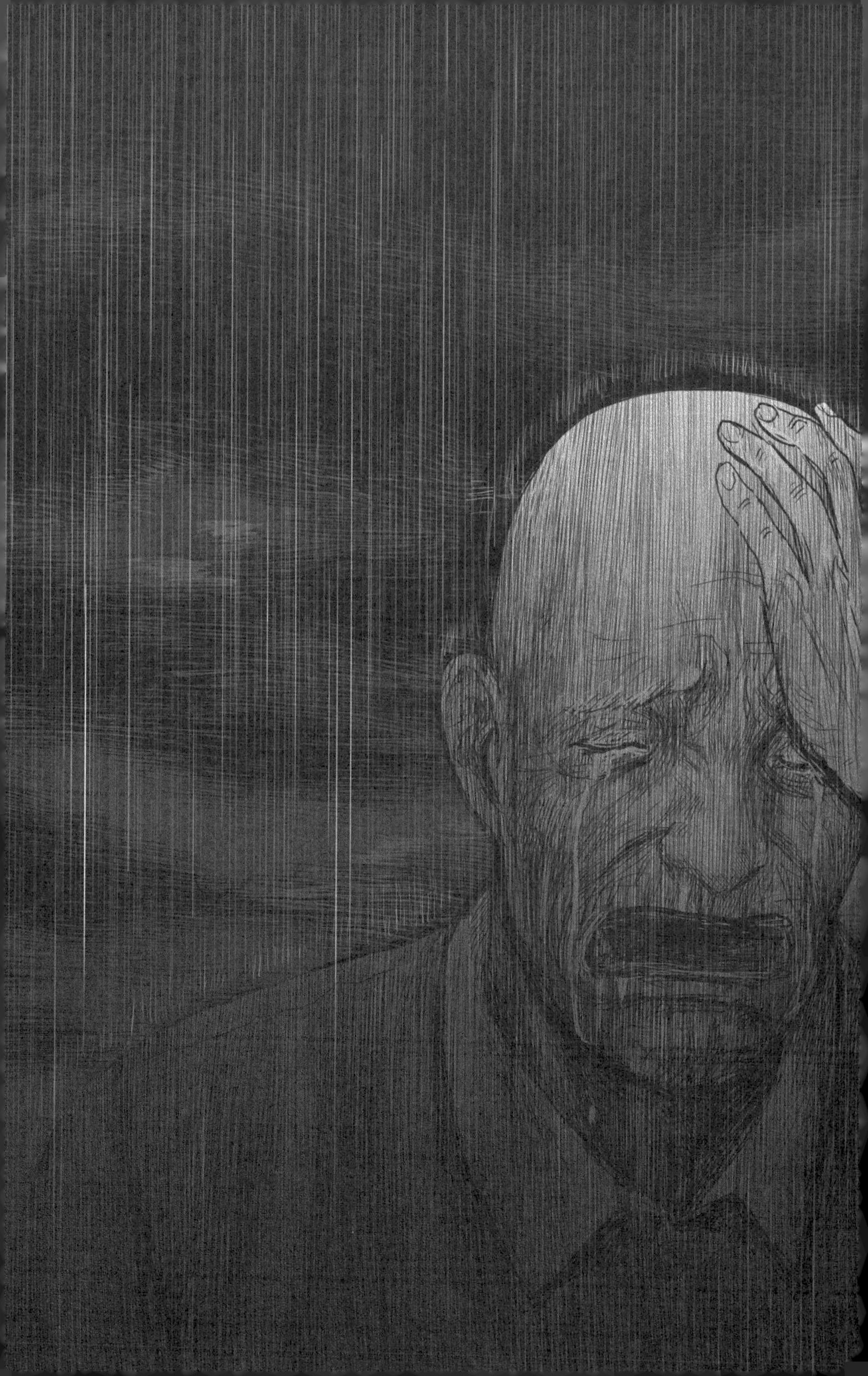

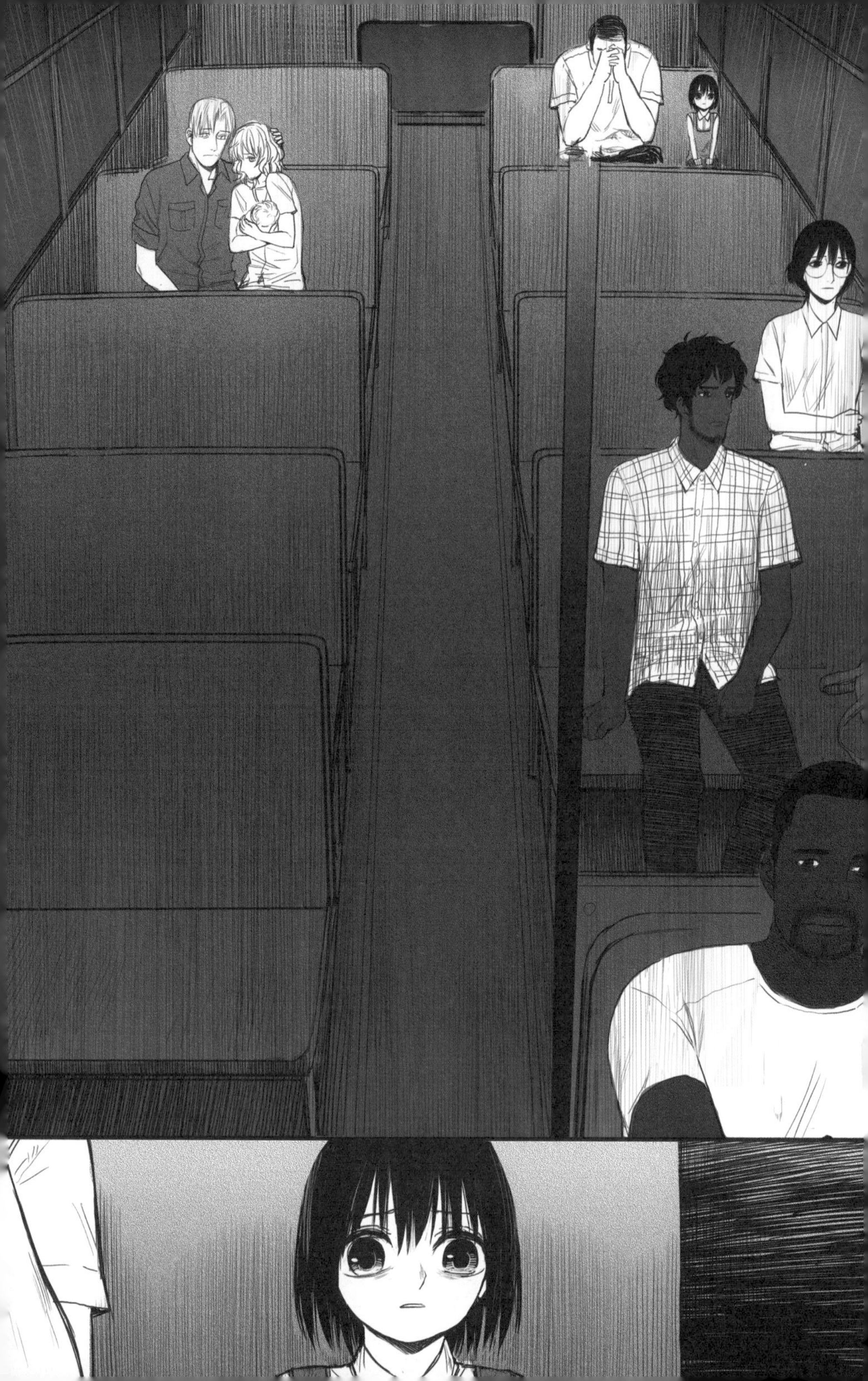

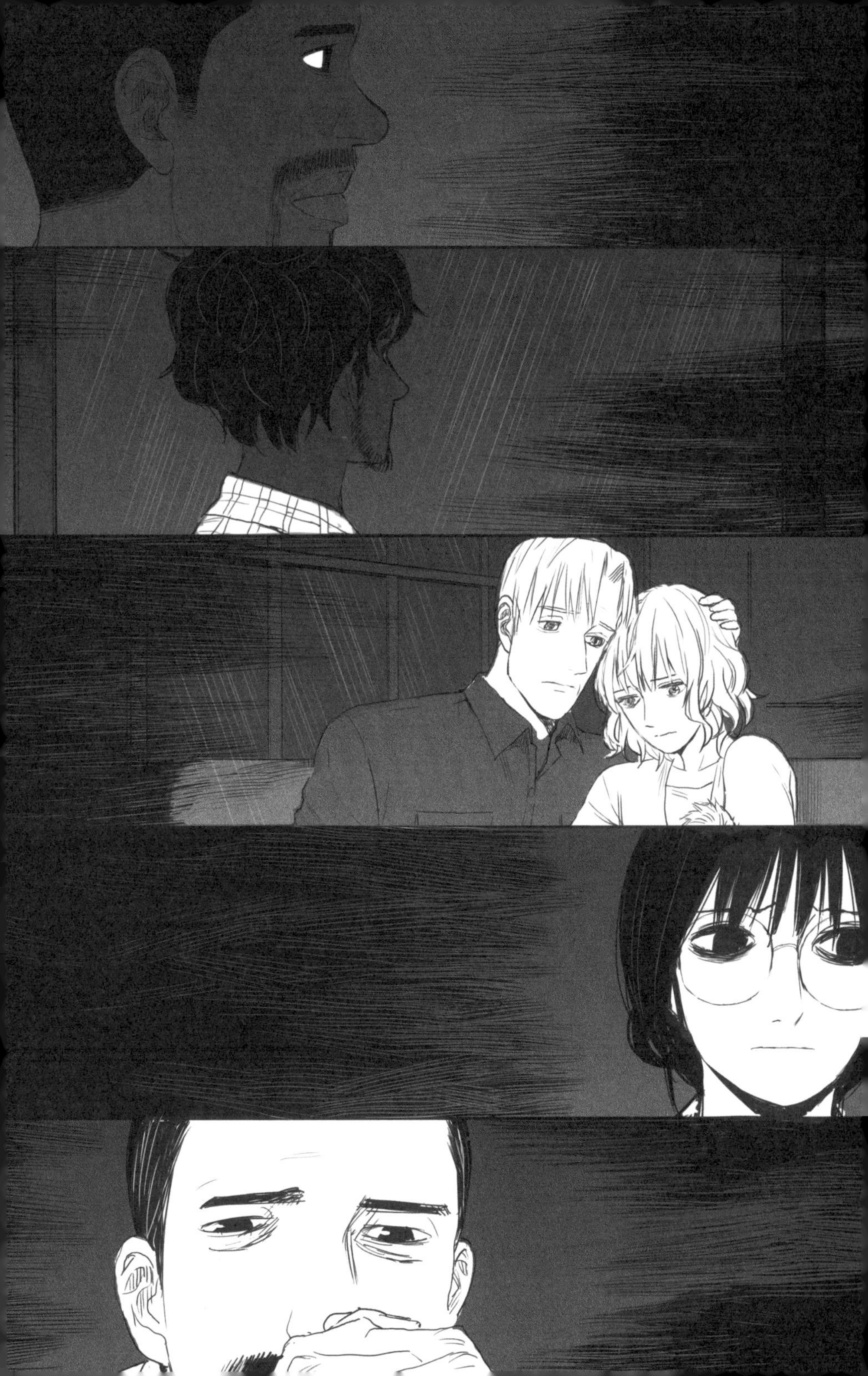

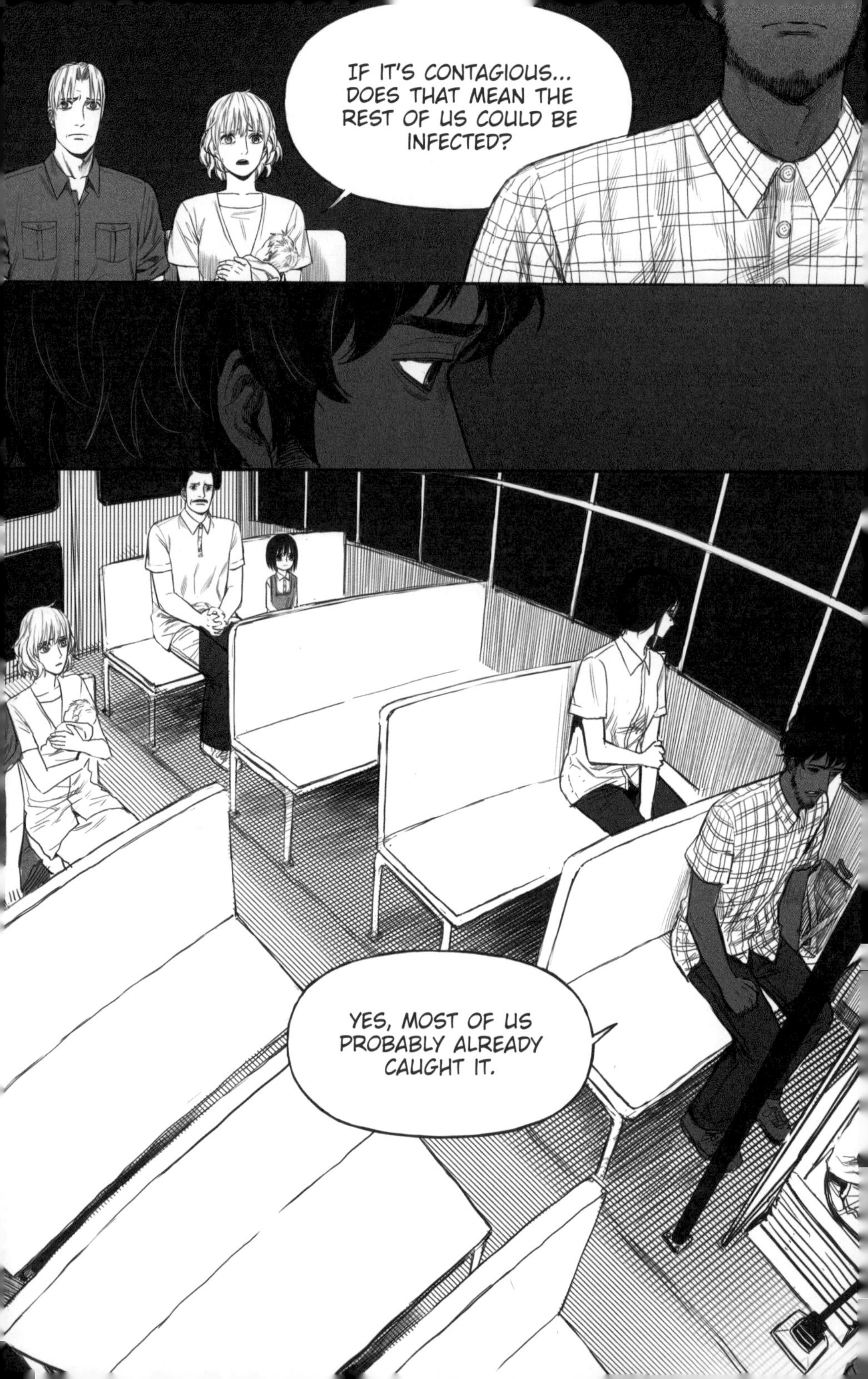
IF IT'S CONTAGIOUS... DOES THAT MEAN THE REST OF US COULD BE INFECTED?
YES, MOST OF US PROBABLY ALREADY CAUGHT IT.

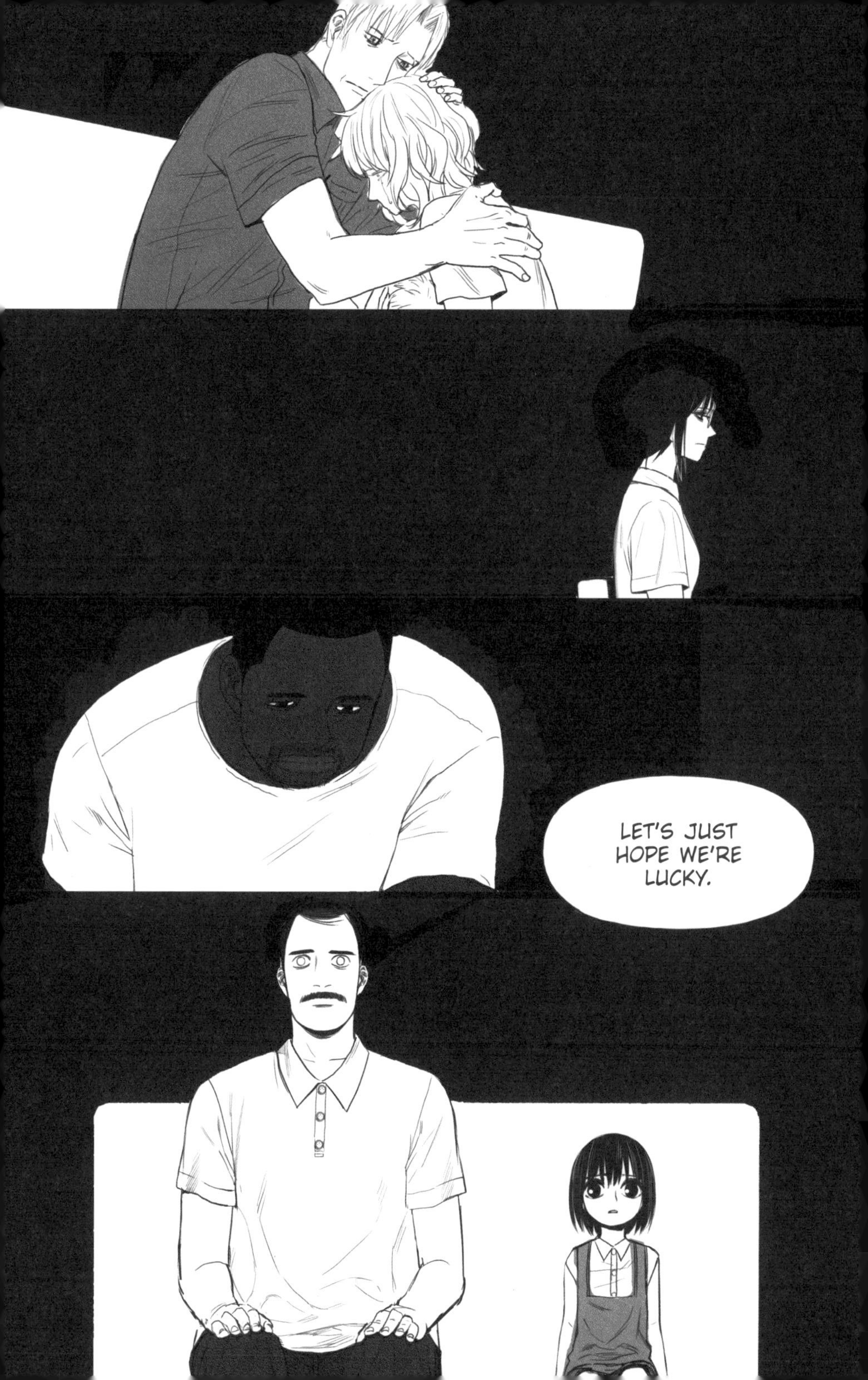
LET'S JUST
HOPE WE'RE
LUCKY.

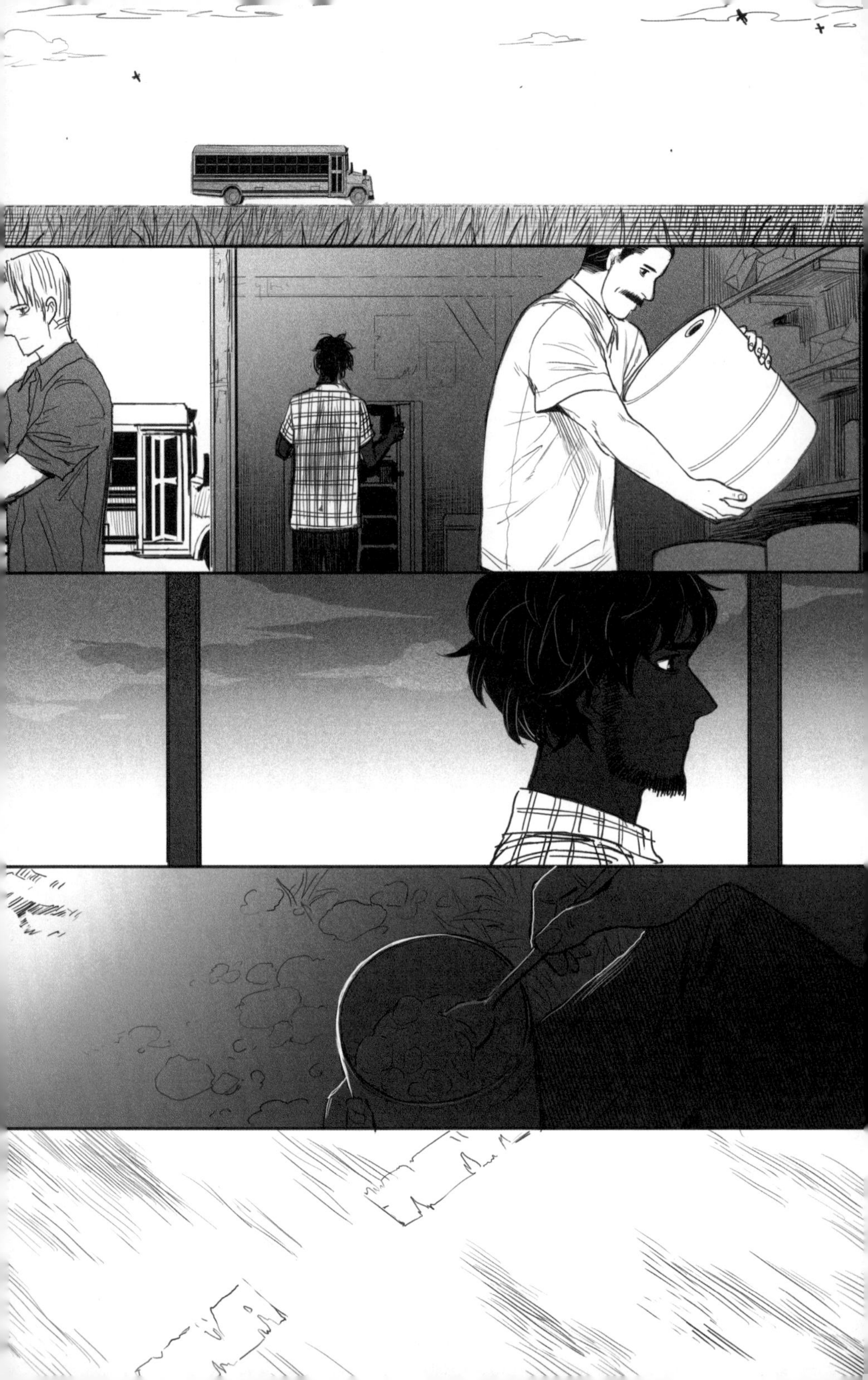

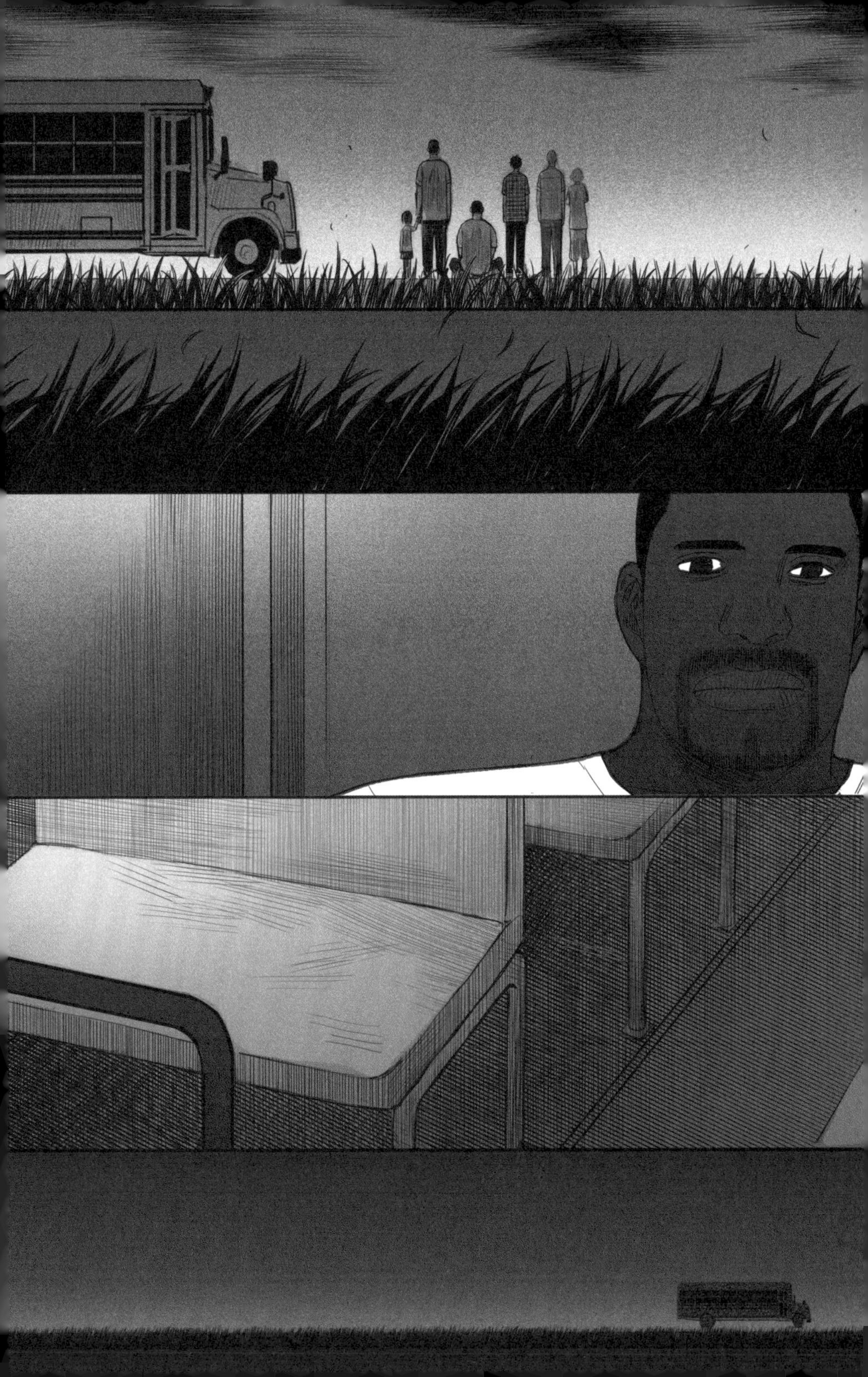

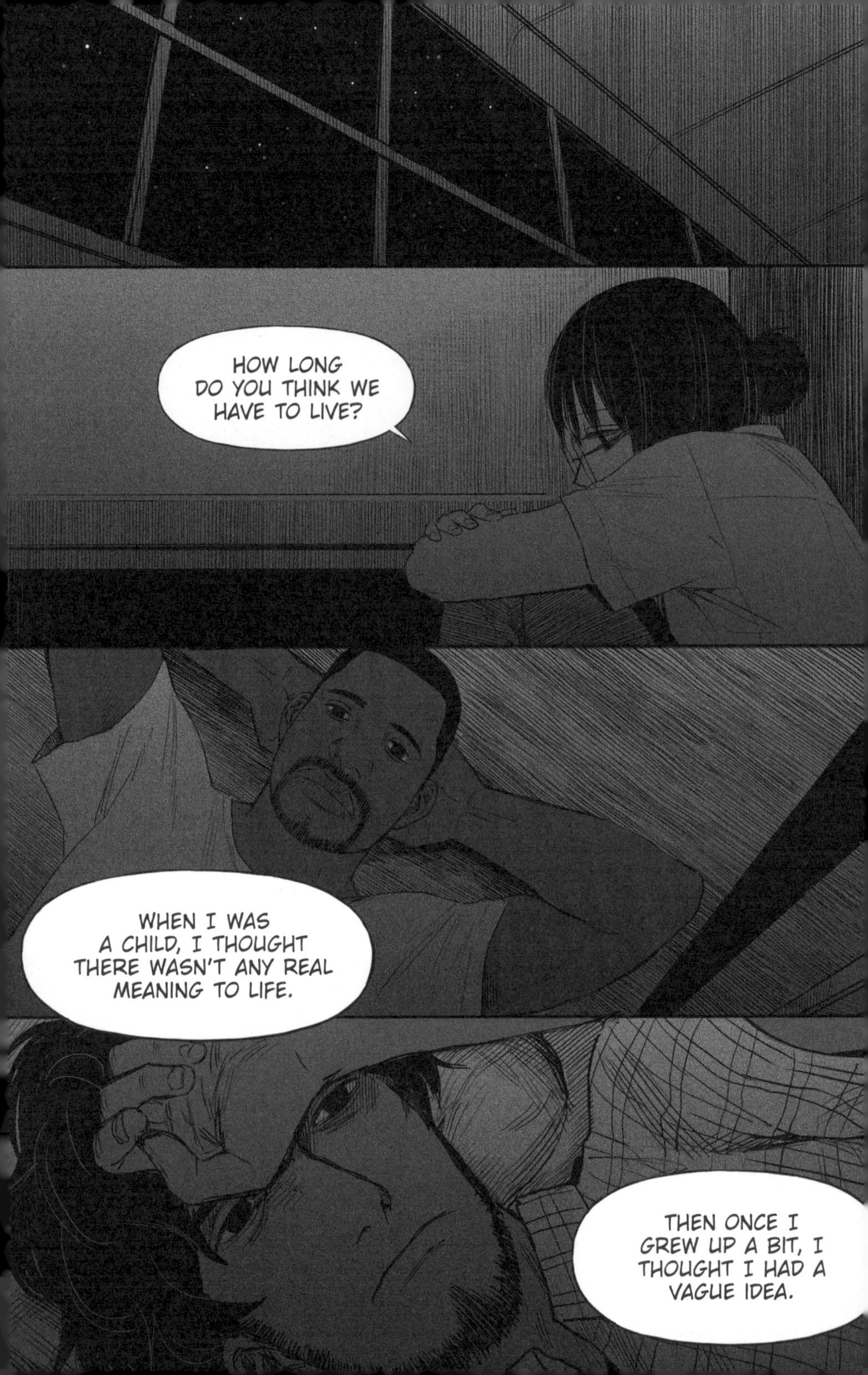
HOW LONG DO YOU THINK WE HAVE TO LIVE?
WHEN I WAS A CHILD, I THOUGHT THERE WASN'T ANY REAL MEANING TO LIFE.
THEN ONCE I GREW UP A BIT, I THOUGHT I HAD A VAGUE IDEA.

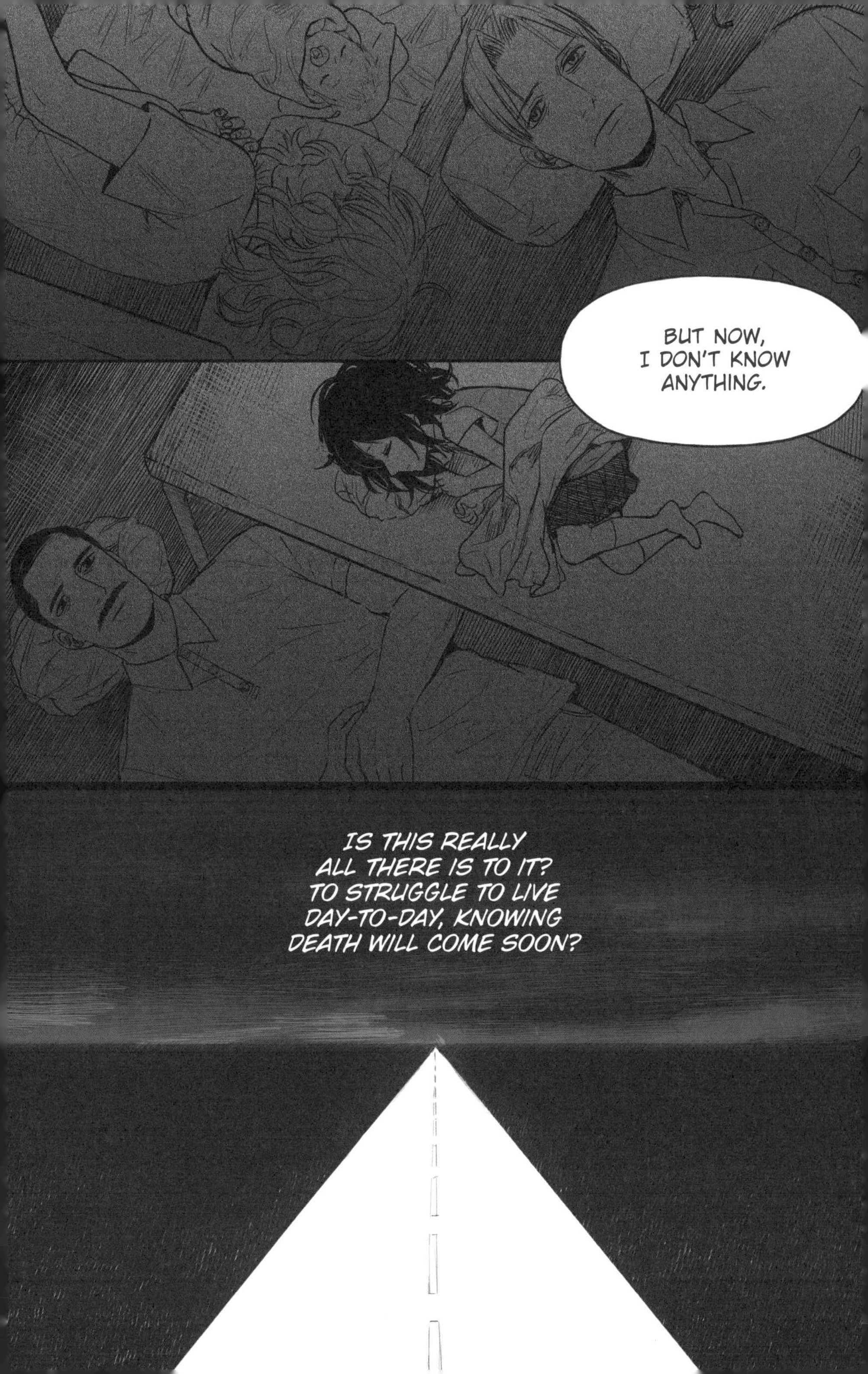
BUT NOW, I DON'T KNOW ANYTHING.
IS THIS REALLY ALL THERE IS TO IT? TO STRUGGLE TO LIVE DAY-TO-DAY, KNOWING DEATH WILL COME SOON?

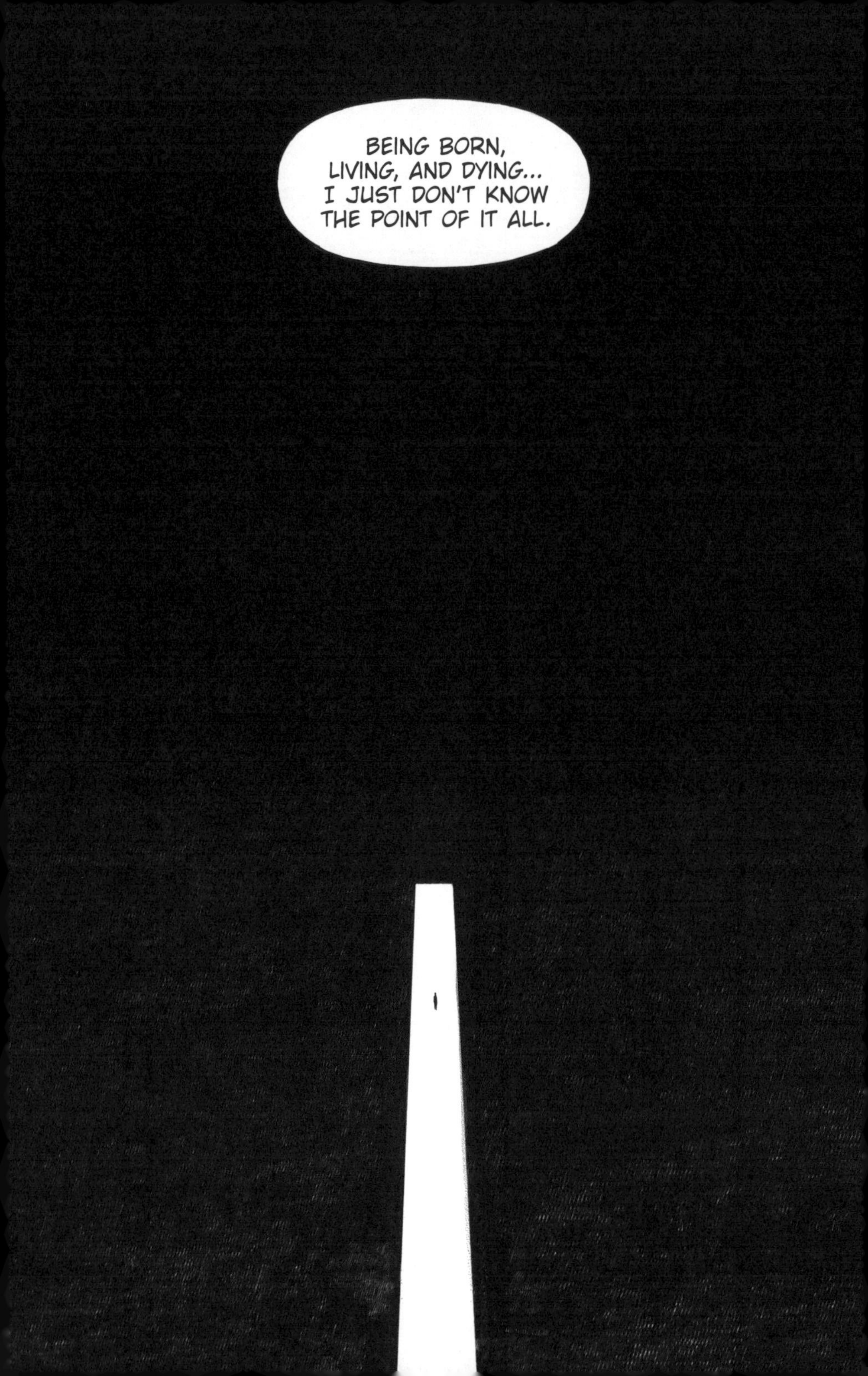
BEING BORN, LIVING, AND DYING... I JUST DON'T KNOW THE POINT OF IT ALL.

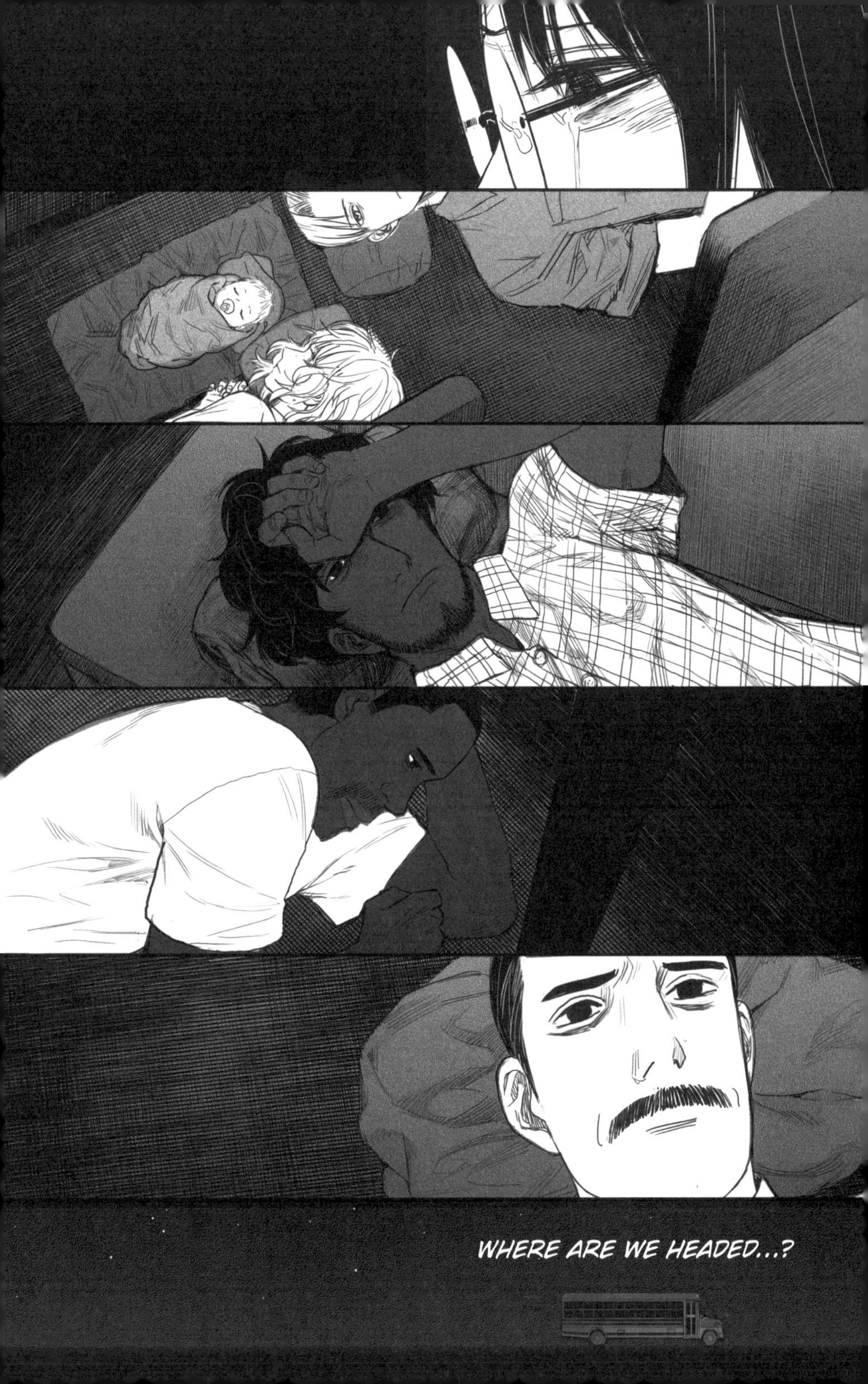
WHERE ARE WE HEADED...?

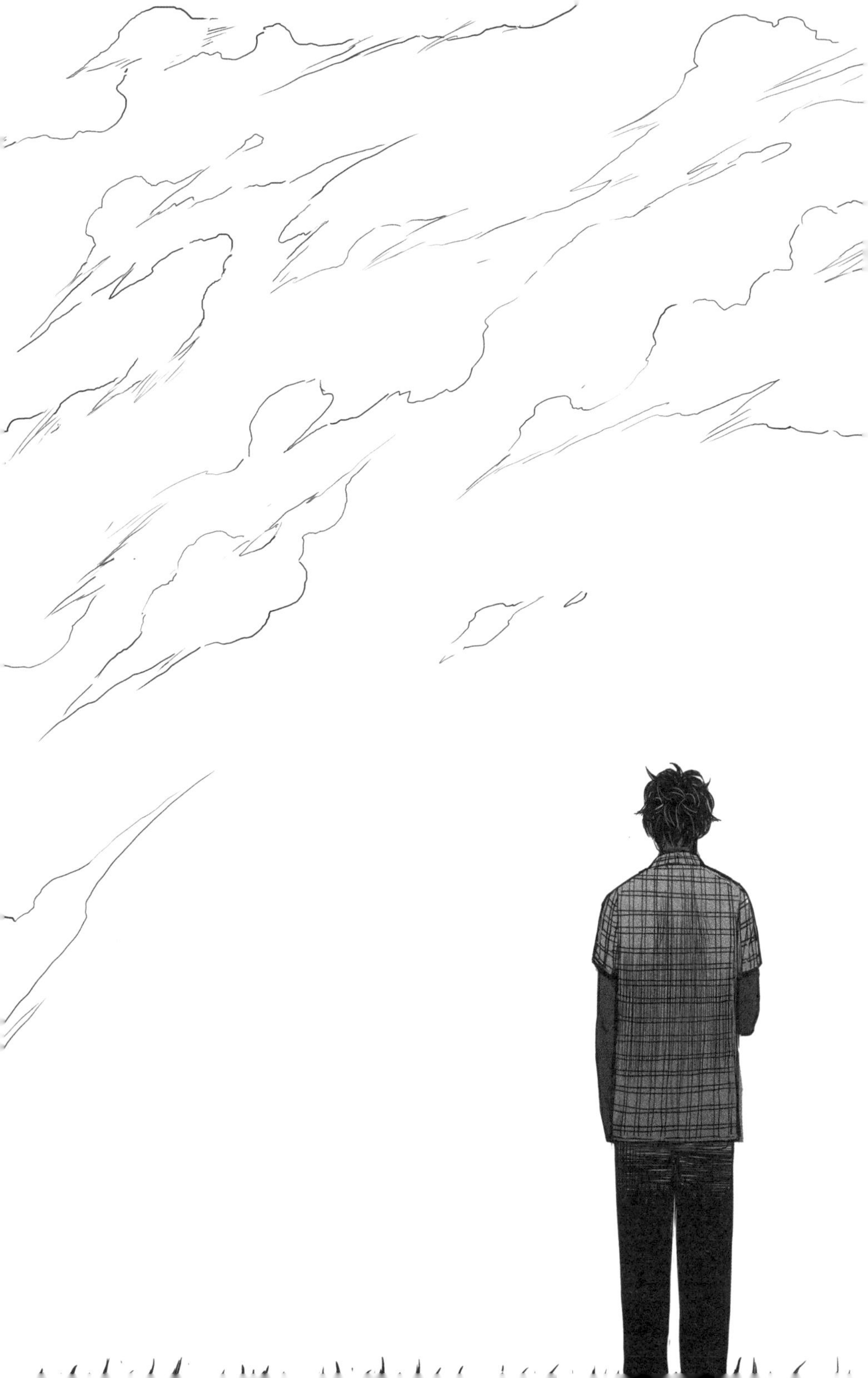

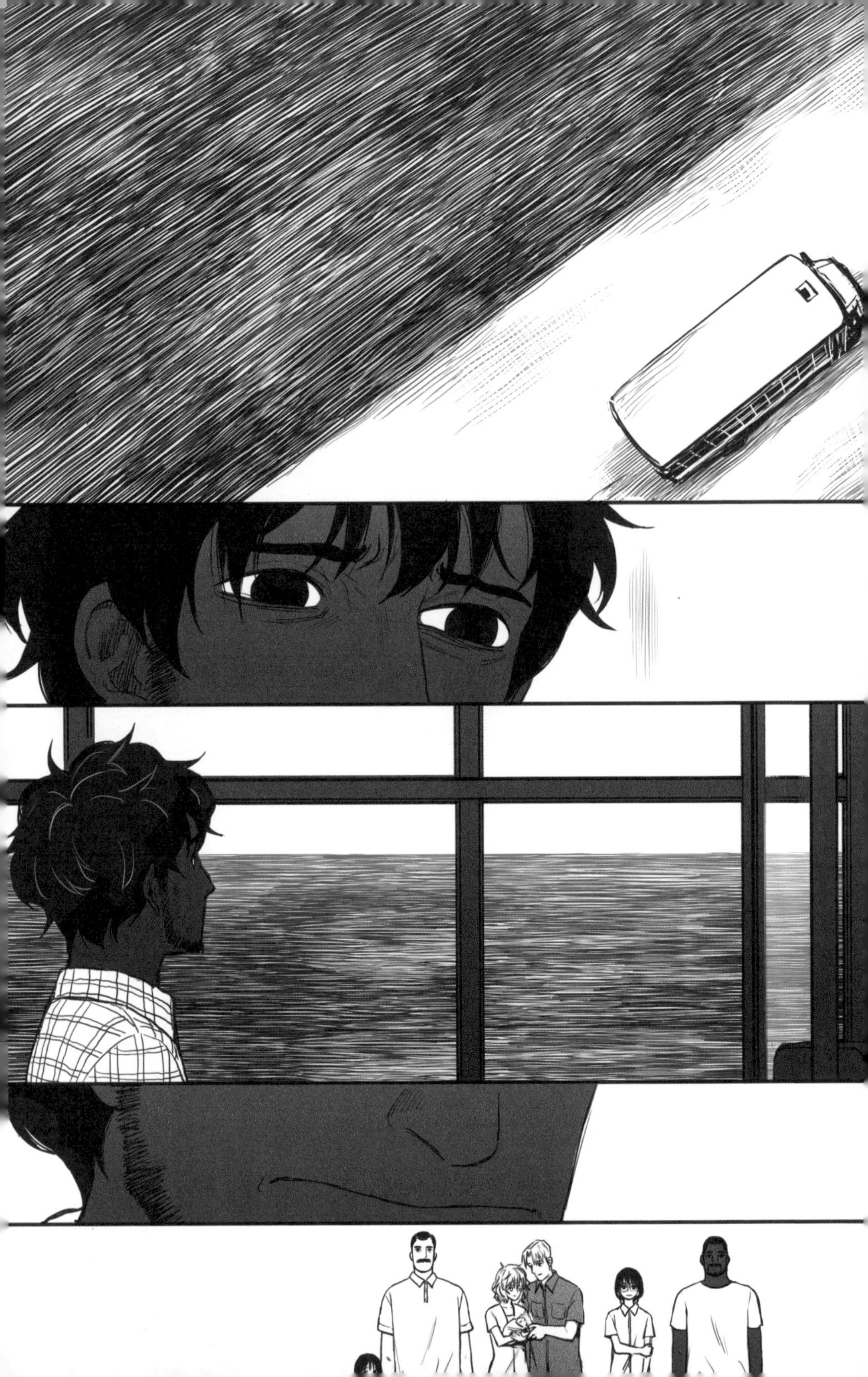

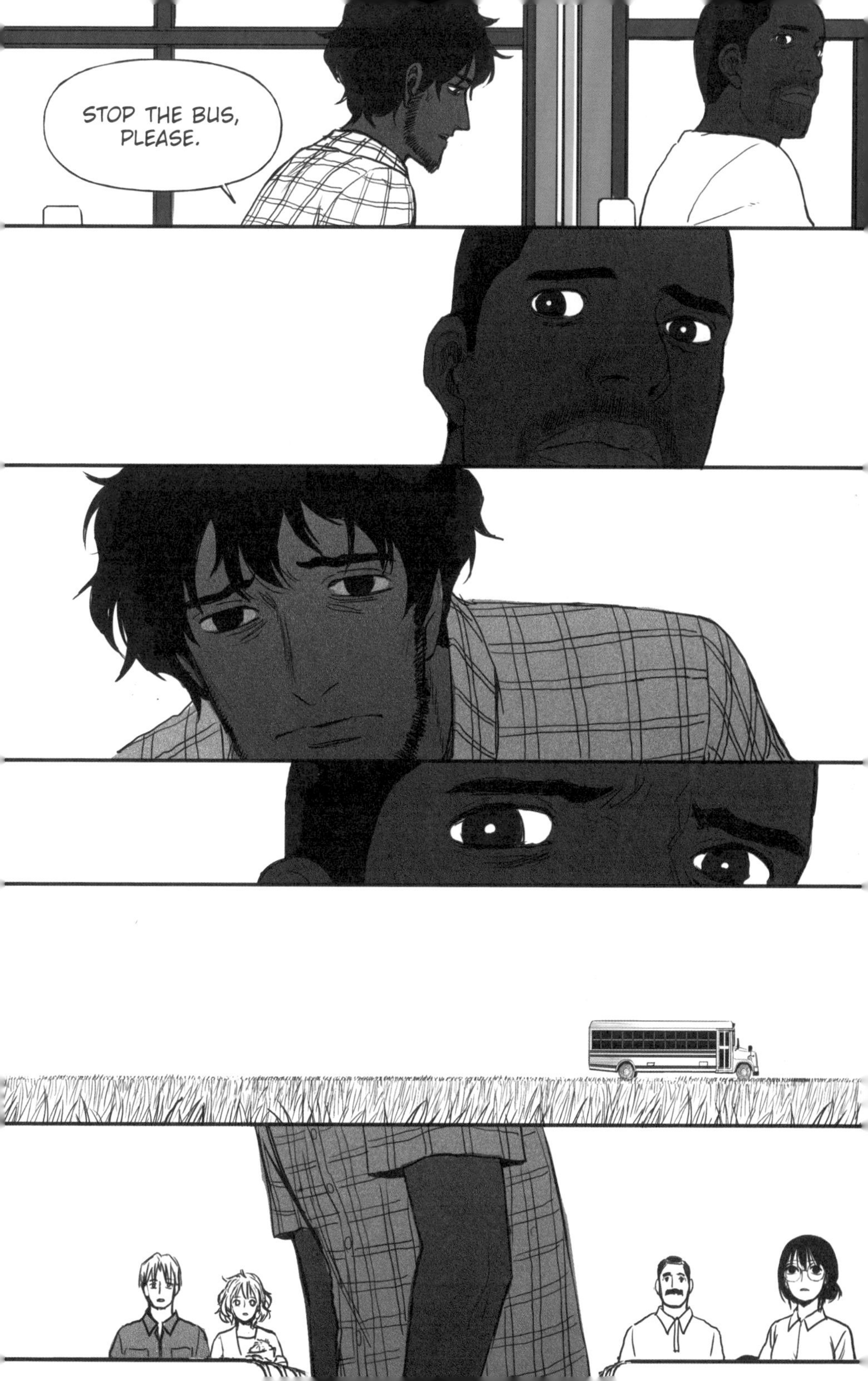
STOP THE BUS, PLEASE.

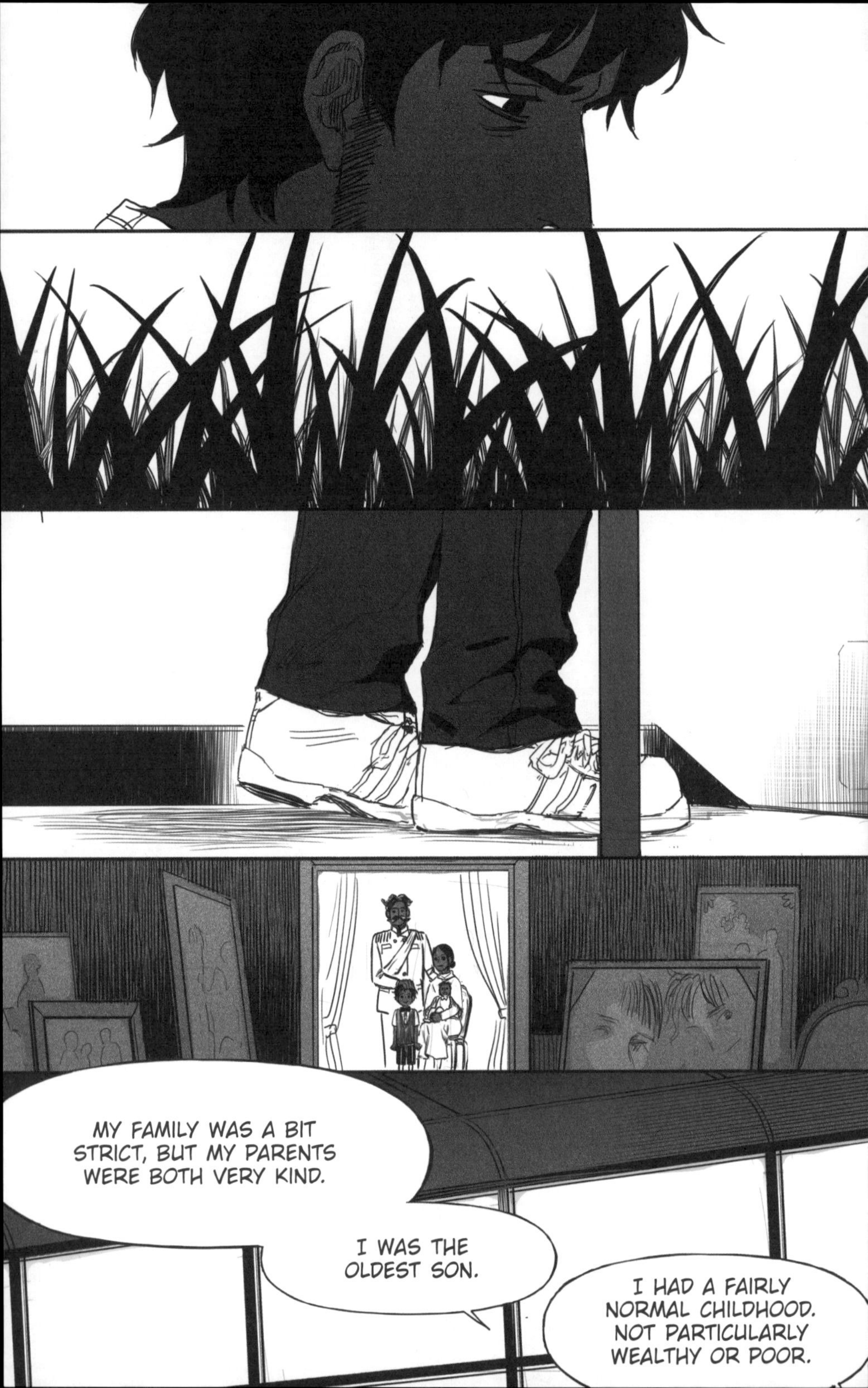
MY FAMILY WAS A BIT STRICT, BUT MY PARENTS WERE BOTH VERY KIND.
I WAS THE OLDEST SON.
I HAD A FAIRLY NORMAL CHILDHOOD. NOT PARTICULARLY WEALTHY OR POOR.

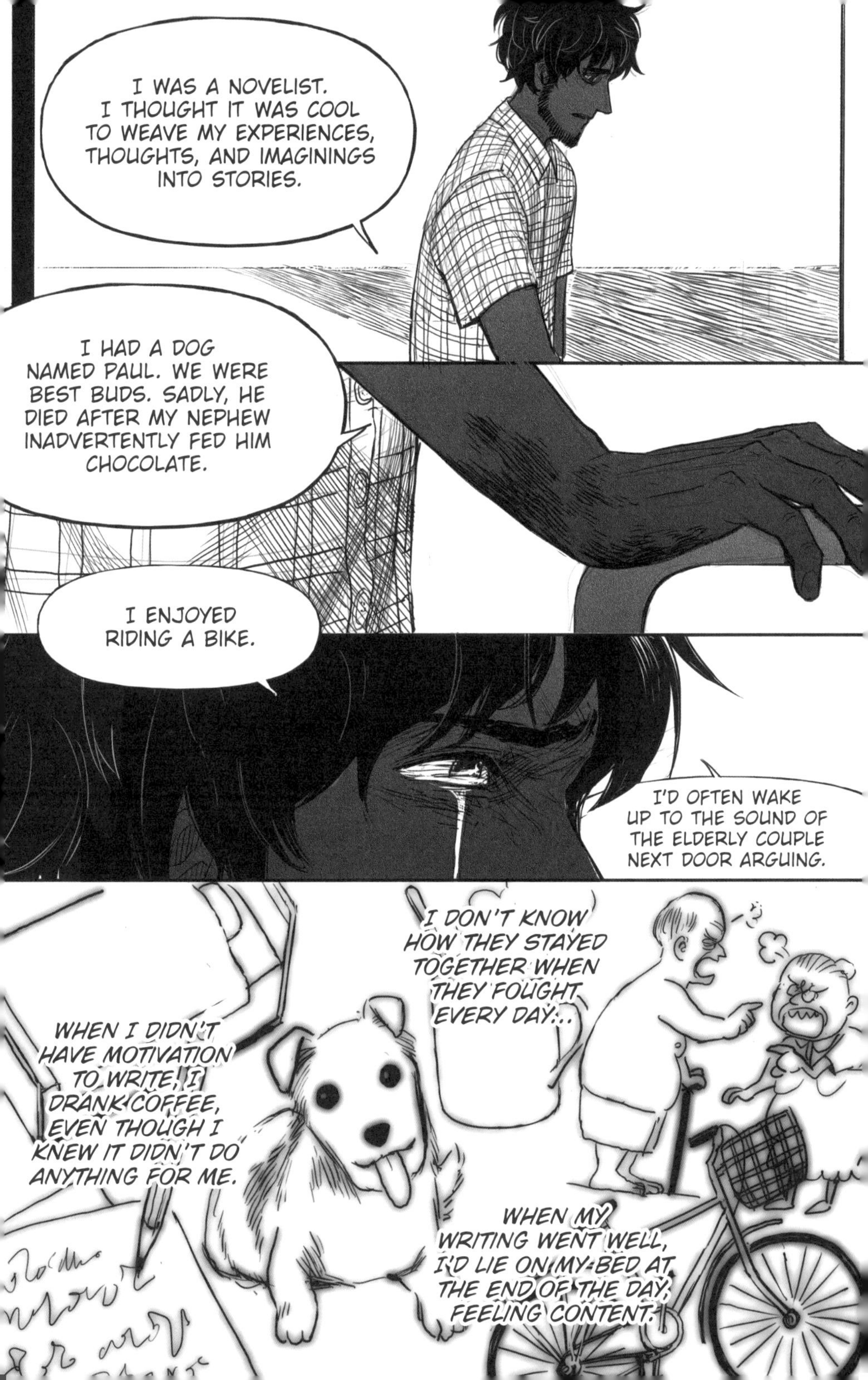
I WAS A NOVELIST. I THOUGHT IT WAS COOL TO WEAVE MY EXPERIENCES, THOUGHTS, AND IMAGININGS INTO STORIES.
I HAD A DOG NAMED PAUL. WE WERE BEST BUDS. SADLY, HE DIED AFTER MY NEPHEW INADVERTENTLY FED HIM CHOCOLATE.
I ENJOYED RIDING A BIKE.
I'D OFTEN WAKE UP TO THE SOUND OF THE ELDERLY COUPLE NEXT DOOR ARGUING.
I DON'T KNOW HOW THEY STAYED TOGETHER WHEN THEY FOUGHT EVERY DAY...
WHEN I DIDN'T HAVE MOTIVATION TO WRITE, I DRANK COFFEE, EVEN THOUGH I KNEW IT DIDN'T DO ANYTHING FOR ME.
WHEN MY WRITING WENT WELL, I'D LIE ON MY BED AT THE END OF THE DAY, FEELING CONTENT.

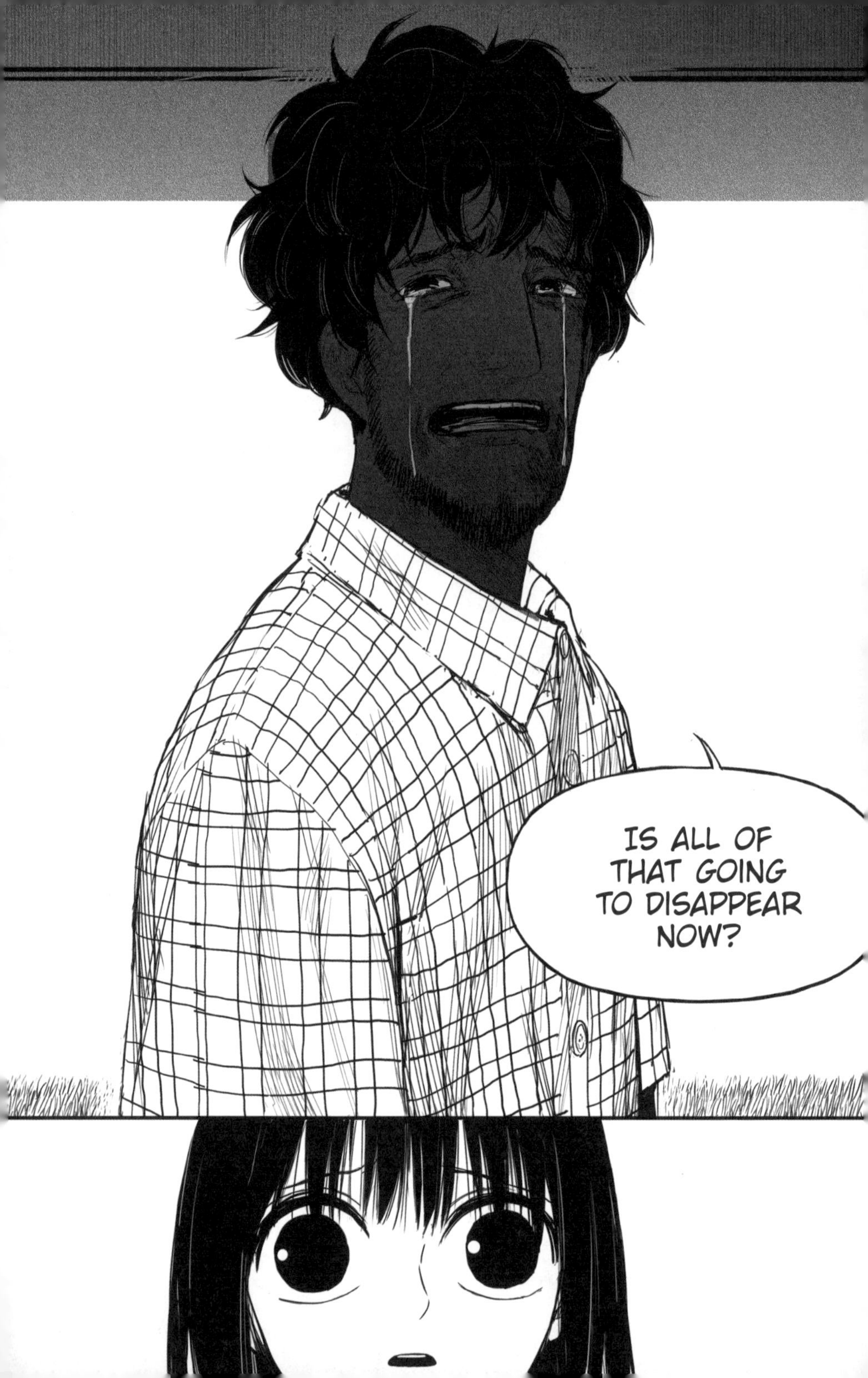
IS ALL OF THAT GOING TO DISAPPEAR NOW?

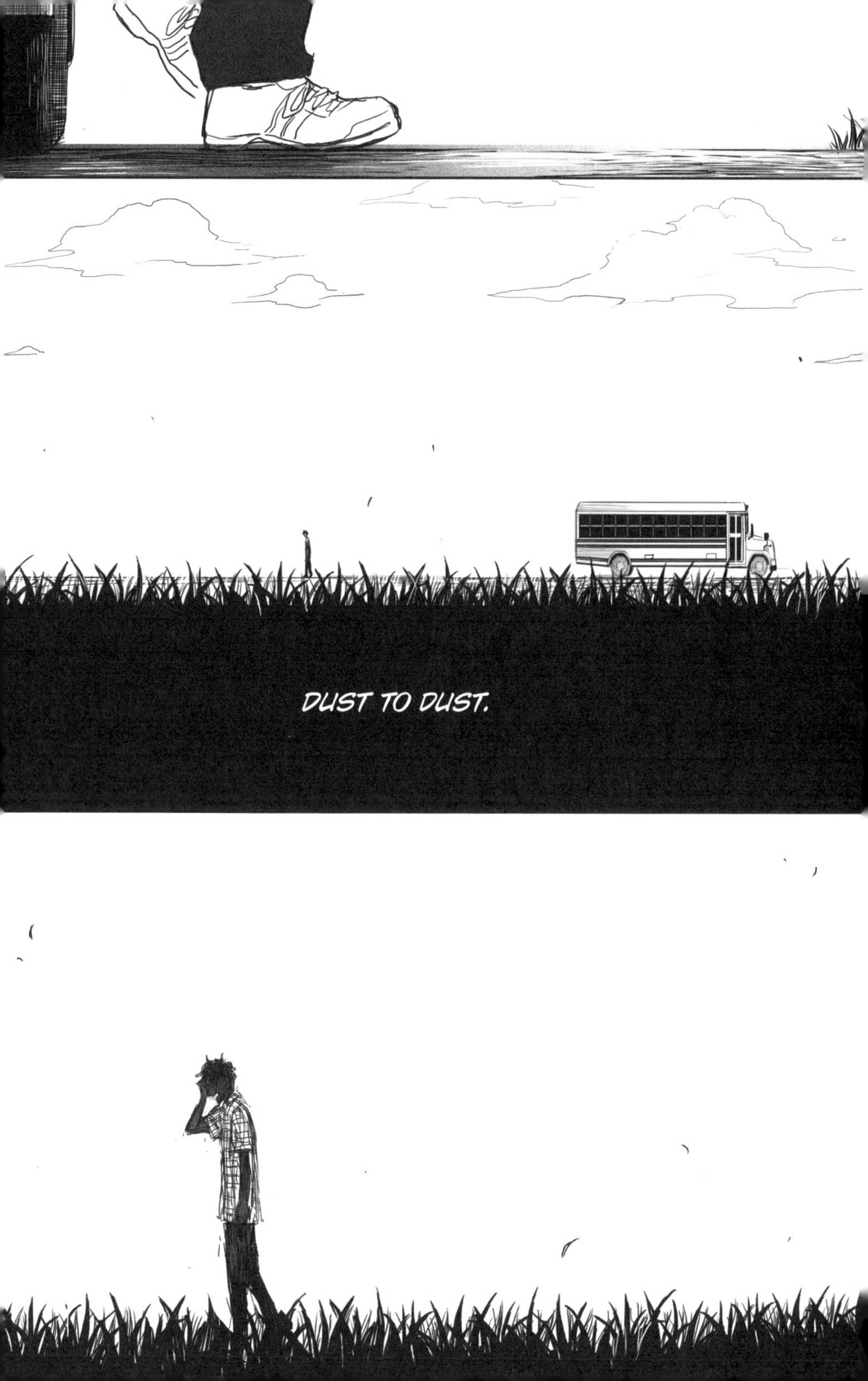
DUST TO DUST.

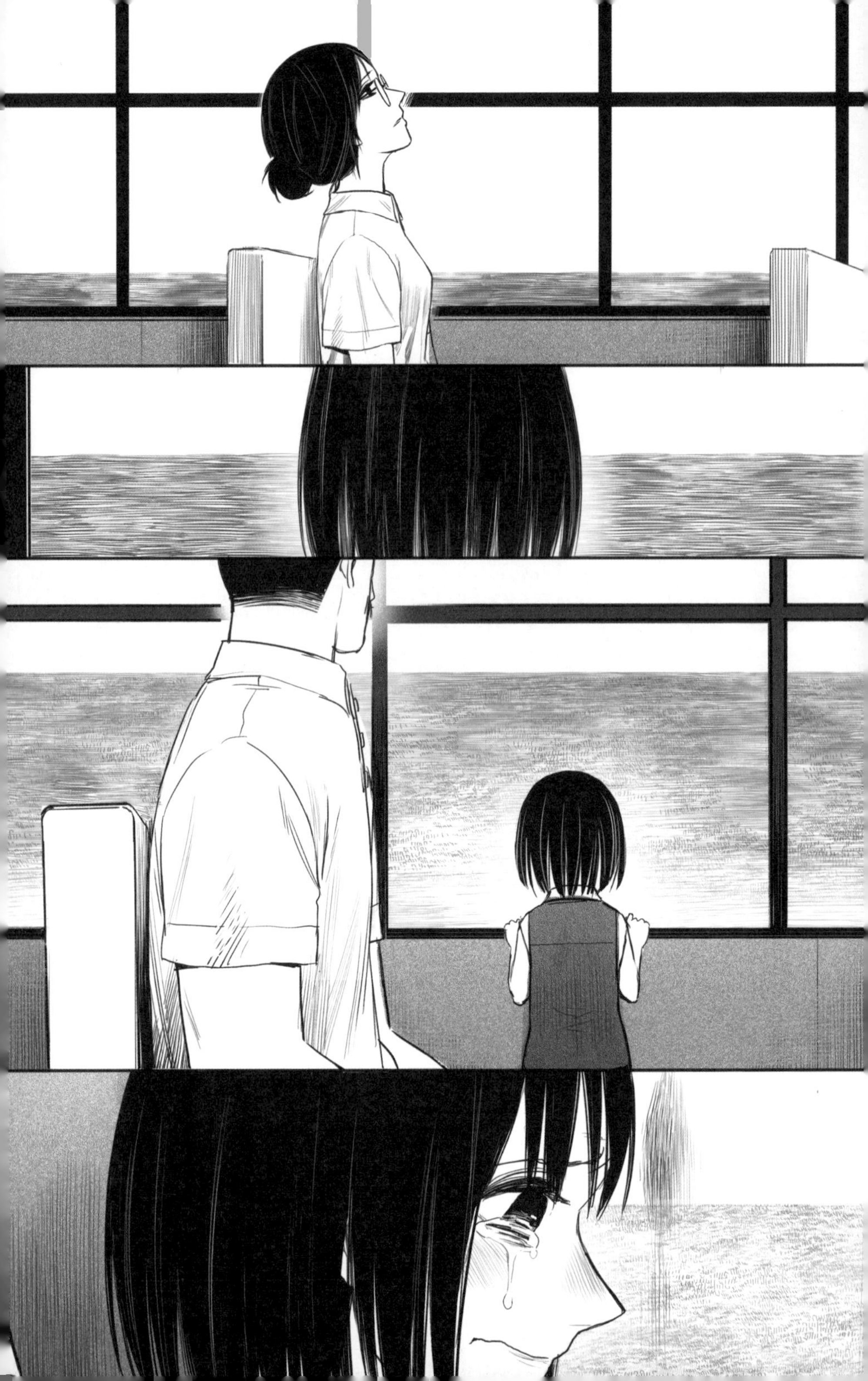

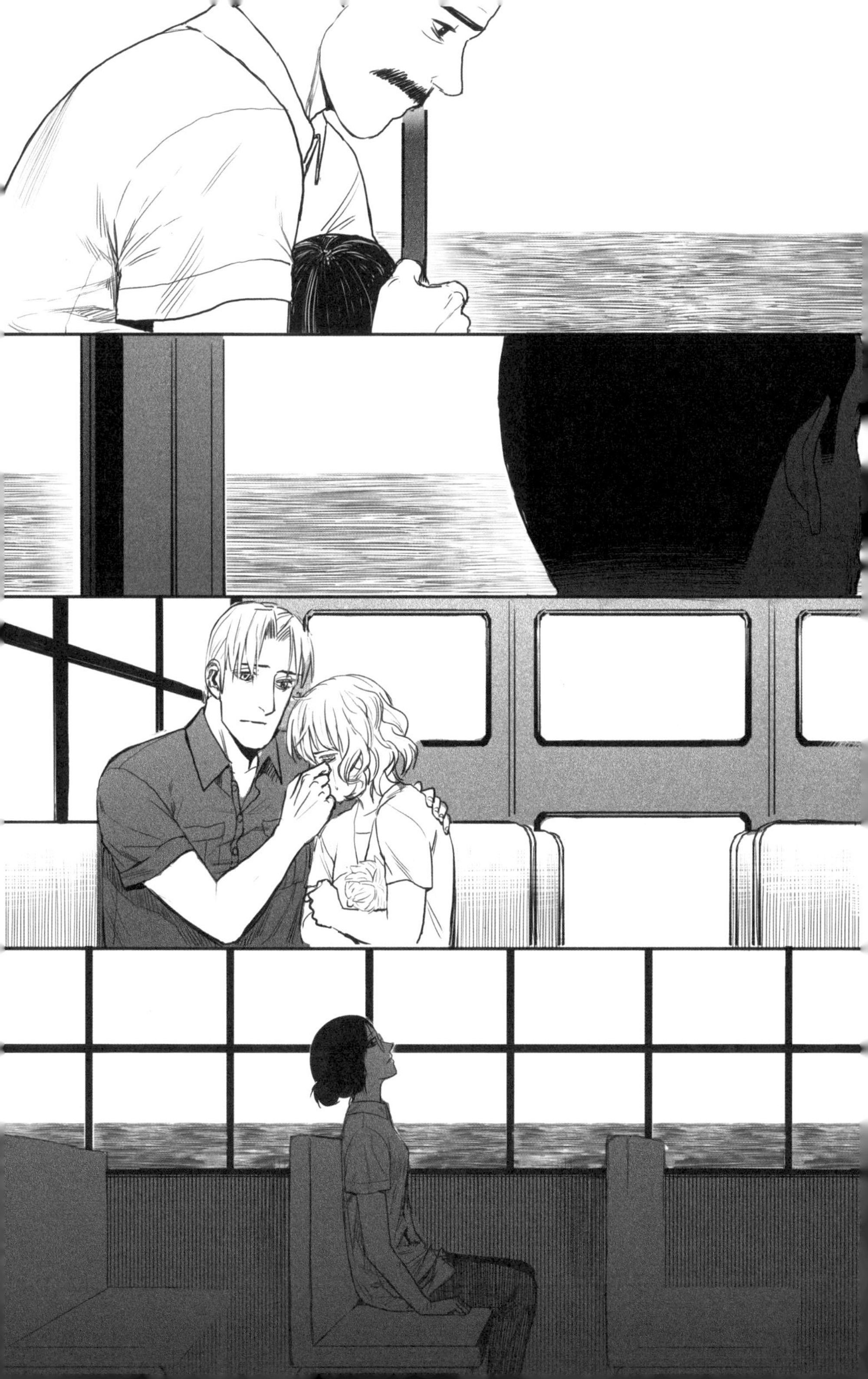

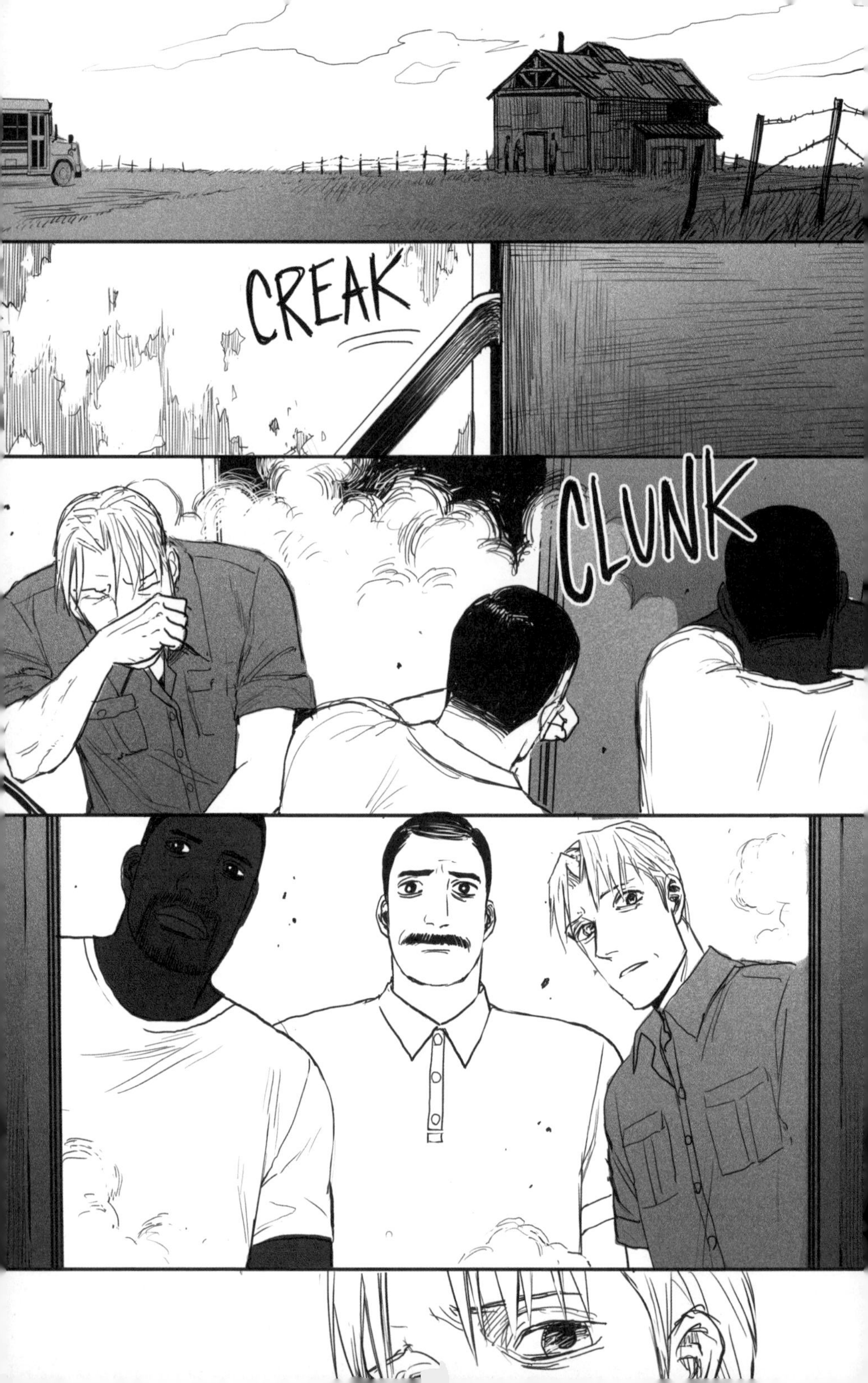
CREAK
CLUNK

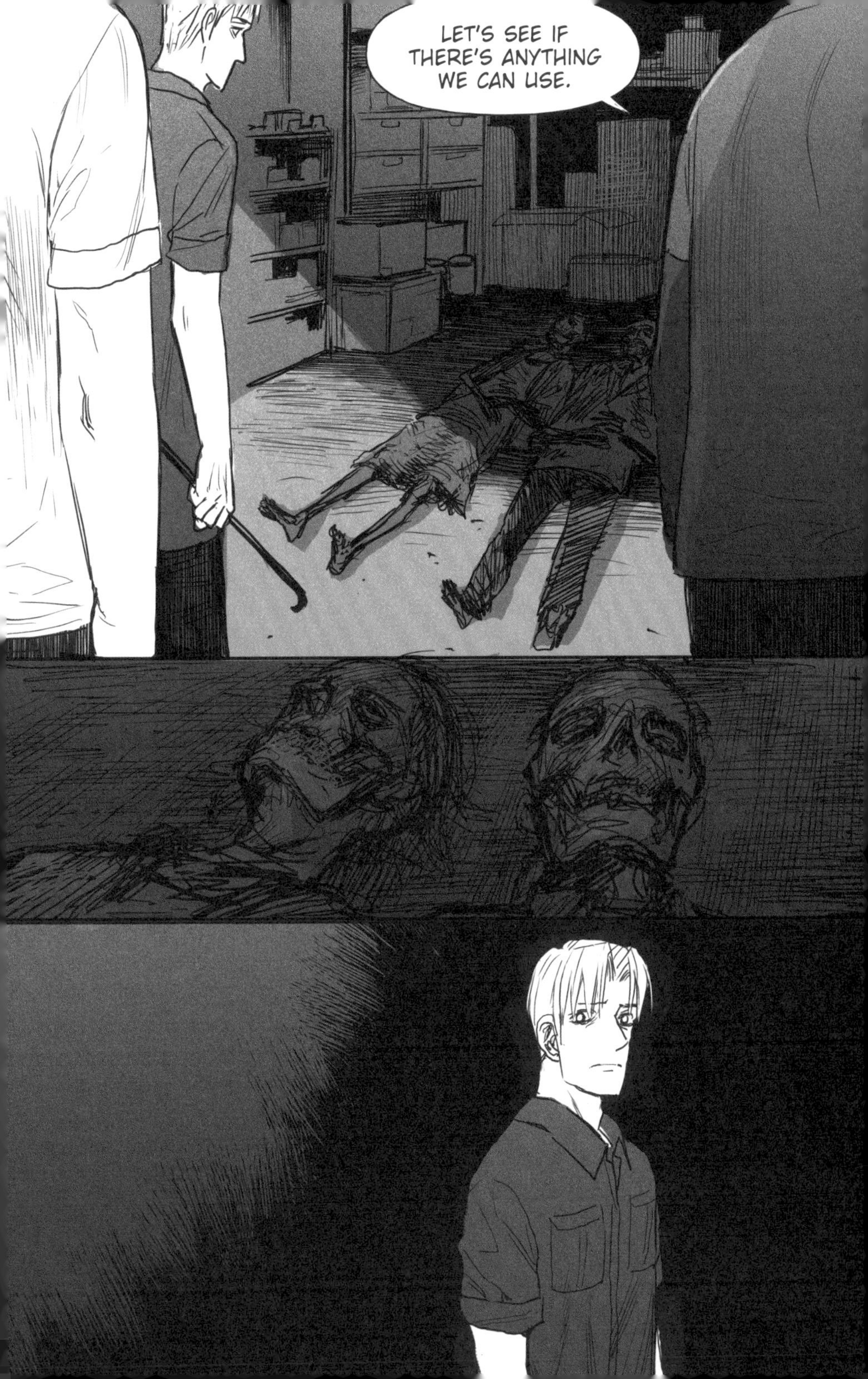
LET'S SEE IF THERE'S ANYTHING WE CAN USE.

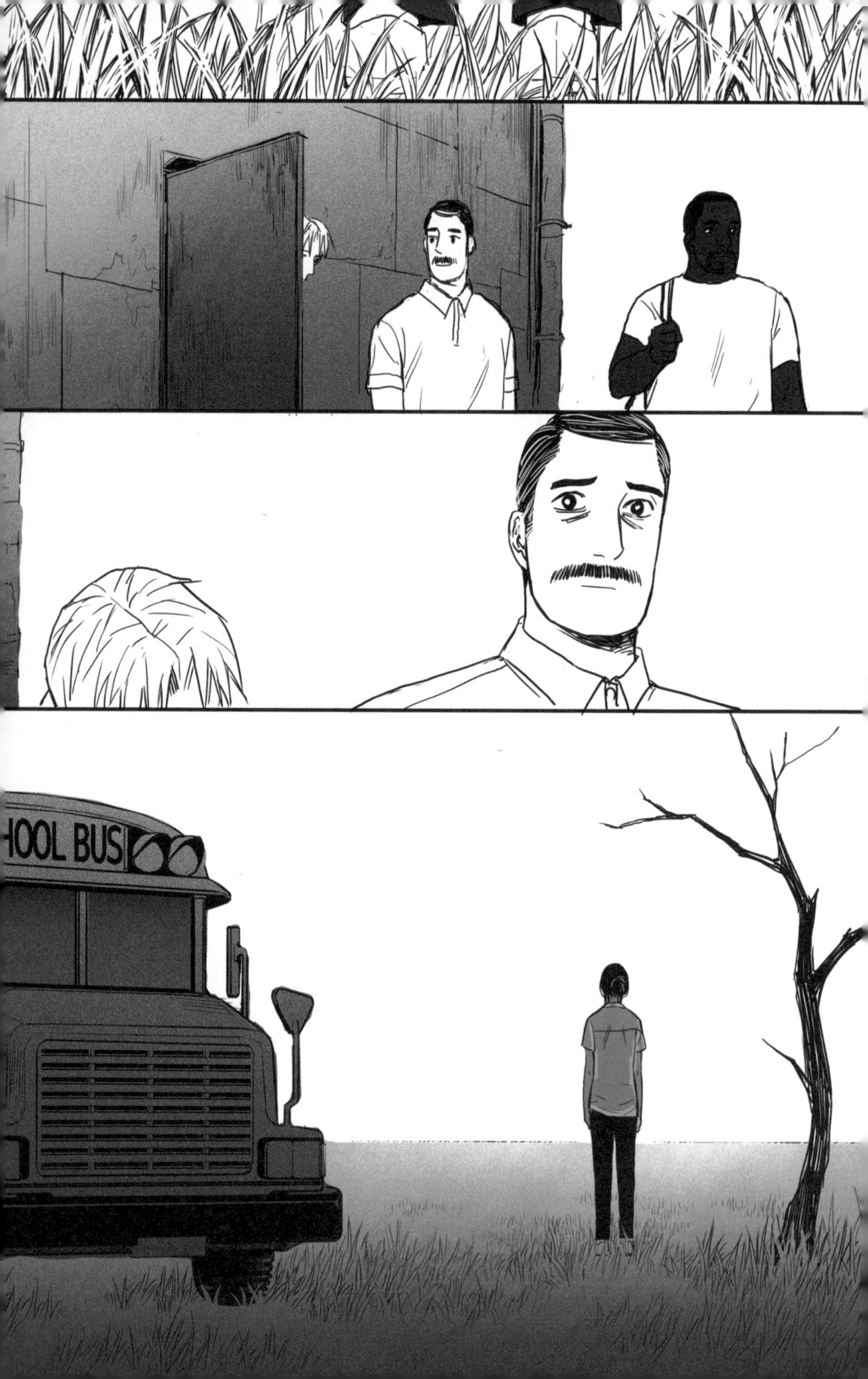
HOOL BUS

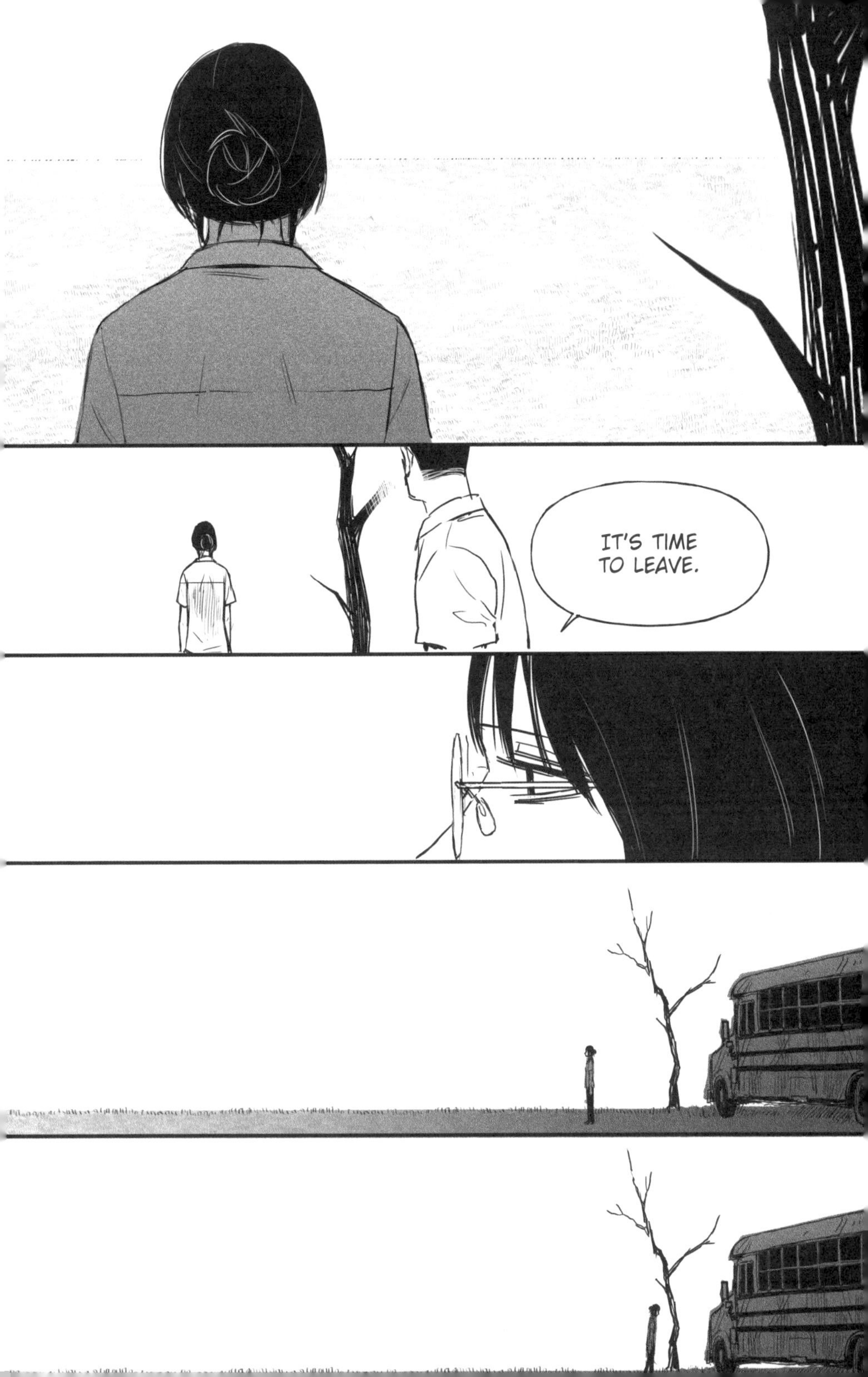
IT'S TIME TO LEAVE.

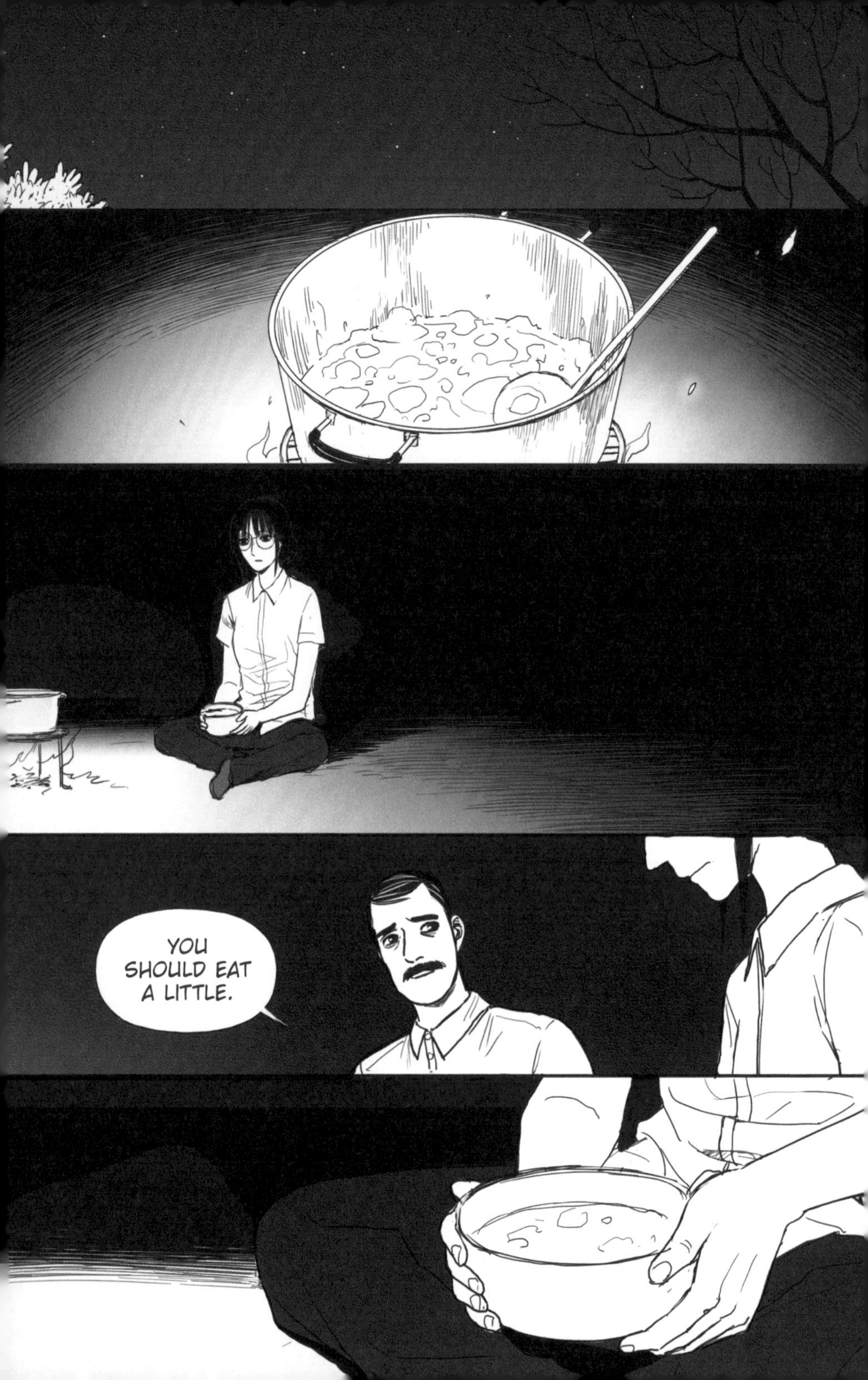
YOU SHOULD EAT A LITTLE.

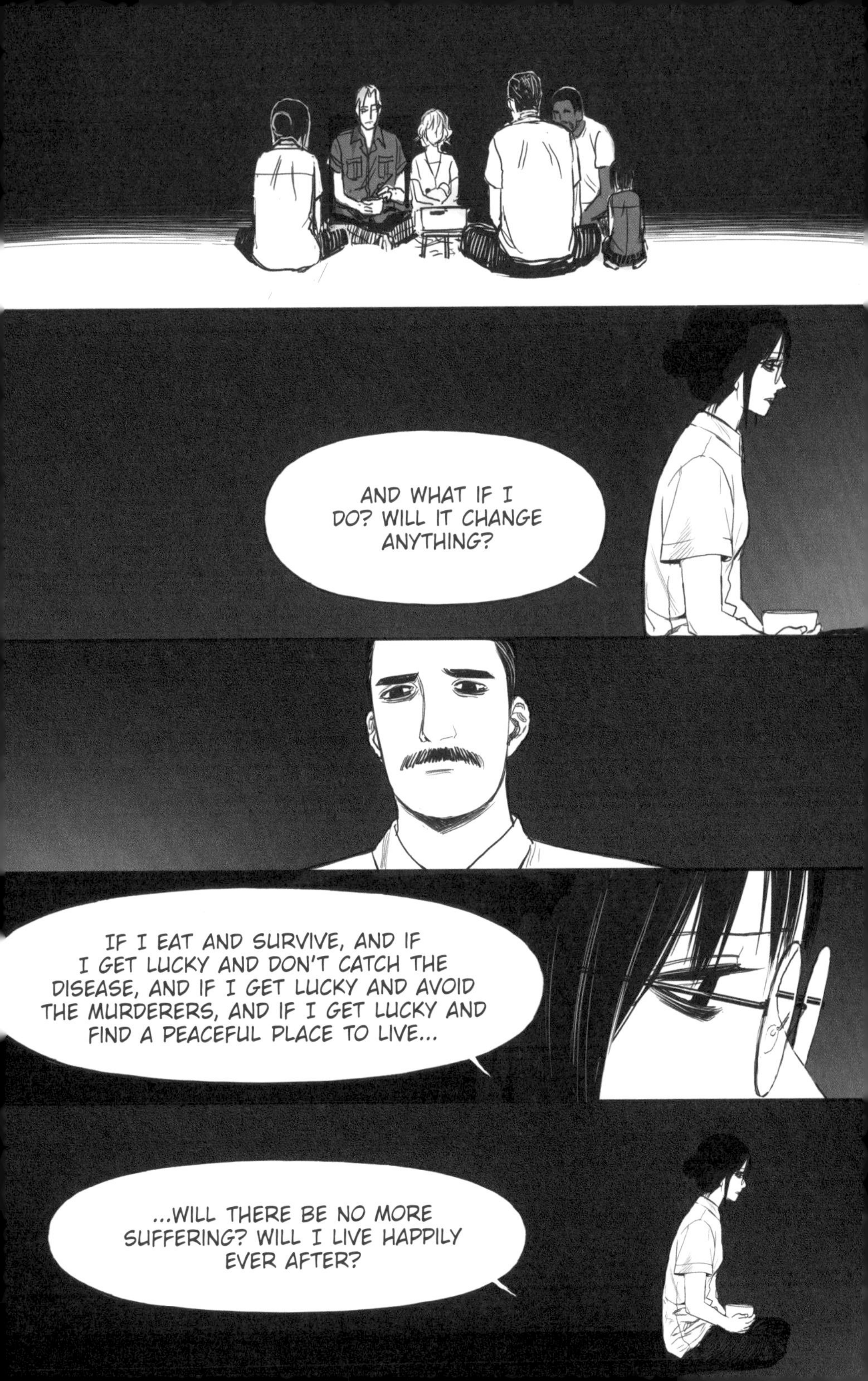
AND WHAT IF I DO? WILL IT CHANGE ANYTHING?
IF I EAT AND SURVIVE, AND IF I GET LUCKY AND DON'T CATCH THE DISEASE, AND IF I GET LUCKY AND AVOID THE MURDERERS, AND IF I GET LUCKY AND FIND A PEACEFUL PLACE TO LIVE...
...WILL THERE BE NO MORE SUFFERING? WILL I LIVE HAPPILY EVER AFTER?

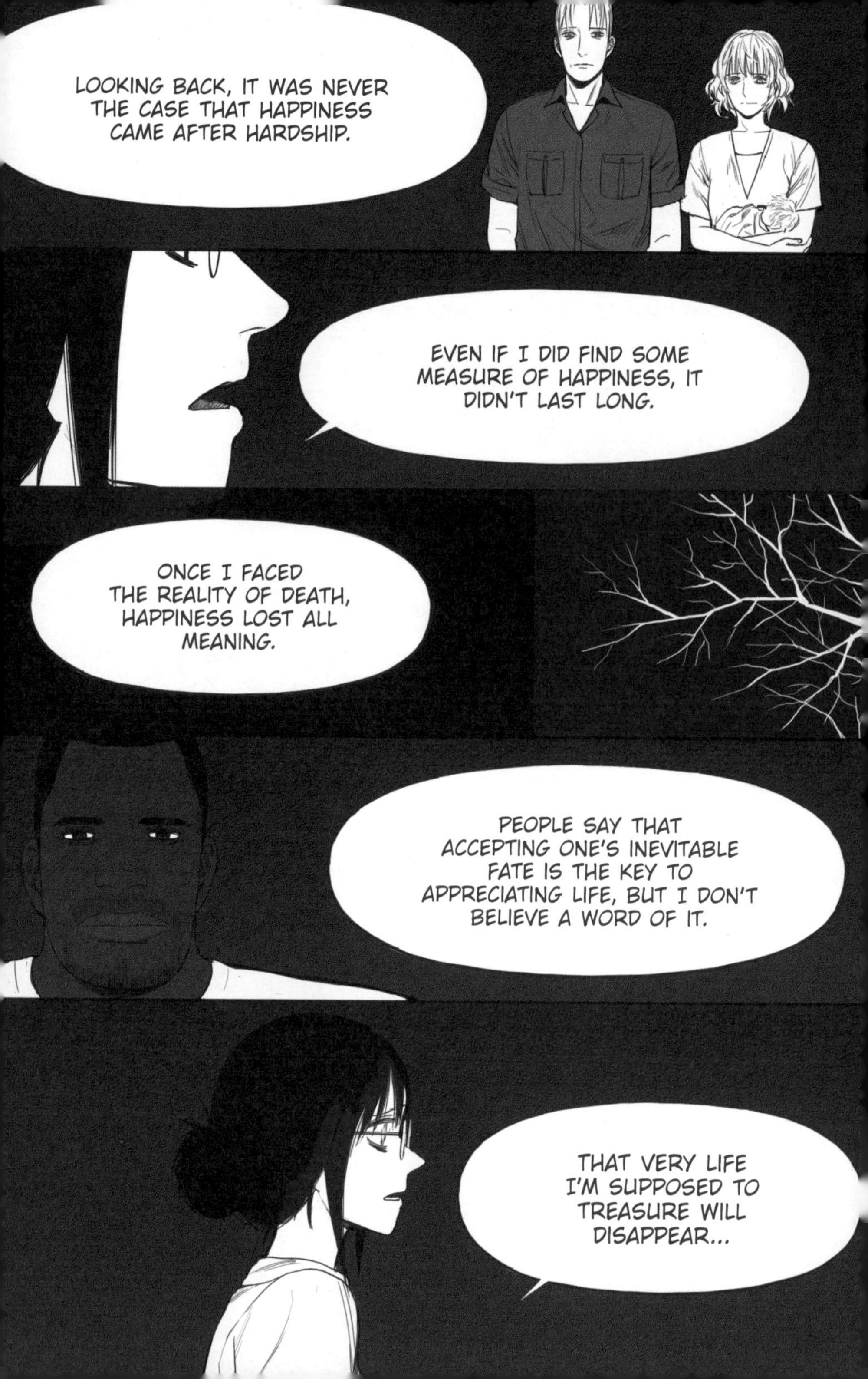
LOOKING BACK, IT WAS NEVER THE CASE THAT HAPPINESS CAME AFTER HARDSHIP.
EVEN IF I DID FIND SOME MEASURE OF HAPPINESS, IT DIDN'T LAST LONG.
ONCE I FACED THE REALITY OF DEATH, HAPPINESS LOST ALL MEANING.
PEOPLE SAY THAT ACCEPTING ONE'S INEVITABLE FATE IS THE KEY TO APPRECIATING LIFE, BUT I DON'T BELIEVE A WORD OF IT.
THAT VERY LIFE I'M SUPPOSED TO TREASURE WILL DISAPPEAR...

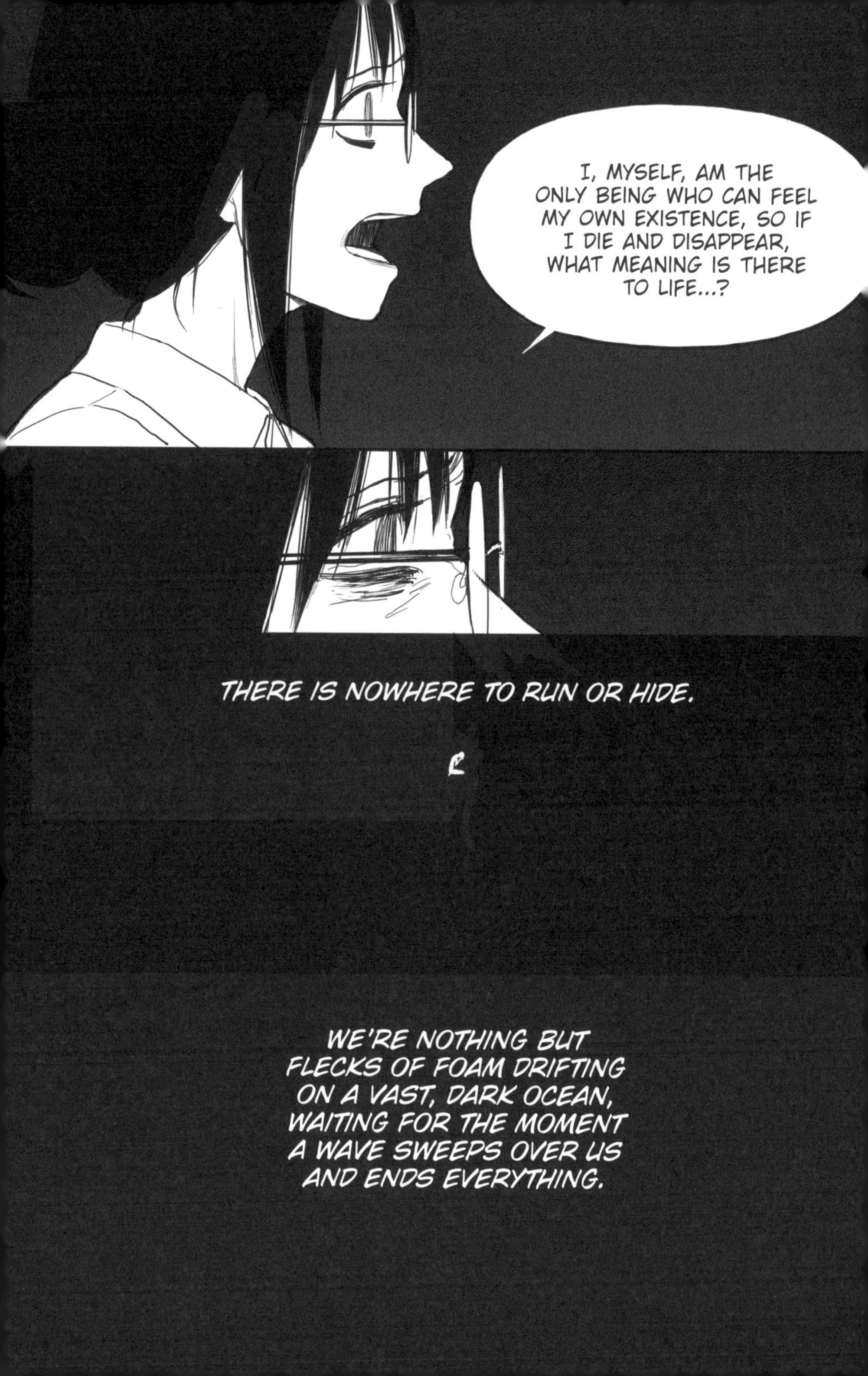
I, MYSELF, AM THE ONLY BEING WHO CAN FEEL MY OWN EXISTENCE, SO IF I DIE AND DISAPPEAR, WHAT MEANING IS THERE TO LIFE...?
THERE IS NOWHERE TO RUN OR HIDE.
WE'RE NOTHING BUT FLECKS OF FOAM DRIFTING ON A VAST, DARK OCEAN, WAITING FOR THE MOMENT A WAVE SWEEPS OVER US AND ENDS EVERYTHING.

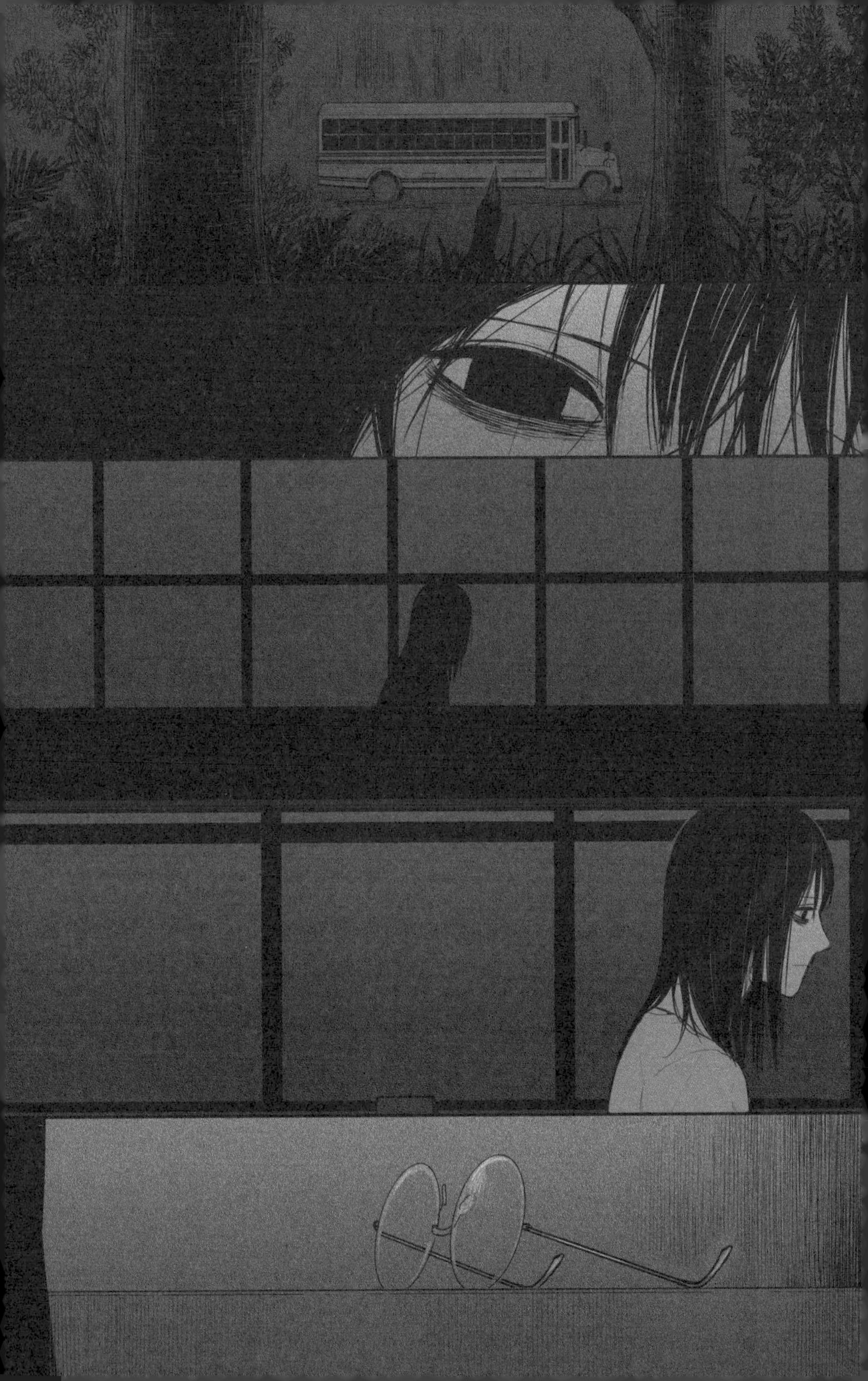

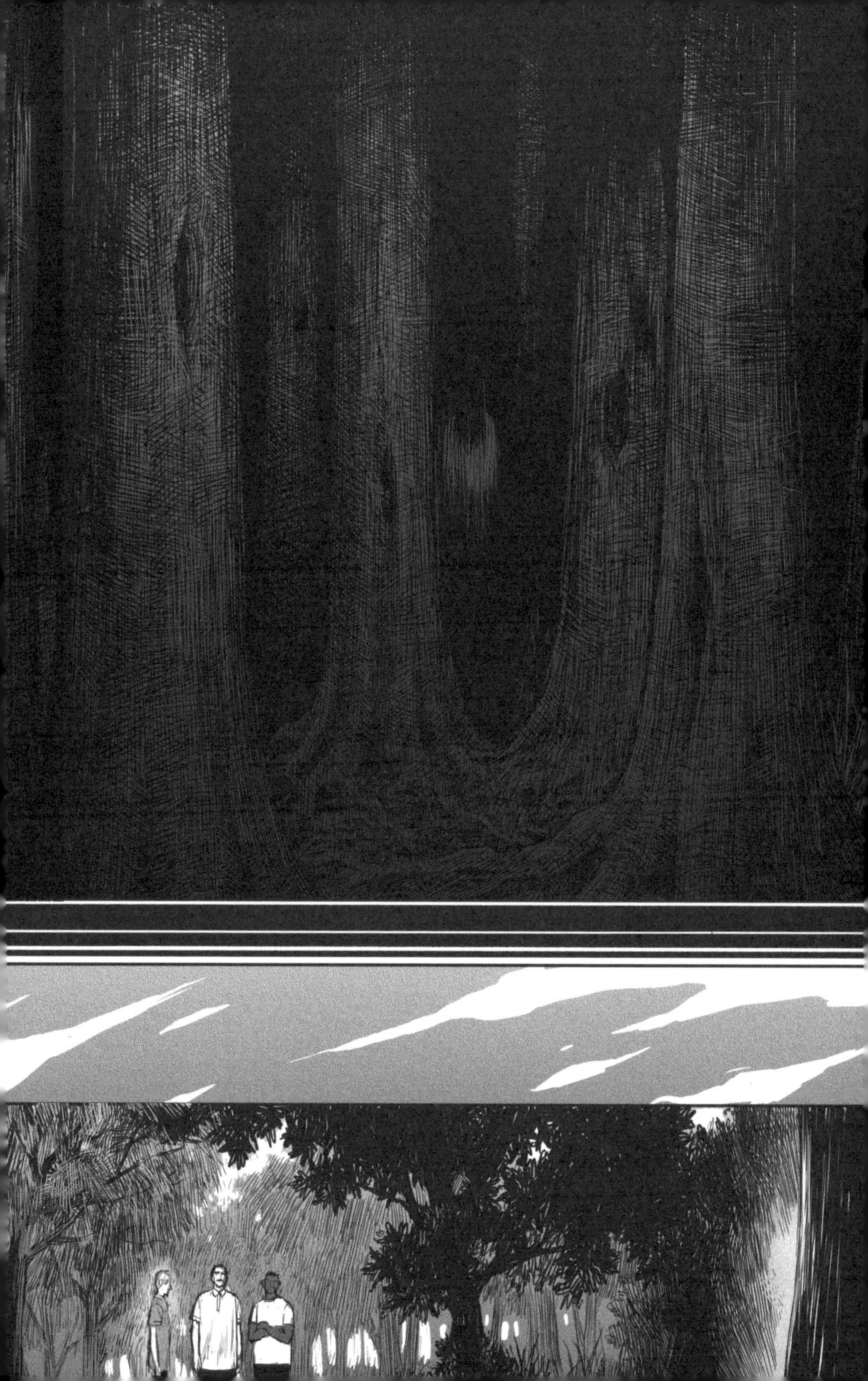

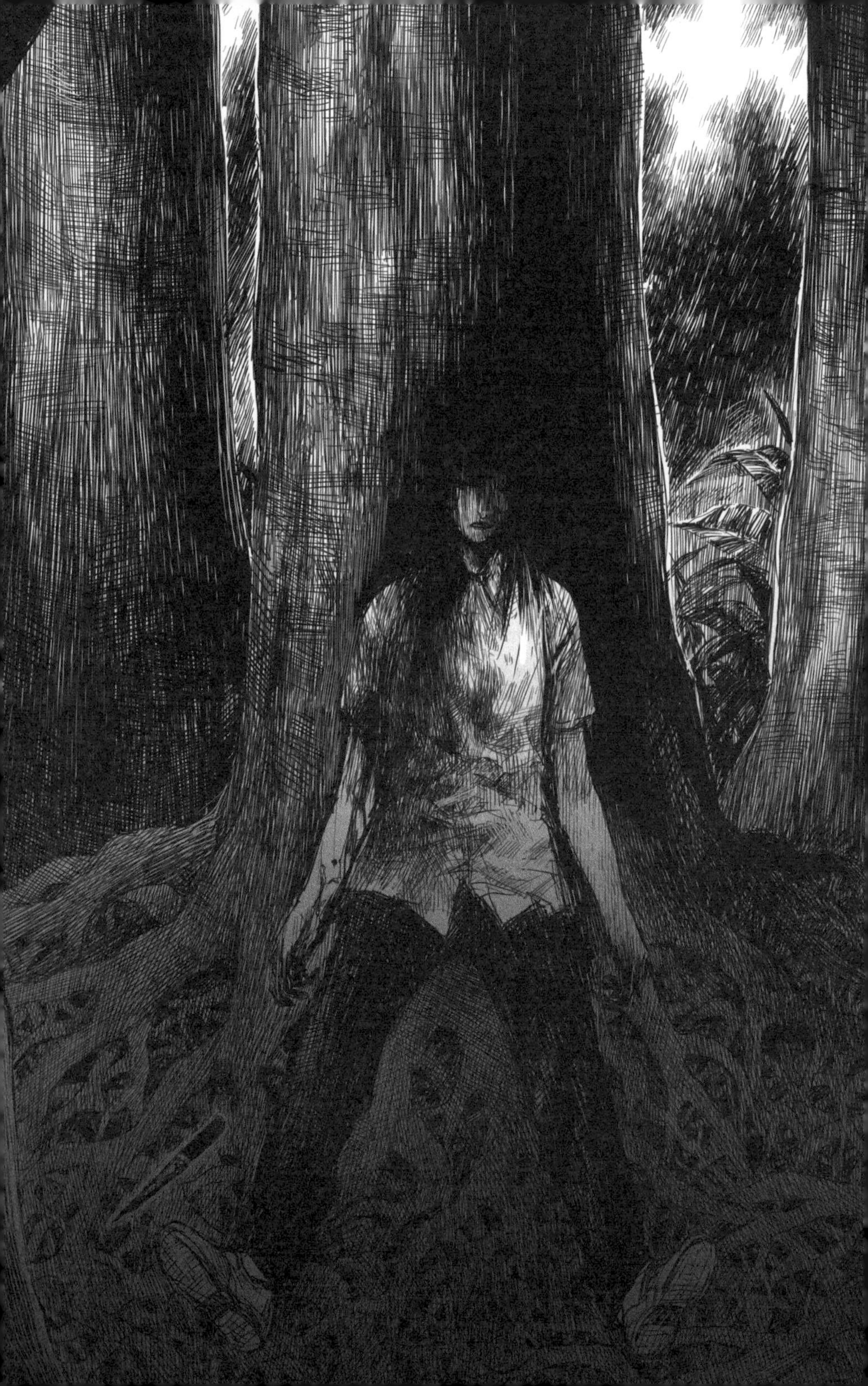

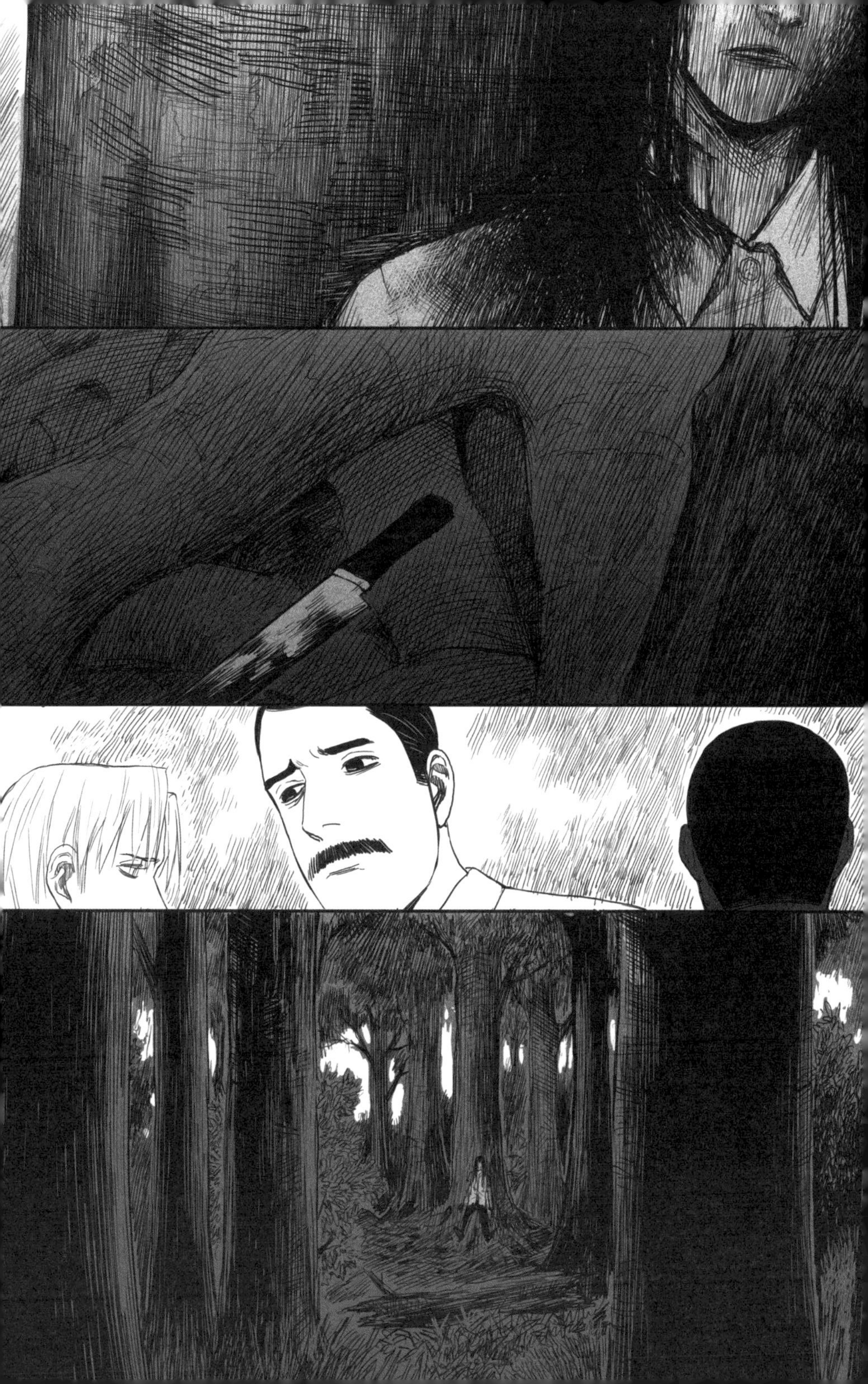

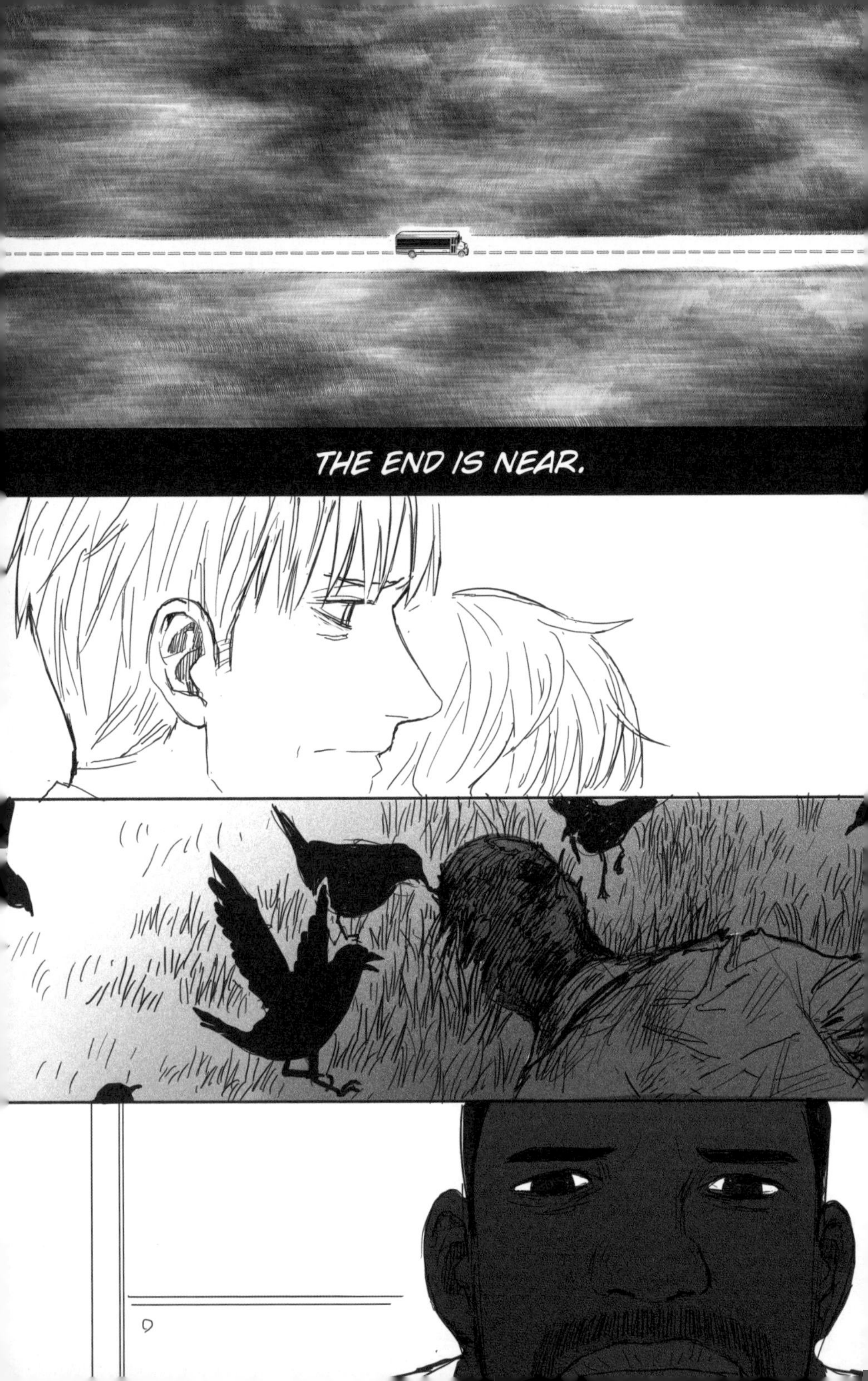
THE END IS NEAR.

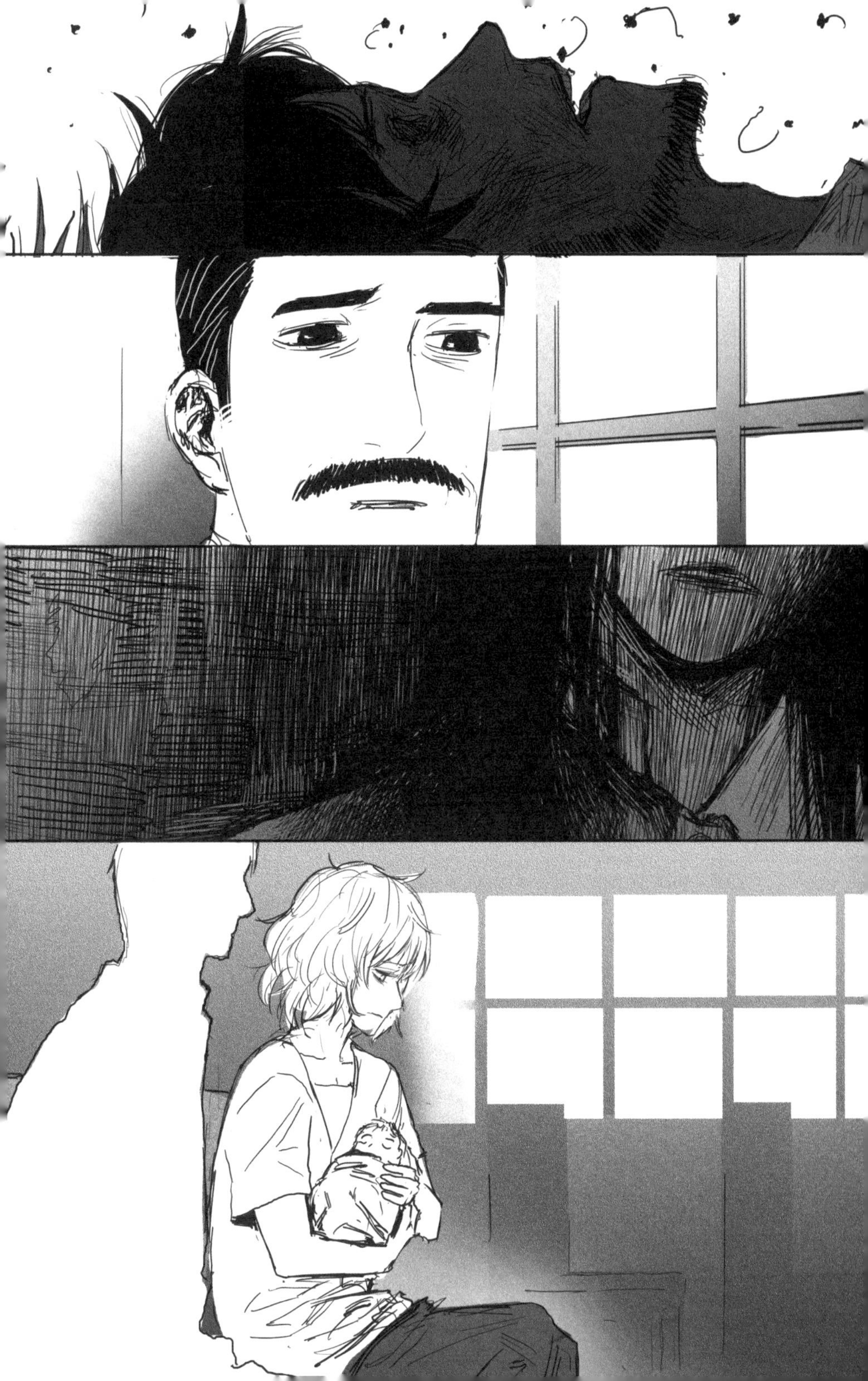

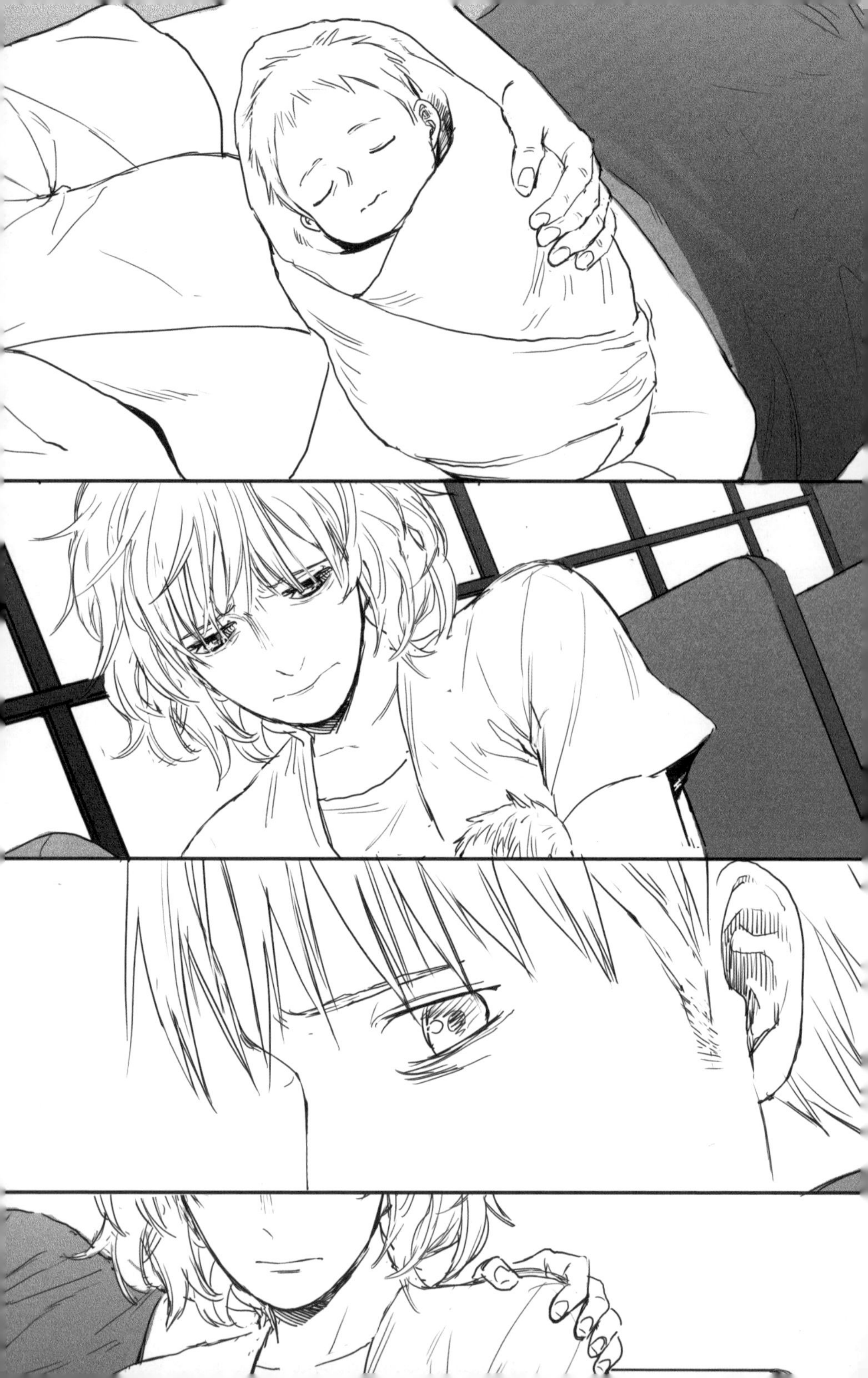

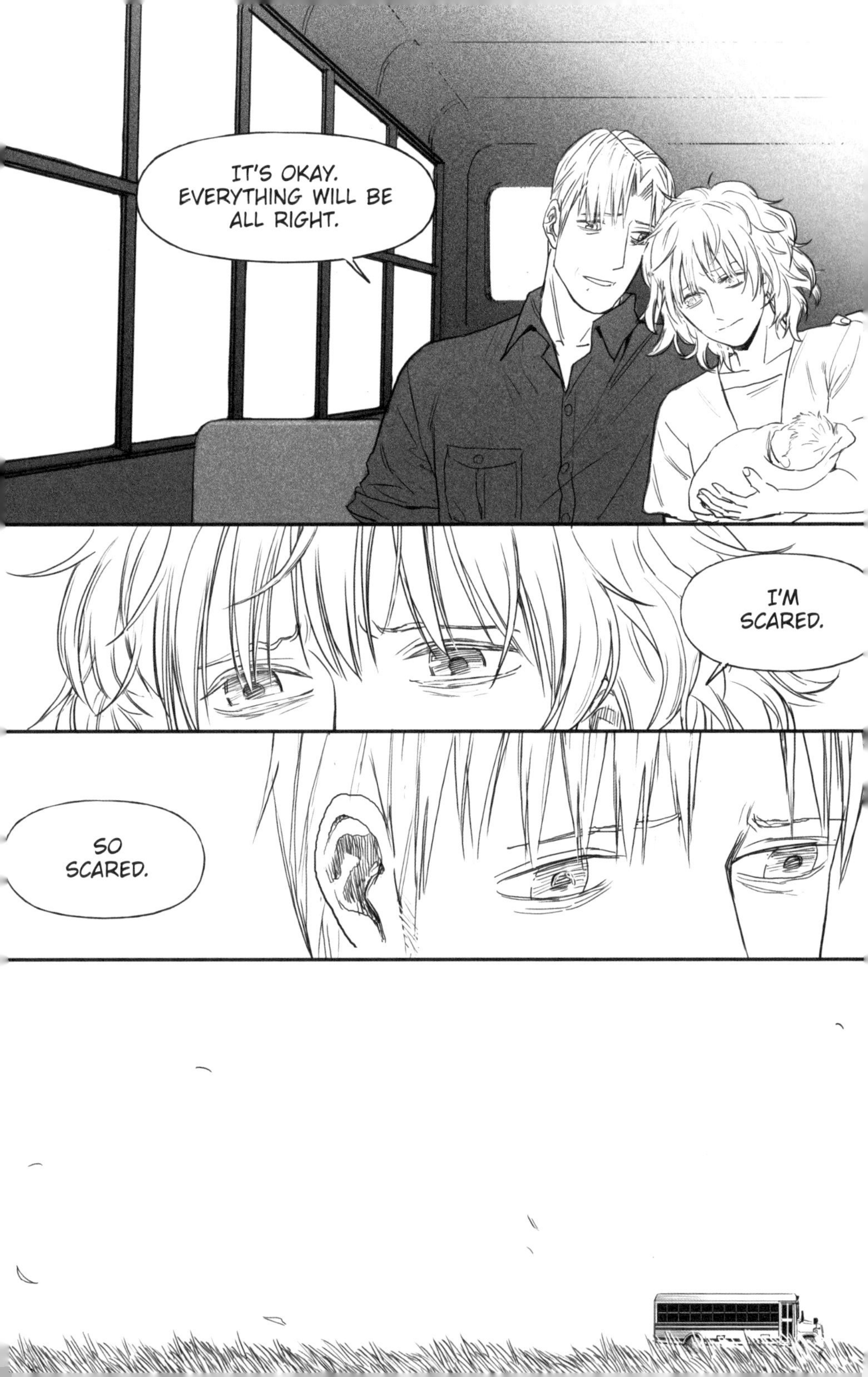
IT'S OKAY. EVERYTHING WILL BE ALL RIGHT.
I'M SCARED.
SO SCARED.

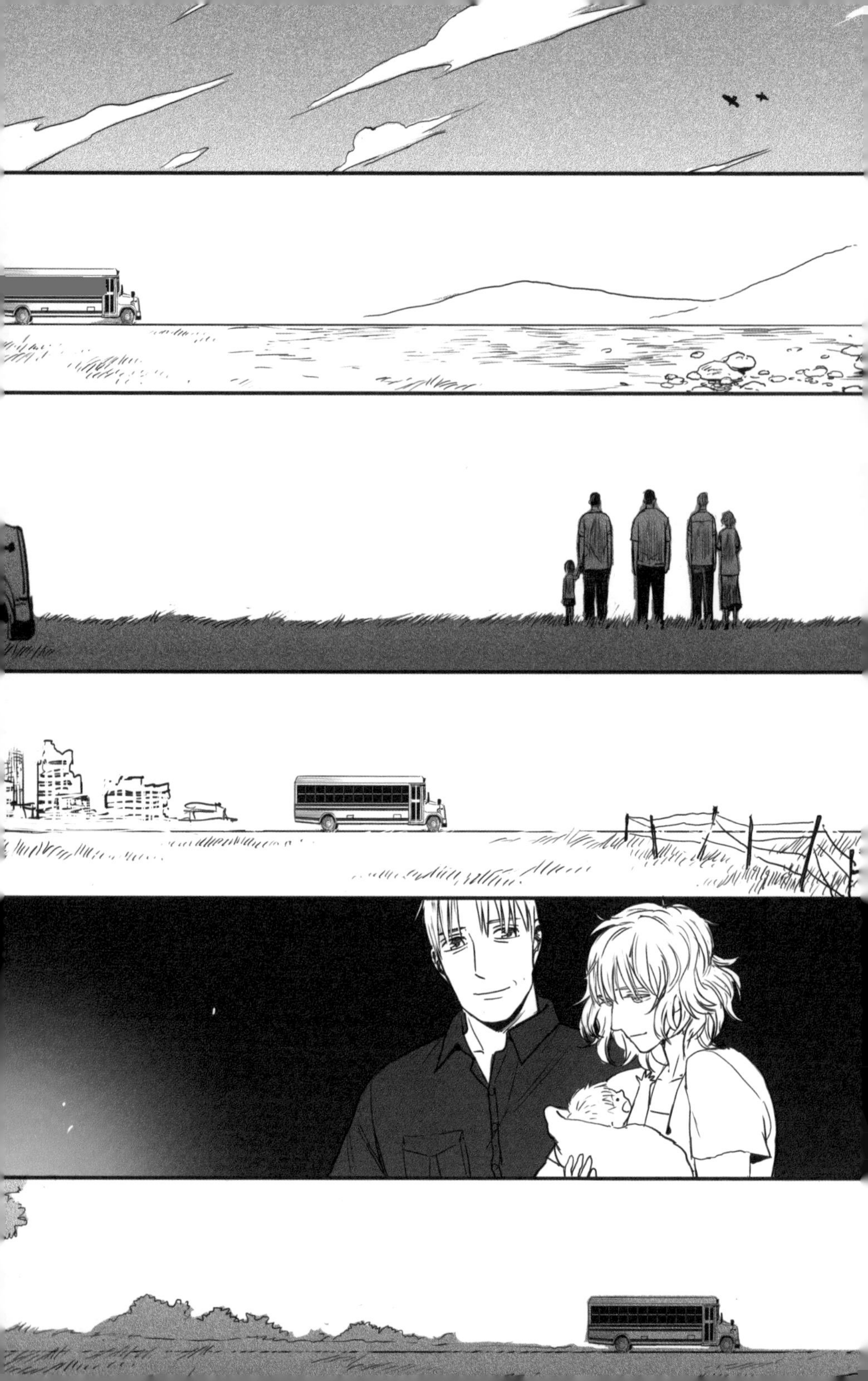

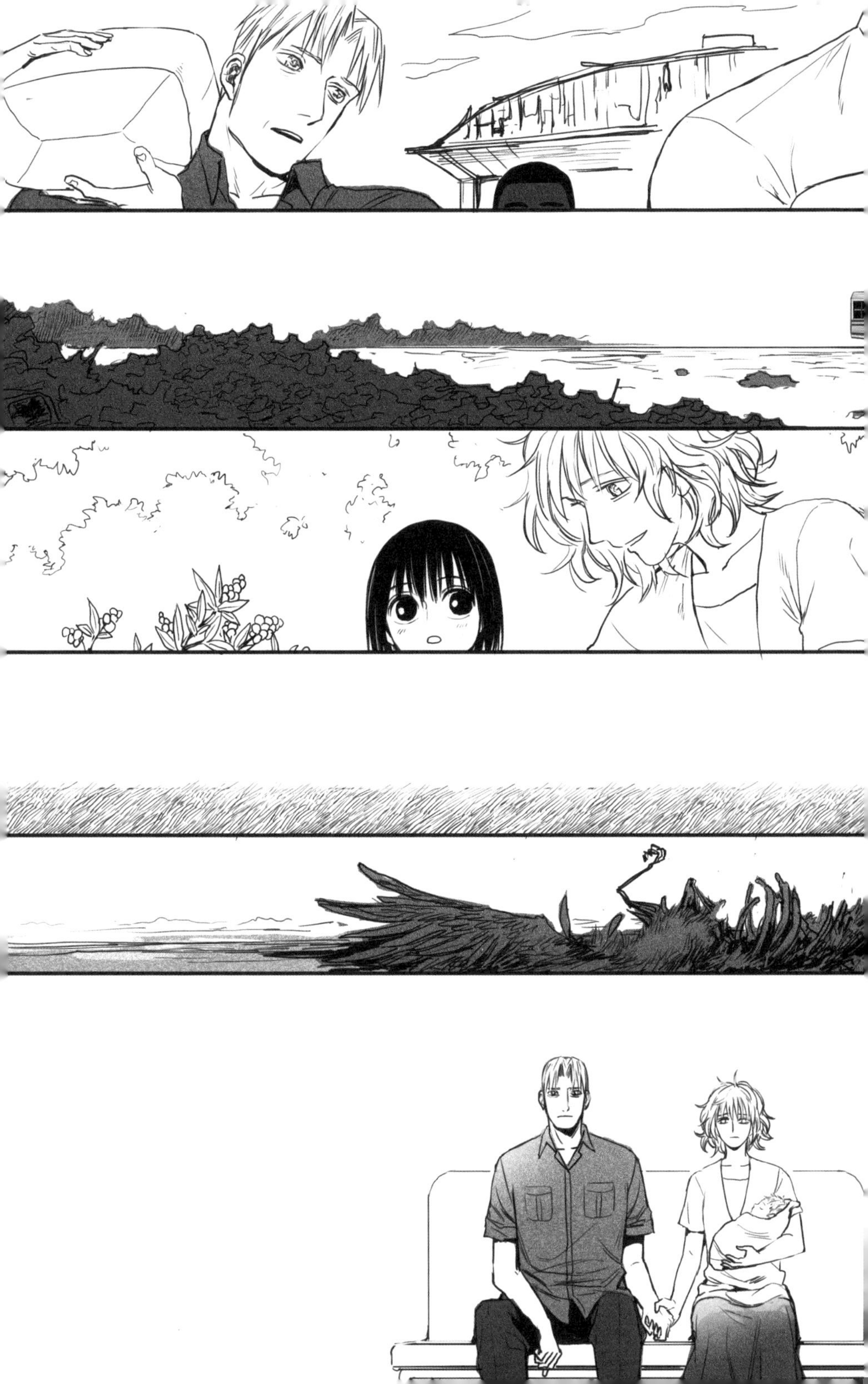

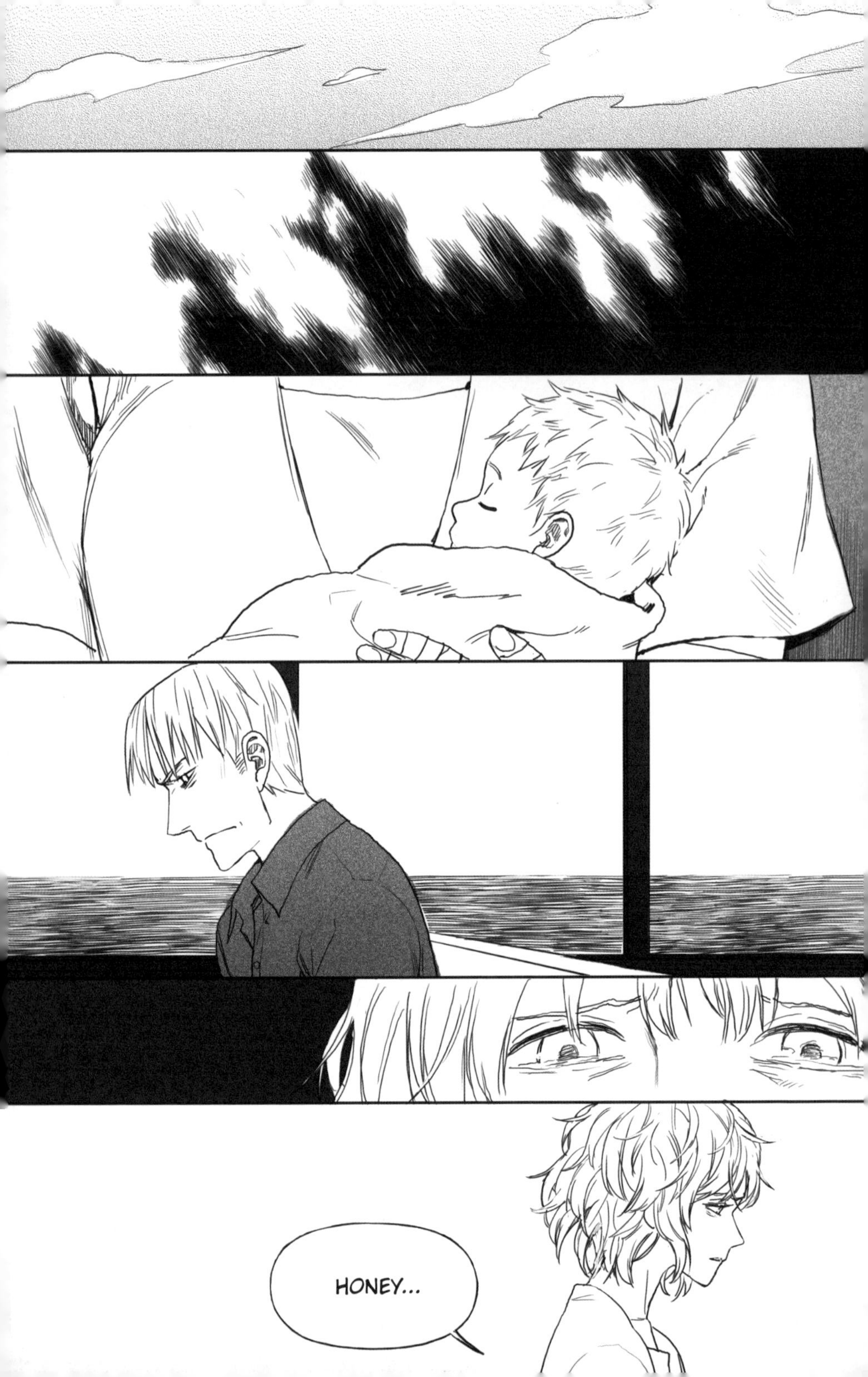
HONEY...

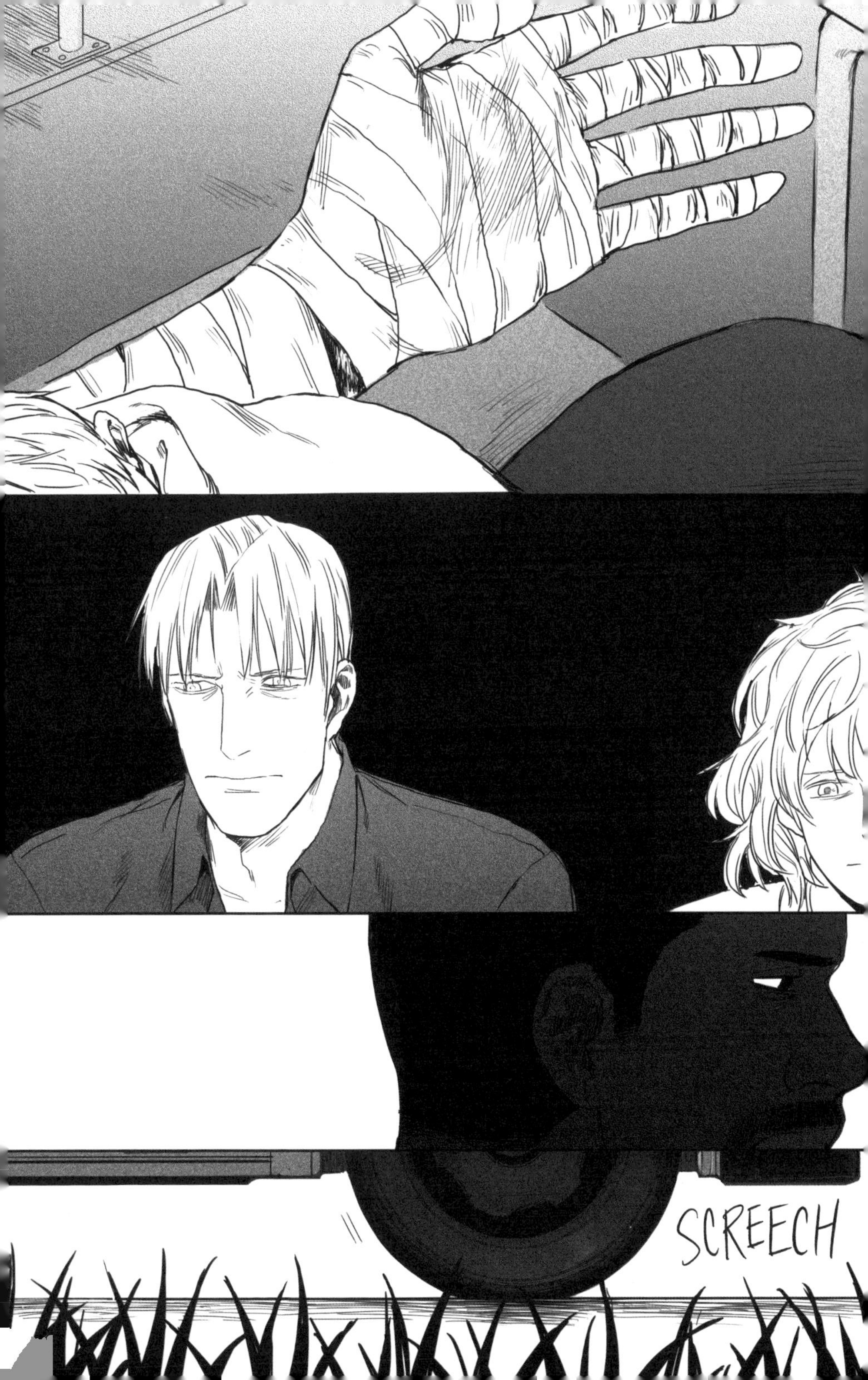
SCREECH

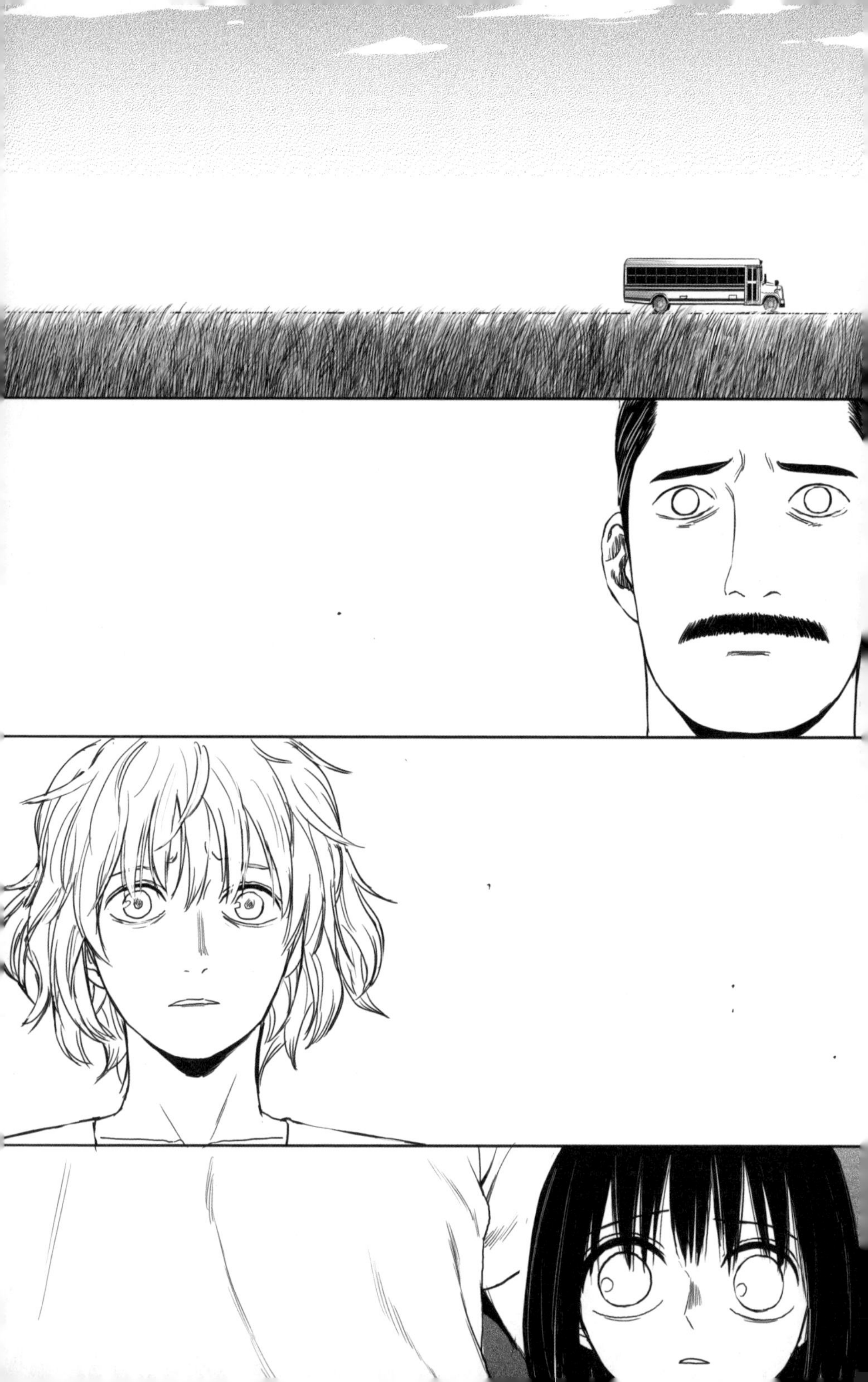

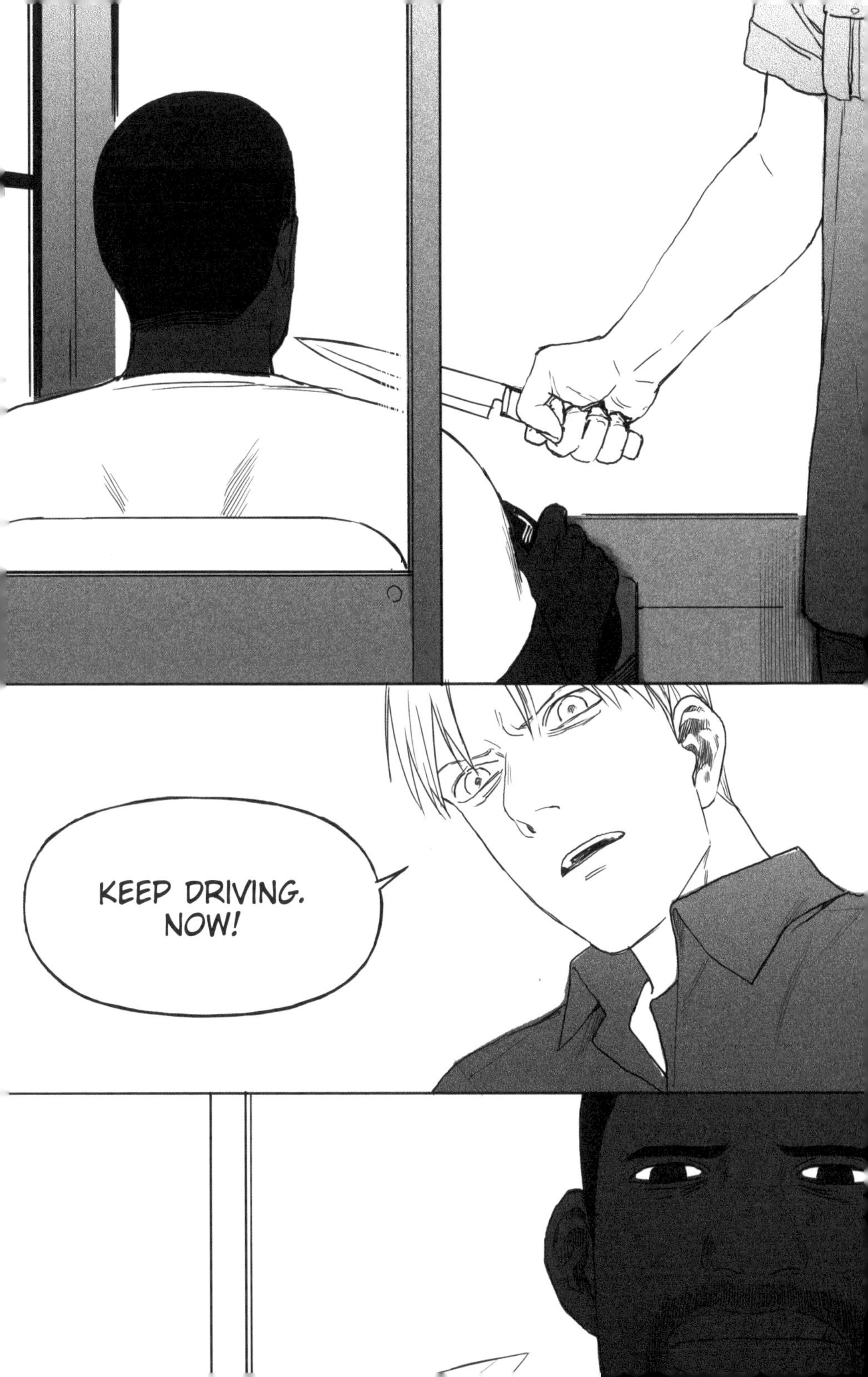
KEEP DRIVING.
NOW!

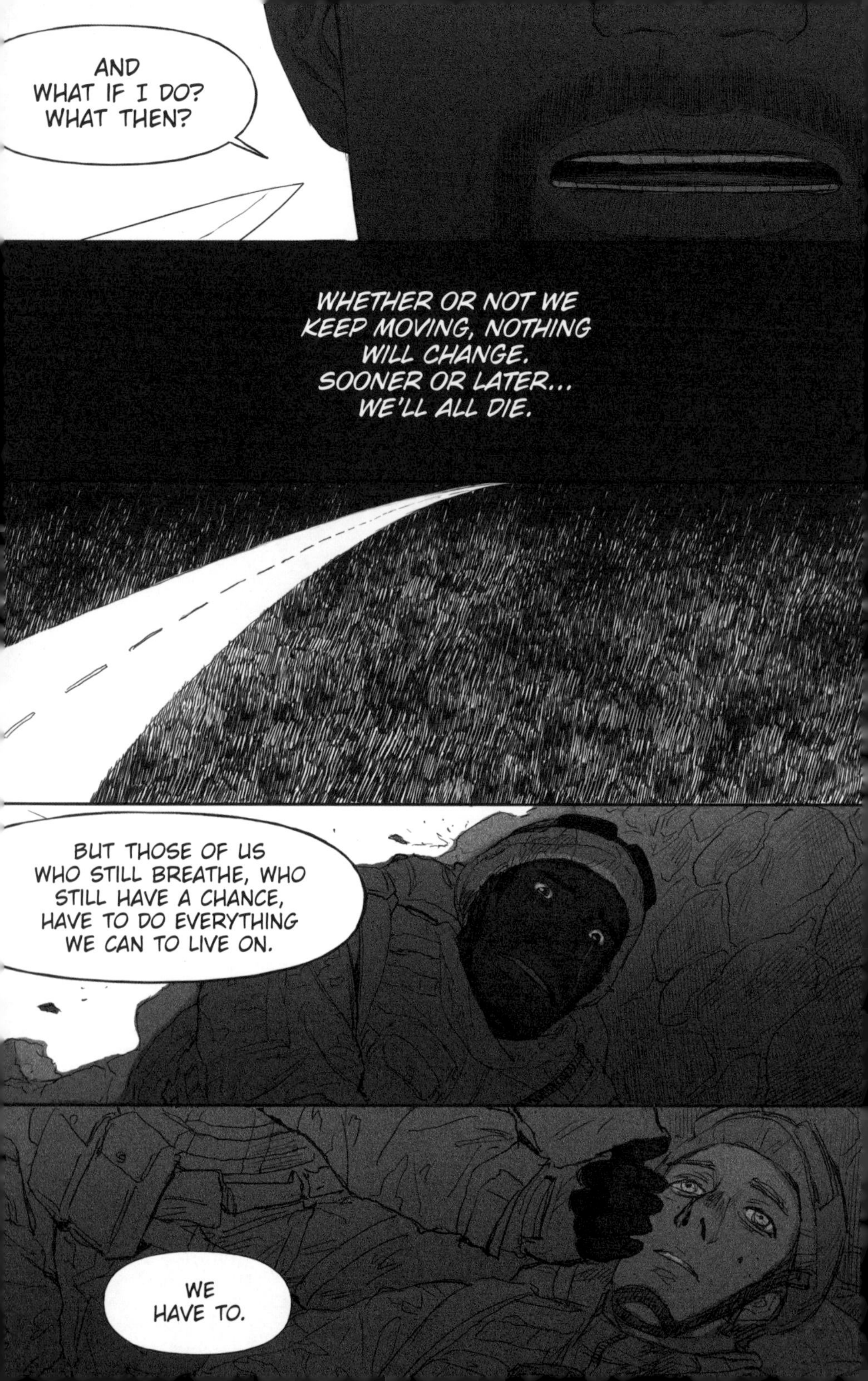
AND WHAT IF I DO? WHAT THEN?
WHETHER OR NOT WE KEEP MOVING, NOTHING WILL CHANGE. SOONER OR LATER... WE'LL ALL DIE.
BUT THOSE OF US WHO STILL BREATHE, WHO STILL HAVE A CHANCE, HAVE TO DO EVERYTHING WE CAN TO LIVE ON.
WE HAVE TO.

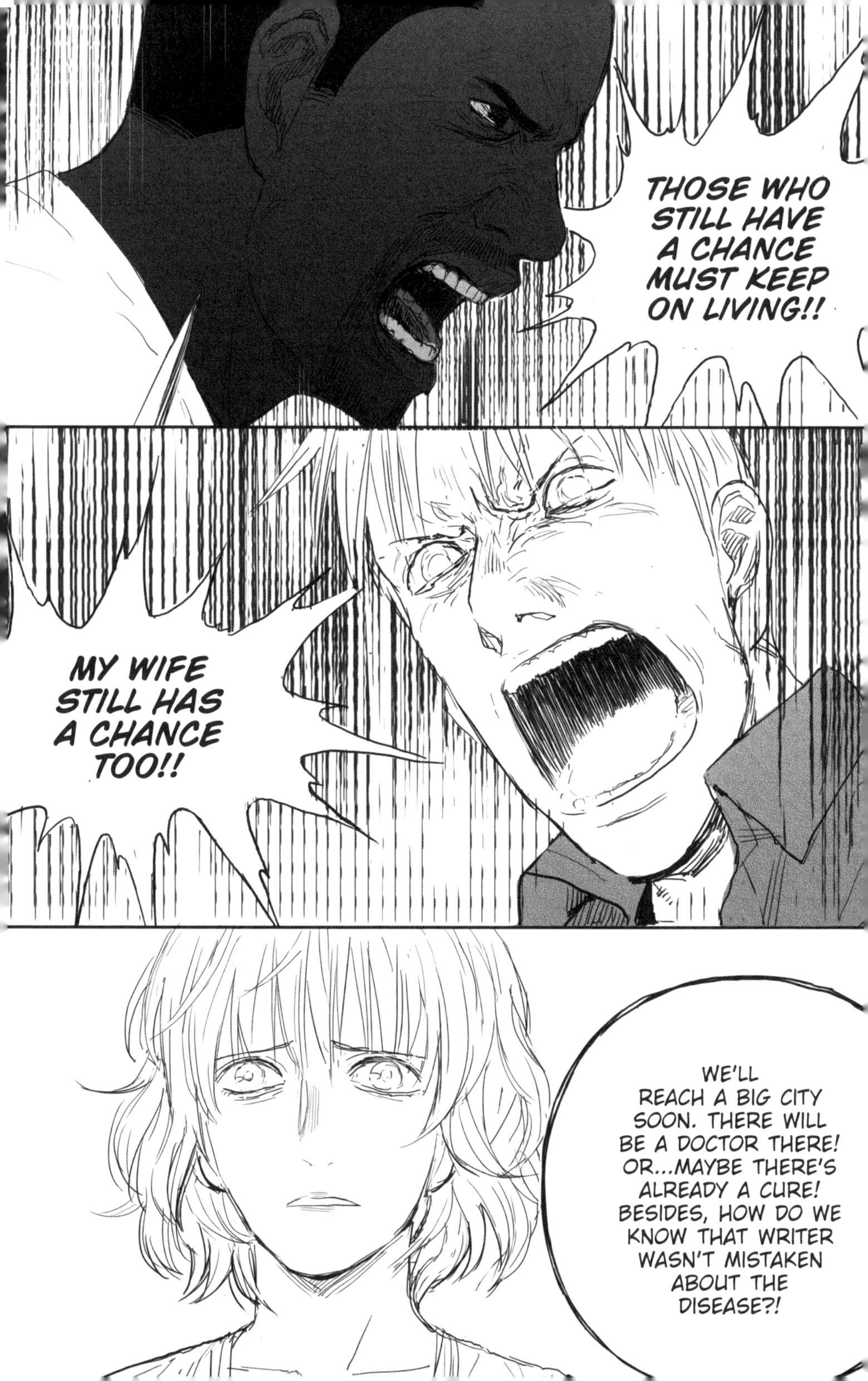
THOSE WHO STILL HAVE A CHANCE MUST KEEP ON LIVING!!
MY WIFE STILL HAS A CHANCE TOO!!
WE'LL REACH A BIG CITY SOON. THERE WILL BE A DOCTOR THERE! OR...MAYBE THERE'S ALREADY A CURE! BESIDES, HOW DO WE KNOW THAT WRITER WASN'T MISTAKEN ABOUT THE DISEASE?!

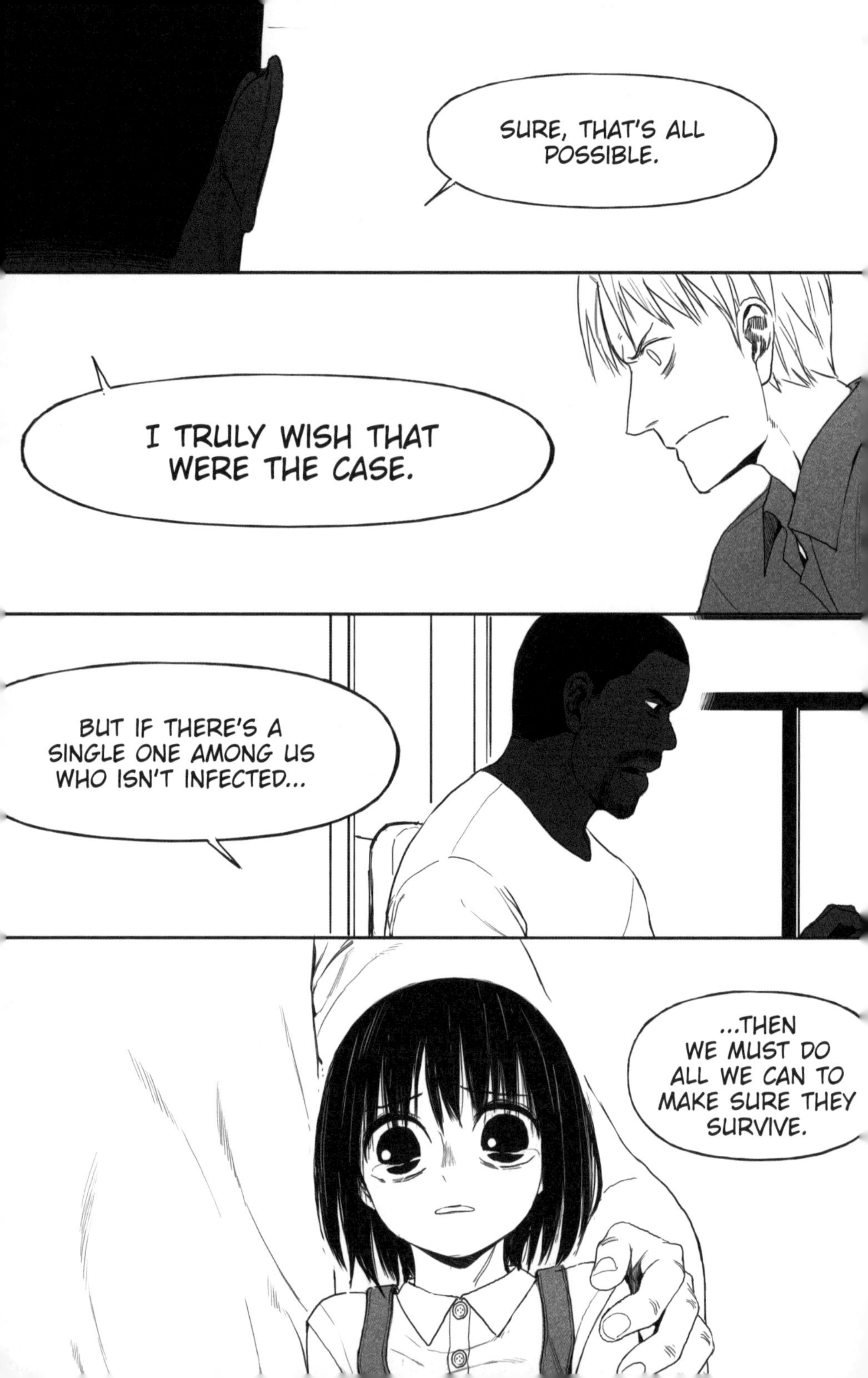
SURE, THAT'S ALL POSSIBLE.
I TRULY WISH THAT WERE THE CASE.
BUT IF THERE'S A SINGLE ONE AMONG US WHO ISN'T INFECTED...
...THEN WE MUST DO ALL WE CAN TO MAKE SURE THEY SURVIVE.

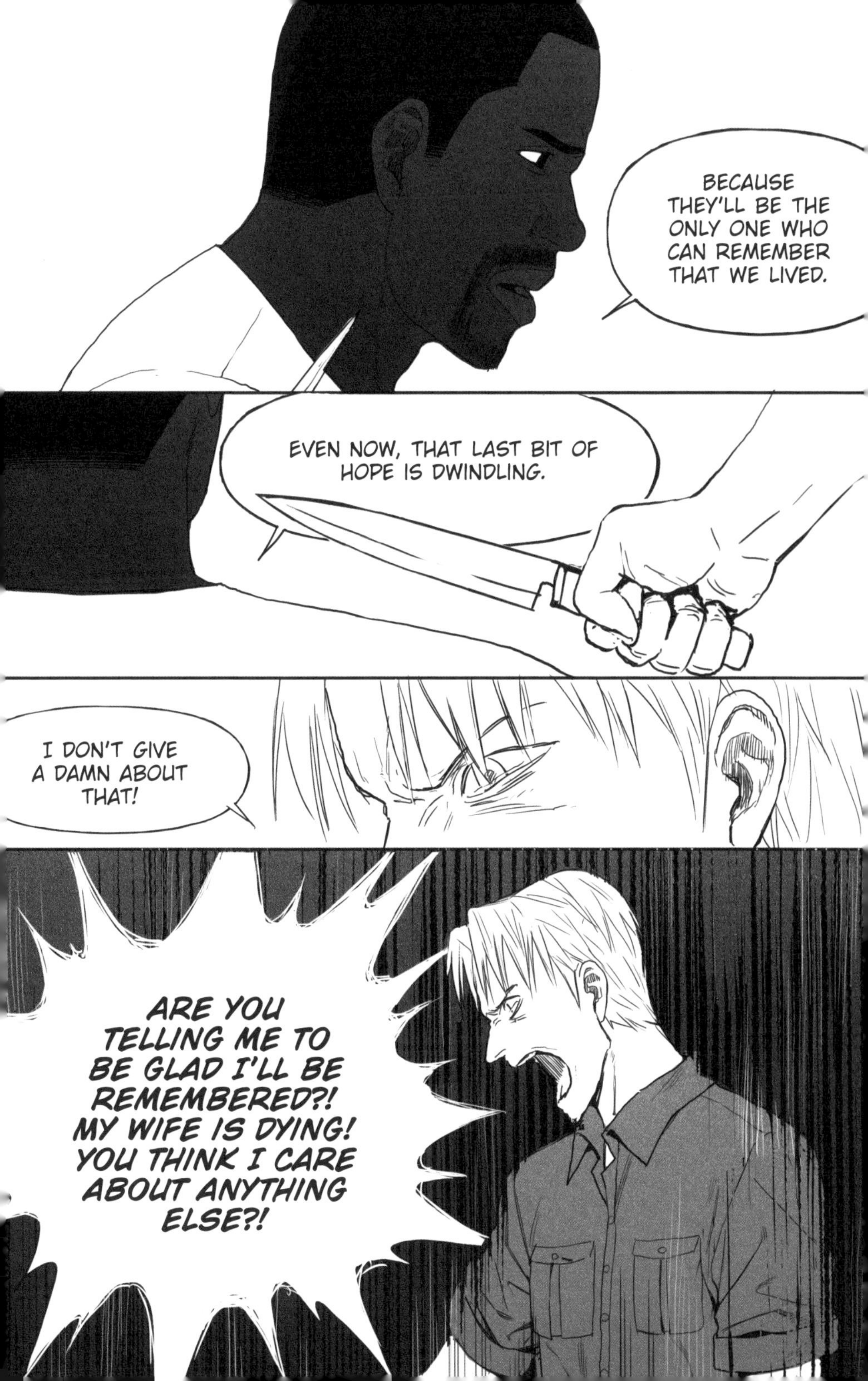
BECAUSE THEY'LL BE THE ONLY ONE WHO CAN REMEMBER THAT WE LIVED.
EVEN NOW, THAT LAST BIT OF HOPE IS DWINDLING.
I DON'T GIVE A DAMN ABOUT THAT!
ARE YOU TELLING ME TO BE GLAD I'LL BE REMEMBERED?! MY WIFE IS DYING! YOU THINK I CARE ABOUT ANYTHING ELSE?!

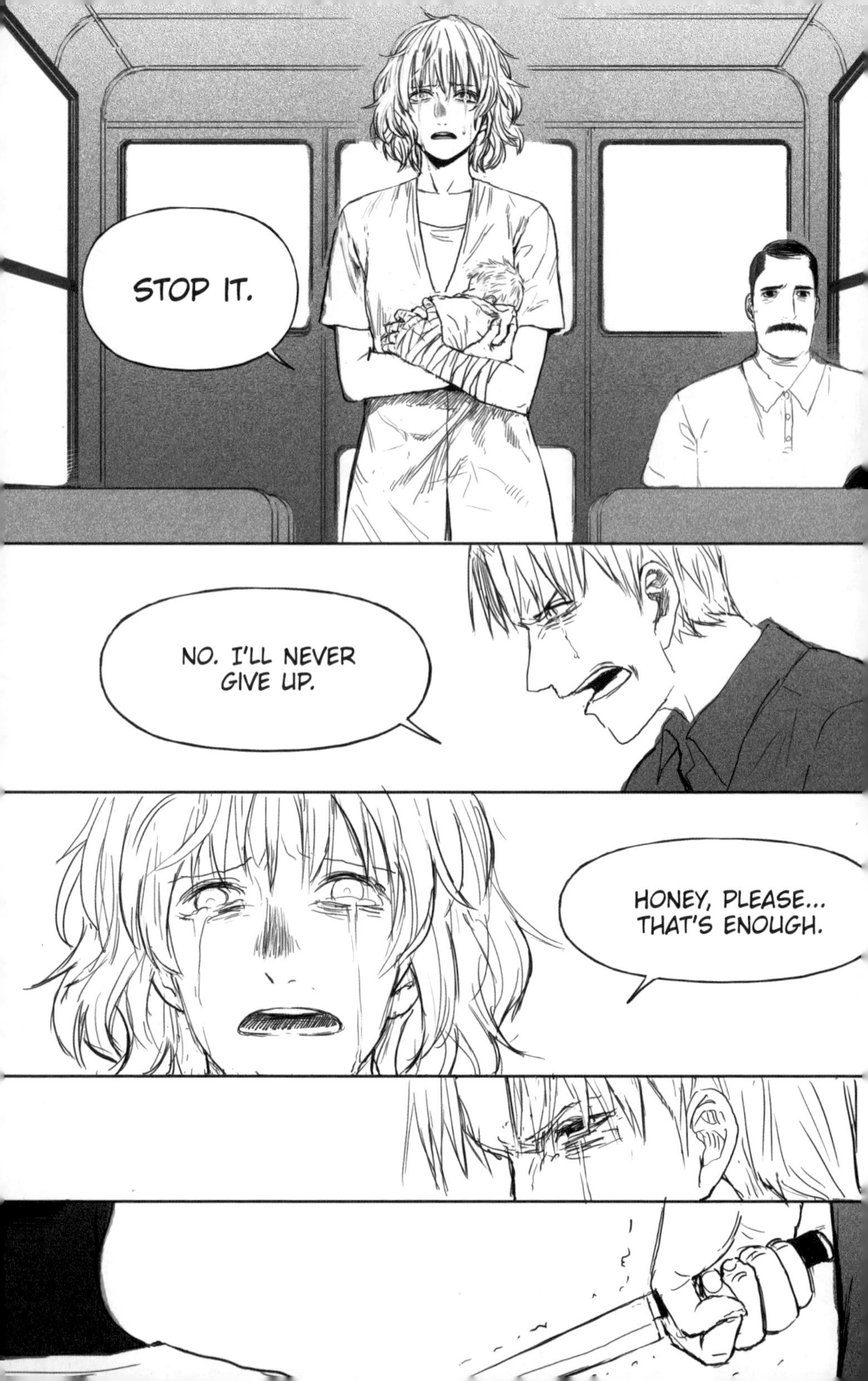
STOP IT.
NO. I'LL NEVER GIVE UP.
HONEY, PLEASE... THAT'S ENOUGH.

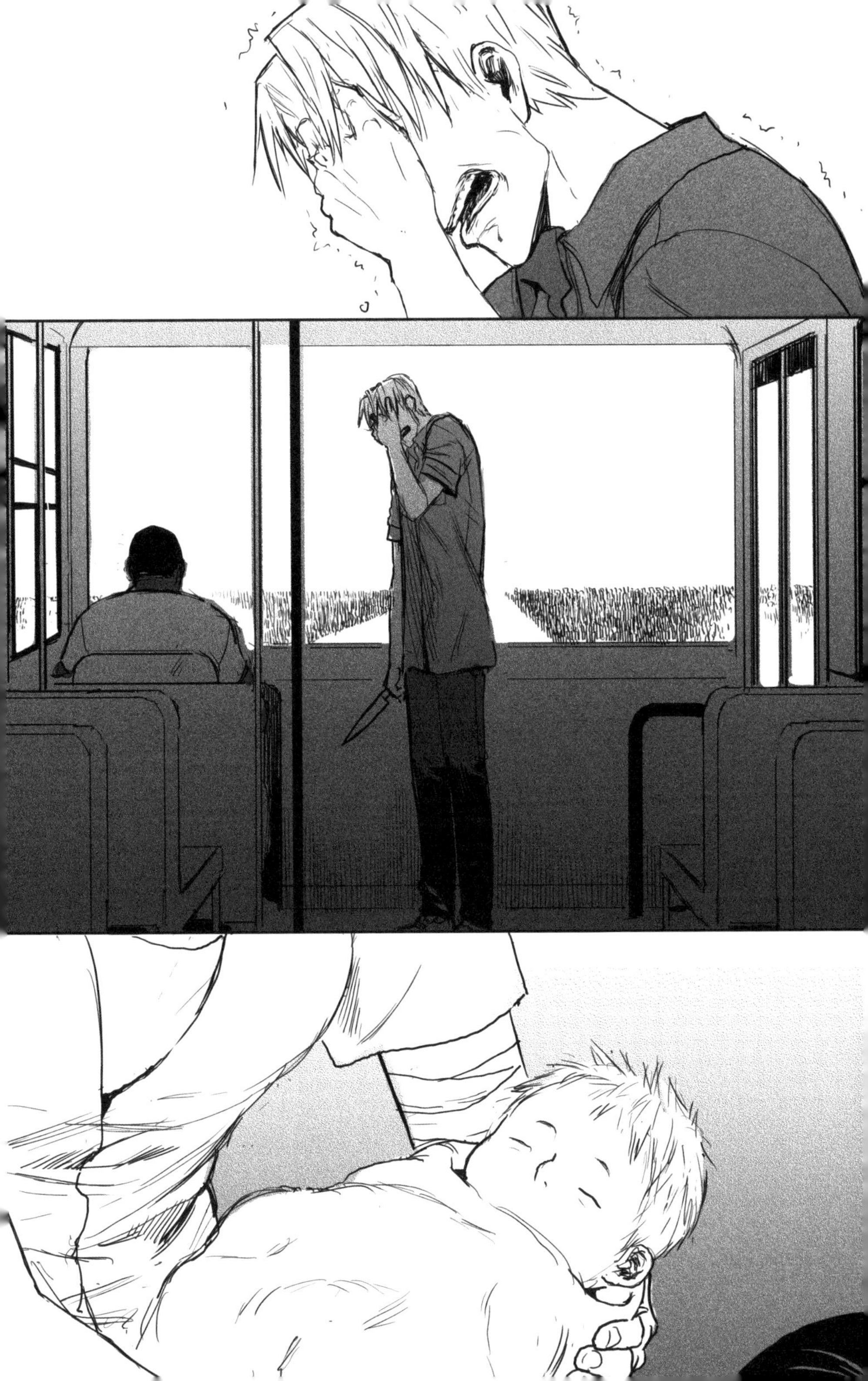

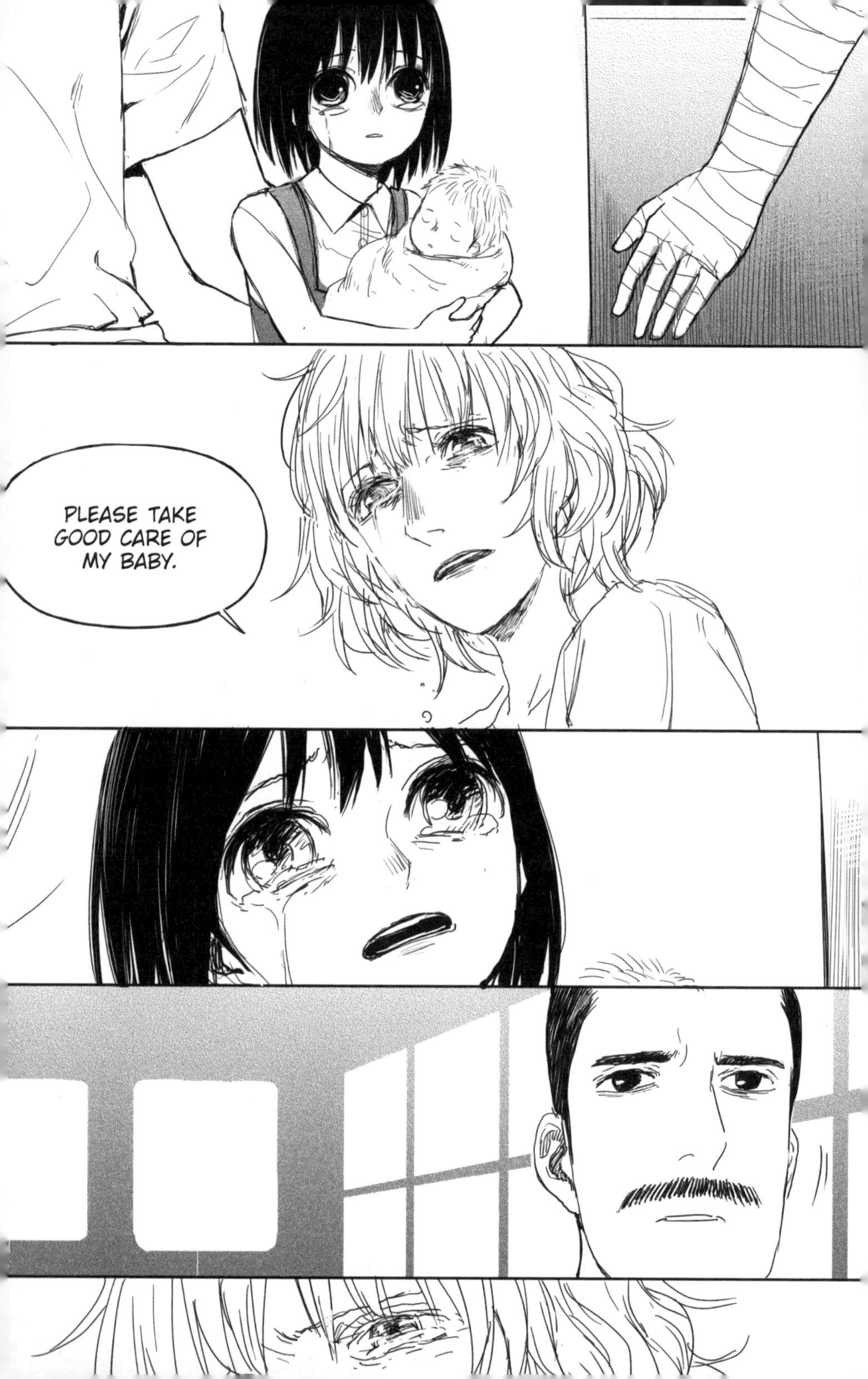
PLEASE TAKE GOOD CARE OF MY BABY.

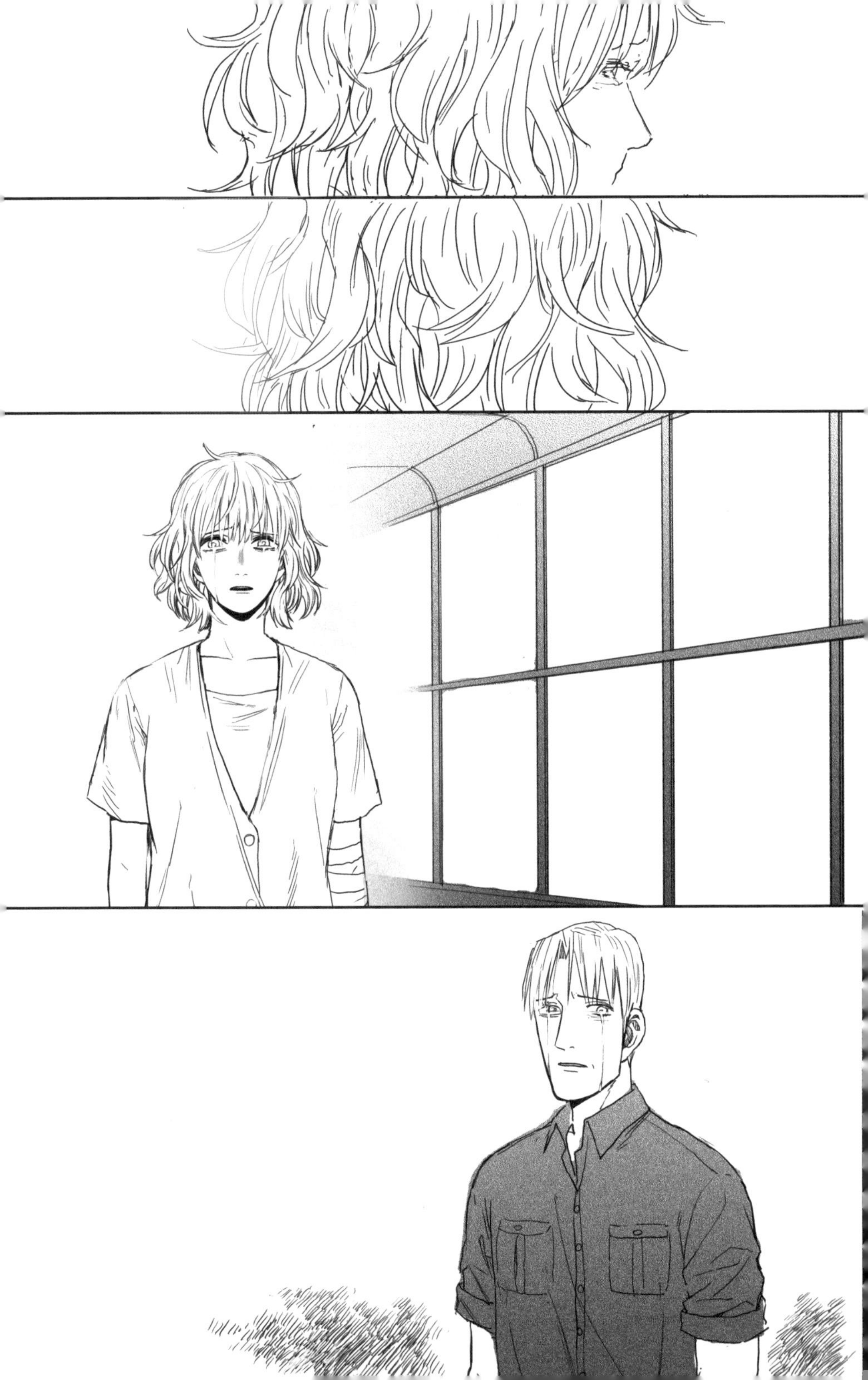

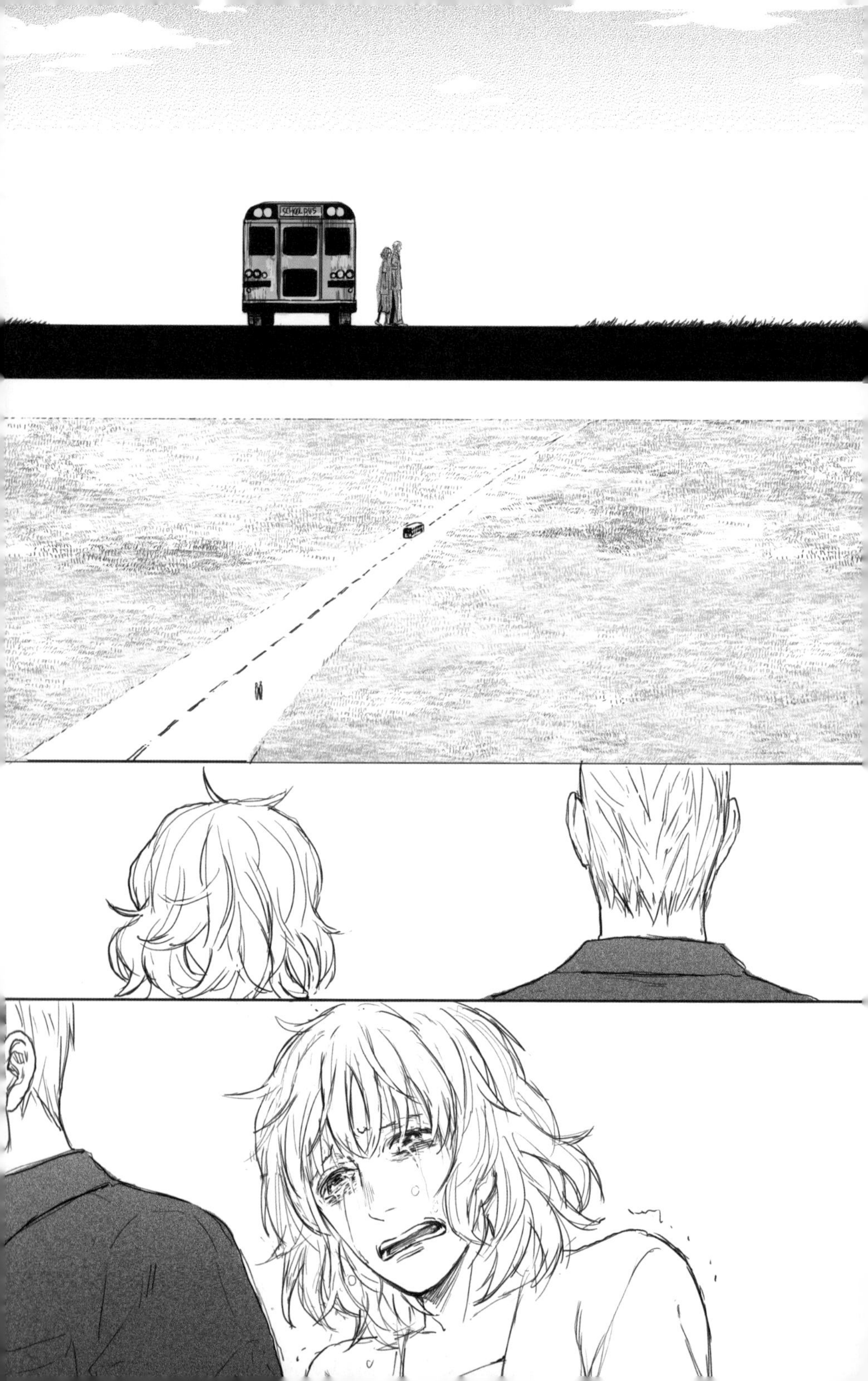
SCHOOL BUS

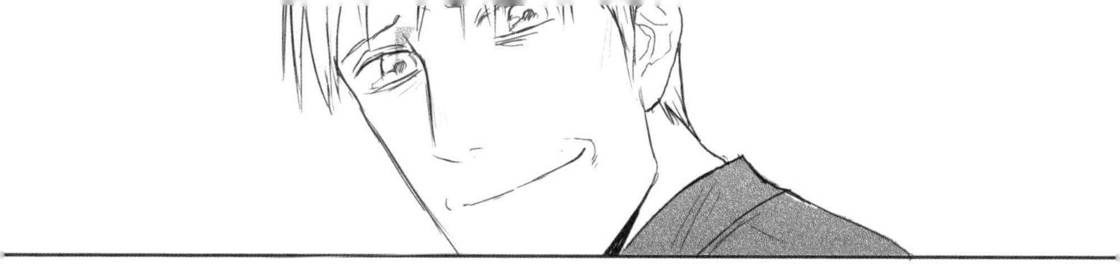
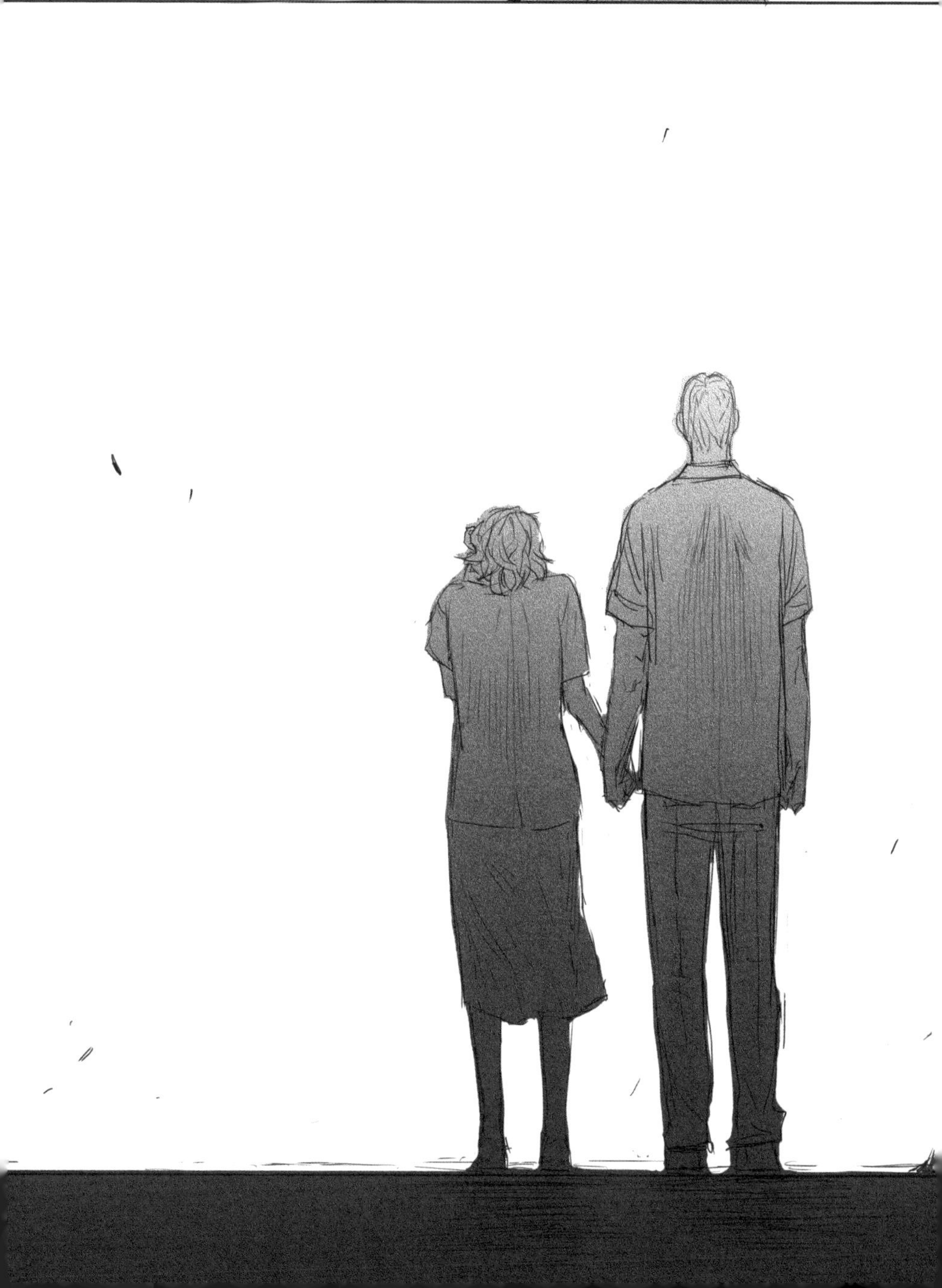

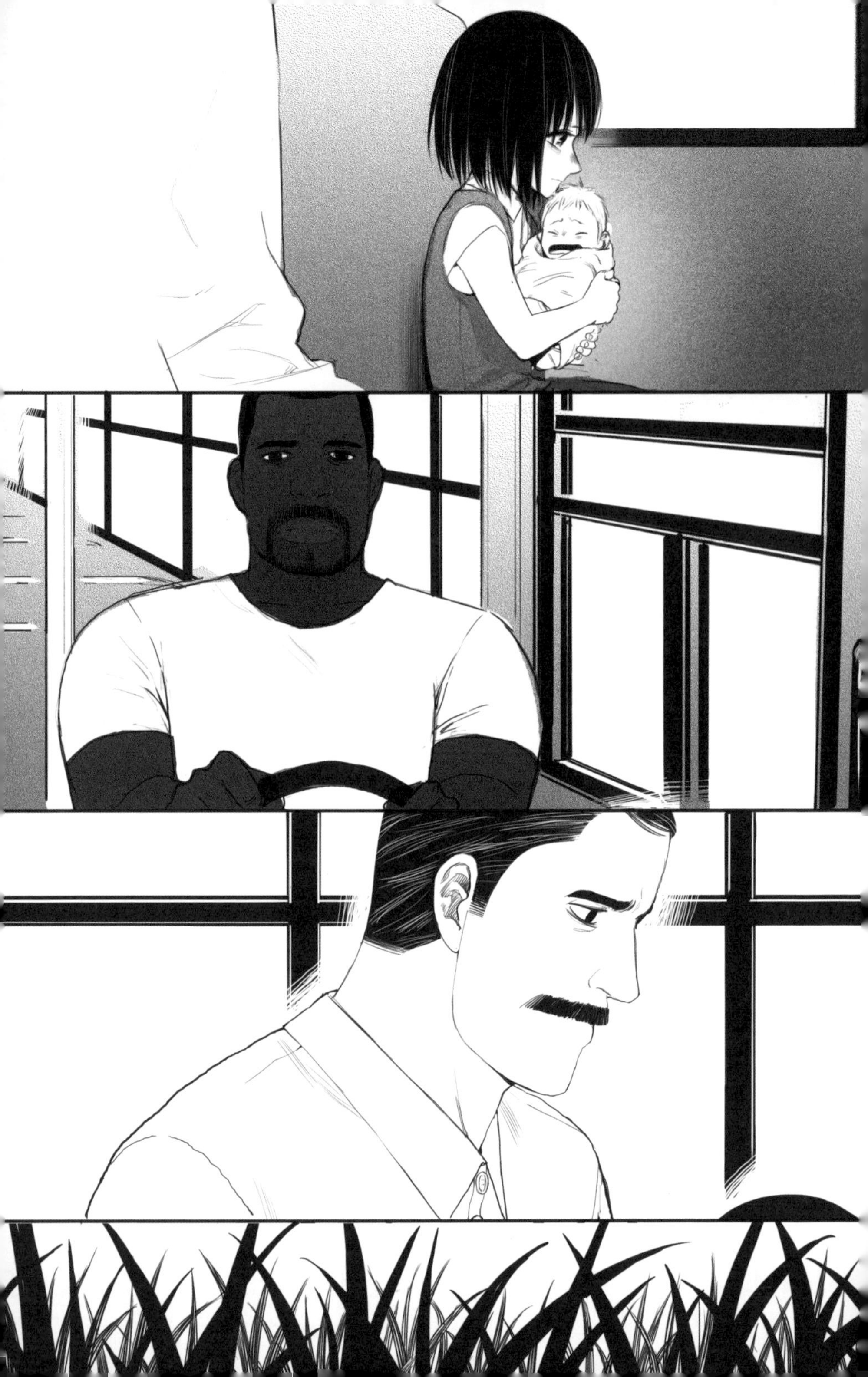

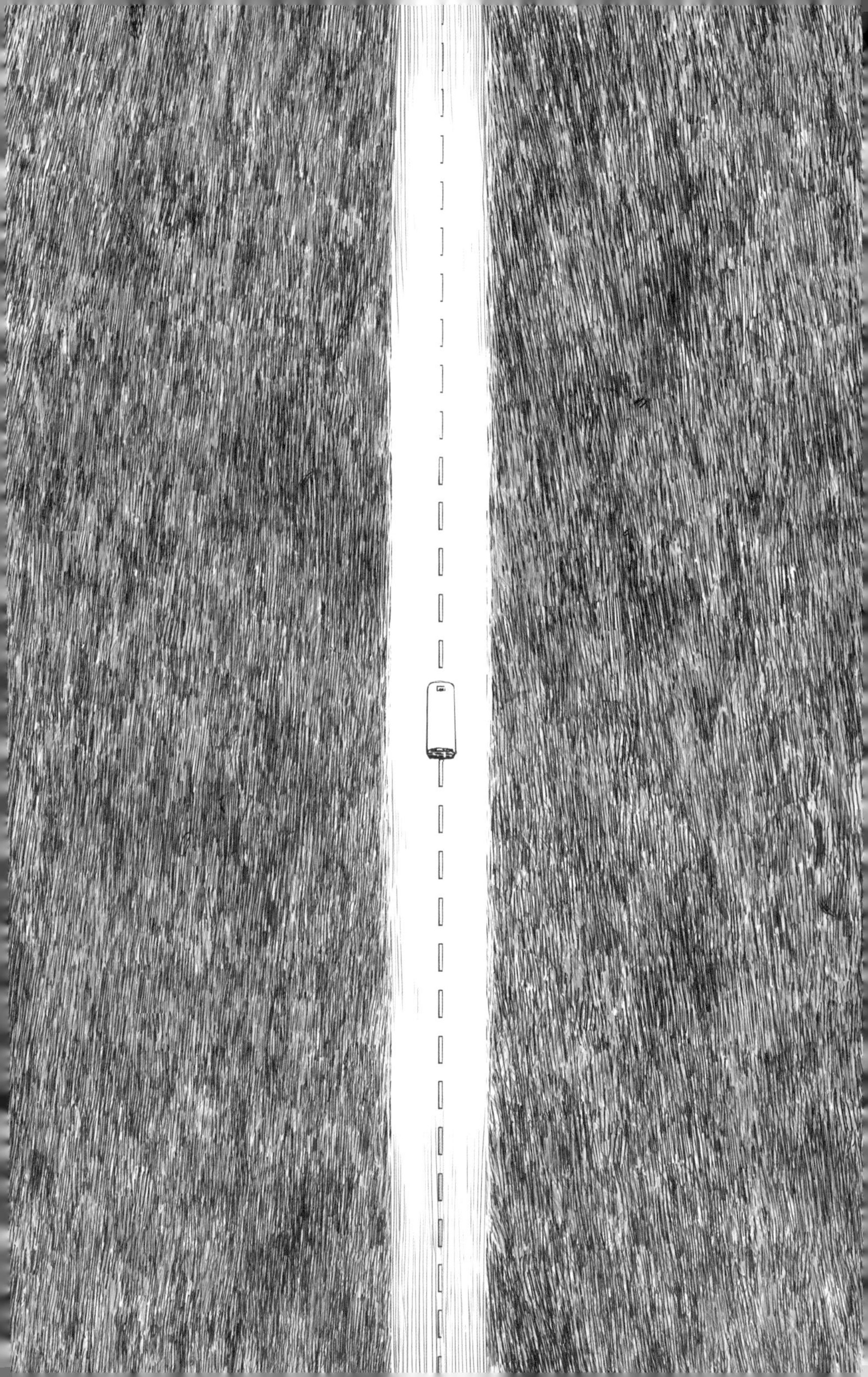

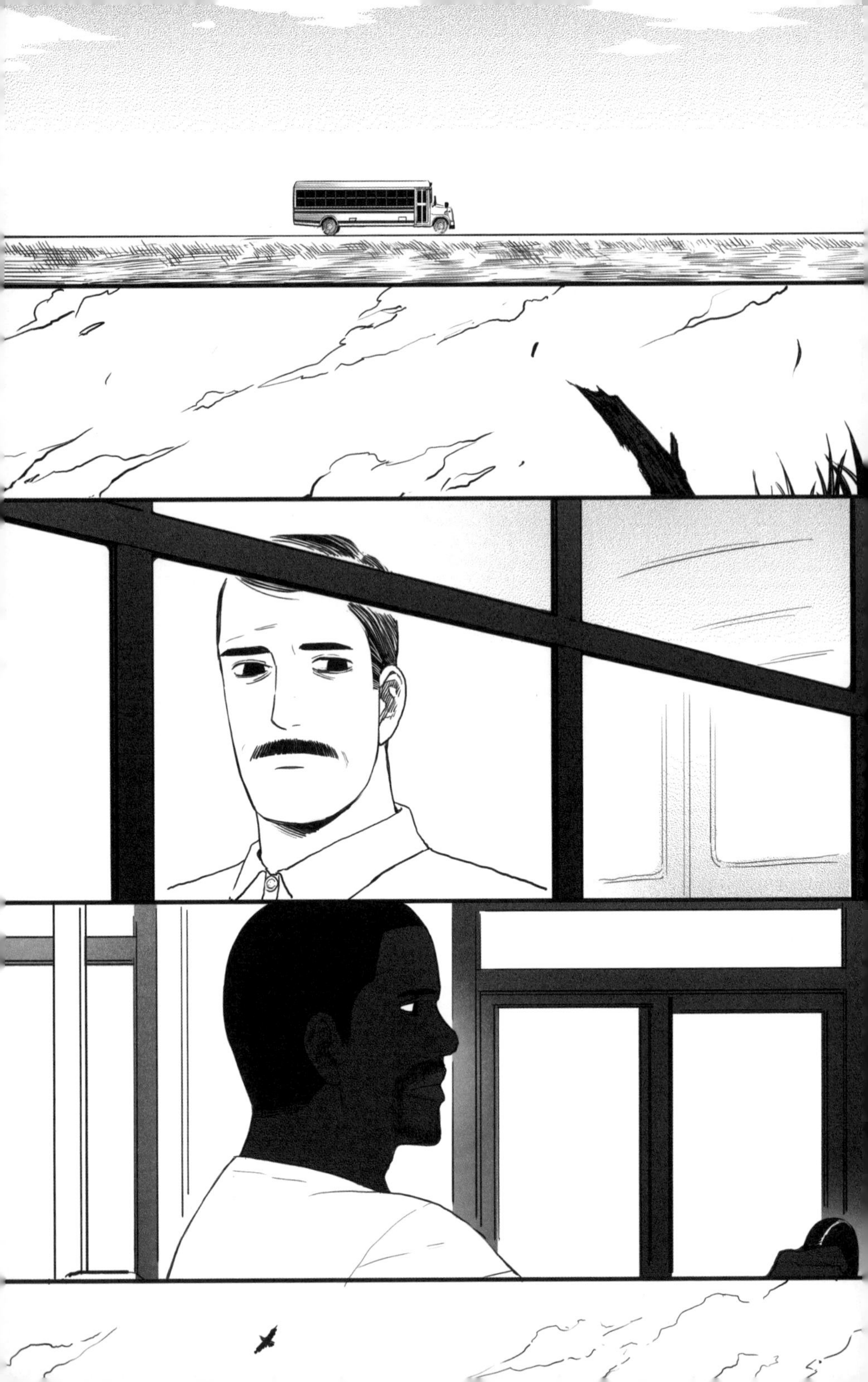

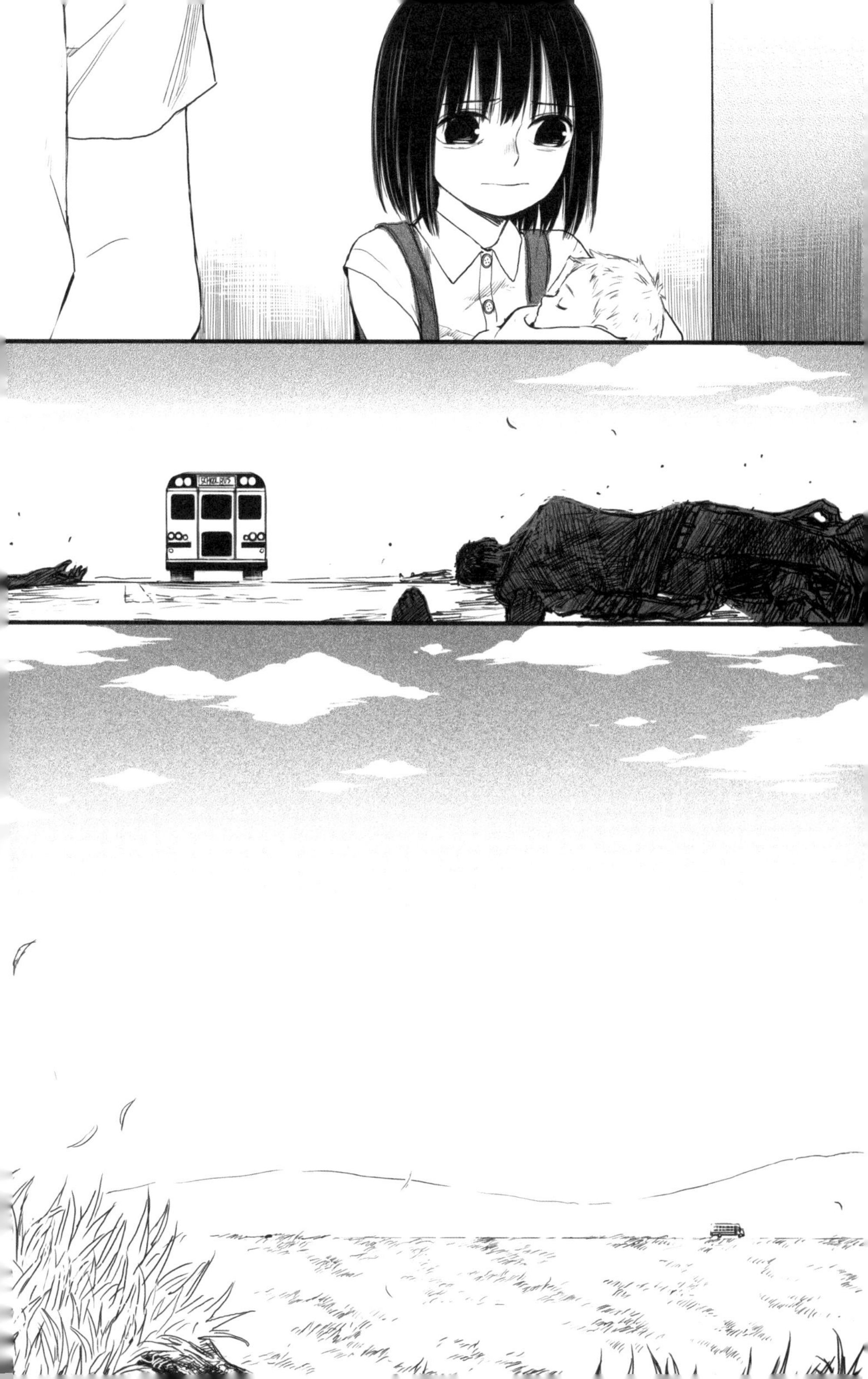
SCHOOL BUS

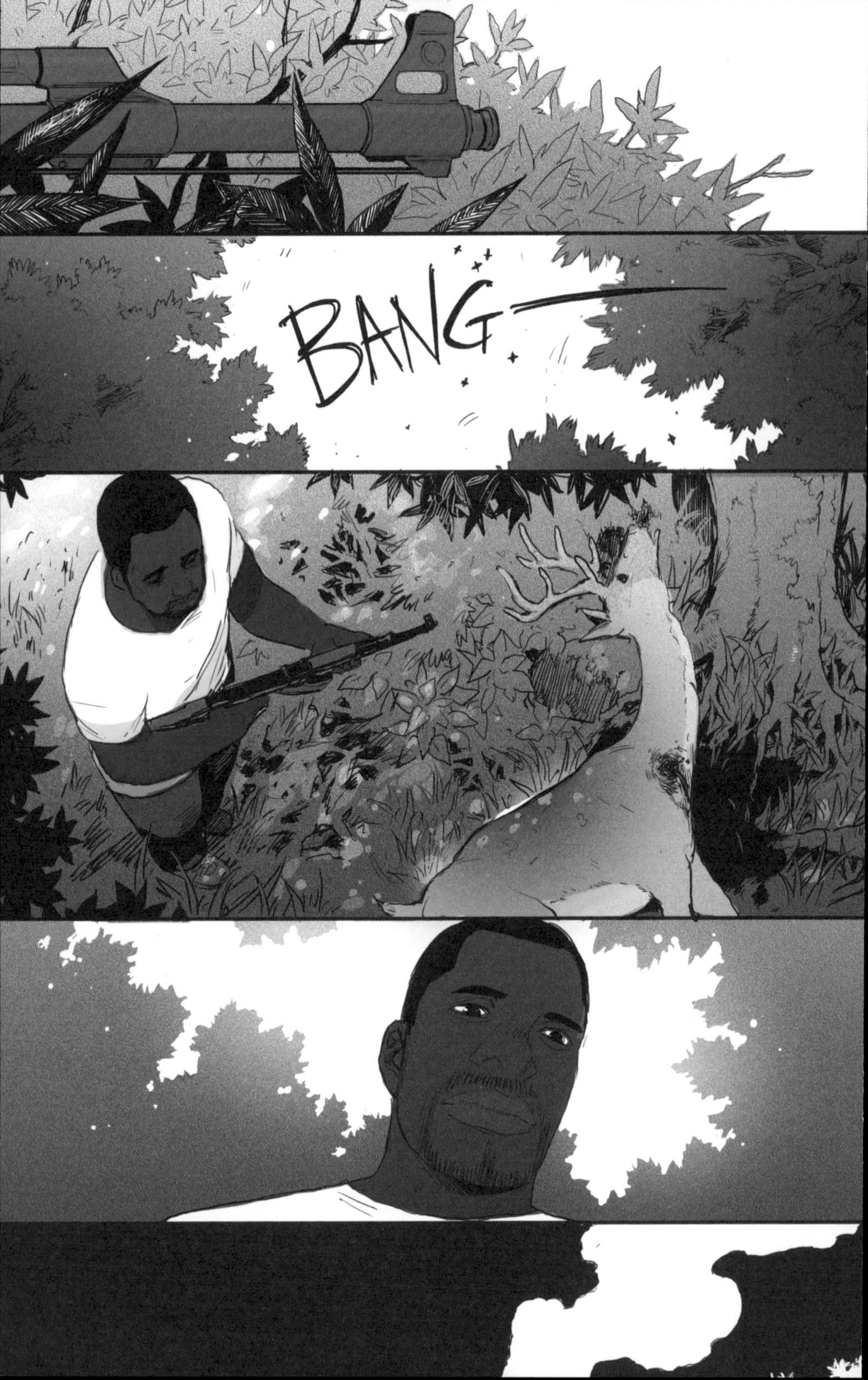
BANG

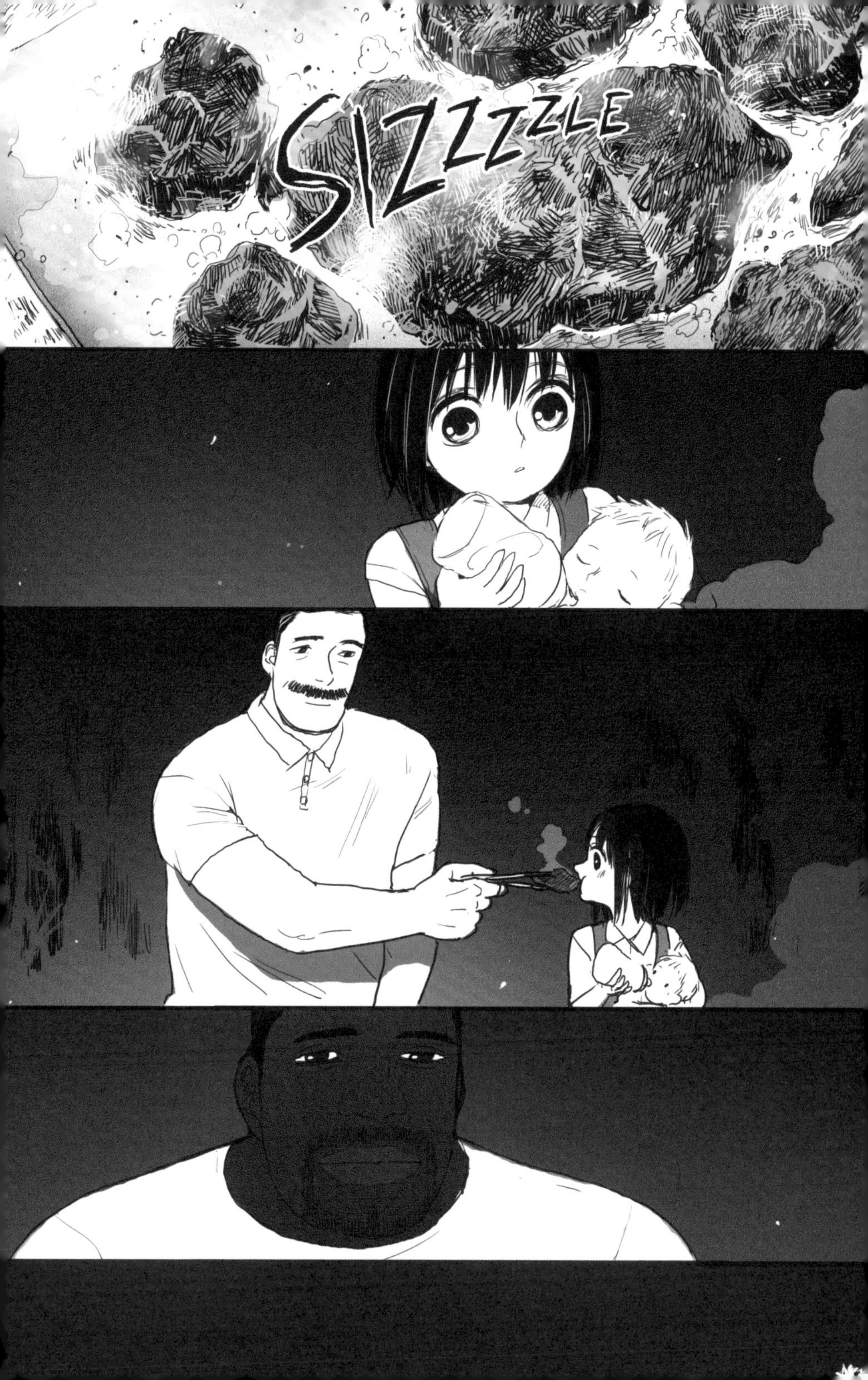
SIZZZZZLE

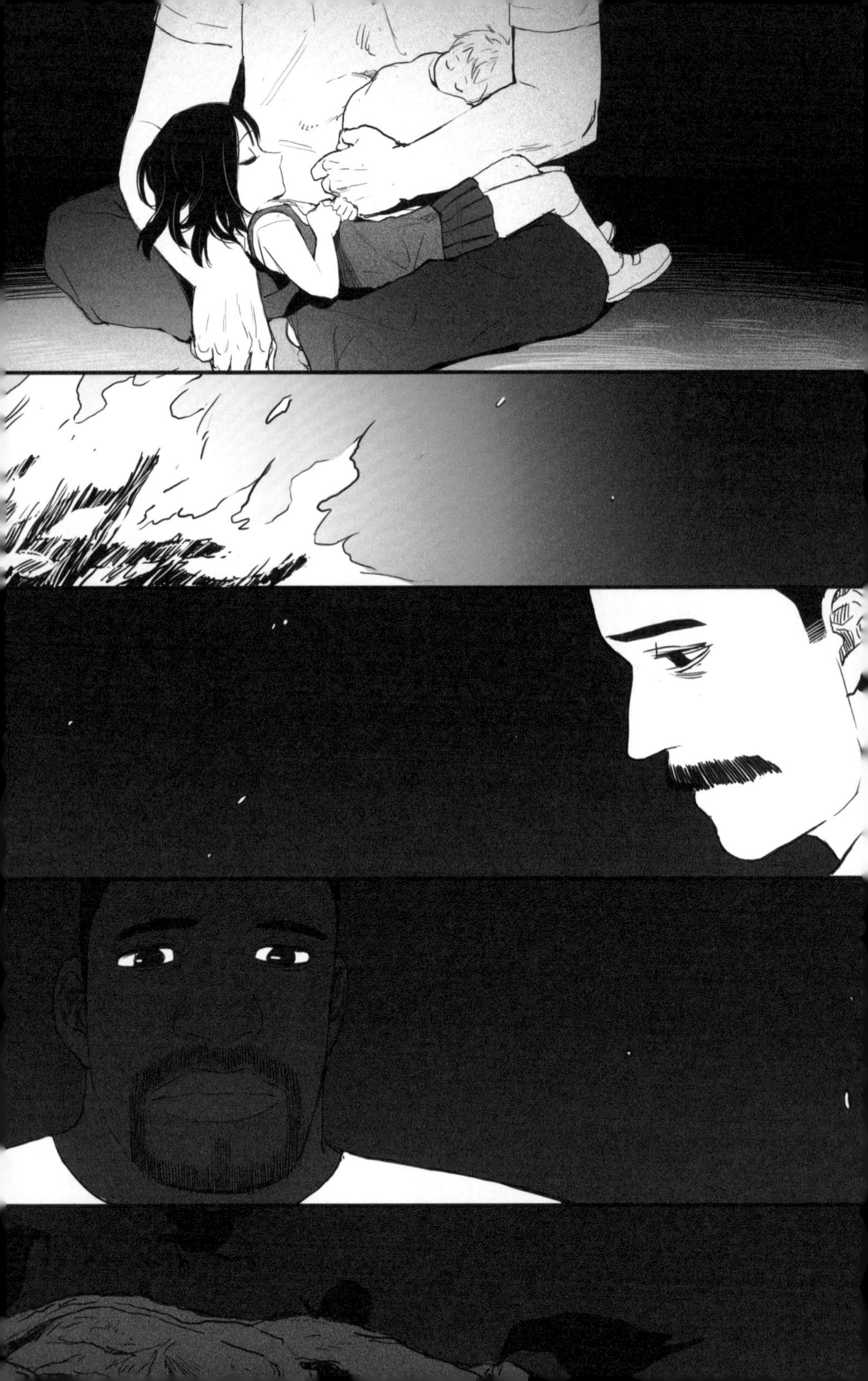

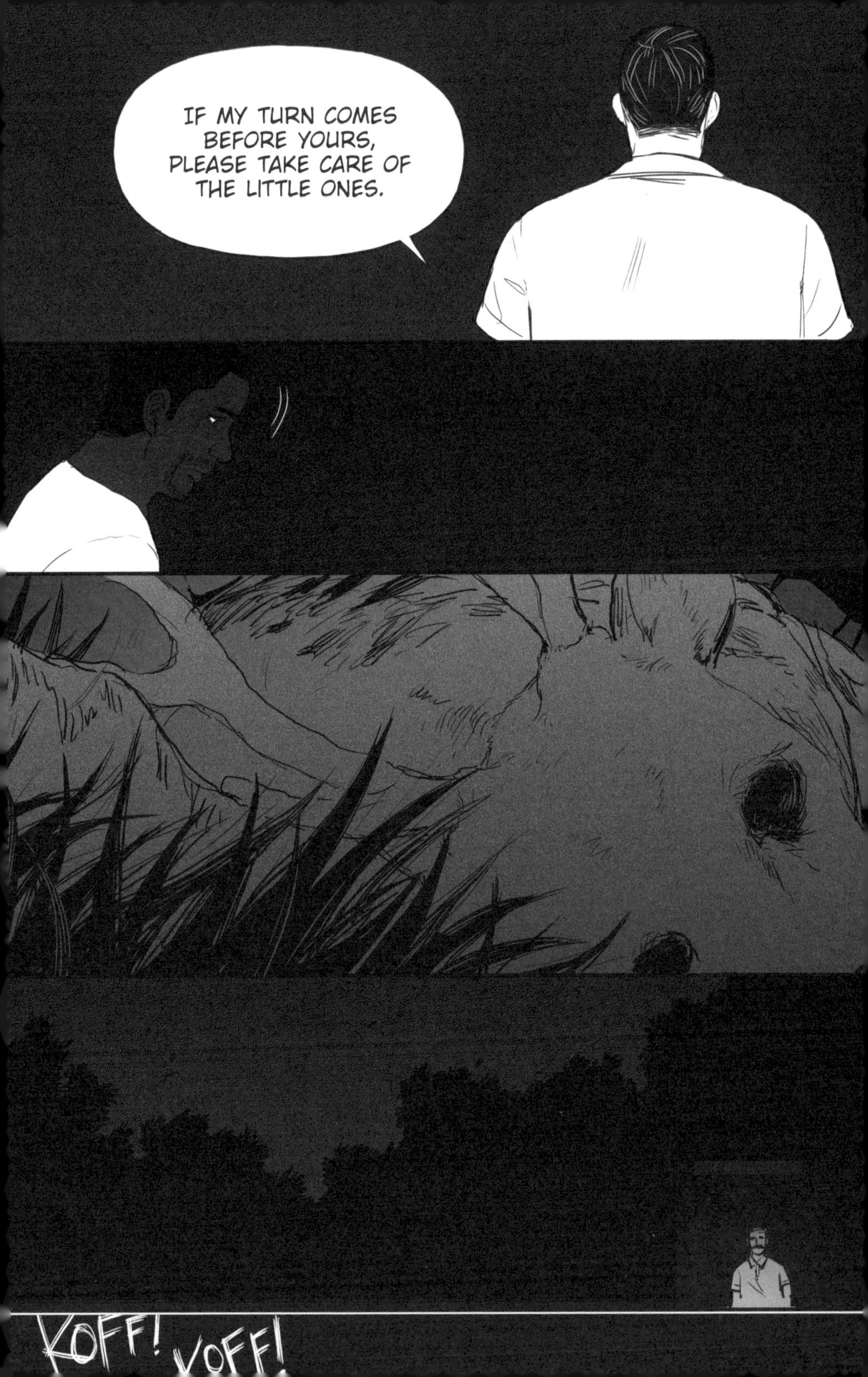
IF MY TURN COMES BEFORE YOURS, PLEASE TAKE CARE OF THE LITTLE ONES.
KOFF! KOFF!

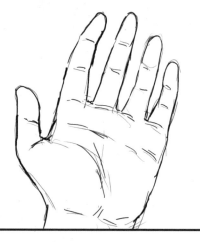

I.

ME.

MYSELF.

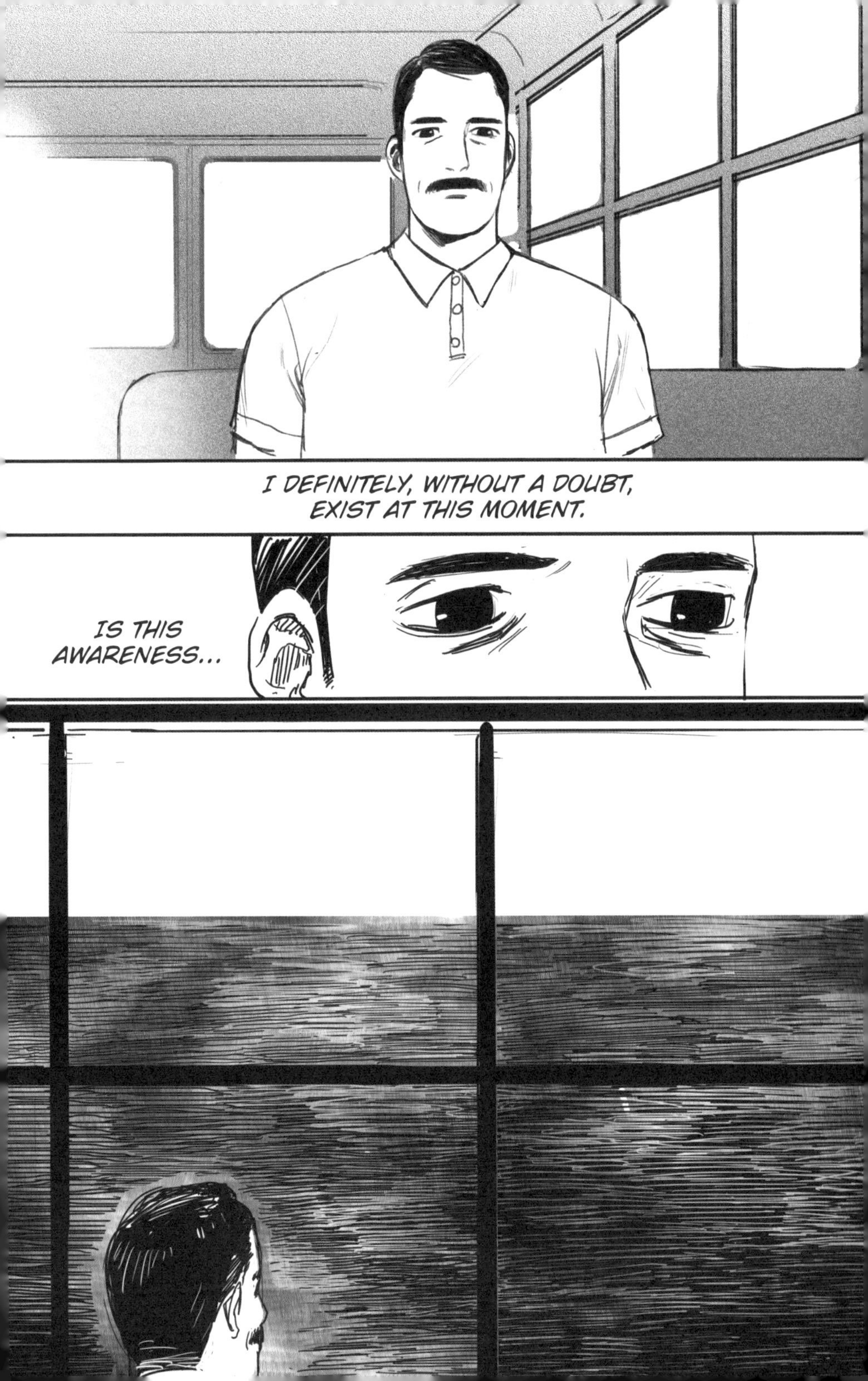
I DEFINITELY, WITHOUT A DOUBT,
EXIST AT THIS MOMENT.
IS THIS
AWARENESS...

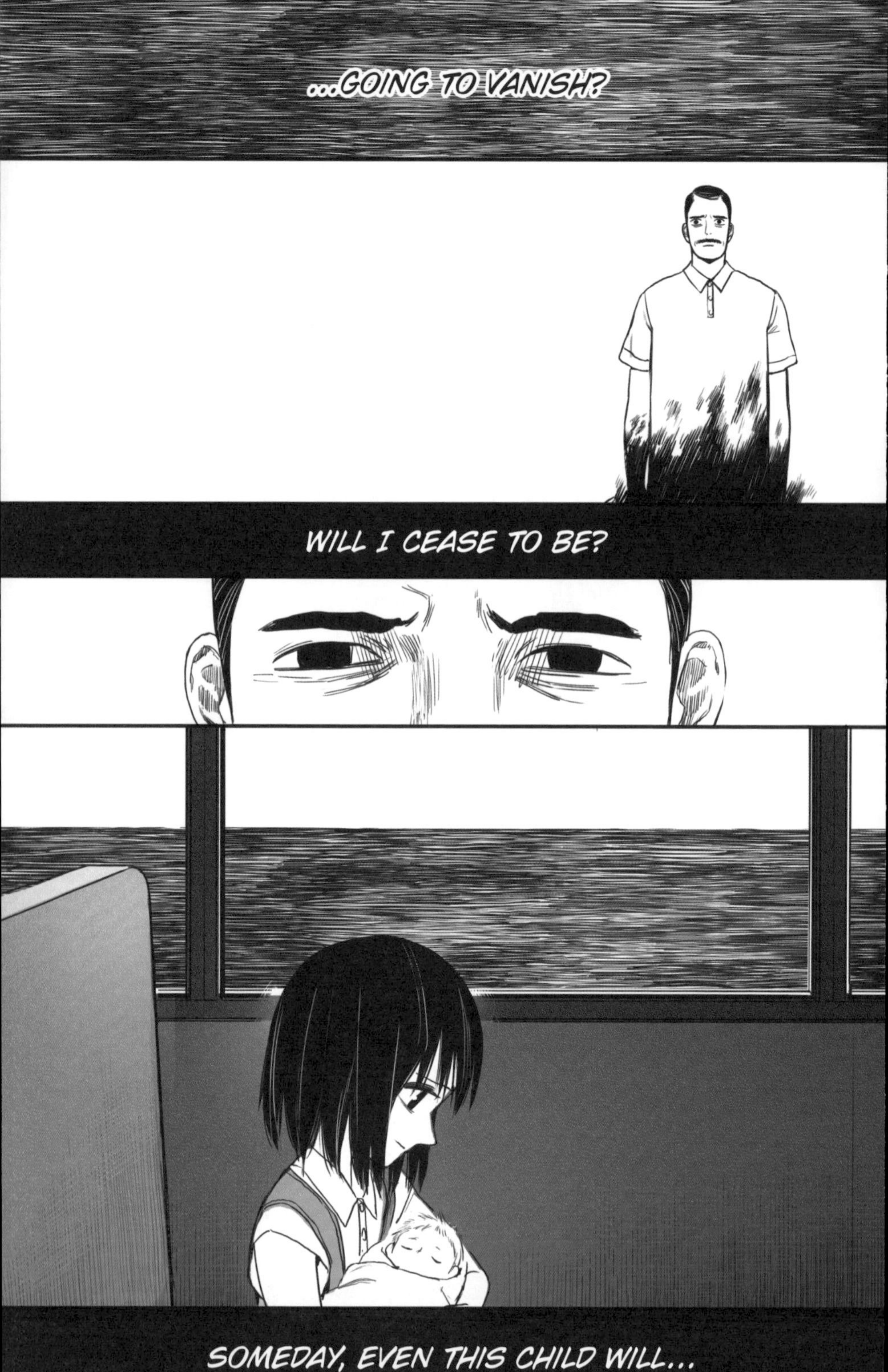
...GOING TO VANISH?
WILL I CEASE TO BE?
SOMEDAY, EVEN THIS CHILD WILL...

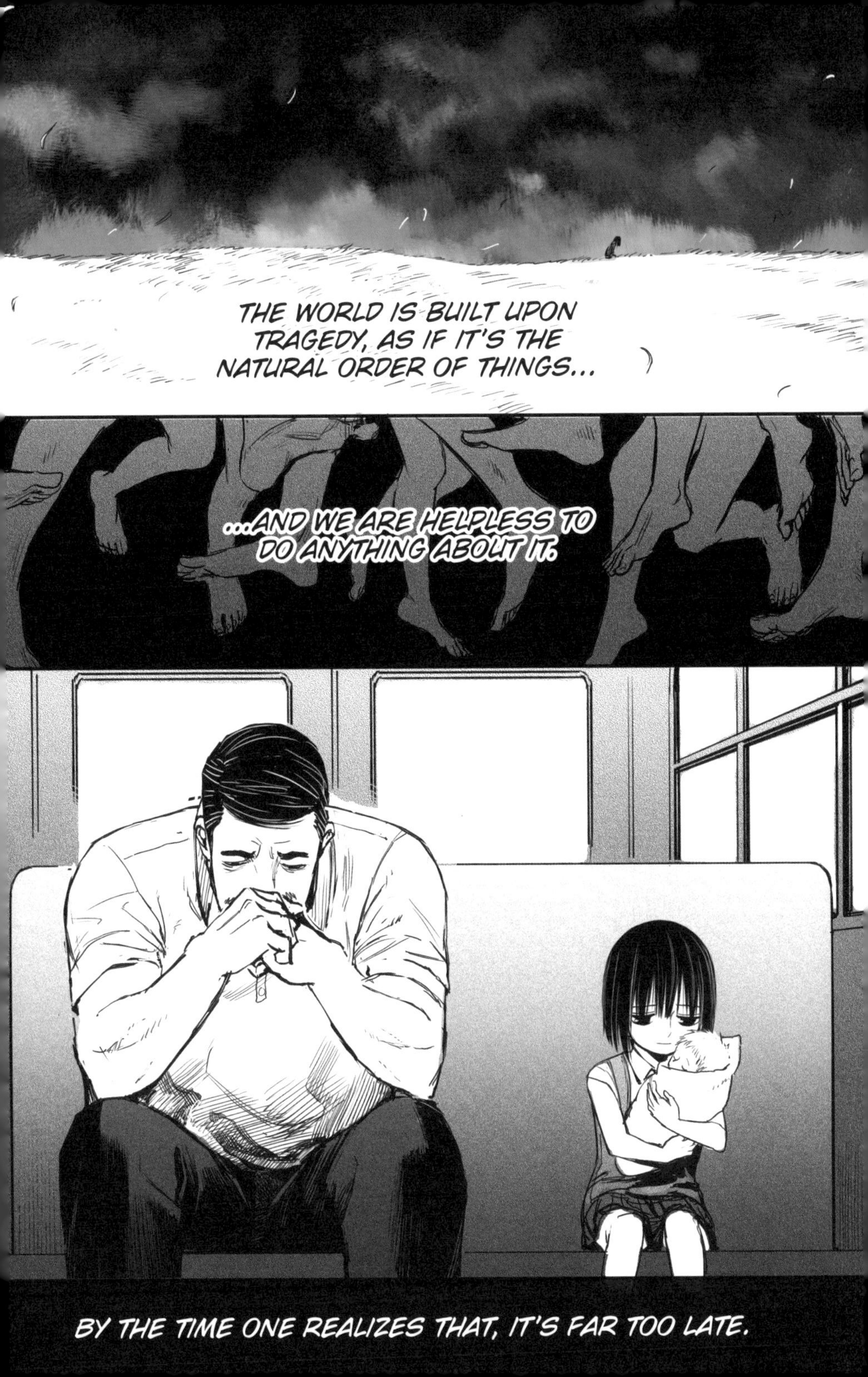
THE WORLD IS BUILT UPON TRAGEDY, AS IF IT'S THE NATURAL ORDER OF THINGS...
...AND WE ARE HELPLESS TO DO ANYTHING ABOUT IT.
BY THE TIME ONE REALIZES THAT, IT'S FAR TOO LATE.

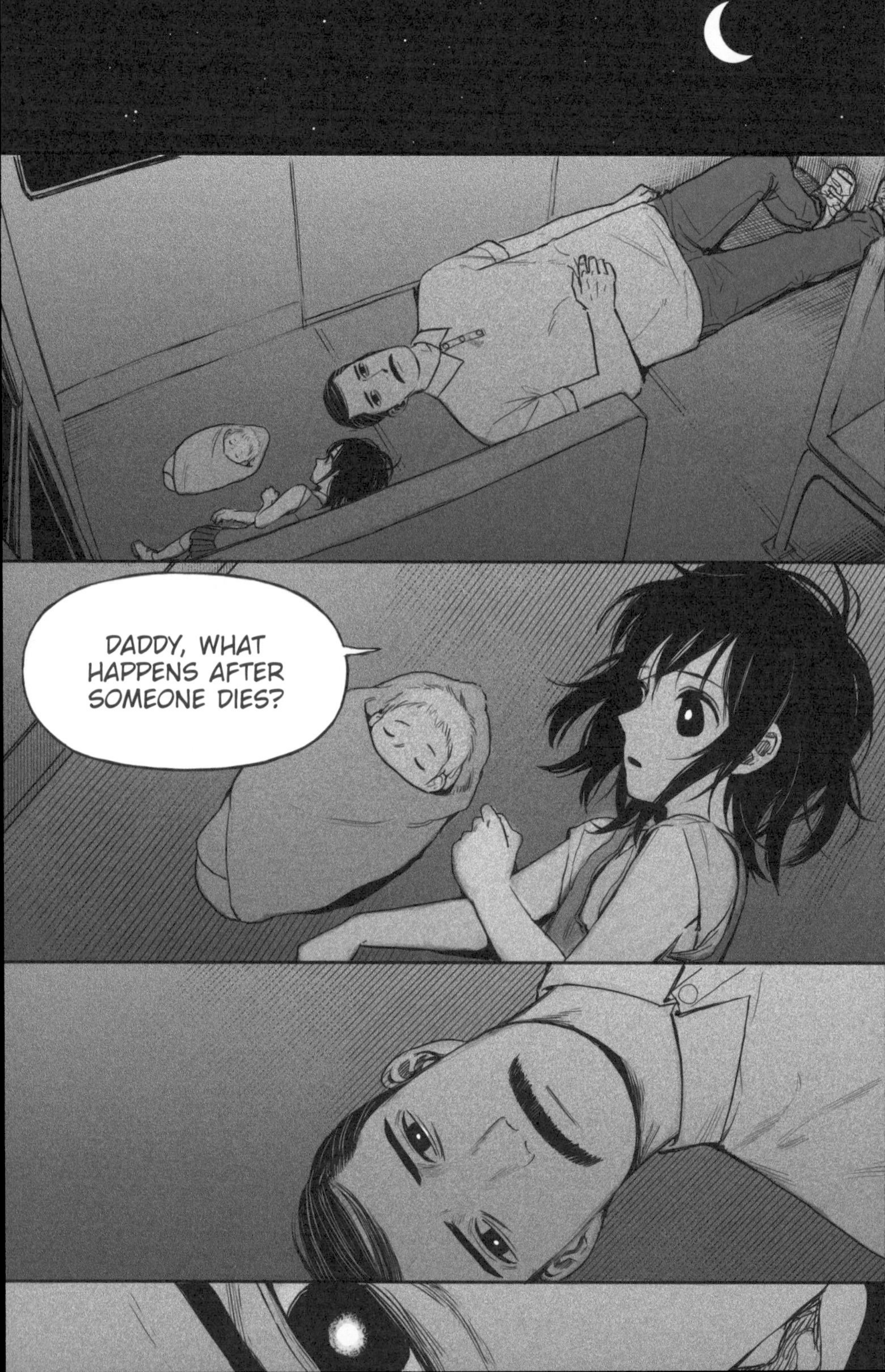
DADDY, WHAT HAPPENS AFTER SOMEONE DIES?

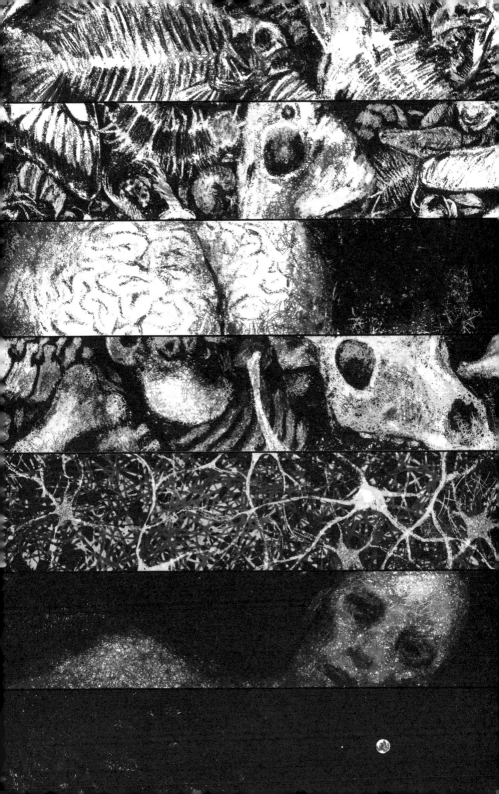

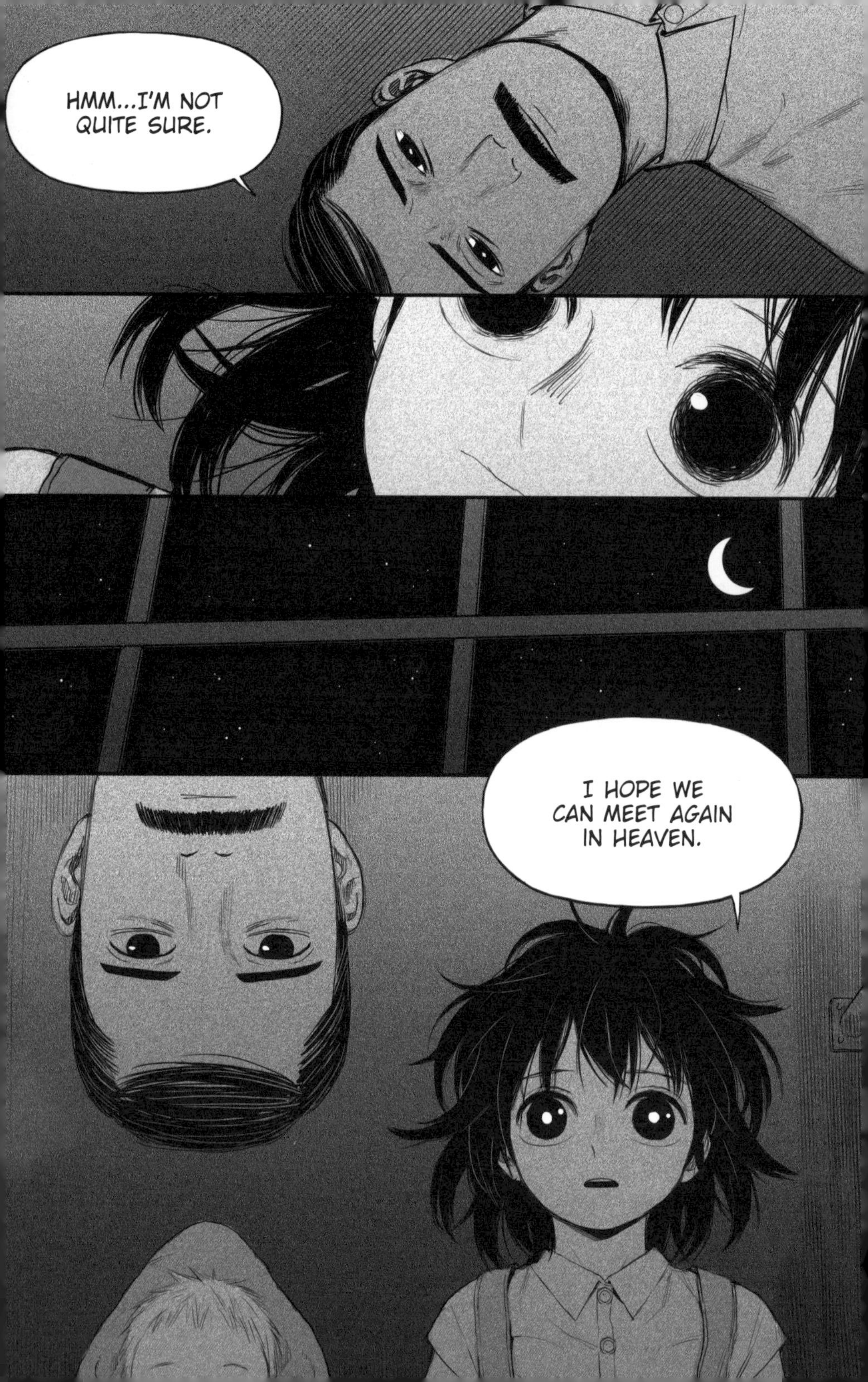
HMM...I'M NOT QUITE SURE.
I HOPE WE CAN MEET AGAIN IN HEAVEN.

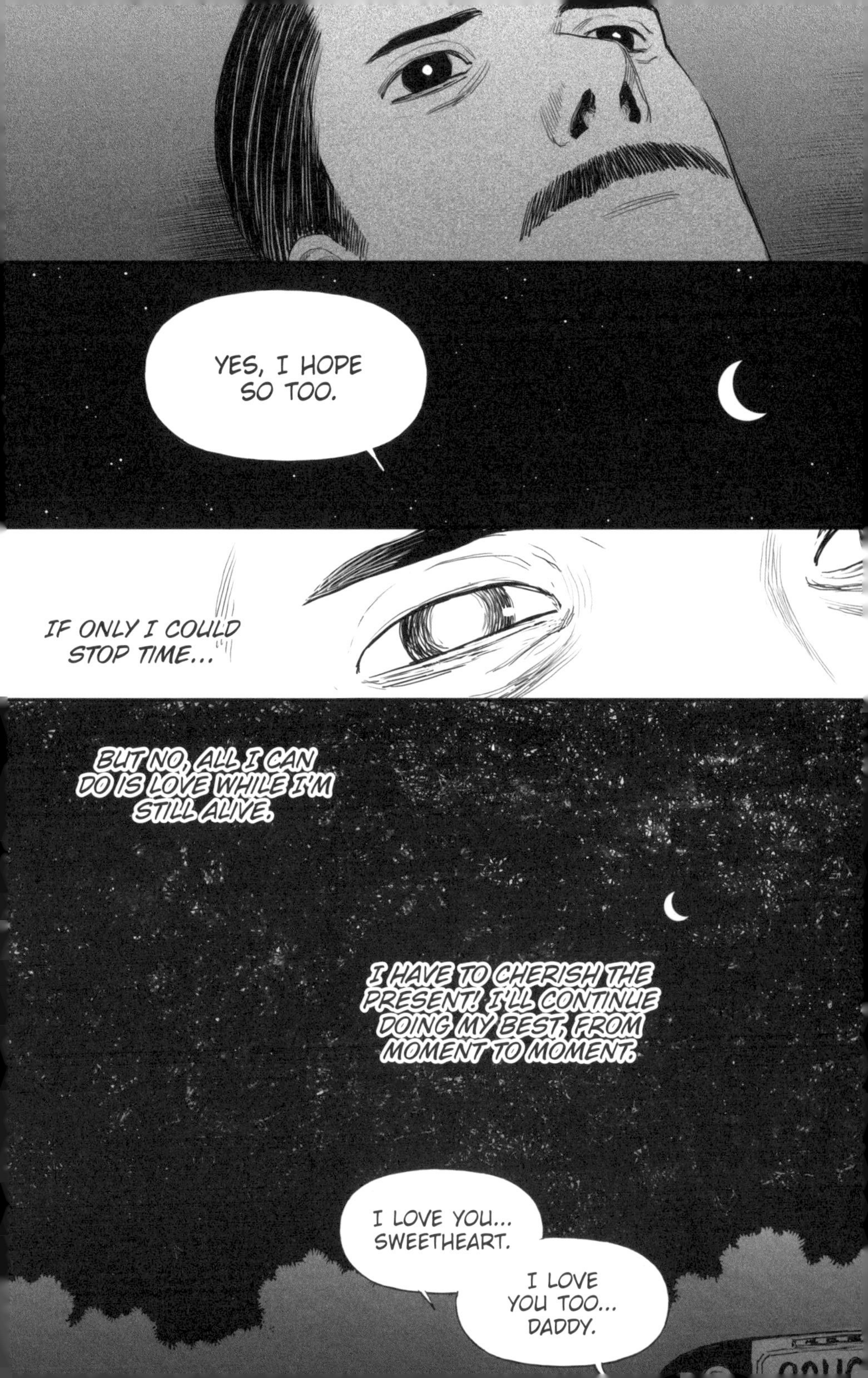
YES, I HOPE SO TOO.
IF ONLY I COULD STOP TIME...
BUT NO, ALL I CAN DO IS LOVE WHILE I'M STILL ALIVE.
I HAVE TO CHERISH THE PRESENT! I'LL CONTINUE DOING MY BEST, FROM MOMENT TO MOMENT.
I LOVE YOU... SWEETHEART.
I LOVE YOU TOO... DADDY.

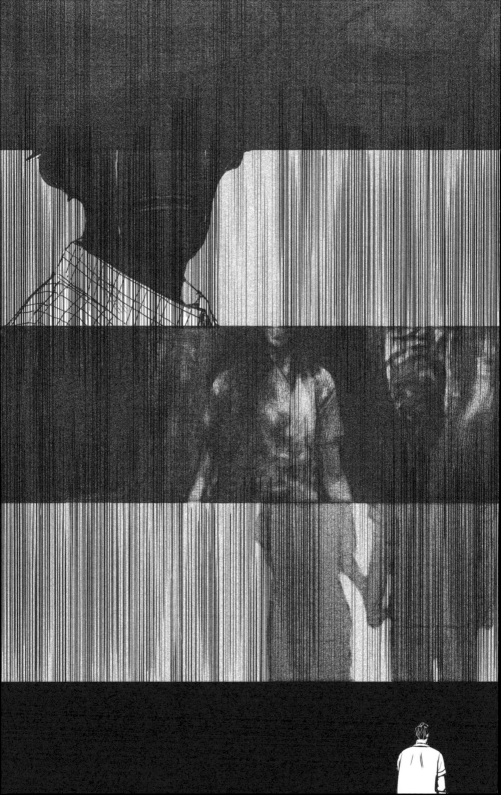

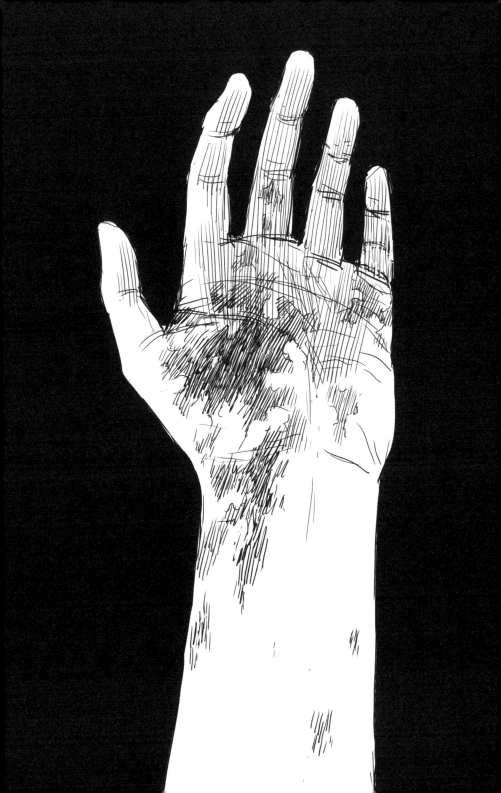

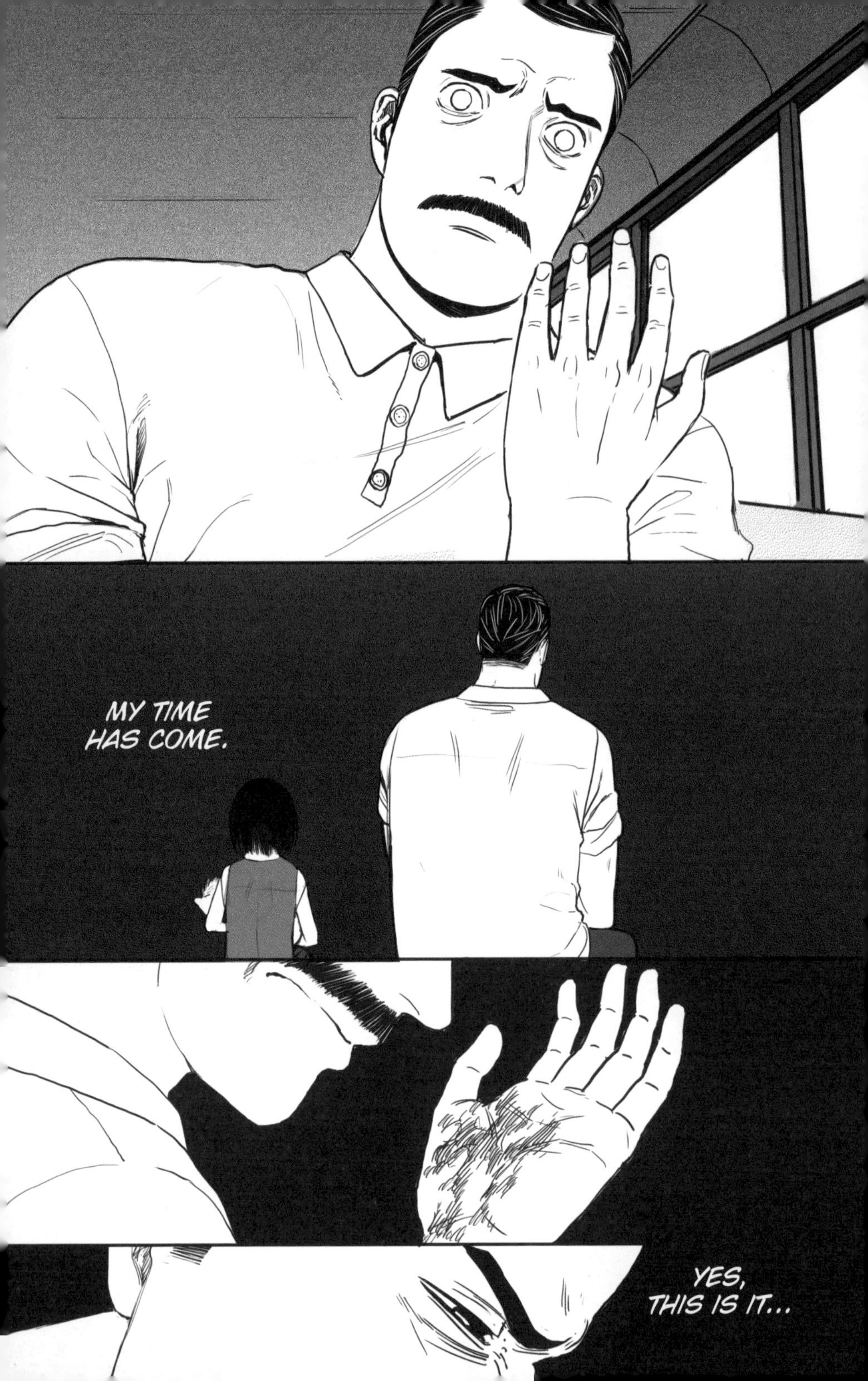
MY TIME HAS COME.
YES, THIS IS IT...

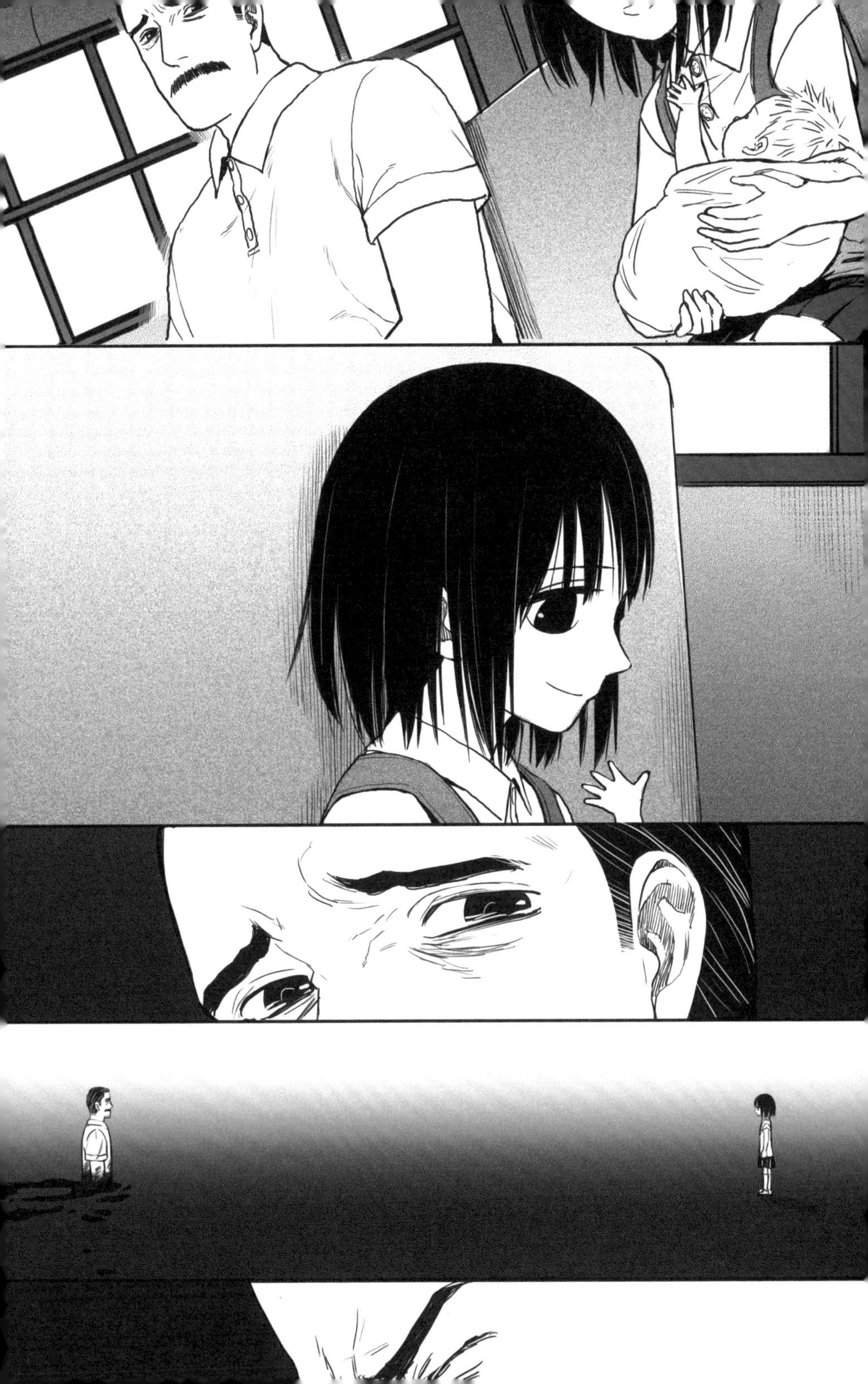

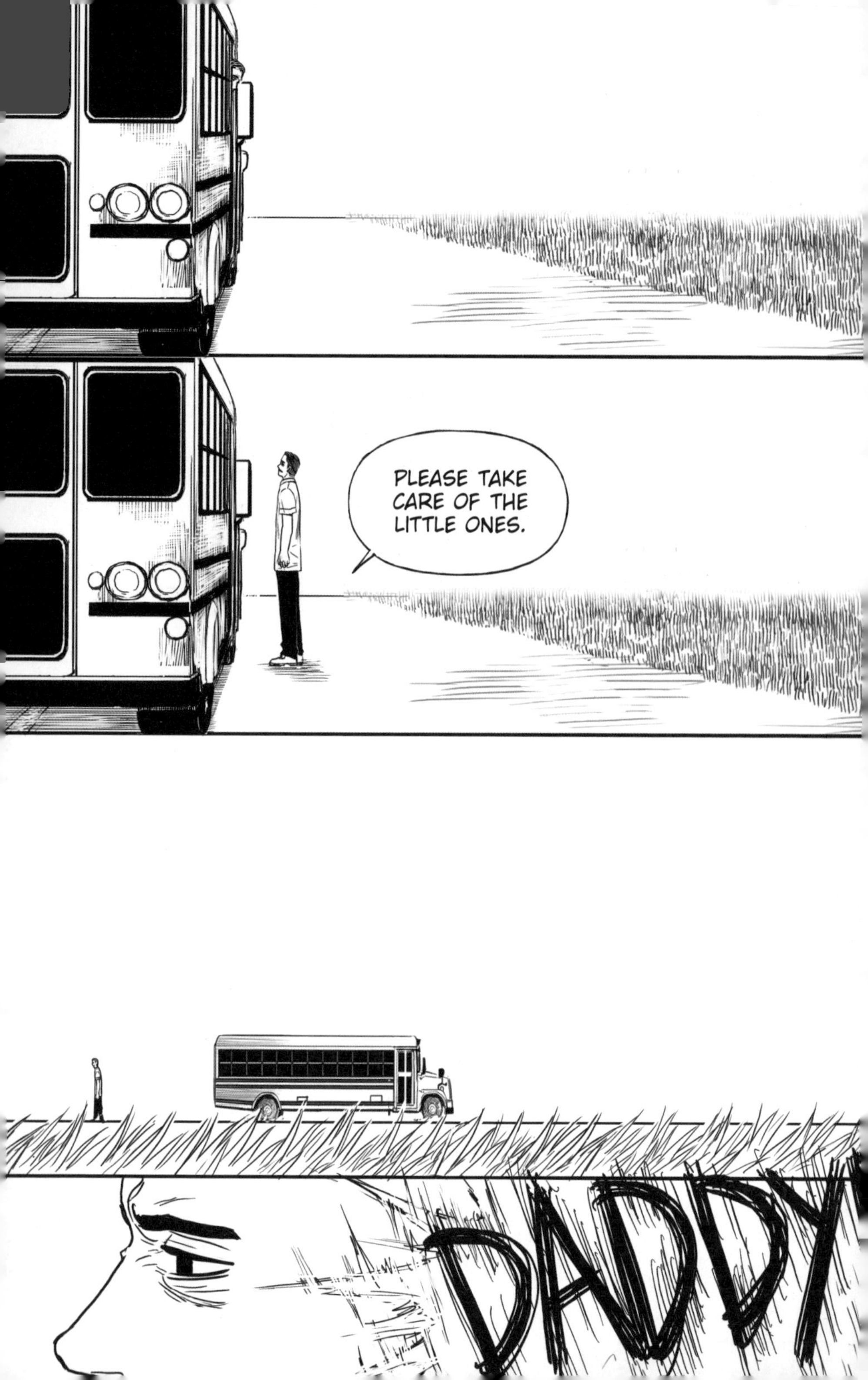
PLEASE TAKE CARE OF THE LITTLE ONES.
DADDY

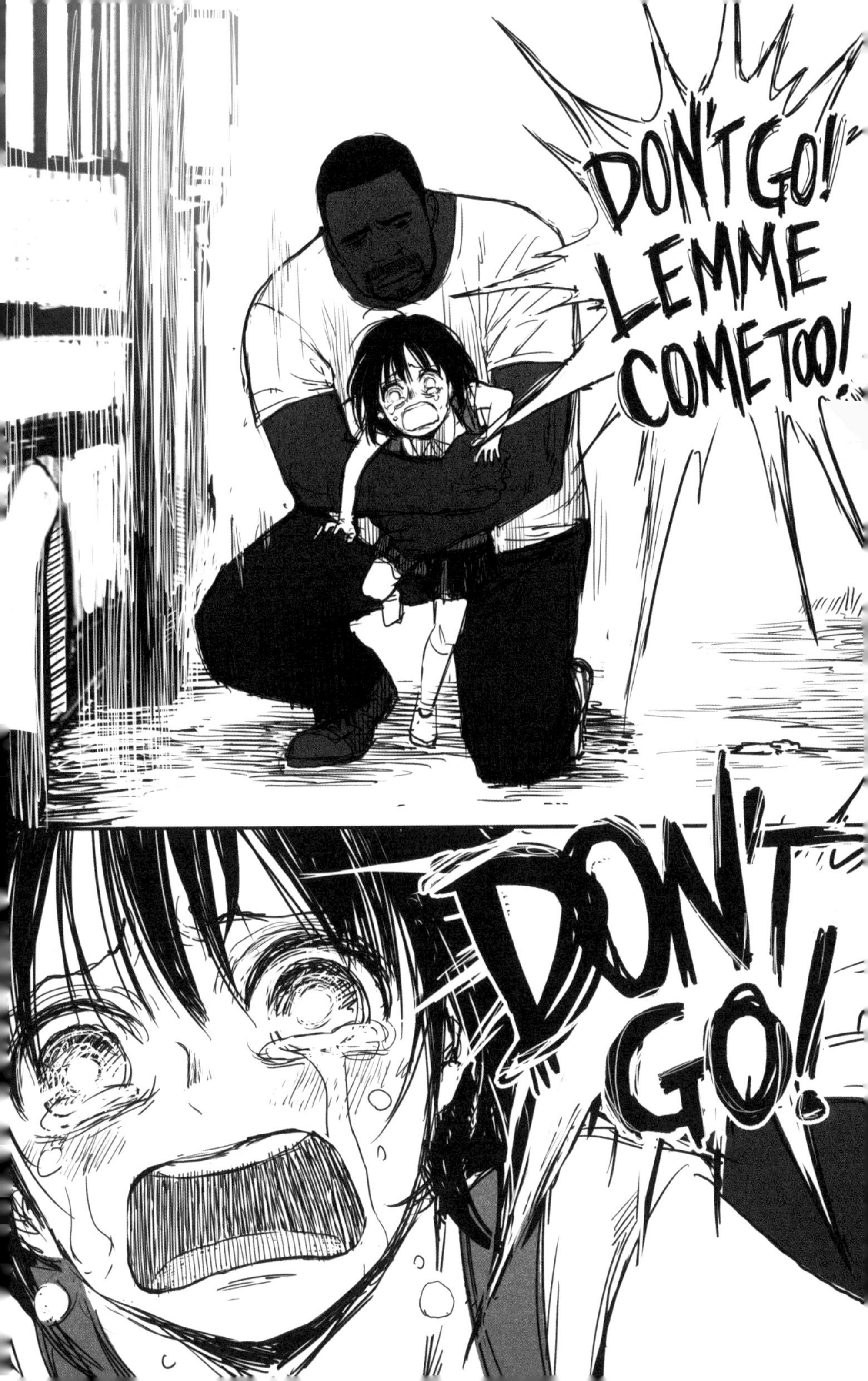
DON'T GO! LEMME COME TOO!
DON'T GO!

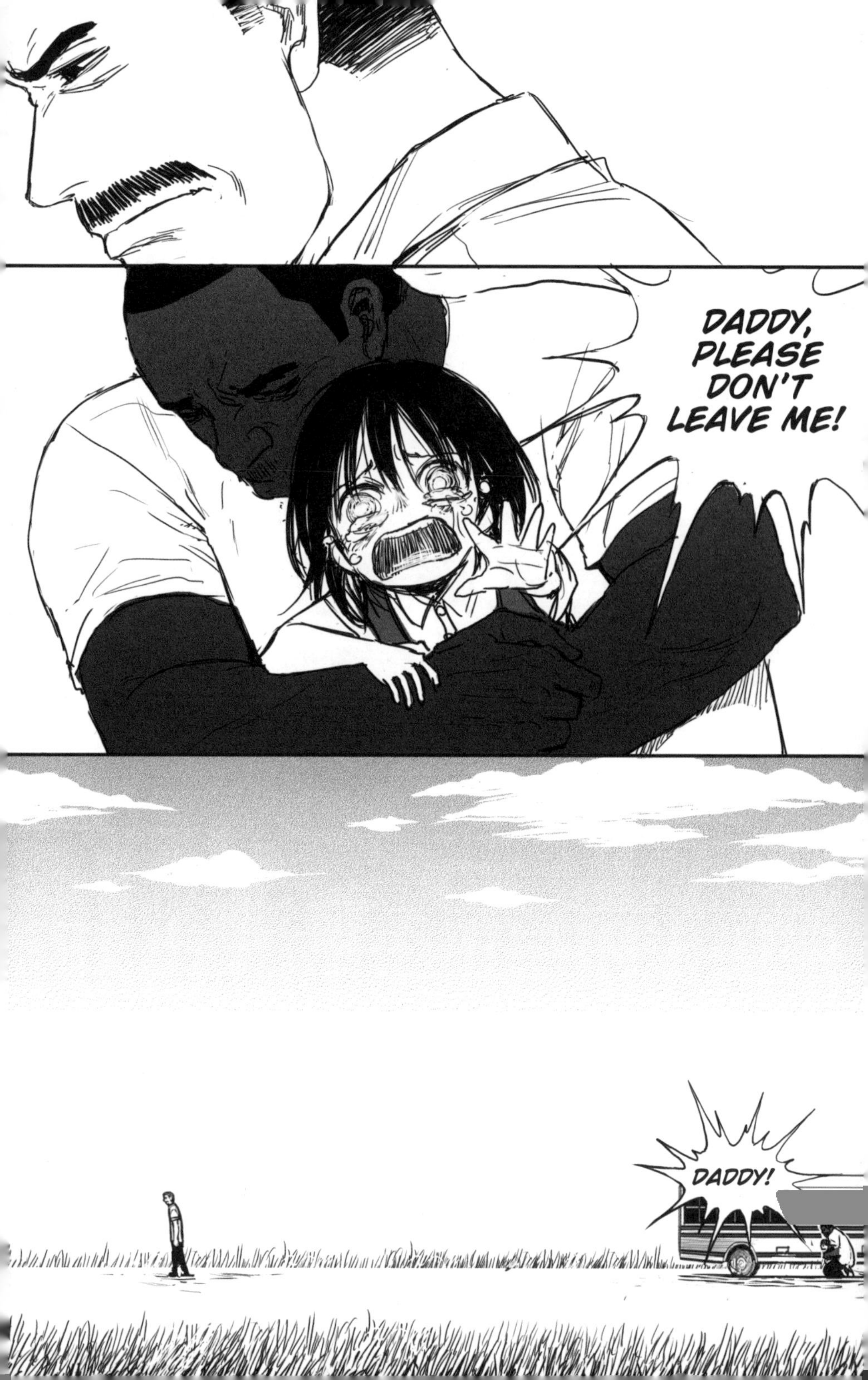
DADDY, PLEASE DON'T LEAVE ME!
DADDY!

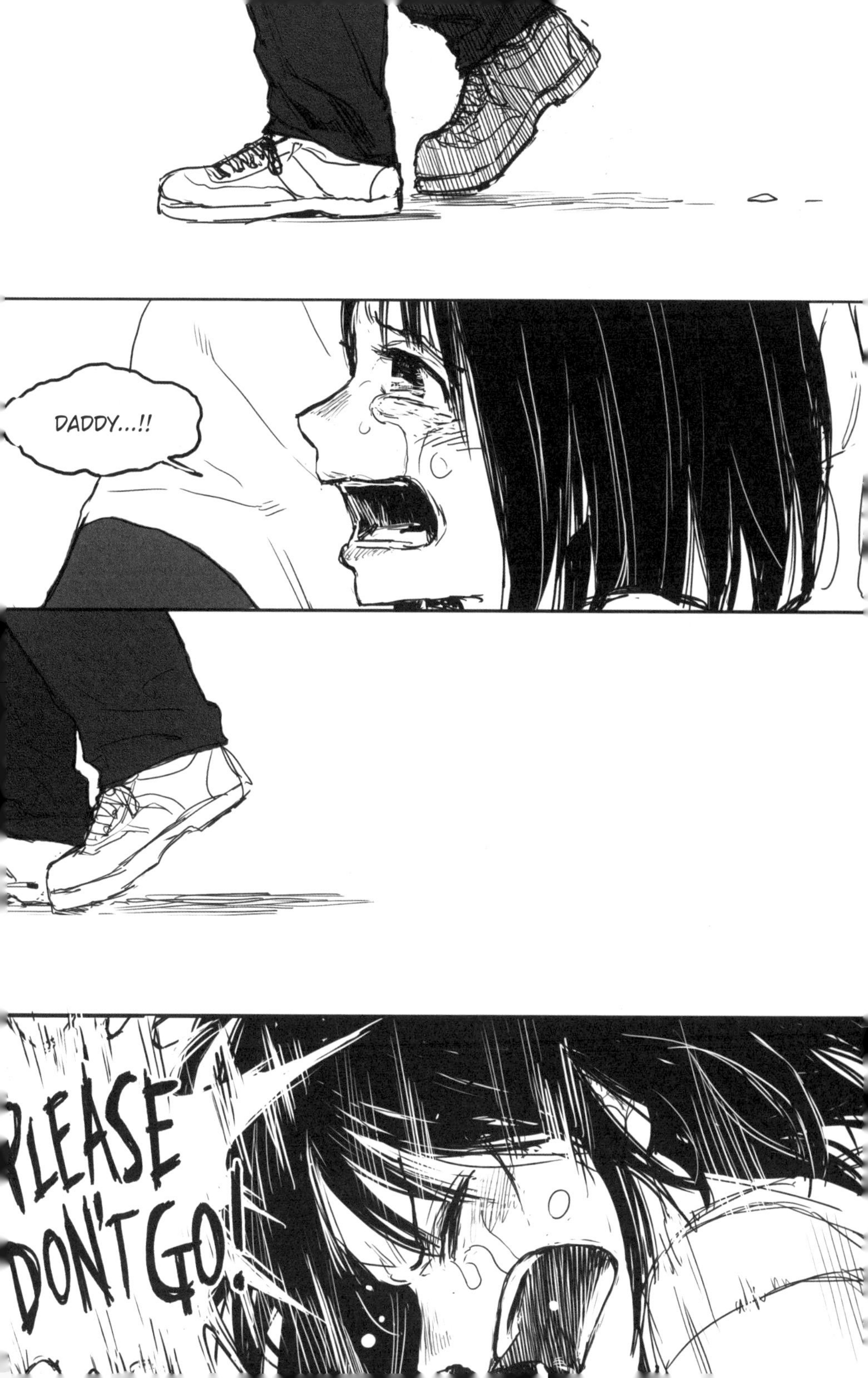
DADDY...!!
PLEASE DON'T GO!!

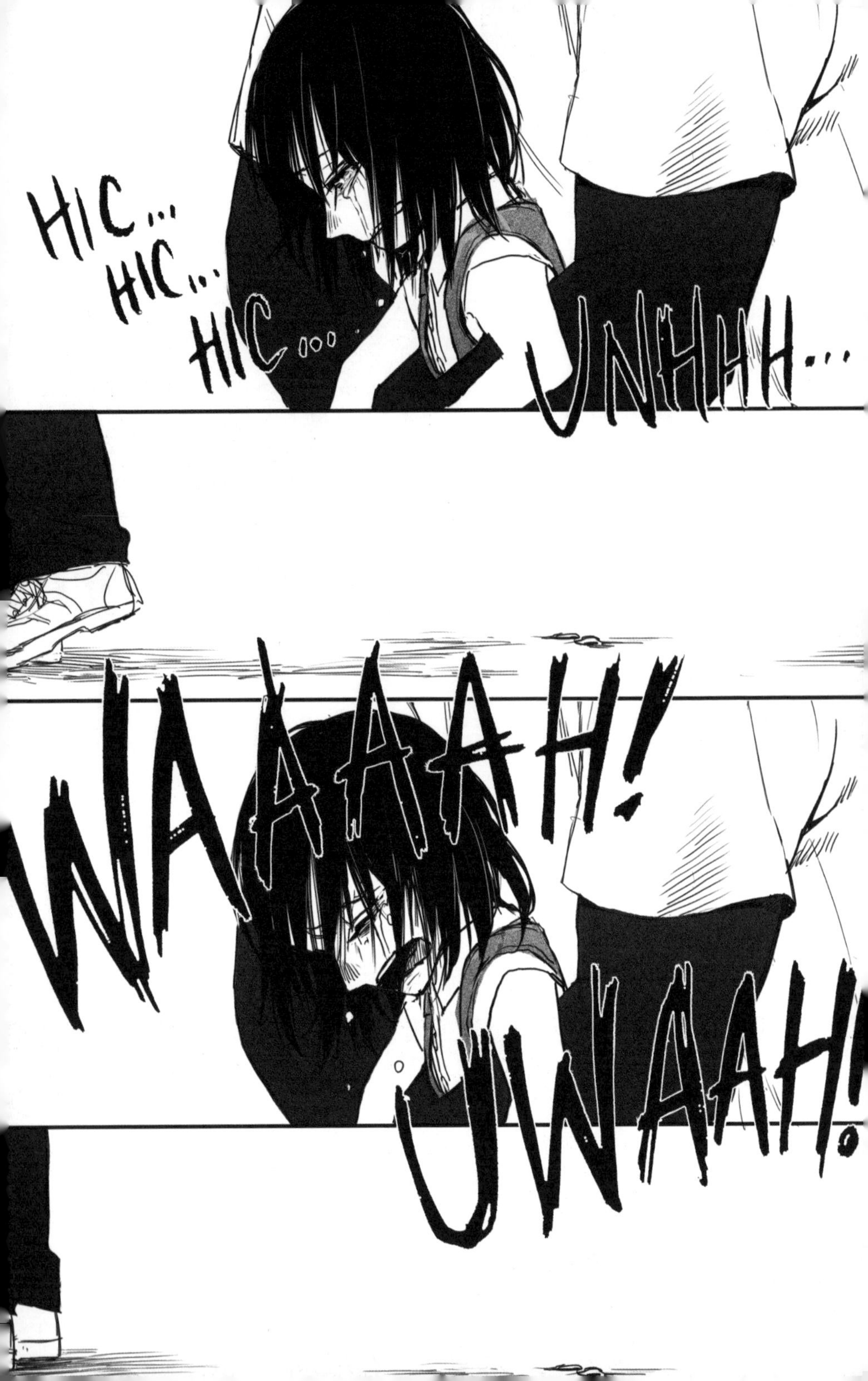

HIC...
HIC...
HIC...
UNHHH...
WAAAAH!
UWAAH!

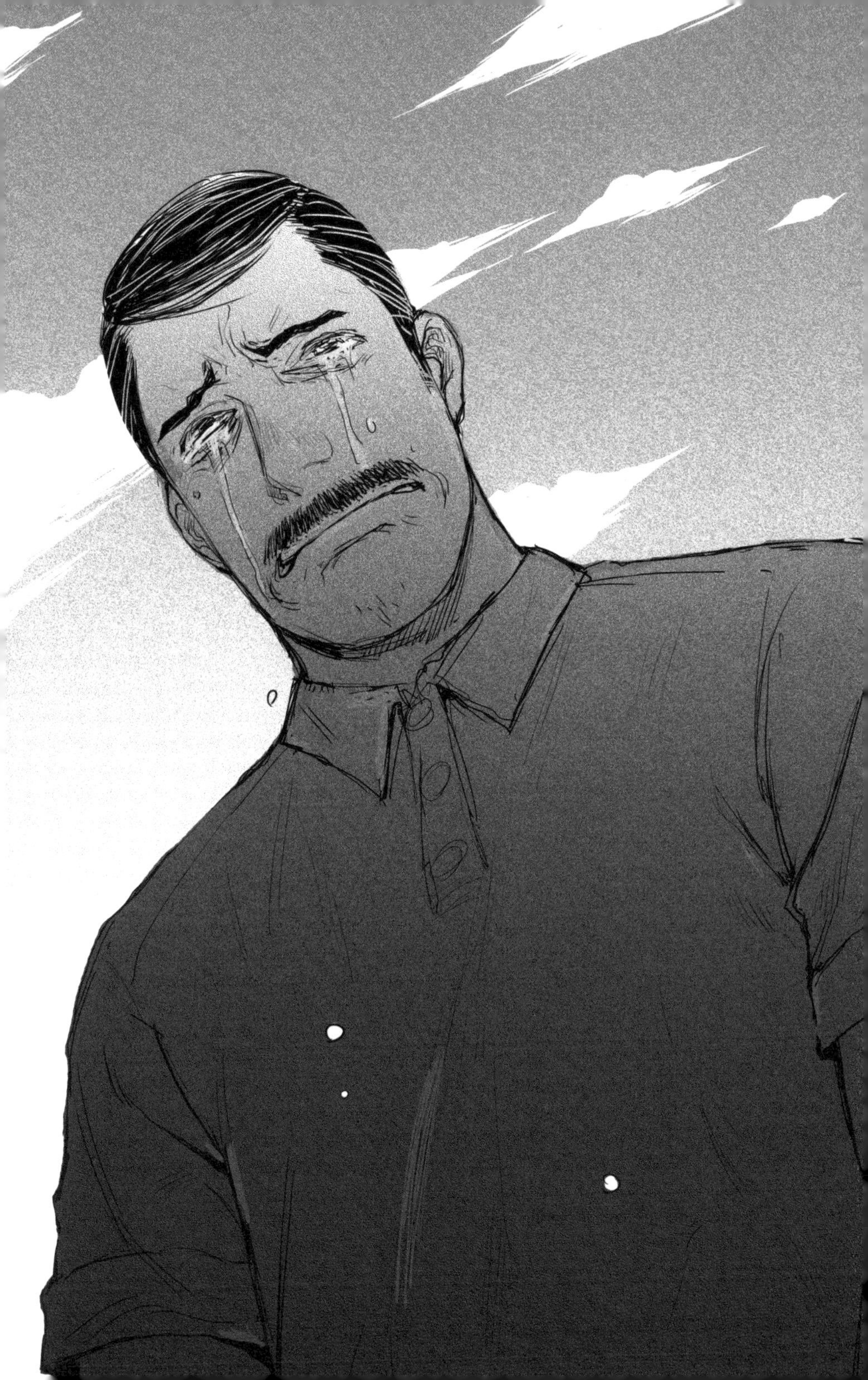

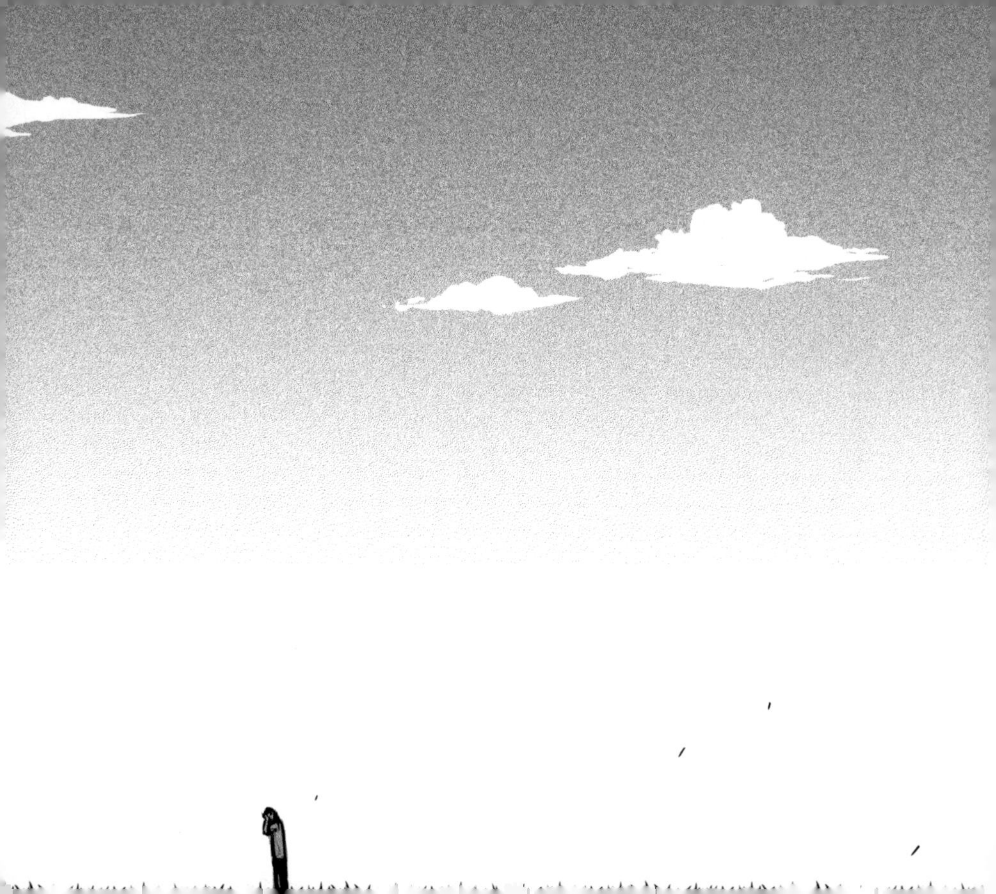

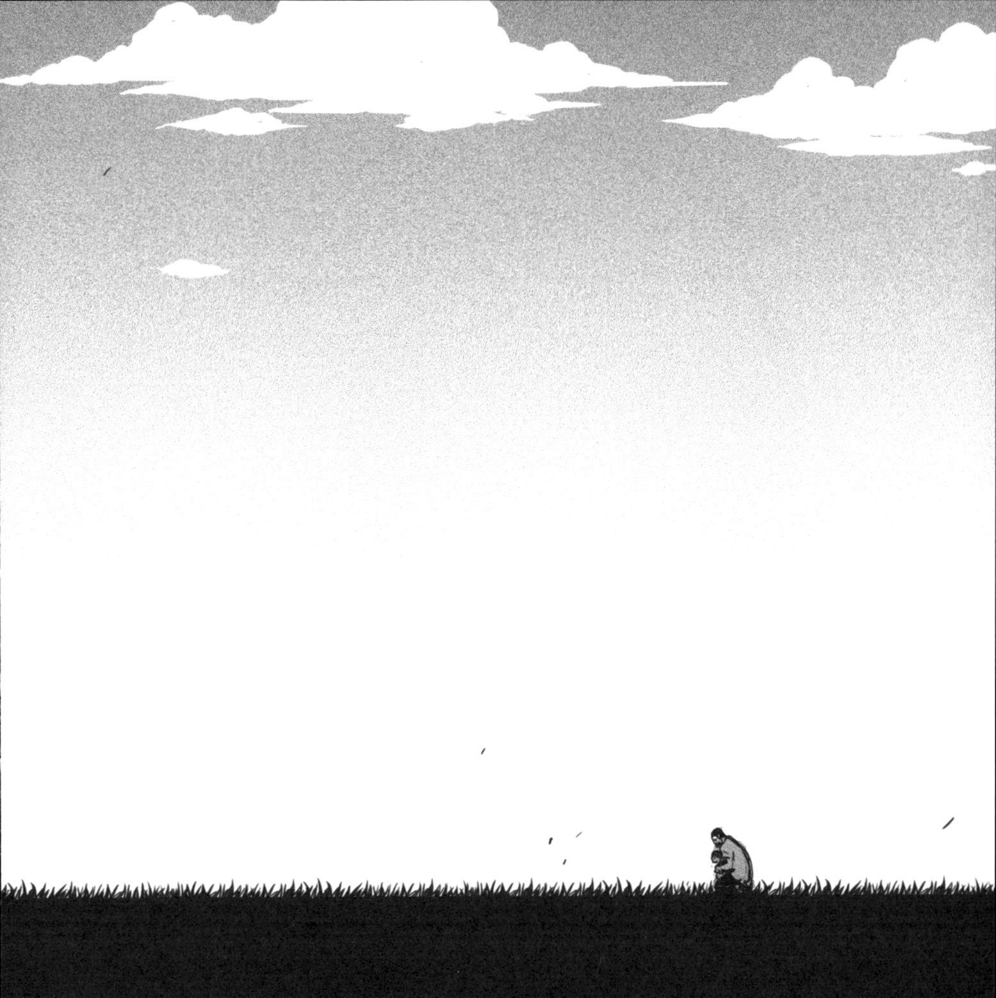

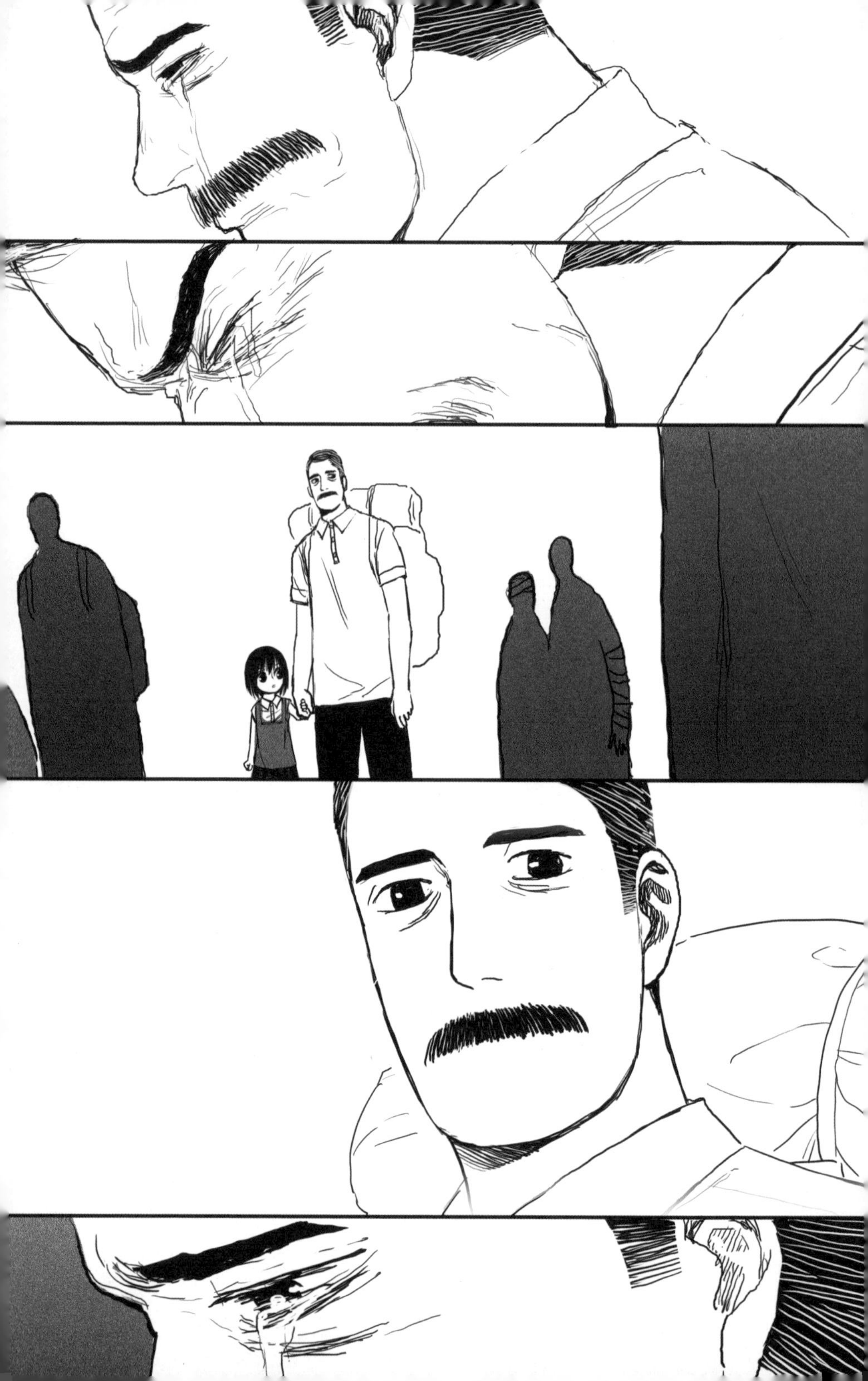

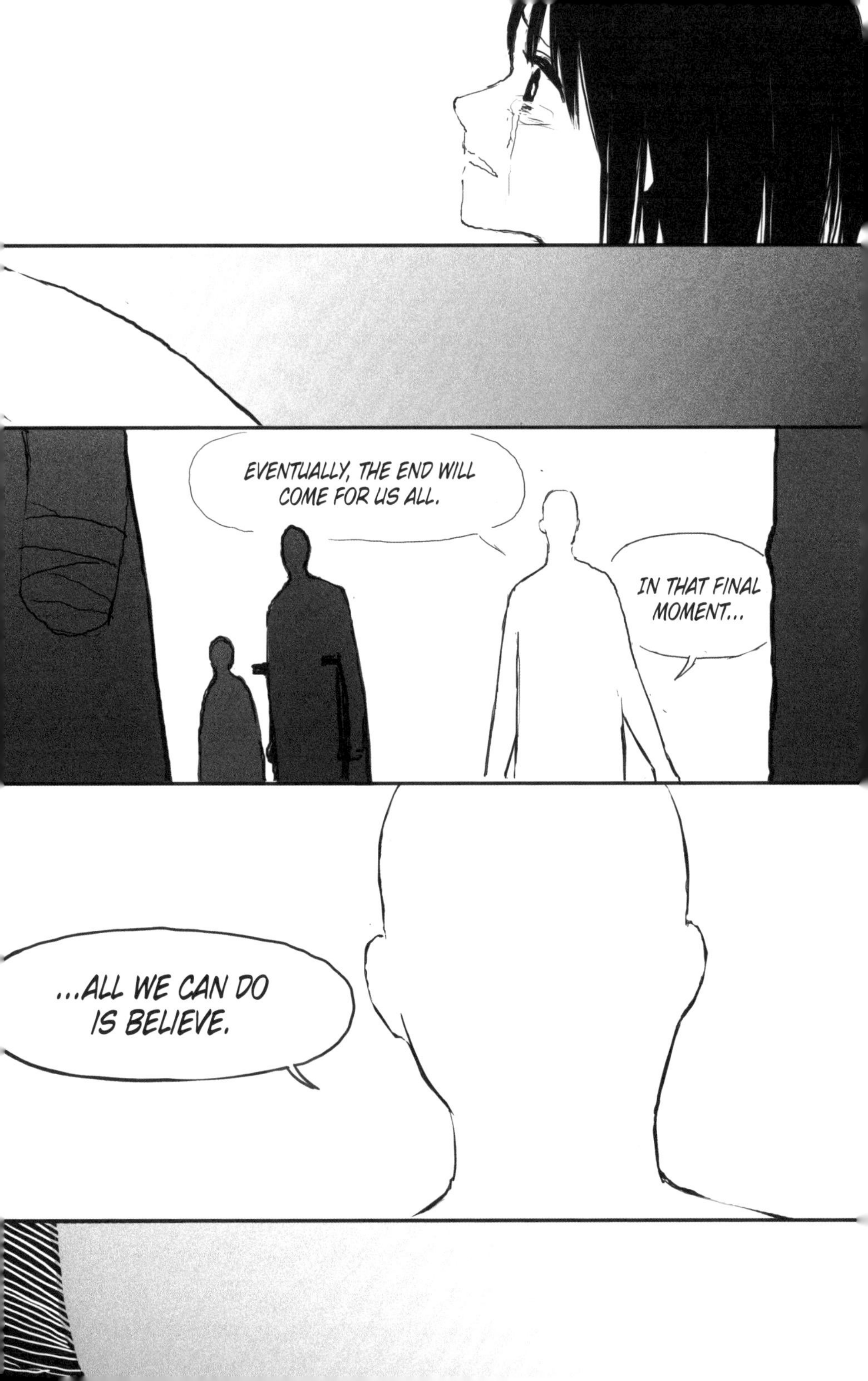
EVENTUALLY, THE END WILL COME FOR US ALL.
IN THAT FINAL MOMENT...
...ALL WE CAN DO IS BELIEVE.

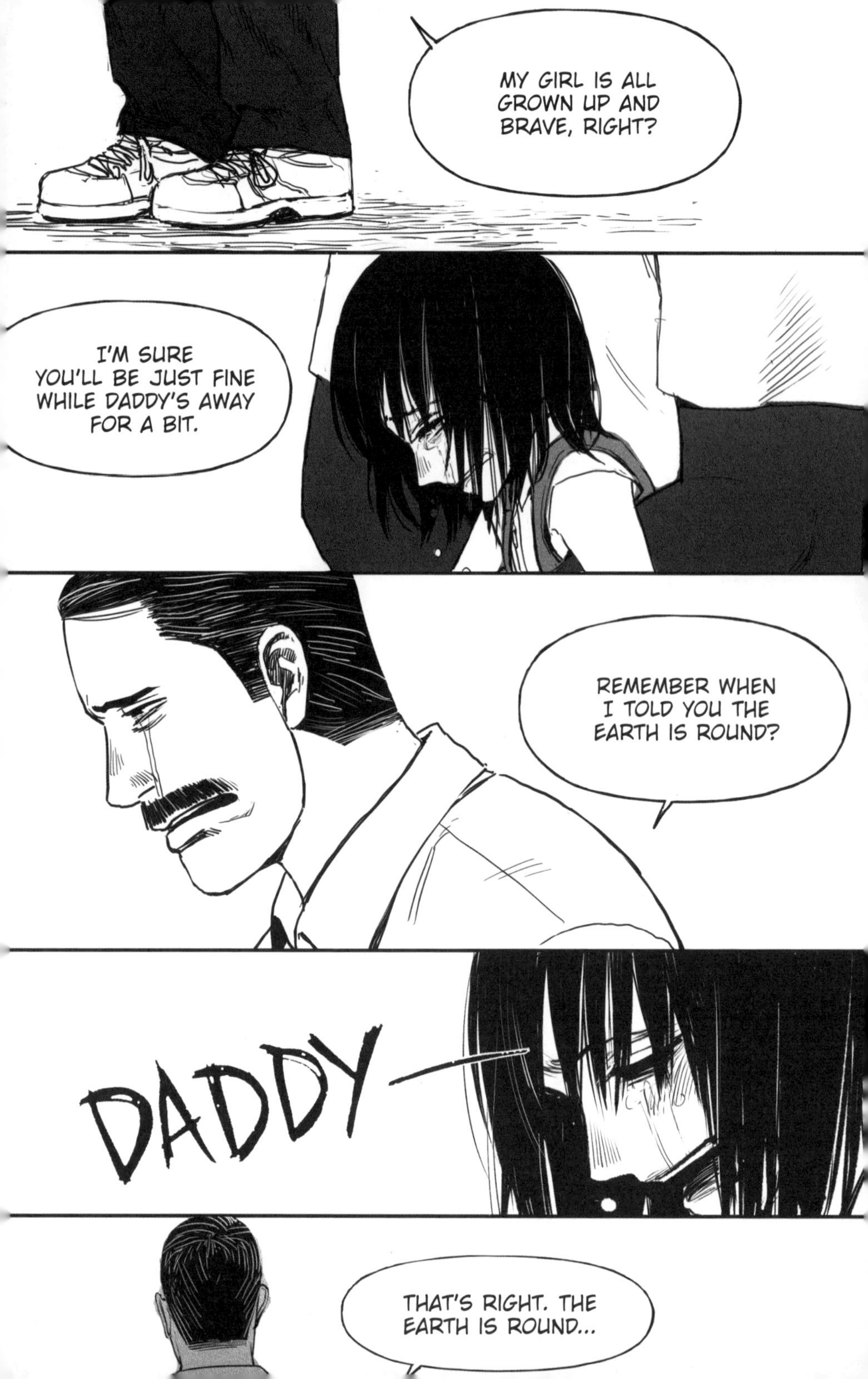
MY GIRL IS ALL GROWN UP AND BRAVE, RIGHT?
I'M SURE YOU'LL BE JUST FINE WHILE DADDY'S AWAY FOR A BIT.
REMEMBER WHEN I TOLD YOU THE EARTH IS ROUND?
DADDY—
THAT'S RIGHT. THE EARTH IS ROUND...

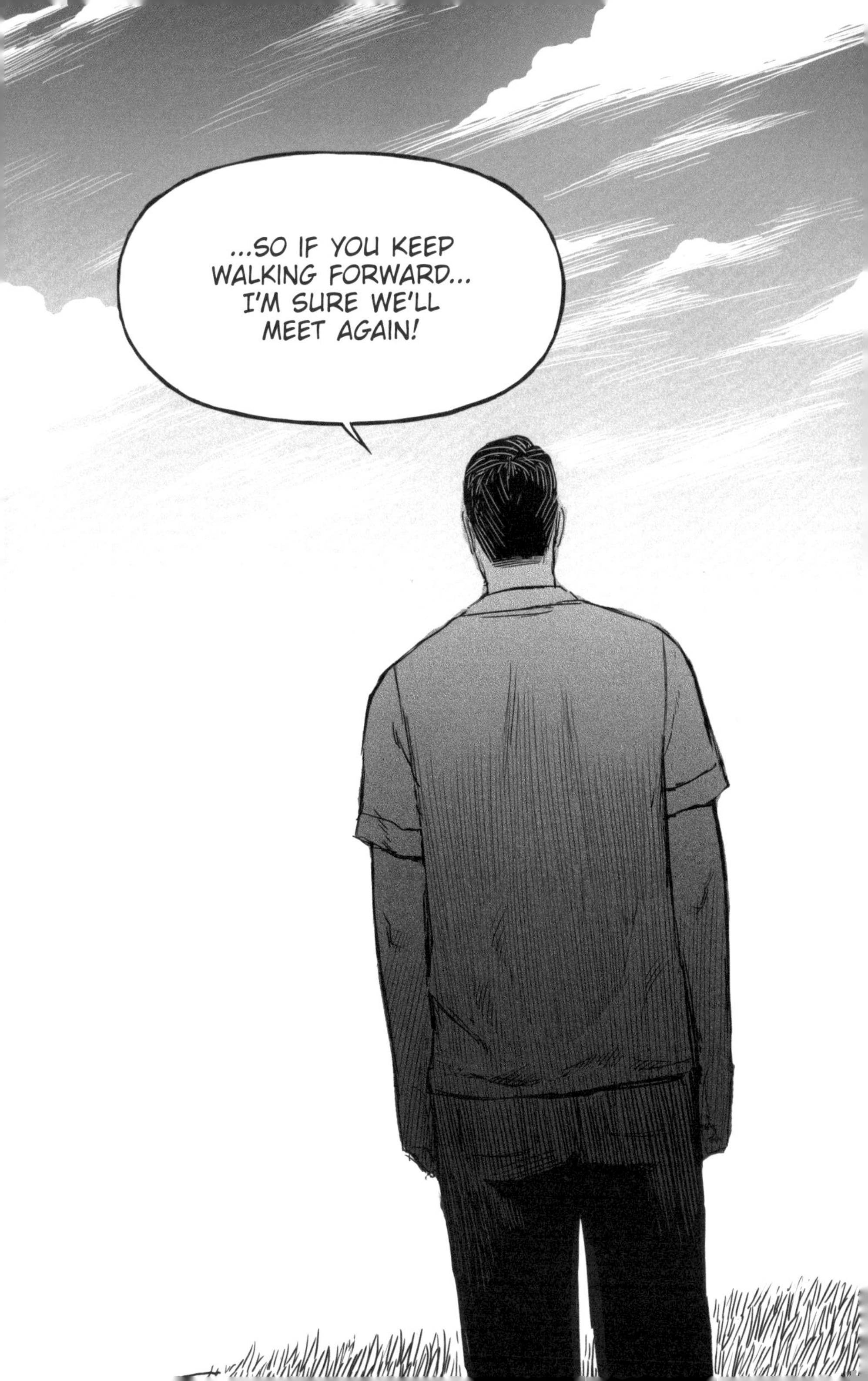
...SO IF YOU KEEP WALKING FORWARD... I'M SURE WE'LL MEET AGAIN!

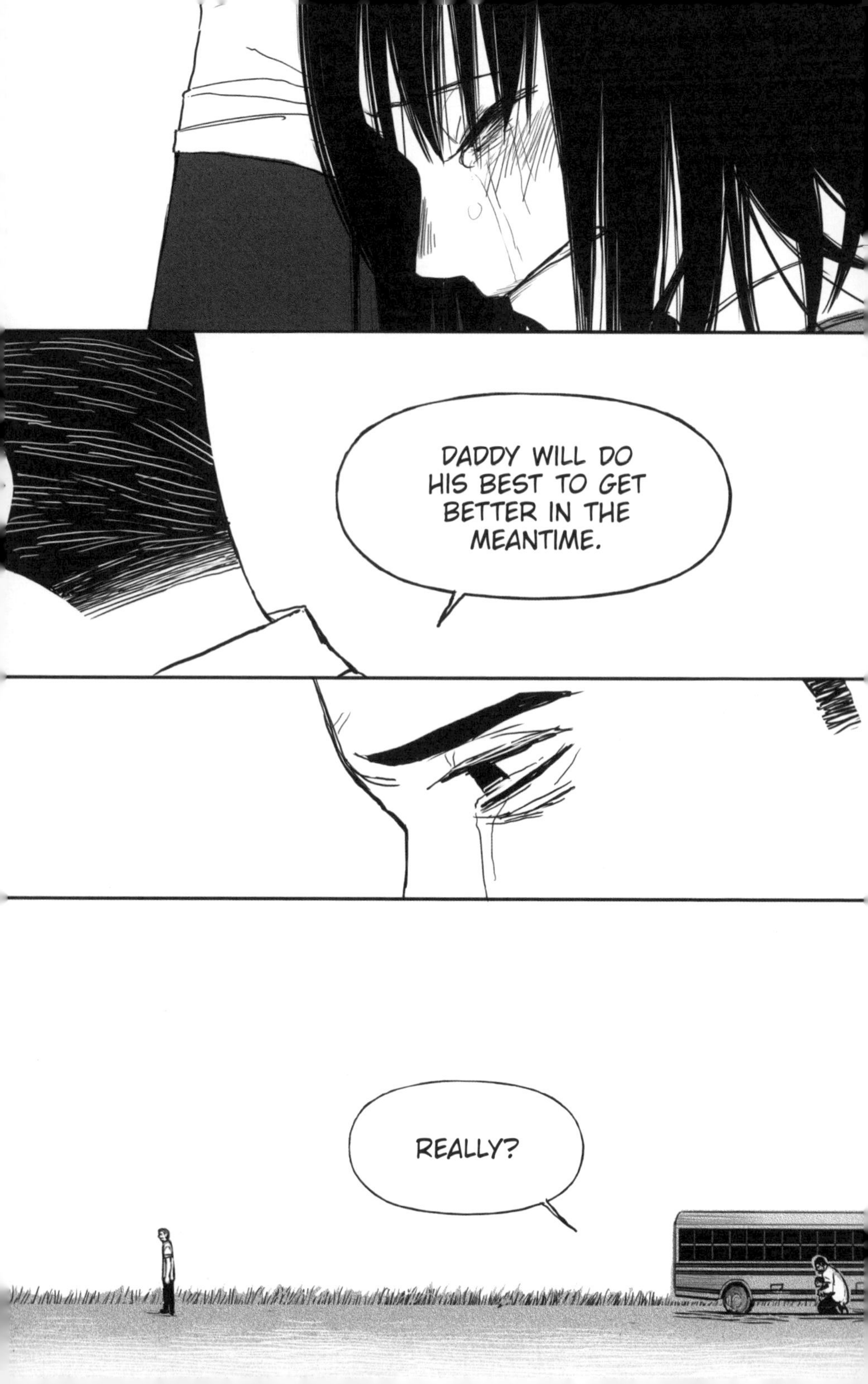
DADDY WILL DO HIS BEST TO GET BETTER IN THE MEANTIME.
REALLY?

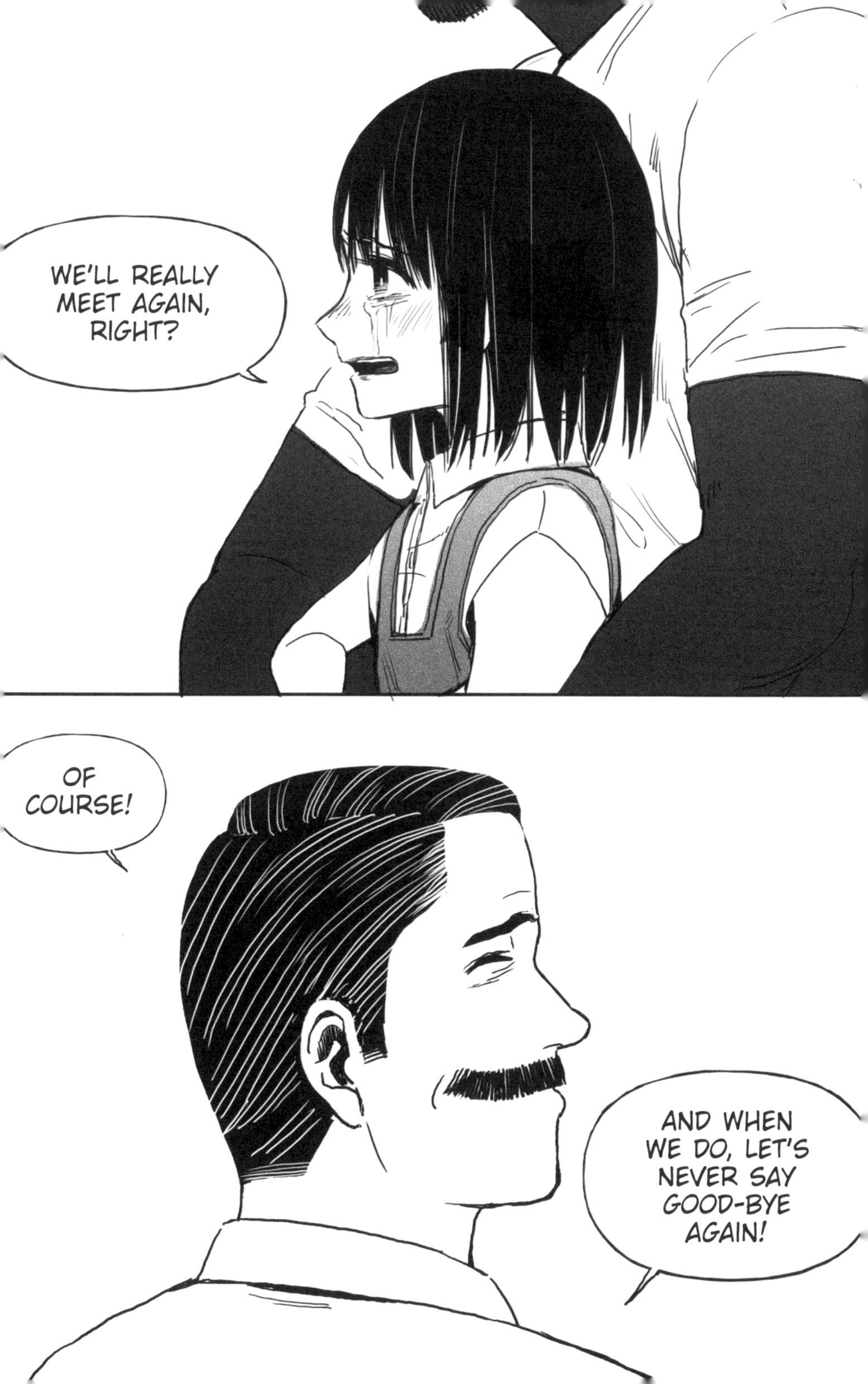
WE'LL REALLY MEET AGAIN, RIGHT?
OF COURSE!
AND WHEN WE DO, LET'S NEVER SAY GOOD-BYE AGAIN!

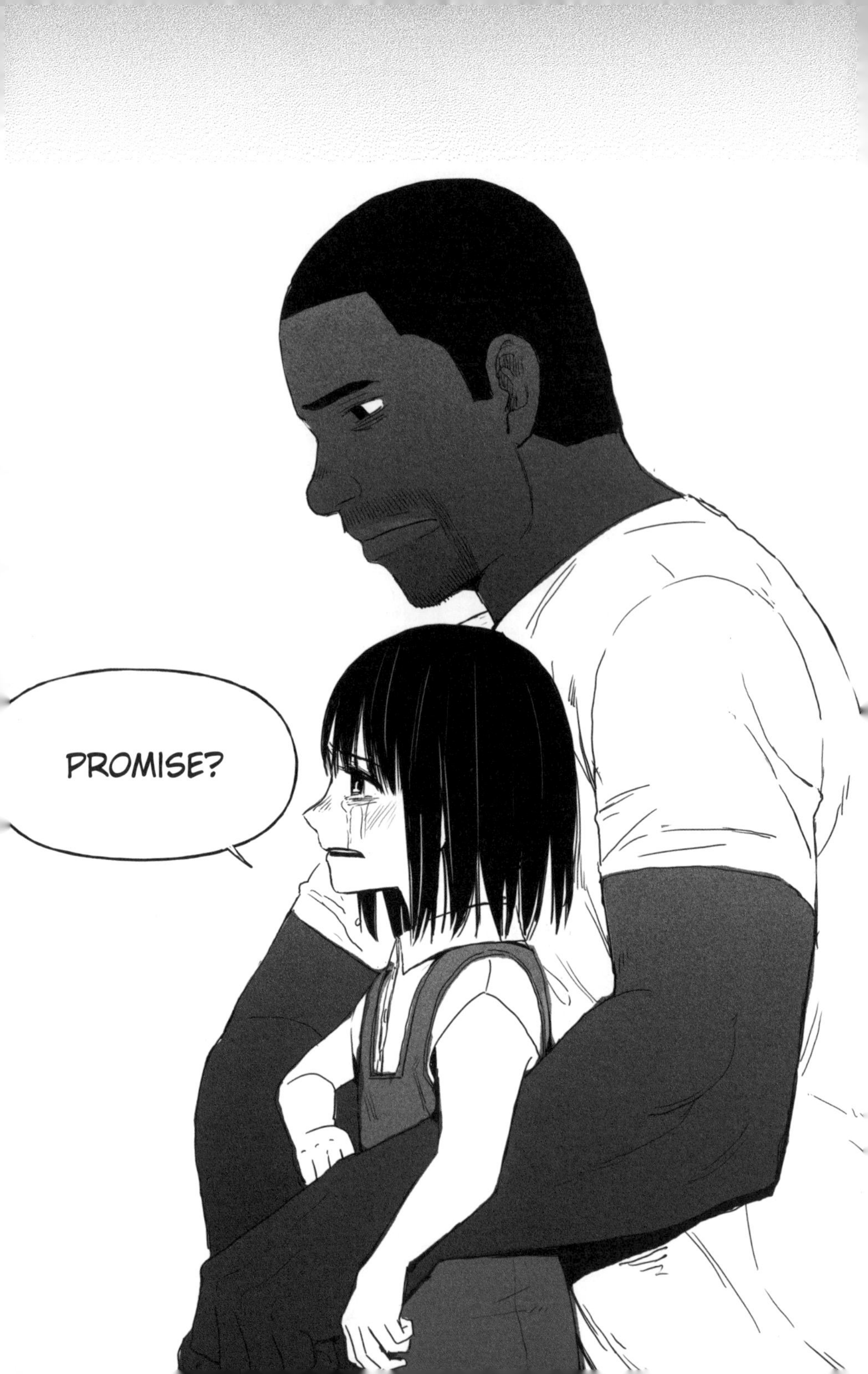
PROMISE?

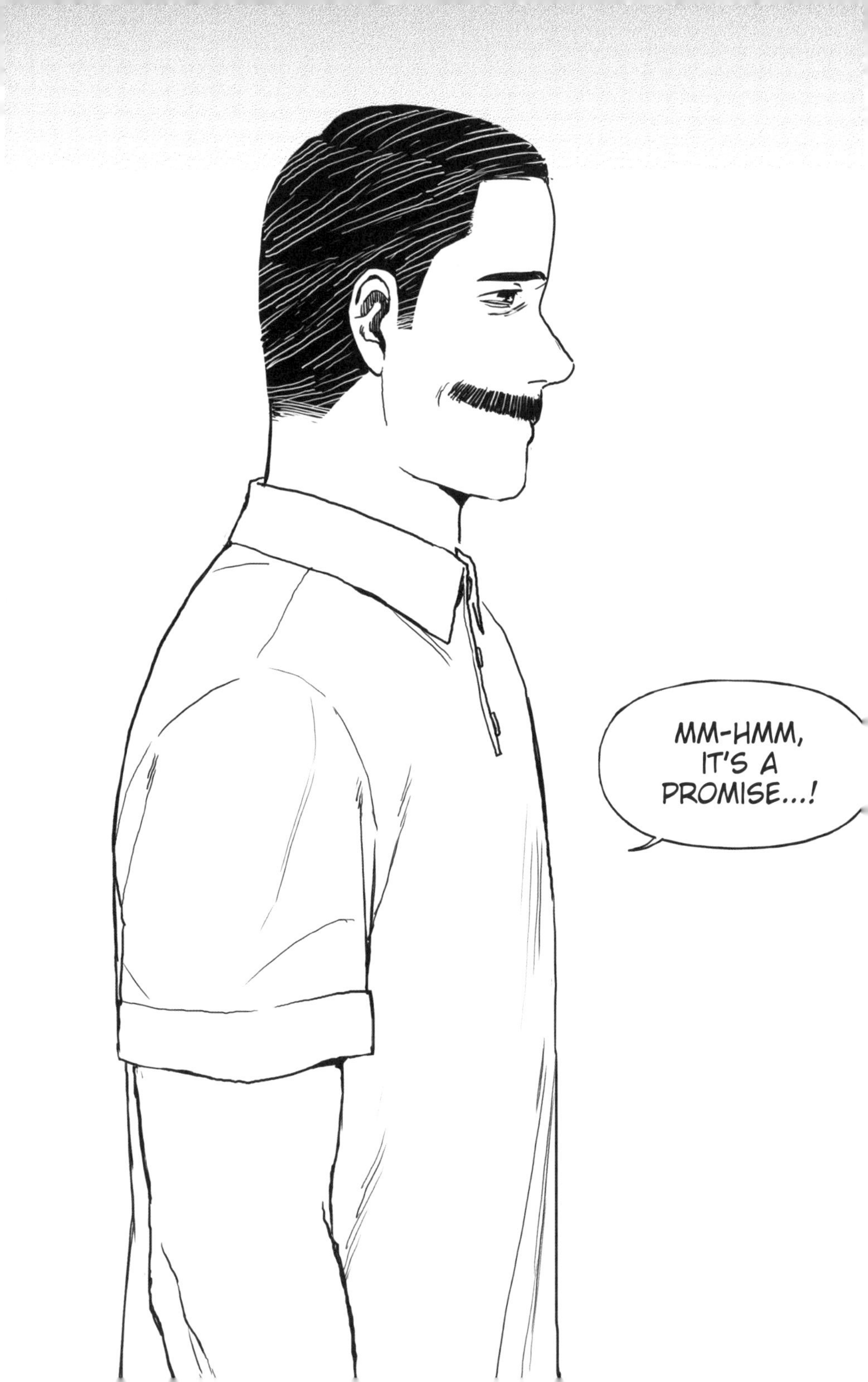
MM-HMM, IT'S A PROMISE...!

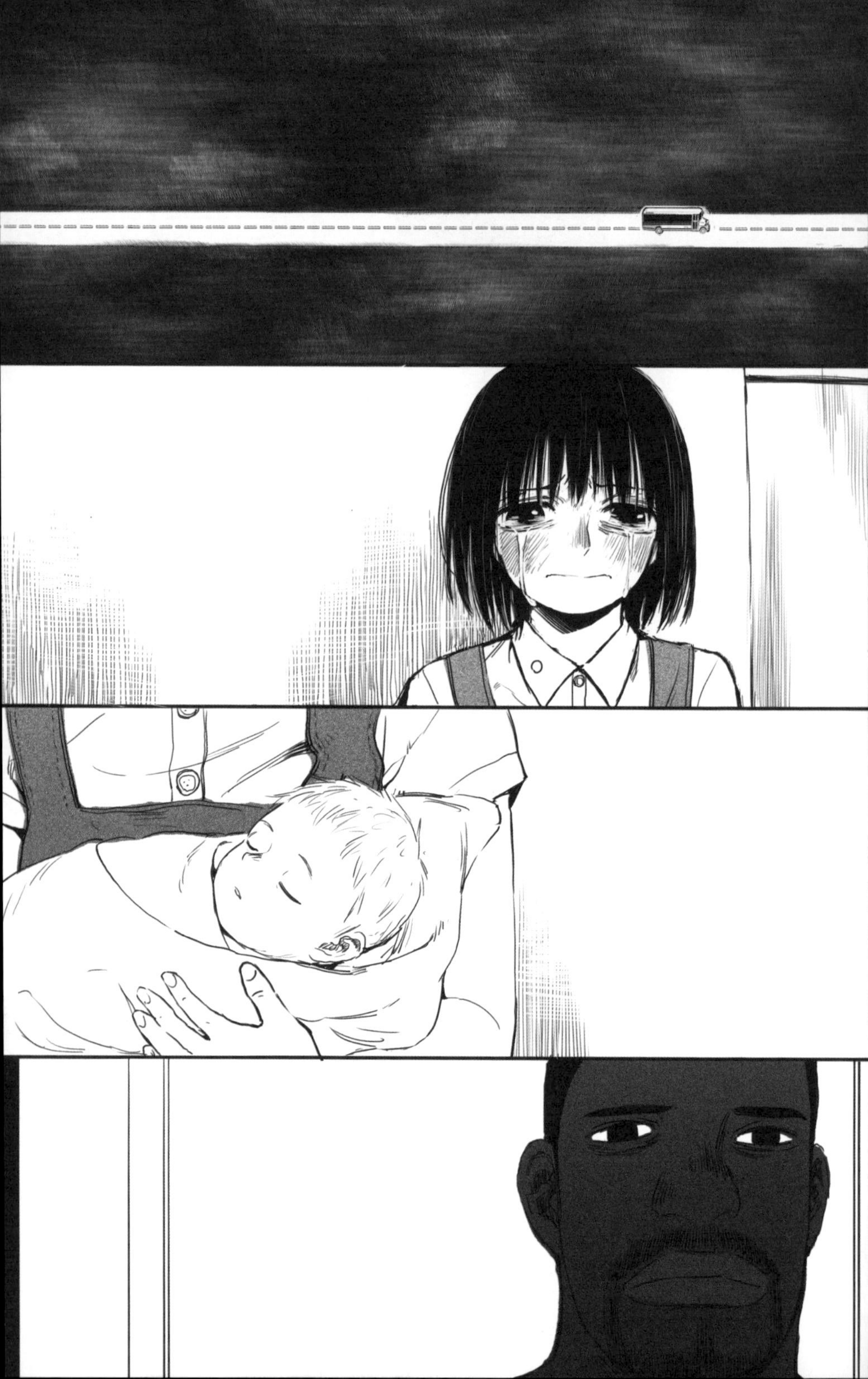

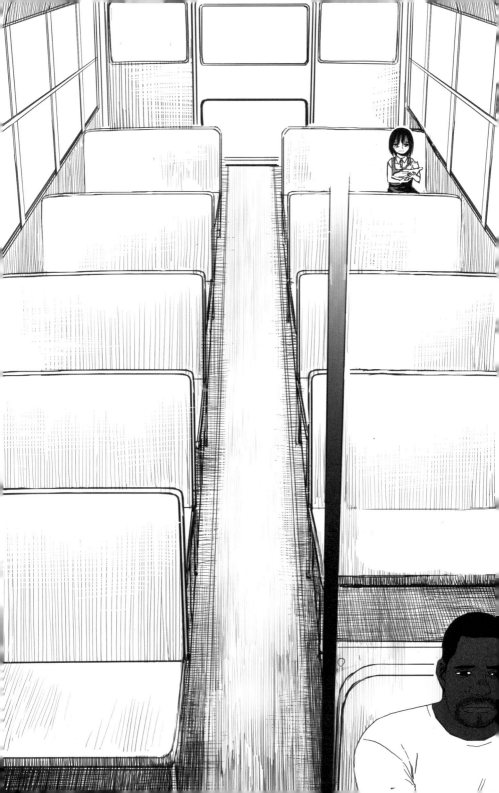

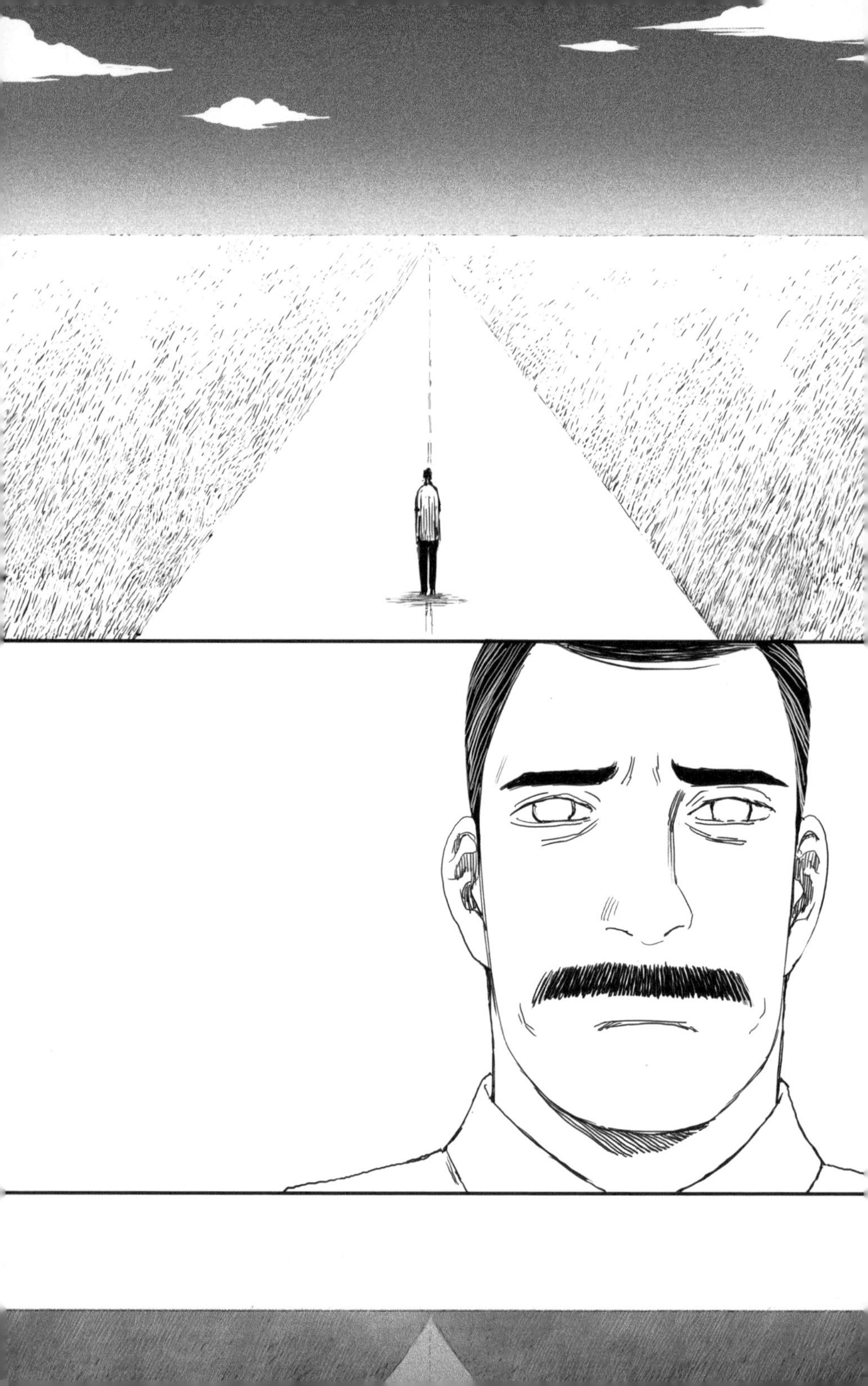

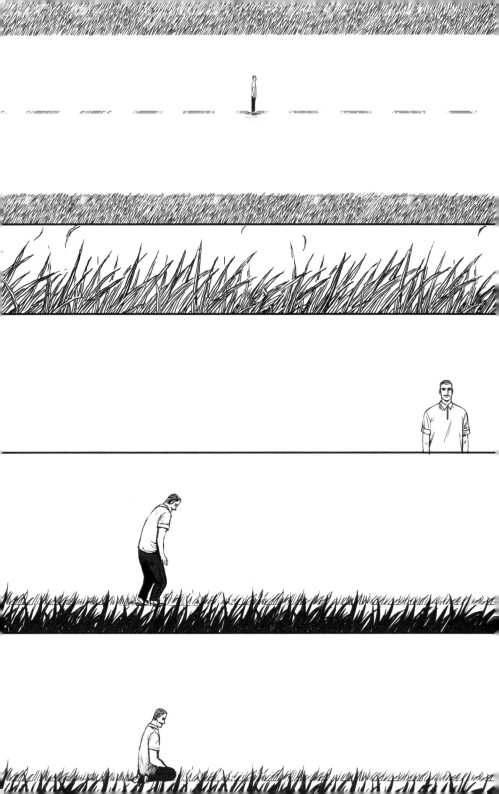

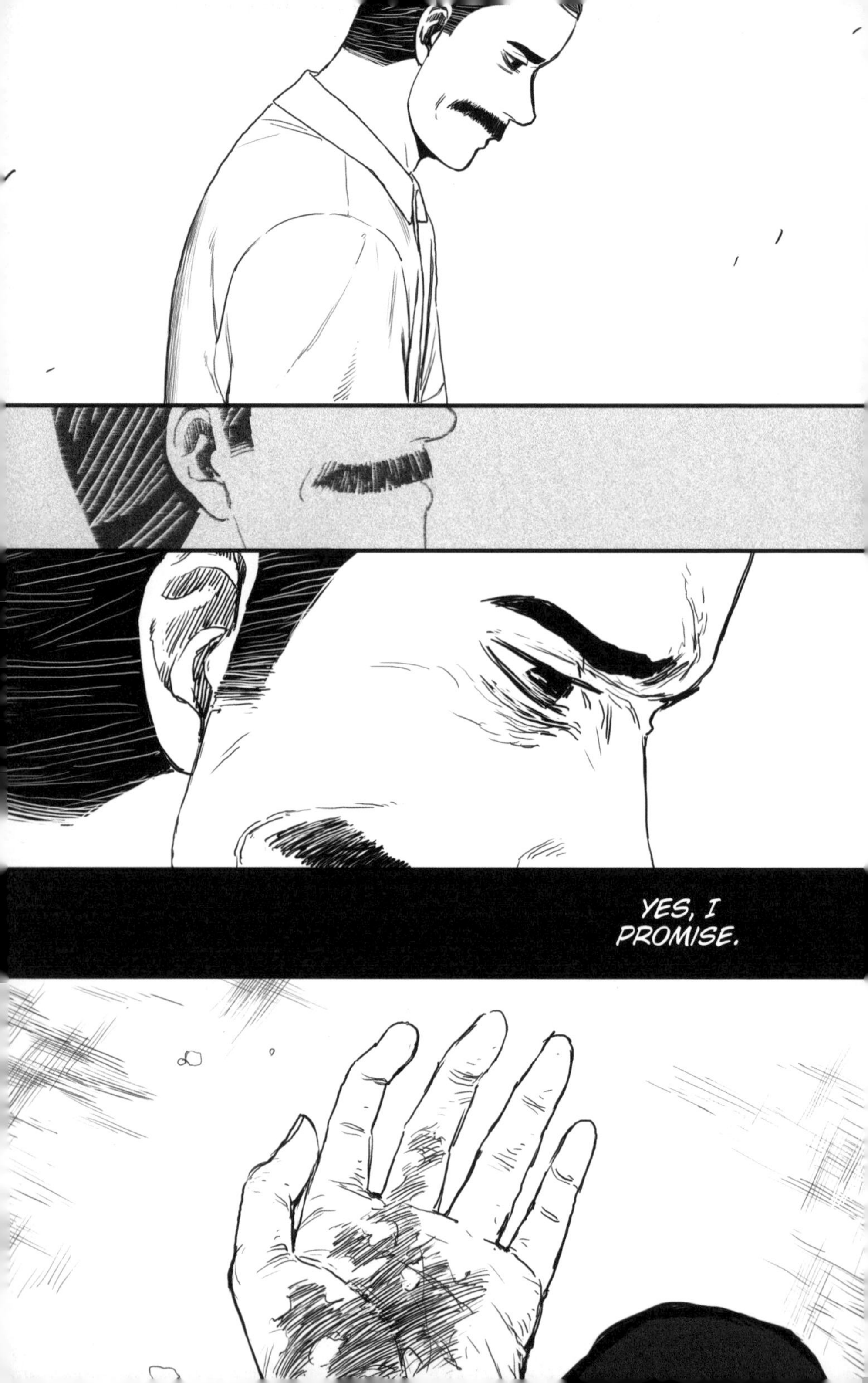
YES, I PROMISE.

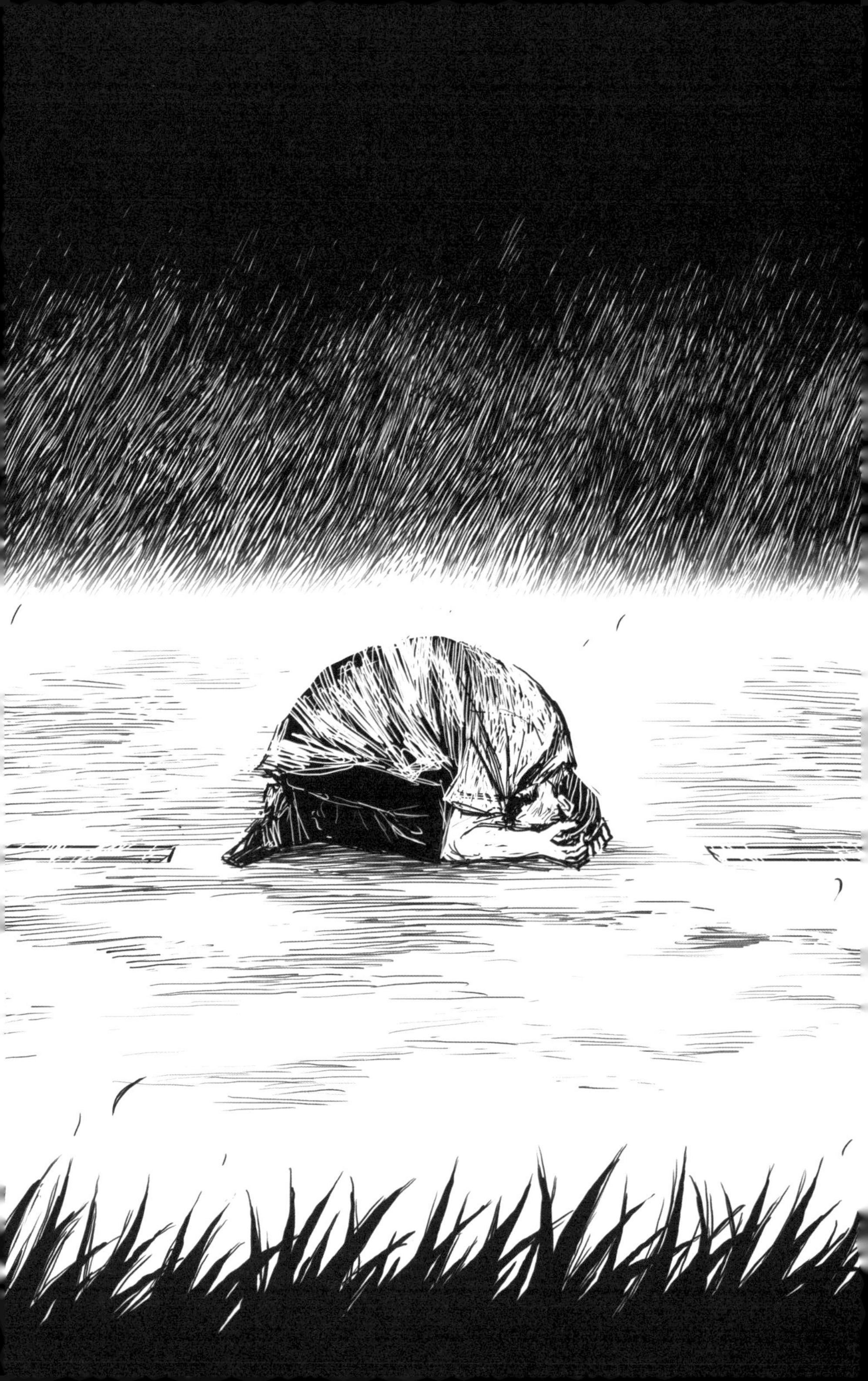

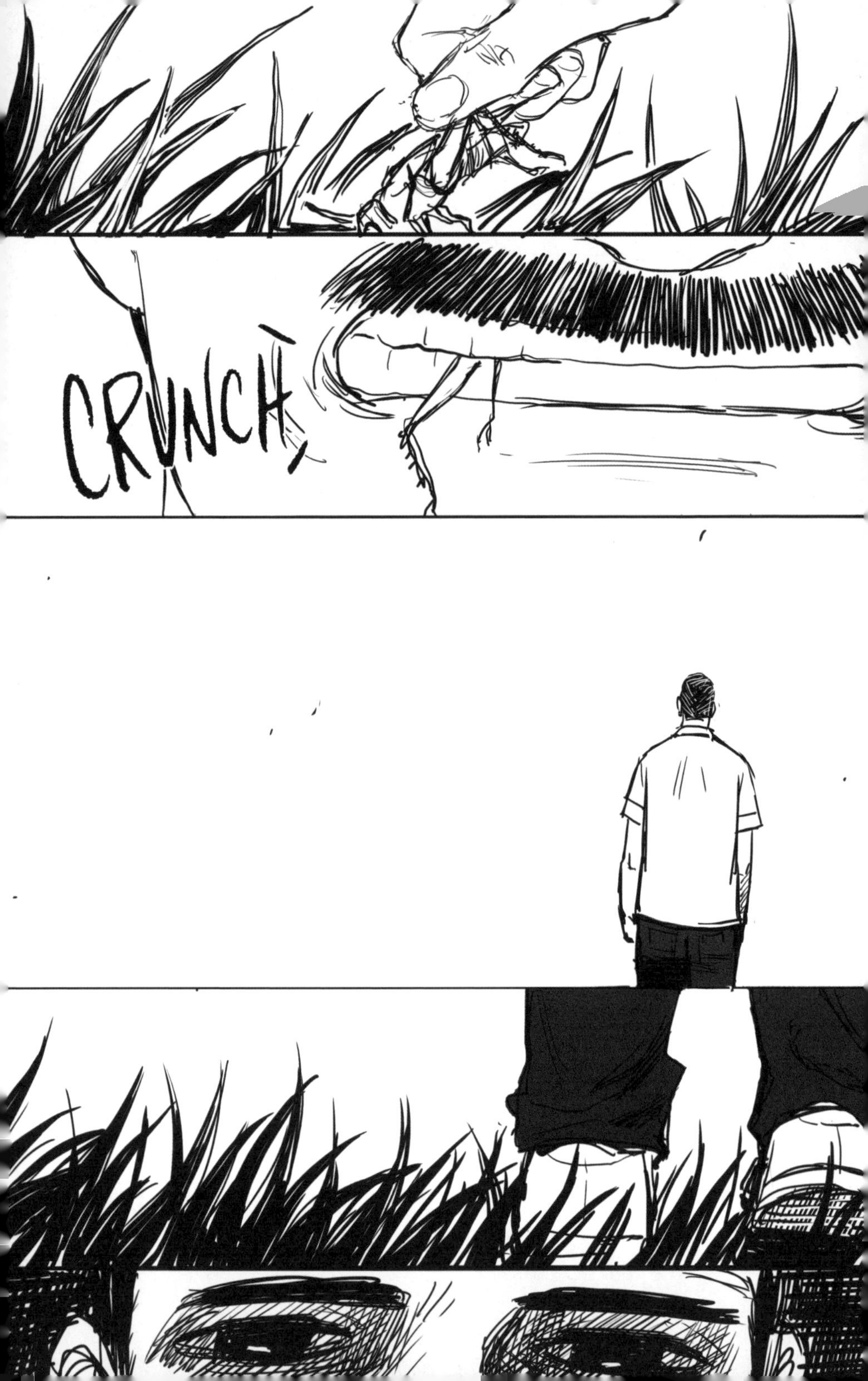
CRUNCH

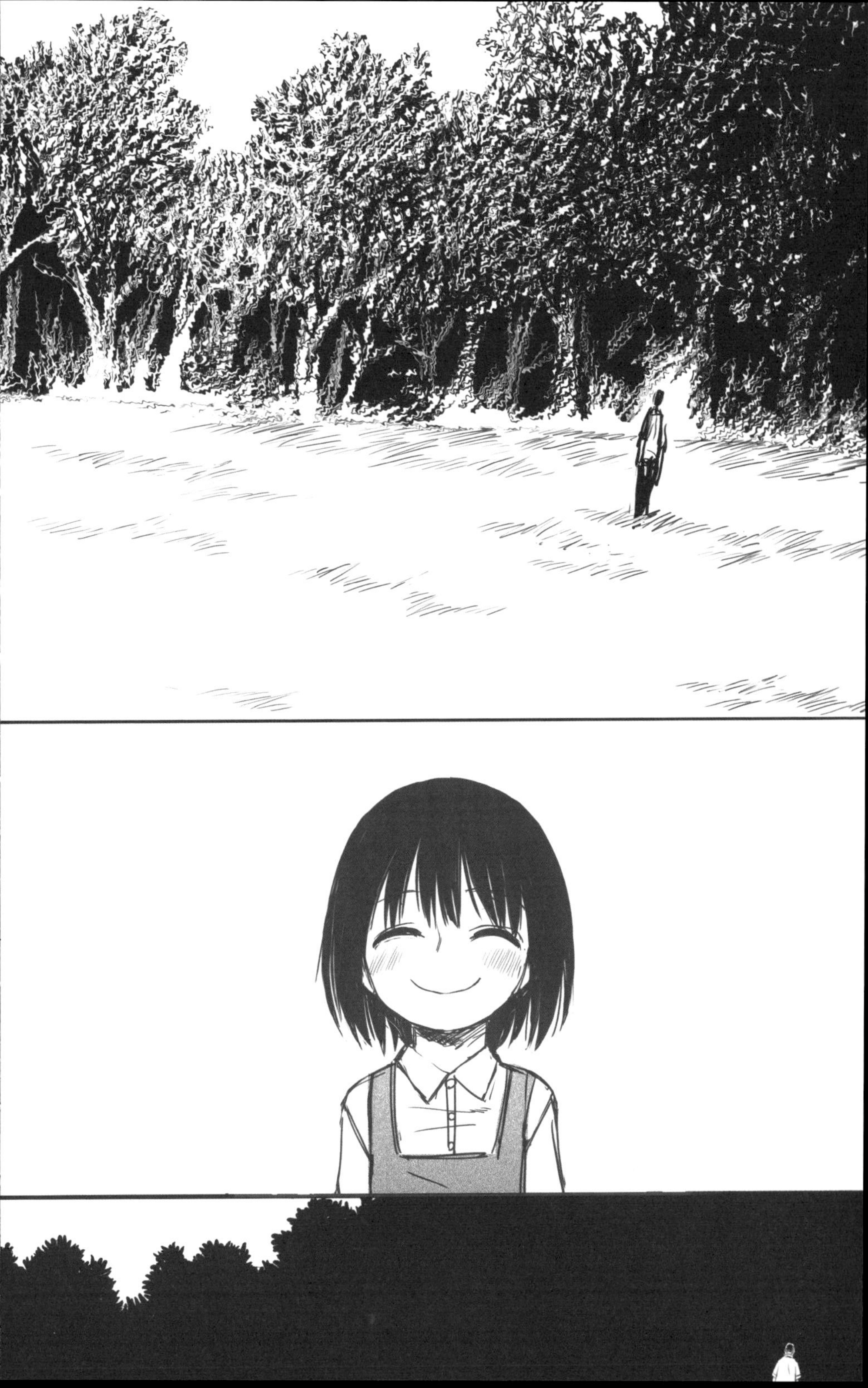

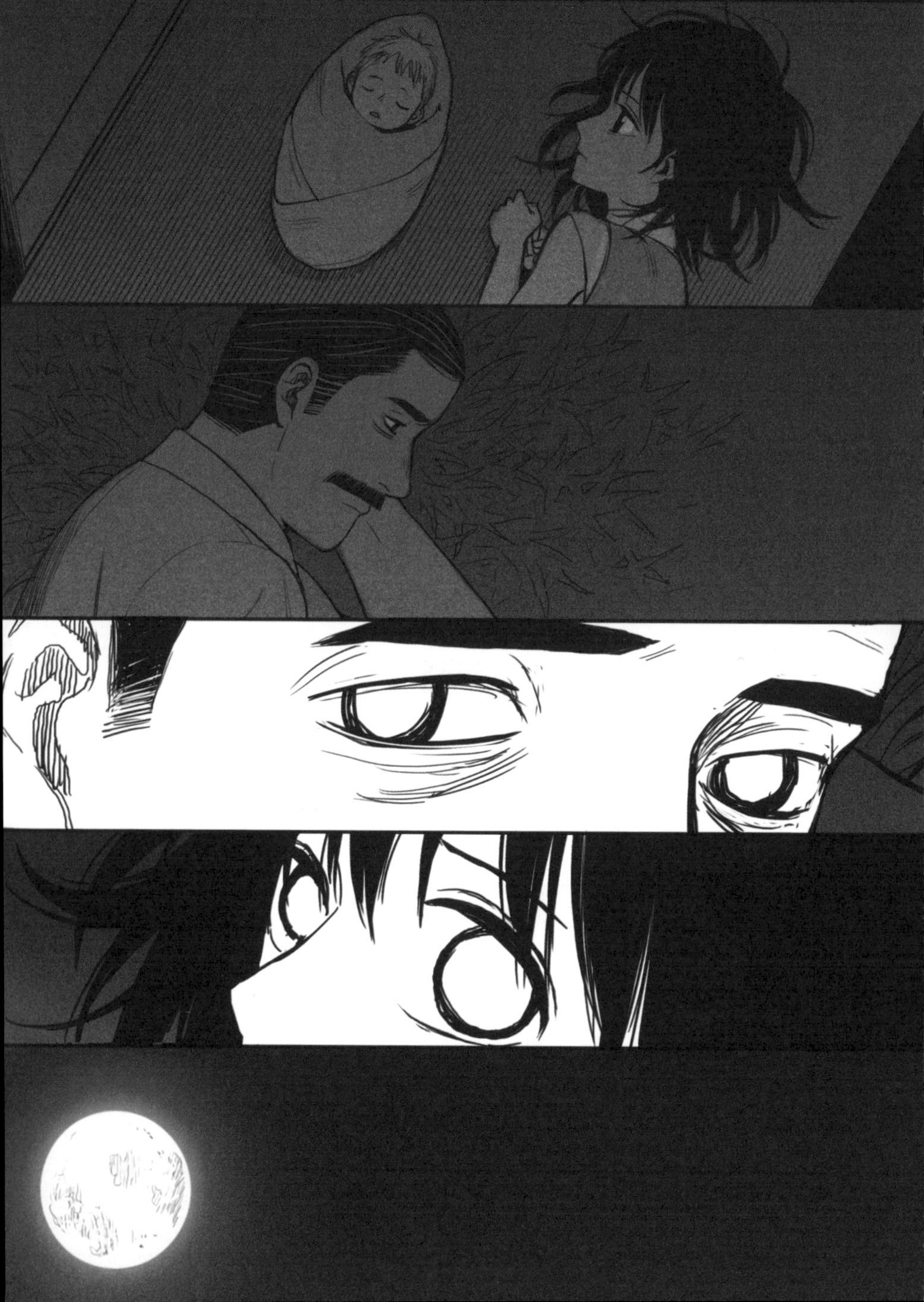

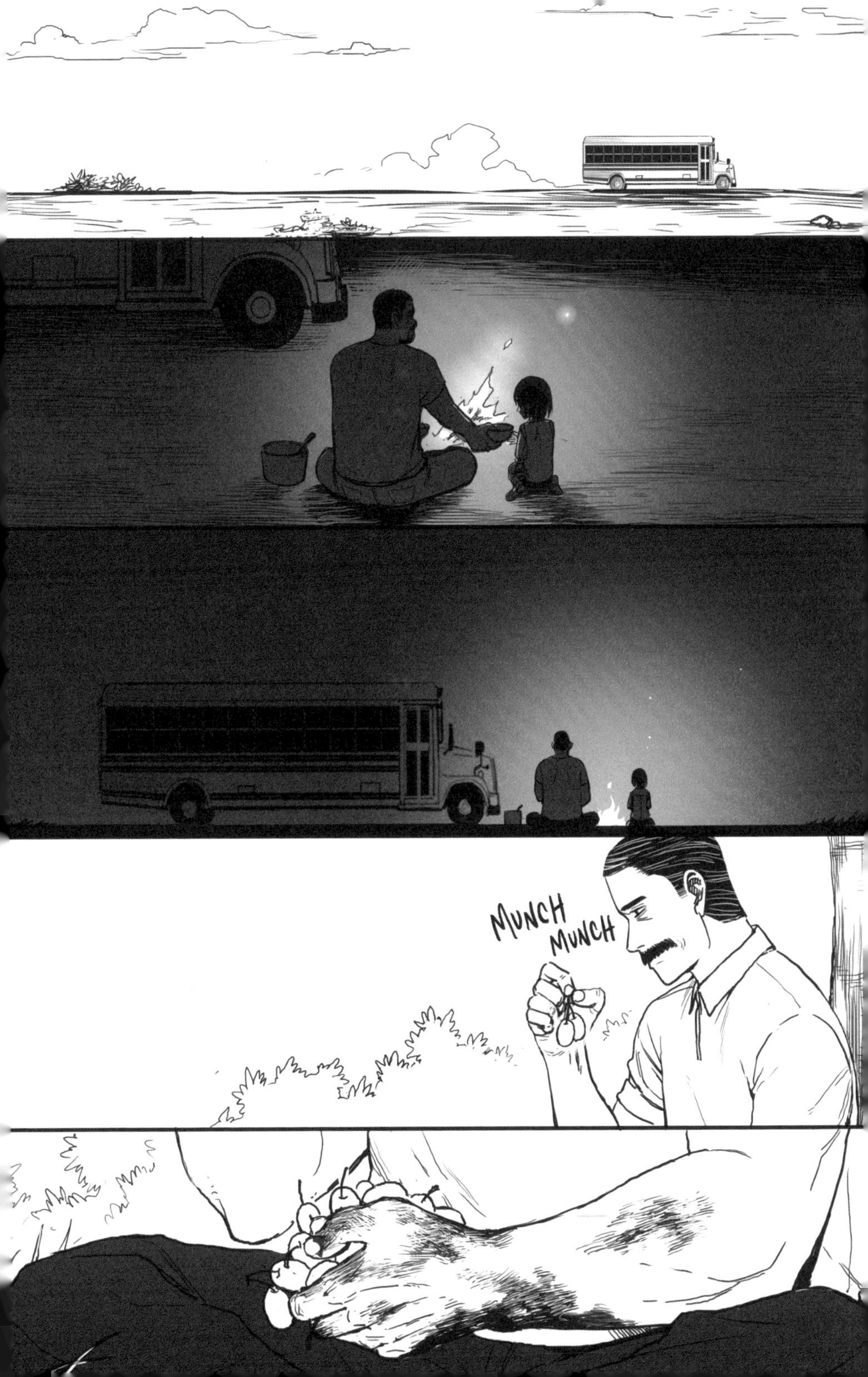
MUNCH
MUNCH

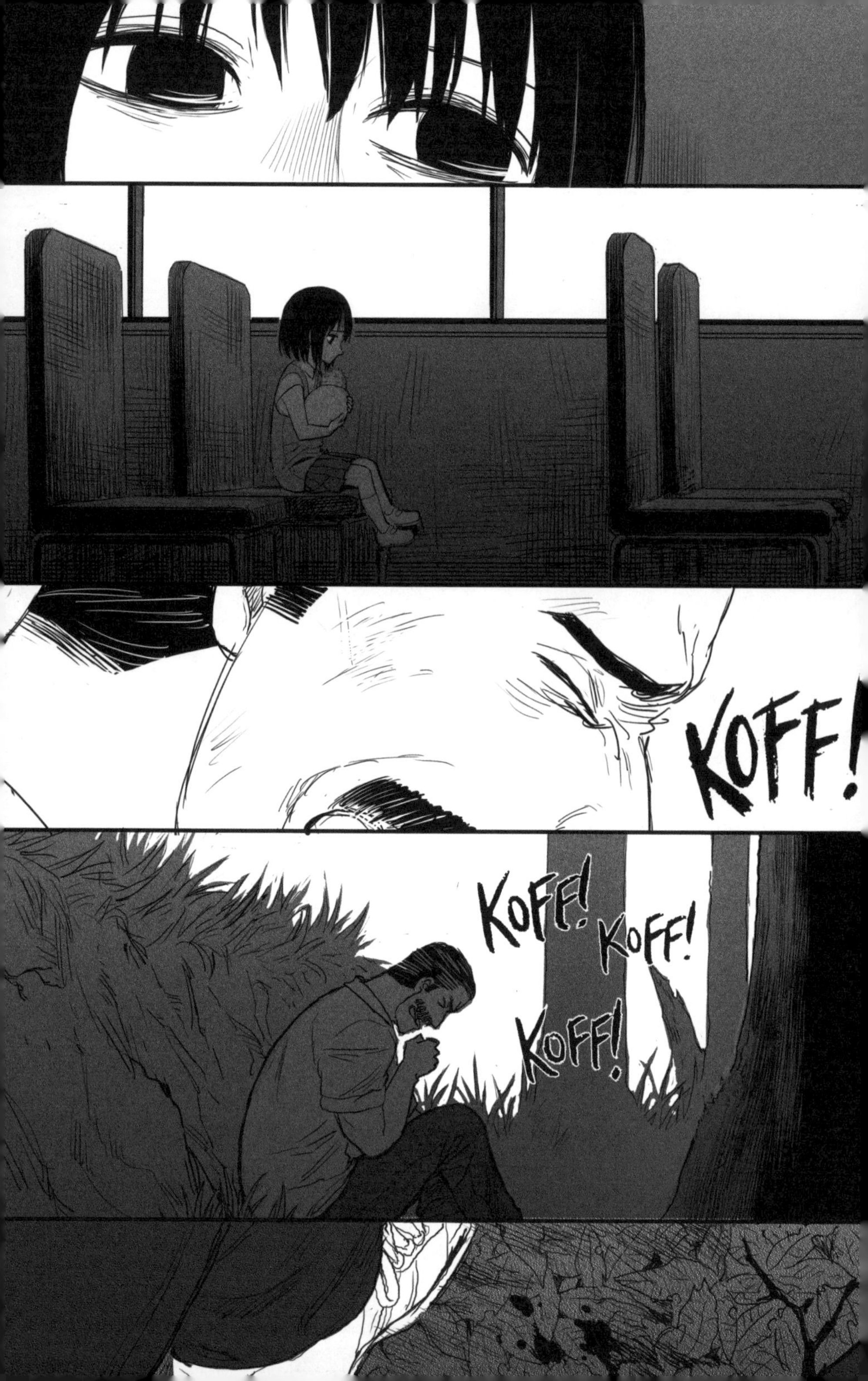
KOFF!
KOFF!
KOFF!
KOFF!

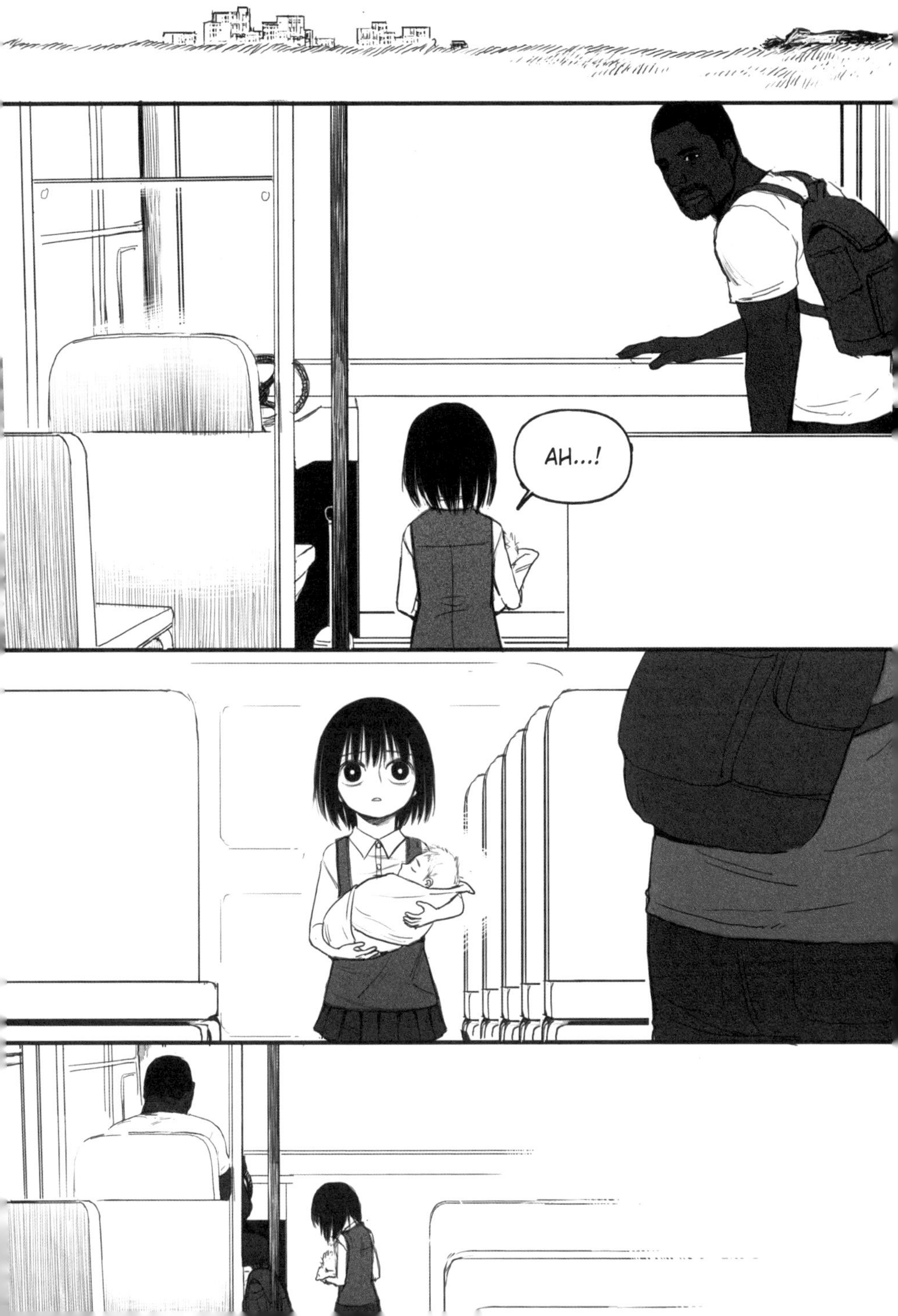
AH...!

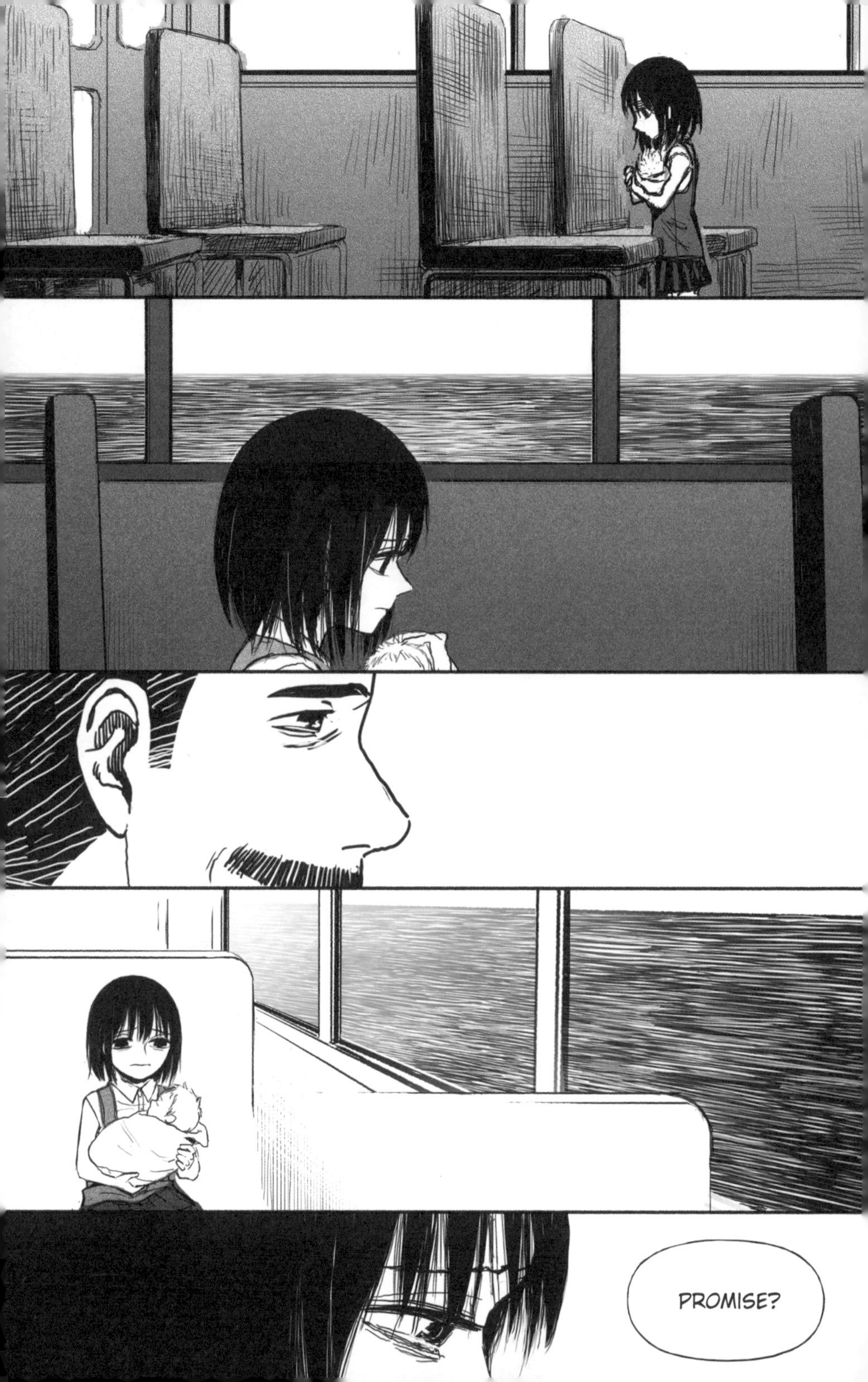
PROMISE?

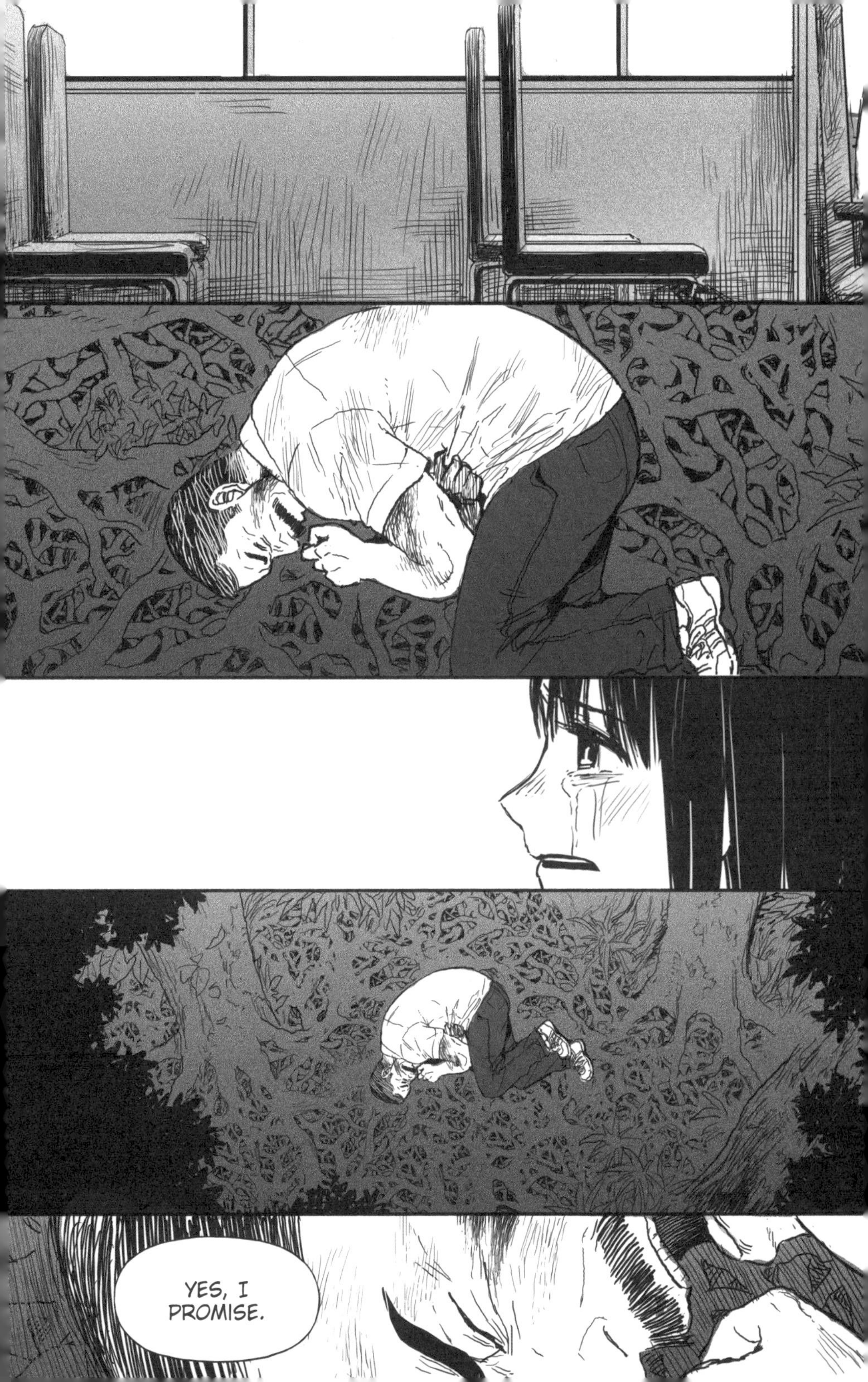
YES, I PROMISE.

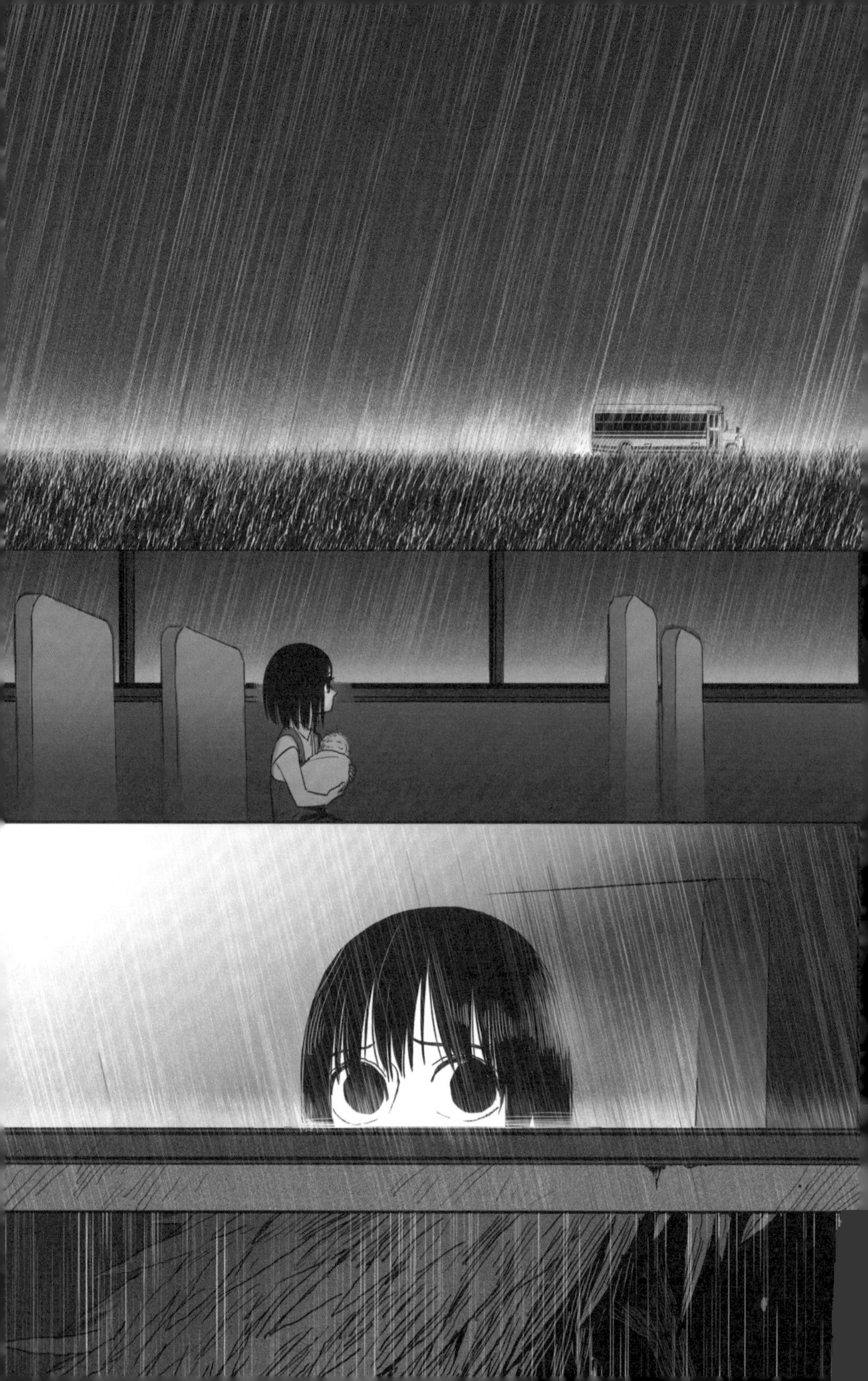

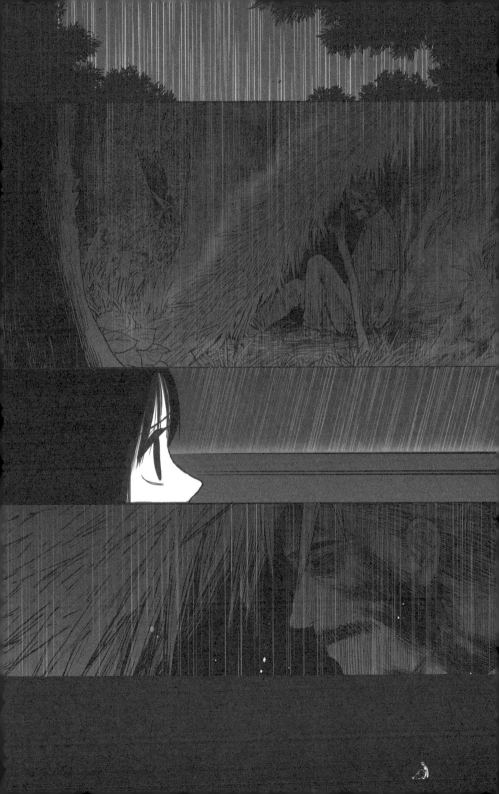

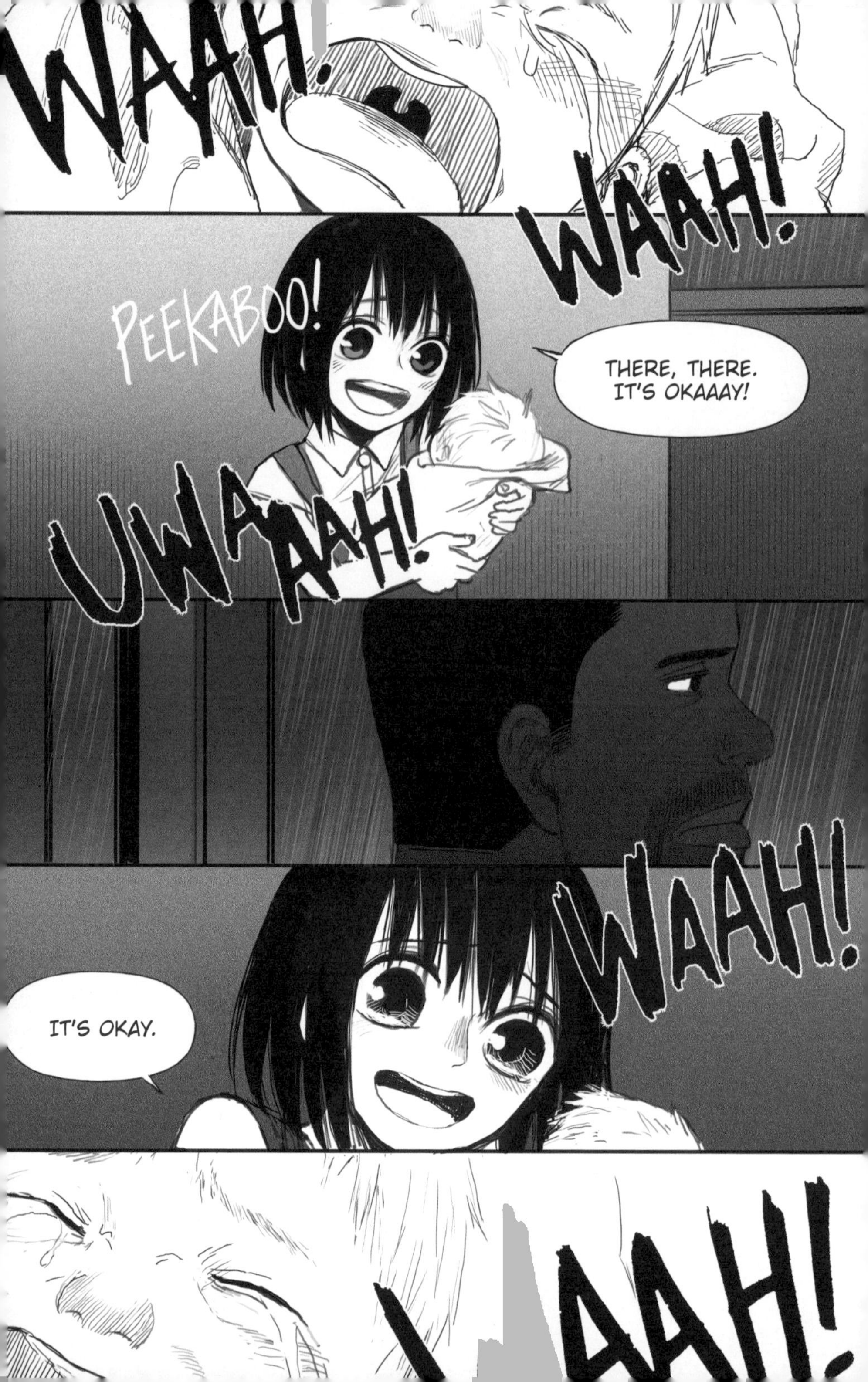
WAAH!
WAAH!
PEEKABOO!
THERE, THERE. IT'S OKAAAY!
UWAAAH!
WAAH!
IT'S OKAY.
AAAH!

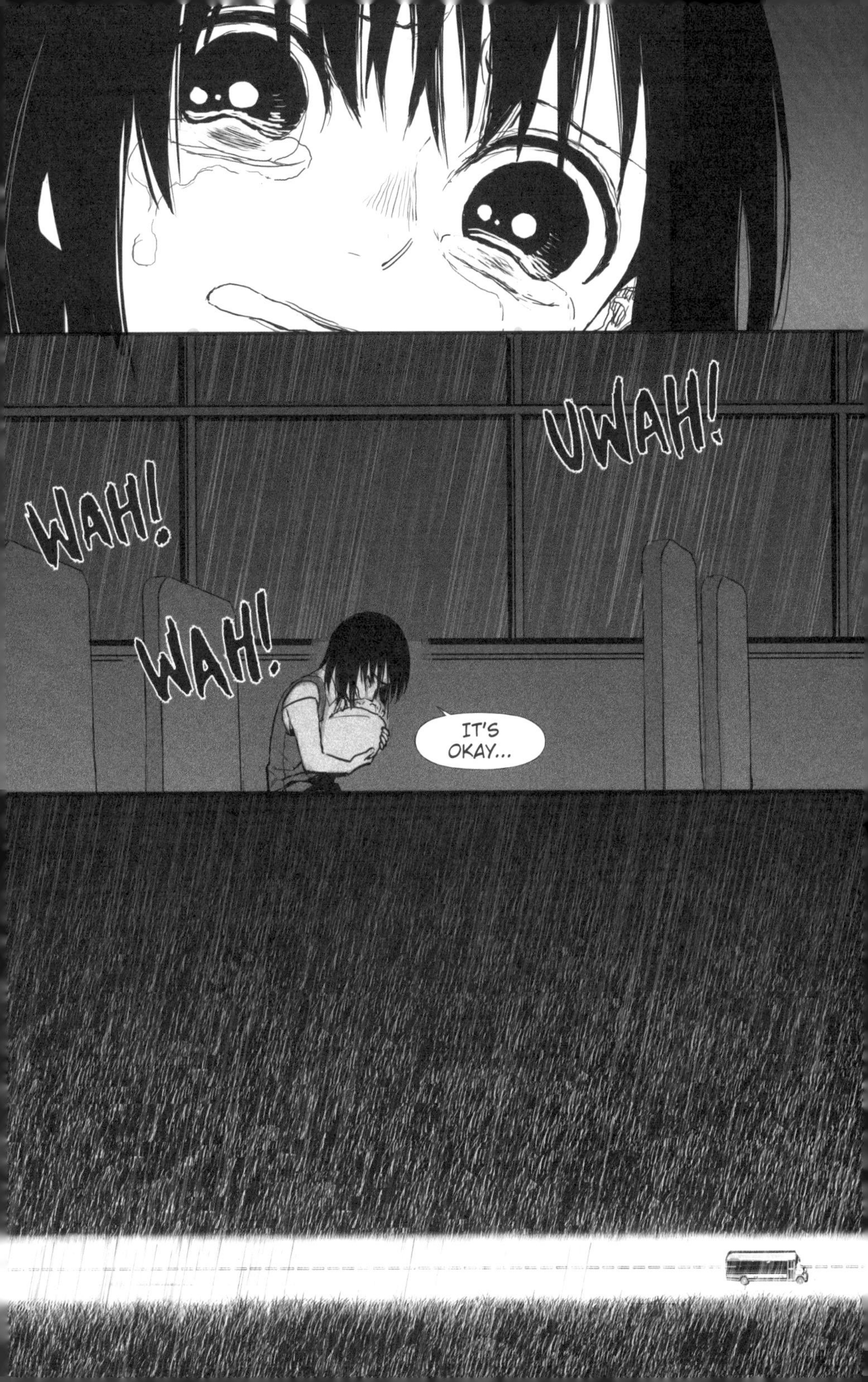
UWAH!
WAH!
WAH!
IT'S OKAY...

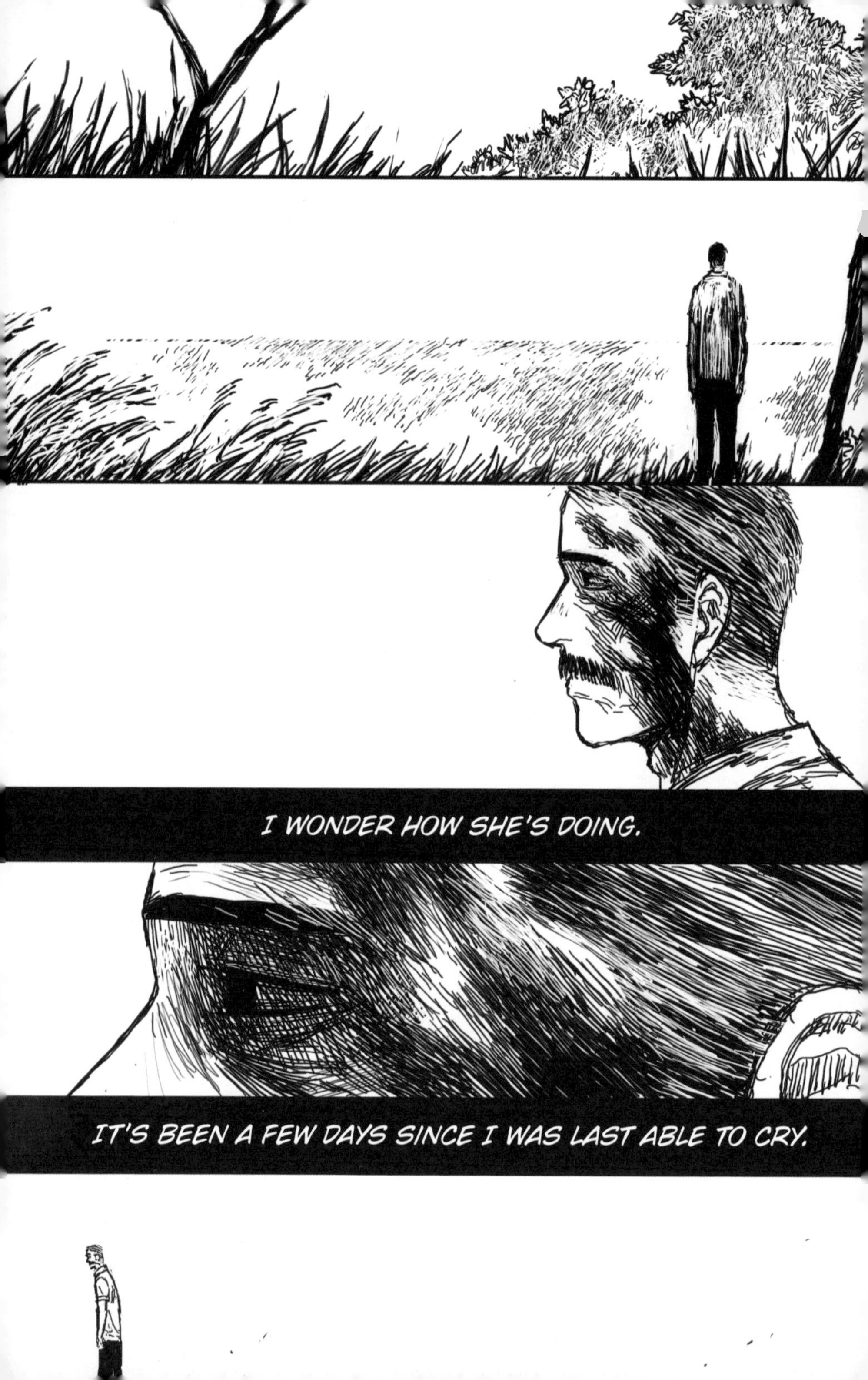
I WONDER HOW SHE'S DOING.
IT'S BEEN A FEW DAYS SINCE I WAS LAST ABLE TO CRY.

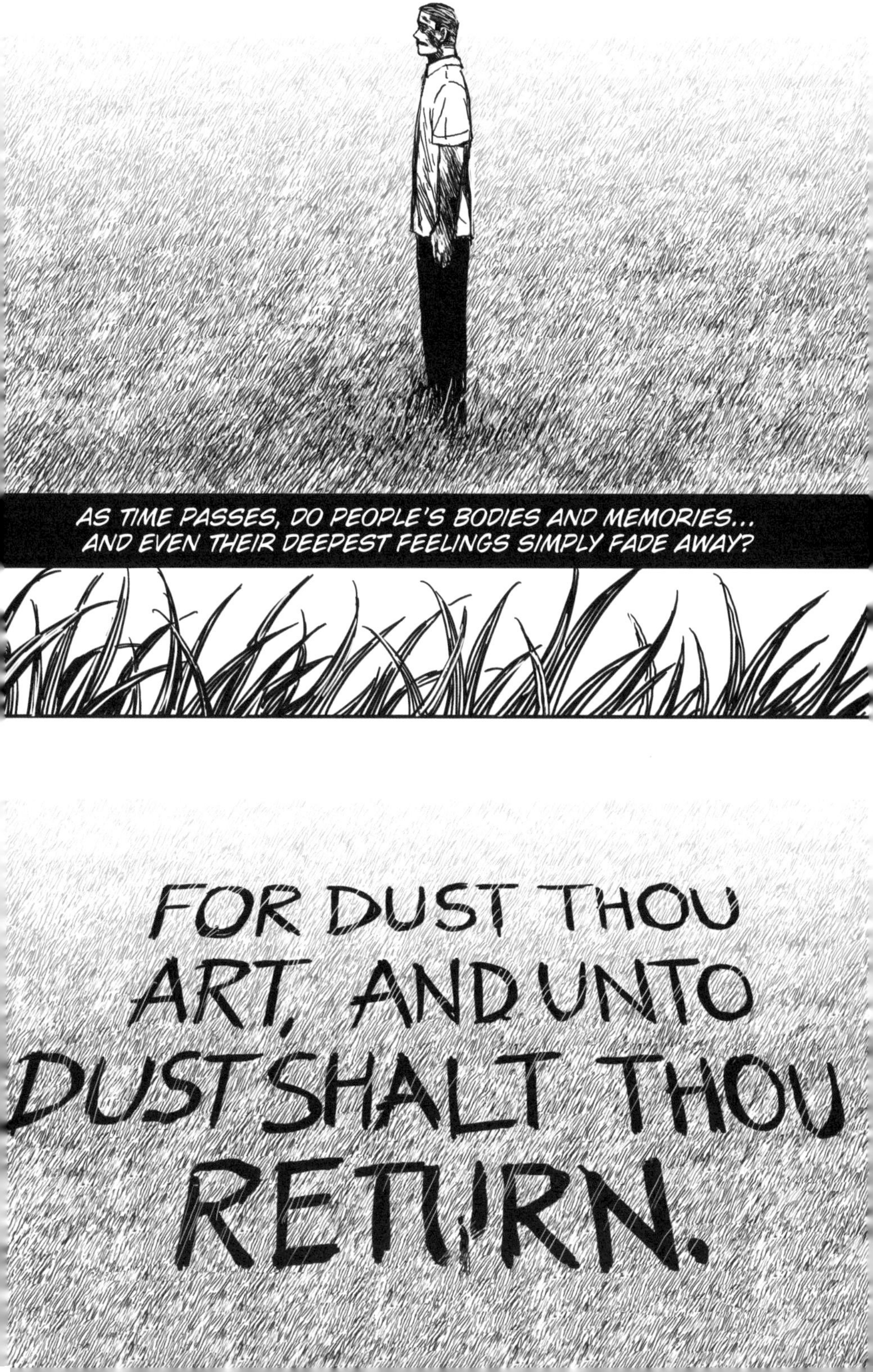
AS TIME PASSES, DO PEOPLE'S BODIES AND MEMORIES... AND EVEN THEIR DEEPEST FEELINGS SIMPLY FADE AWAY?
FOR DUST THOU ART, AND UNTO DUST SHALT THOU RETURN.

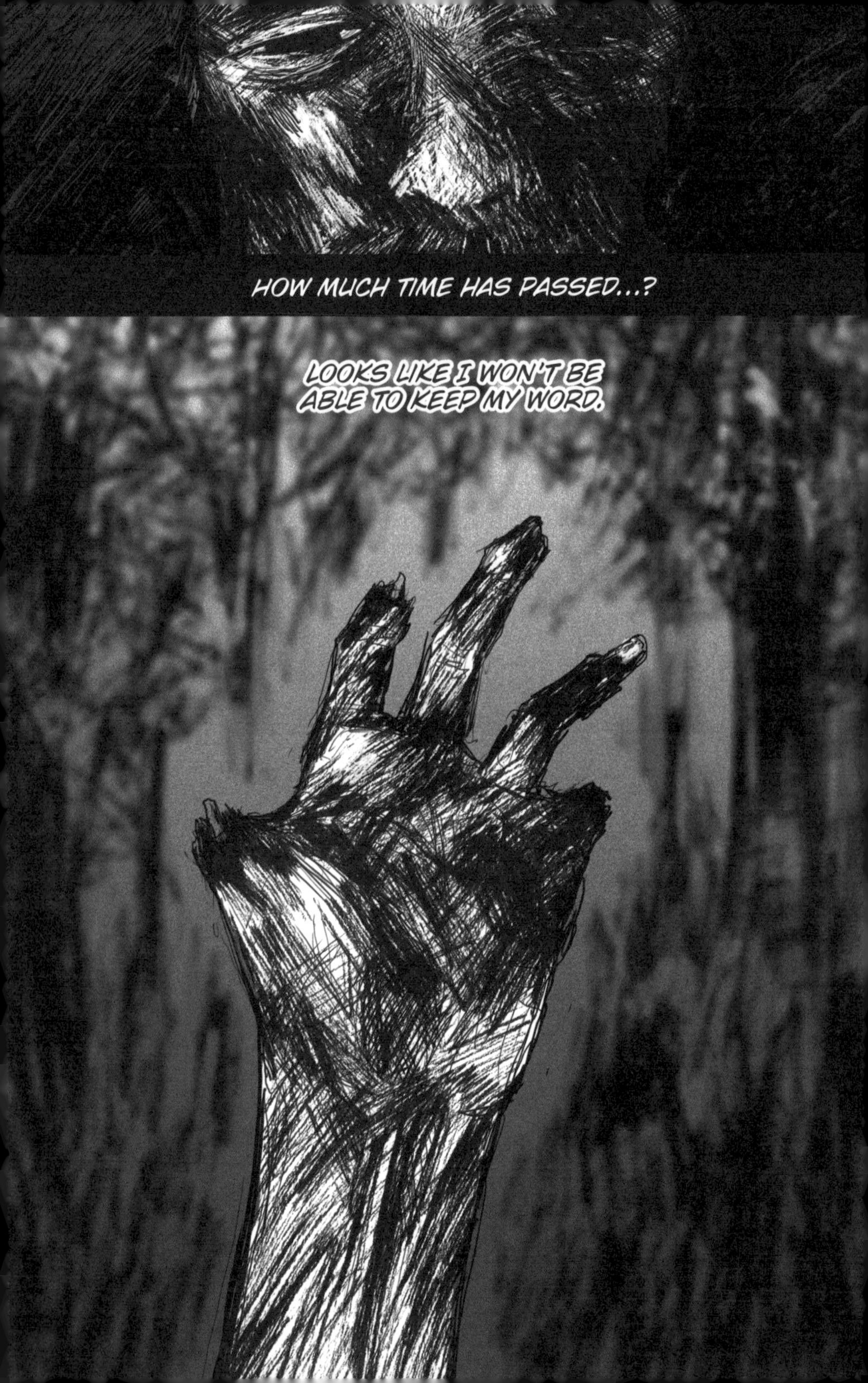
HOW MUCH TIME HAS PASSED...?
LOOKS LIKE I WON'T BE ABLE TO KEEP MY WORD.

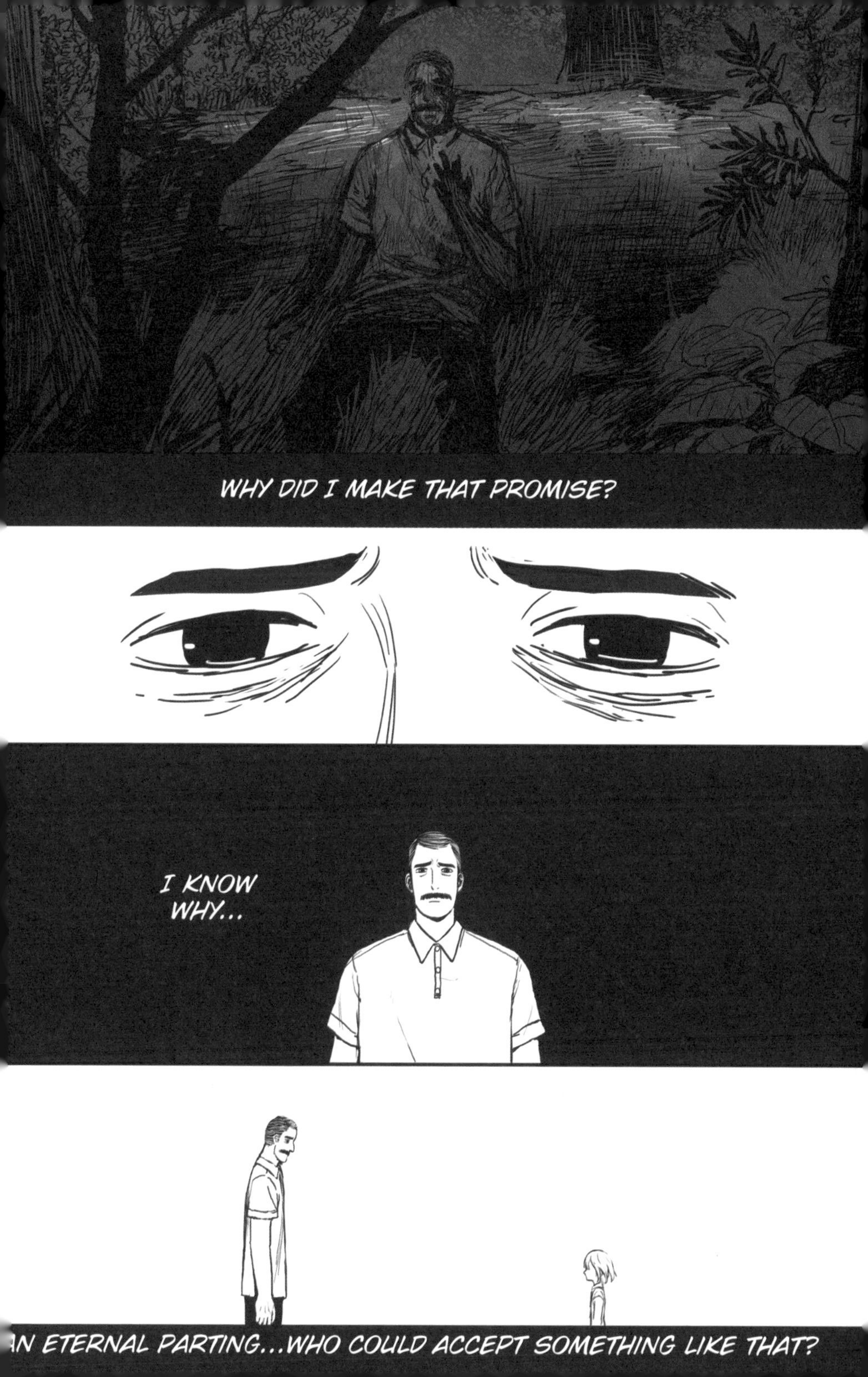
WHY DID I MAKE THAT PROMISE?
I KNOW WHY...
AN ETERNAL PARTING...WHO COULD ACCEPT SOMETHING LIKE THAT?

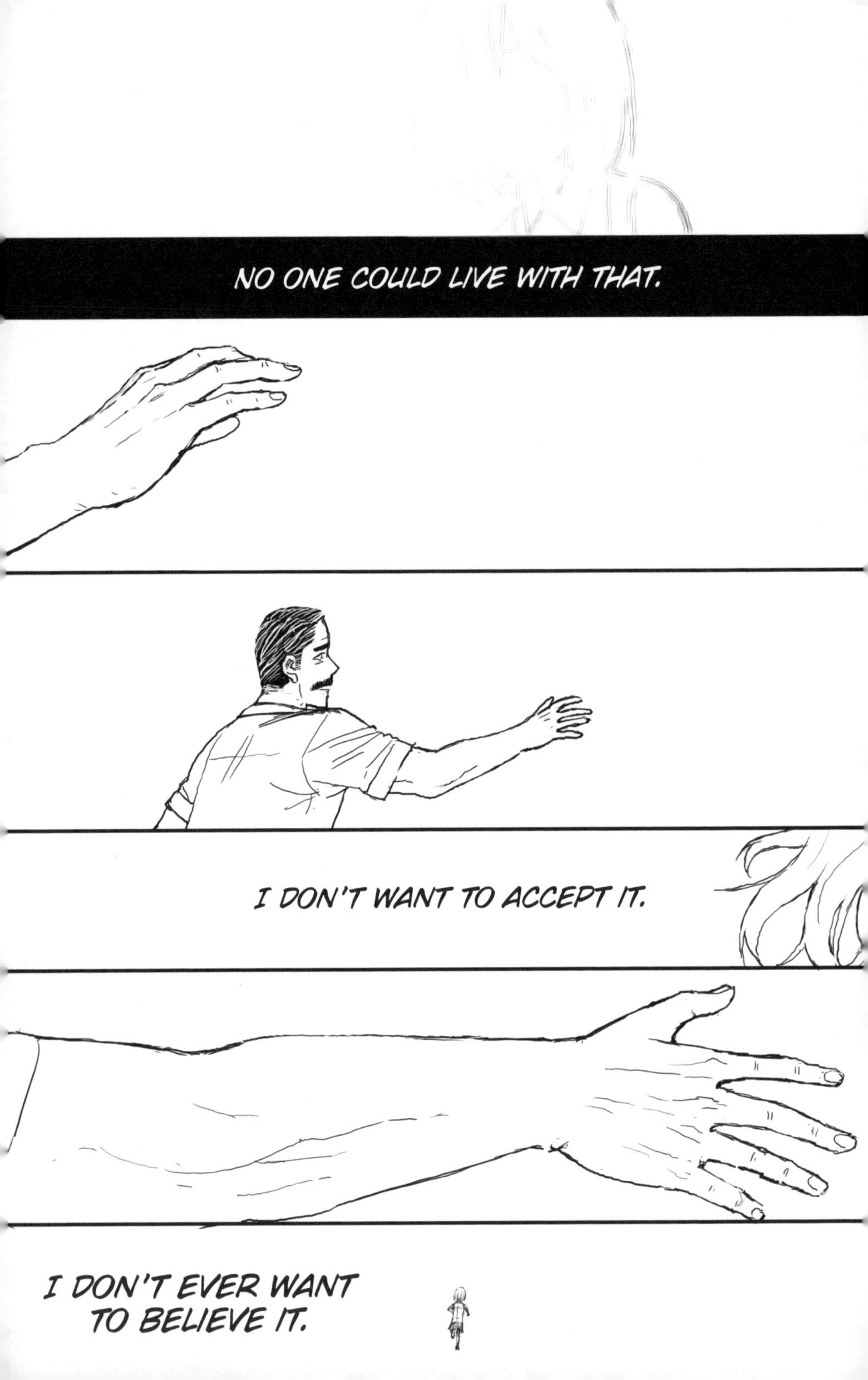

NO ONE COULD LIVE WITH THAT.

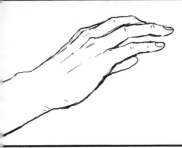

I DON'T WANT TO ACCEPT IT.

I DON'T EVER WANT TO BELIEVE IT.

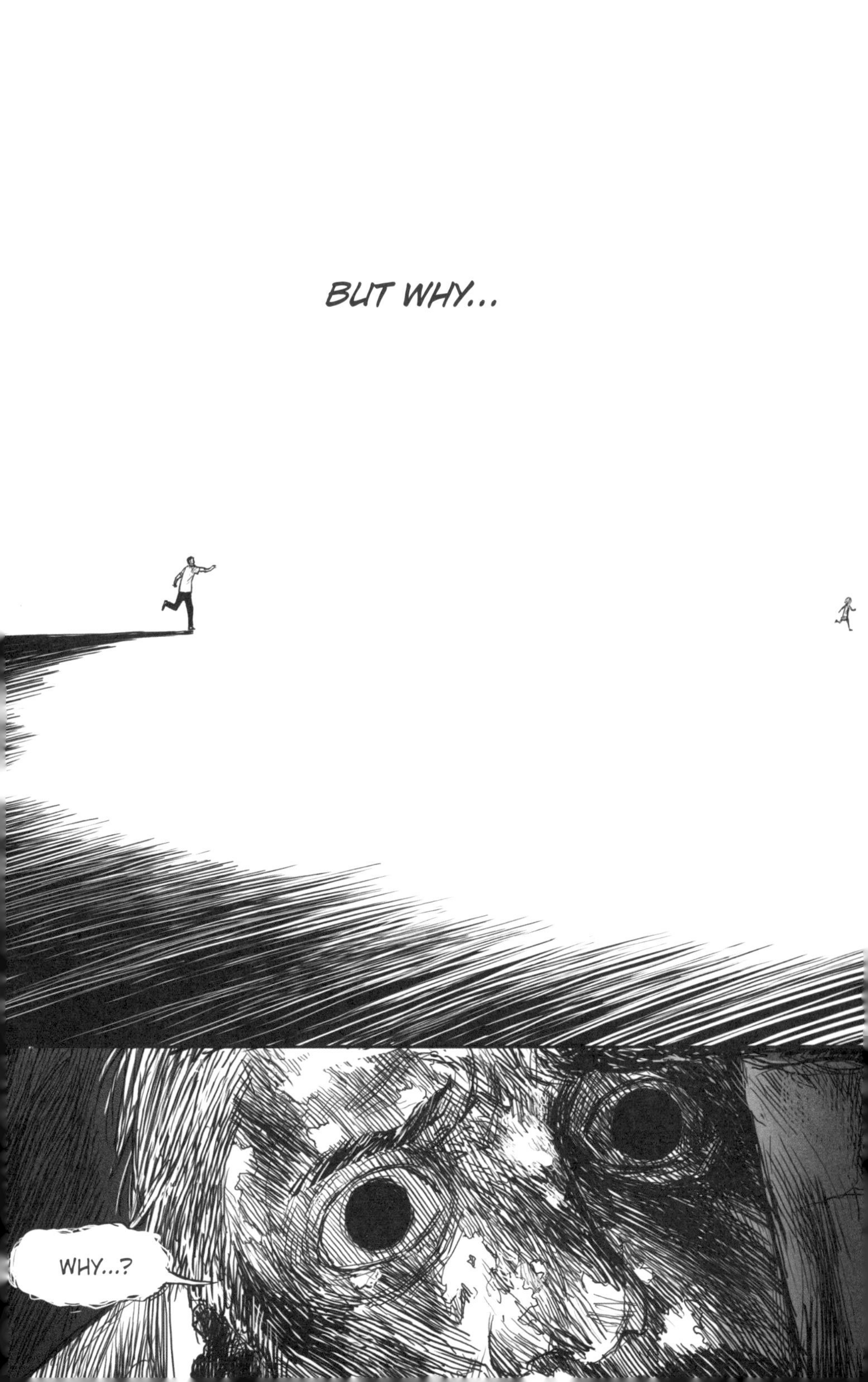
BUT WHY...
WHY...?

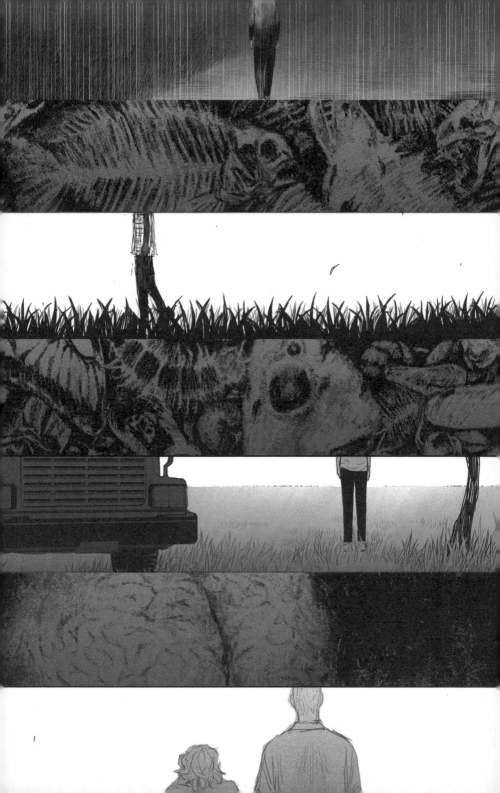

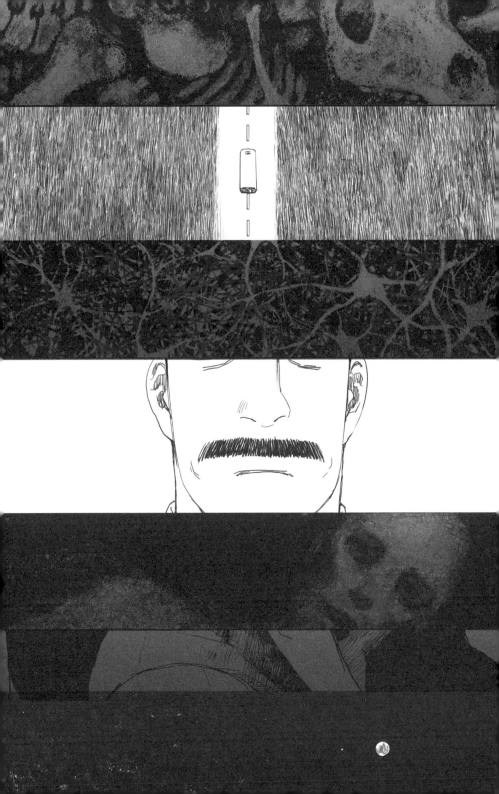

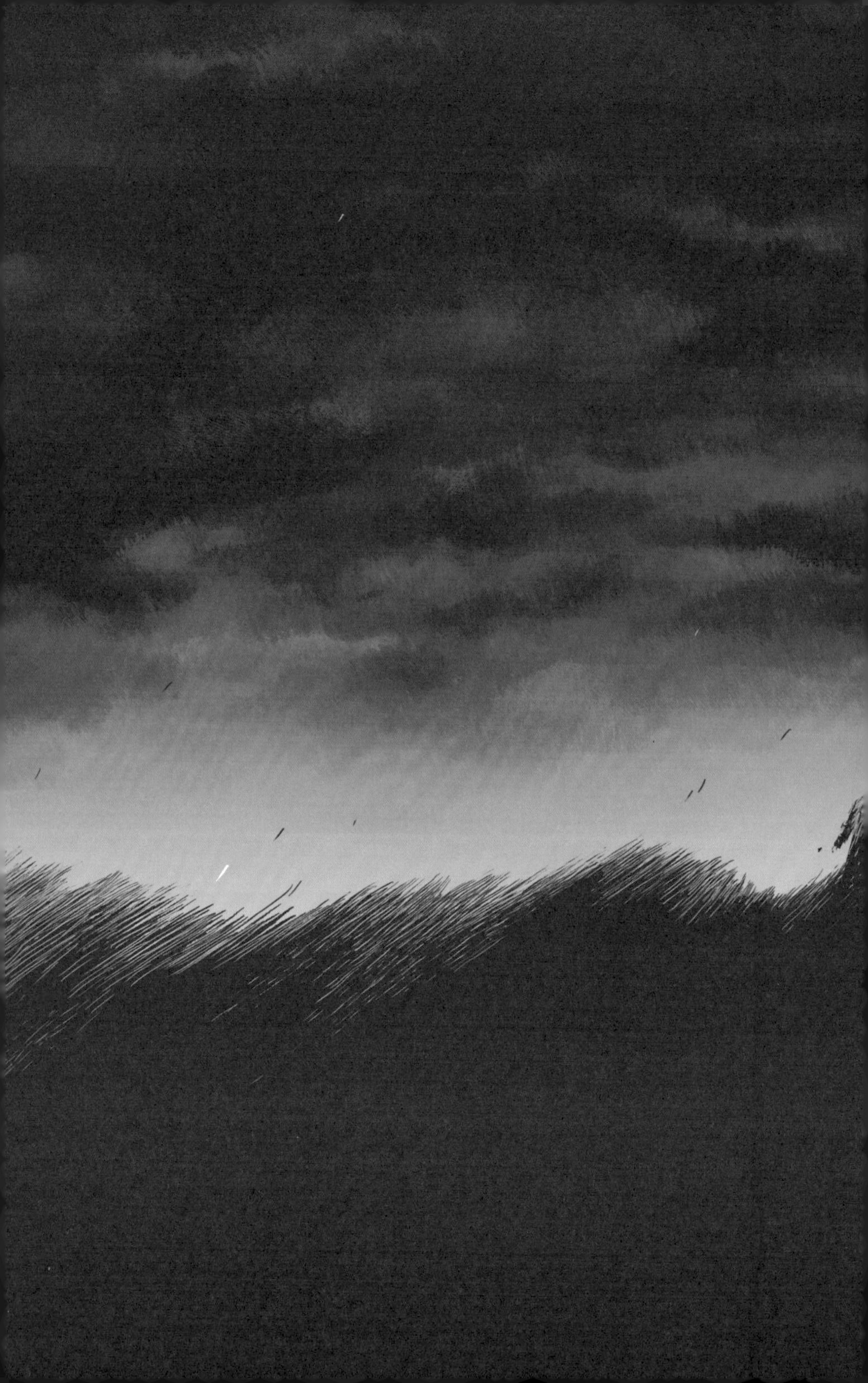

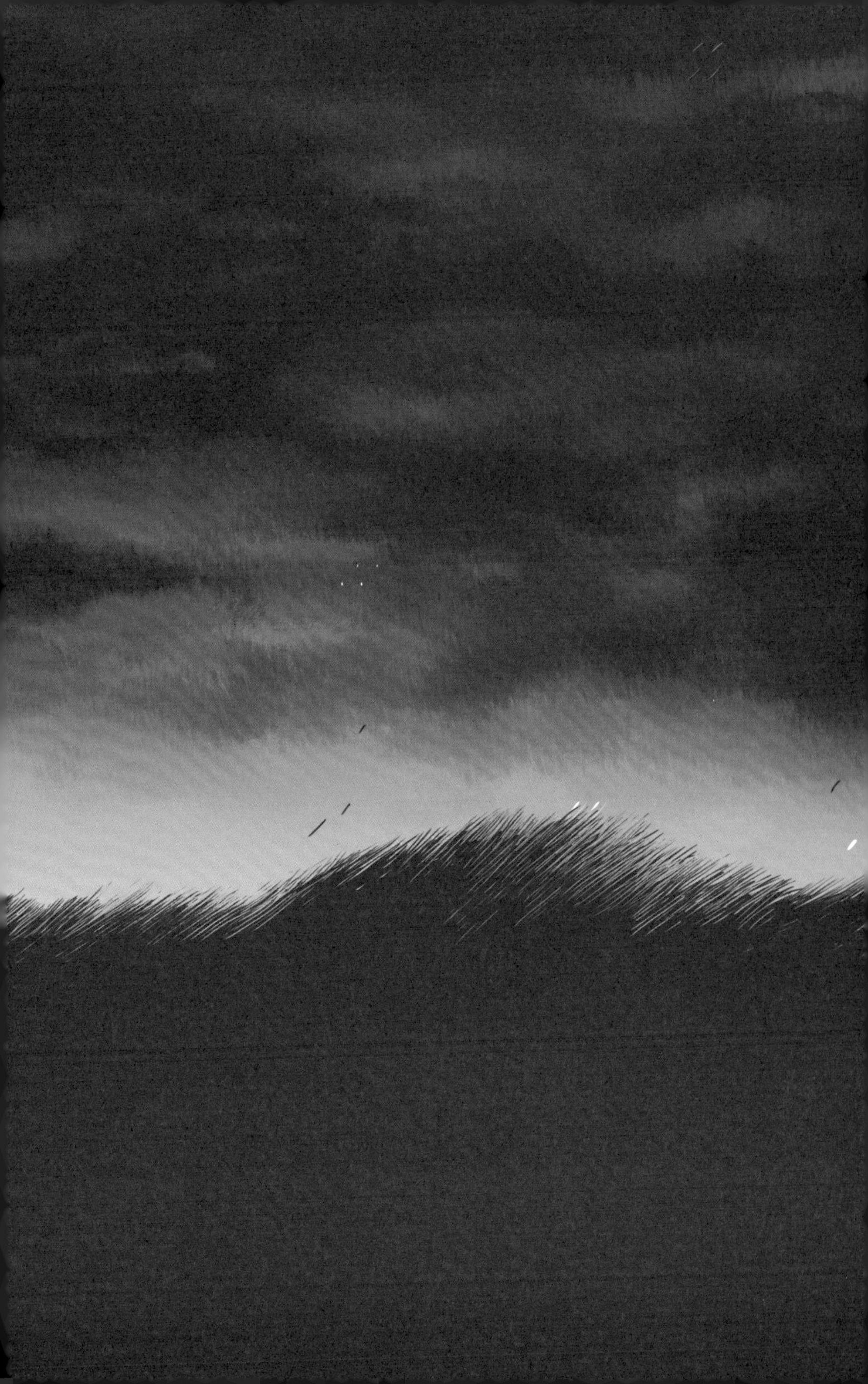

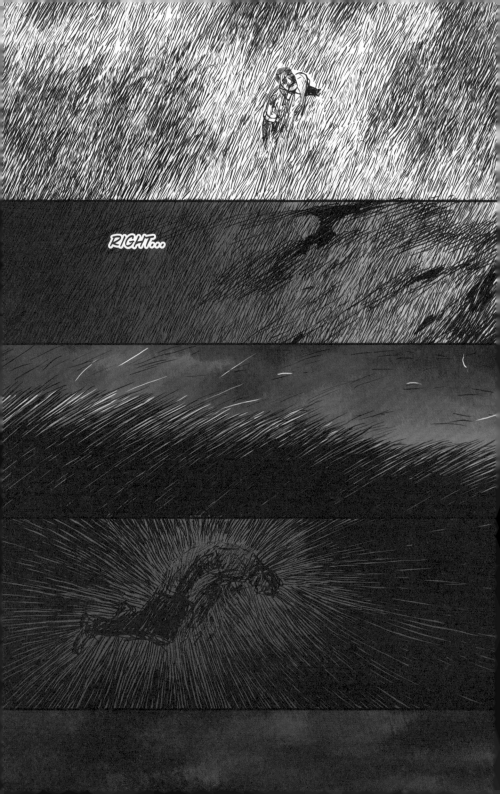

RIGHT...

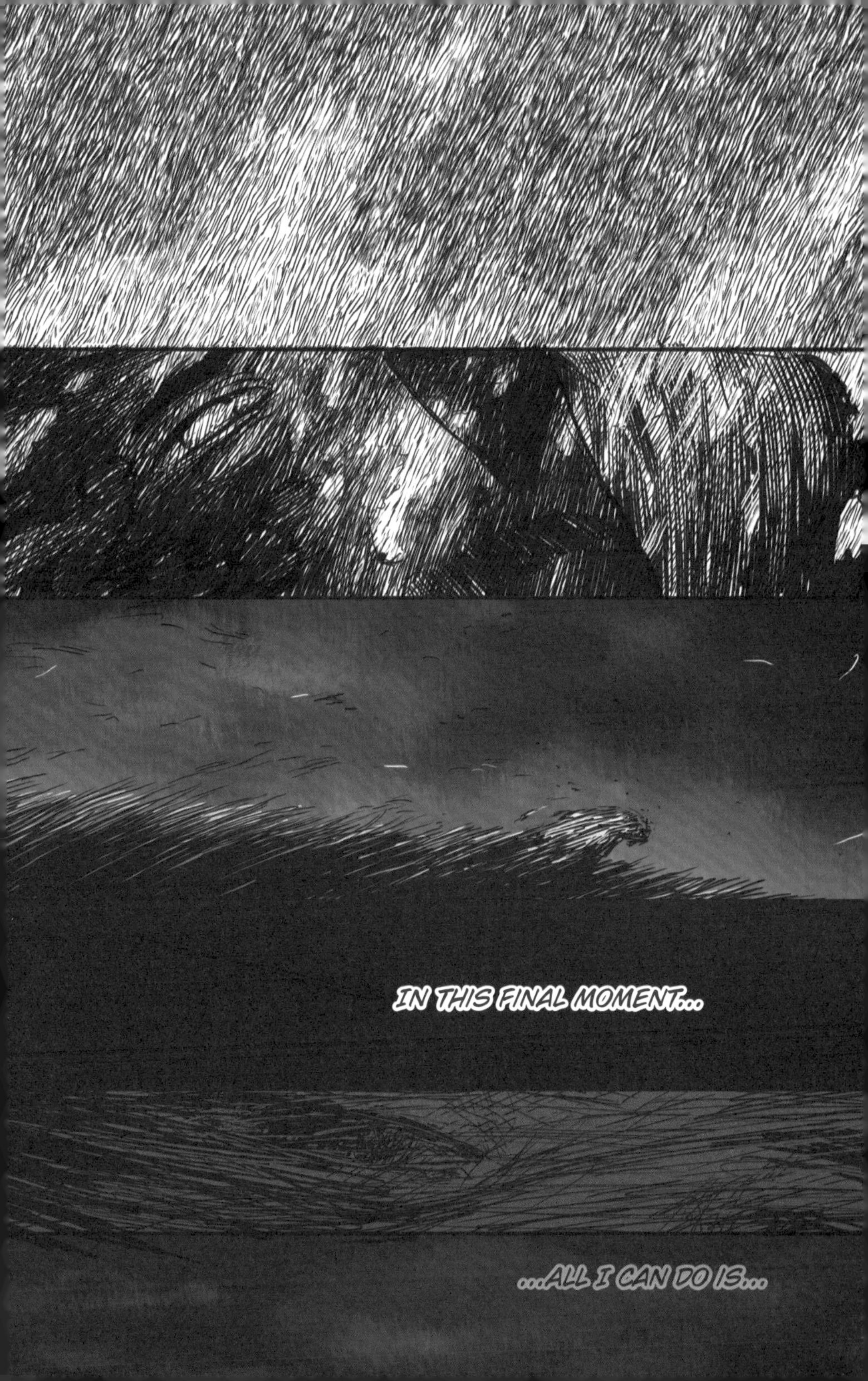
IN THIS FINAL MOMENT...
...ALL I CAN DO IS...

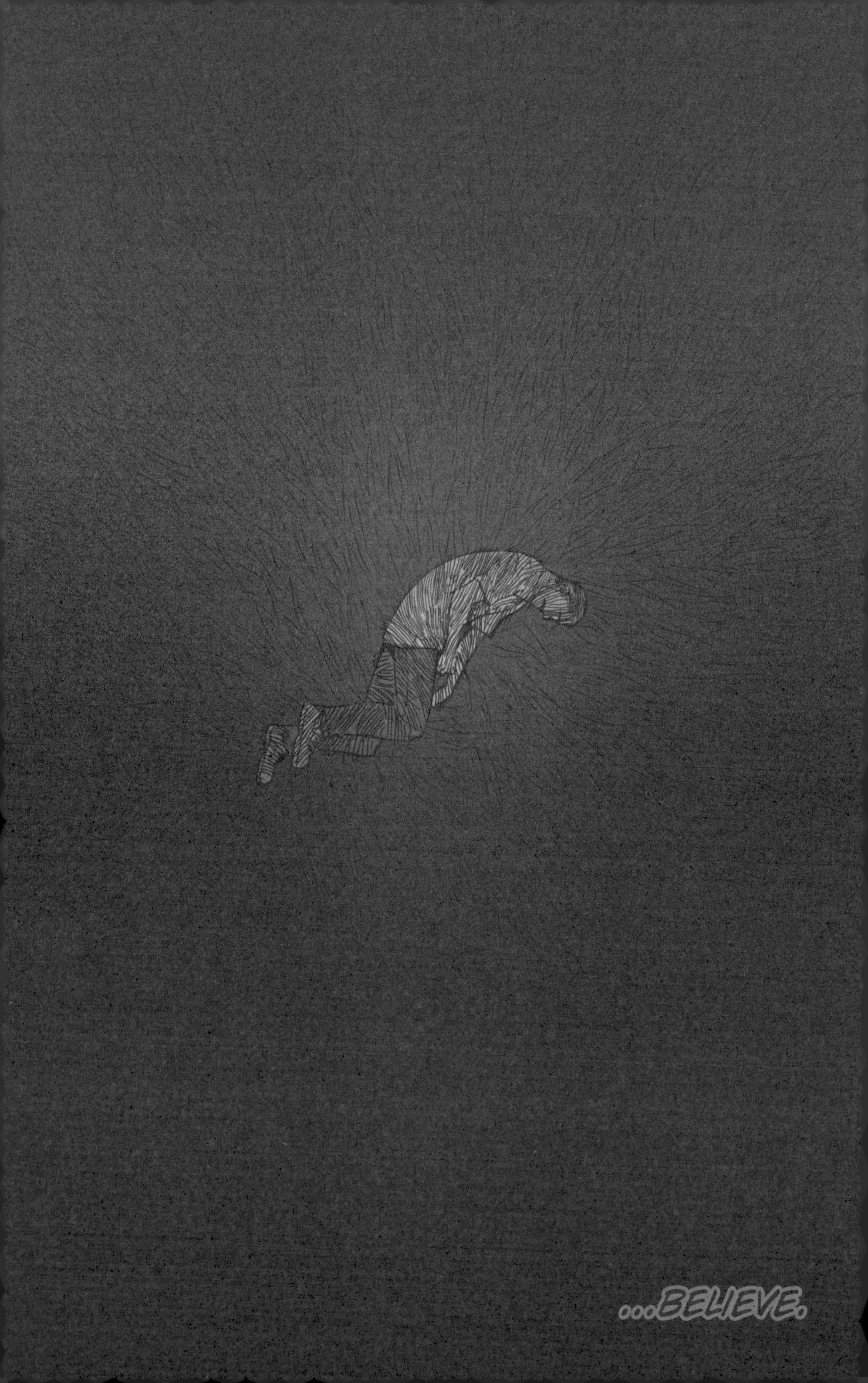
...BELIEVE.

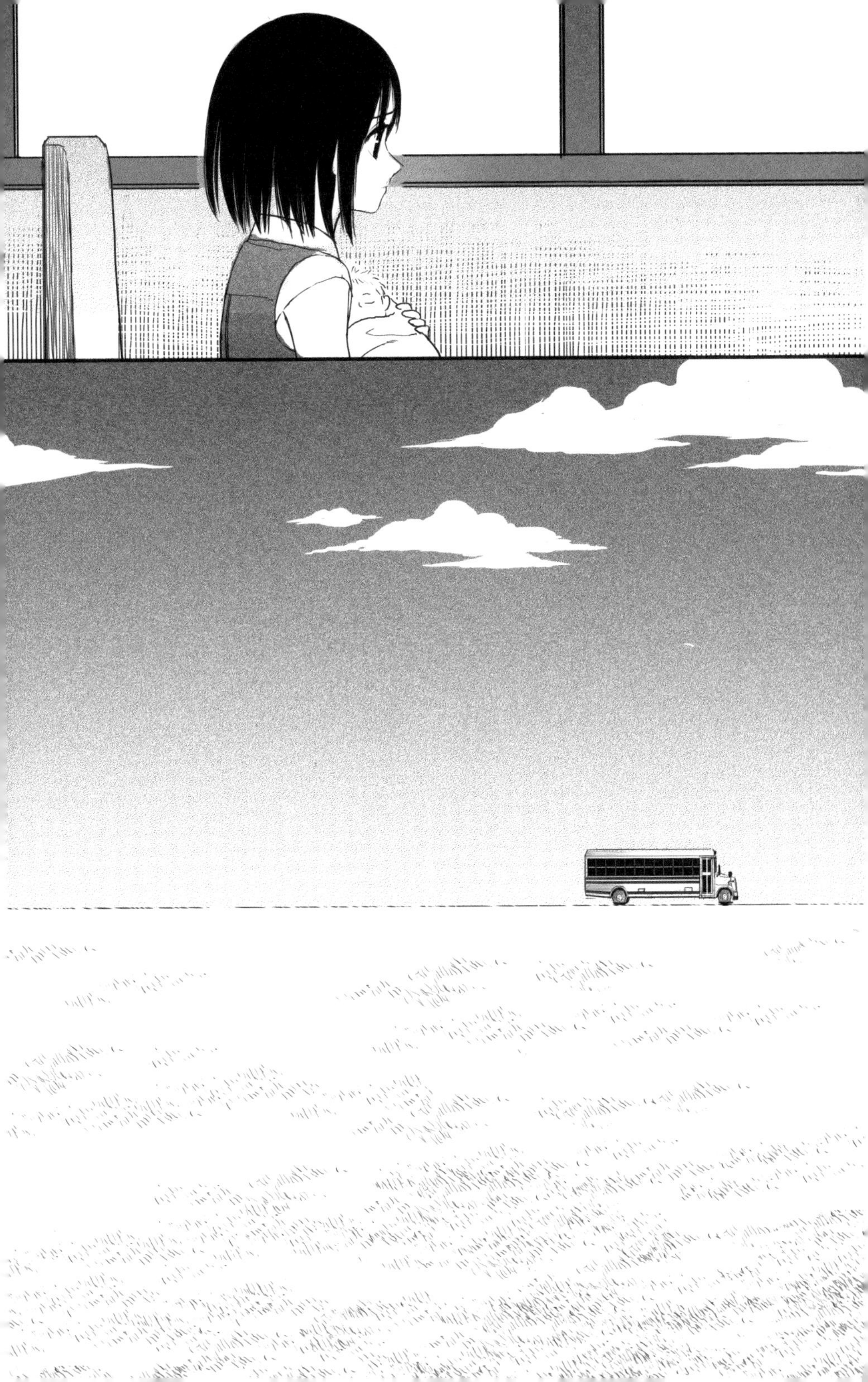